INTELLECTUALS AND POETS
IN MEDIEVAL EUROPE

BY THE SAME AUTHOR

Medieval Latin and the Rise of European Love-Lyric (2 vols., 2nd ed., Oxford 1968)

The Medieval Lyric (2nd ed., London-New York 1977)

Poetic Individuality in the Middle Ages: New Departures in Poetry 1000-1150 (2nd ed., London 1986)

Fabula: Explorations into the Uses of Myth in Medieval Platonism (Leiden-Köln 1974)

(with Ursula Dronke) *Barbara et antiquissima carmina* (Barcelona 1977)

Bernardus Silvestris, Cosmographia, edited with Introduction and Notes (Leiden 1978)

Francesco Colonna, Hypnerotomachia Poliphili: Introduction (Zaragoza 1981)

Women Writers of the Middle Ages: A Critical Study of Texts from Perpetua (✝ 203) to Marguerite Porete (✝ 1310) (Cambridge 1984)

The Medieval Poet and his World (Roma 1984)

Dante and Medieval Latin Traditions (Cambridge 1986)

Rosvita, Dialoghi drammatici, a cura di Ferruccio Bertini: *Introduzione* (Milano 1986)

(ed.) *A History of Twelfth-Century Western Philosophy* (Cambridge 1988)

Latin and Vernacular Poets of the Middle Ages (London 1991)

STAMPATO CON IL CONTRIBUTO
DELL'ASSOCIAZIONE DON GIUSEPPE DE LUCA

STORIA E LETTERATURA
RACCOLTA DI STUDI E TESTI

183

PETER DRONKE

INTELLECTUALS AND POETS
IN MEDIEVAL EUROPE

ROMA 1992

EDIZIONI DI STORIA E LETTERATURA

EDIZIONI DI STORIA E LETTERATURA
Roma - Via Lancellotti, 18

CONTENTS

IV *The Medieval* Planctus

Indices

PREFACE

In June 1989 I received with enormous pleasure a letter from
Maddalena De Luca, suggesting the possibility of publishing another
volume in her "Storia e Letteratura" series. The present collection,
Intellectuals and Poets in Medieval Europe, is the result.

The essays in the first two sections concern diverse attempts, by
philosophers, poets and mystics, to find fresh images for the realm
of the supernatural and the divine — images by which the natural
and the human too are illuminated in new ways. The first three focus
on aspects of the Platonic tradition, especially in the twelfth century
— in order to define the individuality of some of the brilliant
thinkers associated with Chartres (1), of Bernard Silvestris in his creation of "goddess Natura" and other feminine personified beings (2),
and of Abelard, and again Bernard, in their Christian but more-
than-half-Platonic interpretation of Vergil (3).

The theme of the third essay, "Integumenta Virgilii", links particularly with that of two in the next section — on "The Prologue
of the Prose *Edda*" (4) and "Hermes and the Sibyls" (8). In each,
the central problem is the re-affirmation of pre-Christian poetry and
wisdom, its re-creation as something unique and still cherishable under a Christian dispensation. Other essays here show different ways
in which images from the visible world — allegorical and symbolic
trees (5) or animals (7) — can both enrich human speculation and
lead to perceptions of the *invisibilia dei.* Similar concerns underlie
the essay on Hildegard of Bingen (6) — though to a large extent her
concepts and images elude known categories. The earlier parts of this
essay dwell on technical questions, of manuscript trasmission and
sources, the later parts present some of Hildegard's unpublished
writings. The aim throughout is to contribute to a fuller understanding of her achievements both as intellectual and as poet.

Another woman writer, Heloise, is the focus of the third section. Here two earlier essays (9, 10) have been complemented by a
new one written expressly for this volume (11), to confirm — and occasionally to modify — my previous suggestions in the light of recent
scholarly debate. These essays offer evidence in support of three con-

clusions: that we have, extant, a group of genuine writings of Heloise to Abelard; that their genuineness is corroborated by a number of independent contemporary testimonies; and that they are distinctive not only in their content but also in their verbal artistry.

These three essays link with the one that opens the final section, on "The Lament of Jephtha's Daughter" (12). This began as an enquiry into the genesis of Abelard's lyrical-dramatic masterpiece, the *Planctus* of the girls of Israel over Seila, daughter of Jephtha, whose sacrifice and heroism Abelard portrays with deliberate echoes of his depiction of Heloise in the *Historia calamitatum*. Work on the essay gradually uncovered a wide range of poetic constants in the laments of young girls, and laments for young girls, in European poetry, popular as well as learned, from ancient Greek tragedies to the twelfth century and beyond. Other aspects of medieval *planctus* are explored in the essays on laments with classical and biblical themes (13, 15, 16), and on the cycle of love-laments by a deeply original woman poet from Provence, Castelloza (14).

As in my earlier volume, *The Medieval Poet and his World* (1984), minor revisions in the texts and notes of the essays have been made silently, and supplementary notes signalling some more recent studies and editions have been added in square brackets.

I should like to express my thanks to the editors of journals and the publishers who have allowed me to reprint, and lightly revise, fifteen of these essays, and above all to Ursula Dronke, with whom I wrote the fourth essay, and Margaret Alexiou, with whom I wrote the twelfth. Neither of these could have been written without the contributions and insights of such collaborators.

Cambridge, 30 May 1991

PETER DRONKE

LIST OF ABBREVIATIONS

A.G.	*Anthologia Graeca*
A.H.	*Analecta Hymnica*
AHDLMA	*Archives d'histoire doctrinale et littéraire du moyen âge*
ALMA	*Archivum Latinitatis Medii Aevi*
CC (CM)	Corpus Christianorum (Continuatio Mediaevalis)
CCM	*Cahiers de civilisation médiévale*
EETS	Early English Text Society
Hofmann-Szantyr	J.B. Hofmann, A. Szantyr, *Lateinische Syntax und Stilistik* (*Handbuch der Altertumswissenschaft* II 2, München 1965)
IMU	*Italia medioevale e umanistica*
MARS	*Mediaeval and Renaissance Studies*
MGH	Monumenta Germaniae Historica
Mlat. Jb.	*Mittellateinisches Jahrbuch*
MS	*Mediaeval Studies*
Novum Glossarium	*Novum Glossarium Mediae Latinitatis*, ed. F. Blatt et al. (København 1957 ff.)
PBB	*Beiträge zur Geschichte der deutschen Sprache und Literatur* (Paul und Brauns Beiträge)
P.G.	Patrologia Graeca
P.L.	Patrologia Latina
RAC	*Reallexikon für Antike und Christentum*
RMAL	*Revue du moyen âge latin*
RTAM	*Recherches de théologie ancienne et médiévale*
SC	Sources Chrétiennes
SO	*Sibylline Oracles* (ed. J. Geffcken, *Die Oracula Sibyllina*, Berlin 1902; ed. A. Kurfess, *Sibyllinische Weissagungen*, München 1951)
TLL	*Thesaurus Linguae Latinae*
ZfdA	*Zeitschrift für deutsches Altertum*
ZfdPh	*Zeitschrift für deutsche Philologie*

I

FORMS OF MEDIEVAL PLATONISM

1

NEW APPROACHES TO THE SCHOOL OF CHARTRES *

I

What is the meaning of «the school of Chartres»? To me it has always stood for what is freshest in thought, richest and most adventurous in learning, in northern Europe in the earlier twelfth century. The character of this school, skilfully defined in a brief essay by Klibansky, seemed in recent years to have been unfolded in the fine studies and editions of Jeauneau, Gregory, Garin, Häring and others [1]. Most recently, however, the historical basis of what is commonly understood by «the school of Chartres» has been scrutinised afresh by the Oxford historian R. W. Southern [2]. Carefully he probes once more the historical testimonies as to who really taught at

* *Anuario de Estudios Medievales* VI (1969, publ. 1971) 117-140.

[1] Cf. particularly E. Garin, *Studi sul platonismo medievale*, Firenze, 1958, pp. 15-87; T. Gregory, *Anima Mundi*, Firenze, 1955; Id., *Platonismo medievale*, Roma, 1958, pp. 53-150; Id., *L'idea di natura*, «Atti del III Congresso internazionale di filosofia medievale» (Milano, 1966), pp. 27-65; N.M. Häring, *The Life and Works of Clarembald of Arras*, Toronto, 1965, and the articles listed *ibid.*, p. ix; Id., *The Commentaries on Boethius by Gilbert of Poitiers*, Toronto, 1966, and the articles listed *ibid.*, pp. ix-x; E. Jeauneau, *Note sur l'École de Chartres*, «Studi medievali», 3ª serie, VI (1964), pp. 821-865; Id., *Guillaume de Conches, Glosae super Platonem*, Paris, 1965; Id., articles in «Sophia», XXIII (1955), pp. 172-183; «AHDLMA», XXIV (1957), pp. 35-100; XXVII (1960), pp. 17-28; «RTAM», XXVII (1960), pp. 212-247; «Vivarium», V (1967), pp. 79-99; and in R.R. Bolgar (ed.), *Classical Influences in European Culture*, Cambridge, 1970, pp. 95-102; R. Klibansky, «The School of Chartres», in *Twelfth-Century Europe and the Foundations of Modern Society* (ed. M. Clagett *et al.*, Madison, 1961), pp. 3-14; R. Lemay, *Abu Ma'shar and Latin Aristotelianism in the Twelfth Century*, Beirut, 1962; H. Schipperges, *Die Schulen von Chartres unter dem Einfluss des Arabismus*, «Archiv. f. Gesch. d. Medizin», XL (1956), pp. 193-210; Id., *Einflüsse arabischer Medizin auf die Mikrokosmosliteratur des 12. Jahrhunderts*, «Miscellanea Mediaevalia», I (1962), pp. 129-153. One or two reservations about details in Lemay's and Schipperges' work, as well as about Häring's treatment of Thierry of Chartres, will emerge in the course of this essay.

[2] *Medieval Humanism and Other Studies*, Oxford, 1970, pp. 61-85.

Chartres, who was taught there and when. He shows that much that had been accepted as evidence for a brilliant school at Chartres by an earlier generation of scholars, notably by Clerval and Poole, is not evidence at all but speculation, flimsy or misguided. After analysing what we know of the careers of the most outstanding men in the earlier twelfth century who have traditionally been linked with Chartres, he comes to the conclusion that

> William of Conches must join Thierry and Gilbert de la Porrée among the masters who can be found teaching at Paris, but so far as we know, not at Chartres. And John of Salisbury must join the many students who studied at Paris but not, so far as we know, at Chartres. And if he goes, who is left? It is very difficult to say [3].

At the same time, Southern argues that the high qualities and originality of the «Chartrain» thinkers have been overrated. Bernard of Chartres «was in his time somewhat old-fashioned. His type of learning no longer held the imagination or satisfied the ambition of younger men». William of Conches and Thierry of Chartres

> are the last representatives of the generation which had derived its knowledge of the world of men and nature mainly from the tradition of the Latin world — from Ovid and Virgil, from Macrobius and Martianus Capella, from Boethius and Cassiodorus. However eager they might be for new texts, their range of competence scarcely extended beyond the sources that had long been familiar.

Of «the three masters», Bernard, Thierry, and William, the verdict is:

> All their thoughts were old thoughts. They had the strength to make old thoughts live again, but they could not add to them [4].

After this swift and expertly directed fusillade, what positions remain for defence? To sketch the possibility of a new evaluation, taking into account Southern's important investigations as well as the other major contributions of recent years, is the purpose of this essay. I shall briefly reconsider the factual question: whom and what is it legitimate to associate with Chartres in the earlier twelfth century? What is the precise nature and significance of the link with Chartres in each context? After that, I shall try to give some succinct indica-

---

[3] *Ibid.*, p. 73.
[4] *Ibid.*, pp. 75, 77, 83.

tions of how I would wish to answer the qualitative questions: are there traces of real brilliance in the thought of Bernard, Thierry and William? In what, if anything, does their originality consist?

Let us begin with the most solid information available: Bernard of Chartres is attested as both teacher (*magister scolae*) at Chartres (from 1114) and as chancellor there (1124); Gilbert de la Porrée is attested as another chancellor of Chartres (1126); Thierry of Chartres as yet another (1141). Southern suggests that of these three only Bernard is known for certain to have taught in the cathedral school. «The existence of a famous man as chancellor of the cathedral cannot be accepted as proof that this famous man was teaching in the school... His own learning cannot be taken as an index of the learning of the school» [5].

This is a salutary comment. At the same time I believe it would be wrong to infer from it that the chancellor's intellectual influence on the school would have been negligible. Quite the contrary: an analogy may help to make this clear. In Oxford and Cambridge today the head of a College (the community of learning most comparable in size) is a scholar whose duties in relation to the College are administrative. He rarely teaches the undergraduates in his College, and quite often does not give any lectures. Nevertheless, he will associate regularly with the Fellows of his College (in Chartres we might say, with the *magistri* and *canonici*); he will talk with them at meals, and they are likely to be influenced by his ideas. Especially if he has come to his new appointment from a teaching chair in another town (like Thierry coming from Paris), where he has devised an admirable and comprehensive teaching syllabus (the *Heptateuchon*), it seems to me unlikely that he would hide this syllabus from his new colleagues, or that it would remain without influence on their teaching. Above all, if this scholar-administrator happens, like Thierry, to be world-famous, a man to whom leading scholars elsewhere in Europe send their works with glowing dedications, is it conceivable that the intellectual community he administers will be quite cut off from his own range of intellectual activities? His influence may well be even more far-reaching in taking less direct forms than the imparting of classroom information. This is the likelier if, like the Chartrain chan-

---

[5] *Ibid.*, pp. 67-69. D. E. Luscombe, *The School of Peter Abelard*, Cambridge, 1969, pp. 57-58, has recently pointed out that there are special difficulties involved in the assumption that Thierry was associated with Chartres earlier in his career. [But cf. now K. M. Fredborg (ed.), *The Latin Rhetorical Commentaries by Thierry of Chartres*, Toronto, 1988, p. 5].

cellor and unlike modern heads of Colleges, it was also a part of his duty to «look after the library and archives» [6].

For Gilbert de la Porrée, on the other hand, we have an explicit testimony of his lecturing at Chartres, though this too raises some delicate questions of detailed interpretation. In the *Dialogus Ratii et Everardi*, Everard of Ypres says «Audivi quia auditor ipsius [Gilleberti] fuisti», and Ratius (probably a fictitious *persona* of the author) replies:

> Fui equidem. Unde et gaudeo et semper gaudebo. Ad quem audiendum mater mea, cuius nomen Ratio Atheniensis, consilio Sophiae, meae sororis, me in Franciam misit. Cui Carnoti quartus in lectionem, Parisius in aula episcopi fere tercentesimus assedi. Et ipsi episcopo Pictavis adhaesi usque ad ipsius obitum, qui me docente Graecam noverat linguam, ego quoque ipso Latinam. Cui sepulto superscripsi hoc breve epitaphium: *Irriguum fontem siccat aquosa dies.* In mense enim aquarii, quod terrae gesserat, terrae reddidit, quod caeli caelo[7].

Häring wrote of Everard:

> He knows the background of Gilbert's doctrine so well that we may believe his claim to have studied under Gilbert at Chartres and Poitiers, though this assumption is somehow weakened by the fact that his epitaph gives the wrong month for Gilbert's death, since he died in November (1154) and not during the time of the aquarius (January or February) [8].

Everard wrote the *Dialogus* late in life, between 1191 and 1198, in the years after he had become a Cistercian monk. Even then he remained a loyal adherent to Gilbert and, four decades after his death, was writing to vindicate his master's memory. I believe, unlike Häring, that only the pentameter (italicised above) constitutes the «brief epitaph», and that the prose sentence «In mense enim aquarii...» is the author's explanation of why he had used the phrase «aquosa dies». Here we might have to reckon with an old man's lapse of memory or faulty rationalisation, four decades after the event.

---

[6] Southern, p. 67.

[7] Ed. N. M. Häring, *A Latin Dialogue on the Doctrine of Gilbert of Poitiers*, «Mediaeval Studies», XV (1953), p. 252. I am indebted to my colleague Dr. Luscombe for drawing my attention to this passage, and for a number of valuable comments on the present article.

[8] *Ibid.*, p. 244; on the date of the *Dialogus*, p. 243; on the chronology of Everard's career, Id., «Mediaeval Studies», XVII (1955), pp. 143-172, especially p. 161.

The epitaph itself, with its conventional «watery day» (cf. Geoffrey of Vinsauf's *lacrimosa dies*, *Poetria Nova*, 375), gives no indication of the month of death.

But Everard's age has a further implication: if we accept that he heard Gilbert lecture at Chartres, it must surely have been in the years Gilbert was chancellor there: it is very unlikely that a man still active in the 1190s would have gone to lectures before 1126.

Does the fact that the *Dialogus* mentions an audience of four for Gilbert in Chartres, and of nearly three hundred in Paris, indicate the relative importance of the two centres? Certainly in terms of quantity, but by no means necessarily in terms of quality or intellectual achievement. The main point of the contrast between Chartres and Paris here may rather be a more personal one: what the speaker wishes to emphasise seems to be «I have been a follower of Gilbert's all my life: I knew and admired him already before he became world-famous». The relative audience sizes, again, may have something to do with the kind of *lectio* in question — clearly an open lecture course in Paris, more probably a «seminar for advanced students» in Chartres.

More problematic is the question, in what ways was William of Conches associated with the school of Chartres? Southern admits «a quite strong presumption that he was a pupil of Bernard of Chartres», for, according to John of Salisbury, «William followed the same method of teaching as Bernard» [9]. But he denies any evidence that William ever taught at Chartres.

On the question of whether William was Bernard's pupil, even the touch of scepticism seems to me unjustified: if we look at John's wording:

> Ad huius magistri [Bernardi] formam preceptores mei in gramatica, Willelmus de Conchis et Ricardus... suos discipulos aliquandiu informaverunt [10].

I think it is stronger than merely saying that William followed the same method of teaching: rather, it suggests that in teaching he was able to form his pupils on the model of his master Bernard. The wording «ad huius magistri formam... informaverunt», playing as it does on the philosophical associations of *forma*, could hardly be used of someone who had not himself experienced this «formation».

Did William also teach at Chartres? The only detailed argu-

[9] *Ibid.*, p. 71.
[10] *Metalogicon*, I, 24 (ed. C. C. J. Webb, Oxford, 1929, p. 57, 23-27).

ments that have ever been advanced for this are those of Schaarschmidt in 1862; all subsequent scholars have adopted the idea from
him [11]. It turns on the interpretation of John of Salisbury's account
of his studies. John, in Southern's words,

> tells us that he left England in 1136 and studied logic on Mont Sainte
> Geneviève, in the suburbs of Paris, from 1136 to 1138. Then he left
> the Mount and followed the lectures of William of Conches and
> others for three years from 1138 to 1141. Finally in 1141 he returned
> and studied logic and theology under Gilbert de la Porrée [12].

Where was John when he heard William of Conches's lectures?
Schaarschmidt argued, in Chartres. One of his arguments — that
John's description of Bernard of Chartres's teaching is an eyewitness
account — is demonstrably false, and has been rejected by all modern
scholars. But do «Schaarschmidt's other arguments amount to nothing» [13]? One vital paragraph of Schaarschmidt's discussion, I believe,
retains its validity:

> That John [at the time of his studies] was well known in Chartres

---

[11] It is worth noting, however, that Clerval was an exception: he argued, long
before Southern, that William taught in Paris and that John of Salisbury heard him
there (*Les écoles de Chartres au moyen-âge*, Paris, 1895, p. 181).

[12] Southern, p. 72, summarizing *Metal.*, II, 10. There are a number of chrono-
logical difficulties in this chapter of the *Metalogicon*, which I do not know how to
resolve. John writes: «consulto me ad gramaticum de Conchis transtuli, ipsumque
triennio docentem audivi. Interim legi plura, nec me umquam penitebit temporis
eius. Postmodum vero Ricardum cognomento Episcopum... secutus sum».

The passage states that John studied with William for three years; we have no
evidence that William was peripatetic during this time. However, if the period of
being Richard's pupil followed rather than overlapped with that of being William's,
as *postmodum* suggests, how was it possible for John to return to Paris *in fine triennii*
to learn from yet another master? The account as it stands gives the impression that
the time with Richard was a separate period, after William and before the return
to Gilbert in Paris, yet the seemingly careful wording *triennio... in fine triennii* would
appear to preclude this. So too, the relative dates of John's learning from Thierry
and from Petrus Helias, of his teaching of aristocratic children, and of his friendship
with the Parisian master Adam du Petit Pont, seem tantalisingly vague. But the fact
that John mentions these details between his remarks on William and Richard and
his account of returning to Paris does not imply that they too must be placed «during the years from 1138 to 1141» (thus Southern, p. 73). As R. L. Poole noted perceptively, «EHR», XXXV (1920), p. 335, in this passage John «speaks of the masters
and friends with whom he came into relations both earlier and later... After this interlude John reverts to the strict order of events».

[13] *Loc. cit.*

is shown by an observation of his (*Metal.* I 5) about Gilbert de la Porrée, who was later to be his teacher: «Gilbert, who at that time was
chancellor at Chartres, was wont to say...» — a turn of phrase which
surely indicates that John had personal relations with Gilbert in
Chartres. Then we also understand why John could express himself as
follows (*Metal.* II 10): «having returned to Paris I met Gilbert again»
— namely in that Gilbert, whom he already knew from Chartres, had
preceded him to Paris [14].

Southern argues (i) that Gilbert need not have given up his
chancellorship at Chartres in order to lecture in Paris; (ii) that John
need not have left Paris, but could simply have transferred from the
Mont Sainte Geneviève, outside the city walls, to the schools by the
river, and then back again [15]. These are indeed possibilities, not cer-
tainties, but they can be granted for the sake of argument. What I
cannot believe is that Gilbert was in or near Paris at the time John
refers to in his anecdotal reminiscing:

> Solebat magister Gilebertus, tunc quidem cancellarius Carnoten-
> sis et postmodum venerabilis episcopus Pictavorum, temporis eius nes-
> cio ridens aut dolens insaniam, cum eos videbat ad studia, que predic-
> ta sunt, evolare, eis artem pistoriam polliceri; quoniam illa est, ut aie-
> bat, in gente sua que sola accipere consuevit omnes aliis operibus aut
> artificio destitutos... [16]

This, as Schaarschmidt saw, suggests that John had known Gilbert at Chartres: for is it likely that John would have written later
in his book «Reversus itaque in fine triennii repperi magistrum Gile-
bertum» [17] if he could have called on Gilbert at any time during
those three years simply by taking a ten-minute walk, from the Seine
to the Mont Sainte-Geneviève [18]? The unforced interpretation of the
two passages taken together seems to me to be that John heard Gilbert's ironic sayings at Chartres; that *repperi* refers to a reunion, not
to a first encounter; and that *reversus* refers to a return from some
distance, not to a ten-minute walk. If I am right in this, then John
was at Chartres in the years before 1141, the years, that is, in which

---

[14] C. Schaarschmidt, *Johannes Saresberiensis nach Leben und Studien, Schriften
und Philosophie*, Leipzig, 1862, p. 22.

[15] Southern, pp. 67, 73.

[16] *Metalogicon*, I, 5 (ed. Webb, p. 16, 7-13).

[17] *Metalogicon*, II, 10 (ed. Webb, p. 82, 6-7).

[18] The distance between the schools within the city walls and those outside
was rather less than a kilometer.

he heard William of Conches's lectures. William's lectures, therefore, will have taken place at Chartres. The evidence, admittedly, is circumstantial and a little complicated ; but of evidence that he ever taught in Paris there is not one trace.

II

Our sense of the intellectual richness of the school of Chartres is enhanced by considering the range of unusual works that were read at Chartres, or read by Gilbert, Thierry or William in the course of their careers. The extent of the Chartrain range of reading has been gradually established by various scholars, but in extremely diverse contexts and in a host of scattered publications. I shall first recall and bring together some of the more striking testimonies, attempting to set them down as specifically as possible. In this it may also be helpful to distinguish precisely between what texts we *know* to have been read at Chartres or by the Chartrain thinkers, and what other texts we have reason to think *may* have been read by them. Such gathering of information is of course only a minor prolegomenon: the important questions are the qualitative ones — how the Chartrains read such texts, how they assimilated them, transformed them in their own writings and built on them afresh. We know, for instance, that Thierry read the Hermetic *Asclepius* — but no one has tried to characterise and assess the imaginative impact of this treatise on Thierry's cosmological speculation. It is problems of this kind that I shall touch on, however swiftly and inadequately, in section III.

William of Conches, already in his youthful work the *Philosophia Mundi*, cites some medical treatises that had reached him by way of translations from the Arabic: the *Pantegni* of ʿAlī Ibn al ʿAbbās, in the translation of Constantine of Africa (*Phil. Mundi* I 21, *P.L.*, 172, cc. 48-49, and passim [*Philosophia*, ed. G. Maurach, Pretoria, 1980, p. 27]), the *Isagoge in Artem Parvam Galeni* of Johannicius (*P.L.* 172, cc. 50, 93 [Maurach pp. 28, 104]), and a treatise *De Urinis* by the ninth century Byzantine writer Theophilus Protospatharius, translated from the Greek (*P.L.* 172, c. 93 [Maurach p. 103]). It is also probable that William's philosophical-scientific notion of man received some stimulus from Nemesius' *De Natura Hominis*, in the eleventh century translation (the «Premnon Physicon») of Alphanus of Salerno [19].

---

[19] Cf. the parallels adduced by Jeauneau, *Glosae*, pp. 129 (d), 130 (d), 141 (a), 241 (b); cf. also Th. Silverstein, *Guillaume de Conches and Nemesius of Emesa*, «Harry Austryn Wolfson Jubilee Volume» (Jerusalem, 1965), II, pp. 719-734.

Would William have had access to such works at Chartres itself? There is every likelihood that the strong medical tradition which we can document for Chartres in the late tenth and early eleventh centuries persisted and was renewed in the twelfth. Two famous pre-Carolingian manuscripts, B.N. lat. 10233, containing Oribasius, and Rufus' *De Podagra*, and B. N. lat. 9332, containing, besides Oribasius, Alexander of Tralles's *Therapeutica* and Dioscorides' *Materia Medica*, were probably brought to Chartres before the end of the tenth century [20]. In 991 Richer of Reims (*Historiae*, IV, 50) tells how he left Reims for Chartres in order to study Hippocrates' *Aphorismi* and a book *De Concordia Yppocratis Galieni et Surani*, which were available there [21]. In the Chartres library there was, until the destruction of manuscripts in the Second World War, a twelfth century manuscript (171) containing «Commentarii in Ysagogas Johannicii; Commentarii in Aphorismos; Commentarii in Pronostica Ypocratis; Commentarii in librum urinarum, qui dicitur a voce Theophili; Commentarii in librum pulsuum qui est Phylareti». There was also a twelfth century manuscript of Alexander of Tralles (342) [22]. As both of these were manuscripts of the cathedral chapter, the presumption is against their having reached Chartres only at a later period.

It is possible, as Jeauneau has suggested, that William not only cited various Arabic and Byzantine medical treatises but also wrote a commentry on one or other of them [23]. New work on the anonymous commentaries still in manuscript may well enable attributions

[20] See L. C. MacKinney, *Early Medieval Medicine, with special Reference to France and Chartres*, Baltimore, 1937, pp. 112-114.

[21] *P. L.* 138, cc. 145-147, cf. MacKinney p. 122. I have not, on the other hand, seen evidence for the existence of Hippocrates' *Prognostica* at Chartres in the tenth century (thus Schipperges, *Die Schulen*, p. 195 n. 4). This seems to me to rest on a misunderstanding of a passage in Richer (147 B) — «in aphorismis Yppocratis vigilanter studui apud domnum Herbrandum magnae liberalitatis atque scientiae virum. In quibus cum tantum prognostica morborum accepissem, et simplex egritudinum cognitio cupienti non sufficeret, petii etiam...» — where *prognostica* clearly refers to matter contained in the *Aphorismi* themselves. So too, for the later period, I am dubious about the influence of Abū Ma'shar's *Introductorium* on either William of Conches or Thierry of Chartres (Lemay, *op. cit.*, pp. 157 ff., 285 ff.).

[22] *Catalogue général des manuscrits des Bibliothèques Publiques des Départements*, XI (1890) ad loc. For the Chartres manuscripts destroyed in 1939-1945, cf. «Speculum», XXIX (1954), pp. 336-337.

[23] Jeauneau, *Note*, p. 851. The existence of very early commentaries (though not by William himself) on both Johannitius and Theophilus, «made in the schools at the beginning of the twelfth century», is noted by R. Klibansky, E. Panofsky and F. Saxl, *Saturn and Melancholy*, London, 1964, p. 104.

to be made. At all events William's exceptional interest in medical theory and the exceptional resources for the study of medicine at Chartres are suggestive, and would tend to corroborate the inferences we have drawn from the *Metalogicon* regarding William's association with Chartres.

So, too, Thierry's interest in mathematics and astronomy takes on a special significance in the context of the tradition we can document at Chartres itself. Already at the time of Fulbert of Chartres († 1028) we know that the cathedral school's library included two rare mathematical works: a treatise on geometry by Albinus (a mathematician whom Boethius mentions), and the *Podismus* of Iunius Nipsius (second century A.D.) [24]. Later, as Haskins showed, «at Chartres a manuscript of the cathedral preserves a treatise on astrology containing Arabic words which dates from 1135, with notes added from 1137 to 1141; and another manuscript of the twelfth century contains Adelard's version of the Khorasmian tables» [25]. It was during his chancellorship at Chartres that Thierry received, dedicated to him, Bernard Silvestris' *Cosmographia* and the translation of Ptolemy's *Planisphaerium*. The second of these dedications, often referred to, seems seldom to have been read. Thus it is still possible for scholars to debate whether it is by Hermann of Carinthia or Rudolf of Brugge [26], when the text, in which Hermann refers explicitly to his own major work the *De Essentiis*, places the authorship beyond a doubt. The use of a perfect or present tense and a future in the same phrase (*ut in eo, quod de essentiis instituimus, plenius patebit*), accords with the fact that the translation and the original work were being written in the same year, but the translation completed slightly earlier [27]. In the long dedication, Hermann outlines his notion of the philosophical principles that form the basis of astronomy, using a conceptual framework that clearly shows its debt to Thierry's

---

[24] Cf. L. C. MacKinney, *Bishop Fulbert and Education at the School of Chartres*, Notre Dame, 1957, pp. 56-57.

[25] *Studies in the History of Mediaeval Science* (2nd ed., repr. New York, 1960), p. 90.

[26] E.g. M. Manitius, *Geschichte der lateinischen Literatur des Mittelalters*, III, München, 1931, pp. 200, 202; N.M. Häring, *Clarembald*, p. 25, n. 17; Schipperges, *Die Schulen*, p. 199, writes as though two separate translations were in question. The dedication is printed by J. L. Heiberg, *Ptolemaei Opera Astronomica Minora*, Leipzig, 1907, pp. clxxxiii ff., who also observed that the attribution to Rudolf is based on the erroneous superscription in the *editio princeps* (*Sphaerae atque astrorum coelestium ratio, natura et motus*, Basel, 1536, p. 227). The preface in this text retains the sentence referring to the *De Essentiis* (*ibid.*, p. 229), but reads *planius* for *plenius*.

[27] Heiberg, p. clxxxv; cf. Haskins, *Studies*, pp. 47-48.

teaching, to the approach formulated in Thierry's *Expositio in Hexameron*. Hermann's high praise of Thierry as his *preceptor* can here be verified — it was indeed no empty flattery [28].

Thus we have some precise testimonies of the ways in which Chartres was open to the new Arabic learning. While some of the Parisian schools may have shown a comparable enthusiasm, we cannot point to any positive evidence for this of the kind we can associate with Chartres: collections of manuscripts from Paris before the late twelfth century have unfortunately not come down to us. What of the new wave of Aristotelian translations from the Greek, which begin to be made in the second quarter of the twelfth century? As Lorenzo Minio-Paluello showed in his pioneer article on James of Venice [29], the oldest manuscript of the «vulgate» translation of the *Posterior Analytics*, almost certainly by James, was a Chartrain one (the twelfth-century codex 92). Again, John of Salisbury, writing probably in 1167, was asking for new translations of Aristotelian works outside the *Organon*. This could refer to any of the following: *Physics, Metaphysics, Nicomachean Ethics, De Anima, De Memoria, De Intelligentia, De Generatione et Corruptione*, all of which were translated, directly from the Greek, by about this time. The earliest manuscript tradition of these translations points to northern France — though admittedly not to Chartres itself [30]. Did John succeed in obtaining the works for which he wrote? And if so, did he bring some of them with him when, nine years later, he was elected bishop of Chartres? It is an attractive conjecture [31].

---

[28] A detailed study of Hermann's vocabulary and concepts here and in his translations, as well as in his *De Essentiis*, to determine the nature and extent of the pre-Arabic and the Arabic-influenced elements, would provide vital evidence towards the most important intellectual transitions in the twelfth century. Until we have a substantial body of such detailed evidence, all contrasts using terms such as «Platonic», «Aristotelian», «old learning», «new learning», «neoplatonism», «scholasticism», will remain superficial. [Cf. now C. Burnett, *Hermann of Carinthia, De Essentiis. A Critical Edition with Translation and Commentary*, Leiden-Köln, 1982].

[29] *Iacobus Veneticus Grecus*, «Traditio», VIII (1952), pp. 265-304.

[30] Cf. L. Minio-Paluello, *art. cit.*, especially pp. 284, 291-294; Id., *Aristotele dal mondo arabo a quello latino*, «L'Occidente e l'Islam nell'alto medioevo» (Spoleto, 1965), especially pp. 611-612.

[31] There are, however, no Aristotelian texts among the books mentioned in the Necrology as John's bequest to the Chartres library (cf. C. C. J. Webb, «MARS», I [1943], pp. 128-129). In fact this list includes little except theological works: apart from John's own *Policraticus*, only a handful of secular books are mentioned, and these are all of a moral or didactic kind. There is no poetry, no logic, speculative philosophy or science (if we except the Senecan *Quaestiones Naturales*). As we can-

For Gilbert de la Porrée, too, we have some evidence of unusual reading. Gilbert, of whom his cautious and erudite editor N.M. Häring wrote, «his equal is not found in Latin theology from Saint Augustine to the most celebrated theologians of the thirteenth century», is known to have studied thoroughly some writings of the Greek Fathers Theodoret and Sophronius (in Latin versions) [32]. More problematic is the question of the forms that Gilbert's influence took. It seems clear that some links were made between the ideas of Gilbert and those of Avicenna, as Avicenna's works reached northern Europe in translations — yet the precise beginnings and the extent of these links remain obscure. As M. H. Vicaire showed in an adventurous and still valuable older article, there is at least one work, the *De Causis Primis et Secundis* (probably late twelfth century), that is indubitably both Porretan and Avicennist in its inspiration. Here there is a conscious attempt to conjoin the logical (Boethian-Porretan) notion of *unitas* with the quasimystical conception of Avicenna [33]. Whether or not this was an isolated phenomenon is still difficult to determine in our present state of knowledge [34].

Southern has valuably reminded us that Chartres did not have the monopoly of Thierry or of Gilbert: Thierry's influence must also have radiated from Paris, that of Gilbert both from Paris and Poitiers. At the same time, I would query his suggestion that Paris, not

not suppose that John had no books whatever in such fields, are we to infer that he disposed of the rest of his library in other ways, or that in the context of a Necrology it was thought appropriate to specify only the more edifying books in the bequest?

[32] N. M. Häring, *The Commentaries on Boethius by Gilbert of Poitiers*, p. 4; Id., *The Porretans and the Greek Fathers*, «Mediaeval Studies», XXIV (1962), p. 188.

[33] Cf. M. H. Vicaire, *Les porrétains et l'avicennisme avant 1215*, «Revue des sciences philosophiques et théologiques», XXVI (1937), pp. 449-482, especially p. 472.

[34] Henry Corbin, in the context of his admirable discussion of Latin Avicennism (*Avicenna and the Visionary Recital*, transl. W. R. Trask, London, 1961, pp. 101-122), mentions two other works: the *De Anima* attributed to Gundissalinus, and a late twelfth century treatise on the wanderings of the soul in the otherworld (ed. M.-Th. d'Alverny, «AHDLMA», XV-XVII [1940-1942], pp. 239-299). But to the best of my knowledge neither of these shows direct links with the thought of Gilbert de la Porrée. The relations between Gundissalinus' works and those of Thierry of Chartres pose another problem that requires further study: I am not, for example, convinced by Häring's arguments suggesting that Thierry wrote his commentary on the *De Inventione* in old age and plagiarised the work of his younger contemporary Gundissalinus (*Thierry of Chartres and Dominicus Gundissalinus*, «Mediaeval Studies», XXVI (1964), pp. 271-286. [Cf. most recently Fredborg (cit. n. 5), pp. 17-20].

Chartres, was the incomparable intellectual centre:

> the number of masters and the wide choice open to students gave
> Paris a position quite different from that of any other city in northern
> Europe. In the years between 1137 and 1147, when John of Salisbury
> was a student, he was able to hear the lectures of ten or twelve
> masters, of whom six or seven were men of the first importance in
> their subject. This simple fact gave Paris an overwhelming advantage
> over every other centre of study in the North [35].

This is precisely the myth of Paris that had reached the ears of
a young Englishman, Daniel of Morley, who came there on his first
trip abroad, around 1160, in search of wisdom. The reality, as he saw
it, was sadly different:

> Cum dudum ab Anglia me causa studii excepissem et Parisius ali-
> quamdiu moram fecissem, videbam quosdam bestiales in scolis gravi
> auctoritate sedes occupare... Qui, dum propter inscitiam suam locum
> statuae tenerent, tamen volebant sola taciturnitate videri sapientes,
> sed tales, cum aliquid dicere conabantur, infantissimos repperiebam.
> Cum hec, inquam, in hunc modum se habere deprehenderem, ne et
> ego simile damnum incurrerem, artes, que scripturas illuminant, non
> in transitu salutandas vel sub compendio pretereundas mecum sollicita
> deliberatione tractabam. Sed quoniam doctrina Arabum, que in quad-
> ruvio fere tota existit, maxime his diebus apud Toletum celebratur, il-
> luc, ut sapientiores mundi philosophos audirem, festinanter
> properavi [36].

In northern Europe it was Chartres, rather than Paris, that first
showed itself exceptionally receptive to the *doctrina Arabum*, the
knowledge being furthered *apud Toletum*. If it had occurred to
Daniel to visit Chartres, he would have found, not all the riches of
Toledo, but certainly some books of Arab science and some open-
minded men to discuss them with.

III

Some far-reaching questions about originality and influences in
twelfth century thought are provoked by the word *elementatum*.

---

[35] Southern, p. 75.

[36] *Liber de Naturis Inferiorum et Superiorum* (ed. K. Sudhoff, «Archiv f. d. Gesch.
d. Naturwiss. u. Technik», VIII [1917], p. 6); corrections from another ms. by Birken-
majer, *ibid.*, IX (1918), pp. 45-51 [Ed. G. Maurach, *Mlat. Jb.* XIV (1979), pp. 204-55].

There has been much debate as to where the term first occurs [37]. Silverstein, assembling a range of early instances, left the problem undecided; in two later articles, however, he appears to suggest that the word originates with William of Conches, though he gives no reasons to support such a suggestion [38]. Lemay, on the other hand, argued that the term is first found in John of Seville's translation of Abū Ma'shar's *Introductorium*, where he has to make a distinction between the Aristotelian concepts *stoicheia* and *sômatika*. When William of Conches uses it, «William's source must have been John's version of the *Introductorium*» [39]. Most recently, Marie-Thérèse d'Alverny has given her assent, though cautiously, to Lemay's suggestion, even if «il faudrait en ce cas retarder les dates présentées jusqu'ici pour la rédaction de la *Philosophia* et des gloses» [40].

A later dating of William's *Philosophia* has its own problems, however: John of Seville translated the *Introductorium* in 1133 [41], and it is not easy to put the composition of William's work after that date. In his late work, the *Dragmaticon*, which we know to have been composed between 1144 and 1149 [42], there are two passages that help to establish an approximate date for the *Philosophia*. One is in the touching and ironic autobiographical sketch that he gives at the opening of Book VI:

> iam que per viginti annos et eo amplius alios docui, adhuc vix plene et perfecte intelligo [43].

[37] Cf. especially, Th. Silverstein, *Elementatum*, «Mediaeval Studies», XVI (1954), pp. 156-162; Id., *Guillaume de Conches and the Elements, ibid.* XXVI (1964), p. 364; Id., *Guillaume de Conches and Nemesius of Emesa*, «Harry Austryn Wolfson Jubilee Volume» (Jerusalem, 1965), II, p. 722; R. McKeon, *Medicine and Philosophy in the Eleventh and Twelfth Centuries: the Problem of Elements*, «The Thomist», XXIV (1961), pp. 211-256; R. Lemay, *op. cit.*, pp. 74-5, 176-179 and *passim*; M.-Th. d'Alverny, «Mélanges offerts à M.-D. Chenu», Paris, 1967, p. 42; Ead., «CCM», XIII (1970), pp. 170-171.

[38] In «Mediaeval Studies», XXVI (1964), p. 364, Silverstein has the mysterious (misprinted?) sentence: «Thus Guillaume seems to be the first to use, if indeed he did not invent, *elementum-elementata* as a noun to designate the four basic kinds of matter...» And in the Wolfson «Festschrift», II, p. 722, speaking of William's definition of the elements, «Not only does it [read "he"?] invent the noun *elementatum* to express its essential distinctions, but... it displays a considerable philosophic talent».

[39] Lemay, pp. 74, 176 n. 4.

[40] «CCM», XIII (1970), pp. 170-171.

[41] Lemay, p. 13.

[42] Evidence in T. Gregory, *Anima Mundi*, p. 7 n. 5.

[43] *Dragmaticon*, ed. G. Gratarolus (repr. Frankfurt a. M., 1967), p. 210; cf. also A. Wilmart, *Analecta Reginensia*, Città del Vaticano, 1933, p. 264.

«Twenty years and more» is admittedly a round figure, but its literal meaning cannot well be *less* than twenty years. Thus when at the opening of the work William refers to the *Philosophia* as an *oeuvre de jeunesse*—

> libellus noster, qui philosophia inscribitur, quem in iuventute nostra imperfectum, utpote imperfecti, composuimus— [44]

even if the concept *iuventus* is generally quite flexible in the twelfth century, we must in this case, bearing in mind the other passage, associate the *Philosophia* with the beginnings of William's teaching career. A date c. 1125 would seem probable [45]; any date after 1130 would be implausible.

A closer examination of William's text, however, strongly suggests to me not only that his is the first attested instance of the term *elementatum*, but that he was perfectly conscious of having coined it himself. Tullio Gregory, who has shown admirably what is original in William's whole theory of the elements, has also pointed out how William was aware of his originality in this: as he makes his interlocutor say in the *Dragmaticon*, «nec in aliquo authore diligenter de illis scriptum invenitur» [46]. If we turn to the context where *elementatum* is first used in the *Philosophia*, the consciousness of innovation seems to me similarly unmistakable. While William takes a definition from Constantine of Africa as his point of departure, his development of the definition is very different from Constantine's [47]:

> Thus elements are simple, minimal particles; the four that we see [earth, water, air, fire] are composed of these particles. The elements themselves are never seen, but are understood through a rational process of division [i.e. through arriving by reasoning at particles that are not further reducible]...

> Someone will ask, where are the elements, then? We say, in the composition of the human body, and of other things, just as a letter exists in the composition of a syllable rather than in its own right...

> Since those simple and minimal particles are the elements, a particle that is cold and dry is earth, a cold and moist one, water, a hot and moist one, air, a hot and dry one, fire.

---

[44] *Dragmaticon*, p. 5.
[45] This is the date suggested by Southern, p. 79.
[46] *Dragmaticon*, p. 22 (cit. Gregory, *Anima Mundi*, p. 202).
[47] Cf. *Anima Mundi*, pp. 204 ff.

Thus, since the four things that are seen are composed of those particles, the one in which cold and dry particles predominate gets called «earth», in virtue of the name of the element; the one where cold and moist particles predominate gets called «water»; where hot and moist predominate, «air»; where hot and dry predominate, «fire».

If, therefore, we should like to impose fitting names, let us call the particles «elements», and the four things that we see, «elementated things». *Si ergo illis digna velimus imponere nomina, particulas predictas dicamus «elementa», ista quatuor que videntur, «elementata»* [48].

I find it hard to avoid the conclusion that an original term is here being coined to express an original conception.

What stimulated William to his distinction between *elementa* and *elementata*? Tullio Gregory, who has most perceptively discussed the intellectual background of William's theory of the elements, has not touched on this particular point. If, as I believe, William made his distinction too early to have been influenced here by the translation of Abū Ma'shar, I would suggest an inspiration nearer home — in a distinction that had been made by his teacher Bernard of Chartres.

John of Salisbury reports some verses written by Bernard:

Non dico esse quod est, gemina quod parte coactum

---

[48] *Philosophia Mundi*, I, 21. Since the passage as printed in Migne (both in *P.L.* 172, c. 49 and *P.L.* 90 cc. 1132-1133) contains errors that affect the sense, I give below a text based on the London ms. B. M. Add. 11676 (s. xiii) f 4 v, omitting the section-headings inserted in this and other mss. I have compared also B. M. Egerton 935 (s. xii) f 5 r, and B. M. Royal 9.A.XIV (s. xiii) f 259 r., in which the text is less satisfactory at several points (e.g. for *ratione divisionis* the Egerton has *ratione divinitatis*, the Royal *ratione diffinitionis*):

Elementa ergo sunt simple et minime particule, quibus hec quatuor constant que videmus; que elementa nunquam videntur, sed ratione divisionis intelliguntur...

Sed queret aliquis ubi sint elementa. Nos dicimus, in compositione humani corporis, et aliorum, sicut littera in compositione sillabe, etsi non per se...

Cum ergo ille simple et minime particule elementa sint, que est frigida et sicca est terra, que frigida et humida, aqua, que calida et humida, aer, que calida et sicca, ignis.

Cum igitur hec quatuor que videntur ex illis composita sint, illud in quo dominantur particule frigide et sicce, nomine illius elementi dicitur "terra"; in quo frigide et humide, "aqua"; in quo calide et humide, "aer"; in quo calide et sicce, "ignis".

Si ergo illis digna velimus imponere nomina, particulas predictas dicamus "elementa", ista quatuor que videntur, "elementata". [Maurach's text, ed. cit. pp. 27-28, omits the phrase about the component particles of air].

> materie formam continet implicitam;
> sed dico esse quod est, una quod constat earum;
> hoc vocat Idean, illud Acheus ilen.

John also traces the train of thought that had led Bernard to formulating these lines [49]. For Bernard it was important to distinguish between the ideas, which are the objects of the divine mind, and the forms (*formae nativae*), reflecting those ideas, which are compounded with matter in the process of creation. Only the ideas are eternal and truly immutable, only they, therefore, are truly «what is». William, it seems to me, wants to parallel Bernard's thought, extending it by analogy to the physical sphere. Where Bernard had said: men imagine that «what is» is what we see — the things compounded of matter and form — but the philosopher knows that «what is» is the pure idea; William says: so too men imagine that the elements are what we see — the earth, water, air and fire around us — but the *physicus* knows that an element is pure, irreducible, *cuius non sunt contrarie qualitates* [50]. He is aware that many philosophers also use

---

[49] *Metalogicon*, IV, 35 (ed. Webb, pp. 204-207). It seems to me that Southern underrates Bernard when he speaks of Bernard's «conservatism of outlook and aim»: «His teaching, so far as we can reconstruct it, kept strictly within the framework of the arts as they had been known in Europe since the tenth century» (p. 79). Garin has shown in an illuminating chapter *Su una tesi di Bernardo di Chartres* («Studi», pp. 50-53) the subtlety and sophistication that underlie Bernard's distinction between *ideae* and *formae nativae*, and also its fecundity; this distinction became vital in the thought of Gilbert de la Porrée, who developed its implications. So too, it seems to me, Bernard's other original distinctions, reported by John of Salisbury in the same chapter of the *Metalogicon*, are exceptionally profound and fruitful: the distinction between *coeternitas (solae tres personae)*, *eternitas (idea... manens in archano consilii, extrinseca causa non indigens)*, and «concreatio» (*quod de subiecta materia creat aut quod ei concreatur*), made possible, and provided a philosophical basis for, the whole poetic mythology of the creative process elaborated by Bernard Silvestris and Alan of Lille. *Coeternitas*, as in Bernard of Chartres, is the realm of the transcendent triune God; *eternitas*, that of Noys and the *ideae (exemplaria)*; *concreatio* that of Natura, Prudentia and the *formae nativae*, the «imagines exemplarium», as Bernard of Chartres had called them, and as the goddesses of Bernard's and Alan's poetry execute them.

[50] *P.L.* 172, c. 49 A [Maurach p. 26]. (B. M. Add. 11676, f 4 r; B. M. Egerton 935, f 4 v, reads *diverse*). Notwithstanding the fine work already done on William's thought by Gregory, Garin and Jeauneau, William's originality in other directions still needs further investigation. I have made some brief suggestions elsewhere («Studi medievali», 3ª serie, VI-1 [1965], especially pp. 410-413) about what is unusual in William's conception of the *anima mundi*. Another aspect of his thought that shows the radical, challenging qualities of his mind can be found in his theory of the funcions of *fabula*, as it emerges in the unpublished commentary on Macro-

elementum in its «everyday» sense, and does not censure this, provided men realise that they are not speaking *ut physicus, de naturis corporum* (*P.L.* 172, 50 [Maurach p. 29]).

The originality here, it seems to me, lies in William's perception that the analysis of the constituents of the empirical world involves a non-empiric «construct», arrived at *ratione divisionis*. Just as for William the *anima mundi* is a physical principle — the *naturalis vigor* in the empirical world — and at the same time a metaphysical construct, a divine first principle for what is created, so too in his treatment of the elements there is a conscious attempt to unite a «physical» discussion with an inquiry into the epistemological basis for such discussion, an inquiry that necessarily reaches beyond the physical.

In what does the originality of Thierry of Chartres's cosmological thought consist? Klibansky has given a brief but perceptive comment:

> Naïve as his account may seem to the modern scholar and scientist, this first systematic attempt to withdraw cosmology from the realm of the miraculous, and to win for physical theory a relative independence from theology, gives Thierry an outstanding place among philosophers [51].

I should like to make some fresh detailed observations of Thierry's

bius (*in Somn.* I, 2-3). Overtly an exposition of Macrobius' thought, it goes far beyond Macrobius (and the entire Platonic tradition) in the ways in which it defends fable and mythopoeic fiction. Thus, for instance, where Macrobius (I 2, 11) allows philosophers only that «genus figmenti» which is chaste in matter and words, and reveals «sacrarum rerum notio sub pio figmentorum velamine», rejecting, like Plato before him (*Republic*, 377-378), the kind of fable which «per turpia et indigna numinibus ac monstro similia componitur, ut di adulteri», William reverses this decision in his discussion of the passage: «*ut di adulteri*: hec verba sunt turpia, sed tamen per illud adulterium aliquod honestum et pulcrum revera habet significari, utpote de adulterio Iovis legitur cum Cybele, et huiusmodi aliis que in loco suo exponentur» (Vat. Urb. lat. 1140, fol. 10 r.).

It is an «apologie for poetrie», a challenge undermining the Macrobian-Platonic position from within. [Cf. P. Dronke, *Fabula*, Leiden-Köln, 1974, Ch. I].

[51] *Art. cit.* p. 8. I am not wholly happy, however, when Klibansky, seeking to show Thierry's originality, stresses his reference «to experiments which everybody could perform and test» (*loc. cit.*). Thierry's homely examples of vaporization (*sicut in fumo caldarii apparet, Expositio* 7, and more fully in 9) seem to me to have a literary source: they are a picturesque rephrasing of Cicero's account of vaporization in *De Natura Deorum* II 27 (cf. particularly *quam similitudinem cernere possumus in iis aquis quae effervescunt subditis ignibus*).

approach in his *Expositio in Hexameron*, to confirm and develop this appraisal.

Thierry accepts the notion that God created matter — that is, the four elements — in the first moment of time [52]. But this is the only premise that he shares with traditional theological accounts of creation. From that first moment onwards, in his view, everything evolved by physical laws, *secundum physicam*, without any suggestion of a divine intervention. *Consequebatur naturaliter... ordo naturalis exigebat... contingebat naturaliter...* — these refrain-like phrases are the guiding principle for his account of the emergence of sky, earth, sea and stars.

What of the emergence of life? —

> When the stars had been created and were moving in the firmament, the heat that resulted from their motion increased and, proceeding to a vital heat, first rested on the waters, that is, on the element higher than earth, and through this the living creatures of the water and the birds were created. And the space [of time] of this fifth turning [of the fire above the air] was called «the fifth day».

> But by way of moisture [from the water] that vital heat naturally reached land, and through this the living creatures of the earth were created, in whose number man was made to the image and likeness of God [53].

---

[52] *Expositio* (ed. N. M. Häring, «AHDLMA», XXII [1955], pp. 184-200), sects. 3 and 5: «Nam cum dicit: *In principio creavit Deus caelum et terram*, ostendit efficientem causam, scilicet Deum. Ostendit etiam materialem, scilicet quattuor elementa, quae nomine "caeli et terrae" appellat...

«*In principio* igitur *creavit Deus caelum et terram*, i. e. materiam in primo momento temporum creavit».

Despite this latter sentence, Thierry soon afterwards quotes with approval the «fuit deus et hyle» passage from *Asclepius*, 14 (Häring, p. 193).

[53] *Expositio* 14: «Stellis autem creatis et motum in firmamento facientibus, ex earum motu calor adauctus et ad vitalem usque calorem procedens aquis primo incubuit, elemento videlicet terra superiori. Et inde animalia aquae et volatilia creata sunt. Et spatium huius quintae conversionis "quinta dies" appellatum est.

«Mediante vero humore, vitalis ille calor naturaliter usque ad terrena pervenit et inde animalia terrae creata sunt, in quorum numero homo ad imaginem et similitudinem Dei factus est».

Häring (p. 189) puts a full stop, not a comma, after *creata sunt*. But this is syntactically faulty — the clause beginning *in quorum numero* is a subordinate clause — and also gives a misleading impression of separateness to the statement about man.

It is interesting to observe that Thierry's disciple Clarenbaldus must have perceived the originality of his master's thought here, and that to him it must have

Two things are striking about this passage: there was no separate creation of animate beings; rather, the animate evolved *naturaliter* from the inanimate, the physical heat, intensifying, proceeded to a *calor vitalis* [54]. Second, there is no essential differentiation here between the emergence of animals and men: though the scriptural notion of man as made in God's image and likeness is retained, man, like all the other *animalia terrae*, emerges through the passing of the *vitalis calor* from water to earth — that is, through a natural process.

Thus I cannot agree with Häring's comment on this passage (*ed. cit.* p. 156):

> He says nothing about the creation of the soul, though we may assume that he shared the Augustinian view of the pre-existence of souls, a theory derived from the premise that God created all things simultaneously.

As Thierry's whole treatise constitutes a rejection of this premise, he cannot very well have shared the Augustinian view of the pre-existence of souls. On the contrary, the passage I have cited compels us to assume that he saw the soul as a *physicus* or *medicus* would have to see it — as a function and product of the *vitalis calor.* Did Thierry ever confront the problem — crucial to a thinker like Avicenna, who was both scientist and mystic — how such a physical conception of the soul was compatible with the religious notion of a separate, immortal soul? Would he have attempted to reconcile these by seeing the *anima mundi* as a kind of immortal sustainer of human souls? We cannot be certain. But the independence of Thierry's stance in this passage is evident.

A moment later Thierry, having completed his account of the process of evolution, hints at an even more radical conception of this process. Where previously he had spoken of God as the efficient cause of the world — *si quis igitur subtiliter consideret mundi fabricam,*

---

seemed over-daring and dangerous. For Clarenbaldus in his «appendix» to the *Expositio* deliberately rephrases this passage so as to restore the more conventional disjunction (ed. Häring, p. 215, italics mine): «calore incumbente terrae, terra produxit herbas et arbores et sua animalia, *et homo creatus est et in paradiso positus*».

[54] Thierry derives his concept of the *calor vitalis* from Cicero, *De Natura Deorum*, II, 23 ff. (esp. 27 *ad fin.*). I am indebted to Dr. Michael Lapidge for pointing this out to me, as well as for other valuable suggestions. For Cicero, however (or for his speaker, the Stoic Balbus), this *calor vitalis* is a principle of growth and nourishment that sustains the world around us, not a creative principle that brought about the primordial world. Thierry's originality, I believe, lies in transferring the Stoic concept from the sphere of physics to that of cosmogony.

efficientem ipsius causam Deum cognoscet — [55] now this role of efficient cause is virtually (*quasi*) transferred to one of the elements:

> Fire is entirely active, earth entirely passive... Therefore fire is as it were the artificer and efficient cause, and earth is subject to it, as it were the material cause [56].

This comes remarkably close to a completely «materialistic» explanation of creation. If a particular physical force is the «efficient cause», then God as efficient cause virtually disappears from the picture. At most he remains «une chiquenaude, pour mettre le monde en mouvement», as Pascal was to reproach Descartes.

Yet Thierry's conception is not quite materialistic: for we must reckon with the continuous active shaping power — *virtus artifex operatrix* — within the universe; and for Thierry this shaping power is divine:

> The philosophers have called this power diverse names. Mercury, in the book entitled *Trismegistus* [i.e. *Asclepius*], calls this power «spirit» in these words: «There was God and Hyle — which is what in Greek we call the material world. And the spirit was with the world, or inhered in the world» ... Plato in his *Timaeus* calls that same spirit «world-soul». Virgil speaks of that spirit thus: «From the beginning oceans and lands, the deep heaven, the lucent ball of the moon and the stars of the firmament, are sustained by the spirit within». The Hebrews indeed speak of the operative spirit in this way: Moses speaks thus: «The spirit of God was borne over the waters»; David thus: «By the word of God the heavens were established»; Solomon, too, speaks of that spirit thus: «The spirit of God filled the universe». And the Christians call that same being «holy spirit» [57].

---

[55] *Expositio* 2 (Häring, p. 185).

[56] *Expositio* 17 (Häring, p. 189): «Nam ignis tantum agit. Terra vero tantum patitur... Ita igitur ignis est quasi artifex et efficiens causa; terra vero subiecta quasi materialis causa».

On the Hermetic and Stoic background of the *ignis artifex*, and the diffusion of the concept in the twelfth century, see Tullio Gregory, *L'idea di natura*, pp. 44-45, where the influence of the *De Natura Deorum* is briefly indicated. It is interesting to note in this connection that two of the earliest MSS of the *De Natura Deorum* would most probably have been accessible to Thierry's friend Bernard Silvestris at Tours (cf. C. H. Beeson, *Class. Philol.*, XL [1945], pp. 219-220; *De Natura Deorum*, ed. A. S. Pease, Cambridge Mass., 1955, I, p. 64).

[57] *Expositio* 25-27 (Häring, p. 193). I have translated Thierry's paraphrase of the Virgilian lines, not the text of *Aen.* VI, 724-726.

Clearly Thierry was not the first to make such identifications. But others had made them more cautiously, hedging them with qualifications, seeing them as approximative likenesses rather than as identities. What is distinctive in Thierry's lines is the unreserved, exultant tone, his dramatic sense of «standing on the shoulders of the giants» [58]. This syncretism has its own particular spirit: the wholehearted acceptance of moments in pagan thought, because of a deep conviction that they were pointing, by the same images, to the same realities as the Jewish and Christian traditions. Here the enormous reverence for antiquity, and the exhilarating sense that it is not distant but contemporary, are inseparable.

The contemporaneity is emphasised by the choice of verbs: while the topic is introduced by a perfect (*appellaverunt*), during the calling of witnesses it is the present tense that makes all the links, being used throughout: not «they spoke», but «they speak». Such summoning of witnesses, biblical and pagan, may suggest an analogy with the various versions, homiletic and dramatic, of the *Ordo Prophetarum* [59]. I would think it almost certain that Thierry, like any *clerc* in twelfth century France, would have met with the *Ordo* in one form or another. But the analogy makes the differences seem the more astonishing: in the *Ordo* the biblical witnesses (at least ten, and once as many as twenty-five), always vastly outnumber the pagan ones (three), and always precede them in being called. Here there are three *philosophi* (Hermes, Plato, Virgil), and three *Hebraei* (Moses, David, Solomon) — and the *philosophi* take precedence. (Thus, in the mosaic of the Duomo at Siena three centuries later, it is Hermes Trismegistus who hands to Moses the tables of the law). *

The particular fervour in Thierry's exposition, the sense that a divine presence has imbued the thought even of a remote period with profound truth, surely owes something to the *montage* of the *Asclepius* itself:

> Hammone etiam adytum ingresso sanctoque illo quattuor virorum religione et divina dei completo praesentia, conpetenti venerabiliter silentio ex ore Hermu animis singulorum mentibusque pendentibus, divinus Cupido sic est orsus dicere... [60]

---

[58] On the range of connotations of this famous phrase, cf. E. Jeauneau, *Nani gigantum humeris insidentes*, «Vivarium», V (1967), pp. 79-99.

[59] See Karl Young, *The Drama of the Medieval Church*, Oxford, 1933, II, pp. 125-171, for the various texts of the *Ordo* and the history of their diffusion.

[60] *Asclepius* 1 (ed. A. D. Nock and A. J. Festugière, *Corpus Hermeticum*, 2nd ed. Paris, 1960, II, p. 297).

* [This interpretation of the mosaic — possible though by no means certain — is discussed further in *Hermes and the Sibyls* (*infra*, no. 8)].

It is divine love that speaks the discourse through Hermes' lips; so too we might say for Thierry, it is the one «holy spirit» that inspires the utterances of his *philosophi* and his *Hebraei*. For Thierry the *Asclepius* was no mere source for quotations; we can recognise that he had been moved by its tone and imaginative scope.

Paradoxically, Thierry's most original gesture may well lie in having chosen to present his cosmology in the most conventional form available to him: the treatise, as the title in one manuscript gives it, is an «Expositio in Hexameron», a commentary on the first chapter of Genesis. Many of Thierry's contemporaries were convinced that the opening of Genesis, read literally, invalidated any attempt at a scientific explanation of creation: creation was a miracle of God's goodness, unaccountable and inaccessible to human reasoning. The divine narrative revealed to Moses is binding, and sets the concepts of philosophers at naught. Thus for instance, in an unpublished poem, the *Flosculus* of Rahewin of Freising, written between 1133 and 1140 [61].

> *Quod unum est principium, non plura.*
> Quorumdam opinio coeterna tria
> Exstitisse, pariter putant principía:
> Hec sunt deus opifex, forma, matería.
> At tu ne incesseris caveas hac via!
>
> *Quod quidam dicebant mundum eternum.*
> Fuerunt et alii deo derogantes,
> Auctorem hunc omnium esse denegantes,
> Mundum eternaliter fuisse putantes
> Et sempiternaliter futurum firmantes.
>
> *Quod deus non tam factor quam creator.*
> Hos utrosque reprobat noster legislator,
> Dicens, in principio deus dominator
> Celum, terram condidit — non ut propagator
> Nec solummodo factor, sed vere creator.
>
> *Quod ex nichilo cuncta, non de preiacente materia.*
> Non yles preiacuit in formas vocanda,
> Nec ydea prefuit ad exemplar danda:
> Ab eterno conditor cognovit creanda
> Que, de quo, vel qualia forent suscitanda.
>
> *Secundum quam rationem dicuntur de deo huiusmodi agere, facere.*

---

[61] On Rahewin, see M. Manitius, *op. cit.* III, pp. 388-392. The dating of the poem is secured by the dedication to Hartmann, provost of Klosterneuburg: cf. W. Wattenbach, «Sitzb. d. bayer. Akad.», III (1873), p. 687.

At hec verba, facere, agere, creare,
Nullo motu faciunt deum laborare,
Nec actus hunc poterit plus exagitare
Quam solem qui operans nescit se mutare.

Eius erit facere nil quam voluisse
Ut res nove fierent, idque decrevisse
Non nisi gratuita sua bonitate,
Nulla indigentia seu necessitate [62].

So too the Cistercian Arnald of Bonneval wrote:

> Nihil apud deum confusum, nihil informe in illa antiquitate fuit, quia rerum materia, ubi facta est, statim in congruas sibi species est formata. Quidquid de mundi aeternitate, quidquid de hyle, vel ideis, vel de illa mundi anima, quam noym dicunt, sensere philosophi, plura inducentes principia, primum Geneseos capitulum abolet et confundit, unum praefigens omnis creaturae principium, scilicet deum... Omnium igitur quae sunt sola causa est bonitas, non necessitas...
>
> Inconveniens omnino et nimis absurdum est credere globum mundi informem et artificem simul ab aeterno fuisse... Aperta est ianua, et egressa est de illa antiqua arca testamenti multitudo innumerabilis visibilium et invisibilium... Circa illam ineffabilem et immensurabilem magnitudinem vane cogitat homo loca vel tempora, omnino minor est autore universitas [63].

Thierry's position is not identical with those attacked by Rahewin and Arnald, whose allusions to the cosmological speculations of their contemporaries in any case have the caricaturing crudity of polemic. Thierry did not teach the eternity of matter or form (though he also, as we saw, adopts a passage from the *Asclepius* — *fuit deus et hyle...* — that clearly implies it). Moreover, Thierry acknowledges God's goodness as his motive for creating: *oportet ut ea, quae creat, ex sola benignitate et caritate creet* [64]. Yet is there not something playful and ironic in the use of *oportet* precisely in this context? In any case, a moment later, Thierry continues: *oportuit aliquid inordinatum praecedere* [65] — at the threshold of the scientific exposition, that is, the notion of necessity is introduced.

Where Rahewin and Arnald see the first chapter of Genesis as

---

[62] München, Clm 19488 (s. xii ex.) p. 104. The complete poem, entitled *Flosculus* in the MS, is on pp. 95-110.
[63] *P.L.* 189, cc. 1515-1516.
[64] *Expositio* 2 (Häring, p. 184).
[65] *Ibid.* (Häring, p. 185).

confuting independent cosmological speculation, Thierry presents his speculations as the literal reading of the sacred text:

> primam Geneseos partem secundum physicam et ad litteram ego expositurus ...ad sensum litterae historialem exponendum veniam... [66]

Only a scientist's interpretation of Genesis, he is saying, can be a truly literal one. Was this said ironically? Or to guard against hostile criticism? Or out of full conviction? Perhaps these alternatives are not exclusive. At all events Thierry was conscious of his paradox, and saw that his gesture of conformity was the safeguard of his astonishing independence.

IV

These notes on William and Thierry can give only the barest indication of the kinds of challenge that the writings of the school of Chartres still set medievalists. There is a considerable range of still unpublished and scarcely studied works that reflect something of the «Chartrain spirit» — for instance, those briefly signalled by Grabmann in 1935, in his «Handschriftliche Forschungen und Mitteilungen zum Schrifttum des Wilhelm von Conches und zu Bearbeitungen seiner naturwissenschaftlichen Werke» [67]. Others, again, are published, but have not yet been provided with a satisfying historical or literary context — for instance, the De Mundi Constitutione *, printed in Migne among the works of Bede, the De Septem Septenis, which Migne prints as a work of John of Salisbury, or the difficult and mysterious De Causis Primis et Secundis that I mentioned earlier. Detailed attention so far has been given chiefly to works composed before 1150; but a comprehensive survey will one day pursue the Chartrain writings right into the thirteenth century — where indeed the greater part of the manuscript evidence lies.

On the sources available to the Chartrain thinkers, much valuable work has been done. Yet in the last resort it is not wholly possible to characterise or assess the contributions of these men in terms of the sources that they knew. This will almost inevitably lead to underrating their achievements [68]. For a truly penetrating insight into

---

[66] Expositio 1 (Häring, p. 184).

[67] «Sitzb. d. bayer. Akad.» (1935), Heft 10.

* [Pseudo-Bede, ed. and tr. C. Burnett (Warburg Institute Surveys and Texts X), London, 1985].

[68] It is significant that in a standard work such as Etienne Gilson's History of

the Chartrain thinkers, one that will do justice to their intellectual stature, the historian of thought must strive to bring to bear on their writings the approach of an exacting literary criticism. He must ask, what imaginative response did the twelfth century writers make to the materials at their disposal? What did the *Timaeus* or the *Asclepius*, Galen or Ptolemy, mean to them? Where did they adopt their materials uncritically, and where and how and why did they transform them? He must trace the subtle ways in which transformation gives rise to fresh creative insights. Some of the finest recent scholarship has broached questions of just this kind. I believe it is along these lines that we shall arrive at a satisfying picture of the school of Chartres.

Postscript

In the two decades since this essay was published, the careers of the masters associated with Chartres, as well as the nature and extent of their originality, have been much discussed. On the question of who taught at Chartres, see especially E. Jeauneau's Introduction to his collected essays, *Lectio Philosophorum. Recherches sur l'École de Chartres*, Amsterdam, 1973, pp. xi-xvi; R. Giacone, *Masters, Books and Library at Chartres*, «Vivarium», XII (1974), pp. 30-51; N.[M.] Häring, *Chartres and Paris Revisited*, in *Essays in Honour of Anton Charles Pegis*, ed. J.R. O'Donnell, Toronto, 1974, pp. 268-329; R.W. Southern, *The Schools of Paris and the School of Chartres*, in *Renaissance and Renewal in the Twelfth Century*, ed. R.L. Benson and G. Constable, Cambridge Mass., 1982, pp. 113-137; O. Weijers, *The Chronology of John of Salisbury's Studies in France*, in *The World of John of Salisbury*, ed. M. Wilks, Oxford, 1984, pp. 109-116; K.S.B. Keats-Rohan, *The Chronology of John of Salisbury's Studies in France*, «Studi medievali», 3ª serie, XXVIII (1987), pp. 193-203; K.M. Fredborg (ed.), *The Latin Rhetorical Commentaries by Thierry of Chartres*, Toronto, 1988, pp. 1-30.

For diverse perspectives on the originality of the Chartrain thinkers, see especially P. Dronke, *Fabula. Explorations into the Uses of Myth in Medieval Platonism*, Leiden-Köln, 1974; R.W. Southern, *Platonism, Scholastic Method and the School of Chartres*, Reading, 1979; E. Maccagnolo, *Il divino e il megacosmo. Testi filosofici e scientifici della scuola di Chartres*, Milano, 1980; P. Dronke (ed.), *A History of Twelfth-Century Western Philosophy*, Cambridge, 1988: in particular the Introduction (pp. 1-18), the panorama offered by W. Wetherbee (pp. 21-53), D. Elford's chapter on William of Conches (pp. 308-327), J. Marenbon's on Gilbert of Poitiers [Gilbert de la Porrée] and the Porretani (pp. 328-357), and the editor's on Thierry of Chartres (pp. 328-357). The bibliographical sections of the volume (pp. 443-486) give a range of further references to recent editions and studies.

Christian Philosophy in the Middle Ages (English ed., London, 1955), «Platonism in the Twelfth Century» is given 14 pages (pp. 139-153), while thirteenth century scholasticism is given 181 (pp. 246-427).

2

BERNARD SILVESTRIS, NATURA, AND PERSONIFICATION *

What kind of reality do the principal allegorical personages in the *Cosmographia* of Bernard Silvestris have? In particular, the figure whom scholars call "the goddess Natura": how far is she a believable, and believed in, being, rather than a rhetorically personified abstraction? What is it that makes Natura (or her mother, Noys) different from such personifications as the Virtues and Vices in Prudentius' *Psychomachia*? And there is a palpable difference, at least in this: the behaviour of antagonists such as Pudicitia and Libido, or Pax and Discordia, follows clearly from the concepts which they embody; the thoughts and actions of Bernard's Natura and her kindred, by contrast, can be mysterious and surprising — they are not conceptually predictable.

It was the great merit of Ernst Robert Curtius to recognize, in the case of Natura, that more could be involved than a rhetorical stratagem:

> Natura is a cosmic power... She is one of the last religious experiences of the late-pagan world. She possesses an inexhaustible vitality... (Her) power over men's souls is proved by the Christian polemic against her [1].

In the twelfth century, Curtius suggests, St. Bernard's notion of Mary the Mother of God as mediatrix, who intervenes actively in the divinely ordered cosmic drama, is comparable to Bernard Silvestris' figure, *Natura plangens*: both are projections of a specific "archetype of the unconscious", that Jung called Anima — a feminine potentiality within the godhead: "The human imagination is bound by this motif, and is strongly prompted in all periods and places to project it time and again" [2].

---

* *Journal of the Warburg and Courtauld Institutes* XLIII (1980) 16-31.
[1] *European Literature and the Latin Middle Ages* (tr. W. R. Trask), London 1953, pp. 106-7.
[2] *Zeitschrift für romanische Philologie*, lviii, 1938, p. 196 (citing Jung).

"The pagan Natura", says Curtius, "never entirely vanishes from consciousness" [3]. This has led a number of later scholars, such as Economou, to speak of "the tradition of the goddess Natura", "a tradition stretching from Claudian in the fourth century to Chaucer in the fourteenth and beyond" [4]. Clearly Curtius, like Economou, was aware of differences of context — aware that Natura may be no more than a rhetorical commonplace or *façon de parler* in one instance while she may be a vividly imagined goddess in another — yet the very concept of a *tradition* of the goddess Natura seems to me questionable, at least for late antique and medieval Europe. Here it is important to draw a number of distinctions, to relate certain phenomena and to isolate others — to observe discontinuities as well as continuities.

First — to put the matter in terms that may sound dramatic or provocative, but are intended as sober fact — I know of no evidence of a *goddess* Natura (as against a personified Natura) in the Latin world before the twelfth century. In the Greek there are testimonies that Physis was invoked as a goddess — in a number of magical papyri, and above all in the so-called Orphic hymn to Physis [5]. This is one of a group of eighty-seven hymns composed, according to the latest scholarship, "not earlier than the second century A.D., for the use of a cult community probably in Asia Minor" [6]. That this hymn to Physis was meant to be used in ritual worship, and was not simply a metaphysical or poetic effusion (as we might suppose, for instance, with the hymns of the neoplatonist Proclus), is indicated even by the prescription over it, that when the hymn is performed the incense-offering should be aromatic spices (θυμίαμα ἀρώματα). Yet neither this Greek hymn nor anything comparable was transmitted to the Latin Middle Ages. The Orphic hymns were first translated into Latin by the young Marsilio Ficino, who did not dare publish them, he wrote, lest he "seem to call readers back to the old cult of gods and *daemones*" [7].

By contrast, it seems to me, everything we have in Latin in late antiquity concerning Natura shows itself unmistakably as involving

---

[3] *European Literature* (*cit.* n. 1), p. 108.

[4] G. D. Economou, *The Goddess Natura in Medieval Literature*, (Cambridge, Mass. 1972), pp. vii, 2.

[5] K. Preisendanz, *Papyri Graecae Magicae* I, Stuttgart ² 1973, i, 310 (ὁρκίζω Φύσιν αὐτοφυῆ); iv, 2833, 2917 (Φύσι παμμήτωρ); G. Quandt (ed.), *Orphei Hymni*, Berlin 1955, 10 (pp. 10-12).

[6] Thus K. Ziegler, in *Der Kleine Pauly*, iv, Munich 1975, col. 357.

[7] "Ne forte lectores ad priscum deorum daemonumque cultum... revocare viderer" (*Epist.* xi, *cit.* G. Faggin, *Inni Orfici*, Florence 1949, p. 22).

either a conscious technique of personification, or else a philosophical concept of *natura* (better written without a capital). This is why, in the Latin material, Curtius' hypostatizations tend to be misleading. To illustrate: Claudian, in his poem *Phoenix*, has the following verses (59-64):

> Fervet odoratus telis caelestibus agger,
> Consumitque senem: nitidos stupefacta iuvencos
> Luna premit, pigrosque polus non concitat axes.
> Parturiente rogo, cunis Natura laborat,
> Aeternam ne perdat avem, flammasque fideles
> Admonet, ut rerum decus immortale remittant.

> [The aromatic mound is set ablaze by heavenly shafts
> and consumes the ancient Phoenix; Luna, stupefied,
> holds back her shining bullocks; heaven does not urge on the sluggish poles.
> As the pyre gives birth, Natura works at the nest,
> lest she lose the immortal bird: she bids the loyal flames
> to deliver that deathless glory of the world.]

On the basis of nothing more than these lines, Curtius, listing the various functions of the goddess Natura in late antiquity, distinguishes one that he calls *Natura de Phoenicis avis immortalitate laborans* [8]. I do not think such a passage warrants the inference that the poet really thought of Natura as a goddess, or imagined reviving the Phoenix to be one of that goddess's powers. The rhetorical texture here shows that not only Natura but much else is being personified: the stupefied Luna is on the same level of rhetoric as the toiling Natura; to some extent even the heaven that does not urge its poles, the funeral-pyre that gives birth, and the loyal flames, are poetically similar to the moon and nature.

Again, Curtius, citing from Tiberianus' prayer to the *Omnipotens* —

> Tu genus omne deum, tu rerum causa vigorque,
> Tu Natura omnis, deus innumerabilis unus...

claims that a comparison of such lines with Bernard Silvestris shows "how near Bernard stands to late-antique paganism" [9]. But I cannot see that Curtius is even justified to print *Natura* with a capital here:

---

[8] *Zeitschrift* (cit. n. 2), p. 185.
[9] *Ibid.*, p. 190.

the lines are saying that the Almighty God comprises the entire race
of gods, the cause and force of things, and the whole of nature, while
still remaining one God, beyond number. This could indeed have
been interpreted pantheistically, yet there is no reason either why a
Christian should not have interpreted it sacramentally: in Hopkins'
words, "The world is charged with the grandeur of God".

Prudentius, according to Curtius [10], "reckons Natura among the
false deities overcome" by the Christian God. Yet again, in the passage adduced, Prudentius does not speak of a goddess Natura, nor
even of nature, but of *elementorum naturam:*

> Nil egit prohibendo vagas ne pristinus error
> Crederet esse deum nigrante sub aëre formas,
> Aut elementorum naturam, quae Patris ars est
> Omnigeni, summa pro maiestate sacraret...? [11]

> [Did he (Theodosius) accomplish nothing by forbidding old error to
> believe that shapes floating in the darkening air were forms of gods,
> or forbidding him to hallow the nature of the elements — which is
> the skill of the all-begetting Father — in place of the supreme
> majesty?]

If there is a personification in these lines, it is old Error, not Natura.

In general, when Latin Church Fathers attack those who make
a *dea* of *natura*, what they have in mind — the contexts show — is
not worshippers such as may have chanted the hymn to Physis and
offered her incense in Asia Minor: what they are combating, rather,
is a kind of materialistic outlook, that sees nature as a first principle,
because for the Fathers this first principle in the cosmos can be nothing but the Christian God. As Lactantius declares: *Deus ipsa natura
est* [12]. His words are strikingly close to those of the pagan Tiberianus
— but his meaning is, beyond any doubt, the sacramental one. I
know of no Fathers, at least in the Latin West, who attacked a pagan
religious manifestation of Natura, or who were even aware that she
could be (in Curtius' terms) a "religious experience".

Admittedly there is a passage in Claudian where Natura is
depicted ordering the ancient chaos, and another where she appears

---

[10] *Ibid.,* p. 184.

[11] *Contra Orationem Symmachi,* i, 10-13.

[12] *Divinae Institutiones,* ii, 8. Lactantius and Tiberianus have a common source
for this utterance in Seneca, *De beneficiis,* iv, 7. I am indebted to Charles Burnett
for the reference.

complaining before Jove [13], and these were known to Bernard Silvestris. So, too, Bernard will have remembered certain moments in Statius' *Thebaid* where nature is personified — as when she is reproached by her daughter, Pietas [14]. Yet to look more closely at such examples is to see that the difference between these poets and Bernard is profound. As Economou aptly notes: "If their Naturas are placed beside those of Bernard, Alan, Jean (de Meun), and Chaucer, they seem like shadows, vaguer and less detailed".

Curtius had written: "Natura in Claudian is far more than a poetic image or pallid personification: she is a mighty divine being" [15]. I would suggest, Claudian's Natura is not a pallid but a colourful personification — almost, we might say, a rococo fantasy — yet this does not make her, in any basic religious sense, a divine being. That is, Claudian would not have addressed a hymn to Natura, or conceived of her as a being who could or should be invoked in hymns. What is more, nowhere in Claudian's poetry do I have the sense of a divine or cosmic Natura in the way that is manifest in Bernard: quite simply, that such a being *matters* to Bernard, is integral to his view of the world.

As the entry *natura* in the *Novum Glossarium* can show, such expressions as *mater natura*, *natura opifex* and *natura creatrix* are not altogether rare in Latin writings from the ninth century onwards [16]. When the fascicule containing *physis* appears, a comparable range of examples will be found attested. The degree of imaginative life that such expressions had must be sensitively assessed for each occurrence. The variations in the spectrum from dead metaphor to vibrant imaginative reality can be enormous — just as there is a gulf, for instance, between our commonplace "Necessity is the mother of invention" and the awesome embodied Necessity ('Ανάγκη) of Aeschylus or Empedocles. But one thing seems clear: however expressively *natura* may feature in medieval Latin writings before Bernard Silvestris, there is no question of a fully-fledged "goddess Natura". The Physis of Greek magical texts and the Orphic hymn did not impinge

---

[13] *De raptu Proserpinae*, i, 248ff., iii, 33ff.

[14] *Thebais*, XI, 457-70. It is perhaps worth recalling that Bernard and his contemporaries will not have known Statius' *Silvae*, a work that both Curtius (*Zeitschrift*, *cit.* n. 2, p. 181) and Economou (*cit.* n. 4, pp. 43-44) discuss as if it had been part of the common medieval Latin inheritance. The *Silvae* were "rediscovered" by the humanists, especially Poggio and Poliziano; the earliest extant MS is *c.* 1430.

[15] Economou (*cit.* n. 4), p. 51; Curtius, *Zeitschrift* (*cit.* n. 2), p. 184.

[16] *Novum Glossarium Mediae Latinitatis*, fasc. "Mox-Nazaza", Copenhagen 1965, *esp.* cols. 1090-1.

on the Latin world before Ficino; thus the "tradition of the goddess Natura" in the Latin West is a modern scholarly myth. Plainly there are numerous contexts from Republican Rome to the twelfth century where a more or less fully personified *natura* occurs. Yet nowhere can we find the being who was created by Bernard Silvestris.

Here there is no tradition or continuity, but a poetic feat of great originality. Nowhere before Bernard, for instance, is Natura seen as "the blessed fecundity of the womb" of the goddess Noys [17]; nowhere previously had Natura been distinguished from Physis, whom Bernard presents as a more modest cosmic artisan. Nowhere before Bernard is Urania, who was known as the Muse of astronomy, transformed into a higher cosmic *creatrix* — Natura's empyrean double. Nor can I trace before Bernard his triad of nature-goddesses (Urania, Natura, Physis), creating man with three different instruments (mirror of providence, tablet of destiny, book of memory); nor do I know any Western account of creation in which the heavenly artificers meet with unexpected difficulties in their task, or even, like Physis, grumble at the task itself [18]. The whole conception of a feminine *trinitas creatrix*, a counterpart to the celestial Christian trinity, working at the fabrication of man in an earthly paradise, is unparalleled. So, too, are the complex relations Bernard depicts between this creating triad and the goddesses Noys and Silva (not to speak, for the moment, of the subsidiary characters or the *exsuperantissimus deus*).

None the less we may ask, what lay behind Bernard's imaginative feat, what might have impelled him towards it? Here I should like to venture some new suggestions. For there was at least one figure widely prevalent in the earlier Middle Ages who is not primarily a philosophical or theological concept, or a personification or allegory, but who is first and foremost a goddess. I am not thinking of the various embodiments of divine Wisdom as a feminine being, important as these are for understanding not only Bernard but a whole range of medieval allegoric poetry [19]. The Sophia-Sapientia of the Wisdom literature is essentially closer to Bernard's portrayal of

---

[17] *Cosmographia* (ed. P. Dronke), Leiden 1978, Megacosmus ii, 1: "Noys... 'Vere', inquit, 'et tu, Natura, uteri mei beata fecunditas...'".

[18] *Ibid.*, Microcosmus xii, 7ff.: "Sed Physis, nil questa palam, taciturna moleste/Murmura mentis habet...".

[19] See especially the perceptive studies of M.-Th. d'Alverny: "Le symbolisme de la Sagesse et le Christ de Saint Dunstan", *Bodleian Library Record*, v, 1956, pp. 232-44; "La Sagesse et ses sept filles", *Mélanges Félix Grat*, i, Paris, 1946, pp. 245-78; "Notes sur Dante et la Sagesse", *Revue des Etudes Italiennes*, n.s., xi, 1965, pp. 5-24.

Noys than Natura: Sapientia, unlike Natura, never has to plead with God, she is wholly at one with him, his untarnished mirror. But when in early medieval thought Sapientia becomes identified with the Logos, or with Wisdom the mother of the seven Liberal Arts, the sense of a cosmic *goddess* quite disappears. Nor, again, has the Boethian Philosophia the functions of a *creatrix*. Only once, perhaps, before the *Cosmographia*, is Boethius' womanly embodiment of philosophy given an imaginative, dramatic aliveness comparable with that of the heroines in Bernard's poem. This is in the eleventh-century Provençal poetic fragment *Boecis* [20]. There, too, there are hints of her divine power — yet she is *revelatrix* rather than *creatrix*: her function is not the shaping of the universe but the loving illumination of her devotee, Boethius.

The one figure who was invoked as goddess in Roman antiquity and continued to be invoked and represented as goddess well into the thirteenth century was not known by the philosophical name Natura, but by that of Earth: Terra, Tellus, Gaia. Here too there were many possibilities: there could be a more or less far-reaching symbiosis of the cult of Terra with Christian cult; again, the goddess could become a personification, vivid or conventionalized, among writers and artists in the learned world. Yet there can be no doubt that Terra, unlike Natura, at least in the Latin West, began life as a goddess, not a personification, and that this was never wholly forgotten.

Thus it is legitimate to speak of a *tradition* of the goddess Terra. The best known examples of this tradition are the widely diffused pair of incantations known as the *Precatio Terrae Matris* and *Invocatio omnium herbarum* [21]. In their volume of the *Corpus Medicorum Latinorum*, Howald and Sigerist listed 27 of the β group of manuscripts, "per totum orbem terrarum paene innumerabiles", and 8 of the γ group; in both groups the two prayers were added to a collection of medical writings, at least from the sixth century onwards [22]. Art historians are agreed that the picture of Tellus, being reverently approached by the author of the incantations, pseudo-Musa, as we find it e.g. in the early thirteenth-century Italian

---

[20] The best edition is that of R. Lavaud and G. Machicot, *Boecis*, Toulouse 1950. See *esp.* the *laisses* xxiii-xxvii (*ed. cit.*, pp. 24-26).

[21] The most recent edition (with many reconstructions) is in G. B. Pighi, *La poesia religiosa romana*, Bologna 1958, pp. 208-10; cf. also M. J. Vermaseren and C. C. Van Essen, *The Excavations in the Mithraeum of the Church of Santa Prisca in Rome*, Leiden 1965, pp. 187-92. Below, in the last line of the second prayer, I translate the MS reading *quae* (Pighi *qui*).

[22] *Corpus Medicorum Latinorum*, iv, Leipzig-Berlin 1927, pp. x-xvii.

manuscript Vienna 93, fol. 33 (Figure 1), is a faithful copy of a late-antique original [23]. The cornucopia in Tellus' right hand, the snake on which she perches, the trees and plants around her, and the water in the foreground, with its god and aquatic monster, all serve to bring out, as in the prayer, that Tellus is "the parent of the nature of the universe", she who "generates and regenerates all things". She alone can preserve, balance, and give life to all. She is the source of order and change in the cosmos, day and night, calm and storm. She "clothes the shades of Dis and measureless Chaos". She nurtures the human race, with perpetual loyalty, and men find refuge in her as the soul departs. She is the Magna Mater of gods and men [24]. The suppliant goes on to implore her to give healing power to the herbs he is about to use. The companion prayer is addressed to the herbs themselves: they, whom Mother Earth has generated (*quas Tellus parens/Generavit*), must be mindful of their divine origin. She who created them has allowed them to be used by men, "in the name of her who bade you to be born".

In the same groups of manuscripts as contain these prayers diverse practical recipes are added in which Earth is likewise summoned: when wild cucumber is gathered, for help against gout, the prayer is directed to Hygia, goddess of health and "supreme nurse of

---

[23] *Reallexikon zur deutschen Kunstgeschichte*, v, Stuttgart 1967, "Erde", cols. 997-1104 (by Karl-August Wirth); see *esp.* cols. 1028-9; cf. also G. Swarzenski, "Mittelalterliche Kopien einer antiken medizinischen Bilderhandschrift", *Jahrbuch des Deutschen Archäologischen Instituts*, xvii, 1902, pp. 45-53.

[24] Dea sancta Tellus, rerum naturae parens,
    Quae cuncta generas et regeneras in dies
    Quod sola praestas *tuam* tutelam gentibus
    Caeli ac maris diva arbitra rerumque omnium,
    Per quam silet natura et somnos capit,
    Itemque lucem reparas et noctem fugas;
    Tu Ditis umbras tegis et inmensum chaos
    Ventosque et imbres tempestive contines
    Et cum libet dimittis et misces freta
    Fugasque solem et procellas concitas,
    Itemque, cum vis, hilarem promittis diem.
    Alimenta vitae tribuis perpetua fide
    Et, cum recesserit anima, in te refugimus:
    Ita quicquid tribuis, in te cuncta recidunt.
    Merito vocaris Magna tu Mater deum,
    Pietate quia vicisti divum numina.
    Tu illa vere gentium et divum parens,
    Sine qua nil maturatur nec nasci potest;
    Tu es magna, tuque divum regina *ac* dea.

                                           (Ed. G. B. Pighi, 1-19)

Fig. 1. Pseudo-Musa praying to Tellus.
Vienna, Österreichische Nationalbibliothek, MS 93, fol. 33

Fig. 2. Tellus and Ecclesia. Montecassino Exultet Roll.
London, B.L., MS Add. 30337, images 4 and 5

Fig. 3. The Eriugenian cosmos. Honorius, *Clavis Physicae*.
Paris, B.N., MS lat. 6734, fol. 3v

Fig. 4. Natura suckling Sciencia.
English enamel casket, 1190/1200. London, V. and A.

dragons", yet she is "adjured in the name of Mother Earth": "Ygia, summa nutrix draconum, per matrem Terram te adiuro..." The herb basil (*ocimum*) is asked to heal "per summam divinitatem, quae te iussit nasci", and when *basilisca*, a herb that cures serpent-bites, is plucked, one must pray "Domina sancta Tellus, et cetera" — the reference appears to be to the *Precatio Terrae Matris* [25].

The functions ascribed to Terra in these pieces are distributed differently in Bernard: in the *Cosmographia*, herbs are the special concern of Physis, not Natura [26], and it is Noys as much as Natura who clothes the measureless chaos with form. I am not suggesting that the *Precatio* or any similar incantation was a specific source for Bernard, but that, while it has been customary to speak of *Das Fortleben der antiken Götter im mittelalterlichen Humanismus* (the title of Bezold's monograph in 1922), this less intellectual, magical-religious aspect of their survival is one that has been largely — and unjustly — ignored. It should perhaps be stressed that when prayers to effect healing were copied in the eleventh and twelfth centuries, it cannot have been for folkloristic or antiquarian reasons: the copyists were not compiling a Bächtold-Stäubli. The texts remained influential because they were still close enough to certain modes of thought of the time to remain usable. The goddess Terra continued to be invoked with practical intent — as we can see from such works as the *Incantamenta* collected by Richard Heim, or from Marie-Thérèse d'Alverny's fine sketch "La survivance de la magie antique" [27]. D'Alverny published for the first time an invocation to help against shooting-pains, from the flyleaf of a twelfth-century manuscript from Moissac: it begins "In nomine Domini", and after dwelling on Christ and calling upon the Trinity and the evangelists, it concludes:

Terra Mater, que creasti   (qui creatis MS)
herbas cum floribus,
suscipe dolores [28].

---

[25] *Corpus Medicorum Latinorum*, iv, pp. 295, 298.

[26] *Cosmographia*, Microcosmus ix, 7. Tellus is personified only three times, somewhat fleetingly, in the *Cosmographia* (Megacosmus iv, 2; Microcosmus ii, 17-18, viii, 21), but more extensively in the *De mundi philosophia* (*c.* 1150) of Milo, who was probably a disciple of Bernard's: see the text and discussion in my book *Fabula*, Leiden-Cologne 1974, pp. 88-94, 160-1. [Milo's poem has now been edited in full by R. A. Pack, *Proceedings of the American Philosophical Society*, cxxvi, 2, 1982, pp. 155-82].

[27] R. Heim (ed.), *Incantamenta Magica Graeca Latina*, Leipzig 1892; M.-Th. d'Alverny, *Miscellanea Mediaevalia*, i, 1962, pp. 154-78.

[28] *Ibid.*, p. 160.

Likewise copied in the twelfth century is the famous Anglo-Saxon ritual for improving the fertility of fields, in which the Christian God and Mary are invoked along with Terra [29]:

> I pray to the holy guardian of heaven's kingdom,
> to Earth and Sky
> and to the true Sancta Maria
> and to the power and court of heaven,
> that by the grace of the Lord I may
> pronounce this charm...

Here the goddess Terra becomes almost the bride of the Christian God:

> Hail to you, Earth, mother of men:
> may you be fruitful in God's embrace,
> filled with food for the benefit of men.

Bernard Silvestris' notion of earth receiving back all she brings forth, his cyclic view of generation and decay —

> a thing's form flows away, its being remains: the power of death
> destroys nothing, only severs what was joined — [30]

his sense that immortality belongs to the cycle and to the species, not to the individual human beings, likewise has ancient popular roots in the Roman world, as some of the formulae in verse epitaphs show [31]. That inscribed for the *sancta puella* Vitalis, who died at the age of ten, ends with the words:

> I am ash, ash is earth, Earth is a goddess, therefore I am not
> dead [32].

In another, the girl herself speaks:

[29] The complete text of the ritual, with a translation and commentary, in G. Storms, *Anglo-Saxon Magic*, The Hague 1948, pp. 172-186. The lines cited below are in my own translation.

[30] *Microcosmus* viii, 45-46.

[31] *Microcosmus* xiv, 157-78. This observation is intended to complement, not negate, the perceptions of learned influence in Bernard's expression of such ideas (see especially the texts cited in my edition, pp. 70-91).

[32] *Anthologia Latina* ii, 2 (ed. F. Buecheler), no. 974:
Cinis sum, cinis terra est, terra dea est, ergo ego mortua non sum.

> I lived dear to my own, I gave up my life, a virgin...
> If Earth is a goddess, I am a goddess, I am not dead [33].

In these brief, uneducated compositions of the late Roman Empire we are not far in spirit from the close of the *Cosmographia*.

Quite apart from such examples of magical syncretism as those in the Anglo-Saxon ritual or the Moissac spell, there were diverse ways, in the centuries before Bernard, in which an image of Terra, personified with greater or less vivacity, could be assimilated into the Christian cosmos. From the early ninth century onwards, there is a profuse tradition of depicting Terra in connexion with certain passages of Scripture. The illustrations seem for the most part to have been directly stimulated by the occurrence of the word *terra* in the text. Often a biblical moment is translated with striking directness into a pictorial gloss — as for instance on Apocalypse 12, 16:

> et adiuvit terra mulierem
> et aperuit terra os suum
> et absorbuit flumen quod misit draco de ore suo...

where a Trier manuscript shortly after 800 shows Terra opening her mouth and swallowing the stream spewed by the dragon [34]. Even a phrase as plain as "qui firmavit terram super aquas" (Psalm cxxxv, 6) is illuminated (e.g. in the early ninth-century Stuttgart Psalter) by an image of Terra as a womanly, numinous being, a nimbus round her head and vine-tendrils growing out of her mouth [35]. While the iconography of Terra in Carolingian biblical manuscripts can be accounted for in terms of attempts at literal interpretation, by artists who had access to ancient models, the sheer abundance of Terra imagery, its persistence from the ninth century to the thirteenth, and its rich iconographic variety, do not suggest that a dead metaphor is being repeated mechanically over and over again. The imaginative stature and importance that a depiction of Earth could still have in the eleventh and twelfth centuries is perhaps best seen in the Exultet Rolls of southern Italy in this period [36]. The verbal parallelism in

---

[33] *Ibid.*, no. 1532:
   Cara mieis vixi, virgo vitam reddidi...
   sein est terra dea, ego sum dea, mortua non sum.
(Cf. also the fragmentary hexameter, II, i, no. 809: "mater genuit materq(ue) recepit").

[34] "Erde" (*cit.* n. 23), pl. 2, col. 1001.

[35] *Ibid.*, pl. 3, cols. 1003-4.

[36] M. Avery, *The Exultet Rolls of South Italy II: Plates*, Princeton 1936. Cf. also

which the joys of earth and church are expressed in the Exultet of
the Easter Saturday rite:

Gaudeat se tellus, tantis irradiata fulgoribus...
totius orbis se sentiat amisisse caliginem.
Laetetur et mater ecclesia, tanti luminis adornata fulgoribus...

prompted the visual pairing of the womanly Tellus and Ecclesia. The
late eleventh-century Montecassino Roll, B.L. Add. 30337 (Figure
2), offers an outstanding instance. In her note to this example, Myr-
tilla Avery mentioned that in costume and attitude the personification of Mater Ecclesia resembles that of the Tellus in the Bari Roll
(c. 1000) [37]. There Tellus grasps two trees on the left and right of her,
just as Ecclesia grasps the vault above the two pillars at her sides; the
Bari Tellus, like the Montecassino Ecclesia, wears a splendid full-
length robe; she has a flowering headdress, just as the later Ecclesia
has vestiges of flowers in her hair. Equally noteworthy is the comparison, hinted at by Avery, of the Montecassino Tellus image with an
earlier, tenth-century Tellus in MS Vat. lat. 9820 [38]. There Tellus,
with a nimbus round her head, receives light on her beautiful face
from a divine hand pouring it out of a triple circle; she holds a cornucopia in her right hand, while with her left she wards off Caligo,
a dark woman who sits nearby in an attitude of mourning.

The reason Tellus can have such nearness to divinity, and can
become deeply comparable to Ecclesia, is that the sense of a whole
Christian cosmos brought to renewed life — which the shining words
of the Exultet convey — transfigures Tellus and Ecclesia equally.
Their connotations, that is, move as far as possible from bare concepts ("the surface studied by the geographer" or "the community
of the faithful") and as close as possible to those of rejoicing living
beings.

Once more it is not a question of arguing that Bernard Silvestris
was influenced by a particular iconographic tradition. Yet it is important to remember, when observing the individuality of Bernard's creation, Natura, in what varied ways the memory of the pre-Christian
goddess who is closest in conception to Natura had been preserved,
and what multifarious artistic craft had been used to integrate her

E. Bertaux, *L'art dans l'Italie méridionale* (3 vols.), repr. Paris-Rome 1968, i, pp.
213-40, and iii (the comparative iconographic tables); J. P. Gilson, *An Exultet Roll...
Reproduced from Add. MS 30337*, London 1929.
[37] Avery, p. 20 and pl. vi.
[38] Avery, pl. cxxxix.

in a Christian world-picture. It seems unlikely that Bernard could have been wholly unaware of either the personification Terra or the goddess Terra. She may well have provided some stimulus to the freedom of invention he assumed.

Another stimulus came from the profoundest intellectual achievement of the earlier Middle Ages, John Scotus Eriugena's *Periphyseon*. One cannot, in my view, fully understand the roles of Bernard's goddesses without seeing the extent to which they are, in Scotus' terms, primordial causes, or primal theophanies [39]. Bernard's goddesses cannot be *reduced* to primordial causes in Scotus' sense, any more than his Natura can be reduced to an Earth-goddess. But Bernard's sense of a divinely ordained dialectic, unfolding physically through principles who are also celestial beings, projections of the unknown God, is in some measure Scotus' inspiration.

If we consider the picture of Scotus' universe in a twelfth-century manuscript of Honorius' adaptation of the *Periphyseon* (Figure 3) [40], we can say that the goddesses in the *Cosmographia* are the equivalent of the first level of beings in the picture, the *primordiales cause*. In Scotus' phrase, they constitute "Nature that both creates and is created" [41] — is created, inasmuch as the unknown God creates himself in them. Presiding over the *primordiales cause* is Bonitas, the Form of the Good — which we might see as the supreme expression of the "superessential" God, just as in Bernard the Good (*Tugaton, suprema divinitas*) has a higher or presiding role over the goddesses Noys, Urania, Natura, Physis, Silva and the rest. In the picture seven feminine theophanies are portrayed; but as the names and the number of primordial causes vary throughout Scotus' work, so too with the divine creative forces in Bernard: there are, we might say, five protagonists — Noys, Silva, and the three Nature-goddesses — but, as the context demands, other names for embodied divine

---

[39] On the concept, see especially T. Gregory, "Note sulla dottrina delle 'teofanie' in Giovanni Scoto Eriugena", *Studi medievali*, 3ª Serie, iv, 1963, pp. 75-91.

[40] The illustration is from Paris, B.N. lat. 6734, fol. 3v. The *Clavis Physicae* of Honorius is now accessible in an excellent critical edition by Paolo Lucentini, Rome 1974. The *Clavis* survives in nine MSS, as well as being listed in numerous medieval catalogues (Lucentini, p. viii). Cf. also the penetrating study of the text by M.-Th. d'Alverny, "Le cosmos symbolique du XIIᵉ siècle", *Archives d'histoire doctrinale et littéraire du moyen âge*, xxviii, 1953, pp. 31-81.

[41] *Clavis* (ed. Lucentini), chs. 68, 82, 90-91, 101, 116-18, 148-51, 165, 300, 308; *Periphyseon*, PL cxxii, cols. 529, 546-8, 561-6, 576-8, 615-26, 662-5, 681-3, 858, 876. The passages up to col. 665 are available in a better text in *Periphyseon* II, ed. I. P. Sheldon-Williams and L. Bieler, Dublin 1972.

forces (such as Endelichia, Imarmene, or Fetura) are introduced [42].

It is worth noting that, when Scotus speaks of the primordial causes as "Nature that both creates and is created", he often inclines to personification. He speaks of the causes "in the most secret recesses of Natura's breasts" (*in secretissimis Naturae sinibus*), or of "Natura's most secret and intimate breasts" (*secretissimos intimosque Naturae sinus*) — this last phrase also signifying for him the midpoint of Paradise. Such expressions, which do not originate with Scotus, but which he developed with a flair and abundance previously unparalleled, have been admirably studied recently by Edouard Jeauneau [43].

In the picture, the primordial causes shape *materia informis*, just as in Bernard Mundus is nursed by Silva and is fashioned and polished by Noys and Natura. *Materia informis* is still disordered, confused, but all its eyes are potentialities looking towards formation. Yet the picture presents that matter as if it were an *effectus causarum* — whereas in Scotus' text inchoate matter is called the "first progression" (*prima progressio*) of the divine nature itself [44]. Here Scotus' thought is closer to Bernard's conception of Silva (also named Ylê): the two ultimate first principles, says Bernard, echoing the Hermetic treatise *Asclepius*, were unity and diversity — that is, God and Ylê. The emphasis in Scotus, as in the pagan *Asclepius* and often in Bernard, is on matter's latent divinity [45].

The next level in the picture shows the ordering of the universe, the separation of the elements and the emergence of beings appropriate to each: the first and highest element, fire or ether, is the realm of the intelligences, angels and *daemones*, and of the stars. Then air is shown, filled with birds, water with fish, earth with animals and — at the far right — with man and woman. This is the completion, in Scotus' vision, of "Natura creata, non creans". It is also, in his thought, which here is profoundly neoplatonic, the turning-point (*conversio*) where the return (*reditus*) of all nature to God begins. The end (*finis*), on the last plane of the picture, shows God "drawing all

---

[42] Complete references for these in the *Cosmographia* can be found in the "Index nominum et verborum" in my edition (pp. 183-96).

[43] *Quatre thèmes érigéniens*, Montreal-Paris 1978, pp. 37-43; full references for the expressions cited above on pp. 41, 43.

[44] Cf. d'Alverny, *art. cit.* (n. 40), pp. 58-60; I leave the complex questions concerning Tempus and Locus and their representation out of consideration here, as they are not directly relevant to the figures treated in this study. D'Alverny discusses Tempus and Locus, *art. cit.*, pp. 61-64; cf. also M. Cristiani, "Lo spazio e il tempo nell'opera dell'Eriugena", *Studi medievali*, 3ª Serie, xiv, 1973, pp. 39-136.

[45] Cf. *Cosmographia* (ed. Dronke), pp. 29-30.

things to himself", so that the cosmic drama may be concluded, the curtain finally drawn. For Scotus, the unique, decisive moment of *conversio* in the universe, which makes this *reditus* possible, is the Incarnation. Bernard in his poem acknowledges the Incarnation as one of many patterns set in the stars — divinely ordained, that is, for the cosmic history [46]; yet it is less central, less crucial to his thought. This, I suggest, is because his cosmology is not, like that of Scotus, oriented to a *finis*, an ultimate and complete return of all things to their original divine perfection, but rather is conceived in terms of cycles or aeons. At the end of a cosmic cycle, there will again be *materia informis* waiting to be made beautiful; the whole battle against formlessness will have to be waged once more [47]. Hence Bernard's emphasis at the end of the *Cosmographia* (Microcosmus xiv, 163-78) is far more on a limited, earthly survival, in one's children, than on Christian immortality in the beyond, or on Scotus' neoplatonic myth, in which the physical world is transfigured and perfected in the divine. With such a close Bernard's conception moves far from any generally admitted Christian belief. One must try to distinguish his individuality here, not blur it so as to "save" him for orthodoxy, nor award blame (or, for that matter, praise) on ideological grounds.

Though Bernard does not use Scotus' word *theophania* (as Alan of Lille was often to do) [48], I think that in his picture of the universe Natura and her kindred occupy the same plane as the "primal theophanies" in that of Scotus, and have comparable roles in the process of creation.

In Scotus the *primordiales cause,* or *prime theophanie,* are more than a convenient device for expressing certain insights into the unfolding and working of the cosmos — more than one possible model or *integumentum,* that could (at least on a nominalist view) be discarded at will in favour of another. That the names and number of primordial causes are variable in Scotus' thought suggests that for

---

[46] Megacosmus iii, 47-54:
   In stellis lepidum dictat Maro, Milo figurat,
      Fulgurat in Lacia nobilitate Nero...
   Exemplar speciemque dei virguncula Christum
      Parturit, et verum secula numen habent.

[47] Cf. *e.g.* Megacosmus i, 35-36:
   Rursus et ecce cupit res antiquissima nasci
   Ortu Silva novo...

[48] Alan uses *theophania* on numerous occasions throughout his work, sometimes with explicit acknowledgement to John Scotus: cf. *e.g. Textes inédits,* ed. M.-Th. d'Alverny, Paris 1965, pp. 203-10, 226-35; *Distinctiones, PL* ccx, col. 971C; *Anticlaudianus,* ed. R. Bossuat, Paris 1955, Prologus, p. 56.

him they are not, taken individually, intrinsic to the structure of the universe. Yet they are a real way of understanding the universe, not just a helpful way of talking about it. And often it seems that Scotus is so deeply, by temperament, a Platonist that he sees the primordial causes as the source of all human apprehension of the real, as (to borrow Shelley's phrase) the "forms more real than living man". At that point one can no longer distinguish in practice between saying: "the theophanies are a construct of the human mind" and "they belong to the structure of reality".

This seems to me as true for Bernard's goddesses as for Scotus' primal theophanies. That is why I cannot accept the view (basically Gilson's [49], though there are still traces of it about today) that Bernard's construction is essentially an elaborate poetic fiction, the truthful counterpart of which is the opening of the Book of Genesis. This is to misunderstand the nature of his *integumentum*: it was no "mere" fable or model, but the expression of a commitment, the affirmation of a world-view in which so much was individual, or individually transformed from elsewhere, that it could not be reduced to a body of beliefs — Christian or pagan or syncretistic.

This said, it must also be admitted that in matters of medieval personification many questions of the degree of reality remain unclear, and may never be decidable with certainty. When churches were built to divine Wisdom (Hagia Sophia), for instance, it would be misleading to say they were being built to Christ, but just as misleading to say they were built to a metaphor. To say positively what was involved is far more difficult. When Abelard, some two decades before the *Cosmographia* was written, dedicated his chapel to the Paraclete — was the Paraclete as *real* as Christ or Mary, who had lived on earth? At all events, chapels could be dedicated to Christ or to Mary with impunity, but Abelard caused a furore by his unusual dedication.

Again, there had existed, since the infancy of the Church, various beliefs about "guardian angels" assigned to human souls [50]. The widely influential second-century text, *Pastor Hermas*, affirmed that two angels, a good and an evil one, accompany each soul; Beatus (d. 798), in his commentary on the Apocalypse, saw the guardian angel allegorically, as a man's own soul; yet the view which gained ascen-

---

[49] E. Gilson, "La cosmogonie de Bernardus Silvestris", *Archives d'histoire doctrinale et littéraire du moyen âge*, iii, 1928, pp. 5-24; cf. also G. D. Economou, *op. cit.* (n. 4), pp. 58-72.

[50] See esp. *Dictionnaire de spiritualité*, i, cols. 586ff. ("Les anges gardiens"), 598ff. ("La dévotion aux anges").

dancy was that of Jerome, echoed in the twelfth century by Honorius and others, that each soul was at the moment of birth entrusted to the care of an individual good angel. While Ambrose, among the Fathers, recommends praying to the angels that guard us, the notion of intimacy with one's guardian angel appears to be found for the first time in the twelfth century, in writings of St. Bernard [51]. The sense of a warm but reverent bond with one's own angel (*in quovis angulo, angelo tuo reverentiam habe*), the loving and familiar tone (*affectuose diligamus angelos... habetote familiares angelos*), the exhortations to "invoke your guardian, your guide, your helper", are something new. Thus it would be wrong to see twelfth-century Christians who prayed to their guardian angel as indulging in a kind of exalted make-believe [52] — and yet, could such prayer ever have been of precisely the same kind as prayer to Christ, or indeed to a saint whose life was still locally remembered? It is perhaps significant that a *Festum angelorum custodum* was not celebrated before the fifteenth century, nor papally sanctioned before 1518, and that, while numerous hymns and sequences at every period are addressed to Michael and to angels in general, there seem to be none to the individual guardian before the fourteenth century [53]. Thus, when Bernard Silvestris (Microcosmus vii, 7) describes a tutelary *Genius* assigned to each human being *in eius custodiam*, should this be seen as a reflexion of the new cult so warmly propagated by St. Bernard? Or are these *Genii* of the same order of *integumentum* as the spirits Bernard knew from Calcidius and Martianus Capella? Or does he, with a poet's delight in mystery, leave the matter open?

[51] Hermas, *Mand.* vi, 2; Beatus, *in Apoc.* i, 5, 44; Jerome, *PL* xxvi, 130B; Ambrose, *De viduis* ix, 55 (*PL* xvi, 251 B); Honorius, *Elucid.* ii, 31 (*PL* clxxii, 1154B); the citations from St. Bernard are from Sermon xii on Ps. xc (*PL* clxxxiii, cols. 233-5).

[52] Elisabeth of Schönau, in a letter describing her ecstatic visions to Hildegard of Bingen, claims that an angel who often visited her whipped her for disobedience, and that she lay sick for three days with five of his whip-marks on her body:

> elevavit super me flagellum, quod quasi in ira magna quinquies mihi amarissime inflixit, ita ut per triduum in toto corpore meo ex illa percussione languerem (*PL* cxcvii, 215C).

Apart from this detail, however, the whole of Elisabeth's account of her angel seems heavily indebted to *Pastor Hermas*, and it is perhaps significant that Hildegard, in her reply to this letter (*PL* cxcvii, 216-18), completely ignores Elisabeth's claim that the angel had been physically present.

[53] The earliest known to me are by Guillaume de Deguilleville († after 1358), "O angele, custos meus" (A.H. xlviii, pp. 342-3), and Konrad of Haimburg († 1360), "Salve mi angelice/Spiritus beate" (A.H. iii, pp. 46-47).

The plot of the *Cosmographia* did not allow Bernard the poet to address a personal prayer to Natura within the epic. However, he endowed her with such poetic life that his follower, Alan of Lille, or the dreamer in Alan's *De planctu Naturae*, invokes her in the Sapphic stanzas "O dei proles genitrixque rerum", which would seem to be the first hymn to Natura since the ancient Orphic one [54]. A further development occurs in John of Hauvilla's epic, *Architrenius*: where, in Bernard and Alan, Natura is portrayed as *plangens*, in John it is the poet-narrator who complains *against* Natura. At first, when he has found her and falls weeping at her feet, she does not let him speak, but discourses to him at length on the cosmic harmony, with vast astronomic detail. When she has done, he bursts out, accusing her:

> Do you, Natura, show any pity that your children are scourged by crimes? What winter has ravaged your motherly serenity towards your little ones? Has a mother's love learnt stepmotherly hate? Alas, you breasts that mean never to offer sweet honey! Alas, you children that will always taste bitter food!

Natura in her answer says:

> You, though aged, still pant to be suckled at the breasts of your nurse, breasts moist with virtues, you, boy full of years and yet not old in heart, senescent with beardless mind. Now an apt age will come upon your spirit... the sweetness that you seek shall be given you, the thirsty nursling shall drink it to satiety, so that base childishness shall leave his spirit [55].

Amid the wide range of traditional imagery in which human beings have (in the words of Juliet's Nurse) "sucked Wisdom from the teat", the notion of Natura offering this drink from her breasts is most unusual. Already the First Epistle of Peter (ii, 2) has the figure of newborn children longing for "the guileless milk of reason" (*rationale sine dolo lac*), and Augustine uses the personification, *Mater Sapientia lactescens* [56]. Representations of Terra giving suck either to beasts or to humans abound in the earlier Middle Ages; Alan of Lille, in his *Distinctiones*, codifies the figurative meanings of *lac, lactare,*

---

[54] *De planctu Naturae*, ed. N. M. Häring (*Studi medievali*, 3ª Serie, xix, 1978) vii (pp. 831-2).

[55] *Architrenius*, ed. P. G. Schmidt, Munich 1974, ix, 178-83, 234-40.

[56] *Tractatus in Joannis Evangelium* 98, 6 ("Mater ipsa Sapientia, quae, cum sit in excelsis angelorum solidus cibus, dignata est quodammodo lactescere parvulis").

mamma and *ubera* in terms of spiritual nourishment [57]. Yet that this nourishment should come from the breasts not of Ecclesia, Sapientia or Grammatica, but from those of Natura, would seem to be new. Very soon after the *Architrenius*, however, we have a visual analogue.

John of Hauvilla's poem was dedicated to the Archbishop of Rouen, Walter of Coutances, in 1184/5. In England in the decade 1190/1200, an artist portrayed Natura giving suck to a crouching young woman named Sciencia (Figure 4). This constitutes one end of the "Liberal Arts" casket in the Victoria and Albert Museum [58]. The opposite end shows Philosophia enthroned, a sceptre in her right hand, an orb in her left. The two sides of the casket show the seven Liberal Arts in the tradition of "La Sagesse et ses sept filles", a tradition that had been given renewed poetic life in Alan of Lille's second epic, *Anticlaudianus* [59]. In the *Anticlaudianus*, too, it is Natura who, in her paradisal dwelling, preserves the sum of cosmic knowledge, the forms in their changeless perfection. The manuscript tradition shows that the *Anticlaudianus*, like the *Architrenius* and *Cosmographia*, was swiftly diffused in the Anglo-Norman world. It seems likely that the designer of the casket was acquainted with the Natura of the cosmological epics; he may even have had the "Natura lactans" passage in the *Architrenius* in mind. On the other hand, while Natura there clearly imparts understanding to her tearful *alumnus*, I have not met a text where the nursling at Natura's breasts — like Architrenius no babe, but fully grown — is called Sciencia.

* * *

The problem of the shifting degrees of reality in personifications is one that poets have handled with knowing freedom from very ancient times. Many of the figures in Hesiod, for instance, oc-

---

[57] "Erde" (*cit.* n. 23), *passim*; Alan of Lille, *Distinctiones* (PL ccx), cols. 825-7, 848, 983-4. Cf. also K. Lange, "Geistliche Speise", *Zeitschrift für deutsches Altertum*, xcv, 1966, pp. 81-122; L. Möller, "Nahrmutter Weisheit", *Deutsche Vierteljahrsschrift*, xxiv, 1950, pp. 347-59.

[58] On this casket, see especially M.-M. Gauthier, *Emaux du moyen âge occidental*, Fribourg 1972, pp. 14, 315; H. Swarzenski, *Monuments of Romanesque Art*, London 1954, pp. 79-80 (no. 488), and pl. 209 (showing four of the Liberal Arts). I am most grateful to Marian Campbell, of the Victoria and Albert Museum, for referring me to Gauthier's work, and for her help in obtaining a photograph of the Natura-Sciencia side of the casket. Neither this image nor anything closely comparable is discussed in W. Kemp, *Natura. Ikonographische Studien...* (*Diss.*, Tübingen 1973).

[59] Cf. M.-Th. d'Alverny's essay (*cit.* n. 19); *Anticlaudianus*, ed. R. Bossuat, Paris 1955, ii, 325-iv, 69.

cupy an undefined ground between the conceptual and the symbolic,
the rationalizing and the imaginative. Among the daughters of
Night [60] are some such as Sleep, Blame and Woe, whom we would
incline to see as no more than personified abstractions; others such
as Clotho, Lachesis and Atropos, where we might hesitate; others
again such as the Hesperides, who do not appear to personify a concept at all. And what of Night herself? Is she an abstraction, or a being of the same order as the Cyclopes or the Giants Cottus and Bri-
areus? It seems scarcely possible to stratify Hesiod's personages, and
he might well not have wished us to try. Nor is there any reason to
suppose that the more abstract figures, the ones that are more patently personified, are later, more artificial creations than the Giants or
the Hesperides. I think that, both early and late, we must reckon
with the possibility of a two-way passage between divine (or daimon-
ic) beings and personifications. Karl Reinhardt, in his brilliant essay
"Personifikation und Allegorie" [61], suggests that in Greece a period
when personifications were great was followed by one when they
dwindled into *façons de parler*, that are used selfconsciously by
philosophers and poets. Yet in Hesiod's *Theogony* alone the two
kinds co-exist imperturbably; and if we reconsider one of Reinhardt's own most striking examples, where in an ode of Pindar
(*Olymp.* xiv) he suggests that the Graces are genuinely made divine
through the poet's intense imagination — [62]

> Without the grave Graces, not the gods even
> marshal their dances, their festivals; mistresses of all
> heavenly action, they who have set their thrones
> beside Pythian Apollo of the bow of gold
> keep eternal the great way of the father Olympian —

it seems to me that the lines immediately before those which Reinhardt cites show Pindar creating the opposite — or complementary
— effect:

> By your means all delight,
> all that is sweet, is given to mankind.
> If a man be wise, or beautiful, or splendid, it is you [63].

---

[60] *Theogony* 211ff., ed. M. L. West, Oxford 1966, p. 120; cf. also pp. 35-36,
227-32.
[61] K. Reinhardt, *Vermächtnis der Antike*, Göttingen 1960, pp. 7-40.
[62] *Ibid.*, pp. 25-26.
[63] I cite from the translation of R. Lattimore, *The Odes of Pindar*, Chicago
1947, p. 42.

Here the Graces seem far more of an abstraction, an epitome of human graciousness and gracefulness. The artistic selfconsciousness is, in my view, equally present in the conceptual and the mythopoeic lines.

Gods may become abstractions, and abstractions can be genuinely deified. To cite Burckhardt's observation about personified concepts in Roman religion:

> Without meaning to, one might arrive at the idea that to the dry, prosaic Romans such things came fairly easily. But the temple of Fear and Pallor (Pavor et Pallor) was consecrated by King Tullus Hostilius amid mortal danger of battle... that of Honour and Valour by the great Marcus Marcellus in the midst of the fearful Punic war. So the deification of such beings must have been hedged with a more profound seriousness [64].

The degree of seriousness, commitment or belief — and, in literary works, the degree of imaginative reality — must be gauged sensitively in each context.

In Bernard's treatment of goddesses there is an element of play as well as of seriousness. He is at times as conscious of fabulating as Plato had been in the *Timaeus*: he too can people his cosmos by feats of joyous, unfettered creation. The mythical dimension of Natura is something for which Bernard could have found only the barest hint in the Latin sources, and he had no access to the Greek: that was a dimension he re-invented afresh, giving to Natura some of the imaginative power which the Earth-goddess could still at times possess in medieval Europe. It is because of this same imaginative power that the *goddess* Silva in Bernard is so different from the concept *silva* in Calcidius, even though that was clearly Bernard's point of departure. So, too, if Urania has her origin in the Muse of Astronomy, she becomes a very different being in Bernard's poem. Bernard's heroines, in short, have their individual functions in his universe and its cycle of generation and decay. They speak and are addressed, they act and suffer and move, with a fullness of life that could not have been gleaned from the earlier learned materials. That is why Bernard's allegory can hardly be accounted for in terms of a tradition, or of continuities. It was an unforeseeable achievement.

---

[64] "Die Allegorie in den Künsten", in Jacob Burckhardt, *Vorträge*, ed. E. Dürr (Gesamtausgabe xiv), Stuttgart 1933, pp. 430-1.

Additional note (*cf.* p. 54, n. 43): It is noteworthy that, in a passage (*De trin.* iii, 9, 16) where Augustine speaks of *ea quae secreto Naturae sinu abdita continentur*, there is also an implicit Terra Mater: *Nam sicut matres gravidae sunt fetibus, sic ipse mundus gravidus est causis nascentium.*

3

INTEGUMENTA VIRGILII *

Macrobe, évoquant l'*Énéide* dans ses *Saturnales*, y parle du
«sanctuaire profond du poème sacré» (*adyta sacri poematis*) [1]. Dans
son commentaire sur le *Songe de Scipion*, il affirme que Virgile avait
donné en même temps une fiction poétique et une vérité philosophique (*et poeticae figmentum et philosophiae veritatem*) [2]. Au XIIᵉ siècle, ces conceptions sont rappelées par Bernard Silvestre, dans son
commentaire sur l'*Énéide*, où il ajoute la notion d'*integumentum* ou
involucrum: le sens profond est enveloppé par la narration fabuleuse
— c'est donc au commentateur de le découvrir [3]. Une génération plus
tard, Jean de Salisbury, qui connaissait bien non seulement les ouvrages de Macrobe mais aussi le commentaire de Bernard, esquissant à
son tour une lecture allégorique de l'*Énéide* au cours de son *Policraticus* (1159), parle d'une sagesse divine (*divina prudentia*) qui a permis
à Virgile de suggérer, sous l'*involucrum* d'expressions fictives, une
image des étapes de la vie humaine [4].

Avant Jean, il y avait deux principaux modes visant à signaler
des significations profondes et voilées dans la pensée de Virgile. Ils
sont distincts, bien qu'il s'agisse de phénomènes apparentés et dans
un certain sens complémentaires. Tous les deux ont leurs racines dans
l'antiquité tardive. L'un procède d'une façon éclectique, voire atomis-
tique; l'autre s'approche d'un système. Le premier, que l'on trouve
chez les philosophes platonisants, surtout au XIIᵉ siècle, consiste à

---

* *Lectures médiévales de Virgile* (Collection de l'École Française de Rome, 80,
Rome, 1985), pp. 313-329.
  [1] *Sat.* I, xxiv, 13.
  [2] *In Somn. Scip.* I, ix, 8.
  [3] *The Commentary on the First Six Books of the Aeneid of Vergil Commonly Attributed to Bernardus Silvestris* (éd. J. W. Jones et E. F. Jones), Lincoln-Londres, 1977,
p. 3. Au sujet des concepts *integumentum* et *involucrum*, cf. É. Jeauneau, *Lectio
philosophorum*, Amsterdam 1973, pp. 127-193, et P. Dronke, *Fabula*, Leyde-Cologne,
1974, surtout pp. 23-28, 48-52, 56-57, 61-64, 119-122.
  [4] *Policraticus* (éd. C. C. J. Webb), Oxford, 1909, VIII, 24 (p. 415).

choisir quelques moments-clé, souvent de la IVe *Églogue* ou du VIe livre de l'*Énéide*, afin de les interpréter comme témoignages de vérités de la pensée chrétienne. Le second, plus systématique, est plus rare: il y en a quelques éléments chez Fulgence, mais c'est surtout Bernard Silvestre, et après lui, d'une manière plus rapide et allusive, Jean de Salisbury, qui ont essayé de voir une signification voilée dans la trame de l'épopée virgilienne, plutôt que dans des passages isolés cueillis dans toutes les poésies de Virgile. Après quelques aperçus généraux sur l'utilisation philosophique de Virgile, je voudrais regarder de plus près un exemple de chacun de ces deux modes de lecture. Pour le premier, je vais considérer la *Theologia* «Scholarium» de Pierre Abélard, qui éclaire d'une façon remarquable ce que pouvait signifier Virgile pour un intellectuel du XIIe siècle. Pour le second, le choix s'impose presque de lui-même: notre témoin le plus fécond de l'allégorèse systématique est le commentaire de l'*Énéide* attribué à Bernard Silvestre — attribution quelquefois contestée, mais jamais, à mon avis, avec des raisons convaincantes [5].

Thierry de Chartres, dans son «interprétation des six jours de la création», essaie d'expliquer le verset de la Genèse *Et spiritus Domini ferebatur super aquas* («Et l'Esprit du Seigneur planait sur les eaux») par une méthode qu'il appelle scientifique et littérale (*secundum phisicam et ad litteram*) [6]. Pour lui, cela veut dire l'expliquer en admettant la possibilité que la matière primordiale soit sans commencement — car Thierry prend au sérieux la phrase hermétique de l'*Asclepius, fuit deus et hyle*: il y avait Dieu et Hylé [7]. Il commence en disant que cette Hylé était le plus semblable à l'eau; ainsi l'eau (sur laquelle planait l'Esprit de Dieu) peut signifier toute la matière primordiale. Nous voyons, ajoute-t-il, que selon les plus anciens philosophes l'humidité était le principe matériel le plus important pour toute création. L'humidité est la source de la croissance, de la vie animée, de l'apparition des pierres et des métaux, et même des étoiles. C'est selon cette doctrine, conclut Thierry, que Virgile a désigné Océanus père de toutes les choses: *Oceanumque patrem rerum* (*Georg.* IV 380) [8].

C'est-à-dire que pour Thierry la libation, que propose la nymphe Cyrène à Océanus comme père universel, exprime d'une façon

---

[5] Voir mon article *Bernardo Silvestre*, dans *Enciclopedia Virgiliana*, I, Rome, 1984, pp. 497-500.

[6] *Commentaries on Boethius by Thierry of Chartres and his School* (éd. N. M. Häring), Toronto, 1971, p. 555.

[7] *Ibid.*, p. 566.

[8] *Ibid.*, p. 567.

mythopoétique la même doctrine de la primauté de l'eau comme principe cosmique qu'enseignaient les anciens philosophes. Et Thierry suggère en même temps que, tout comme Virgile, l'auteur du libre de la Genèse se servait d'un mythe, pour exprimer la même réalité cosmologique: les eaux fécondées par le Saint-Esprit, et Océanus père de l'univers, sont deux expressions voilées de l'aperçu physique d'un Thalès.

De même, l'auteur anonyme d'un commentaire, composé peut-être vers 1100, sur le chant *O qui perpetua* de Boèce, justifie le choix boécien du terme «semeur» (*sator*) pour Dieu en invoquant le chant cosmologique de Silène dans la VIe Églogue:

> Car il chantait comment, au sein du vide immense,
> Les éléments mêlés (*coacta semina*), la terre et l'onde et l'air
> Et le feu se pressaient, ces principes de tout... (31-33) [9]

On peut parler sans absurdité, dit l'anonyme, des débuts des éléments (*exordia elementorum*) comme semences, puisqu'il y avait des couches de semences pour l'univers qui allait naître. Mais il insiste sur le fait que le mot *sator* n'est qu'une métaphore, bien qu'elle soit pertinente. Encore une fois c'est sur le mode mythopoétique que Virgile appuie la conception physique d'un substrat préexistant.

Mais le moment cosmologique le plus important pour les platoniciens médiévaux est sans aucun doute le début du discours d'Anchise dans le VIe livre de l'*Énéide*. Et là on hésitait beaucoup: ces vers étaient-ils métaphoriques ou non? Jusqu'à quel point Anchise parlait-il dans le mode couvert (*integumentum, involucrum*), de sorte qu'il fallait interpréter ses paroles, les dépouiller de leur voile fabuleux afin de révéler ce qu'elles exprimaient en vérité sur l'esprit divin et l'univers et les âmes humaines? Et jusqu'à quel point les paroles mêmes décrivaient-elles cette *veritas* que Virgile avait vue par une intuition directe et inspirée? —

> Au commencement le ciel, la terre, les champs liquides, le globe lumineux de la lune, le soleil et les étoiles sont vivifiés de l'intérieur par un esprit: répandu dans les membres du monde, cet esprit en fait mouvoir la masse entière et transforme en s'y mêlant ce vaste corps. C'est de lui que naissent les races des hommes, des animaux, des oiseaux et de tous les monstres que porte l'océan sous sa surface de marbre. Ces semences ont la vigueur du feu et sont d'origine céleste,

---

[9] Le commentaire est édité par É. Jeauneau, *op. cit.* (n. 3), pp. 311-331 (ici p. 325). Je cite les vers virgiliens d'après la traduction de Paul Valéry, *Bucoliques*, Paris, 1956, p. 99.

en ce que les corps impurs ne les alourdissent pas et que les membres terrestres, voués à la mort, ne les ont pas atrophiées [10].

Comme a bien noté Édouard Jeauneau, on peut retracer l'histoire des allusions à ces vers dès l'antiquité tardive (Macrobe, saint Jérôme, Fulgence, et Virgile le Grammairien), à travers la Renaissance carolingienne (Jean Scot Érigène, Remi d'Auxerre), à Bovon de Corvey et Gunzon de Novare au Xe siècle, jusqu'aux philosophes chartrains du XIIe, et bien au-delà [11]. Toutefois, dans l'application qu'on faisait de ce texte-clé, il y avait beaucoup de nuances.

Dans l'argumentation de Jean Scot, par exemple, qui est suivie de très près par son adaptateur Honorius au début du XIIe siècle [12], il n'y a aucune trace d'allégorèse: il s'agit simplement de comparer deux hypothèses physiques qui visaient à expliquer les causes du mouvement et du repos dans l'univers. Selon Platon et Virgile [13], dit Jean Scot, le monde est un grand être vivant, formé par l'union des éléments, dont le mouvement et le repos dépendent de l'âme du monde. Il cite les vers virgiliens pour confirmer que c'est dans tous les quatre — le firmament de feu céleste, la terre, les champs de l'eau, et la région aérienne de la lune et des étoiles —, que l'âme, principe universel de vie (*generalis vita*), anime et meut tout ce qui est en mouvement ou en repos. Par contre, poursuit-il, Grégoire de Nysse avait une autre explication de ces phénomènes, selon laquelle le Créateur a placé deux forces contraires, la lourde et la légère, comme les principes déterminant par leurs proportions les degrés divers de mouvement — du plus rapide, le feu, jusqu'à l'immobilité complète de la terre. Tandis que la théorie de Platon et de Virgile, dit Jean, est pénétrante et vraisemblable, et donc n'est pas à mépriser, je m'incline pourtant devant celle de Grégoire, «puisqu'il a un argument très subtil» (*subtilissime disputat*).

Pour Thierry de Chartres, par contre, quand il vient à l'âme du monde, il s'agit plutôt d'un archétype constant dans la pensée humaine que d'une hypothèse purement physique. La physique avait montré à Thierry que la matière primordiale resterait en chaos, que

---

[10] *Énéide*, VI, 724-732; traduction adaptée de l'édition de la *Collection des universités de France*.

[11] *Guillaume de Conches, Glosae super Platonem* (éd. É. Jeauneau), Paris, 1965, p. 145 n. (b).

[12] Johannes Scottus Eriugena, *Periphyseon* I (éd. I. P. Sheldon-Williams), Dublin, 1968, ch. 29 (pp. 114-116); cf. Honorius Augustodunensis, *Clavis Physicae* (éd. P. Lucentini), Rome, 1974, pp. 25-26.

[13] Jean n'ajoute Virgile que dans la dernière rédaction du *Periphyseon* (cf. Sheldon-Williams, éd. cit., p. 114).

rien ne subsisterait, si Hylé n'était pas informée et ordonnée de l'intérieur, par ce qu'il appelle «la puissance de l'artiste» (*virtus artificis*). Or il constate que ce qui a été révélé aux chrétiens sur cette *virtus artificis*, et ce qu'en ont deviné les prophètes de l'Ancien Testament, s'accorde à merveille avec la pensée des grands païens [14]. C'est cette puissance, dit-il, que Moïse visait à exprimer par son image de l'esprit de Dieu au-dessus des eaux, et, malgré certaines différences d'expression, les philosophes ont toujours pensé à cette même énergie vitale, formatrice au-dedans de la matière: ils l'ont appelée l'esprit qui remplit toutes les choses (ainsi Hermès); l'âme du monde (ainsi Platon); l'esprit qui vivifie de l'intérieur (ainsi Virgile). Les témoins païens expriment donc la même conviction que les Hébreux (Moïse, David — parlant du Verbe du Seigneur qui ferme les cieux — et Salomon), et la même conviction aussi que les chrétiens qui parlent du Saint-Esprit.

Guillaume de Conches cite à plusieurs reprises dans son commentaire sur le *Timée* les paroles d'Anchise, *quantum non noxia corpora tardant*: c'est pour autoriser une distinction entre les diverses fonctions de l'âme du monde dans l'univers [15]. Guillaume avait commencé, tout comme Thierry, par identifier l'âme du monde platonicienne avec le Saint-Esprit ou l'amour divin. Mais il a été attaqué pour son audace, notamment par Guillaume de Saint-Thierry; alors, par prudence, il a apporté des réserves à l'identification, et enfin, dans son dernier chef-d'œuvre, *Dragmaticon*, il n'en parle plus [16]. Ce qui compte pour lui, pourtant, c'est que l'esprit inhérent, qui donne le mouvement et la vie, agit diversement selon la capacité des divers corps, dont les uns peuvent retarder sa force plus que les autres.

Cependant, l'usage le plus original que fait Guillaume du discours d'Anchise se trouve dans une allusion moins directe, où il interprète quelques autres vers de Virgile [17]. Au début du *Timée*, quand Platon parle de la fondation d'Athènes, Guillaume dans son commentaire rappelle le mythe d'Érichthonius, le roi d'Athènes qui était né avec des pieds de serpent. Il cite les vers de la IIIe *Géorgique* (113 et s.): «Érichthonius osa le premier atteler quatre chevaux à un char, et se tenir debout sur des roues, vainqueur à la course rapide». Or il

---

[14] *Op. cit.* (n. 6), pp. 566-567.

[15] *Glosae* (cit. n. 11), pp. 145, 152, 157, 174.

[16] *Glosae* p. 145 n; cf. Tullio Gregory, *Anima mundi*, Florence, 1955, pp. 123-174; P. Dronke, «*L'amor che move il sole e l'altre stelle*», dans *Studi medievali*, 3ª serie, VI, 1965, 389-422 (ici pp. 410-413).

[17] *Glosae* pp. 93-94. Je cite les vers d'après la traduction dans l'édition de la *Collection des universités de France.*

existait déjà une interprétation allégorique moralisante et banale de
ces vers, par Fulgence. Fulgence avait raconté qu'Érichthonius était
né de l'union non consommée de Vulcain et de Minerve: Vulcain, le
feu de la fureur (*furiae ignis*), assaillit Minerve (*sapientia*), qui se
défend contre son assaut. Le résultat est Érichthonius — qui, par un
jeu étymologique, signifierait *eris phthonos*, la lutte de l'envie. C'est
ainsi, dit Fulgence, que, selon Virgile, Érichthonius a inventé le cirque (voilà son interprétation de *currus*, le char) — parce qu'au cirque
il y a toujours une lutte pleine d'envie (*invidiae semper certamen*) [18].

Pour Guillaume le sens allégorique devient tout autre. Selon lui,
Vulcain, dieu du feu, signifie la «clarté d'envol» (cette fois le jeu de
mots va de *Vulcanus* à *volans candor*): c'est l'ardeur de l'imagination
(*fervor ingenii*) qui veut se joindre à la Sagesse (Pallas). Il n'atteint pas
l'union parfaite — irréalisable dans la vie mortelle — donc sa
semence tombe sur la terre, parce que le corps fragile et terrestre la
rend pesante. L'expression dont se sert Guillaume ici — *semen illud
cadit, quia ex fragili et terreno corpore gravatur* — rappelle subtilement
à la fois l'origine céleste des semences (*caelestis origo seminibus*) et
combien elles sont alourdies par les corps (*corpora tardant terrenique
hebetant artus*).

Ainsi Guillaume développe son allégorie: de cette semence sur
la terre est né Érichthonius. Il a donc une origine à la fois élevée et
basse: il est né de la Sagesse divine (Pallas) et de l'aspiration aux choses célestes, cette clarté d'envol que signifie Vulcain. En même temps
il est né avec des pieds de serpent (*habens draguntinos pedes*), parce
qu'il a aussi la préoccupation des choses temporelles, préoccupation
utile et avisée comme l'est le serpent (*utilis est et astuta ut draco*).
Mais l'aspiration céleste est plus digne que la temporelle. Et puisque
celle-ci ne se trouve guère, ou même jamais (*vix aut nunquam*), sans
quelque trait ignoble, pour cacher ce trait, Érichthonius invente le
char — qui signifie la raison, l'intellect et les vertus.

Ce char avait pour Guillaume toutes les connotations platoni-
ciennes du char de l'âme. Il avait déjà commenté les «chars légers»
dont parle Boèce dans sa prière philosophique *O qui perpetua* [19], et
Guillaume revient à ce thème quand il commente dans le *Timée* le
retour des âmes à leurs étoiles. Là il s'appuie de nouveau sur une citation virgilienne — les paroles de Déiphébus à Énée, quand il le
quitte: «Je compléterai le nombre [des âmes] en retournant aux ténè-

---

[18] Fulgentius (éd. R. Helm), Stuttgart, 1970², *Mitol.*, II, 11 (pp. 51-52).
[19] Cf. P. Courcelle, *La Consolation de Philosophie dans la tradition littéraire*,
Paris, 1967, p. 310.

bres» (VI 545) [20]. Érichthonius, selon Guillaume, avait inventé son char spirituel afin de cacher la partie moins noble, l'aspect serpentin, de son corps. C'est un beau geste, mais peut-être est-ce aussi un geste ambigu. L'homme ne peut pas nier son aspect terrestre — devrait-il le cacher? Cet aspect est utile et sagace, affirme Guillaume, même s'il n'est presque jamais noble jusqu'au fond. Mais Érichthonius cache ce défaut de la meilleure façon: il invente le char de raison, intellect et vertus. C'est-à-dire que pour Guillaume la condition corporelle elle-même peut devenir la source d'une découverte qui mène au ciel: l'homme en tant que terrestre peut inventer ses propres moyens d'ascension céleste. Ici, comme souvent, Guillaume apporte un optimisme humain très individuel au cœur de la pensée platonicienne, il renverse la tendance trop facile de la plupart des platonisants de mépriser le monde d'ici-bas.

La mise en valeur de moments virgiliens au service du platonisme chrétien va beaucoup plus loin chez Pierre Abélard. Abélard paraît avoir développé des intérêts cosmologiques relativement tard dans sa carrière, et on ne peut pas exclure qu'il ait été influencé sous cet aspect par la tradition chartraine, voire par Guillaume de Conches lui-même [21]. C'est dans la dernière version de sa *Theologia*, dite «Scholarium», qui remonte aux années 1135-1139, que l'on voit le plein épanouissement des réflexions d'Abélard sur Virgile [22].

Abélard s'approche du discours d'Anchise à travers la pensée de Macrobe. C'est Macrobe, selon lui, qui a deviné dans le texte virgilien sur l'âme du monde presque tout ce que les chrétiens croient au sujet du Saint-Esprit. L'âme du monde chez Macrobe est, elle aussi, le Créateur: elle procède de Dieu le Père et du Nous, qui est Dieu le Fils [23]. Virgile et Macrobe appelaient l'âme du monde *mens*, pour signaler l'unité substantielle de l'Esprit et du Fils [24]. C'est la dignité de l'âme du monde que Virgile voulait exprimer par *Mens agitat molem*; sa puissance créatrice et vivifiante par *Hinc hominum pecudumque genus*. On peut harmoniser facilement, dit Abélard, toutes

---

[20] *Glosae*, p. 211.

[21] Cf. *Fabula* (cit. n. 3), pp. 55-60.

[22] *Theologia «Scholarium»* [= *Introductio in Theologiam*], PL 178, col. 1024-1032 [*Petri Abaelardi Opera Theologica* III (éd. E.M. Buytaert et C.J. Mews, CC, CM XIII, 1987), pp. 388-402]; cf. *Theologia Christiana*, dans *Petri Abaelardi Opera Theologica* II (éd. E. M. Buytaert, CC, CM XII), I, 110-129 (pp. 117-128).

[23] Abélard ajoute que, même si les philosophes parlent quelquefois de la «création» ou de la «naissance» de l'âme du monde, cela n'est qu'une façon de parler qui équivaut à la procession, telle que la conçoivent les théologiens.

[24] Cette dernière observation ne se trouve que dans la *Theologia Christiana* (éd. cit.), I, 110.

les paroles de Virgile et de Macrobe avec la teneur de notre foi: ainsi, quand les membres s'affaiblissent (*hebetant artus*), cela montre comment la grâce du Saint-Esprit est moins efficace parmi les hommes plus sensuels. De l'abondance de la fontaine divine — le Nous — sont animés les corps célestes et les étoiles: ce sont les anges et les esprits qui furent créés avant l'homme. Ici Virgile et Macrobe s'accordent avec les paroles de saint Jean (I 16): «C'est de sa plénitude que nous avons tous reçu».

En se basant sur un passage de saint Jérôme, Abélard affirme que Virgile, qui suivait la pensée stoïcenne de Zénon, avait même compris la double présence de Dieu dans sa création, dont saint Paul écrit: *per omnia*, et *in omnibus*. Virgile voit que Dieu traverse *per omnes* quand il écrit dans la IVe *Géorgique*:

> deum namque ire per omnes
> terras tractusque maris caelumque profundum (221-2)

(«en effet, Dieu se répand partout, dans les terres, dans les espaces de la mer et dans les profondeurs du ciel» [25]); de même, Virgile exprime la présence de l'Esprit *in omnibus* par le vers d'Anchise, *spiritus intus alit*.

Puis Abélard affronte l'objection qu'on pourrait lui faire: qu'il donne aux textes des «philosophes» — Virgile et Macrobe — un sens qui est loin de leur intention, qu'il détourne leurs expressions vers la foi chrétienne. Et pourtant, répond-il, les mots peuvent avoir un sens caché dont celui qui parle n'est pas conscient. Tel était le cas quand Caïphe dit: «il est opportun qu'un seul meure pour le peuple, afin que toute la race ne périsse» (Jean XI 50), ne sachant point comment la mort du Christ sauverait la race humaine. Mais les prophètes eux non plus ne comprennent pas le plein sens ou la pleine portée de ce qu'ils disent, puisque c'est le Saint-Esprit qui parle au moyen d'eux. D'ailleurs, Macrobe lui-même souligne que ce que les philosophes disent de l'âme du monde doit être interprété selon son sens caché (*mystice interpretanda*).

Le monde païen avait, lui aussi, ses vrais prophètes: ce sont les Sibylles, qui — selon des textes qui au XIIe siècle étaient encore acceptés comme remontant dans leur intégralité à l'époque préchrétienne — avaient préconisé la divinité et l'humanité du Verbe, la Passion, et le Jugement dernier.

Abélard croit vraisemblable que Virgile ait connu une telle prophétie sibylline, car, dans la IVe *Églogue*, quand il présage la nais-

---

[25] Traduction de l'édition de la *Collection des universités de France*.

sance merveilleuse d'un enfant qui descendra du ciel à la terre, qui ôtera les péchés du monde et instaurera un nouvel âge, Virgile lui-même signale qu'un chant *Cumaei carminis* — de la Sibylle de Cumes — l'a poussé à écrire. Le poète, dit Abélard, ne savait peut-être pas (*fortassis poeta ignorante*) ce que la Sibylle, ou le Saint-Esprit, proclamait par sa bouche. Mais on peut démontrer, à cause des événements qui suivirent, que les paroles de Virgile, qui seraient fausses prises au pied de la lettre, et ineptes si elles n'étaient que panégyrique humain, ne sauraient se référer en vérité qu'à la naissance du Fils de Dieu. D'ailleurs, dans une autre *Églogue*, la VIIIᵉ, Virgile fait allusion à la Trinité divine:

> D'une triple couleur, je ceins ton effigie
> Et trois fois la promène autour de cet autel;
> Trois fois, c'est que le Dieu goûte le nombre impair. (73-75) [26]

Abélard concède tout de suite que le contexte littéral est celui d'un rite de sortilège, pour contraindre Daphnis, l'amant rebelle. Mais, demande-t-il, d'où vient la force mystérieuse du triple, que reconnaît aussi Salomon quand il écrit *Funiculus triplex difficile rumpitur* («le fil triple ne rompt pas facilement», *Eccl.* IV 12)? Le fil avec sa triple couleur, le triple circuit de l'autel, sont efficaces dans le rite parce que Dieu se réjouit du nombre impair: c'est, ajoute Abélard, comme si Virgile avait dit que Dieu voulait faire décrire sa propre perfection selon la Trinité des personnes — de la même substance, comme la laine, et avec des propriétés diverses, comme les trois couleurs des torons.

Je n'ai esquissé que quelques mouvements de pensée dans l'argumentation riche et un peu labyrinthique d'Abélard. La rapidité de cette esquisse pourrait donner l'impression qu'Abélard se servait de Virgile seulement comme *auctoritas*, pour appuyer une série de thèses qu'il chérissait. Mais ce serait une impression fausse. Les références que fait Abélard à Macrobe montrent que Macrobe est, pour ainsi dire, la première clef à la lecture des moments philosophiques qui se trouvent en Virgile — une clef néoplatonicienne, par laquelle les aperçus virgiliens sont enfermés dans un ensemble déterminé, dans une image du monde. Puis, Abélard invoque saint Jérôme pour suggérer les parallèles étroits qui existent entre l'enseignement stoïcien sur Dieu et le monde et le schéma chrétien. De la même façon, Abélard essaie de montrer que la lecture macrobienne de Virgile, bien qu'elle soit indépendante du christianisme, permet une autre lecture,

---

26 Traduction de Paul Valéry, *Bucoliques* (cit. n. 9), p. 123.

ésotérique (*mystice interpretanda*), qui révèle un sens latent pleinement chrétien.

La structure verbale est triple (comme le fil d'Alphésibée dans l'Églogue): il y a 1) les vers du poète inspiré, le *vates* dont les expressions cachent une signification profonde et cohérente — comme l'avait déjà vu Macrobe; 2) l'interprétation de Macrobe, qui rend explicite cette signification que souvent la langue poétique voilait; et 3) l'inteprétation chrétienne, qui débarrasse la macrobienne de tout ce qui, pour un chrétien, restait imprécis sur la nature de la divinité, et lui donne son sens le plus approprié et le plus pleinement lumineux, le sens que l'on peut voir enfin comme l'achèvement idéal de ce que le *vates* et le néoplatonicien voulaient exprimer.

On pourrait soupçonner que pour Abélard il y avait même un autre niveau distinct: car, derrière Virgile, il entrevoit la Sibylle. Ses oracles étaient une source énigmatique pour le poète, il les a développés d'une façon «inspirée», mi-consciente mi-inconsciente. Le don du poète est apparenté à celui de la Sibylle, mais il y a chez lui quelque chose de plus voulu. Chaque «lecture» des expressions voilées ou sibyllines — la lecture qu'en donne d'abord Virgile, puis Macrobe, et enfin le philosophe chrétien, rend un peu plus explicite la signification cachée, pour aboutir à la clarté sans voiles.

Dans le même contexte, Abélard donne aussi une longue citation du VIIe livre des *Confessions*: la confrontation détaillée que fait saint Augustin entre les textes néoplatoniciens et le prologue de l'Évangile de saint Jean. Augustin dit avoir reconnu dans les textes païens ce que saint Jean affirme de Dieu le Père et de son Verbe ou Nous — mais, insiste-t-il, ces textes ne contenaient aucune trace de l'incarnation du Verbe [27]. Dans sa lecture de Virgile, Abélard va plus loin: il y voit aussi une perception du Saint-Esprit comme consubstantiel avec le Nous, et enfin il y voit l'incarnation de l'enfant divin — révélée, bien que sous un voile.

Les éléments de la synthèse abélardienne ne sont pas nouveaux: Augustin à part, il y avait parmi les Pères de l'Église des rapprochements entre l'âme du monde et le Saint-Esprit, et il y avait, bien sûr, l'interprétation messianique de la IVe *Églogue*. Mais Abélard prend ces éléments et en fait pour ainsi dire une réponse nouvelle à saint Augustin. Là où Augustin dit de la vérité spécifiquement chrétienne, je ne l'ai pas trouvée là, parmi les païens — *non ibi legi, non est ibi* [28] — Abélard, se référant à Virgile, dit en effet: *ibi legi, est ibi*. Tout

---

[27] *Conf.*, VII, ix, 13-14. [Voir la discussion plus détaillée dans *Hermes and the Sibyls* (*infra*, no. 8)].
[28] *Ibid.*

est là, si on sait le lire: il faut seulement prendre dans ses justes conséquences la lecture révélatrice que Virgile apporte à l'oracle sibyllin, et Macrobe au texte de Virgile.

Bien que la lecture de l'*Énéide* de Bernard Silvestre soit la plus étendue et la plus cohérente qui nous reste du Moyen Âge, ce qui nous en reste s'arrête avant la fin du VIe livre; donc nous ne pouvons plus lire son interprétation du discours d'Anchise. Mais il y a des raisons de croire que cela allait être le plus haut point de son exégèse. Dans ce commentaire nous voyons, en fait, un «pèlerinage de la vie humaine», par lequel Énée (qui signifie l'esprit humain, *humanus spiritus*) s'achemine peu à peu vers la suprême science, la connaissance περὶ ἀρχῆς, que lui révèle Anchise (qui signifie le Père universel, *Pater omnium*). Pour Bernard, le VIe livre était celui où Virgile «déclare la vérité philosophique plus profondément qu'ailleurs» [29], et méritait donc un commentaire beaucoup plus ample que les autres livres. Il est probable que l'explication des livres VII à XII, que Bernard avait promise au début de son exposé, était aussi brève que celle des livres I à V; d'autre part, on ne peut pas exclure que Bernard ait changé son projet à mi-chemin, ou qu'il l'ait laissé inachevé.

Le commentaire, tel qu'il nous est parvenu, est non seulement fragmentaire mais montre des divergences significatives entre les quatre manuscrits — à vrai dire, quatre versions — qui restent toujours accessibles. Les variations, aussi bien que les répétitions fréquentes de détails, dans toutes les versions, montreraient, comme a bien observé Manlio Stocchi, que «le testimonianze manoscritte giunte fino a noi risalebbero a... distinte *recollectae* riproducenti un medesimo corso pubblico di lezioni quale fu registrato separatamente da differenti uditori» [30].

Malgré ces défauts dans la transmission du commentaire, on peut discerner un dessein lucidement conçu. Le nom d'Énée, dit Bernard, peut être analysé comme s'il était *ennos demas*. Cela signifie *habitator corporis*, l'habitant du corps — c'est-à-dire, l'âme. En réalité, ajoute-t-il, le deuxième mot, δέμα, signifie une chaîne (*vinculum*), parce que le corps est la prison de l'âme [31]. Ce jeu étymologique, que

---

[29] *The Commentary* (cit. n. 3), p. 28 (*profundius philosophicam veritatem in hoc volumine declarat Virgilius*).

[30] M. P. Stocchi, *Per il commento virgiliano di Bernardo Silvestre*, dans *Lettere italiane*, XXVII, 1975, 72-82 (ici p. 81). [Le fragment d'un commentaire dans le manuscrit Cambridge, Peterhouse 158, publié par C. Baswell, dans *Traditio*, XLI, 1985, 181-237, me paraît avoir un rapport moins étroit avec le commentaire bernardien].

[31] *The Commentary*, p. 10.

l'on rencontre pour la première fois chez Bernard, lui permet de voir l'âme, Énée, comme fils d'Anchise (le Créateur) et de Vénus, l'harmonie de l'amour cosmique. (En bon platonicien, Bernard distingue cette «Vénus céleste» de la Vénus lascive, qui est terrestre). Les six premiers livres de l'Énéide contiennent, voilées (*sub integumento*), des allusions aux étapes de la vie de l'âme: allusions à la naissance et à l'enfance dans le premier livre, à la première jeunesse dans le deuxième, à l'adolescence dans le troisième; les livres IV et V nous suggèrent la *iuventus* et la *virilis etas* d'Énée; enfin, dans le sixième livre, Énée atteint la compréhension philosophique, au moyen de sa descente aux enfers.

Le premier livre est rempli d'allégories physiologiques et morales. Le dieu des vents, Éole, signifie la naissance: il suscite les vents — les vices — qui assaillent la mer, qui est le corps. L'enfant Énée se nourrit de vaines images (*pictura pascit inani*): il est encore trop jeune pour comprendre la nature de la vraie félicité [32]. Puis, au IIᵉ livre, quand il raconte la fin de Troie, c'est une image de l'enfant commençant à parler: le récit d'Énée est un mélange d'histoire et de légende — tout comme l'enfant ne sait distinguer à fond entre vérité et fiction. (Pour Bernard, la source troyenne la plus digne de confiance était Darès). Pendant ses voyages, au IIIᵉ livre, Énée arrive en Crète — c'est-à-dire, à sa nature charnelle. Il n'atteint pas encore l'Italie, qui est sa nature céleste. Ainsi, au cours de sa jeunesse virile, que figure le IVᵉ livre, il cède à la *caverna* de la passion sexuelle; mais ensuite l'éloquence (le dieu Mercure) le persuade d'abandonner la sensualité (Didon) et de s'acheminer vers la sagesse. La sensualité, quand elle se trouve délaissée, se consume jusqu'aux cendres — Didon se réduit à la seule pensée. Dans le Vᵉ livre, Énée révère la mémoire d'Anchise, son père divin, par quatre concours: ce sont les quatre vertus cardinales. Alors il perd Palinure, qui signifie sa propre perception imparfaite (*errabunda visio*); enfin il peut voir que l'image de son père l'enjoint à la descente aux enfers. Ces enfers ne sont pas au-dessous de la terre: ils sont le monde visible, le seul monde par lequel l'esprit humain peut arriver à la connaissance du Père Créateur.

L'exposition du VIᵉ livre explique en détail comment tout le séjour aux enfers peut être interprété comme le voyage vers Dieu, au travers de réalités physiques et d'expériences intérieures. Le voyage commence par une conception imaginaire (*cogitatio imaginaria*), l'image humaine du père que nous retirons du monde sensible. Mais la gnose s'accomplit avec l'aide de la Sibylle, qui est le conseil divin

[32] *Ibid.*, p. 12.

(le jeu de mots ici est *Sibylla/scibile* — ce qu'il est possible de savoir) [33]. C'est elle qui guide l'esprit vers le rameau d'or de la philosophie, vers les *Triviae lucos* («les bois d'Hécate») qui représentent le Trivium, et vers les toits dorés (*aurea tecta*) du Quadrivium.

Telles sont les grandes lignes de la lecture allégorique. Cette lecture est souvent interrompue, surtout au cours du VIe livre, par des explications verbales et par des excursus philosophiques et physiologiques — une discussion complexe de l'ordre du savoir, par exemple, ou des renseignements sur les chambres du cerveau.

Les excursus à part, le schéma de Bernard est-il original? Bernard connaissait, évidemment, les ouvrages de Macrobe et de Fulgence. À Macrobe il doit quelques aspects de l'allégorèse psychologique des enfers virgiliens — de sorte que Phlégéthon, par exemple, signifie l'ardeur de la colère, Styx la haine, et Achéron la tristesse [34]. À Fulgence remontent les premières indications que le progrès d'Énée correspond aux âges de l'homme — bien que Bernard développe cette correspondance par une foule de subtilités nouvelles. Fulgence avait laissé entendre aussi que l'*Énéide* cachait des secrets de la nature (*secreta phisica*) [35], et il avait fourni à Bernard quelques jeux étymologiques significatifs — notamment ceux qui regardent les noms d'Éole, d'Anchise et de Palinure. Dans beaucoup de détails sur les mythes, et dans ses efforts de démythologiser, Bernard se sera sans doute servi d'une *koiné* mythographique où souvent on ne peut plus préciser la source directe — s'il s'agit, par exemple, de Servius ou d'Isidore ou de Remi d'Auxerre.

Enfin il faut se demander si, au moment où Bernard écrivait son commentaire (peut-être vers 1125-30), existait déjà le commentaire sur l'*Énéide* de Guillaume de Conches. Ce commentaire était conservé, à côté de celui de Bernard et de trois traités anonymes sur l'*Énéide*, dans un manuscrit de la Bibliotheca Amploniana d'Erfurt, qui aujourd'hui est malheureusement perdu [36]. Les deux savants, Bernard et Guillaume, s'intéressaient aux mêmes textes, y compris les nouveaux textes sur la médecine et l'astronomie traduits de l'arabe; ils donnaient souvent des cours sur les mêmes auteurs; dans l'état actuel de nos connaissances, la question de priorité ou d'influences

---

[33] *Ibid.*, p. 31. [La variante *siobole* (cf. Jones *ad loc.*) suggérerait plutôt l'étymologie isidorienne, à partir des mots grecs σιός et βουλή].

[34] *In Somn. Scip.* I, x, 11. Cf. P. Courcelle, *Les Pères de l'Église devant les enfers virgiliens*, dans *AHDLMA*, XXII, 1955, 5-74.

[35] Fulgentius (éd. cit.n. 18), *Virg. Cont.*, p. 83.

[36] Voir les détails fournis par G. Padoan, *Il pio Enea, l'empio Ulisse*, Ravenne, 1977, pp. 215-216.

réciproques ne peut pas se résoudre. Néanmoins il me paraît fort probable que la *conjointure* de Bernard (si je peux me servir de l'expression de Chrétien de Troyes) est une conjointure qui est vraiment la sienne. D'une façon soigneuse, presque émouvante, il oriente l'*Énéide* vers l'idéal humaniste chartrain — ou bien tourangeau, parce que Bernard est également conscient d'une tradition libérale tourangelle, qui comprenait déjà de grands noms comme Bérenger, Hildebert, et Adélard [37]. La conception dominante — lire l'*Énéide* comme le pèlerinage du savant, qui voit le progrès spirituel en termes d'un progrès dans les arts libéraux, pour aboutir à la profondeur métaphysique — peut bien être la contribution individuelle de Bernard.

Certes, on pourrait lui objecter qu'il y a quelque chose de trop forcé, de trop artificiel, dans une telle tentative de faire du héros virgilien le «nouvel homme» (*novus homo*) des humanistes du XIIe siècle. Cet Énée, en effet, n'est autre que l'image, humaine et divine à la fois, que les déesses reçoivent du Dieu suprême et qu'elles fabriquent dans un paradis terrestre — dans la *Cosmographia* de Bernard et ensuite dans l'*Anticlaudianus* d'Alain de Lille [38]. Même si on peut apercevoir des éléments d'un progrès spirituel chez l'Énée de Virgile, la carrière d'Énée, après tout, n'est pas celle d'*homo Carnotensis*.

On pourrait répondre que pour Bernard l'*Énéide* était en grande partie un prétexte. En tant que professeur, il devait inculquer beaucoup d'information sur la mythologie, la physique, et la morale, et souvent ce n'est que par un tour de force qu'il rapproche cette information du texte de Virgile. Mais il y avait aussi chez lui quelque chose de plus engagé. Bernard l'exprime dans un autre commentaire, celui sur Martianus, où il esquisse un parallèle structural entre l'*Énéide*, les *De nuptiis* de Martianus, et la *Consolation de Philosophie* de Boèce:

> Car, tout comme chez Virgile, Énée est guidé à travers les enfers, par la Sibylle qui l'accompagne, jusqu'à Anchise, ici, chez Martianus, Mercure est guidé à travers les régions du monde, par la vertu qui l'accompagne, jusqu'à Jupiter. C'est ainsi, également, que dans sa *Consolation* Boèce voyage à travers les faux biens jusqu'au bien suprême, guidé par Philosophia. Les trois images expriment presque la même réalité [39].

---

[37] Cf. Bernardus Silvestris, *Cosmographia* (éd. P. Dronke), Leyde, 1978, pp. 7-12.

[38] *Cosmographia* (éd. cit.), *Microcosmus* V-XII; *Anticlaudianus* (éd. R. Bossuat), Paris, 1955, VI-VII.

[39] Extrait du *Commentaire sur Martianus Capella*, éd. É. Jeauneau, dans *Lectio Philosophorum* (cit. n. 3), p. 41.

Le voyage de Natura dans la *Cosmographia* de Bernard — Natura, guidée par sa sœur céleste, Urania, jusqu'à Tugaton, le bien suprême — s'inscrirait aussi dans cette perspective. Cela veut dire qu'en fin de compte Bernard est plus proche de Virgile qu'il ne l'est de Macrobe: pour son héroïne, Natura, comme pour Énée, la tâche qui est son destin doit se réaliser sur la terre. C'est ainsi que, selon Bernard, le voyage d'Énée aux enfers est le voyage terrestre, le pèlerinage de la vie humaine — comme il explique: «Bien que le père, le Créateur, ne soit pas dans les créatures, on le rejoint pourtant par la connaissance des créatures».

L'influence du commentaire bernardien dépasse ce que les manuscrits seuls laissent soupçonner. Le plus ancien, de la première moitié du XIIIe siècle, provient de Saint-Martial de Limoges, un autre de Cambrai [40]; le troisième, bien que copié en France, inclut des commentaires italiens, et fut acheté par la Bibliothèque Jagellonienne à Cracovie en 1447 [41]. La version abrégée dans l'Ambrosiana (copiée vers 1400) est de provenance italienne; nous ne savons pas où fut copié le manuscrit perdu d'Erfurt, celui d'Amplonius. Mais il est certain que l'attrait d'une lecture «intégumentale» de l'*Éneide*, telle que Bernard l'a abordée, s'est fait sentir jusque dans les milieux humanistes, non seulement en Allemagne et en Pologne, mais aussi en Italie et en Espagne. Ainsi, par exemple, il y a une longue citation de Bernard dans le *De laboribus Herculis* de Coluccio Salutati, qui fait allusion à Bernard comme «l'allégoriste sérieux» de Virgile (*serius allegorizator*) [42]; et, au début du XVe siècle, le polygraphe espagnol Enrique de Villena munit sa traduction de l'*Énéide* d'un tas de gloses qui remontent souvent aux allégorèses de Bernard [43].

En Europe septentrionale, les premiers lecteurs du commentaire de Bernard étaient Jean de Salisbury et le troisième Mythographe (qu'il s'appelle ou non Albéric de Londres) [44]. Après eux, le problème des influences devient plus délicat. On avait désormais une convention — disons une grille — pour la lecture allégorique de l'*Énéide*, et tandis qu'on peut voir facilement, par exemple, que cette grille était connue de Dante, comme a montré Theodore Silverstein dans

---

[40] Cf. T. Silverstein, compte rendu de *The Commentary* (cit. n. 3), dans *Speculum* LIV, 1970, pp. 154-157.

[41] *The Commentary*, p. xvi.

[42] Cf. *Colucii Salutati de laboribus Herculis* (éd. B. L. Ullman), 2 t., Zurich, 1951, I, p. 193, 5-19, où Coluccio cite *The Commentary*, p. 71, 19-29. Voir aussi les autres références bernardiennes dans l'*Index Auctorum* d'Ullman, II, p. 644.

[43] Voir l'édition de Pedro M. Cátedra: *Enrique de Villena, Traducción y glosas de la Eneida*, 2 t., Salamanca, 1989.

[44] Cf. *Bernardo Silvestre* (cit. n. 5) p. 500.

une étude fondamentale, *Dante and Virgil the Mystic* [45], publiée il y a déjà un demi-siècle, la question de savoir si Dante dépend quelquefois directement de Bernard — comme l'a affirmé Ernst Robert Curtius [46] — reste très incertaine. Cependant avec Boccace, dans ses *Esposizioni sopra la Comedia di Dante*, nous pouvons en être presque sûrs. Boccace, qui avait copié lui-même la *Cosmographia* de Bernard, et qui la cite dans ses *Esposizioni*, y ajoute une allégorie très bernardienne de l'antre d'Éole [47], et là ce sont surtout les allusions physiologiques qui laissent croire qu'il adaptait Bernard — à moins que le commentaire perdu de Guillaume de Conches ait beaucoup ressemblé au bernardien sous cet aspect.

Enfin, je voudrais suggérer qu'en dehors de l'influence directe et indirecte de la lecture virgilienne de Bernard, on peut y voir le signe et la promesse d'un phénomène qui va s'épanouir en Europe au cours du XIIIe siècle. Je pense à toute la tendance à intérioriser la narration épique, qui peut prendre des formes très diverses. Dans le monde persan du XIIe et du XIIIe siècle, comme l'a montré Henry Corbin dans une belle étude, il y avait un véritable passage «de l'épopée héroïque à l'épopée mystique»: de grands penseurs et poètes, tels que Sohrawardî, ont transformé la vieille épopée des rois, le *Shâh-Nâmeh* de Ferdawsî, en évocations des aventures et des conquêtes à l'intérieur de l'âme, en récits d'initiations [48]. En Occident, on pourrait comparer la façon dont l'auteur de la *Queste del Saint Graal*, écrite vers 1225, a abordé ses sources plutôt romanesques, pour leur donner la puissance d'une fable spirituelle — ou bien l'immense commentaire ésotérique que constitue le poème *Der Jüngere Titurel* d'Albrecht von Scharfenberg sur le fragment *Titurel* de son grand prédécesseur, Wolfram von Eschenbach. En Europe c'était peut-être la conviction que l'*Énéide* cachait des sens intérieurs, qu'on pouvait dévoiler, qui a ouvert la voie à l'interprétation spirituelle de la matière épique et romanesque dans les langues vulgaires, même s'il ne s'agit plus d'un commentaire scolastique mais de créations nouvelles.

---

[45] *Harvard Studies and Notes*, XIV, 1932, 51-82.

[46] *Europäische Literatur und Lateinisches Mittelalter*, 2e éd., Berne, 1954, p. 359 n.

[47] Éd. G. Padoan (*Tutte le opere di Giovanni Boccaccio*, t. VI, Verona, 1965), pp. 134-136, 809-810.

[48] H. Corbin, *En Islam iranien*, II, Paris, 1971, surtout p. 211 et s.

II

IMAGINING THE DIVINE

4

THE PROLOGUE OF THE PROSE *EDDA*:
EXPLORATIONS OF A LATIN BACKGROUND *

I

We possess Snorri's mythological work in a state of disharmony: passages in *Ynglinga Saga* are at variance with passages in the Prose *Edda*; statements in the Prologue to the Prose *Edda* do not always tally perfectly with statements in *Gylfaginning*. We must suppose that Snorri's mind was — perhaps over many years — seeking different ways of presenting Norse heathen tradition. In *Ynglinga Saga* he presented traditions of the Norse gods as a form of history, a prelude to the lives of the Kings of Norway. In *Gylfaginning* he presented a fuller picture of heathen cosmology and myth as a tale within a tale; deliberately, that is, *not* as history. Why should such a master of the art of realistic historical narrative as Snorri value so highly, and return so often to, the fictions about the heathen gods — grotesque as they often were, and sometimes confused even beyond his power of repair? Was it only native piety that led him to record the ancestral traditions to ensure that they did not fall out of memory, or did he attribute to them a significance beyond the antiquarian? It is still commonly said that Snorri "apologized" for his native Norse mythology by presenting it as a devilish illusion [1]. We should like to suggest that, on the contrary, Snorri was convinced that the heathen traditions had a positive intellectual value for a Christian Norseman, and that he could have found confirmation for his conviction in certain Christian writings. We offer an examination of the opening paragraphs of the Prologue to the Prose *Edda* and a comparison with some Latin analogues to show the basis of our suggestion.

---

* Written with Ursula Dronke. *Sjötíu Ritgerthir helgathar Jakobi Benediktssyni* (2 vols., Reykjavík 1977), I 153-176.

[1] Cf. W. Baetke, *Die Götterlehre der Snorra-Edda* (Berichte... Sächs. Akad. 97, 3, Berlin 1952), pp. 37ff.; A. Holtsmark, *Studier i Snorres Mytologi* (Norske Videnskaps-Akad., II, Hist.-Filos. Kl. N.S. 4, Oslo 1964), pp. 15, 23ff.

II

For the beginning of Snorri's Prologue [2] scholars have signalled a parallel and possible source. This is in Martin of Braga's epistolary sermon *De correctione rusticorum*, a work that was utilized and in part adapted by later homilists, in Latin, Anglo-Saxon and Norse [3]. The precise nature and significance of the parallels between Martin and Snorri, however, have not hitherto been investigated.

First it should be said that the sequence of thought is close to Snorri only in the original Latin text of Martin, not in the later homilies deriving from it. Let us compare with Snorri, *Prologus* 1, the following paragraphs from Martin:

> When God in the beginning made heaven and earth, in the celestial dwelling he made spiritual creatures, that is, angels, to praise him as they stood before his gaze...
>
> After the angels' downfall, it pleased God to fashion a human being from the clay of the earth and set him in paradise...
>
> The first man was named Adam, and his wife, whom God created from Adam's flesh, was named Eve. From these two the whole race of mankind was propagated. But mankind, forgetting their creator, God, committing many crimes, stirred God to wrath. Because of this he sent a flood and destroyed them all, save for one just man named Noah, whom he preserved with his children in order to renew the human race.
>
> After the flood the race of men was restored by the three sons of Noah, who had been spared together with their wives. And when

---

[2] *Edda Snorra Sturlusonar*, ed. Finnur Jónsson (Copenhagen 1931), p. 1, ll. 1-16; all our citations are based on this edition. On the question of Snorri's authorship of the Prologue, see especially W. Baetke, op. cit. pp. 46ff., who also summarizes earlier discussions; A. Holtsmark, op. cit. pp. 6ff.

[3] C. P. Caspari's edition, *Martin von Bracara's Schrift de correctione rusticorum* (Christiania 1883), is still valuable for its extensive commentary and discussion of the various adaptations. There is a modern text in C. W. Barlow (ed.), *Martini Episcopi Bracarensis opera omnia* (New Haven 1950), pp. 159-203. On the relationships among the vernacular versions, see J. C. Pope (ed.), *Homilies of Ælfric: A Supplementary Collection* II (EETS, Oxford 1968), 669-70, who argues that "there can hardly be further question" that Ælfric's homily *De falsis diis* is the direct source for the Norse homily in *Hauksbók*: "The Norse writer is very free, but he follows Ælfric's order exactly aside from certain understandable omissions, and he moves through the same sequence of Biblical examples to the conclusion of the Daniel Story". See also the more detailed discussion by A. Taylor, *Leeds Studies in English*, N. S. III (1969), 101-9. On Wulfstan's homily, see D. Bethurum (ed.), *The Homilies of Wulfstan* (Oxford 1957), pp. 333ff., who says that in *De falsis dies* (sic) Wulfstan rewrote Ælfric's homily, but that there is no evidence that Wulfstan consulted Martin's Latin text.

an increasing multitude began to fill the world, once more mankind, forgetting the world's creator, began, in disregard of him, to worship creatures. Some adored the sun, some the moon or stars, others fire, others again the watery depth or welling springs, believing not that all these were made by God for mankind's use, but that they had emerged of their own accord and were gods.

Then the devil or his minions — the demons who were cast out of heaven — seeing that ignorant men, in disregard of the creator, were led astray by creatures, began to show themselves to men in diverse forms, to speak with them and ask that they should offer them sacrifices, on high mountains and in leafy woods, and worship them instead of God. The demons gave themselves the names of human malefactors, men who had spent their lives in every crime and misdeed, so that one demon called himself Jupiter, who had been a magician and tainted by monstrous adulteries... Another demon called himself Mars, who had been the instigator of quarrels and discord... [4]

The thought first moves from the creation, by way of the fall of the angels (which Snorri does not mention), to the fall of man. The next lines, both here and in Snorri [5], are essentially a recapitulation from *Genesis*: the multiplication of Adam and Eve's descendants over the earth, sinfulness and the forgetting of God, the destruction of the human race in the flood and its restoration through Noah. Then both Martin and Snorri say what *Genesis* does not: for a second time mankind, having again multiplied, neglected the worship of God and forgot the knowledge of the true God. In Martin this forgetting is seen as the origin of idolatry: the worship of creatures instead of the creator. Here Snorri diverges from the homilist, or indeed — if he knew this particular homily — deliberately contradicts him. For Snorri, the forgetting of God (*víthast um veröldina fanz eigi sá mathr, er deili kunni á skapara sínum*) is the beginning of a new dialectic, a process in which, aided by a divinely conferred earthly understanding, mankind recovers the knowledge of God, gradually and at first imperfectly, by way of observing created things. When, after the flood, men forgot God a second time, Snorri does not say as Martin does that they were deceived by demons. On the contrary, it is precisely then that the true God imparts new wisdom to mankind [6]. It is earthly wisdom, not spiritual; yet it is wisdom

---

[4] *De corr. rust.* 3-7. Here and below we cite both Latin and Icelandic texts in translation, in order to have a common denominator for comparisons; certain key phrases are also cited in the original languages.

[5] Ed. cit. p. 1, ll. 4-10.

[6] Ed. cit. p. 1, ll. 16ff.

enough for them to attain, by contemplating the created world, a glimmering of the nature of its creator, enough for them to renew their belief in his omnipotent presence behind earthly phenomena. The gift that, in Snorri's Prologue, God gives mankind after the flood is the power to observe cosmic design, and thence to understand what the philosophers and theologians call "the argument from design" for God's existence [7].

The Bible tells of God blessing Noah and his descendants after the flood, and of how God provided them with nourishment and fertility in the physical world; it also tells of the conditions God then laid down [8]. But neither in the Bible nor in commentaries on *Genesis* is there a trace of Snorri's assertion that at this time God "also conferred on them such wisdom, that they understood all terrestrial matters" (*mithlathi hann ok spekthina, svá at their skilthu alla jarthliga hluti*). As for the preoccupation of Martin, and of early exegetes of *Genesis*, with evil magic and idolatry — of these Snorri says not a word [9].

Martin does not refer to the tower of Babel in his sermon. On the other hand the two Old English homilies that derive from Martin — those of Ælfric [10] and Wulfstan [11] — make a link between the biblical Babel episode, after the flood, and the cult of different gods. This link has a certain counterpart in Snorri, yet Snorri is devoid of the polemical tone that the Anglo-Saxons exhibit. To cite Ælfric:

> Now we do not read in books that man started idolatry
> in all the time before Noah's flood,
> till the giants fashioned the wondrous tower [12]
> after Noah's flood, and God there granted them
> as many languages as there were builders.
> When they then travelled to distant lands
> and mankind multiplied, they were deceived
> by that ancient fiend who had tricked Adam before,

---

[7] Cf. Carl van Endert, *Der Gottesbeweis in der patristischen Zeit* (Freiburg i. Br. 1869).

[8] *Genesis* IX 1ff.

[9] In the Prologue (p. 5), "foresight" (*spádómr*) is attributed to the human Óthinn and Frigg; in *Gylfaginning* itself (pp. 8f.), Gylfi is said to be "wise" (*vitr*) and his knowledge of magic is not reprehensible; the human Æsir have "foresight", and the illusions (*sjónhverfingar*) they practise upon Gylfi are not said to be evil.

[10] Ed. Pope, II, 680, 72-81.

[11] Ed. Bethurum, p. 261.

[12] On the legend that the tower of Babel was built by giants, see J. C. Pope, ed. cit. II 713-714.

so that perversely they fashioned themselves gods
and failed to recognize the creator who had made them men.

When Snorri says that the belief in God, and the concept of
God, which men after the flood arrived at through their intuitive
"argument from design"

> changed in many respects, according as the peoples dispersed and
> their languages branched off from one another (*á marga lund breyz, svá
> sem thjóthirnar skiptuz ok tungurnar greinduz*) —

he is indeed alluding to Babel, and to the varying religious beliefs
that followed the differentiation of languages. But he does not make
this allusion in order to condemn. Despite the diversities that appeared, he goes on to suggest, the essential intuition underlying
them remained unchanged: the intuition that this world is an ordered world, and hence presupposes an orderer.

In Snorri, what leads Noah's descendants to the "argument
from design" is a series of observations of parallels between the earth
and living creatures, parallels that would seem to belong to the tradition of macrocosm-microcosm speculation [13], yet for the details of
which in Snorri we can suggest no precise source. In addition, says
Snorri, men's observations of the universe, of the balance between
an unchanging earth and sun and stars and the changing motions
amongst them, as these insights gained force through being handed
down over generations, prompted the inference to a "governor of the
heavenly bodies" (*stjórnari himintunglanna*). The sentences about astronomy form the transition to the "argument from design" itself,
and to this we now turn.

III

Many theologians have stated explicitly what Snorri supposes to
be true of mankind after the flood — that it is an essentially human
attribute to be able to see the "argument from design", to make an
inference from the order and beauty of the visible world to a divine
orderer. To cite at least one testimony, from Augustine, that specifically refers to mankind before the Christian revelation, mankind at
the time when, in Snorri's words, "They did not know where his

---

[13] On this tradition see especially R. Allers, *Traditio* II (1944) 319-407; M.
Kurdzialek, *Miscellanea Mediaevalia* VIII (1971) 35-75; F. Rico, *El pequeño mundo
del hombre* (Madrid 1970).

kingdom was, and yet believed that he ruled all things on earth and in the air of heaven". Augustine says:

> Since God is proclaimed to all creation, even to all pagan peoples, before they could believe in Christ, the name of God could not have remained utterly unknown. For this is the power of true divinity: it cannot be absolutely and completely hidden from a rational creature that uses its reason. Except for a few men in whom nature is too much corrupted, the whole human race affirms that God is the author of this world [14].

The "argument from design", of which there is already a trace in the biblical *Book of Wisdom* [15], can be found elaborated in many places in the Latin tradition, from Cicero and Seneca to the major Church Fathers, down to numerous theologians of Snorri's time. It would be pointless to try to suggest a specific source here. We should like, however, to compare in some detail with Snorri one of the earliest Christian Latin testimonies, in Minucius Felix's dialogue *Octavius*. Though this work enjoyed scant diffusion [16], it shows a movement of thought that has clear affinities with Snorri's, it has an eloquence and intellectual command worthy to set beside his, and of all the testimonies from the early Church it is the one closest to Snorri in seeing the positive elements in pagan belief as outweighing the negative. —

---

[14] *In Joannis Evangelium* CVI (Corpus Christianorum XXXVI 610). An even more far-reaching claim had been made by Tertullian (*Adv. Marcionem* I 10, Corpus Christianorum I 451): it was the God of Moses who was known, through innate conscience, by the greater part of mankind, who had not even heard the name of Moses, even those beclouded by idolatry:

> Denique maior popularitas generis humani, ne nominis quidem Moysei compotes, nedum instrumenti, deum Moysei tamen norunt; etiam tantam idolatria dominationem obumbrante... Ante anima quam prophetia. Animae enim a primordio conscientia dei dos est; eadem nec alia in Aegyptiis et in Syris et in Ponticis.

[15] *Sap.* XIII 1ff. — but the point of this passage is invective against those who do not see the force of the "argument from design", or who, while seeming to see it, infer from it a plurality of gods. So, too, the discussion of the origins of idolatry in *Sap.* XIV, while clearly it will have been known to Snorri, and may have been at the back of his mind when he wrote of kings who become taken for gods, is too hostile in tone to be aptly compared with the Prologue.

[16] Only one early (ninth-century) manuscript survives, and no allusions to the work were found in the medieval library catalogues investigated by Max Manitius (*Handschriften antiker Autoren in mittelalterlichen Bibliothekskatalogen*, Leipzig 1935).

All men, without distinction of age, sex or rank, were created with the capacity and skill both of reason and sense: they do not acquire wisdom through fortune — no, it is implanted in them by nature...

What can be so evident, so manifest and clear, when you raise your eyes to heaven and gaze on what is below and round about, than that there is some divinity of surpassing intellect by whom all nature is inspired, moved, nurtured, governed?

Look at the heaven, how far it is outstretched, how swiftly it is whirled — studded with stars at night or irradiated by the sun by day — then you will recognize how wondrous and divine a balance is set in it by a supreme moderator. Look at the year, brought about by the circling of the sun, the month, determined by the waxing, waning and effort of the moon... Or again, when the order of the seasons and their stable variety of fruits is recognized, does not spring proclaim his divine author and parent by his flowers, summer by her harvests, autumn by his happy ripeness, and winter by her vital olive-crop? This order would be easily overthrown, were it not held fast by the highest reason... Look at the ocean: it ebbs and floods in reciprocal tides...

Thus in this house of the universe, when you see heaven and earth as providence, order, law, you may be sure that the lord and parent of the whole is more beautiful than any of the parts, more beautiful even than the stars themselves.

In this do I not have the assent of all mankind? I hear the crowd, when they stretch out their hands to heaven, say nothing but "God", "God is great", "God is true", and "if God wills". Is this the natural speech of ordinary people, or the prayer of a professing Christian? Those who would see Jupiter as the all-ruler are mistaken in the name, yet they agree there is a single highest power...

I have expounded the opinions of almost all the more illustrious and glorious philosophers: they designated the one God, though under many names, in such a way that one would think either that Christians now are philosophers, or that already then the philosophers were Christians.

But if the world is ruled by providence and governed by the will of the one God, then the ancient tradition of the ignorant, delighted or captivated by fairy-tales, must not drag us into a mistaken agreement: that realm of fantasy is refuted by the arguments of its own philosophers, helped by the authority of reason and great age. For our ancestors believed so readily in fictions, that rashly they gave credence even to monsters, mere miracles: Scylla with her many coils, the multiform Chimaera ... Before the world was opened up by commerce and peoples syncretized their rites and customs, each nation venerated its founder, or an illustrious chieftain, or a virtuous queen brave beyond her sex, or the inventor of some useful gift or art, as a citizen good to commemorate: thus it was a tribute to the dead and an exemplar to those who were to come...

> Euhemerus records those who were held to be gods on account
> of the excellence of their virtue or their gift... Prodicus tells of those
> who were adopted into the pantheon, who by their voyaging and by
> the new fruits they discovered bestowed social benefits on mankind [17].

The Christian God, says Octavius, is invisible, and yet Christians can
perceive him (*sentire*) by way of the visible world, just as did the men
of ancient times:

> For in his works and in all the motions of the universe we per-
> ceive his ever-present power, when he thunders, flashes forth or ful-
> minates, and when he is serene. Do not be amazed if you do not see
> him: all things are impelled, stirred, whirled by wind and tempests,
> yet wind and tempests are not seen by the eyes [18].

In the later part of the dialogue, when Octavius turns to the
forms of cult by which the ancient benefactors of mankind are worshipped, he uses invective and ridicule, as became customary among
the later Fathers. But both in his "argument from design" — possible, as he claims, for all mankind to see — and in his exposition of
euhemerism, what is remarkable is the temperate tone. The ancients
were credulous in seeing their dead kings and *héros civilisateurs* as divine, yet with their credulity went a laudable reverence for heroic virtue and a gratitude for great benefits.

Several points of comparison with Snorri seem particularly
noteworthy. The power to see the "argument from design" is not the
prerogative of philosophers (even if they, according to Minucius Felix, have voiced it most articulately): men know it with a "wisdom
implanted by nature" (*natura insitos esse sapientiam*) in Minucius'
words; "they knew it by earthly wisdom" (*skildu their jarthligri skilningu*) in Snorri's.

Snorri passed from this intuition to an account of the world as
it was in those days, and thence, at length, to the Æsir, suggesting
how they came to be taken for gods. The Æsir were specially
favoured human beings, favoured in their wisdom and strength and
beauty, and they were benefactors to the peoples among whom they
travelled: "Such well-being accompanied their travels, that wherever
they stayed in any countries, there were then good seasons and peace,

---

[17] *Octavius* XVI 5; XVII 4ff.; XVIII 4, 10-11; XX 1-3, 6; XXI 1-2. The Budé
edition (ed. J. Beaujeu, Paris 1964) is particularly valuable for its detailed commentary and classical parallels; the editor, however, is very much *parti pris* in seeing
Minucius Felix as later than Tertullian and deriving from him.

[18] *Octavius* XXXII 4-5.

and all believed it was they who determined this" (*ok sa timi fylgthi ferth theira, at hvar sem their dvölthuz ilöndum, tha var thar ar ok frithr, ok truthu allir, at their væri thes rathande*) [19]. Octavius, too, knows of such primeval benefactors, of surpassing strength and skill and fame, who travelled and brought fertility and social blessings. Unlike Snorri, he begins by tilting at the credulity of later generations, who mistook such ancient benefactors for gods; but like him he realizes that this reverence for the strangers, the travellers who bring blessings, must belong to a particular stage of history, when communities and languages were cut off from one another, and hence these strangers could have an exceptional aura for those whom they visited and favoured. In Snorri's words, "wherever they travelled throughout the lands, many glorious things were said concerning them, so that they were thought to be more like gods than men" (*hvar sem their foru ifir lönd, tha var agæti mikit fra theim sagt, sva at their thottu likari gothum en monnum*) [20]: Snorri, that is, differentiates like Octavius between a first stage, of admiring veneration, and a second, of complete deification. Both Octavius and Snorri see the apotheosis of outstanding human beings as an illusion of communities too much cut off from one another in space and time. It is a mistake, but an understandable one.

IV

In the opening paragraphs of the Prologue, Snorri has some striking passages concerned with naming. When men became evil again after the flood, they no longer wanted to name God (*vildu eigi nefna guth*); thus they could no longer tell their children of the creator's mighty deeds, and at last they lost the name of God (*týndu guths nafni*). But when they recovered a knowledge of the creator, through contemplation of created things, they gave names to all things out of their own minds, in order to describe the creator's power the better. Then, as races separated and languages diverged, "this belief" (*thessi átrúnathr*) also altered in many respects. The implication seems to be that naming was the essential first stage of communicating understanding and, dependent upon understanding, belief.

[19] Ed. cit. p. 6, ll. 16-18. In this respect both Minucius Felix and Snorri contrast sharply in their view with Martin of Braga, who speaks of the demons taking the names of primordial human malefactors (*inponentes sibi vocabula sceleratorum hominum, qui in omnibus criminibus et sceleribus suam egerant vitam — De corr. rust. 7*).

[20] Ed. cit. p. 5, ll. 10-12.

Such a preoccupation with preserving and handing down the name of God correctly could be paralleled in certain Hellenistic Gnostic texts, but we know of nothing comparable in the main-stream of the Latin tradition. Belief in the validity, or quasi-numinous force, of the primordial naming of peoples and things, however, has both Germanic and Christian roots. Tacitus mentions the distinction that was made by the Germans of his day between a "recent and lately added" name (*recens et nuper additum*) such as that of "German" and the "true and ancient names" (*vera et antiqua nomina*) of the individual Germanic peoples [21]. In the Christian con-text, the significance of naming emerges most clearly in discussions of *Genesis* II 19, where Adam names the animals. Bede for instance, who follows Augustine in the main features of his exposition, con-trasts this moment of archetypal naming with the multifarious nam-ing that replaces it after Babel, which, though at first still God-given, became eventually a random naming:

> It is clear that Adam bestowed names on the living creatures of the earth and the birds of the sky in the language that the whole hu-man race spoke till the building of the tower. But at the fall of the tower, when God gave each nation its own distinct tongue, he must be thought to have given the nations distinct names for animals as for other things, in accordance with each language. It is obvious, however, that later mankind gave new names at will, to new phenomena and to living creatures, throughout the peoples; they continue to do so even now [22].

All the commentators on the *Genesis* passage agree that Adam's summons by God to name the animals was a special divine favour, given in order to show man that he surpassed all the rest of crea-tion [23]. The divine aspect of the naming is emphasized strikingly by Remigius of Auxerre in his commentary:

> Adam bestowed names on all things in Hebrew. But when the languages were divided, the various nations called everything accord-ing to their own nature and pleasure. God made all things come to Adam, that he should impose names according to his own decision,

---

[21] *Germania* 2, 2f.; cf. A. Borst, *Der Turmbau von Babel* II i (Stuttgart 1958), 439.

[22] *Hexaemeron* II 19-20 (Corpus Christianorum CXVIII A 55); cf. Augustine, *De Genesi ad litteram* IX 12 (Corpus Script. Eccl. Lat. XXVIII i, 281-2).

[23] Apart from Augustine and Bede (loc. cit.), cf. for instance Claude of Turin (Patrologia Latina 50, 908-9) and Angelom of Luxeuil (P.L. 115, 134).

that through this he might recognize that he was held dearer and worthier than the rest, being granted such a power by the Lord. Figuratively Adam signifies Christ... who imposed a name on all creation —
that is, on mankind, whom, through regeneration, he transmuted
(*transtulit*) into a new creation, for he wanted them to be called by his
own name, Christian [24].

The redemption is a new act of speech, a new "metaphor" (*transtulit*
in the technical sense), as well as a transformation, making new the
face of the earth.

The commentators on *Genesis* speak of the separation of tongues
at Babel in a condemnatory way: it was a punishment for man's *superbia*; the attempt to build the tower was "the self-exaltation of heret-
ics" (*elatio haereticorum*) [25]. Once more Snorri stands in contrast
with the theological tradition: he alludes only to a diversification of
language and belief; in tone his allusion remains neutral. At the close
of *Gylfaginning* he states that the Æsir applied to historical persons
and places ("to the men and places that were there"), that is to men
in their own community and places familiar to them, the mythological names in the legends they had recounted to Gylfi, so that people
should not doubt that the two Æsir, the mythological and the historical, were identical [26]. This somewhat puzzling procedure (the moral
implications of which we discuss later) is illuminated by an argument
such as Lactantius develops — if for the moment we disregard his
fierce polemic framework — when he speaks of the gods of the
Graeco-Roman world. The purpose of Lactantius' euhemerism is to
show that the poets' myths are garbled, but not wholly false: there
is a substratum of historical truth. Similarly, the names of the gods
are not arbitrary: once upon a time, *in illo tempore*, there existed a
great king who named his parents Heaven and Earth, Ouranos and
Gaia. To Lactantius, of course, he was no god, but

> One could argue thus: Saturn, since he was a most mighty king,
> to perpetuate his parents' memory, gave them the names Heaven and
> Earth, though previously they were called by other names. It is for the
> same reason that we know names (of venerated human beings) have
> been given to mountains and to rivers... It is no wonder, then, that
> the names Heaven and Earth were given to those who had brought
> forth the mightiest of kings [27].

[24] *Comm. in Gen.* II 19 (P.L. 131, 62-63).
[25] Ibid. XI 9 (P.L. 131, 81).
[26] Ed. cit. pp. 76f.
[27] *Divinae Institutiones* I xi.

V

In the ninth century, it was probably Remigius of Auxerre who compiled a systematic, synoptic account of the Graeco-Roman gods and their stories, the little treatise that goes under the name of the Second Vatican Mythographer. It begins with a prologue that is instructive to compare and contrast with Snorri's: [28].

> Those whom the pagans venerate, claiming that they are gods, turn out to have been men of former times: the pagans began to worship them after their deaths, on account of the life or merits of each one. Thus Isis came to be worshipped in Egypt, Jupiter in Crete, Juba among the Moors, Faunus in Latium, Quirinus among the Romans, Minerva in Athens, Juno in Samos, Venus among the Paphians, Vulcan among the Lemnians, Liber among the people of Naxos and Apollo among those of Delos.
>
> The poets, too, embarked upon their praises, and exalted these mortals to the skies by the songs they composed. They are given names according to their deeds, as for instance Mercury because he is set over merchandise, and Liber's name derives from liberty. There were also brave men, or founders of cities, of whom people made statues when they were dead, because they loved them, and that they themselves might have solace for the loss of these heroes by contemplating their images. Here an error crept upon their descendants, through the persuasive influence of demons, so that those whom the ancestors had honoured only to commemorate their name, the descendants took to be gods and worshipped them.
>
> The Stoics say there is only one god and goddess, alike in power, and by reason of their offices and acts they are called by various names. It is the same god who is called now Sol, now Liber, now Apollo; the same goddess who is called now Luna, now Diana, now Ceres, now Juno, now Proserpina. The divinities, however, seem to comprehend both sexes, in that they are incorporeal.

The first two paragraphs of Remigius' prologue are taken over, with light alterations, from the opening of Isidore of Seville's chapter on pagan gods in his *Etymologiae* (VIII xi); the whole of this chapter was incorporated in the ninth century in Hrabanus Maurus' encyclopaedic compilation *De universo* [29] and thereby enjoyed even wider

---

[28] Ed. G. H. Bode, *Scriptores rerum mythicarum Latini tres* (Cellis 1834), I 74ff. On the identification of the second mythographer with Remigius of Auxerre, cf. P. Courcelle, *La Consolation de Philosophie dans la tradition littéraire* (Paris 1967), pp. 244-8.

[29] XV vi (P.L. 111, 426-436).

diffusion. Here we meet a relatively sympathetic account of the principle of euhemerism [30] — only the notion that a laudable veneration of ancestors was replaced by a false ancestor-worship, through the influence of demons, reveals its Patristic past. With the euhemeristic principle Isidore and Remigius combine an etymological principle, attempting to relate the names of gods to their natures and functions or to the benefits they confer. For such etymologizing of divine names, Cicero's *De natura deorum* is of special importance in the pre-Christian Latin tradition [31]. While its influence in the Middle Ages never matched that of Isidore's work, the *De natura deorum* is read again with special interest in twelfth-century France, particularly at Tours and at Chartres.

The etymologies of names of gods in Snorri's Prologue, however, have a somewhat different character, and have evidently undergone another influence. The importance Snorri attaches to Troy, and his efforts to relate the Norse names to Trojan ones, suggest rather an attempt to give his people's ancestors the same Trojan aura as writers such as Nennius, and above all Geoffrey of Monmouth, had conjured up for the Kings of Britain [32]. Here it is less a question of finding a meaningful element in the name than of finding approximate parallels of sound that will suggest a link with names from the Homeric world. Not *Liber a libertate*, but Brutus-Brito, would seem to be the inspiration behind such links as Snorri makes: Trór-Thórr, Trákiá-Thrúthheim, or Síbíl-Sif.

The final paragraph of Remigius' prologue is his own. The notion that a single god is the reality underlying the many different divine names, comes close to Snorri's idea both of mankind's inference to an all-ruler and the diversification in their naming of him. Remigius, however, adds that it is the same with the names of goddesses: he does not, that is, suggest there is a fundamental human

---

[30] On Graeco-Roman euhemerism and its early Christian reception, see K. Thraede's admirable account, "Euhemerismus", in *Reallexikon für Antike und Christentum* VI 877-890. For later medieval variations on euhemerism, cf. J. D. Cooke, *Speculum* II (1927) 396-410.

[31] On the etymologizing of divine names, cf. R. Klinck, *Die lateinische Etymologie des Mittelalters* (München 1970), pp. 177ff.; for instances of the twelfth-century influence of *De natura deorum*, cf. P. Dronke, *Fabula* (Leiden-Köln 1974), pp. 22, 29, 37, 91, 176; id., "New Approaches to the School of Chartres", *Anuario de Estudios Medievales* VI (1969) 133-5 [*supra*, no. 1, pp. 32-35; cf. also "Problemata Hildegardiana", *infra*, no. 6, pp. 162-4].

[32] See especially E. Faral, *La légende arthurienne* II (Paris 1929) 69-92; A. Heusler, "Die gelehrte Urgeschichte im isländischen Schrifttum" (1908, reprinted in his *Kleine Schriften* II, Berlin 1969, 80ff.).

intuition of monotheism, even though he moves a step nearer such a suggestion with his final sentence, where he says that the one god and the one goddess comprehend both sexes.

The step that Remigius does not take was taken by his successor, the so-called Third Vatican Mythographer, in his prologue to a similar didactic work on stories of gods and goddesses. While an attempt has been made to identify this mythographer as Alberic of London [33] (which would mean he was a slightly older contemporary of Snorri's), this identification, and the author's date and milieu, still remain uncertain. At all events, in his prologue he makes the thought of Remigius more lucid and consistent; and while he here utilizes predecessors both pagan and Christian — Servius, Augustine, Fulgentius, Remigius himself [34] — his reverence for pagan philosophers (and indeed his dismissal of the ignorant multitude) indicates that this author has undergone the influence of twelfth-century humanism:

> ... ignorance did not envelop all mankind, nor did everyone think the rites of idolatry should be accepted. For philosophers, whose authority has in many cases handed down either a way to truth or an affirmation of reason, say that there is a single god, undoubtedly the creator of heaven and earth and of all things. Yet they call him many names, on account of the manifold ordering principle of the world. He is called Vitumnus in that he grants life, Sentinus in that he bestows sense-perception. He is called Jove or Jupiter in the ether, Juno in the air, Diana in the earth, and there are many other names of the same god, as though they were names of many gods. And often one and the same god is not only spoken of by diverse names, but is said to be of varied sex... [35]

This passage raises the fascinating and difficult question, to what extent could Snorri have been influenced by twelfth-century Latin thought, as against Patristic thought? R.M. Meyer, who has the merit of first suggesting some points of comparison between

[33] Cf. E. Rathbone, *Mediaeval and Renaissance Studies* I (1941) 35-38. Miss Rathbone's thesis depends on citations in Helinand's *Chronicon* from a "Magister Albericus Lundoniensis in poetario suo"; but she has, in my view, given no evidence to show that this "poetarius" is fully identical with the text of Mythographus Tertius, rather than being simply a work which draws upon the mythographic text.

[34] Apart from the explicit references in the mythographer's prologue, the opening story, about Syrophanes, is adapted from Fulgentius, *Mitol.* 1, 1; the verses of Valerius Soranus and the citation of Varro go back to Augustine, *Civ.* VII ix and VII vi respectively; the other anonymous verses are cited from Servius, *in Aen.* IV 638.

[35] *Scriptores rerum mythicarum* I 152.

Snorri and the Third Vatican Mythographer [36], was careful to stress that he had in mind the influence not of this particular Latin text but of a text *of this type* (perhaps one lost today). Nonetheless, Meyer believed it was a question of direct influence, of Snorri's having had access to a particular Latin mythographic text. In what follows we would not wish to go so far: it may well be a question of indirect rather than direct influences. But we would suggest that some of the emphases Snorri gives in his Prologue are akin to those given by some of the greatest twelfth-century Christian platonists — by William of Conches, Thierry of Chartres, Hugh of Saint-Victor, Bernard Silvestris, and Alan of Lille. There is nothing in Snorri's Prologue to show that he had works by these men at his elbow (though that he had read some of their writings cannot of course be ruled out). Much, however, suggests to us that Snorri had become familiar with some of their most remarkable ideas — perhaps through conversations with scholars who had studied in France, or through teachers who had undergone this platonizing influence. Above all, we believe a certain influence, direct or indirect, was possible because Snorri would have found in twelfth-century Latin humanist speculation much that was congenial to him, much that he could absorb because of its kinship with his own attitude to myth and the temperament with which he approached mythological speculation.

VI

The suggestions that follow must remain brief and tentative. If one compares, for instance, the approaches to pagan myth of Snorri and the Chartres humanist William of Conches [37], it will be at once apparent how much these two men have in common that sets them apart from the entire Patristic tradition, even from Minucius Felix, who was perhaps its most humanistic representative, at least in the Latin world. It should go without saying that Snorri and William are not neo-pagans [38]: their attitude to the myths they relate is intellec-

---

[36] "Snorri als Mythograph", *Arkiv för nordisk Filologi* XXVIII, N.F. XXIV (1912) 109-121.

[37] On William's approach to pagan myth, see especially E. Jeauneau, "L'usage de la notion d'*integumentum* à travers les gloses de Guillaume de Conches", (1957, reprinted in his *Lectio Philosophorum*, Amsterdam 1973, pp. 127-192); P. Dronke, *Fabula*, chs. I and III, and Appendix B.

[38] This is unfortunately the suggestion made regarding Bernard Silvestris' use of pagan elements in his *De mundi universitate* (or *Cosmographia*), in E. R. Curtius' otherwise admirable chapter "Die Göttin Natura", *Europäische Literatur und*

tually alert, often witty and ingenious, at times even sardonic, yet there is never any underlying hatred or scorn such as the Church Fathers showed, no trace of the pervasive Patristic belief that the myths are diabolically inspired, and that hence they must be either redeemed (exorcized) or rejected.

With the unpolemical attitude to pagan myths the twelfth-century humanists combined a more positive attitude to earthly wisdom, an attitude that Snorri shares. The distinction between earthly and spiritual wisdom continued to be made — just as Snorri makes it (*En alla hluti skildu their jarthligri skilningu, thvíat theim var eigi gefin andlig spekthin*) [39]. But where in previous centuries the principal purpose of such a distinction tended to the disparagement of earthly — merely earthly — wisdom, in the twelfth century it far more often led to the exaltation of such wisdom. Even when the distinction was made in Pauline terms, the emphasis was far less on the darkness of what can be seen *per speculum in aenigmate* than on the wonder of seeing *invisibilia dei per ea quae facta sunt* [40] — the wonder Snorri celebrates in his own way in *Prologus* 1.

Boethius had already shown how sensory knowledge is integrated in the knowledge of imagination, reason, and intellectuality, and for mankind forms the necessary base for these [41]. It is this sense of the vital need of earthly understanding, as the base of all human understanding, however high, that underlies the new myths fashioned by the twelfth-century platonists: Bernard Silvestris' account of man's creation, by goddesses of nature, in an earthly paradise [42]; Alan of Lille's chariot that ascends the spheres guided by human understanding and drawn by horses who are the five senses [43]; or his fable of the four spheres, that culminates in revealing the lowest, sensory sphere as the centre of the highest, the divine sphere, whose midpoint is "the handiwork, creation" [44]. While the Chartres platonists and Bernard and Alan also emphasize the element of divine favour, the gift of knowledge that comes from on high, the precise way in which they exalt specifically human understanding might be seen as epitomized by Snorri's words:

lateinisches Mittelalter (2nd ed., Bern 1954), ch. VI, esp. pp. 121-2 ("ein heidnischer Humanismus... von der Atmosphäre eines Fruchtbarkeitskultus durchdrungen").

[39] Ed. cit. p. 3, ll. 4-6.
[40] See especially *Fabula* pp. 32-47.
[41] *Consolatio Philosophiae* V pr. 4-5.
[42] [*Cosmographia* (ed. P. Dronke, Leiden 1978) II ix-xii].
[43] *Anticlaudianus* (ed. R. Bossuat, Paris 1954) IV-V.
[44] *Alain de Lille: Textes inédits*, ed. M.-Th. d'Alverny (Paris 1965), pp. 297-306; cf. P. Dronke, *Fabula* pp. 144-153.

God also conferred on mankind such wisdom, that they understood all terrestrial matters, and all the varied phenomena which they
could see in the air and the earth (*mithlathi hann ok spekthina, svá at
their skilthu alla jarthliga hluti ok allar greinir, thær er sjá mátti lopts ok
jarthar*).

What was mankind able to understand with the wisdom of the
earth, without spiritual understanding? According to Snorri, "that
all things were fashioned of some substance" (*at allir hlutir væri
smíthathir af nökkuru efni*) [45]. Anne Holtsmark would see this as
typifying erroneous understanding, the carnal or heretical belief of
those who lack spiritual knowledge [46]. As Snorri has already emphasized that this wisdom is God-given, such an interpretation cannot
be correct. On the contrary, we suggest that what Snorri here evokes
is the fundamental understanding of creation as the twelfth-century
Christian platonists saw it, and it is an understanding of this kind,
however limited, that he attributes to his pre-Christian ancestors.

Was the notion that "all things were fashioned of some substance" incompatible with the notion which had long established itself as orthodox, that God created all things out of nothing? In the
twelfth century, as in most periods, there were fundamentalists about
who held that *creatio ex nihilo*, or else the *Genesis* account of creation, invalidated the whole of the platonic cosmological speculations
and made them heretical [47]. Yet despite the attempts to silence such

[45] Ed. cit. p. 3, ll. 6f. Note the text of the Uppsala MS: *trutho, at allt veri af
nockuro efni skapat ethr smithat*. Anne Holtsmark (op. cit. p. 23) would wish to contrast *skapa*, which she sees as the orthodox Christian conception, against *smítha*,
which she sees as designating the specifically pagan error:
> "We should note that the word *skapa* is not used; *smítha* presupposes that
> there is a substance out of which to 'fashion', and it is in fact heathenism to
> believe that 'all things were fashioned from some substance'".

Clearly the Uppsala copyist was unaware of such a distinction. That Holtsmark's contrast is in any case untenable can be seen from such passages as the Vulgate text of *Ps.* LXXIII 16-17, where the verbs *fabricari* (*smítha*) and *facere* (*skapa*)
are used synonymously of the divine creative action:

Tu fabricatus es auroram et solem.

Tu fecisti omnes terminos terrae;

Aestatem et ver tu plasmasti ea.

[46] Op. cit. p. 22f. It should be noted that Augustine himself renders the biblical phrase, addressed to God in *Sap.* XI 18, as *Qui fecisti mundum ex materia informi*,
both in *De Genesi imperfectus liber* III 10 and *De Genesi ad litteram* I xiv, 28 (the
Vulgate has *quae [omnipotens manus] creavit orbem terrarum ex materia invisa*). Augustine, moreover, suggests that this *materia informis* existed before time (*Conf.* XII
xxix, 40; cf. Hrabanus Maurus *in Genesim*, P.L. 107, 446).

[47] On this and on Thierry of Chartres's interpretation of the opening of *Gene-*

brilliant teachers as Abelard and William of Conches, the narrowly
orthodox did not succeed in suppressing the thought of the Christian platonists. There were two principal ways in which these could
present their speculations in a manner compatible with orthodoxy:

1) God created primordial matter (Hyle, or Silva), or a primordial substance (Usia), out of nothing, with the creation of time, and
informed the substrate with a principle of development by which an
ordered universe was able to unfold. (Thierry of Chartres indeed
presented an account of this kind as being the literal meaning of the
Genesis story).

2) The primordial substrate could be seen as having no beginning, as being perpetual — but this did not mean it was eternal in
the same sense as God was eternal. For such a distinction, between
the perpetuity of the world and an eternity that is unique to God,
a "complete possession of limitless life all at once", the twelfth-
century platonists had the high authority of Boethius [48]. Only to
claim for matter the same kind of eternal life as for God would have
been generally deemed heretical.

Thus the earthly wisdom of the pre-Christian world, the idea
that all things were created out of some substance, far from being a
failure of true understanding, brings out precisely that bond between
the finest pagan speculation and Christian thought which the
twelfth-century platonists stressed over and over again in their writings. The earthly wisdom that God gave the pagans was a true divine
gift. He gave it, among others, to Plato, whose account of the divine
artificer, and of the way he created out of the primordial substance,
Plato's twelfth-century Christian disciples harmonized with *Genesis*
and with the *creatio ex nihilo*.

VII

Finally, there is one remarkable feature about Snorri's account
of how men arrived at the "argument from design" which has not,
it seems, been noted hitherto, and which may owe something to
another moment in twelfth-century speculation. From men's macro-
cosmic observations, "The thought stirred within them (*grunathi*)
that there might be some governor of the heavenly bodies"; "in order that one might the better describe these matters, and root them

sis, see P. Dronke, "New Approaches to the School of Chartres" pp. 133-9 [*supra*,
no. 1, pp. 32-39].

[48] *Consolatio Philosophiae* V pr. 6; cf. P. Courcelle, *La Consolation de
Philosophie* pp. 221-231.

fast in the memory, they then gave names out of their own minds (*meth sjálfum sér*) to all things" [49]. Does it not look as if, in addition to the inference men make from observable phenomena, Snorri is suggesting that there is latent in the human mind an idea of the divine ruler of created things, and that the reason the names given are worthy of remembrance, and that the memory is not delusive, is because the mind which bestows the names is aware that it is naming things of divine origin? In the human mind itself there is something that allows the inference to God the designer to be realized, and allows the names to reflect the truth that things *are* designed. It is just such a "psychological" element that was introduced into the "argument from design", for the first time in the twelfth century, in Hugh of Saint-Victor's *De sacramentis* [50]. It is in the human mind, Hugh argues, that the notions of invisible as against visible, infinite as against finite, take shape, by a process of introspection, and it is this that enables the mind to make its leap to the invisible designer. Five centuries later such a line of thought was to be developed (almost certainly without reference to Hugh) in an original and elegant way by Descartes. Snorri of course is far from such philosophizing. And yet his hint of a psychological element, both behind the "argument from design" and behind the naming that flows from it, seems still another of the features that prompts us to see the train of thought in his Prologue as so much in the spirit of the finest twelfth-century humanism.

VIII

Snorri has tried to show in his native traditions of cosmology and mythology a far-reaching anticipation of Christian thought. Had he read treatises in which "naming" is discussed, such as we have adduced for comparison with his own statements, he could have confirmed much of their teaching from Norse tradition. The gods and goddesses have many variant names, reflecting different aspects of their divine nature. Already in the names of Óthinn recorded in poems that Snorri, at least, would have regarded as heathen, there are gleams of Christian nomenclature. His names *Thrithi* and *Jafnhár* (*Grímnismál* 46, 49) evoke the Trinity and may indeed have inspired the Trinity of *Hár, Jafnhár* and *Thrithi* in *Gylfaginning* [51]. The com-

---

[49] Ed. cit. p. 2, ll. 17-18; p. 3, ll. 1-3.
[50] *De sacramentis* I iii, 6-10 (P.L. 176, 219-220).
[51] Attempts to see foreshadowings or equivalents of the Christian Trinity in pagan thought were common in early twelfth-century speculation. Abelard in his

moner "All-Father" and "High One" celebrate a paternal omnipotence comparable to that of the Christian God, and this parallel too Snorri exploits in *Gylfaginning*. Diversity of mythical variants in heathen tradition — earth lifted out of ocean, or carved from a giant corpse; divine acquisition of knowledge as runes, or as honeyed mead, or (as in *Sigrdrífumál*) a swirling blend of both; Thórr's killing, or *not* killing, of the World Serpent — could well exemplify the diversity of belief (*átrúnathr*) that followed upon the dispersal of nations. If Snorri knew Christian speculations about the creation of the universe out of matter, he could have seen them prefigured in the Norse myth of the primordial giant, whose body formed itself out of the venomous icy drops — *eitrdropar* — flung up by the stormy currents of Élivágar. Perhaps it is because such speculations were known to him that Snorri elaborated his explanation of the creation of those life-bearing drops in physical terms of the conjunction of hot and cold air-currents (*Gylfaginning* ch. 5).

As if to underline the value he placed upon heathen tradition, Snorri chose for his most complex presentation of Norse myth a framework that he found in native sources. Here the "historical" mirrors the "mythical": the good-humoured deluding of Gylfi by the human Æsir mirrors the equally good-humoured tricking of Thórr by Útgartha-Loki and his giants. Gylfi's visit to the human Æsir re-enacts the visits of Óthinn to the giants (as in *Vafthrúthnismál*) to gain their wise secrets from them. That Gylfi calls himself by one of Óthinn's own disguise-names, *Gangleri*, reinforces the parallel [52].

---

three *Theologiae* found the Trinity in the divine powers depicted by Plato in the *Timaeus* (cf. *Fabula* pp. 61ff.); Bernard Silvestris, in his commentary on Martianus Capella, went even further and saw an equivalent to the Trinity not only in the *philosophica pagina* with its *pater, nois,* and *anima mundi,* but also in the "hidden" (i.e. symbolic) utterance of pagan mythology: *In mistico autem Iovis est nomen divine potentie, Pallas divine sapientie, Iuno divine voluntatis* (*Fabula* p. 181). This equivalence — almost certainly Bernard's own invention — was spurred by a phrase in Martianus (ed. Dick, p. 22, 5) in which Jupiter consults Juno as to what might be her will.

Hár, Jafnhár, Thrithi all occur among the Óthinn names in *Grímnismál*, but are not there brought into any relation with one another. All MSS of the Prose *Edda* cite the lines containing these three names (ed. cit. p. 27f.); it seems somewhat unlikely, therefore, that *Jafnhár* should have been interpolated into the text of *Grímnismál* by a copyist who knew *Gylfaginning* (as suggested by Sijmons and Gering, *Kommentar zu den Liedern der Edda,* I 214). On Óthinn as one of a triad of gods, cf. J. de Vries, *Altgermanische Religionsgeschichte* (2nd ed. Berlin 1956-7) section 399.

[52] *Gangleri,* "Footweary", listed as one of Óthinn's names in *Grímnismál* 46, is comparable with *Vegtamr,* "Road-Tamed", Óthinn's disguise-name in *Baldrs Draumar.* On Óthinn's dissimulations, cf. J. de Vries, op. cit. section 396.

One could almost say that Snorri is implying that Óthinn was a *figura* of Gylfi, the historical questioner. So, too, the giants in Útgartha-Loki's hall could be *figurae* of the Æsir having their intellectual skills put to the test. As Thórr tests the giants, so Gylfi tests the Æsir, and both explorers are left on the edge of the unknown — *ser tha onga höll ok onga borg*. Snorri appears deliberately to invent nothing, but to take all he needs for the articulation of his thought from native matter. When he makes the Æsir all sit together in talk after Gylfi's departure, recalling the legends they have told him (*en æsir setiaz tha atal ok ratha rathum sinum ok minnaz athesar frasagnir allar*) [53], is Snorri borrowing a scene from *Völuspá* 60? After the upsurge of the new green earth, the Æsir meet again on their old plain and talk of the mighty World Serpent, and recall there (*minnaz thar*) the great issues (*megindóma*), and the ancient secrets (*fornar rúnar*) of Óthinn. The poet of *Völuspá* does not tell us why they renew the memory of the past in the new present. Snorri makes his human Æsir perpetuate the old memories by a new naming. Does he really imply that they are enacting an evil deed when they attribute the legendary adventures of the gods to historical men, or does he envisage them as the first euhemerists: *thar var tha Thorr kallathr ok er sa Asathorr hinn gamli?* [54]

Every reader of Snorri's mythographic work senses both his scholarly intelligence, alert to all the Christian attitudes that will greet his writings, and his intellectual addiction to native tradition. Though not himself a great poet, he can see what great poetry — that of Egill, or of *Völuspá* — has sprung from that tradition. He has tried in the *Edda* to affirm the values he attributes to both sides of

---

[53] Ed. cit. p. 76, ll. 23f.

[54] Ed. cit. p. 77, ll. 4f. As Snorri here makes no adverse criticism of the Æsir's behaviour, one could well interpret his lines to mean that by attributing marvellous deeds to known historical persons (namely themselves), the Æsir intended to ensure their future fame as humans. Gylfi's recounting of what they had told him (*kemr heim iriki sitt ok segir tha tithindi, er hann hefir sét ok heyrt, ok eptir honum sagthi hverr mathr authrum thessar sögur*) could, similarly, be the beginning of that kind of veneration of humans which, as both Snorri and Minucius Felix suggest, culminates in apotheosis. The view that the identification of the mythical and the historical Æsir was a wicked act of falsification designed to mislead mankind (cf. A. Holtsmark, op. cit. p. 57) is found in the Prose *Edda* only in *Skáldskaparmál* ch. 8 (ed. cit. p. 86, ll. 19ff), in a passage that does not occur in the Uppsala MS. To infer (as Holtsmark does, op. cit. p. 24) that Snorri attributed a devilish nature to the Æsir from the statement by Hár in *Gylfaginning* (ed. cit. p. 11, l. 6) that Óthinn was with the frost-giants (*Tha var hann meth hrimthusum*) before heaven and earth were made, seems far-fetched.

his inheritance, but, like the lion of *Physiologus* who, with a sweep
of his tail, wipes away the marks of his footprints as he descends to
the valley of the Incarnation, Snorri has left us few vestiges by which
we can trace the Christian origins of his work [55].

[55] [On the problem of the authenticity of the Prologue, see Gottfried Lorenz,
Snorri Sturluson, Gylfaginning: Texte, Übersetzung, Kommentar, Darmstadt 1984, pp.
24-28; on Snorri in relation to learned traditions, see also Margaret Clunies Ross,
Skáldskaparmál: Snorri Sturluson's ars poetica *and medieval theories of language*
(Odense 1987)].

5

ARBOR CARITATIS *

An eloquent chapter in Huizinga's *The Waning of the Middle Ages* is entitled "Symbolism in its Decline". Symbolism dwindled — into allegory:

> Symbolism expresses a mysterious connection between two ideas, allegory gives a visible form to the conception of such a connection. Symbolism is a very profound function of the mind, allegory is a superficial one... The force of the symbol is easily lost in the allegory... Allegory seldom loses an air of elderliness and pedantry. Still, the use of it supplied a very earnest craving of the medieval mind.
>
> In the later Middle Ages the decline of [the symbolic] mode of thought had already long set in... Symbolism was, in fact, played out [1].

Huizinga's formulations clearly betray their descent from Goethe's sharp distinction between symbol and allegory, and reflect exactly Goethe's value-judgement [2]. Allegory is seen as the anaemic, intellectually limited, unpoetic poor relation of symbolism.

In 1924, the year *The Waning of the Middle Ages* was published,

---

* *Medieval Studies for J. A. W. Bennett*, ed. P. L. Heyworth (Clarendon Press, Oxford, 1981), pp. 207-53.

For reasons of space, the notes and references are strictly limited. Most of the texts discussed in the course of the essay (from Hermas to Pico) have a large secondary literature devoted to them, including much on which I should have liked to comment. Generally, however, I have referred only to secondary sources that are of special importance to my argument, or that offer extensive further bibliography in their subject.

[1] Penguin edn. (Harmondsworth, 1955), pp. 206-10. (The original Dutch edition, *Herfsttijd der Middeleeuwen*, was published in Haarlem, 1919; the first English version, *The Waning of the Middle Ages*, adapted and revised by the author, in London, 1924).

[2] *Maximen und Reflexionen*, 749-50 (*Goethes Werke, Hamburger Ausgabe* (5th impr., 1963), xii. 470-1). Like Goethe in these maxims, Huizinga associates symbolism with *Idee*, allegory with *Begriff* ("conception"). I have discussed Goethe's dicta in *Fabula* (Leiden-Cologne, 1974), pp. 120-2.

Walter Benjamin was writing his *Ursprung des deutschen Trauerspiels*; it appeared three years later. In order to evaluate historically the overriding use of allegory in German baroque tragedy, Benjamin began by challenging the notion and the judgement that had remained virtual dogma since Goethe. Benjamin wanted to comprehend allegory rather than disparage it — to see it as a poetic language with its own existential validity:

> Allegory... is not a game with images, manipulating them, but a mode of expression, in the way language is expression, indeed in the way writing is.
> Its antinomies must be analysed dialectically... Each person, each thing, each condition can signify any other. This possibility implies that the profane world... is characterized as a world whose detailed features are not all that important... And yet... as the necessary means of signifying and pointing to something other, these features win a power which allows them to appear incommensurable with profane objects, raises them to a higher plane, and can even sanctify them [3].

Where Huizinga had seen as "the general and essential tendency of the spirit of the expiring Middle Ages, that of accentuating every detail, of developing every thought and every image to the end, of giving concrete form to every concept of the mind" [4], Benjamin — here thinking primarily of baroque rather than late medieval allegory — stresses an element of fluidity and unpredictability:

> Around the figural centre... the whole mass of emblems groups itself. They seem capricious in their ordering: "The disordered court" — the title of a Spanish tragedy — could be taken as indicating the scheme of allegory. The laws of this court are "scattering" and "gathering". Things are gathered according to their signification; the lack of concern for their reality scatters them again. The disorder of the allegorical scenery corresponds to that of the boudoir of the gallant [5].

It is this "disorder of the allegorical scenery" that I should like to examine more closely, by way of a motif particularly cherished in the later Middle Ages: the *arbor caritatis*. Here is a motif where one might expect an excess of schematization, "of accentuating every de-

---

[3] W. Benjamin, *Ursprung des deutschen Trauerspiels* (Suhrkamp Taschenbuch, Frankfurt A. M., 1972), pp. 178, 193. On the period of composition, see ibid., p. 273.

[4] *The Waning*, pp. 278-9.

[5] *Ursprung*, p. 210.

tail, of developing every thought... to the end", and indeed in some
of the thirteenth- and fourteenth-century trees of love, both sacred
and profane, this can be found, relentlessly. Yet there was also the
possibility of disordered — or not rigidly ordered — scenery, and I
believe that some of the finest poets and prose-writers saw this as a
creative possibility and chose it consciously. For them Goethe's
dichotomy between symbol and allegory was by no means necessary:
what Goethe himself called "true symbolism" — "the living momentary revelation of what is unanalysable" [6] — could and did occur in
the midst of their allegories.

In the twelfth century Bernard Silvestris, discussing *figura* and
involucrum, makes no demarcation between the realm of hidden inner meaning — all that is evocative, enigmatic, the dark utterances
of the Sibyl — and that of explicitly distinguishable meanings, the
realm of the allegorists [7]. For Bernard these were complementary and
continuous — in his theory as in his own poetry. For him *involucrum*
comprehended the whole spectrum of explicit and implicit meaning,
allegory and symbol, concept and image. It is the interplay of these,
and the continuities between them, that deserve special attention as
we turn to some trees of love.

For English readers, perhaps the best-known instance is the tree
of charity in *Piers Plowman* [8]; I shall take this as a point of departure
for my reflections. I shall not be concerned here with the place of
Langland's tree in the vibrating web of the whole poem. Every absorbed reader is aware of the seemingly unpremeditated interplay of
vegetal notions throughout the poem, and the constant interchange
of echoes between the physical and the spiritual worlds. There is the
planting of seeds — whether of corn or of virtues; the ripening of
crops — of apples or of humanity; the incursion of weeds and
wormes of synne; the hastening of the harvest of the world, which
gives the poem its urgency. I shall concentrate on certain fluctuations
between the abstract and the dramatic within the image of the tree
itself.

As Passus XVI opens, the figure Anima explains to the poet-

---

[6] *Maximen und Reflexionen*, 752 (*Goethes Werke*, loc. cit.).

[7] See *Fabula*, pp. 119-26.

[8] *Piers Plowman: The B Version*, ed. George Kane and E. Talbot Donaldson
(London, 1975). All my Langland citations are from this edition. For an account of
the principal recent discussions of Langland's tree, see David Aers, *Piers Plowman
and Christian Allegory* (London, 1975), pp. 79-109; to Aers's bibliography I would
add especially Morton W. Bloomfield, "Piers Plowman and the Three Grades of
Chastity", *Anglia*, lxxvi (1958), 245-53; Pietro Calì, *Allegory and Vision in Dante and
Langland* (Cork, 1971), pp. 135-43.

dreamer that charity is a most steadfast tree; its root is mercy, its trunk, pity. The next lines show Langland's characteristic movement through different degrees of abstraction and reality, different kinds of causal nexus: on the tree of charity, the leaves are loyal words, the law of Holy Church; the blossoms are gently acquiescent speech and looks; the tree is called patience and the poor who are simple of heart; its fruit is charity, which grows there through God and good men. Words, law, looks, patience, poor people, charity, God, good men — all these are conjoined, in effortless transitions, to convey aspects of the tree.

Next, the tree becomes microcosmic: it grows in a garden fashioned by God — the human being. The root is of that stock (the poet leaves open whether *that stokke* is the human trunk or the human race). The arbour of the garden is the heart, and the land must be raked and weeded by free will — *liberum arbitrium* — under Piers Plowman. Later in the vision, *liberum arbitrium* is interpreted as the Holy Ghost, active in human beings as their principle of freedom: free will, proceeding from the Father and the Son, *is the holy goost of alle* [9] — a daring as well as difficult conception. Piers yields even less to a simple allegoresis, yet he evokes an ideal of human life, whether as realized by Christ in his time on earth, by Peter in his role as trustee of salvation, or by any man or woman, at any time, in so far as they incarnate that ideal form.

Now follows the dream within the vision, the *louedreem*, as Langland calls it (20). Here Piers shows the dreamer the tree supported by three props, so that it may stand upright against the winds. The emissary of the first wind, the world, is covetousness, who creeps among the leaves. Piers beats him down with the first prop — the power of God the Father. The second corrosive wind, carnality, Piers beats down with the second prop, the wisdom of God, till he sees the tree to some extent ripen and fill with fruit. Then the fiend tries to destroy the fruit, shaking the tree's root and throwing up to the top unkind neighbours, strife-brewing backbiters, and others, as if they were so many sticks aimed at bringing fruit down. He sets a ladder of lies against the tree, to fetch away Piers's flowers. Piers's

---

[9] XVI.224. Whilst Donaldson (*Piers Plowman: The C-Text and Its Poet* (New Haven, 1949), p. 189) quotes an extremely pertinent passage from Bernard of Clairvaux, who sees free will as the aspect of man by which he is *imago dei*, Langland's wording — *fre wille of bothe/ Spiritus procedens a patre & filio & c,/ Which is the holy goost of alle, and alle is but o god* — suggests something more radical: not an image of God but a "human form divine", for which the essential parallel, I believe, is to be found less in Bernard than in Joachim (see esp. the passage from the *Concordia* cited in n. 19 below).

lieutenant, *liberum arbitrium*, hinders him for a while, and at last, against a concerted attack, uses the third prop as a weapon.

Once more these brief indications will suggest the strange spectrum of realities: the wind of the world, creeping covetousness, human backbiters flung up at the tree, the fiend's ladder of lies, the lieutenant *liberum arbitrium*, the three divine props. The dreamer, his eyes fascinated by those props, questions further, and Piers seems to give a purposely tantalizing reply: I shall tell you at once, he says, what this tree is called. The ground where it grows is called goodness. And I've told you the name of the tree. It means the Trinity. As Piers looks at him sharply, the dreamer stops himself from asking more about this. Yet through Piers's half-refusal to answer, alluding to his earlier answer, the identity of the tree in the *louedreem* with that in the framing vision is established.

From now on the transformations of concepts and images become swifter and more insistent. The tree has three fruits: the lowest, matrimony; the second, near the top, continence (later called widowhood); the third, at the summit, maidenhood. The dreamer asks Piers to pull down an apple for him, and Piers — like the fiend previously — flings something to the top of the tree and also shakes the tree. All its three fruits begin to cry lamentably. As the fruits drop, they reveal themselves as human beings of the pre-Christian world; they are gathered by the devil and hoarded in limbo. Piers, in sheer rage at this, takes up *filius* — the second prop — to hit out at the devil and get his fruit back. At that moment *spiritus sanctus* spoke in Gabriel's mouth: *filius* must dwell in Mary's chamber till the fruit of Piers flowers and ripens; Jesus will have to joust, by judgement of arms, to carry off Piers's fruit, if he wins his tourney against the fiend.

The dreamer's quest for the meaning of charity is crowned by this enigmatic scene. To understand the charity that is consummated in the incarnation and redemption — to win an apple of the tree — it would appear, he must first understand the condition of dying for which that charity is a remedy, he must hear the death-cry of the fruits, and Piers must make the fruits fall just as the devil does — though with another end in view.

Later the poet, awake again, meets Abraham, or meets faith, a herald of Abraham's house (this ambiguity is sustained also in later Passus). The herald is looking for a knight whose blazon is three equal persons in one limb. He explains: that there can be three such persons, who none the less are one, is shown in the threefold human condition — marriage, widowhood, and virginity — which "was taken out of one man", and which betokens, respectively, Father,

Son, and Spirit. Here, that is, the conception of higher and lower fruits — marriage as the lowest, virginity as the highest — which Piers, in conformity with ascetic writers, had propounded earlier, is corrected: now each of the three states signifies one of the three equal divine persons.

It is clear that these shifts and fluctuations are deliberate, that the "disordered scenery" was Langland's poetic choice. Moreover, as I hope to indicate, the most memorable allegoric trees had always been presented with the help of disordered scenery. The processes of transformation — often as unpredictable, astounding, or bizarre as some of the scene-changes required in Benjamin's baroque tragedies — had been, at least since the second century AD, recurring features in the visionary tradition. What we have in Langland, I believe, is less a toleration of inconsistencies than a number of instinctive contraventions of the norms of allegoresis, in order to achieve a richness not fully explicable, a whole that is greater than the sum of its explicit parts. It is the new links — the logically unforeseeable ones — that are poetically among the most profound. Thus for instance the transition from the violent gesture of Piers, hitting out at the fiend with the prop *filius* (by the will and generosity of Father and Spirit) — *To go robbe that Rageman and reue the fruyt fro hym* (89) — to the serene words

> And thanne spak *spiritus sanctus* in Gabrielis mouthe...

brings about a poetic fusion — fury and love, the divine prop and the divine child, the human fruit of love, the theft that is an act of love, even (if we insist on the bizarre) the third prop of the tree becoming the angel's words — such as no purely allegorical juxtaposition could have achieved. And it is not a confusion but a flash of light.

Again, the comparison of the Son to the widow (or state of widowhood) — itself a daring, original thought — is made luminous by the biblical text that is not so much a justification of the likeness as a moving intuition, bringing disparate realms of sorrow together for the first time:

> The sone, if I dorste seye, resembleth wel the widewe:
> *Deus meus, deus meus, ut quid dereliquisti me?*
>
> (213-14)

None of the figurative elements that went to form these scenes in Langland is wholly new. An allegorical tree of charity is already used as something familiar by Augustine in his commentary on the first Epistle of John:

> God finds the hearts of mankind like a field... There he wants to plant the tree: charity.
>
> Let each of us test our action, to see whether it emanates from the vein of charity, whether, from the root of love, boughs of good works sprout forth.
>
> Love and do what you will... If the root of love is within, nothing but what is good can come from that root [10].

Again, the image of a tree with three fruits — marriage, widowhood, and virginity — had been widely expounded and presented pictorially, especially in the treatise *Speculum virginum* [11]. The twelfth and thirteenth centuries had seen the growth of a veritable forest of trees of virtues and trees of vices. From the late thirteenth century onwards, we find frequent homiletic and visual use of an *Arbor amoris* [12] — a tree of divine love, though there is also a profane counterpart, a tree of courtly love, in the *Romans du Vergier et de l'Arbre d'Amors* [13].

---

[10] *PL* 35. 1993, 2020, 2033:

Quasi agrum invenit [deus] corda hominum... Plantare ibi vult arborem: caritatem.

Opus ergo suum probet unusquisque nostrum, utrum de vena caritatis emanet, utrum de radice dilectionis rami bonorum operum pullulent.

Dilige, et quod vis fac... radix sit intus dilectionis, non potest de ista radice nisi bonum existere.

Langland scholars hitherto have not, as far as I can discover, noted these vital passages.

[11] The *Speculum virginum* was composed *c.* 1130-40 and diffused in nearly sixty MSS, including those of a Dutch and a Swedish translation. See esp. E. S. Greenhill, *Die geistigen Voraussetzungen der Bilderreihe des Speculum virginum* (Münster, 1962); Matthäus Bernards, *Speculum virginum* (Cologne-Graz, 1955); on Patristic sources for the three fruits of the tree, Bernards, pp. 40-4.

[12] *Arbor amoris/Der Minnebaum*, ed. Urs Kamber (Berlin, 1964). The *Arbor amoris* was popular in various Latin redactions from 1300 onwards, and later also in German ones. On some earlier, secular analogues in medieval German poetry, see H. J. Weigand, "Arbor amoris", in *Essays on European Literature in Honor of Liselotte Dieckmann* (St. Louis, 1972), pp. 167-77.

[13] Ed. A. Långfors, *Neuphilologische Mitteilungen*, xxix (1928), 3-33. Långfors (p. 4) mentions the existence of two other poems on the same subject; I would also signal the somewhat later ballade, "J'ay ung arbre de la plante d'amours/Enraciné en mon cueur proprement", which is generally printed in the older editions of François Villon among the "poésies attribuées" (though without any serious grounds for the attribution).

The *Arbor amoris* gives a mystical interpretation of the tree that
Nebuchadnezzar saw in his dream (Daniel 4):

> What is this tree if not the love of God? God planted his love
> at the centre of the earth, wanting it to grow luxuriantly on every side.
> The centre of the earth is the heart of man, from which the power
> both of earthly and of heavenly action proceeds. And as the tree be-
> gins on earth and, growing, tends heavenwards, so the love of God,
> leaving earthly things, always seeks the heavenly [14].

The beautiful, healing leaves are divine words; the fruit is indescrib-
able and unimaginable: the joy of divine union.

The courtly *Arbre d'Amors* was likewise planted in the orchard
of the human heart. Its root is *conoissance*, it is watered by *volentés*;
the branches are *loiautés, largesce, proësce*, and *courtoisie*, and from
each branch spring little twigs of further qualities. The leaves trembling in the wind are the talk of beloved and lover, the flowers are
valorous deeds, the fruits, honour and excellence. The crown of the
tree is *mesure* — with that, love becomes perfect.

As Langland's tree is threatened by *vnkynde Neighebores,/ Bak-
biteris brewecheste, brawleris and chideris* [15], this *Arbre d'Amors* is attacked by all who are loveless or who betray love:

> I vendront et mari jalous
> Et mesdisant et envious,
> Jangleour et losengeour,
> Cordelier et preechour,
> O fausses begines vendront,
> Et ipocrites i seront... [16]

Yet after the battles waged against these by true lovers, the tree remains intact, victorious.

Such tree-allegories, however elaborate in their detail, are imaginatively simple compared with Langland's. And that there had
been many crudely didactic tree-allegories in the century before *Piers
Plowman* is undeniable. In this period, the art of preaching itself
came to be likened to a tree. *Praedicare est arborizare*: the well-grown
sermon must be rooted in a theme, that flourishes in the trunk of a
biblical *auctoritas*, and thence grows into its branches and twigs: the

---

[14] Ed. cit., p. 44.
[15] XVI. 42-3.
[16] Ed. cit., pp. 19-20.

divisions and subdivisions whereby the preacher extends his subject-matter [17].

Yet subtler and more complex uses of the tree for image or analogy existed, especially in certain contexts where it came to be a figure of the Trinity. Joachim of Fiore, in the late twelfth century, depicted a tree of the Trinity in his *Liber figurarum* [18]; in his writings, on the other hand, he tends to speak rather of three trees growing each out of the other. In his *Concordia* he explains that this threefold tree means first the Trinity, and secondarily, by participation, mankind: mankind who progress from the first tree, of the ancient world, to the second — the incarnational world that grows out of it — towards the third, the world of the Holy Spirit. Here the affinity between Joachim and Langland seems to me closest — for to Joachim the world of the Holy Spirit is the world of free will and of charity:

> The Holy Spirit manifests liberty, for it is love. Where there was fear, there was servitude; where there was teaching, there was discipline; and where there is love, there is liberty [19].

[17] Urs Kamber, *Arbor amoris*, p. 73 (the phrase *praedicare est arborizare* itself, however, appears not to occur before the fifteenth century). The structural-homiletic use of a tree is also strikingly exemplifed in such a text as the prologue of Ubertino da Casale's *Arbor Vitae Crucifixae Iesu*, completed in 1305 and widely influential thereafter: see the facs. of the Venice 1485 edition, with introduction and bibliography by Charles T. Davis (Torino, 1961), fol. a iii.

An interesting range of material relating to allegorical trees is assembled by Leo Spitzer, *Essays in Historical Semantics* (New York, 1948), pp. 67-133, and by E. S. Greenhill, "The Child in the Tree", *Traditio*, x (1954), 323-71. On the earlier Christian traditions, the bibliographies in the (collaborative) article "Baum" in *Reallexikon für Antike und Christentum*, ii (1954), 1-34, in J. Flemming's article "Baum, Bäume" in *Lexikon der christlichen Ikonographie* i (1968), 258-68, and most recently in Manfred Lurker's *Der Baum in Glauben und Kunst* (2nd edn., Baden-Baden, 1976), pp. 163-70, are indispensable.

[18] The attribution of the *Liber figurarum* to Joachim himself has been cogently argued by M. Reeves and B. Hirsch-Reich, *The Figurae of Joachim of Fiore* (Oxford, 1972). The use of tree-imagery in connection with the Trinity can be found already at the beginnings of Christian Latin poetry, in Marius Victorinus' *Hymnus de Trinitate*, III 87-90:

Semen,
Arbor,
Fructus,
    O beata trinitas.

(Ed. P. Henry and P. Hadot, Sources chrétiennes (1960), i.640).

[19] *Concordia Novi ac Veteris Testamenti*, ii.1-4 (ed. Venice, 1519), fols. 19rb—20vb, with some corrections (in ⟨ ⟩ brackets) and modified punctuation:

The conjunction of the final tree, the Holy Spirit, both with liberty and with the Christian ideal of *amor*, which is charity, illuminates one of the most remarkable aspects of Langland's vision. Yet other parallels too are suggestive. In an Anglo-Norman bestiary of *c.* 1210 a poet, Guillaume le Clerc, presents the Indian tree, Peridexion, of the *Physiologus* tradition [20]:

> In its branches dwell doves that feed to satiety on the tree's fruit [21] and rest in its shadow. A hostile dragon lurks to devour those doves that desert the tree, yet the dragon can never come within the shadow, or else he would die.
>
> The tree is God the Father, the shadow is the Spirit, the fruit the Son. It was the Spirit that overshadowed Mary at the incarnation. The doves are all mankind, who can be saved by eating the fruit of the tree and never straying beyond its shadow.

The trinitarian trees both of Joachim and of the bestiaries

Has, inquam, duas arbores sublimes et condensas ponamus ante oculos mentis: et sic in eis patrem et filium, quorum alius ex alio est, principaliter intelligamus — ut tamen cum eis genus hominum secundarie accipiamus, quia, etsi disiuncti sumus a bono deo conditione nature, gratie ipsius participatione coniuncti...

In prima itaque cedro, de cuius medulla et ramorum vertice nata est arbor secunda, haud dubium quod similis ei populus ille antiquus intelligendus est, qui (sicut iam superius diximus) creatus est spiritualis ad imaginem patris, sicut et sequens populus ad imaginem filii...

In tertia vero arbore, aliquid omnino simile, aliquid dissimile est... Diximus primam arborem proprietate mysterii pertinere ad patrem; secunda⟨m⟩ ad filium; tertia⟨m⟩ ad spiritum sanctum. Et scimus quia primus ordo, qui institutus est primo, vocatus est ad laborem legalium preceptorum; secundus, qui institutus est secundo, vocatus est ad laborem passionis; tertius, qui procedit ex utroque, electus est ad libertatem contemplationis, scriptura attestante qu⟨e⟩ ait: "Ubi spiritus domini, ibi libertas". ...Significat enim idem tempus tertium illum statum felicitatis extreme...

Spiritus sanctus exhibet libertatem, quia amor est. Ubi enim timor, ibi servitus; et ubi magisterium, ibi disciplina; et ubi amor, ibi libertas.

On Joachim's tree-imagery, see M. Reeves, "The *Arbores* of Joachim of Fiore", *Papers of the British School at Rome*, xxiv (1956), 124-36, and *The Figurae*, Part III, Chs. v-ix.

[20] Guillaume le Clerc, *Le Bestiaire*, ed. R. Reinsch (1892; repr. Wiesbaden, 1967), vv. 2965-3104 (pp. 352-8). Reinsch edited the *Bestiaire* from twenty MSS (pp. 13ff.). Guillaume's precise source here is not easy to determine. While much in the *Bestiaire*, as Reinsch noted, corresponds with ps-Hugh of St. Victor, *De bestiis et aliis rebus*, the Peridexion passage (III.39 in the printed text of ps-Hugh, *PL* 177.99-100) is too garbled to ascertain whether Guillaume was using a better and fuller MS of this text, or other sources of *Physiologus* material. On ps-Hugh, cf. most recently N. Henkel, *Studien zum Physiologus im Mittelalter* (Tübingen, 1976), pp. 156-7.

[21] With Guillaume's expression, *saolez* (2979), compare Langland's *saulee* ("satisfaction of appetite", XVI.11).

might well have formed part of Langland's inheritance. Yet it is in mystical vernacular poets of the thirteenth century, whose work Langland could scarcely have known, that we perceive something approaching the speed of his own imaginative transitions and accumulations. Thus for instance in the *Revelations* of Mechthild of Magdeburg (*c.* 1250), God in a dialogue says to the soul:

> I am in myself, in all places and in all things,
> as I was before all beginning;
> I am waiting for you in the arbour of love,
> plucking the flowers of sweet union for you
> and making a bed for you there
> with the delectable grass of holy intimacy...
> and there I bend down for you the highest tree
> of my holy Trinity,
> and you will then pluck the green, white and red apples
> of my madescent humanity,
> and the shadow of my Holy Spirit shades you
> from all earthly grief [22].

Here the divine lover inclines the tree for Mechthild, to let her take apples, whereas Piers brings the fruit down painfully at the dreamer's request. The plucking of flowers and making a bed in the grass echo moments of human love in songs of Walther von der Vogelweide [23]; the tree of the Trinity, whose fruit is Christ and whose shadow is the Spirit, must echo a divine bestiary akin to Guillaume's. Yet this cannot account for the particular fusion of images and allegories here, the fresh combinations — delectable grass of intimacy, apples rich with the sap of Christ's human nature — or the tone of tender rhapsody.

---

[22] Mechthild von Magdeburg, *Offenbarungen, oder Das fliessende Licht der Gottheit*, ed. P. Gall Morel (1869; repr. Darmstadt, 1963), ii.25. With Mechthild's expression *oepfel miner saftigen menscheit* (for the reading, see the note in Margot Schmidt's translation (Einsiedeln, 1955), p. 403 n. 76), compare Langland's image for matrimony (XVI.68): *a moiste fruyt withalle*. [Cf. now *Mechthild von Magdeburg. "Das fliessende Licht der Gottheit"*, Bd. I: Text, ed. H. Neumann (Munich, 1990)].

In the MHG treatise of the *Maibaum* (ed. A. Birlinger, *Alemannia*, viii. 109-17, xiii. 285 ff.), Christ on the cross is the May-tree, his body and limbs the trunk and branches. His blood flows into the soil of the loving heart, that it too may grow and bear fruit. The tree gives shade to all; a fountain of life wells from its trunk. Birds — phoenix, eagle, nightingale, and parakeet — nest in its branches, and human souls must fly after them: *Also vindet yeder vogel sein genist in dem mayen.*

[23] Especially the songs "Under der linden" and "Nemt, frowe, disen kranz" (ed. Lachmann-Kraus-Kuhn, 39,11 and 74,20).

In Italy around 1290 the Franciscan poet and mystic Jacopone develops, in three of his *laude* [24], tree-allegories with a complication and logical perplexity comparable to Langland's, though his imagery can also be less controlled, his conceptual frame less cogent. Thus in one (84), for instance, there are three trees — faith, hope, and charity — and the branches of each tree are at the same time three planetary heavens and three hierarchies of angels. God commands Jacopone to mount his steed, so as to climb the branches of the tree of charity. Jacopone takes light as his shield and darkness as his lance, to joust against the vices as he climbs the branches of that tree.

We can see, then, that what is new in Langland's vision lies not so much in the components as in the movement and structure: within his *conjointure*, certain combinations of motifs and images are original, or have a dramatic force they had never had before. The scope of Langland's transgressions of known, systematic allegory, fusing traditional elements unpredictably, is startling. This is true also of Mechthild and Jacopone, though in rather different ways. Whether we view the transgressions as so many sins against an allegorical norm, or as imaginatively valid ways of stepping beyond that norm, is something each reader, in each context, must decide.

I should now like to consider a few instances of tree-imagery in greater detail. The examples, necessarily much restricted in number, have been chosen because they display some transformational processes comparable to those of Langland, and because they reach unusual heights of subtlety and intensity, especially, as we shall see, in the later Middle Ages. The texts are ones that show the imaginative potential of the "disordered scenery" — where a writer, drawing on varied motifs and images, is aware of their power of transformation, not only into one another but also into the conceptual realm and then back into images again [25].

---

[24] Iacopone da Todi, *Laude*, ed. Franco Mancini (Bari, 1974), nos. 77, 78, 84.

[25] It is the nature of these complexities that is my concern here, not the establishing of specific historical relationships. I shall not, for instance, try to determine Langland's precise reading — even though, from what has been mentioned so far, it should be clear that Langland must have been aware of precedents not only for elements in his presentation of the *arbor caritatis*, but also for the remarkably fluid, multivalent mode of presentation.

Much in the tradition of visionary allegory, profane as well as sacred, could be illuminated if the influence of *Pastor Hermas* were studied in detail. As yet, no full recension of the numerous MSS of the "Vulgate" translation has been published (cf. A. Siegmund, *Die Überlieferung der griechischen christlichen Literatur in der lateinischen Kirche* (Munich-Pasing, 1949), pp. 86-7). Among the texts discussed below, a direct influence of *Pastor Hermas* seems to me probable in the case of the sequence *Arbor eterna*, in Lambert's *Liber Floridus*, and in the writings of Hildegard

The first text, the *Pastor Hermas* — composed in Rome in the mid-second century — belongs to the beginnings of Christian visionary writing and helps to establish its poetic foundations [26]. The earliest Latin version of the Greek text, from the second century itself, survives so abundantly in manuscripts that we may be sure it was influential in making Hermas' gentle, tortuous, often puzzling apocalypse familiar to the medieval West. The two protagonists, the Shepherd and Ecclesia, who, in a series of visions, reveal truths to the narrator Hermas, are in their ways as richly elusive as Piers Plowman in Langland's poem. In Hermas' archaic theology, where Christ is called both Holy Spirit and highest of the angels, and human beatitude consists in becoming an angel, the Shepherd, who has been appointed by the highest angel to be Hermas' individual guardian from birth till death, is often also called "the angel of repentance" (ὁ ἄγγελος τῆς μετανοίας) [27]. Hermas does not recognize his angel at first, but then the Shepherd's shape changes, and Hermas realizes the Shepherd is his own guardian angel — for he takes on the appearance of Hermas himself. The angel, we might say, is Hermas' celestial image [28].

and Joachim. It is noteworthy that Lefèvre d'Etaples, publishing the *editio princeps* of *Pastor Hermas* (Paris, 1513), edited it along with Hildegard's *Scivias*, writings of Elisabeth of Schönau and Mechthild of Hackeborn, and the prophecies of a Dominican with Joachite affinities, Robert of Uzès (d. 1296). Lefèvre dedicated the volume *Adelaidi virgini* — to the abbess of Hildegard's Rupertsberg; the letter of dedication shows that he was well aware of the features that linked these texts across the centuries. (On Hildegard and Hermas, see H. Liebeschütz, *Das allegorische Weltbild der heiligen Hildegard von Bingen* (Leipzig, 1930), esp. pp. 51-6.)

On the other hand, Hermas also exercised a considerable indirect influence: many of the texts, for instance, outlined in C. Fritzsche, "Die lateinischen Visionen des Mittelalters bis zur Mitte des 12. Jhdts.", *Romanische Forschungen*, ii (1886), 247-79, iii (1887), 337-69, or in A. Rüegg, *Die Jenseitsvorstellungen vor Dante* (Einsiedeln, 1945), could be seen as testimonies to this. Whether Langland had read Hermas, or later texts in the Hermas tradition, is too large a question to broach here; none the less, certain features in the *Pastor* that are emphasized below should be particularly suggestive to readers familiar with *Piers Plowman*.

[26] For *Pastor Hermas* I have used Robert Joly's edition of the Greek (Sources chrétiennes, 2nd edn., Paris, 1968); there is a text of the Latin "Vulgate" translation in *PG* 2. 891-1012, but for the passages cited below it seemed advisable to follow the Oxford, Bodleian MS Laud misc. 488 (s. xii ²/₄) rather than Migne. On one occasion I have corrected a phrase in this MS with the help of another, Cambridge University Library MS Dd.4.11 (s. xiii). References to the Migne text are given in parentheses.

[27] On Hermas' Christology and angelology, see R. Joly, ed. cit., pp. 31-3, 43, 49-50; the principal "angel of repentance" passages are listed ibid., p. 369.

[28] *Vis.* V (ed. cit., pp. 140-5).

But Hermas likewise meets with several womanly bringers of revelation; chief among these is Ecclesia. Like Sapientia in the Book of Proverbs, Hermas' Ecclesia is seen as the first-born of creation, begotten before all things; for her, the Shepherd declares, the universe was formed [29]. Thus at first she appears to Hermas as a woman immensely ancient; then her face becomes youthful, though she is still white-haired; and at last, in a third vision, she is wholly young and beautiful, her face noble, joyous, and serene [30]. Yet in two of the most elaborate visions in the work Ecclesia is not only a woman but an edifice: "The tower that you see being built, it is I, Ecclesia!" This tower is four-sided (τετραγώνος), and is built with living, human stones: it grows out of the terrestrial Church. Again, in the vision that specially concerns us here, it is hard not to see the immense tree that covers the whole earth and gives shade to all the faithful as — at least implicitly — still another Ecclesia image [31].

This tree, which the Shepherd shows to Hermas, is a willow covering the fields and mountains. All who have been called in the name of the Lord come into its shadow. A sublime angel cuts branches from the tree and hands small twigs from the branches to the people in the shade. Yet when the angel had finished his cutting, the tree remained completely whole, as it had been before. Each human being was then recalled by the angel, to hand back his twig [32].

---

[29] *Vis.* II.4 (ed. cit., p. 96).

[30] *Vis.* III.11-13 (ed. cit., pp. 128-33).

[31] Hugo Rahner, *Greek Myths and Christian Mystery* (English edn., London, 1963), p. 303, goes further and, discussing *The Shepherd*, speaks of "the Church represented, with a wealth of development, as a green willow-tree". But in Rahner's account several surprising inaccuracies follow: e.g. "And immediately all are made to return their twig *which must be grafted anew on to the tree,* and herein is shown the nature of penance, for *most of the Christians can only give back a half-withered twig...*" (italics mine). The two tower-episodes in *Pastor Hermas* are *Vis.* III and *Sim.* IX (Ecclesia's characterization of herself as tower, *Vis.* III.3, p. 106; the tower as tetragonal, *Sim.* IX.2, p. 292). The willow-episode is *Sim.* VIII.

[32] *Sim.* VIII.1: Oxford, Bodleian Laud misc. 488, fols. 55ᵛ—56ʳ (PG 2. 971-2):

Ostendit mihi salicem tegentem campos ac montes, sub cuius umbra venerant omnes qui vocati erant in nomine domini. Et iuxta eam salicem stabat nuntius domini valde preclarus et sublimis, et secabat cum falce magna de ea salice ramos, et populo illi, qui erat sub umbra salicis eiusdem, exiguas ac veluti cubitales virgas porrigebat. Postquam autem accepissent universi, deposuit falcem, et arbor illa integra permansit sicut antea videram eam. Quo nomine mirabar atque intra me disputabam. Ait ad me pastor ille: Desine mirari quod arbor illa tot ramis prescisis permanserit integra; hoc expecta, et tunc demonstrabitur tibi quid significet nuntius ille qui populo porrexerat virgas et rursus eas ab his reposcebat. Quo quisque istas acceperat

The condition of the returned twigs is elaborately described, by means of twelve distinctions: at one extreme are twigs arid and putrid and as if moth-eaten; others show varied proportions of greenness and dryness. But most people bring back their twigs as green as before, and this gives the angel joy. He is joyful too at seeing some whose green twigs have grown tendrils, and most joyful of all when he sees those whose twigs have borne not only tendrils but fruit. These last three groups are given crowns and shining robes, and are admitted into the beautiful tower.

The sublime angel then departs and leaves the scene to the Shepherd, who says to Hermas: Let us take all the other twigs and plant them, to see if they can revive. — My Lord, how can arid twigs grow again? — This tree is a willow, and forever it loves life. If the twigs are watered even a little, many will revive [33].

As the Shepherd instructs Hermas, some aspects of the vision — such as the tree remaining whole after being cut — are left unexplained, but also new details emerge that make the allegoresis more enigmatic than the vision it seeks to explain. Now the tree is said to cover not only fields and mountains but the whole of the earth: it is a cosmic tree, and it is called the law of God, which is given to the whole world. At the next moment, this willow becomes the Son of God. Whilst Hermas often calls the Son of God 'the sublime angel', here, mysteriously, the sublime angel is Michael, and is distinct from Christ [34].

As Hermas and the Shepherd go, some days later, to look at the spoilt twigs they had planted, the twigs are again returned in diverse states. The Shepherd gazes at them and says: As I told you, this tree loves life: you see how many have done penance and won salvation. Once more each condition of a twig is seen to express, in meticulous detail, the condition of a soul. And then Hermas is sent by the Shepherd to proclaim the need for repentance throughout the world

---

ordine, eodem etiam vocabatur ad illum, virgamque reddebat (*sic* C, ad illam virgam que reddebatur O).

[33] *Sim*. VIII.2: fol. 57ᵛ (*PG* 2. 973-4):

Accipiamus ab omnibus virgas et plantemus eas, si possint reviviscere. Dico ei: Domine, iste, que sunt aride virge, quemadmodum possunt reviviscere? Ait mihi: Arbor hec salix est, semperque amat vitam. Si plantate ergo fuerint he virge exiguumque humoris acceperint, plurime ex hiis reviviscunt.

[34] *Sim*. VIII.2: fol. 58ʳ (*PG* 2, loc. cit.):

Arbor hec magna que campos tegit atque montes totamque terram, lex est dei in totum orbem terrarum data. Hec autem lex filius dei est, predicatus in omnibus finibus orbis terre. Populi vero stantes sub umbra, hii sunt qui audierunt predicationes eius et crediderunt. Nuntius autem ille magnus et honestus Michahel est...

— for, even after these twig-testings, hope is still offered afresh to all mankind. The task that the sublime angel had handed over to the Shepherd is now entrusted by the Shepherd to Hermas, narrator of the vision.

Here at the dawn of Christian dream-allegory we already encounter some of that disordered scenery which was to be so versatile later. In Hermas' visions, events take place with an unhurried, magical, ritual solemnity: he has none of Langland's more insistent tempi, and little of his intellectual agility. Yet, as in Langland, there is an abundance of images and concepts that flout the logic of explanation. Where each of the twigs, for instance, has its meaning fixed and made explicit, the branches are never explained, the meaning of the tree itself undergoes several changes, and the Shepherd and the sublime angel, who preside over the episode, remain enigmatic: their precise place in the scheme of salvation is never spelt out. Most complex of all are the transformations of Ecclesia throughout the work: first-born of creation, for whom the universe was made, young and beautiful guide, tetragonal tower of living stones, willow that covers the earth and protects the faithful.

Such transformations — and the imaginative processes that prompted them — have given vitality, I believe, to a number of visionary writings of the Latin Middle Ages. In a scarcely known classical sequence of *c.* 900, copied in an insular hand and only once printed, in garbled fashion, a century ago [35], a series of transformations is evoked that indeed reveals debts to Hermas, yet goes beyond the early Christian work in swift, flamboyant, lyrical language:

Arbor eterna [36], diva, summa, / apostolorum pectora sonans...

[35] The sequence is copied on fol. 55ᵛ of the Welsh Juvencus MS, Cambridge U.L. Ff.4.42. This MS contains both Welsh and Latin glosses (s. ix²-x¹), as well as later glosses (s. x/xi) in an English Caroline minuscule: the MS had been acquired by an English centre by the year 1000 (cf. T. A. M. Bishop, *Trans. Cambridge Bibl. Soc.* iv (1967), 258, and D. N. Dumville's O'Donnell Lectures, *England and the Celtic World in the Ninth and Tenth Centuries* (forthcoming)). The sequence was printed by A. W. Haddan and W. Stubbs, *Councils and Ecclesiastical Documents*, i (Oxford, 1869), pp. 622-3 (giving the MS pressmark as Ff.4.32). They did not recognize the classical sequence form, with syllabic parallelism between the half-strophes; they printed the entire text as a continuous *vers libre*. They also overlooked the contraction-sign to the upper right of the letter b in the first word, "Arbor", and printed the opening phrase thus: "Arbe terna", suggesting an emendation to "Orbe terna". Only one or two of their other misreadings are signalled below.

For knowledge of this text I am indebted to Michael Lapidge, who hopes to prepare a new edition shortly.

[36] Ecclesia is *arbor* at least implicitly in *Pastor Hermas* (see discussion above,

Eternal tree, divine, supreme, echoing the heartbeats of the apostles, summit of the governable heaven [17]... banquet of belief, queen of the East, whirling the courses of the stars: Ecclesia, the one mother, fourfold and undivided.

The opening phrases conjoin a cosmic image and a quasi-human one — an everlasting tree that none the less responds to the beating of men's hearts. This figure then becomes, allegorically, *fidei mensa*, yet at once, with *orientalis regina*, a human *figura* — the bride of the celestial Solomon — emerges again. We see her, like Sapientia at the creation, whirling the stars (*volvens sidera*), and then, identified as Mater Ecclesia, she is both fourfold and one — like Hermas' tower, and like the heavenly Jerusalem.

Near the close of the sequence the cosmic associations, as well as the allegorizing and Solomonic ones, yield to a human anguish:

11a	Tandem derelicta	11b	mater fugitiva,
12a	quae peperit et deflens pignora,	12b	audita denique vox est in Rama...

At last the fugitive mother is abandoned, bewailing the children that she bore; at last a voice was heard in Rama... [38]

and n. 31). In Patristic writings *arbor* is regularly used to denote the mast of the ship Ecclesia (see Hugo Rahner, *Symbole der Kirche* (Salzburg 1964), p. 363). In Gregory the Great's *Moralia* (XIX.1, *PL* 76. 97), the risen Christ is the *arbor magna* that grew from the *granum sinapis*; the boughs of that tree are holy preachers, the birds that nest upon the boughs are blessed souls, who have flown aloft on wings of virtues. Here the allegory begins with the resurrection but is gradually transformed into the "mystical body". Scotus Eriugena unfolds an allegory of incomparable depth and splendour in *Periphyseon*, v. 36 (*PL* 122.978-82), where the whole of human nature returns to paradise — its pristine state — to eat of the *arbor vitae* which is Christ, the centre of that paradise. Compare also the exposition of the tree of life by Scotus' early twelfth-century disciple Honorius, *PL* 172.276-8, and the image of the immense paradisal tree in the *Visio Tnugdali* (ed. A. Wagner, (Erlangen, 1882), pp. 50-51), which is explicitly *typus Ecclesie*: "vidit unam arborem maximam et latissimam, frondibus et floribus viridissimam... in cuius frondibus aves multe diversorum colorum et diversarum vocum cantantes et organizantes morabantur... Erant autem sub eadem arbore multi viri et femine in cellis aureis et eburneis, et ipsi sine cessatione laudabant et benedicebant deum... Anima autem, ad angelum conversa, ait: Que est arbor illa et ille, que sub ea sunt, anime?... Hec arbor typus est sancte Ecclesie, et isti, qui sub ea sunt viri et femine, constructores et defensores erant sanctarum ecclesiarum..."

[37] I read *summa celi regnabilis* (the final word is rare: cf. Du Cange, s.v.); Haddan-Stubbs print *summa/Coeli regna/Bi bis* (without elucidation).

[38] This part of the sequence, in my view, is indebted to Notker's renowned

Ecclesia, after embodying world-tree and allegoric banquet, cosmic principle and Solomonic queen, is the mother bereft — the Rachel of Matthew's gospel and Jeremiah's prophecy, helpless in grief as her innocents perish [39]. Concept and image, allegory, figura, and symbol are gathered — or swept headlong — in this stream of lyrical expression.

In the first years of the twelfth century Lambert of Saint-Omer, who completed his superbly designed *Liber Floridus* in 1120, drew a double tree-image, in which again a subtle interrelation of images and concepts can be observed. To begin with, the good tree, *Arbor bona*, is the loyal Ecclesia, *Ecclesia Fidelis*; the evil tree — "autumnal, fruitless, doubly dead, uprooted" (*autumnalis... infructuosa bis mortua eradicata*; cf. Jude, v. 12) — is Synagoga, whose root had been cupidity (*Cupiditas, id est avaritia*) [40]. But the root of the good tree is Karitas, as the inscription explains: "just as many branches come forth from the one tree-root, so many virtues are generated from the one Karitas". Each of the eleven virtues that sprouts from Karitas is a distinct plant; the stem of the tree grows as holy hope (*Sancta Spes*).

So far the allegory might seem to be largely schematic; but a captivating range of associations is brought within the compass of

"Rachel" sequence, *Quid tu, virgo* (ed. W. von den Steinen, *Notker der Dichter und seine geistige Welt* (Berne, 1948), ii.86); this sequence came to be used as the climax of numerous versions of the dramatic *Ordo Rachelis* (cf. Karl Young, *The Drama of the Medieval Church* (Oxford, 1933), ii.116 ff.).

[39] Matt. 2:17-18; Jer. 31:15; cf. W. von den Steinen, *Notker*, i.399-404.

[40] *Lamberti S. Audomari Canonici Liber Floridus* (facs. ed. A. Derolez, Ghent, 1968): *Arbor bona* and *Arbor mala* occur on fols. 231ᵛ—232ʳ, Derolez's transcription on pp. [102-3]. Derolez is the first scholar to transcribe the title *Ecclesia Fidelis* correctly. It had been misread as *Ecclesia fidelium* by many scholars (e.g. A. Katzenellenbogen, *Allegories of the Virtues and Vices in Mediaeval Art* (London 1939), p. 65; H. de Lubac, *Exégèse médiévale* (Paris, 1959 ff.), ii.2,200; A. Grabar, C. Nordenfalk, *La peinture romane du onzième au treizième siècle* (Geneva, 1958), pp. 158-9, with the further misreading *cupiditas sive avaritia*). The point is of literary importance, as the correct reading marks Lambert's deliberate transition from image to concept, which is discussed below.

Nine further copies of the *Liber Floridus* were executed in the twelfth century (see esp. L. Behling, "Ecclesia als Arbor bona", *Zeitschrift für Kunstwissenschaft* xiii (1959), 139-54; cf. also *Liber Floridus Colloquium*, ed. A. Derolez (Ghent, 1973). Notwithstanding the diffusion of the work, Lambert's tree, whose root is Karitas, has been strangely ignored by Langland scholars who have discussed the tree of charity. Thus for instance, to illustrate Langland's tree, D. W. Robertson, Jr. and B. F. Huppé, *Piers Plowman and Scriptural Tradition* (Princeton, 1951), pp. 192-5, use two drawings from a MS of Hugh of St. Victor's *De fructibus carnis et spiritus*. Yet this is not very apt, as the root of Hugh's tree is Humilitas; Caritas simply features on the trunk between Fides and Spes, and is not given any distinctive emphasis.

the schema, by means of the diverse sacred texts inscribed on the illuminated page [41]. The tree is *Sapientia superna*, filled with good fruits; the fruit is the spirit; its guardians are a thousand peacemakers. Solomon says of Sapientia, "her fruit is more precious than all riches" — and it is Sapientia the bride who replies to her lover: "his fruit is sweet to my throat".

At the foot of the page, the good tree is identified with the resplendent queen of Psalm 44:10, decked with many-coloured embroidery (*varietate circumdata*). She is at the right hand, not of the king anointed by God — as in the Psalm — but of God himself: *a dextris dei*. The image would again suggest Sapientia in her cosmic role, but instead Lambert now equates this queen with *fidelium ecclesia*. The change of expression (from *Ecclesia Fidelis* above) suggests that the image of the loyal bride has become the concept of the community of believers, just as the many-coloured bridal dress here becomes the diversity of virtues (*virtutum diversitate amicta*).

Three decades later, in Hildegard of Bingen's first visionary work, *Scivias*, completed in 1151, images and concepts act upon one another in more intense and less predictable ways. Here too a series of illustrations, prepared, it would seem, at Hildegard's direction, corroborates the visions and gives them greater immediacy, even though the illuminator cannot catch all the complexities suggested in the writing [42].

In the third part of *Scivias*, Hildegard, like Hermas, beholds a tower being built. This tower she calls "the foreshadowing of the will of God" (*precursus voluntatis dei*). Its architecture is laden with mystic meanings. At the northward-facing corner of the tower — the

---

[41] "Iacobus de arbore bona dicit: Sapientia superna plena est fructibus bonis. Hinc Paulus: Fructus autem spiritus est; et dominus: Mille pacifici qui custodiunt fructus eius. David rex: Fructum suum dabit in tempore suo. Hinc Salomon: Fructus eius pretiosior cunctis opibus. Hinc Sapientia dicit: Fructus eius dulcis gutturi meo".

[42] For the complete *Scivias*, one must still resort to the unreliable text in *PL* 197.383-738. [See the "*Additional note*" on p. 133 below]. The illuminations from the *Scivias* MS Wiesbaden Hess. Landesbibl. 1, which today is lost, have been reproduced (from a twentieth-century copy made by the nuns at Eibingen) in Maura Böckeler's German translation, *Wisse die Wege* (2nd edn., Salzburg, 1954). For the extracts of *Scivias* newly edited below, the fundamental extant MS is Vat. Pal. lat. 311, which was copied in Hildegard's own scriptorium, on the Rupertsberg, within her lifetime (cf. M. Schrader and A. Führkötter, *Die Echtheit des Schrifttums der heiligen Hildegard von Bingen* (Cologne-Graz, 1956), pp. 44-5). I have also consulted for these passages the "Riesenkodex", MS Wiesbaden Hess. Landesbibl. 2, prepared, again at the Rupertsberg scriptorium, chiefly in the years 1177-9 [cf. *infra* p. 146, n. 7] — though I adduce its readings only on the very rare occasions when the text of Vat. Pal. lat. 311 is faulty or doubtful.

North has for Hildegard connotations of the demonic and menacing — she sees a column of steely colour, vast and terrible to behold [43]. It was three-sided, each edge sharp as a sword. But from the edge facing East — the direction that suggests the burgeoning of the divine — boughs were growing out of that steely column, from root to summit. On the bough nearest the root Abraham was sitting, on the next, Moses, on the third, Joshua; each of the other patriarchs and prophets, too, has his own bough, in the order in which they had lived on earth. All were facing northwards, looking into the future. Between the edges of the column that faced East and North, it was smooth and round, as if lathed, but wrinkled like the bark of a tree at the places where shoots are wont to grow. A wondrous radiance shone out from the northern towards the southern face, and in the diffusion of light Hildegard perceived hosts of saints walking in joy. This third face of the column was shaped like an archer's bow, tapering at each end. At the summit of the column all was luminous; it was crowned by a dove with a beam of gold in its mouth. When I looked there, says Hildegard, I heard a voice from heaven reproving me, saying: What you are seeing is divine. At that voice I trembled so much that I dared not look further.

Throughout *Scivias*, such visions are followed by explanations, which Hildegard receives from the heavenly voice and records. The column shows the mystery of the divine word, in which all justice, of the New Testament and the Old, is fulfilled. Justice is the key concept in the allegoresis here. The first face of the column looks eastward — towards the dawn that precedes the perfect day of total justice. The second looks to the North, where — despite gospel and precepts — all injustice begins. The third, southward-looking face is the wisdom of the saints, strengthened by justice — the saints who showed in the gospels the bud that they made fruitful, both in good works and in the perception of hidden meanings.

The allegory then becomes more complex. The boughs on the eastern edge of the column show the ages of the patriarchs and prophets, because the sharp column of divinity extended those ages from root to summit — from the good that begins in the minds of the elect to the summit that manifests the Son of Man, who is total justice. In the exposition of the tree-imagery that follows, inner moral meanings, concerning aspects of justice, are constantly interwoven with Old and New Testament allusions, which themselves are related figurally to one another. Thus for instance Moses, on the se-

---

[43] The passages discussed from here onwards are edited in the Appendix below.

cond bough, shows the act of planting that God inspired, by beginning that law-giving which was fulfilled in the Son of the most high.
In the age of each patriarch and prophet, God breathed upwards
towards the height of his laws, a height that — by a succint metaphor
— Hildegard calls "the unique bud of each age". On the northward-
looking face of the column, the patriarchs and prophets see the future: the incarnation, but also Christ's battle against Satan, the ruler
of the North. The smooth bark, with wrinkles where new shoots will
sprout, shows the whole process of prefiguring, that culminates in
"the most just bud" (*rectissimum germen*) of the incarnation.

Hildegard called her poetic and dramatic work a "symphony of
the harmony of heavenly revelations" (*symphonia armonie celestium
revelationum*) [44]; so too, truly to convey the texture of her visionary
prose, one would have to dwell on its symphonic aspect. Only a few
hints, with reference to her tree-imagery, can be ventured here. The
arboreal aspects of the column, for instance, which contrast sur-
realistically with its steely sharpness [45], are already adumbrated in
the preceding vision, the description of the tower. Later visions in
Scivias depict another column — "secret and mighty and purple-
black in colour" (III. 7) [46] — the column of the Trinity, and then
(III. 8) a shadowy column, *obumbrosa* (the word seems to be Hildegard's coinage) [47] — the column of Christ's humanity, with rungs

---

[44] I have discussed Hildegard's *Symphonia* in *Poetic Individuality in the Middle
Ages* (Oxford, 1970), pp. 150-92 (texts with melodies, ibid., pp. 209-31), and in the
essay "The Composition of Hildegard of Bingen's *Symphonia*", *Sacris Erudiri*, xix
(1969-70), 381-93. [Cf. also *Poetic Individuality* (2nd ed., London, 1986), pp.
xxxiii-xlii].

[45] For other images of trees with metallic characteristics, see C. G. Jung, "Der
philosophische Baum", *Verhandlungen der Naturforschenden Gesellschaft in Basel*, lvi
(1945), 411-23 (esp. pp. 412, 418, 420-1).

[46] Vat. Pal. lat. 311, fol. 150[va]:
⟨D⟩einde vidi in angulo occidentali demonstrati edificii mirabilem et secretam
atque fortissimam columpnam, colorem purpuree nigredinis habentem, eidemque
angulo ita impositam, ut et intra et extra ipsum edificium appareret. Que etiam tante
quantitatis erat, ut nec magnitudo nec altitudo ipsius intellectui meo pateret, sed
quod tantum miro modo planissima absque omni ruga fuit. Habebat autem in exteri-
ore sui parte tres angulos calibei coloris, a pede usque ad cacumen ipsius velut
acutissimus gladius incidentes, quorum unus contra affricum respiciebat, ubi plurimum putridi straminis ab eo succisum et dispersum fuerat, et unus contra chorum,
ubi multe pennule per illum discisse ceciderant, atque medius contra occidentem,
ubi plurima putrida ligna ab ipso desecta iacebant — hec singula ab eisdem angulis
propter temeritatem ipsorum succisa...

[47] *Obumbrosus* is not attested in *TLL*, in the *Novum Glossarium*, in A. Blaise's
Dictionnaire latin-français des auteurs chretiens, or in his *Lexicon Latinitatis Medii
Aevi*.

like a ladder reaching from top to bottom. On the rungs all the powers of God, or virtues — the *virtutes dei* — descend and ascend again, laden with stones, having "a keen desire to complete the task of building" the edifice, the heavenly Ecclesia. (Here an echo of Hermas seems to me unmistakable) [48].

To suggest Hildegard's symphonic use of language here: the first of these *virtutes*, Humilitas, both in her emblematic costume and her words, recalls a tree:

> The first image wore a gold crown on her head, with three branches reaching higher, flashing with the beauty of precious stones, green and red, and with white berries. On her breast she wore a lucent mirror, in which appeared, with wondrous brightness, the image of the incarnate Son of God. She said: I am the column of lowly minds... for whoever, when ascending, catches hold of the highest bough of the tree first, most often falls by sudden accident. But he who, wishing to ascend, starts from the root, cannot fall easily...
>
> I was roused to anger in heaven when Lucifer bit himself and beyond himself [again the expression — *semetipsum transmomordit* — is an arresting coinage], in hate and pride... But when man was formed — O O O the noblest seed, O O O the sweetest bud — the Son of God was born, for man's sake, at the end of ages, a human being [49].

If a certain heaviness and repetitiveness is at times felt in these developments, if the concepts seem an anticlimax after the stark, intense images, the tree-pillar, together with its exposition and relation to the cognate visions, none the less shows how little Hildegard's way of writing proceeds in terms of known quantities. Her allegoresis can give rise to wholly unforeseen complexities, and also at moments to daring new metaphors that are not themselves explained. Each of Hildegard's visions can be seen as a totality embracing several modes: it is a divine image with temporal significance, or an earthly image that carries a reflection of the divine; but it also always be-

---

[48] In particular, the *virtutes* as maidenly figures carrying the living stones for the building of Ecclesia offer a striking resemblance to the "blessed spirits", the maidens in *Pastor Hermas, Sim.* IX.4 (cf. my discussion in *Eranos-Jahrbuch*, xli (1972), 62-4).

[49] Text below, p. 138. So, too, *Gratia dei* — another of the *virtutes* — continues this vein of imagery (Vat. Pal. lat. 311, fol. 160[vb]):

Nam bona arbor ut fructum ferat irrigatur, circumciditur, atque circumfoditur, et ab ea vermes, ne fructum eius comedant, abstrahuntur. Quid est hoc? Bonus scilicet homo non sit durus nec malivolus ad iusticiam dei... Sed tamen antequam homo sentiat me in cogitatione sua, aut intellectus ipsius intelligat me intra se, sum ei caput et plantatrix fructuositatis.

comes an image of virtues, seen both as "powers of God", descending the rungs of the pillar or tree, and as human qualities capable of ascending. Through this, Hildegard's images of the divine realm become at the same time reflections concerning the human knowledge by which the divine can be reached and known. This is something that the images alone could scarcely have achieved.

In 1298 another mystic who, like Hildegard, was both poet and cosmologist — Ramón Lull — wrote his *Tree of the Philosophy of Love* [50]. He dedicated the Latin version, in Paris that year, to the king, Philippe le Bel, and a vernacular one — not his own Catalan text but, it would seem, a French adaptation which today is lost — to the queen, Jeanne de Navarre [51]. The *Tree*, he tells us, was made

---

[50] *Arbre de Filosofia d'Amor*, ed. Jordi Rubió, in *Ramon Llull: Obres Essencials* (Barcelona, 1960), ii. 9-84. All references below are to this edition.

[51] *Arbre*, pp. 23, 79; cf. also J. N. Hillgarth, *Ramón Lull and Lullism in Fourteenth-Century France* (Oxford, 1971), pp. 108, 154. It would seem to me plausible to see Ramón's *Arbre* as in some respects a rejoinder to the *albre d'amor* described by Matfre Ermengaud a decade earlier in his *Breviari d'amor* (composed 1288-92). For Matfre's prose description of his tree, see the excellent edition of the Provençal, Catalan, and Castilian versions by P. T. Ricketts, in *Hispanic Studies in Honour of Joseph Manson* (Oxford, 1972), pp. 227-53. Dr Ricketts has in progress a new edn. of the entire *Breviari* (Leiden, 1976 ff.), which will eventually supersede that of G. Azaïs, Béziers, 1862-81).

What Matfre wanted to depict by means of his tree was the whole of love, sacred and profane. Thus, "In the topmost circle of the tree God is inscribed and figured, from whom is born all that is, has been, and will be good. In the next circle, descending from the first, is Natura, whom God appointed to govern all creatures" (ed. Ricketts, art. cit., p. 235). From Natura descend two kinds of law, natural and human. From each of these are born two kinds of love: from the natural come sexual love and love of offspring, which are common to all creatures; from the human come love of God and one's neighbour, and love of earthly goods. Each of these four branches of the tree of love bears its own fruit: love of God and neighbour bears the fruit everlasting life; the fruit of loving earthly goods is pleasure, that of sexual love is children, that of the love of children, joy. The leaves, flowers, and roots of this tree are likewise specified. Like Langland's tree of charity, it is a threatened tree: beside each of its branches stands a figure with iron implement, trying to cut a branch down. At the summit is a lady called Universal Love — *Amors generals* — who comprehends all the loves in herself.

Matfre's allegory, though elaborate, does not go beyond a schematic structure; yet it is a scheme of extraordinary inventiveness, in that it brings concepts into new configurations. To establish his hierarchy of values and their interrelations, Matfre draws on the humanism of twelfth-century Chartrain thought: the relation he depicts between God, Nature, and *Amors generals* shows affinities with Alan of Lille's *De planctu Naturae*; the two branches of law, that of nature and that of man, take up a profound distinction first made by William of Conches (see S. Gagnér, *Studien zur Ideengeschichte der Gesetzgebung* (Uppsala, 1960), esp. pp. 226-46); as in

in order to exalt lady Amor (the love whose form is *caritat*) and the beloved (*amat*), who is God. The lover (*amic*) is the human being who loves God. Like the trees in Ramón's other writings, this one is analysed in every aspect of its roots, trunk, branches, twigs, leaves, flowers, and fruit. To begin with, there are eighteen roots, each showing one of the attributes of love: its goodness, greatness, duration, power, wisdom, and many others. Only two of the roots have a negative potential: *contrarietat* and *menoritat* (contrariness and less-love).

How was it possible for Ramón to transform such diagrammatic artifice into a means of conveying intense emotional experience? I suggest, by way of all that is unpredictable, even deliberately inconsistent, that he introduces. Thus for instance, when Ramón defines the form of love, the first part of the tree-trunk, we see the *amic* suffering from his too-great longing for the beloved:

> "Contrariness", said the lover, "could you help me against greater loving?" Greater concord-of-love overheard this, and related it to greater goodness, duration and power, and to lady Love; and all together bound and captured the lover, and punished him — with loving more.
> The lover sighed, lamented, wept, and railed at lady Love, who was killing him with loving. Contrariness and less-love heard his plaints and weeping; but the other roots of love refused to listen, and as much as they could they tortured the lover with loving [52].

Roots that punish and refuse to listen are strange enough, yet their role soon becomes far more mysterious (or, if you will, illogical) than that. To illustrate by at least one motif: in an interlude set between the leaves and the flowers of the tree, the lover, mortally sick, asks lady Love for a doctor. Yet all the doctor does is done deliberately to inflame the lover more. After taking the patient's pulse and examining his urine, the doctor concludes: this man needs a medicine that will make him mad! The medicine is compounded of the roots of the tree of love — all save contrariness and less-love. A moment later, however, these roots have been transformed into lady Love's page-boys (*donzells d'amor*) — the two treacherous ones, contrariness and less-love, abetting the lover's escape from the sick-room into a forest, the others pursuing, fighting, and at last leaving him imprisoned.

William, Matfre's two branches are still seen as springing from both God and Natura. Where Matfre attempted a subtle integrative synthesis, Ramón devised an *Arbre* from which — at least overtly — all human love was banished.

[52] *Arbre*, p. 31.

The beloved wants to condemn the runaway lover to death, and a trial takes place. Love-life is appointed as the lover's advocate, love-death is retained by the beloved, so that the lover's rights may be established. And here Ramón makes explicit: "The rights of love are the roots of love". [53]

The beloved consults these roots: should the lover die? Only two — contrariness and less-love — say that he should live. Then, to bring about the lover's death, the roots are commanded to take him through the world and show him all those who dishonour the beloved. Then he will die of sorrow:

> Love's pages brought the lover to see the poor, who die of hunger, thirst, disease and cold, who ask alms of greedy, rich, vainglorious men... Then the lover felt great sorrow for the poor, for his beloved was little loved by the rich and greedy; and through that sorrow his sickness multiplied...
>
> "Love-death", said wisdom, "tell the pages to bring the lover to Jerusalem: let them take him through the entire holy land, show him the temple of David and the temple of Solomon, and show him where Jesus Christ was born and died. Then shall the lover die of love!" ...When the lover saw the holy land... and remembered the passion of Christ, his loving multiplied so greatly... that by force of love he cried: "Ah holiness, ah lady Love, ah loving! Forgive Love's pages, who have brought me to this land to die!" [54]

So swift an outline of certain moments, while it cannot do justice to the poetic excitement of the text, at least makes clear that Ramón's is an extreme case of disordered scenery — or better, of disordered drama, as it is the characters themselves who are constantly changing form and function. The roots of the tree of love, who had begun as abstractions, turn into ingredients of a love-philtre, then into messengers, then fighters, and back into a more abstract sphere as the rights of love. Then they become a jury deciding on the lover's fate, and at last one of the roots, *saviea* (wisdom), seals his fate, by showing him the death of Christ and making him echo Christ's dying words ("Father, forgive them...") in his own moment of death. The paradox is this: all that goes to make these roots of love logically incoherent is also what gives them imaginative life. The consistent schema is impaired over and over again, every detail fluctuates, and in these fluctuations the febrile experience is accurately portrayed. The imaginative splendour of Ramón's *Arbre* is inseparable from his

[53] *Arbre*, p. 56.
[54] *Arbre*, p. 63.

numerous and conscious transgressions of allegorical norms; at the same time, the work presupposes those norms and would have been inconceivable without them.

In Ramón Lull's writings, every aspect of knowledge was depicted and analysed in terms of trees and their structure; in his vast *Arbre de Sciencia* Ramón devised no fewer than sixteen such trees, from the elemental tree to the divine. In the words of Pico della Mirandola two centuries later, Ramón's was an *ars combinandi*, and because of this Pico honours it as a *cabala*, a counterpart *apud nostros* of the Jewish cabbalistic works [55]. In 1486 Pico — still only twenty-three years old — included two groups of "cabbalistic" theses among the 900 *Conclusiones* that he set up as a challenge for public disputation in Rome [56]. The previous year he had come in contact with a converted Sicilian Jew, who had assumed the magnificent name Flavius Mithridates. Flavius translated a corpus of cabbalistic writings for Pico, from Hebrew into Latin; his autograph manuscripts survive, unpublished, in the Vatican Library today [57]. One of the works Pico mentions by name in his *Conclusiones* is the book *Bahir* [58]: this is the oldest extant cabbalistic text; it was composed or

---

[55] *Apologia (Giovanni Pico della Mirandola, Gian Francesco Pico: Opera Omnia*, Basle, 1557-73, repr. Hildesheim, 1969) i.180.

[56] Giovanni Pico della Mirandola, *Conclusiones*, ed. B. Kieszkowski (Geneva, 1973). Kieszkowski, however, bases his edition on the Erlangen MS, which, according to Chaim Wirszubski, "is a copy and not the original of the *editio princeps*" ("Francesco Giorgio's Commentary on Giovanni Pico's Kabbalistic Theses", *Journal of the Warburg and Courtauld Institutes*, xxxvii (1974), 145 n. 1).

[57] On Flavius, see especially Chaim Wirszubski (ed.), *Flavius Mithridates, Sermo de Passione Domini* (Jerusalem, 1963). On the relations between Flavius and Pico, see G. Scholem, "Zur Geschichte der Anfänge der christlichen Kabbala", *Essays presented to Leo Baeck* (London, 1954), pp. 158-93; F. Secret, "Nouvelles précisions sur Flavius Mithridates maître de Pic de la Mirandole", in *L'opera e il pensiero di Giovanni Pico della Mirandola nella storia dell'umanesimo* (Florence, 1965), ii.169-82.

[58] Ed. Kieszkowski, p. 78. None the less, as Scholem (art. cit., p. 167) showed, Pico's reference is in fact to fol. 331[v] of the MS, Vat. Ebr. 191—that is, to a series of passages appended to the *Bahir* proper, of which the translation finishes on fol. 326[r]. These additional passages follow the *Bahir* in several of the Hebrew MSS, and were not distinguished from it in the Latin translation. Pico's allusion naturally implies that he had read the work itself as well as the "appendices". On the *Bahir*, see the admirable translation and commentary by G. Scholem, *Das Buch Bahir* (Leipzig, 1923), and his more recent discussion in his *Ursprung und Anfänge der Kabbalah* (Berlin, 1962), pp. 29-70. On the possibility of an earlier direct influence of the *Bahir* on European thought, in Catharist circles in southern France, see Shulamith Shahar, "Le catharisme et le début de la cabale", *Annales Economies Sociétés Civilis-*

redacted in Provence *c.* 1167-80, and translated by Flavius in 1485-6. It is a text pervaded by images and allegories of a mystic tree, as vivid as they are enigmatic. Since this tree not only shows striking affinities with the more complex mystic trees of Christian tradition, especially those of Hildegard and Langland — though naturally there is no question of a direct relationship — but also takes us forward into the thought of one of the most brilliant humanists, it offers an appropriate concluding illustration.

Once more the transitions among diverse imaginative modes are remarkable. For all its daring innovations, the *Bahir,* in Scholem's words, "preserves or imitates the literary form of the *Midrash* — questions to elicit the meaning of difficult or contradictory verses in the Bible" [59]. And indeed the first appearance of the tree in the *Bahir* comes in the midst of a learned discussion of when the angels were created, an exegesis of Psalm 104: 3-4: [60] "All admit that the angels were not created on the first day — lest it should be said that Michael extended in the southern part of the firmament and Gabriel in the north and the holy and blessed God in the middle". To counter this, a verse from Isaiah (44: 24), is adduced: "But I am the Lord, creating all things, extending the heavens alone, making fast the earth — who could have been with me?" Then suddenly, from exegesis and biblical *auctoritas,* we move into a myth, such as can be paralleled in Gnostic writings of the second and third centuries AD: [61] the text continues:

tions, xxix (1974), 1185-1210. The *rapprochements* are not decisive, however, and the author is appropriately cautious in her conclusions.

[59] *Ursprung,* p. 46.

[60] [The Hebrew Psalm 104 = Vulgate 103]. The texts discussed from here on are edited in the Appendix below, from Flavius' autograph. I am deeply grateful to the late Professor Wirszubski for checking my edition of these passages, and for giving me his expert advice about the Hebraisms in the Latin text.

[61] The principal relevant text is the cosmogonic myth of Simon Magus, as expounded in Hippolytus' *Refutatio,* VI.9-18 (ed. P. Wendland (Leipzig, 1916); cf. G. Scholem, *Ursprung,* pp. 63ff.). On the cosmic tree in myth and religion there is a vast literature: in addition to the article "Baum" in *Reallexikon für Antike und Christentum* (see above, n. 17), I have found the following treatments of the mythologem in diverse cultures particularly illuminating: Z. Ameisenowa, "The Tree of Life in Jewish Iconography", *Journal of the Warburg and Courtauld Institutes,* ii (1938-9), 326-45; R. Bauerreis, *Arbor vitae* (Munich, 1938); E. A. S. Butterworth, *The Tree at the Navel of the Earth* (Berlin, 1970); A. K. Coomaraswamy, "The Inverted Tree", *Quarterly Journal of the Mythic Society,* xxix (1938), 111-49; C.-M. Edsman, *"Arbor inversa:* Heiland, Welt und Mensch als Himmelspflanzen", *Festschrift Walter Baetke* (Weimar, 1966), pp. 85-109; Uno Holmberg, *Der Baum des Lebens,* Annales Academiae Scientiarum Fennicae B XVI (Helsinki, 1922); E. O. James, *The Tree of Life*

I indeed, when I planted this tree, so that the delight of the whole world might be found in it, called it by the name *chol*, that is, "all", for all things hang on that tree and all things proceed from it, all stand in need of it, all gaze through it and hope in it; from there the souls fly forth. I was alone when I made it, nor can any angel strut on it and say "I was there before you". And when I made fast the earth in which I planted and rooted this tree, and gave them joy and rejoiced in them [62] — who could have been with me to whom to reveal this secret?

Immediately afterwards we are back with the exegetes: Rabbi Emorai says, this then implies that God created the necessary things of the world even before the heavens. And the Rabbi who had just evoked the grandiose Gnostic myth replies in a different mode. As the narrator in Langland has a dream within a dream, in which the tree of his outer dream is expounded and enriched with new concepts, so here the myth of the cosmic tree is extended by a parable, which none the less continues the myth conceptually. To explain how God could have created the *necessaria mundi* before creating the heavens, we are now told:

It is like a king who wanted to plant a tree in his garden. He searched the whole garden to find out if it had a spring that would keep the tree alive, and did not find one. Then he said: I shall dig for water and bring forth a spring, so that the tree can survive. He dug and brought forth a spring welling with living water, and then planted the tree. And the tree stood firm and bore fruit and prospered in its roots, because men watered it continually by drawing water from the spring.

Here we are not far from the willow of *Pastor Hermas*, which, because it is by the water, forever loves life and brings new life forth.

The next appearance of the tree in the *Bahir* again begins with cosmological — and now, it would seem, astrological — images [63].

(Leiden, 1966); G. Lechler, "The Tree of Life in Indo-European and Islamic Cultures", *Ars Islamica*, iv (1937), 369-416; H. de Lubac, "L'Arbre cosmique", *Mélanges E. Podechard* (Lyons, 1945), pp. 191-8; O. Viennot, *Le culte de l'arbre dans l'Inde ancienne: textes et monuments brâhmaniques et bouddhiques* (Paris, 1954).

[62] The reference here is presumably to tree and earth together. These passages are sects. 14-15 in Scholem's translation. The other passages, in order of citation below, are from sects. 66-7, 71, 85.

[63] See the Latin text in the Appendix below: "The holy and blessed God has a tree traversed by twelve world-boundaries: north-east, south-east, the east of height and depth, north-west, south-west, the west of height and depth, the north

Yet soon these too are transformed into allegories: the tree whose arms are the twelve boundaries of the world, presided over by a series of astral rulers, becomes a tree of justice, a tree of Israel, whose actions are seen as determining the course of the universe; at the same time it is a microcosmic tree, whose heart is the human heart and whose stem is the human spine:

> As Rabbi Rehamai said: Unless there were holy and pious Israelites who exalt me (God) over the whole world through their merits, by whom the heart is nourished and the heart nourishes them, there would be no world [64]; for they are all holy forms, who have been set over every people and race, and saints of Israel have occupied the body of the tree, or rather its pillar and its heart. For as the fruit is the beauty of the body, so Israel has received the fruit of the beautiful tree called citrus; as the palm-tree has branches all around and its heart is at the centre, so Israel has received the beauty of this tree, which is its heart, and corresponding to that beauty is the spinal column in the human being, the central part of the body...

In a later passage we learn that what Flavius here calls *citrus* is that "fruit of the fairest tree" which is mentioned along with the palm in Leviticus 23: 40, in the instructions for plucking festive branches for the Feast of Tabernacles; then the citrus is allegorized as the feminine principle, without which the world cannot subsist; its glory is celebrated in words that are used of the bride in the Song of Songs, and the conjunction of citrus and palm is seen as a *hieros gamos*. In the earlier moment, however, it is the saints of Israel who are the palm and who receive the fruit of the citrus. It is inwardly, in the saints, that the primordial union of the two trees is re-enacted. As in Hildegard, the cosmic tree is also a column: it is the arboreal

of height and depth and the south of height and depth. They are extended and they reach as far as the immeasurable, and they are the arms of the world, and within them is the tree. And in all the world-boundaries there are prefects, corresponding to prefects or governors, and they are twelve. Again, within the (celestial) sphere there are twelve prefects, these... (making) thirty-six in all, including those of the world-boundaries".

Here a lacuna in the MSS, even in the early MS from which Flavius was translating, makes understanding difficult. Scholem (*Das Buch Bahir*, pp. 64-9) would see in the numbers a complex symbolism in which the prefects are celestial powers operating in the cosmos, like the rulers of the thirty-six decans in astrology, and in which the twelve directions correspond to the twelve tribes of Israel, and the twofold series of thirty-six prefects matches the seventy-two names of God.

[64] Here Scholem (*Das Buch Bahir*, p. 70 n. 2) postulates another lacuna; but Flavius translates the sentence without a break.

trunk, and the spinal column in the human being, and, some twenty
lines later in the *Bahir*, it becomes both the world-axis and a moral
allegory of justice:

> It is said there is a pillar reaching from the earth to the firma-
> ment, and it is called *Sadic*, after the just. And when there are just men
> in the world, it is augmented and grows strong; otherwise it grows fee-
> ble. And it supports the whole world, as is written (of the just man):
> "foundation of the world". When it is (completely) enfeebled, it can
> no longer support the world. So, even if there were only one just man
> in the world, he can sustain it.

As in Hildegard's vision, the cosmic and moral and inner law
are apprehended simultaneously. Where in Hildegard the just are
perched on branches growing out of the steely pillar, here they constitute the pillar itself.

In still another modulation, which again recalls Hildegard, the
tree grows in layers that are the *virtutes dei*; it is watered by

> wisdom, the soul of the saints, flying from the spring to the great
> duct, ascending and joining the tree. Through whose hands does that
> soul leap? Through the hands of Israel: when there are just and good
> men, the indweller (Shekinah) [65] dwells in their midst and in their
> works... And justice is that (divine) indweller...

In the diverse moments concerning the tree in the *Bahir* Scholem would see diverse strata of composition: there are "old fragments" that preserve an archaic myth of the cosmic tree, a younger
layer, where the tree has become a figure of the human organism, and
a final redaction in Provence, after 1167, in which Israel becomes the
trunk or heart of the tree whose fruits are souls [66]. However valid
this may be as a historical perspective, I would suggest that imaginatively the most vital aspect of the *Bahir* tree is precisely the synthesis,
the complex interplay of myth and allegory, of image and concept,
that one — presumably late — author, relying on disparate sources,
achieved. Whoever devised those complex transformations of the
tree was no ordinary redactor or compiler, but had an exceptional
power of giving cohesion of a new kind — the kind that depends on
the "disordered scenery" of medieval allegorical visions.

When Pico, within a year of receiving Flavius' translation, came

---

[65] On Shekinah, see especially G. Scholem, *Von der mystischen Gestalt der Gottheit* (Zürich, 1962), Ch. IV (pp. 135-91).

[66] *Ursprung*, pp. 64, 66, 68-70.

to write his *Conclusiones*, he formulated several of his "cabbalistic" theses in arboreal terms:

4. The sin of Adam was the truncation of the kingdom from the other plants.

36. The sin of Sodom came about by the truncation of the ultimate plant.

42. Joseph was buried in bones and not in body, because his bones were the powers (*virtutes*) and host of the tree on high called *Sadic*, flowing to the earth above [67].

These cryptic sentences imply a vision of the world as a living growth, that can be impaired by sin and sustained by even one just man. As in the *Bahir*, Sadic, the pillar of the just, is also the mystic tree; the bones of Joseph the just become the celestial *virtutes*, which are the layers of that tree; and the expression "flowing to the earth above" recalls the numerous *Bahir* images of the watering of the tree, so that it may bear fruit. Why did Pico, a rhetorician with marvellous powers of conceptual explication, here adopt such compressed, riddling language, full of suggestiveness yet not rationally ordered? It would seem that both the matter and the manner of the *Bahir* had stirred a response in him.

---

[67] Ed. Kieszkowski, pp. 51-3. To cite at least one suggestive parallel to the uses of the pillar-tree in Hildegard, the *Bahir*, and Pico—Henri de Lubac, in his "L'Arbre cosmique" (see n. 61), says of the *stûpa* of Sanchi: "Ainsi cette sculpture du *torâna* nord de Sanchi nous offre, unis jusqu'à l'identification, un homme, un arbre, un pilier. Considéré dans son essence suprême, le Bouddha est en même temps le pilier cosmique et l'arbre de la vie".

Additional note: Since this essay was dispatched for publication, a new edn. of Hildegard of Bingen's *Scivias*, ed. A. Führkötter and A. Carlevaris, has appeared (Corpus Christianorum, Cont. Med. xliii-xliii A, Turnhout, 1978). While substantially superior to that in Migne, it still offers a normalized and not always well-chosen text (cf. my discussion, "Problemata Hildegardiana", *Mittellateinisches Jahrbuch* xvi, 1981, 97-131 [no. 6 below]). An important study of the *Liber Floridus* MS has also appeared: A. Derolez, *Lambertus qui librum fecit* (Brussels, 1978). An essay by G. B. Ladner, "Medieval and Modern Understanding of Symbolism: a Comparison", *Speculum* liv (1979), 223-56, includes fine discussion of medieval tree-symbolism, though not specifically of trees of charity. To my pages on Mechthild, finally, I should like to add cross-references to Gertrude of Helfta, *Legatus* iii. 15 (*De arbore amoris*; cf. also iii.17), ed. P. Doyère, Sources chrétiennes 143, pp. 62 ff.; and to Marguerite d'Oingt, *Les oeuvres*, ed. A. Duraffour, P. Gardette and P. Durdilly (Paris, 1965), pp. 144-7. Such tree-visions, it seems, became something of a constant among thirteenth-century women mystics; but there is already a striking use of the tree of charity motif in Dhuoda's *Liber manualis* for her son William (composed 841-3), ed. P. Riché, Sources chrétiennes 225, pp. 268-70.

The complexities that we glimpsed with Langland's tree of charity can lead us to perceive comparable imaginative and conceptual processes in many works of different kinds in different centuries. But whereas to Huizinga these processes seemed regressive, a phenomenon typical of a time of waning, a decline from an age when symbolism had been fresher and more direct, to Benjamin the same phenomenon was elemental: in the baroque tragedies "the disordered court" of allegory could still become an authentic community, could express complex perceptions, which might scarcely have been conveyable any other way. In the late Middle Ages there are, to be sure, many allegories that tend to the mechanical and make one think Huizinga was right. At the same time, a heritage that includes Hildegard and Mechthild, Jacopone, Ramón Lull, and Will Langland, and later the translation that Flavius made for Pico, lends profound support to Benjamin's reassessment of allegory's nature and worth.

APPENDIX

1. From Hildegard of Bingen's *Scivias* (on the manuscripts, see above, n. 42)

127vb

Quarta visio tercie partis.

⟨E⟩t deinde, ultra predictam turrim precursus voluntatis dei, sed cubito uno infra angulum qui respicit ad septentrionem, vidi quasi / columpnam calibei coloris, prefate lucide parti muri eiusdem edificii exterius appositam, valde terribilem aspectu, tanteque magnitudinis ac altitudinis, ut mensuram eius nullomodo discernere possem. Et eadem columpna tres angulos habebat, ab imo usque ad summum quasi gladium acutos, quorum primus respiciebat ad orientem, secundus autem ad septentrionem, et tercius ad meridiem, exterius ipsi edificio aliquantulum coniunctus.

128ra

Ex angulo autem qui respiciebat ad orientem procedebant rami a radice usque ad cacumen eius, iuxta cuius radicem vidi in primo ramo Abraham sedentem, in secundo vero Moysen, et in tercio Iosue, ac deinde reliquos patriarchas et prophetas, ita sursum singulos in singulis ramis ordinate sedentes, secundum tempus quo in hoc seculo sibimet successerant — qui se omnes converterant ad angulum eiusdem columpne qui respiciebat ad septentrionem, admirantes ea que in spiritu futura viderunt in ipsa.

Sed inter hos duos angulos, unum scilicet vergentem ad orientem et alterum ad septentrionem, erat — ante facies ipsorum patriarcharum et prophetarum — eadem columpna ab imo usque ⟨ad⟩ summum [1] quasi tornatilis et rotunda, plenaque rugarum, ut de arboris cortice solet germen pullulare. A secundo vero angulo, respiciente / ad septentrionem, exivit splendor mire claritatis, se extendentis et reflectentis ad angulum qui respiciebat ad meridiem. Et in eodem splendore, in tam magnam latitudinem se diffundente, conspexi apostolos, martires, confessores et virgines, atque alios plurimos sanctos, in magno gaudio deambulantes. Tercius vero angulus, qui respiciebat ad meridiem, erat in medio latus et extentus, in imo autem et in summitate aliquantulum gracilior et constrictus, secundum modum arcus qui extenditur ad sagittas iaciendas. In cacumine autem eiusdem columpne vidi tantam claritatem luminis, ultra quam humana lingua effari possit, in qua apparuit columba, habens in ore suo radium aurei coloris, multo fulgore in eandem

128rb

---

[1] usque summum V usque ad summum R

columpnam radiantem. Cumque illuc aspicerem, audivi vocem
de celo, magno terrore me redarguentem, et dicentem: "Quod
vides, divinum est." Ex qua voce ita contremui, ut amplius illuc
aspicere non auderem.

128vb

... "Quapropter et hec columpna, quam ultra predictam turrim precursus voluntatis dei vides, designat ineffabile misterium verbi dei, quia in vero verbo, id est in filio dei, impleta
est omnis iusticia novi et veteris testamenti...

129ra

"Est quoque valde terribilis aspectu, quoniam iusticia in
verbo dei metuenda est humane scientie...

129rb

"Et primus angulus respicit ad orientem, qui est primus ortus inceptionis cognoscere deum in divina lege, ante perfectum
diem omnis iusticie. Secundus autem ad septentrionem, quoniam, post inceptionem bone et institute operationis, evangelium filii mei et alia precepta in me patre surrexerunt: contra
partem aquilonis, ubi omnis iniusticia orta est. Tertius vero ad
meridiem, exterius ipsi edificio aliquantulum coniunctus, qui
est roboratis operibus iusticie profunda et exquisita sapientia
principalium magistrorum, per calorem spiritus sancti, qui obscura in lege et prophetia aperuerunt, et qui in evangeliis osten-
derunt germen quod fructuosum fecerunt ad intelligendum,
tangentes exteriorem materiam scripturarum in opere bonitatis
patris, et suaviter ruminantes in ea misticam significationem.

129va

"Quod autem / ex angulo qui respicit ad orientem procedunt rami a radice usque ad cacumen eius, hoc est quod in ortu
cognitionis dei per legem iusticie — quasi in angulo orientali
— apparuerunt rami: tempora scilicet patriarcharum et prophetarum, quia illa acuta columpna divinitatis hec omnia extendit
ab initio radicis — id est bone inceptionis in mentibus electorum suorum — usque ad cacumen eius, quod est usque ad ma-
nifestationem filii hominis, qui omnis iusticia est. Unde etiam
iuxta eius radicem vides in primo ramo Abraham sedentem,
quia per acutissimam divinitatem exspirabatur hoc tempus,
quod primitus ortum est in eodem Abraham, cum quieta mente
reliquit patriam suam obediens deo; in secundo vero Moysen,
quoniam deinde plantatio surrexit inspiratione dei, in initio date legis per eundem Moysen, in presignificatione filii altissimi;
et in tercio Iosue, quia ipse postmodum habuit spiritum hunc
a deo, ut consuetudinem legis dei confirmaret robustiorem in
precepto divino.

"Ac deinde vides reliquos patriarchas et prophetas, ita sursum singulos in singulis ramis ordinate sedentes, secundum
tempus quo in hoc seculo sibimet successerant: quoniam, in
unoquoque tempore subsequentium patriarcharum et prophetarum

129vb

exspiravit / deus sursum ad altitudinem preceptorum suorum
— uniuscuiusque singulare germen — cum ipsi in diebus suis
disposite et ordinate in ostensa sibi iusticia quiescebant, divine

maiestati fideliter subiecti, ut in temporibus suis venientes erant.

"Et hii omnes convertunt se ad angulum eiusdem columpne qui respicit ad septentrionem, admirantes ea que in spiritu futura vident in ipsa, quia omnes, admoniti spiritu per spiritum sanctum, se verterunt et viderunt ad evangelicam doctrinam fortitudinis filii dei, diabolo repugnantis — de incarnatione eius loquentes, et admirantes quod ipse, veniens ex corde patris et de utero virginis, in magnis mirabilibus se ostendit in suo opere et sequentium se, qui ipsum in nova gratia mirabiliter imitantes caduca conculcabant, et ad eternorum gaudia fortiter anhelabant.

"Sed quod inter hos duos angulos, unum scilicet vergentem ad orientem et alterum ad septentrionem, est ante faciem ipsorum patriarcharum et prophetarum eadem columpna ab imo usque ad summum quasi tornatilis et rotunda, plenaque rugarum, ut de arboris cortice solet germen pullulare — hoc est quod inter binas summitates, videlicet inter manifestatam cognitionem meam et subsequentem doctrinam filii mei, latuit per tipum prefigurationis in animabus / antiquorum patrum, in legibus meis commorantium, unicum verbum quod est filius meus, a primo electo usque ad ultimum sanctum, in mistica tornatura circumornatus: quia ipse omnia instrumenta sua bene composuit ac limavit, scilicet per volubilem gratiam omnibus se pium manifestans, ut prefigurabatur in rugis circumcisionis, que fuit umbra futurorum in appositis significationibus per austeritatem legis, in se habentis rectissimum germen latens, summe et sanctissime incarnationis."

130ra

156ra

Octava visio tercie partis.

⟨E⟩t deinde, in plaga meridiana in prefato lapideo muro demonstrati edificii, ultra predictam columpnam vere trinitatis, item vidi quasi columpnam magnam et obumbratam, intra et extra idem edificium apparentem, que scilicet visui meo tam obumbrosa apparuit, ut nec magnitudinem nec altitudinem eius cognoscere valerem. Et intra columpnam hanc atque columpnam vere trinitatis, erat interruptus locus longitudinis trium cubitorum, vacuusque absque muro, ut superius ostensum est, fundamento ibi tantum posito. Hec ergo umbrosa columpna in hoc ipso edificio in eodem loco stabat ubi desuper in celestibus misteriis, coram deo, illum magnum et quadratum lucidissimique candoris splendorem prius videram, qui, secretum superni creatoris / designans, in maximo misterio mihi manifestatus est — in quo etiam alius splendor velut aurora, in se aeriam in alto purpuree lucis claritatem habens, fulgebat, per quem mihi in mistica ostensione misterium incarnati filii dei demonstratum fuerat.

156rb

In columpna autem ista, ab imo usque ad summum eius, in modum scale ascensus erat, ubi omnes virtutes dei, descendentes et ascendentes, oneratas lapidibus, ad opus suum ire videbam, acutum studium idem opus perficiendi habentes. Et audivi lucidum illum qui sedebat in throno dicentem: "Isti fortissimi operarii dei sunt."...

156va

Prima imago portabat coronam auream capiti suo impositam, tres ramos altius extantes habentem, atque preciosissimis lapidibus viridis et rubei coloris et albis bacis multo fulgentem ornatu. In pectore vero suo habebat speculum lucidissimum, in quo mira claritate imago incarnati filii dei apparebat. Et ait: "Ego sum columpna humilium mentium, et interfectrix superborum cordium. In minimo incepi, et ad ardua celorum ascendi. Lucifer erexit se sursum super se, et corruit sub se deorsum. Quisquis me vult imitari, filius meus esse desiderans, si me matrem sitit amplecti, opus meum in me perficiendo, hic tangat fundamentum, et leniter ad alta sursum ascendat. Quid est hoc? Ipse primum carnis sue vilitatem inspiciat, et sic sursum de virtute in virtutem suavi et leni animo gradatim proficiat — quia qui summum ramum arboris primum apprehendit ad ascendendum, repentino casu sepissime cadit. Qui autem, volens ascendere, a radice incipit, huic non est tam facile / caden-

156vb

dum, si caute incedit...

"Ego ad indignationem in celo provocabar, cum Lucifer semetipsum odio et superbia transmomordit. Sed o o o, humilitas hoc tolerare noluit. Propter quod etiam ille ruina magna deiectus est. Formato autem homine, o o o, nobilissimum granum, et o o o, dulcissimum germen, filius dei propter hominem in fi-

157ra

ne temporum natus est, homo... O virtutes, ubi est / Lucifer? In inferno est. Surgamus ergo omnes, ad veram lucem appropinquantes, atque edificemus maximas et fortissimas turres in provinciis, ut, cum venerit dies novissimus, plurimum fructum et in spiritalibus et in carnalibus apportemus."

2. From Flavius Mithridates' version of the *Bahir*: MS Vat. Ebr. 191 (1485/6)

290^r
Ps. 104
[103]: 3-4

Dixit Rabi Johanan, "secunda die creati sunt angeli, ut scribitur, 'qui trabificat in aquis ascensus suos, vel edes suas', et scribitur, 'qui facit angelos suos spiritus, ministros eius ignem urentem.'"

290^v

Dixit Rabi / Levitas, filius Tiberie [1], "omnes concedunt, et concedit etiam Rabi Johanan, quod aque iam erant, sed in se-

Ps. 104

cundo 'trabeficavit in aquas ascensus suos, vel edes suas'. Quis-

---

[1] Tiburie MS

[103]: 3 nam? — 'Ille qui ambulat super pennas venti'. Legati [2] tamen non fuerunt creati nisi usque ad diem quintam.

"Et concedunt omnes quod non fuerunt creati die prima, ne diceretur quod Michael extendebat in parte meridionali firmamenti et Gabriel in septentrionali et deus sanctus et benedictus ordinabat in medio. 'Sed ego dominus, faciens omnia, Isa. 44:24 extendens celos solus ego, firmans terra⟨m⟩, mi mecum existente? *

'Ego quidem, quando plantavi hanc arborem ut delectatio totius mundi in ea esset, et firmavi in ea omnia, vocavi nomen eius chol, idest omne, quia omnia pendent in ea et omnia ab ea exeunt, et omnia indigent ea, et per eam speculantur et in ea sperant, et inde volantes anime sunt. Ego solus fui quando feci illam, nec superbiat aliquis angelus in ea, dicere 'ego preveni te'. Etiam quando firmavi terram in qua plantavi et radicavi arborem hanc, et letificavi ea simul et letatus sum in eis — mi mecum existente * cui revelavi hoc secretum?'"

Dixit Rabi Emorai, "A verbis tuis discimus quod necessaria huius mundi creavit deus sanctus et benedictus ante celos". Dixit ei etiam, paradigmaticos, "Res similis est regi qui voluit plantare arborem in horto. Consideravit totum hortum ad sciendum si haberet fontem aquarum subsistere illam [3] facientem, et non invenit. Dixit 'Fodiam aquam et educam fontem, ut possit subsistere arbor'. Fodit et eduxit fontem scaturientem aquam vivam, et postea plantavit arborem. Et stetit arbor et fecit fructum, et prosperavit in radicibus suis, quia aquarunt eam continuo hauriendo a fonte."

301ʳ Arborem enim habet deus sanctus et benedictus, in qua sunt duodecim termini diametrales: scilicet terminus orientalis septentrionalis, terminus orientalis meridionalis, terminus orientalis celsitudinis, terminus orientalis profunditatis, terminus occidentalis septentrionalis, terminus occidentalis meridionalis, terminus occidentalis celsitudinis, terminus occidentalis profunditatis, terminus septentrionalis celsitudinis, terminus septentrionalis profunditatis, terminus meridionalis celsitudinis, terminus meridionalis profunditatis.

Et ampliantur et eunt usque ad "adead", et sunt brachia mundi, et intus eos est arbor. Et in omnibus his diametralibus sunt prefecti e regione prefectorum, sive comissarii, et su⟨n⟩t duodecim. Etiam intus in spera sunt duodecim prefecti, hi [4]

---

[2] vel nuntii MS (*in margin*)
[3] illum MS
* mi mecum existente = quis mecum existebat
[4] *Lacuna after* hi (cf. G. Scholem, *Das Buch Bahir,* p. 66 n. 3); triginta duo *deleted before* triginta sex MS

301ᵛ ⟨..⟩ triginta sex quidem cum diametralibus. Et / unicuique est
Eccl. 5:7 unus, ut scribitur, "quia alcior altiore custode custos est".

302ʳ Ut dixit Rabi Rahamai, "nisi essent sancti et pii Israelite qui
sublevant me super toto mundo per suos meritos, a quibus ali-
tur cor et cor alit eos, mundus non esset — nam omnes sunt
forme sancte que prefecte sunt super quemcumque populum et
gentem, et Israel sancti ceperunt corpus arboris, seu cippum
eius et cor eius. Quemadmodum enim fructus est decor corporis, sic Israel acceperunt fructum arboris decore que dicitur citrus; quemadmodum arbor palme habet ramos circumcirca et
cor eius in medio est, sic Israel acceperunt decorem huius arboris, qui est cor eius, e cuius decoris regione est filus spine dorsi
in homine, qui est principale corporis.".…

303ʳ Traditum est, una columna est a terra usque ad firmamentum,
et vocatur Sadic, nomine iustorum. Et quando sunt iusti in
mundo, augetur et roboratur; sin autem, debilitatur. Et sustinet
Prov. 10:26 totum mundum, ut scribitur, "fundamentum seculi". Quando
enim debilitatur, non potest sustinere mundum. Ideo, quamvis
in mundo non esset nisi unus iustus, potest substentare
seculum.

307ʳ Quenam est ⟨radix⟩ arboris quam dixisti? Dixit ei, omnes virtutes dei sancti et benedicti sunt una super alia, et similes sunt
arbori. Quemadmodum arbor hec per aquas educit fructus
suos, sic deus sanctus et benedictus per manus aquarum multi-
plicat virtutes arboris. Quenam sunt aque dei sancti et benedicti? Sapientia est, et hec est anima sanctorum que vol*at* [5] a
fonte ad magnum syphona, et ascendit et coniungit se in arbore. Et per manus cuius volat? Per manus Israel: quando sunt iusti et boni, habitatrix habitat in medio eorum, et habitat in
operibus eorum… Et iusticia est habitatrix…

317ʳ Quidnam est latus tabernaculi? Aut, numquid latus in eis est?
Dixit quidem, "latus est in eo tabernaculo paradigmaticos. Res
similis est regi qui cogitavit in corde suo plantare novem arbores masculas in paradiso suo, et erant omnes palme mascule que
dicuntur dacalim. Quidnam fecit? Dixit, postquam sunt tantum unius speciei, non poterunt durare. Igitur in medio eorum
plantavit citrum, et est una de illis novem que ascenderant in
317ᵛ cogitatione sua / ut essent masculi. Et quenam est citrus? Equi-
Lev. 23:40 dem citrus femina est, et hoc quod scribitur, 'fructus arboris
gloriose et palme palmarum'. Quidnam est fructus arboris gloriose? Equidem ut dicit glossa Chaldaica, 'fructus arboris citri

───────────

⁵ volant MS

et palmarum cordis'. Quidnam gloriose? Quia gloria omnium est, et est hec illa gloriosa que dicitur in cantico canticorum, Cant. 6:10 ubi scribitur, 'que est zoth * que oritur ut aurora, pulchra ut luna, clara ut sol, venerabilis ut turmate?' Et hoc quidem e regione femine est, et secundum nomen suum capta est femina ab Adam, quia inpossibile est mundus tam superior quam inferior permanere sine femina."

Quare igitur vocatur femina Hebraice necheba, idest perforata? Quia poros habet et foramina lata, et habet etiam plura foramina quam habeat vir. Quenam sunt? — sunt quidem foramina uberum et matricis et loci receptionis. Quidnam est illud quod dixisti, quod canticum canticorum est gloriosum? Equidem gloriosum est omnium voluminum sanctorum. Sic enim dixit Rabi Johanan: "omnes libri textus sunt sancti, et lex etiam sancta, sed canticum canticorum est sanctum sanctorum."...

Quidnam est hoc sanctum? — est quidem citrus, que est gloria omnium. Quare vocatur gloriosa, idest hadar? — Equidem quia hec hadar est citrus que est gloria omnium, separata scilicet a fasciculo cordis palme. Non preceptum cordis palme adinpletur nisi per eam, et ipsa citrus connexa est in eo cum omnibus, quia cum omnibus unum est, et cum omnibus simul est cor palme. Quemnam representat cor palme? — filum scili-
Lev. 23:40 cet spine dorsi. Et ita est "folium autem arboris myrthi". Quem-
318ʳ nam representat?/ ⟨...⟩ Quia scilicet oportet ut folium arboris myrthi habeat folia coperiencia maiorem partem sui. Si enim folia non coperiunt maiorem partem sui, nihil est. Quare? Paradigmaticos: res est similis homini habenti brachia quibus protegit caput suum; sunt quidem brachia duo, et cum capite tria, et sic sunt hic folium ad sinistram, myrthi vero ad dextram, arbor vero in medio. Quare dicta est arbor? — quia est radix arboris.

6

PROBLEMATA HILDEGARDIANA *

I

The new "Scivias"

1978 saw a major contribution to the understanding of Hildegard of Bingen's writing, with the appearance, in the "Corpus Christianorum", of a new text of "Scivias". Till now, for a complete text of Hildegard's first extensive work, all readers who have not had access to a manuscript have perforce been confined to basically one and the same edition — that of Jacques Lefèvre d'Etaples in 1513. It was this text, reprinted anonymously in 1628, that was incorporated — with a sprinkling of new errors — in Migne's "Patrologia Latina", vol. 197 [1]. The differences between Lefèvre's text and the new one can be seen in all clarity: the recent editors, Adelgundis Führkötter and Angela Carlevaris, have helpfully set the Lefèvre readings (**f**), with those of the sixteenth-century manuscript copied from Lefèvre (**m**), in a separate apparatus at the foot of each page. Lefèvre's divergences from the original ranged from minor departures and rephrasings throughout "Scivias" to at times elaborate rewriting, especially

---

* *Mittellateinisches Jahrbuch* XVI (1981) 97-131.

[1] See *Hildegardis Scivias*, ed. A. Führkötter/A. Carlevaris (Corpus Christianorum, Cont. Med. XLIII-XLIII A), Turnhout 1978, lvi-lx. References to "Scivias" below, if two arabic numbers are separated by a comma, indicate page and line in this edition. When citing "Scivias" I follow the new edition in its (normalized) spelling, punctuation, and — in poetic passages — line arrangement. For all other citations from Hildegard's works I give the spelling of the MS(S) indicated (except that I distinguish *u* and *v*, and capitalize names), adding my own punctuation and, where appropriate, line-divisions. When two MSS are adduced, in the case of minor orthographic differences, the spelling followed is that of the first mentioned. For precise scholarly enquiry into Hildegard's writings, it is still necessary to control all the earlier editions with the help of MSS. This was well seen by Hans Liebeschütz, *Das allegorische Weltbild der heiligen Hildegard von Bingen*, Leipzig 1930 — still incomparably the finest study of her works —, who corrected the printed texts of her visionary trilogy throughout by use of the Wiesbaden "Riesenkodex" (**R**).

in the first two visions of Part II. Clearly the humanist was discon-
certed by some of Hildegard's strikingly individual images and expressions. Thus in II 2, chapters 6 and 7, where Hildegard's text —
it would seem in all extant manuscripts before 1513 — characterizes
one of the three "powers of the flame" as *purpureus viror*, and this
(quintessentially Hildegardian) image recurs, in brief space, seven
times, Lefèvre changed it systematically to *insitus vigor*. In the same
two chapters, he altered Hildegard's expression *viriditas* (a leitmotif
throughout her writings) to *virtus* at each occurrence.

Now at last we have a text based on the early manuscripts, not
on Lefèvre. The text is preceded by a description of the codices,
which summarizes and at times extends the admirable work that Sister Führkötter, together with Sister Schrader, had done in 1956,
which indeed laid the foundations for serious textual study of Hildegard's works [2]. After the text of "Scivias" come not only a Scriptural and liturgical index, but also a brave attempt at an «Index Auctorum». As Hildegard names no "auctores" whatever within
"Scivias", the question of her sources is particularly difficult and
delicate. The ten pages of references (653-62) given here — even if
many suggested sources and analogues can and should be questioned
anew [3] — make some notable advances. (A few illustrations of source
problems that are still elusive or unresolved will be given in section
III below). The volumes conclude with a vast «Index verborum et
elocutionum» (666-913) — a precious aid to future study of Hildegard's diction. Her language and style, unfortunately — in view of
the deep acquaintance the editors show with Hildegard's writing —
receive no discussion whatever in the introduction to the edition.

[2] M. Schrader/A. Führkötter, *Die Echtheit des Schrifttums der heiligen Hildegard
von Bingen*, Köln/Graz 1956.

[3] For instance, I can see no point in a parallel such as that (p. 661) between
Minucius Felix and Scivias I 3 (55, 518): the resemblance is only between the expression *cautelam dare* in Hildegard and *dant cautelam* in Octavius 7, 6. There the
context is the wholly different one of pagan Roman religion. Moreover, it should
be remembered that the "Octavius" survives in only one ninth and one sixteenth
century MS, and can hardly have been accessible to Hildegard or to her intellectual
environment. So, too, the alleged parallel (p. 660) in I 6 (103, 99) between Hildegard
and Scotus Eriugena's "Expos. super hierarchiam" is tenuous in the extreme. The
diffusion of this work, as the recent Corpus Christianorum edition (by J. Barbet)
indicates, is likewise scant: there is only one complete continuous MS and four incomplete ones (though there are also thirteen MSS of the "Corpus Dionysiacum"
with passages of Scotus' commentary interspersed). More problematic is whether
Hildegard's angelology is in any way indebted to the "Caelestis hierarchia", which
— it may be significant — was known to Elisabeth of Schönau. Yet again the Diony-
sian parallel adduced here (p. 655) is too vague to establish a debt.

Despite much fine work, and a text incomparably closer to the original than was available hitherto, the new edition has some serious flaws. I should like to comment briefly on these, in a constructive spirit, in the hope that, in future volumes of Hildegard's writings in the "Corpus Christianorum", certain things will be done (as they so easily could be done) in a philologically more acceptable way.

Although the MSS are described in careful detail, there is no attempt to state how they are related to one another. There is neither a MS stemma nor a reasoned discussion of why no stemma is feasible, or required [4]. There is no indication which MS is being followed at any time as a base [5]. If the apparatus of MS variants is meant to imply that, with the sole exception of the variants noted, the MSS are unanimous in their testimony, then, at least for passages I have collated in three MSS, this again and again is not the case [6]. Finally, the

[4] The editors have only a brief aside (li, n. 103) that, in accordance with advice from Bernhard Bischoff, "wurde von einem Stemma — nach Lage der Hss. — abgesehen".

[5] The editors' phrase about the lost Wiesbaden MS — "Weil die Hs. seit 1945 verschollen ist, kommt der Fotokopie von **W** (in Originalgröße), die für die Edition benutzt wurde, eine eminente Bedeutung zu" (xxxv-xxxvi) — is somewhat ambiguous. Clearly it was appropriate to use this photocopy, along with the surviving MSS, in preparing the edition; or was the photocopy used as the base MS for the entire text? One hopes not, for, despite the assurance (ibid.) that "auf ihr sind die auf Rasur stehenden Texte... und vieles andere deutlich erkennbar", the problems of corrections, and of which ink is the corrector's, must surely be difficult to determine with certainty from photographs. That is, the evidence of these (or of the handmade facsimile copy made in 1927-33) should not carry a weight comparable to that of the extant MS **V**, which was copied in Hildegard's scriptorium within her lifetime.

[6] A few examples (the faulty recording and evaluating of readings from **R**[s] — the "Symphonia" in **R** — will be discussed separately below): I 3 (41, 81) *Sed ab ipso aethere quidam flatus*: the editors state in the apparatus that *et* appears after *Sed* in the 1513 printed text. This would make the reading easily discountable. They did not note that the *et* occurs also in one of the key-witnesses, **V**, which they themselves acknowledge (p. xxxviii) "besonders sorgfältig geschrieben und weist relativ wenige Fehler auf". — I 6 (100, 23) *in acie alia*: the absence of a note in the apparatus suggests the codices are unanimous; *in alia acie* V. — II 2 (128, 124-6) *sic et homo... perit in fide*: the editors should have noted that VR both read *infide*, and should have considered whether an adverbial form ("faithlessly") might here be possible. — III 3 (372, 42-3) *pallio albo, inferius in duabus oris ipsius purpura contexto: horis* V should have been noted, even if it is only a spelling variant. — III 4 (390, 54-5) *tres angulos habebat ab imo usque ad summum quasi gladios acutos*: V not only articulates the sentence, setting a comma after *habebat*, but reads *usque summum* (not noted ed.). — In III 13, among readings not noted are: 620, 189 *querebatur: quęrebatur* (i.e. *quaerebatur*) O 205 *fons*: corr. from *frons* V 214 *maiori: maiore* O 257 *et o suavis vita*: corr. from *et suavis vita* V 272 *queritur: quęritur* (i.e. *quaeritur*) O 279 *debilis*: corr. from *flebilis* V 285 *ad eandem anima: animam* VRO (misprint in edition?) 320 *ad re-*

edition offers a normalized text. This might in general be defensible
in a series such as "Corpus Christianorum", but is, in the exceptional
circumstances of Hildegard's MS transmission, a tragic mistake.

Briefly, the MS situation for "Scivias" is as follows [7]. Of the
eleven complete MSS of the work, three were written in Hildegard's
scriptorium on the Rupertsberg: two of these — **V** and ***W** (lost
since 1945) — still within her lifetime, the third (**R**) completed just
after her death. Of the remaining MSS, at least two (**H**, **Br**, and possibly also the lost ***E**) still belong to the twelfth century, but were
copied at other centres; two others belong to the first years of the
thirteenth (**C** was copied at Trier in 1210; **O**, of unknown
provenance, is not merely thirteenth century, as the editors state, but
— as Powicke rightly observed — early thirteenth). Finally, there are
two later MSS — **F** (copied from **H** and perhaps ***E**) and **T** (copied
from **C**) — that have no independent value, and an eleventh MS, **m**,
copied from the 1513 printed text.

The present writer has not been able to see the photos of ***W**,
that are still extant in the Eibingen convent, but has copied numerous chapters of "Scivias" from **V**, often collating **R**, and occasionally
O. The accord of the two Rupertsberg MSS, **V** and **R**, is so far-
reaching, even to minute details of spelling and punctuating, that,
for the passages collated, I would have no hesitation in saying that
in every aspect in which **V** and **R** agree we have the actual text that
Hildegard intended and authorized, including her approved orthography and punctuation. The frequent ignoring of that punctuation in
the new edition means that Hildegard's articulation of her prose —
of its cola and commata, its parallelisms of rhythm and rhyme — is
obscured [8], and often sentences that are lucid in the Rupertsberg

---

quirendum perditam: corr. from *ad requirendam p.* V 355 *fugi*: corr. from *fuge* V 380
indue te arma lucis: armis O 404 *filia*: corr. from *anima* O.

[7] These details are of course based on the Schrader/Führkötter study (note 2),
and on the introduction to the new edition. On the precise date of O, see also F.
M. Powicke, *The Medieval Books of Merton College* (Oxford 1931) 236. Asterisks are
here prefixed to the two lost codices, *W and *E, for clarity: many medievalists
tend to confuse especially the two Wiesbaden codices, *W and R, or to be unsure
which of them is still extant. [The editors' siglum (B) for Brussels B.R. 11568 has
been modified to **Br**, in order to distinguish this MS clearly from Berlin lat. qu. 674,
which is designated **B** in some of the literature on Hildegard and in Sections 3-5
below. Most recently, in his edition, Guiberti Gemblacensis Epistolae, Pars I, CC
(CM) 66, 1988, Albert Derolez has offered codicological reasons for believing that
the main part of **R** must have been copied before, not after, Hildegard's death —
i.e. that, with the exception of one later addition, September 17, 1179 is the *terminus
ante quem* of the "Riesenkodex" (xxx-xxxi)].

[8] E.g. III 13   (621, 238)   *dum ille corruit,*

MSS become hard to follow in the edition [9]. As regards orthography, it is not simply that the testimony of what was favoured by Hildegard and her scriptorium at this moment in time is philologically valuable and should not be discarded in a scholarly edition; it is also that, where certain mistakes *have* crept into the MSS, the actual spelling can allow one to see how the error arose, where the normalized spelling cannot.

An apt illustration is the error at 620, 185: the editors print the wholly improbable *tu circumdata es amplexibus divinorum mysteriorum*. Here only the two copies of Hildegard's "Symphonia" (**D**, **R^s**), where this line also occurs, preserve the correct reading, *divinorum ministeriorum* [10]. If the editors had retained the spelling *misteriorum* (sic **VRO**), the source of the corruption would at once be evident.

There is one other major kind of textual flaw in the new edition. The wording of much of Scivias III 13 is in large measure identical with that of songs in Hildegard's "Symphonia", and with parts of her play, the "Ordo Virtutum". The editors assume without discussion that the lyrical works, both songs and play, derive from and are later than "Scivias" (e.g. xiii, xxxi, li-lii — «Die dem "Scivias" entnommenen Texte»). Thus the two MSS of the "Symphonia' (**D**, **R^s**) are listed simply as «Handschriften der Exzerpten-Überlieferung». I have on two previous occasions suggested how difficult it is to ascertain priority for the prose or lyrical versions of these passages [11]. I shall argue below that in certain respects one can

>   *qui super se volare voluit.*
> (622, 260)   *ad te suspiro,*
>   *et omnes Virtutes invoco.*
> (623, 291)   *O nescio quid faciam,*
>   *aut ubi fugiam.*

In each case **R** draws attention to the homoioteleuta and rhymes, by means of commata, whereas the editors always merge the parallel phrases in a single line, without commata.

[9] E.g. III 8 (478, 50-55) reads: *Haec ergo umbrosa columna in hoc ipso aedificio in eodem loco stabat ubi desuper in caelestibus mysteriis coram Deo illum magnum et quadratum lucidissimique candoris splendorem prius uideram. Qui secretum superni creatoris designans in maximo mysterio mihi manifestatus est.* But the punctuation of **V** — *uideram, qui secretum* — must be retained, if Hildegard is not to be saddled with a sentence that lacks a finite verb.

[10] I have discussed the sense of *ministerium* here, and the precedents for the usage in early Christian Latin, in: *Eranos-Jb.* 41 (1972) 85-88.

[11] See "Hildegard of Bingen as Poetess and Dramatist", in: P. Dronke, *Poetic Individuality in the Middle Ages* (Oxford 1970) 150-179 [cf. also 2nd ed., London 1986, xxxiii-xlii], and The Composition of Hildegard of Bingen's Symphonia, in: *Sacris Erudiri* 19 (1969/70) 381-393. The book includes a critical ed. of the "Ordo

go further: only with a naive and over-dogmatic notion of literary composition could one continue to maintain that lyrics in the "Symphonia", and the "Ordo" itself, are derivatives, not originals. In the case of the "Ordo Virtutum", close attention to the parallel passages can establish that a text of the play was in existence when Scivias III 13 came to be written. One cannot be as certain how much of the remainder of the "Symphonia" was complete before "Scivias" (i.e., before 1151); yet it is important to recall that Hildegard was known for her originality of lyrical composition (*modos novi carminis*) already in 1148, as a letter to her in that year, by Odo of Soissons, affirms [12].

Thus the importance of the MSS **D** and **R**[s] for "Scivias" is enormous, and raises sensitive questions of judgement. In each case of discrepancy between the "Scivias" and "Symphonia" MSS (and there are many, some of real importance), we must ask, did Hildegard revise the one composition in the light of the other, so that there are two "correct" readings, one for each context? Or is there a corruption in either the "Symphonia" or the "Scivias" transmission, and only one "right reading" for a given passage? It is to these questions that I shall now turn.

II

Poetry and prose

The varied music that Hildegard hears in her final vision (III 13) is, as she explains in the surrounding prose (614, 29ff.), of three kinds. It consists (1) *in laudibus civium supernorum gaudiorum* (these are the praises of Mary, the angels, and the diverse ranks of saints, which form chapters 2-7); (2) *in querelis revocatorum* (ch. 8); and (3) *in exhortatione virtutum* (ch. 9).

Praises, laments, exhortation — to the praises of the first movement correspond a group of antiphons and responsories in Hildegard's "Symphonia"; to the second and third correspond parts of

Virtutum" (180-192), and a critical ed. of two of Hildegard's sequences, "De undecim milibus virginum" and "De Sancto Ruperto", 209-231 (with the melodies, ed. by I. Bent). For discussion of further ranges of Hildegard problems, see also P. Dronke, *The Medieval Lyric* (London/New York ²1977) 75-78, 238-240, with critical ed. of *Columba aspexit*, melody ed. by I. Bent; *Fabula* (Leiden/Köln 1974) 96-99, 161-163 and passim; Tradition and Innovation in Medieval Western Colour-Imagery; in: *Eranos-Jb.* 41 (1972) 51-107, esp. 82-88, 98-104; "Arbor Caritatis" [*supra*, no. 5, 103-41].

[12] PL 197, 351-352; cf. *Poetic Individuality* (note 11) 153.

the "Ordo Virtutum". In its lyrical-dramatic form, the "Ordo" is self-contained; here in "Scivias" it is not self-contained, but part of a carefully planned triadic structure within a larger vision. The *querelae* (ch. 8) begin with line 50 of the "Ordo" (ed. Dronke) [13], with the lament which is there given to the Virtues to sing: *O plangens vox est hec maximi doloris* (50-58). This is followed at once in "Scivias" by their summons to joy: *O vivens fons, quam magna est suavitas tua* (= Ordo 198-208), and here it is answered by words of the *Vivens lux* (621, 215-224), scorning the «tortuous serpent» (*tortuosum serpentem*) [14]; with these the *querelae* section concludes. Such an answer could clearly not have existed in the "Ordo", where the divine light never speaks. It has been composed expressly for "Scivias".

The long chapter of *exhortatio* (III 13, 9) begins, after a prose introduction, with the Virtues introducing themselves:

> *Nos uirtutes in Deo sumus*
> *et in Deo manemus.*

Again it is clear that this passage could have had no place in the "Ordo", where the Virtues are introduced dramatically in the prelude, in dialogue with the patriarchs and prophets. It follows that in Scivias III 13, 8 the two "Ordo" passages were not to be thought of as spoken by the Virtues; they are, as the chapter-heading indicates, a *vox harmoniae* (not further identified) emitted from heaven.

Only then, in "Scivias", comes the *querela animarum in carne positarum* (= Ordo 9-15), and a series of passages of pure dialogue. This dialogue corresponds — with only relatively small variants in the lines themselves — to the following parts of the "Ordo":

Scivias (CChr, pp. 622-629)	Ordo (ed. Dronke, pp. 181-191)
245-311	9-49
312-315	159-160

[13] References prefixed by "Ordo" in this section refer to my ed., in: *Poetic Individuality* (note 11) 180-192; it is the only text of the play that utilizes both the extant MSS: not only **R⁵** (as the "Scivias" editors call it), but also the MS that I called **A** (London BL, Add. 15 102), which was copied in 1487. I do not mention the **A** variants in the discussion below.

[14] The phrase is not annotated in the edition. While it may go back to Is 27, 1, the prophecy that the Lord will kill *Leviathan serpentem tortuosum*, the context in Hildegard, and especially her double apostrophe — *o serpens... o turpissime illusor* — suggests to me that she had in mind Prudentius' hymn before sleep, and in particular the strophe that begins *o tortuose serpens* (Cath. VI 141).

316-327	68-75
328-331	156-158
332-349	59-67
350-377	161-178
378-380	183-184
381-386	179-182
387-406	185-197
407-443	209-228
444-454	242-251

The "Ordo" in my edition comprises 269 lines. Of these, fewer than half (127) occur in the dialogued chapter of Scivias (III 13, 9); another twenty had occurred in the previous chapter, but outside any context of dialogue or drama. As the comparative table shows, there are also noteworthy differences in the order of lines: at times the passages in "Scivias" correspond with moments set far apart in the "Ordo".

Before broaching the question of priority, let us consider certain strictly textual problems. That the didascalia in "Scivias" are often longer and more explicit than in the "Ordo" is natural enough, as, when "Scivias" was read by a single reader, listeners would need to have the speakers in a dialogue identified more fully than if they were seeing a number of different performers in the various roles. Yet some of the didascalia in the "Scivias" MSS are, quite simply, wrong. Thus at Scivias 622, 255 the editors print *INVOCATIO FIDELIS ANIMAE*, and so too at 266 *FIDELIS ANIMA*; the "Symphonia" (**R**^{s}) has, in both instances, *FELIX ANIMA*. The whole point of the intrigue is that this soul is, at this moment, happy (cf. *O dulcis divinitas... O libenter veniam ad vos*), but that she is *not* steadfast or loyal. That is, the reading of **R**^{s} must be adopted for "Scivias" also (even if, as the apparatus indicates, the "Scivias" MSS are unanimous against it), for the passage there to make sense. It is noteworthy that at 266, according to the editors, the photograph of *****W** shows an erasure: presumably it was planned to insert the correct reading.

It is the same — happy — soul who a moment later grows depressed [15]. *****W** makes this clear at 623, 272 by reading *ANIMA ILLA*; it is less clear in the reading preferred by the editors — *SED GRAVATA ANIMA QVERITVR* — where it would be better to set *GRAVATA* in parenthesis, by commata, or dashes, or round brackets.

---

[15] I discuss the reasons for *Anima*'s change from joy to sadness in detail in: *Poetic Individuality* (note 11) 172ff.

The Soul laments, it is too harsh for her to fight against the flesh. The Virtues then ask her (Ordo 30-31):

> *quare tam flebilis es*
> *contra hoc quod deus contrivit in virginea natura?*

For *flebilis* the editors print the more banal *debilis* of the "Scivias" MSS [16]. They do not, however, note that **V**, the Rupertsberg "Scivias" still copied in Hildegard's lifetime, shows *flebilis* corrected in another ink to *debilis*.

What has happened? Theoretically, *debilis* might have been what Hildegard intended in "Scivias", *flebilis* in the "Ordo". In that case one would, I think, have to say that the "Ordo" reading represents her revision or improvement. But the correction in **V** suggests that another answer is likelier: namely, that Hildegard originally intended and wrote *flebilis* in both "Scivias" and "Ordo", and that it was one of her secretaries who conventionalized her expression — that is, that we can still see a trace of this secretarial change in **V**, a change which (according to the apparatus in the new edition) the remaining MSS reflect unanimously, whilst only **R**ˢ preserves Hildegard's (in both senses) original phrasing.

So, too, I believe this is what has occurred at Ordo 38-40 (= Scivias 623, 292-4):

> *O ve michi, non possum perficere*
> *hoc quod sum induta.*
> *Certe illud volo abicere!* [17]

The "Scivias" MSS appear to be unanimous in reading *hoc quo sum induta*, and indeed a few lines earlier both Ordo (34) and Scivias (287) have *Vide quid illud sit quo es induta*. Yet as Hildegard a little later does use the double accusative with *induere* (Ordo 184 = Scivias 380) — *indue te arma lucis* [18] — I suspect that she wrote *hoc*

---

[16] As do, with even less excuse, the editors of the "Symphonia" (P. Barth/M. I. Ritscher/J. Schmidt-Görg, *Hildegard von Bingen, Lieder* [Salzburg 1969] 169, 300), where *debilis* has no MS justification.

[17] The editors conclude the first line here with *hoc*; but again the "Scivias" text in **R** signals the rhyme by a comma after *perficere*.

[18] This phrase, as the editors note, echoes Paul (Rom 13, 12). It is noteworthy that constructions of the type *induere aliquem aliquid* are first frequent in the "Itala": e.g. Lev. 8, 7 there reads: *vestivit eum tunicam et praecinxit eum zonam* (where the "Vulgate" has ablatives). On this, see esp. D. Norberg, *Syntaktische Forschungen* (Uppsala 1943) 119f. Norberg points out that, apart from Greek influence on the

quod sum induta (and quite possibly also *illud sit quod es induta*), and that the secretarial tidying of her Latin has effaced what she wrote except at Ordo 39. This, then, not the testimony of the "Scivias" MSS, would represent her actual phrasing.

Exactly the same, I suggest, will have happened at Scivias 624, 320f. (= Ordo 68-70), where **R**[s] has:

> *et enutriam vos*
> *ad requirendam perditam dragmam*
> *et ad coronandum in perseverantia felicem.*

According to the new edition, all "Scivias" MSS here (except one, **Br**, which has *quaerendum* — i.e. presumably *querendum*, or perhaps *quęrendum*) have *requirendum* — the gerund, not the gerundive. Yet this (from my limited work with the MSS) is not quite accurate, since **V** at least shows a correction from *requirendam* to *-um*. Once more it will have been Hildegard's secretary-collaborator who thought the gerund better grammatically and more symmetrical with *ad coronandum* in the next line; it will be the "Ordo" and uncorrected **V** that represent what Hildegard herself wrote.

In other cases a decision is more difficult. Thus at Scivias 307 **R**[s] offers the more vivid expression *Strepitus diaboli* where the "Scivias" MSS have *Suggestio diaboli*; yet they have *Strepitus diaboli* later, at 332, where **R**[s] simply has *Diabolus*. Here, that is, it is not a question of a secretary's having eliminated an unconventional phrase of Hildegard's from her text, only that this phrase is perhaps most aptly used to characterize *Diabolus* at his entry and opening words, rather than later; in this sense the **R**[s] order might be held correct. At Scivias 319, the editors have not noticed that **R**[s] has *Venite ad me, Virtutes* (not *omnes Virtutes*, like the other MSS); here the question of correctness or revision is too slender to determine.

By contrast, there seems to me no doubt that, in the Devil's next speech, the "Scivias" MSS must again be corrected. The editors print (625, 336ff.):

> *Ego autem dico:*
> *«Qui uoluerit me et uoluntatem suam sequi,*
> *dabo illi omnia»;*

biblical language, the primary construction with such verbs is "die passivische, oder richtiger die mediale. Schon Plautus verwendet nämlich das Partizip *indutus* mit einem Akk., z.B. Men. 512". Cf. also Hofmann/Szantyr 45. — Here the scribe of **O** (see above, note 6) "corrected" Hildegard, writing *indue te armis lucis.*

*tu uero cum tuis sequacibus
nihil habes quod dare possis.*

This should read, as in **R⁵** (Ordo 59-61): *Ego autem dico, qui voluerit me et voluntatem meam sequi, dabo illi omnia. Tu vero, tuis sequacibus nichil habes quod dare possis* [19]. The reading *meam* is supported not only by **R⁵** but also by the "Scivias" text itself in **R**. Even more important, the editors do not note that **R⁵** has no *cum*. Here the poetic sense shows that **R⁵** alone preserves the true reading: the contrast between *Diabolus* claiming he will give *his* followers everything, and asserting that the *Virtutes* can give *their* followers nothing, has been foolishly obscured in the "Scivias" MSS.

Almost all other **R⁵** readings (other than didascalia) in the remainder of the dialogue are better than the corresponding readings in the "Scivias" MSS, and hence ought to have their place in a critical edition of "Scivias" [20]. At Ordo 212 (= Scivias 628, 414) *Anima*'s answer to *Diabolus* — *Ego omnes vias meas malas esse cognovi* — is the dramatically appropriate riposte to his allegation *Tu amplexata es me*. The reading in the "Scivias" MSS — *vias tuas* for *vias meas* — may be edifying, but is dramatically pointless [21]. At Scivias 423 (= Ordo 218), the imagery of chivalric campaign in the surrounding lines guarantees the reading of **R⁵** — *cum militibus tuis* — against *cum sodalibus tuis* of the "Scivias" MSS. (Was Hildegard's secretary perhaps shocked by the image of womanly *milites*, or less well acquainted with their prototypes — in Prudentius' "Psychomachia" — than Hildegard herself?) Finally, the **R⁵** reading at Ordo 248 (= Scivias 451) — *ex te fluit fons in igneo amore* — avoids the pleonasm *igneo ardore* of the "Scivias" MSS.

In many respects, then, we can be reasonably certain that **R⁵** represents the wording intended by Hildegard, and that in the copying of "Scivias" we must reckon not only with minor slips but also with occasional secretarial "adjustments" — the medieval equivalent

[19] I print these lines as prose: in the "Ordo", only *Diabolus* has a speaking, not a singing part, and his lines are deliberately made less rhythmic than those of the other protagonists. (In the words of Lorenzo in "The Merchant of Venice": "The man that hath no music in himself.../Is fit for treasons, stratagems and spoils").

[20] One can scarcely choose, however, between very minor variations such as Scivias 419 *Unde* and Ordo 214 *Inde*, or Scivias 449 *laus tibi sit* and Ordo 247 *laus sit tibi*.

[21] Astonishingly, the German editors of the "Symphonia" (*Lieder* [note 16] 197, 310) go to the length of altering the text they are allegedly printing, and insert *tuas* from "Scivias".

of insensitive copy-editing, attempts to make the unexpected in a
text conform to more straightforward habits of expression.

What of the passages where the *sequence* of dialogue diverges
in "Scivias" and the "Ordo"? The two most important disparities in
sequence are revealing. In Scivias 319ff. *Humilitas* summons the *Virtutes* to the quest for *Anima*; they assent, and she says (625,
326-331):

> *Ideo, dilectissimae filiae,*
> *teneo uos in regali thalamo.*
> *O filiae Israel,*
> *sub arbore suscitauit uos Deus,*
> *unde in hoc tempore recordamini plantationis suae.*
> *Gaudete ergo, filiae Sion.*

This is at one followed by *strepitus Diaboli*:

> *Quae est haec potestas,*
> *quod nullus sit praeter Deum?*

The devil's answer does not fit well with the last lines of *Humilitas*, and it is precisely these lines that correspond to a different section of the "Ordo". In "Scivias", we have been told nothing of this
tree, which the opening and close of the "Ordo" establish as the co-
ordinating image of the whole play; and "this power" (*haec potestas*)
is difficult to refer to anything in *Humilitas'* speech. In the "Ordo",
by contrast, it refers to the power of *Innocentia* (*que in pudore bono
integritatem non amisisti, 57*), celebrated by the other *Virtutes,* and it
is this that rouses *Diabolus'* angry challenge, and his claim that he
himself has a greater *potestas*.

Here it seems that Hildegard has tried to abridge and adapt
from the already existent "Ordo", and that her adjustment was not
wholly successful. She wanted to abridge by speeding up the action,
omitting most of the longest scene in the play, the lyrical scene in
which the Virtues one by one reveal their nature. So she has kept
only the opening summons and the final, climactic words of the
scene, which become "Scivias" 328-331, returning at once to the
conflict concerning *Diabolus* and *Anima*. The full beauty of these
lines is indeed hard to perceive in "Scivias" for one who does not
know their reverberations in the parts of the "Ordo" that "Scivias"
cuts.

If this is accepted, then the reason for another change is easy
to see: the sequence which, in the "Ordo", goes as follows (176-85):

Penitens Anima ad Virtutes

Ego peccator qui fugi vitam:
plenus ulceribus veniam ad vos,
ut prebeatis michi scutum redemptionis.
O tu omnis milicia regine,
et o vos, candida lilia ipsius, cum rosea purpura,
inclinate vos ad me, quia peregrina a vobis exulavi,
et adiuvate me, ut in sanguine filii dei possim surgere.

Virtutes

O Anima fugitiva, esto robusta,
et indue te arma lucis.

Anima illa

Et o vera medicina, Humilitas, prebe michi auxilium, —

is changed in "Scivias" to give the order (626, 374ff.):

PAENITENS ANIMA IN CORPORE

Ego peccator qui fugi uitam,
plenus ulceribus ueniam ad uos,
ut praebeatis mihi scutum redemptionis.

VIRTVTES

O anima fugitiua, esto robusta,
et indue te arma lucis.

PAENITENS ANIMA IN CORPORE

O tu omnis militia reginae,
et o uos candida lilia ipsius cum rosea purpura,
inclinate uos ad me,
quia peregrina a uobis exulaui,
et adiuuate me ut in sanguine Filii Dei possim surgere.
Et o uera medicina humilitas,
praebe mihi auxilium. —

The sequence which in the play suggested an impulsive, spontaneous order, where the Virtues and *Anima* each "cut in" on the other's thoughts, is converted to a more logical prosaic order. At Scivias 387, *Et o vera medicina humilitas, praebe mihi auxilium* now connects with and is symmetrical with the clauses immediately preceding: *et adiuuate me ut in sanguine Filii Dei possim surgere.* It has lost the character of excited intervention that it had in the play [22].

With the antiphons and responsories that occur both in the "Symphonia" and in "Scivias", it is not possible to say whether they were first composed with the visionary work or the lyrical cycle in mind. What must be stressed, however, is that, whether for the one context or the other, they were conceived lyrically from the outset. By the intensity and music of their language they stand out from the prose in "Scivias" that surrounds them. Thus there are two objections to the frequent statements that these pieces in the "Symphonia" are "drawn from" "Scivias" ("entnommen"): not only may they well have been planned first for the "Symphonia", or indeed as single lyrical compositions for particular liturgical feasts, but one must at all events dispel the impression that for Hildegard lyrical composition consisted of taking passages from her prose, dividing them into lines of a length suitable for musical phrases, and then adding notes. We may no longer be able to tell in full detail the relations between "Scivias" and the "Symphonia"; at least we can be certain they were not like that.

III

Sources

The "Vita" of Hildegard, begun in her lifetime by her secretary Gottfried († 1175/6) and completed by Theodoric of Echternach in 1181, two years after her death, preserves twelve extended passages of her autobiographic notes *. These are signalled clearly as her own words, and are given in direct speech throughout. The first of these passages, a precious personal testimony to the nature of Hildegard's visionary gift, contains some lines crucial to the question of her sources. In the fullest and best MS of the "Vita", Berlin lat. qu. 674 (= **B**), fol. 7[va], they read:

> *In eadem visione, scripta prophetarum, ewangeliorum, et aliorum sanctorum, et quorumdam philosophorum, sine ulla humana doctrina intellexi, ac quedam ex illis exposui, cum vix noticiam litterarum haberem, sicut indocta mulier me docuerat. Sed et cantum cum melodia in laude*

---

[22] On the use of an opening *Et*, and especially the "prophetic" *Et* at the beginning of Scivias I 1, see the excellent comments of Führkötter/Carlevaris (note 1) xviii.

[* I have given a new edition of a substantial part of these notes in my *Women Writers of the Middle Ages* (Cambridge 1984), 231-241.]

*dei et sanctorum, absque doctrina ullius hominis, protuli, et cantavi, cum
nunquam vel neumam vel cantum aliquem didicissem.*

Through her vision, that is, Hildegard claims to have understood «the writings of the prophets, the gospels, and the writings of
other holy men, and of certain philosophers, without any human instruction». Unfortunately, the text of the "Vita" in **R** (fol. 320ᵛᵃ)
omits the vital *et*, giving *et aliorum sanctorum quorumdam
philosophorum* ("and of other holy certain philosophers» — the collo-
cation of the words is as bizarre in English as in Latin). This is also
the way the passage is printed in the edition of the "Vita" (Migne
PL 197, 104A, garbled here as in many other places). Even Führkötter, in her German translation of the text, though she claims to be
basing this on MSS — on **B** as well as **R** — renders the passage: "In
dieser Schau verstand ich ohne irgendeine menschliche Bildung die
Schriften der Propheten, der Evangelien *und anderer heiliger Lehrer*"
(emphasis mine) [23].

The over-edifying impression created by the corrupt text and
misleading translation must be put right. Hildegard is not speaking
exclusively of religious testimonies — prophets, gospels, and other
holy teachers. What she is saying is that she understood biblical
texts, other holy (i.e. theological) writings, *and those of certain
philosophers*, intuitively — without any formal training in bible
study, theology, or philosophy. It was in just this way that Saint Augustine had claimed that, when young, he had understood Aristotle's
"Categories" and other difficult works in the liberal arts (Conf. IV
16: *nullo hominum tradente... nullo adminiculo humani magisterii tot
nodosissimi libri enodati*): Hildegard may even be recalling this particular chapter in the "Confessions".

On the basis of these writings, Hildegard here adds, she expounded certain ideas, even though she scarcely had literary
knowledge: she did so in the way an «unlearned» woman (her
teacher, Jutta of Sponheim) had taught her to write. Moreover, she
continues, she was able to compose songs and to sing them, even
though she had not learnt to read music (*neumam*) and had not been
trained as a singer.

The two salient points that emerge from the passage are: (1) Hildegard admits that she knew and used certain philosophical works
as well as holy ones; (2) she does not claim to have been "inspired"

[23] Das Leben der heiligen Hildegard von Bingen, transl. A. Führkötter (Düs-
seldorf 1968) 38 n. 2; cf. 66. The passage is also misquoted in Führkötter/Carlevaris
(note 1) xv.

either to knowledge or to lyrical composition *ex nihilo* — in the way, for instance, that Bede relates of Caedmon. If we make allowance for a certain element of modesty-topos, "ad maiorem dei gloriam", we can interpret her as saying that, because of a divinely granted intuitive gift, she could master learned texts without difficulty, notwithstanding her fairly rudimentary schooling. And certainly the gift of composing and singing music without training in notation or sight-reading is a perfectly normal, even if unusual, one. The pluperfect *didicissem* (at the close of the passage cited) does not rule out, indeed may even imply, that she came to understand musical notation at a later stage.

The other key passage in Hildegard's writings that bears on the question of her sources is one in the Berlin Fragment that was published by Schipperges in 1956 [24]. In **B**, fol. 109ra, it reads: *Pagani philosophi, ut Donatus, Lucanus, erant precurrens sucus et precurrens vox philosophorum ecclesie.* The MS preserves this as a self-contained "sententia"; yet it may be possible to see the following one (though it is marked as separate in the MS) as an amplification of this thought: *Sol per totam terram lucet — ita et exspiratio spiritus sancti.* That is, if the sun can shine throughout the whole world, and the breath of the Holy Spirit can reach all realms, pagan and Christian, then pagan philosophers as well as Christian can have true "sap" in their writings, even if their voice is that of a precursor, not of divine Sapientia.

The genuineness of the Berlin Fragment has never been disputed. Even though the attribution of some passages to Hildegard could — and in my view should — be challenged [25], there seems no reason

---

[24] H. Schipperges, "Ein unveröffentlichtes Hildegard-Fragment", in: *Sudhoffs Archiv für Geschichte der Medizin* 40 (1956) 41-77.

[25] The so-called «Hildegard-Fragment» in **B** is in fact a very heterogeneous series of fragments, and some of these, such as the extract from "Causae et Curae", are clearly by Hildegard. But the various excerpts come helter-skelter, and are often repetitive, and among them are a number of absurdities (e.g. that Adam and Eve spoke a Teutonic language, or that angels were not created), which I should be reluctant to ascribe to Hildegard; others again (e.g. a complaint that nowadays women prophesy, to the scandal of men), which it would hardly be possible to ascribe to her. (The context here rules out that the phrase might be ironic). It would seem to me that a collection of Hildegard-excerpts, or Hildegard-"Sententiae", has been contaminated with other apocalyptic utterances (as so often happens in this sphere of writing), and that it would be prudent to accept as genuine only such passages as are clearly compatible with — and comparable with — the undoubted writings of Hildegard. And even then the question, how far an excerptor was copying extracts of Hildegard that have not otherwise survived, and how far he or she was composing in the Hildegardian manner, must remain to some extent open.

to doubt that of the two sentences just cited. Indeed, for one versed in Hildegard's modes of expression, the strange phrase *precurrens sucus* is so distinctively Hildegardian as to leave little room for doubt. It is unfortunate that the editors of the new "Scivias", in their discussion of sources (xiv-xviii), overlooked this passage and these names completely. Neither Lucan nor Donatus (nor any treatise based on Donatus) appears in the "Index auctorum".

With Donatus, it is difficult to proceed in our present state of knowledge: we should have to be able to ascertain with what commentary, or commentaries, Hildegard may have read Donatus — for it is in these, rather than in the jejune doctrine of the "Ars maior" and "Ars minor", that relevant philosophical elements might be traced [26]. With Lucan I would suggest the problem is clearer: the philosophical motif to which Hildegard responded in the "De bello civili" was an aspect of Lucan's Stoicism, it was "Lucan's imagery of cosmic dissolution'" (to cite the title of a recent study) [27]. Like Lucan, Hildegard saw human transgressions reflected on a cosmic scale: thus at the beginning and end of human history she sees disturbances in the universe, the elements portending and expressing in their own ways the disaster, the sickness or evil that befalls mankind: so at the fall of Adam:

> All the elements of the world (*Omnia elementa mundi*), which previously had subsisted in great calm, turning into wildest restlessness, brought hideous terrors forth. For that (elemental) creation, which had been made to serve man, and had been aware of no hostility in itself, when man seized upon rebellion, inflicted many great ad-

---

[26] We should need, for Donatus commentaries, a range of studies comparable to those that R.W. Hunt, and more recently KM. Fredborg, have achieved for commentaries on Priscian. I have not found anything of decisive relevance to Hildegard in the standard older collection of materials, that of Ch. Thurot (*Notices et extraits des manuscrits* 22, 2), Paris 1867. [Certain elements in Smaragdus, "Liber in partibus Donati", ed. B. Löfstedt, L. Holtz, A. Kibre, CC (CM) 68, 1986, are philosophically suggestive: cf. esp. Holtz's observations, li-lii. Smaragdus' treatise, however, was largely forgotten after the tenth century (lxiv).]

[27] M. Lapidge, in: *Hermes* 107 (1979) 344-370, with fine discussion of the key passages and of the earlier Stoic background. On the textual crux in Lucan I 74ff. (cited below), see 360 n. 72. On the "Rezeption" of Lucan in the Middle Ages, see esp. two recent articles by P. von Moos: "Lucans *tragedia* im Hochmittelalter. Pessimismus, *contemptus mundi* und Gegenwartserfahrung", in : *Mlat. Jb.* 14 (1978) 127-186; " 'Poeta' und 'historicus' im Mittelalter", in: *PBB* Tübingen 98 (1976) 93-130. These are rich in insights and in further references. The twelfth-century Lucan commentary cited and discussed by J. Martin, in: *Traditio* 11 (1955) 400-406, is notable for its cosmological interest.,

versities upon him, since he had inclined himself to baser things, so
that he was coerced (*coerceretur*) by elemental forces (Scivias I 2; 32,
660ff.).

Again, in the final stage of the universe:

> After this I saw: and behold, all the elements and all creatures
> were shaken by a dire motion. Fire, air and water burst forth and
> caused earth to be moved, lightnings and thunderbolts clashed, moun-
> tains and forests fell, to make all that was mortal exhale its life. And
> all the elements were cleansed — so that everything which had been
> sordid in them would vanish in such a way as never to appear again...
> And soon all the elements were radiant in utmost serenity, as if
> a deep-black skin had been peeled off them: fire no longer scorched,
> air was no longer murky, water had no more fury (*furorem*), earth no
> more bitterness...
> For just as man, when destined to end, is downcast, forewarned
> by many infirmities, so that in the hour of his death he is dissolved
> in much grief, so too the greatest adversities will herald the world's
> end, and will dissolve (*dissoluent*) the world in diverse terrors at its
> end: for the elements will then display their terrors, since they will not
> be able to practise them afterwards.
> With a sudden, unexpected motion, the elements are let loose
> (*relaxantur*) in the end — all created things are convulsed, fire breaks
> forth, air is released, water flows out, earth is shaken, lightnings
> scorch, thunderbolts din, mountains are cleft, forests fall, and
> whatever is in air or water or earth gives up its life. For fire moves all
> the air and water fills all the earth (Scivias III 12; 604, 31ff.) [28]

So also Lucan, evoking the Roman civil war on a worldwide
scale (*quid pacem excusserit orbi*, I 69), turns to imagery of the dissolution of the universe, the Stoic "ecpyrosis" (I 72-81):

> *sic, cum conpage soluta*
> *saecula tot mundi suprema coegerit hora*
> *antiquum repetens iterum chaos, omnia mixtis*
> *⟨viribus inter se contendent semina mundi⟩,*
> *sidera sideribus concurrent, ignea pontum*
> *astra petent, tellus extendere litora nolet*
> *excutietque fretum, fratri contraria Phoebe*

---

[28] This last sentence, and the notion of the purification of the elements, would
seem closest to a passage in Seneca's "Quaestiones Naturales" (a work discussed in
relation to Hildegard below) III 28, 7, concerning deluge and conflagration: *Utrum-
que fit, cum deo visum ordiri meliora, vetera finiri. Aqua et ignis terrenis dominantur;
ex his ortus, ex his interitus est.*

ibit et obliquum bigas agitare per orbem
indignata diem poscet sibi, totaque discors
machina divolsi turbabit foedera mundi.
In se magna ruunt.

While conpages/compago is used in "Scivias" only figuratively, not
physically (527, 397), in the "Liber divinorum operum" Hildegard
speaks of the *imago* of the cosmic man, in which are perceived, ordered, *vires elementorum... omnesque compagines membrorum hominis*
qui in illo — scilicet mundo — dominatur [29]. Like Lucan, she uses *sol-*
vere, quatere, ruere and their compounds to describe the elemental
disorders. Again, when Lucan evokes the storm during which Caesar
crosses the Adriatic (V 577ff.), the word *furor*, which characterizes
the civil war itself (*Quis furor, o cives*, — I 8) and in particular Caesar's battling, is used of the winds (*furori ventorum*) and of the sea
(*furebat pontus*). *Furor* is also the word Hildegard uses of the element
water, as well as of Satanic, of human, and even of divine rage [30].
Where Lucan speaks of *mundumque coercens... unda*, she sees man,
at the moment of the first sin, «coerced» by the elements.

In Caesar's storm, the connotations are again of the shattering
of elemental harmony: earth yields to water, water is content with no
bounds save the sky (622-4), the air is murky with lightnings, the
vault of the gods trembles, there is thunder on high and the heavens
are in anguish as their frame is moved (*motaque poli conpage laborant*,
633); the elements seem to have burst out of their harmonious sta-
tions (*rupisse videntur concordes elementa moras*, 634-5). Underlying
such imagery there would seem to be the Stoic conception of "cosmic
sympathy" [31]: the elements are influenced by the human warfaring,
the human *furor*, and react accordingly. The notion is equally evident
in a remarkable passage in Hildegard's "Causae et Curae":

> The elements are subject to man and, according as they are
> touched by the actions of men, they at times exercise their functions.
> For when men clash in battles, terrorism, hate and envy and sins of
> discord, the elements overturn themselves, moving into a discordant
> mode of heat or cold, or of great effusions and inundations.
> *Elementa enim subiecta sunt homini, et secundum quod ipsa tangun-*

---

[29] Gent, MS 241 p. 88; **R** fol. 223ra (PL 197, 789).

[30] See the "Index verborum et elocutionum" in Führkötter/Carlevaris (note 1)
761. The passage from Job 21, 17-18 that Hildegard cites in Scivias I 2 (15, 123-5)
might well have suggested to her a link between *furor* and *inundatio*.

[31] K. Reinhardt, *Kosmos und Sympathie. Neue Untersuchungen über Poseidonios*,
München 1926.

tur ab operibus hominum sic officia sua interdum exercent. Nam quando homines se invicem intermiscent, cum preliis, terroribus, odio et invidia, ac in contrariis peccatis, tunc evertunt se in alium et in contrarium modum aut caloris aut frigoris, aut magnarum effusionum et inundationum [32].

In Lucan VI 461-82 the rebellion of each of the elements in turn is evoked — fire disobedient to its law, air and water behaving in unnatural ways (sea-tempests without wind, a transfixed torrent and a diverted river), earth shaking its axle-tree (*concussit*) — though Lucan expresses it all with a wealth of mythological reference that is alien to Hildegard. What she saw in Lucan, however, was how to represent the elements as alive, as if human, responding to the human disturbances, consciously taking part in all aspects of destiny, prefiguring, reflecting and consummating it.

Other aspects of Hildegard's cosmological notions, too, would seem to be of Stoic inspiration: as Liebeschütz suggested half a century ago, Hildegard's conception of a circle of "strong air", which acts as a "nerve" for the cosmos, a nerve that by its tension is responsible for universal cohesiveness, can be traced in Seneca's "Quaestiones Naturales" (II 6). Similarly her notion of air as a principle of motion and life in the higher spheres as well as the sublunary world would seem to reflect the Stoic concept of *pneuma* nourishing and sustaining all parts of the cosmos (Q.N. II 4, VI 16) [33]. The use of Seneca's "Quaestiones" in the mid-twelfth century is not widespread — William of Conches's "Dragmaticon" (c. 1144-49) is a notable exception [34] — and yet, in default of equally compelling parallels in other sources, we must reckon with the possibility of Hildegard's having had access to the Senecan text.

A philosophical text rather better attested in the mid-twelfth century was Cicero's "De natura deorum" [35]. And (again unless truly

---

[32] København, MS N. K.S. 90 b p. 41 (cf. *Causae et Curae*, ed. P. Kaiser [Leipzig 1903] 57).

[33] Cf. Liebeschütz (note 1) 70-71, 80-81.

[34] C. Picard-Parra, "Une utilisation des 'Quaestiones Naturales' de Sénèque au milieu du XIIe siècle", in: RMAL 3 (1949) 115-126.

[35] Cf. P. Dronke, "New Approaches to the School of Chartres", in: *Anuario de Estudios Medievales* 6 (1969), esp. 133-135 [*supra*, no. I, 32-35]. Occurrences of the "De natura deorum" in medieval library catalogues of the German language-area are collected in M. Manitius, *Handschriften antiker Autoren in mal. Bibliothekskatalogen* (Leipzig 1935) 20-26. The sixteenth-century catalogue of St. Eucharius in Trier, a community with which Hildegard had close links, does not, however,

plausible intermediaries were to be discovered) it seems to me that Book II of Cicero's treatise, Balbus' exposition of Stoic beliefs, can best account for Hildegard's most striking transformation of a Stoic concept — her visionary depiction of the cosmic *vis ignea* at the opening of her "Liber divinorum operum":

> *Et vidi velut in medio australis aeris pulcram mirificamque in misterio dei imaginem quasi hominis formam, cuius facies tante pulcritudinis et claritatis erat, ut facilius solem quam ipsam inspicere possem, et circulus amplus aureique coloris caput eiusdem faciei circumdederat...*
>
> *Et imago hec dicebat: Ego summa et ignea vis que omnes viventes scintillas accendi, et nulla mortalia efflavi, sed illa diiudico ut sunt; circueuntem circulum cum superioribus pennis meis — id est cum sapientia — circumvolans, recte ipsum ordinavi. Sed et ego ignea vita substantie divinitatis, super pulcritudinem agrorum flammo, et in aquis luceo, atque in sole, luna et stellis ardeo, et cum aereo vento — quadam invisibili vita que cuncta sustinet — vitaliter omnia suscito.*
>
> *Aer enim in viriditate et in floribus vivit, aque fluunt quasi vivant, sol etiam in lumine suo vivit, et, cum luna ad defectum venerit, a lumine solis accenditur ut quasi denuo vivat; stelle quoque in lumine suo velut vivendo clarescunt.*
>
> *Columpnas etiam, que totum orbem terrarum continent, constitui, id est ventos illos qui pennas sibi subditas — scilicet leniores ventos — habent, qui lenitate sua ipsis fortiores sustinent, ne cum periculo se ostendant — quemadmodum corpus animam tegit et continet, ne exspiret. Sicut etiam spiramen anime corpus firmando colligit ut non deficiat, sic quoque fortiores venti sibi subiectos animant, ut officium suum congruenter exerceant.*
>
> *Ego itaque vis ignea in his lateo ipsique de me flagrant, velut spiramen assidue hominem movet, et ut in igne ventosa flamma est. Hec omnia in essentia sua vivunt nec in morte inventa sunt: quoniam ego vita sum. Racionalitas etiam sum, ventum sonantis verbi habens, per quod omnis creatura facta est, et in omnia hec sufflavi, ita ut nullum eorum in genere suo mortale sit, quia ego vita sum. Integra namque vita sum, que de lapidibus abscisa non est, et de ramis non fronduit, et de virili vi non radicavit — sed omne vitale de me radicatum est* [36].

While the passage as a whole suggests the pervasive physical presence of this fiery force, in the last sentence cited Hildegard

---

mention the "De natura deorum", but only the "Somnium Scipionis" and "De officiis" (ibid. 26).

[36] Gent, MS 241 p. 29-30; **R** fol. 208[rb-va] (PL 197, 741-3). In the first line of the fourth paragraph cited, I have chosen the Gent reading *que* (referring to *Columpnas*) rather than R's *qui* (probably a scribal slip rather than a forward reference to *ventos*).

stresses that the principle itself is not only divine but also in some sense immaterial: I interpret the words as: "I am the fullness of life, not hewn from stones, nor growing shoots from boughs, nor rooted in a man's sexual power — but all that is life-giving takes its root from me». Thus she gives in the end an unmistakably Christian colouring to Balbus' "fiery force", which for him was rational and divine but was also material. In a long series of arguments, Balbus tried to show "that all things which are nourished and grow contain in themselves the force of heat (*vim caloris*); the veins and arteries of our bodies never cease to flash as with a fiery motion (*igneo motu*); it is a vital force pervading the whole world (*vim ... vitalem per omnem mundum pertinentem*). That hot and fiery force is so fused in the whole of nature that the power of procreating and the cause of begetting inhere in it (*calidum illud atque igneum ita in omni fusum esse natura ut in eo insit procreandi vis et causa gignendi*). "In trees and what grows from the earth this principle is thought to inhere in the roots" (*radicibus inesse*). But in other parts of the world sense and reason inhere, and so "the world is a god and the whole *vis* of the world is contained in the divine nature. Moreover, that burning heat (*fervor*) of the world is purer and more pellucid... than this earthly warmth of ours... not stirred by another, nor by any external impulse, it moves of its own accord and spontaneously". Such motion is more divine (*divinius*) than any derived motion. "Therefore... this ardour must be soul (*animus*); through this it comes about that the world is animate" (II 23-32). In III 18, finally, Cotta speaks of Balbus' argument "concerning that fiery force and heat from which you said all things were generated" (*de vi ignea deque eo calore ex quo omnia generari dicebas*): here, that is, Hildegard's actual expression *vis ignea* was used [37].

Much of Hildegard's visionary conception can be seen in these moments of the "De natura deorum". But while she too, in her own way, brings the physical and the divine together, she naturally, as a Christian, does not follow Balbus in his final step, of claiming that the world itself is a god.

Other fruitful, though still difficult, approaches to the problem

---

[37] *Vis ignea* also occurs, however, at several places in Seneca's "Quaestiones Naturales" (e.g. I 15), as well as in Ovid's "Metamorphoses" I 26 (but there as a periphrasis for the element fire). In Lucan (IX 7) it is Pompey's *ignea virtus* that enables his soul at death to unite with the *aether*. In a Christian context, Prudentius seems to echo Stoic language at the opening of his hymn for the burial of the dead (Cath. X 1-2): *Deus, ignee fons animarum, / duo qui socians elementa...* (On the possibility that Hildegard was familiar with the "Cathemerinon", see note 14 above).

of Hildegard's philosophic sources will be through more intensive study of her vocabulary. In the autobiographical notes in Hildegard's "Vita" — to give one instance — I was struck by the words *conglobositas* and *inaquositas* (Migne PL 197, 106D, 123A, 126C): they are not to be found in "Thesaurus Linguae Latinae", and not yet in any of the medieval Latin dictionaries. Can they be traced to a particular medical work, and so shed new light on Hildegard's scientific reading? * Equally delicate is the problem with such a philosophic concept as *prima materia*, which Hildegard uses twice in the opening verses of Scivias III 13 (615, 45ff.): *creavit mundi primam materiam... ut eduxit in prima materia omnes creaturas*. Here the tradition, at least from the Carolingian period onwards [38], is too abundant to allow us to ascertain a specific source. This problem can be perceived from another vantage by reconsidering some — I believe misleading — judgments advanced by Schipperges, when he denied that Hildegard could be responsible for the chapter-headings in "Causae et Curae":

> They do not stem from Hildegard's language, but from the terminology of the thirteenth century. Thus the Aristotelian concept *hyle* for *materia* is found only in the margin [i.e. in headings], not in the text. So too the concepts *generatio* and *corruptio* unmistakably come from the well known Aristotelian book "De generatione et corruptione", which first reached the West by way of Toledo around the middle of the twelfth century. Hildegard in her text speaks not of *generatio* but of *genitura* [39].

[* In 1987, when investigating the sources of Hildegard's vocabulary, in connection with the new edition of her "Liber divinorum operum" (ed. A. Derolez, P. Dronke, CC [CM] 92, in press), I was able to consult the unpublished materials of several dictionaries, including the Mittellateinisches Wörterbuch in Munich. While *inaquositas* is recorded exclusively in Hildegard's writings and would seem to be her coinage, *conglobositas* is one of a group of rare expressions that she derives from Constantinus Africanus: this particular word is recorded only in Constantinus (Panteg. Theor. 6, 8) and in Hildegard. In a recent essay, "Platonic-Christian Allegories in the Homilies of Hildegard of Bingen", in Mélanges Edouard Jeauneau, ed. H.J. Westra, Leiden 1991, note 11, I have given succinct documentation for some of Hildegard's more unusual reading (notably of Aethicus Ister, "Asclepius", Calcidius, Claudianus Mamertus, Constantinus, Filastrius, Lactantius, and Origen); the edition of the "Liber" will bring further details.]

[38] See F. Blatt, *Novum Glossarium*, s.v. *materia*.

[39] Cf. Hildegard von Bingen, *Heilkunde*, transl. H. Schipperges (Salzburg 1957) 41. Schipperges' next sentence, "Likewise Aristotelian is *aether* as a concept for a celestial substance of immaterial nature", is, in this context, misleading in two ways: one, because this Aristotelian notion was diffused to the earlier Middle Ages by Apuleius' version of the pseudo-Aristotelian "De mundo" (see esp. I 291); two,

While I do not wish to claim that all the chapter-headings in the unique (and relatively late) MS of "Causae et Curae" necessarily go back to Hildegard, Schipperges' arguments to the contrary do not hold water. The concept *hyle* is at least as common in the twelfth century as the thirteenth — indeed the use of *hyle* was one of Singer's chief reasons for believing (again I think mistakenly) that Hildegard had been influenced by Bernard Silvestris [40]! My point is that Hildegard might have known the concept and term *hyle* from innumerable sources: as from Augustine (see especially his illuminating discussion of *hyle* in "De natura boni" 18), Ambrose ("Hexameron", I 1), or Calcidius, or — perhaps most probably — from the "Asclepius" [41]. Similarly, the Aristotelian antithesis *generatio-corruptio* could be readily encountered before the new Aristotelian translations — most frequently in the corpus of Boethius' writings on the "De interpretatione" [42].

Finally, we must reckon with the possibility that Hildegard's knowledge of cosmological texts increased over the years, that in particular her late work, "Liber divinorum operum", and perhaps also her medical writings, may show traces of more advanced reading than "Scivias" does. Nonetheless, even though it is chronologically possible, it seems unlikely that Hildegard, at the time of writing the "Liber" (completed in 1173), will have come to know early translations of Aristotelian physical treatises. Yet here too one must be accurate: neither James of Venice's translation of the "Physica", nor the slightly later "Vatican" version — both made direct from the Greek — have anything to do with Toledo [43], and there is a translation, again from the Greek, of "De generatione et corruptione", which survives already in a MS "probably little later than the middle of the twelfth century" [44], which thus may well be older than the one Gerard of Cremona made from Arabic. So here again it is somewhat misleading to see such a text as «reaching the West by way of Toledo».

---

because Hildegard's concept of *aether* is not immaterial: cf. e.g. Causae et Curae (note 32) 7, 1, 21 (*Aether... firmatur*), or Scivias I 3, passim.

[40] C. Singer, *From Magic to Science* (New York 1958) 220, 237.

[41] I have touched on Hildegard's knowledge of the "Asclepius" in: *Poetic Individuality* (note 11) 158. Where the Hermetic treatise mentions an *ignis solum... vivificum* (2), and closes with the prayer *o vitae vera vita, o naturarum omnium fecunda praegnatio* (41), the Holy Spirit for Hildegard, in her sequence *O ignis spiritus paracliti*, is not only *ignis* but *vita vite omnis creature... vivificando formas... spes compaginis membrorum omnium*.

[42] See TLL VI 2, 1784, s.v. *generatio*.

[43] L. Minio-Paluello, *Opuscula. The Latin Aristotle* (Amsterdam 1972) 572.

[44] Minio-Paluello (note 43) 117.

One other text rich in philosophical materials deserves mention here, because it is by one of the few authors whom Hildegard actually names. This is Origen's "De principiis". Hildegard's reference to Origen is admittedly to another work, on the Gospel of Luke, and she makes only the briefest allusion to him [45]. Yet a number of passages in "De principiis" can be seen to reflect some of the same concerns as Hildegard's in the way of cosmology [46]; on the other hand, I have not found any conclusive indications of a debt.

Older attempts at suggesting sources for Hildegard, especially those of Singer, were often based on insufficiently precise command of materials. Thus for instance Singer, calling the *vis ignea* of the opening of "Liber divinorum operum" "this spirit of the Macrocosm, the *Nous* or 'world spirit' of Hermetic and Neoplatonic literature", claims that

> the *anima universalis* of Neoplatonic writings can be identified with the *Nous* of Bernard (Silvestris) ... Hildegard's figure of the spirit of the Macrocosm is identical with Bernard's *Nous*. Hyle, on the other hand, becomes in Hildegard's plan the monstrous form, the emblem of brute matter, on which the spirit of the universe tramples [47].

There are several confusions here. First, in Bernard the divine "Nous" is called *Noys*, and is a feminine being, whereas the figure in the opening vision of Hildegard's "Liber" is explicitly masculine. Second, Bernard distinguishes carefully between *Noys* and the world-soul (*anima mundi*, Endelichia) — as carefully as the ancient Neoplatonists distinguished between Nous and Psyche. But Singer's worst misreading concerns Hildegard's text itself. She speaks of *monstrum horribilis forme*, whose right ear is bitten by a serpent, and this serpent is trodden down by the *summa et ignea vis* (PL 197, 743 A); but Hildegard makes explicit that the monster is *Discordia*, and the serpent, *Diabolus* (748 D). Her notion of matter is very different: matter is not monstrous but beautiful, ablaze with divinity. Later in the vision cited above, the divine fiery force declares: «That I flame across the beauty of fields signifies the earth, which is the matter from which God made man» (*Quod autem super pulcritudinem agro-*

[45] See Expositio Evangeliorum XVII, ed. J. B. Pitra, in: *Analecta Sacra* VIII (Monte Cassino 1882), 293; cf. Führkötter/Carlevaris (note 1) xv n. 22.

[46] Origenes, *Vier Bücher von den Prinzipien*, ed. H. Görgemanns/H. Karpp (Darmstadt 1976) I 3, 3; I 6, 4; II 1-3; II 8, 3; II 9, 1-5; IV 4, 6-7 (160-162, 230, 284-302, 316-322, 390, 400-410, 800-806).

[47] Singer (note 40) 217, 220.

rum flammo, hoc terra est, que materia illa est de qua deus hominem fecit) [48].

One other pseudo-source, indicated by Singer, has found its way into classic modern works in the history of science. In Scivias I 4 (61, 55ff.) Hildegard sees

> men of earth carrying milk in their vessels and making cheeses from it. A part of the milk was thick, and from this firm cheeses were made; a part was thin — from this insipid cheeses were curdled; another part was permeated by decay, and from this bitter cheeses were made.

The vision is explained to her: the men making cheese (75, 494ff.)

> are men and women in the world who have in their bodies the human semen from which different kinds of people are procreated... There are firm cheeses, because the semen in its strength, effectively and well concocted and tempered, brings forth vigorous human beings, who are given a great radiance both of spiritual and physical gifts... The insipid cheeses are curdled because this semen in its frailty, ineffectively half-tempered, brings forth frail offspring, in such a way that often they are stupid, tepid and useless in their achievements, in regard to God and to the world... There are bitter cheeses because that semen, in the feebleness of its mixture, poorly ejaculated and ineffectually mingled, brings about malformed beings, such as frequently have bitterness, difficulty and oppression in their hearts, so that they cannot often raise their minds to higher things.

Such a "cheese analogy of conception" is to be found in Aristotle's "De generatione animalium" and briefly in Clement of Alexandria's "Protrepticus", neither of which had been translated in Hildegard's lifetime. Unfortunately Singer, followed by Needham, suggested that Aristotle's analogy could also be found in two sections, *De perfectione* and *De impeditione*, of Constantine of Africa's treatise "De humana natura" [49]. While today this is regarded as an epitome drawn from Constantine rather than as a genuine work of his [50], it seems chronologically possible for Hildegard to have known it. The

---

[48] Gent, MS 241 p. 30-31; R fol. 208vb (PL 197, 744 B).

[49] Singer (note 40) 228; J. Needham, *A History of Embryology* (Cambridge ²1959) 85.

[50] Cf. H. Schipperges, *Die Assimilation der arabischen Medizin durch das lat. MA.* (Sudhoffs Archiv, Beiheft 3), Wiesbaden 1964, 47.

question whether Hildegard might have been influenced by the Constantinian transmission of Arabic and Aristotelian medical lore is of importance not only here but even more with regard to her "Causae et Curae" and "Physica"; on this particular point, however, a reference to the Constantinian text shows the parallels to be spurious. As the "De humana natura" is not easily accessible, I cite the two sections to which Singer referred in full in the note below [51]; I should add that no mention of a "cheese analogy" occurs anywhere else in the treatise either [52].

From where, then, if not from an Aristotelian tradition, did Hildegard derive her "cheese analogy", with its strangely irreligious physical determinism? The answer can be inferred, I believe, from a recent anthropological study of the "cheese analogy" among the Basques of Sainte-Engrâce, in southern France [53]. Sandra Ott has documented the elaborate and fascinating uses of this analogy in a community where it can owe nothing to a learned tradition. So, too,

---

[51] The text is in: Albucasis, *Methodus medendi* (Basel 1541) 313-321. The last two sections (p. 321) read:

De perfectione

Solet autem natura omnibus membris perfectum ut pluribus embrion apparet generari, plurimumque vero grosso capite, et tenui collo, vel magnis pedibus, et subtilibus cruribus et brachiis perditis, manibus humeris affixus, aut sublatis cruribus, pedibus, genibus applicitis, aut manuum, et pedum singulis, vel duobus digitis perditis hac luce perfrui. Sed duobus modis in embrii compositione contingit. Aut enim natura aequam habens materiam et redarguentem spiritum secundum horum duûm aequitatem moderate, et perfecte informat, aut abundanti materia et spiritu minorato, eiusdem materiei abundantiam alicui addit membro, ex qua vastius caeteris efficitur, vel ampliato spiritu et materia minorata. Aut ex parte extenuat, aut ex toto non dimittit procreari. Et haec omnia autem aequitate utriusque materiei, scilicet et spiritus natura perfecit. Aut augmento vel minoratu horum unius fiunt.

De impeditione

Solet etiam in generatione quibusdam viris illud muliebre, et quibusdam foeminis illud virile membrum quo luxuriantur adiici, sed impedita vel oblita natura fit. Nam cum aliquo eventu impeditur, vel obliviscitur, illud materiei humidum superfluum, quod ad vastitatem vel ad numerum alicuius membri solet disponere, ad alterius naturae membrum sine ratione immittat.

[52] Nor does the "cheese analogy" occur in Aulus Gellius III 10, as is claimed by Needham (note 49) 66, unless it be vaguely implicit in the words *semen... primis septem diebus conglobatur coagulaturque* (III 10, 7). In Hildegard it recurs in: *Causae et curae* (note 32) 109, 165.

[53] Sandra Ott, "Aristotle among the Basques: The 'Cheese Analogy' of Conception", in: *Man* (N.S.) 14 (1979) 699-711.

a reference to the superstitions connected with cheese in Bächtold-Stäubli can document for northern Europe a range of popular beliefs linking the emergence and development of human life with cheese analogies [54]. They are not as "Aristotelian" as among the Basques, for there is less concern with embryology than with the destiny of the child that is born. Thus for instance, in the Swiss Alps, on the day of a child's birth, the villagers inscribe a cheese with the name and year, a cheese that is eaten communally at the burial of that child when it dies. In Treffelstein (in the Bavarian Alps), if the child is a boy, the guests at the christening-party must eat cheese, so that in due course the lad's beard will grow. In northern England, after a child's birth, a hole is cut in the middle of the "groaning-cheese", making of the cheese a ring through which the child is drawn on the day of its christening. Bächtold-Stäubli also recalls ancient analogues to such traditions: thus Athenaeus (II 65) cites archaic verses to the effect that at the Amphidromia, the family festival held five days after an infant's birth, it was the custom to toast a slice of Gallipoli cheese. And among the recipes added to the "Gynaecia" of Soranus we find goat-cheese used as a means of inducing conception:

> *mulier ut concipiat, etiam si nunquam conceperit, capra cum peperit, ante quam haedus eius suffecerit et lac sugere incipiat, mulge et ex eo fac caseolum et in sinistro brachio in linteolo obligatum suspendito ut portet mulier; sed cum in balneum ire voluerit, domi illum munditer reponat; reliquis horis omnibus secum habeat* [55].

I am not suggesting that Hildegard read a Soranus MS which contained this recipe: on the contrary, the recipe is the chance survival, through an early written testimony, of a range of widespread popular lore to which Hildegard's insatiably inquiring mind will have been open — a mind that, as we know from her other writings, was often engaged in problems of women's medicine, and often tempted to the borders of medicine and magic.

Two final smaller points with regard to the written transmission of texts to the Rupertsberg. The new editors of "Scivias" rightly note, among their liturgical parallels (665), two clear echoes of the sequence *Scalam ad caelos*. But they cite this from "Analecta Hymnica", as an anonymous hymn, not knowing that it is the final sequence

---

[54] H. Bächtold-Stäubli/E. Hofmann-Krayer, *Handwörterbuch des dt. Aberglaubens* IV 1062ff., s.v. "Käse".

[55] Sorani Gynaeciorum, ed. V. Rose (Leipzig 1882) 125f. (cf. Bächtold-Stäubli [note 54] IV 1065).

in the "Liber Hymnorum" of Notker Balbulus, poetically one of
Notker's crowning achievements [56]. This raises the question (which
I cannot hope to resolve here) of the transmission of *Scalam ad caelos*
and in what MS Hildegard might have encountered it [57]. Above all,
what further Notker sequences might have been contained in the
MS Hildegard knew? Could she have gained from Notker the sense
of a lyrical liturgical cycle, in which compositions are poetically inter-
related, and was she helped towards shaping her own cycle, her
"Symphonia", by glimpses of Notker's achievement?

The other question concerns Hildegard's access to Lucan. Did
she have a copy available at the Rupertsberg? The Berlin MS of the
"Liber vite meritorum", Theol. lat. fol. 727, written at the Rupertsberg by one of the two copyists who wrote the Gent "Liber divinorum operum" (the MS which incorporates Hildegard's own revisions
and is thus in a sense her autograph) [58], suggests an interesting possibility. The flyleaves and binding of the Berlin "Liber vite meritorum" contain fragments from Horace's "Odes" and "Epodes" in an
eleventh-century hand, as well as the fragmentary words, in capitals:
...IMO CIVILI BELLO FINITO VT AB ALIO ABSTINEA...

Is this the remnant of a colophon to "De bello civili"? And, if
the MS of the "Liber vite meritorum" stems from the Rupertsberg,
did the Lucan text stem from there as well? The Horace fragments,
too, are intriguing: they consist of incomplete lines of Epodes V

---

[56] W. von den Steinen, *Notker der Dichter* (Bern 1948) I 408-413, II 90-91; cf.
The Medieval Lyric (note 11) 41-44.

[57] It is at least worth mentioning that one of the earliest MS testimonies to
Notker's sequences, including *Scalam ad caelos*, existed in Hildegard's immediate vi-
cinity: the MS (today London BL, Add. 19768) copied c. 960 at the monastery of
St. Alban in Mainz (described by von den Steinen [note 56] II 208-10; a briefer
description by H. Husmann, *Tropen- und Sequenzenhss.* [München/Duisburg 1965]
152-4). The prosarium unfortunately does not survive complete (the first 68 pages
of the MS are missing); in its present state it contains 28 sequences, of which 25
form the (incomplete) "Sanctorale"; this group of sequences dedicated to saints includes 15 that von den Steinen ascribes to Notker (see the tables [note 56] II
219-20).

[58] Cf. Schrader/Führkötter (note 2) 50-51; on the Gent MS, see esp. A. Derolez, "The Genesis of Hildegard of Bingen's Liber divinorum operum", in: *Litterae
Textuales (Festschrift G.I. Lieftinck)*, II (Amsterdam 1972) 23-33; (id.), Deux notes
concernant Hildegarde de Bingen, in: *Scriptorium* 27 (1973) 291-295. The Berlin MS
Theol. lat. fol. 727 passed from the Rupertsberg to the monastery of St. James in
Mainz. The suggestion, however (Schrader/Führkötter [note 2] 50), that this could
be established only «nach einem früheren, jetzt nicht mehr vorhandenen Besitzer-
vermerk», is incorrect: the words *Liber sancti Iacobi*, in a hand of s. XV, are still legible on fol. 1ʳ.

91-102 and VI 1-9 (the lines being split between the front and back flyleaves, which once formed a single leaf), VI 10-16 and VII 1-14, and, pasted on the inside of the wooden front cover, Odes III 27, 60-75 and III 28, 1-5, with glosses. That Hildegard knew Lucan is, as we saw, established by the testimony of the Berlin Fragment. That she might also have had access to Horace, and there encountered for instance the detailed description of sorcery in the fifth Epode, is, for the moment, a mere speculation, that would require detailed study. Yet it is worth signalling even this possibility, if only to indicate from still another side what exceptionally complex problems Hildegard's sources raise.

IV

Hildegard's unpublished writings

The Berlin MS Lat. qu. 674 (**B**) was described with admirable fullness by Degering in 1917. He signalled the fact that «the majority of the 54 letters assembled here [fols. 25ra-56rb] are not included in the printed collections of her letters» [59]. In this codex the letters, with only a few exceptions, were furnished with headings (e.g. ep. 12 "De etatibus hominis atque mundi"; ep. 30 "De hominum moribus quadripertitis"), to make of each letter, we might say, a small treatise or homily. Probably for this reason too the "salutationes" of the Berlin letters have (with only one exception, ep. 28) been omitted, so that we can no longer tell to whom they were originally addressed.

In their fine study "Die Echtheit des Schrifttums", Schrader and Führkötter added some further observations and minor corrections to Degering's description [60]. There are in fact 56 letters (Degering's nos. 40 and 42 each consist of two distinct pieces); of these, 12 are contained in other collections (including 9 in the Wiesbaden "Riesenkodex", **R**) [61], and 44 had remained unknown. Schrader and Führkötter were able to deduce the addressees of several of the letters, and in their manuscript study they edited two of the unpublished ones [62]. Yet amazingly, in the six decades and more since De-

---

[59] H. Degering, in: *Mitteilungen der Kgl. Bibl* III (Berlin 1917) 12-18, esp. 13 on the letters.

[60] Schrader/Führkötter (note 2) 79-83.

[61] Schrader/Führkötter (note 2) 158 n. 13.

[62] Degering (note 59) no. 21 — to Abbot Ludwig of Trier — ed. Schrader/Führkötter (note 2) 143; no. 35 — to Frederick Barbarossa — ed. ibid. 130f. In the German anthology of Hildegard's letters, *Hildegard von Bingen, Brief-*

gering's description of the MS, the Latin text of none but these two letters has ever been edited [63].

The Berlin MS, however, which begins with the "Vita" of Hildegard, also offers another precious unpublished testimony. It is the only MS that preserves the text of a ceremony Hildegard devised, for driving away a demon from a young Rhenish noblewoman, Sigewize, who was "obsessed" [64]. While the "Vita" gives details of this episode, including some in Hildegard's own words, and while her letter to Abbot Gedolph of Brauweiler, which contained the invented ceremony, also occurs in the "Vita" in **R,** only **B** has retained — in the margins of the page — the remarkable wording of Hildegard's mimetic magic.

Hildegard's use of magical invocations to effect healing is known from her "Physica". At the close of the book *De elementis* (II) is one in which the personified Earth is addressed in the name of the Christian Trinity: Earth must take up the life-principle, the "greenness", in the sick person, make it grow again, and perfect it:

> *Tu terra, in homine illo viriditatem recipe et cresce et perfice. In nomine patris et filii et spiritus sancti, qui omnipotens et vivens deus est in secula seculorum. Amen* [65].

So, too, the book *De lapidibus* (IV) is full of magical-medical prayers. In a different sphere, we have Hildegard's mimetic depiction of the

---

wechsel (Salzburg 1965), A. Führkötter gave a translation of fourteen of the unknown ones.

[63] Three of these letters (Degering 14, 36, 42) are printed for the first time in Section 5 below. [For eleven others, see my Women Writers of the Middle Ages, Cambridge 1984, 256-264 (translations and commentary ibid. 183-195)].

[64] Cf. Schrader/Führkötter (note 2) 12. Führkötter, *Das Leben* (note 23) 102 and passim, translates *obsessa* as "besessen" throughout; but in twelfth-century usage there was a distinction between *obsessio*, where a demon attacks, lays siege, from without, and *possessio*, where he takes possession of a soul and lodges in it (see A. Blaise, *Lexicon Latinitatis Medii Aevi*, 629, s.v. *obsessio*). This particular demon was thought to have afflicted the woman's private parts (see note 81 below).

[65] Brussels, MS 2551, fol. 37ᵛ (PL 197, 1214 D). I have discussed medieval, and especially twelfth-century, invocations to *Terra*, in: "Bernard Silvestris, Natura and Personification", in: *Journal of the Warburg and Courtauld Institutes* 43 (1980) 16-31 [*supra*, no. 2]. There are some fine observations on "Magische Wirkungen" in Hildegard's medical writing in: I. Müller, Krankheit und Heilmittel im Werk Hildegards von Bingen, in: *Hildegard von Bingen 1179-1979 (Festschrift)*, ed. A. Ph. Brück (Mainz 1979) 311-49, esp. 340-342; on Hildegard's magical use of gems, see P. Riethe, "Die medizinische Lithologie der Hildegard von Bingen", ibid. 351-370.

deliverance of *Anima* from *Diabolus* in the "Ordo Virtutum". What is fascinating to observe in the relatively late testimony of the mimetic ritual she composed for Sigewize (1169) [66] is how the two kinds of inspiration, from magic and from poetic drama, come together [67].

Seven priests — she tells the Abbot of Brauweiler in her letter [68] — are to be chosen "in the name and order" (*in nomine et ordine*) of Abel, Noah, Abraham, Melchisedech, Jacob, Aaron, and Christ. After doing penance, the seven shall approach the patient (*patientem*) and encircle her. Each shall hold a rod in his hand, "as a figura of the rod with which Moses, at God's command, struck the Red Sea and the rock", so that, now as then, a miracle of divine deliverance may be performed. The seven priests themselves shall be a figura of the seven gifts of the Holy Spirit, so that the Spirit who was borne across the waters and breathed life into man may now breathe out (*exsufflet*) the unclean spirit from the exhausted person (*ab homine fatigato*). "Let the first priest, who will bear the name Abel, say: 'Hear, you malignant and foolish spirit, whoever you be that dwell in this person [69], hear these words — words not thought out by man but manifested by him who is and lives'".

From here onwards, only the Berlin MS preserves the text. It is written on three edges of fol. 21^r, and not only some letters and words but entire lines have been cut away. (The MS was rebound in the eighteenth century). Yet even though incomplete [70], it is worth setting out all that survives [71], in the hope that, with the text available, historians of medieval liturgy will be able to provide a commentary and illuminate Hildegard's sources and analogues.

[66] On the date, and the evidence for the woman's name, see Führkötter, *Das Leben* (note 23) 143 n. 50.

[67] On the ancient and ecclesiological background, see esp. K. Thraede, "Exorzismus", in: *RAC* VII (1969) 44-117. I have not been able to find a comparably documented discussion of twelfth-century material.

[68] PL 197, 280 AB.

[69] In **B**, fol 21ra, *N.* has been added (superscript) after the words *in homine isto* (280 C), thus making the imprecation more generally usable.

[70] Also in the sense that, through Hildegard's biographer, we know of at least one passage it contained at the close, of which there is no trace whatever in the Berlin margins (**B** fol. 21^{rab}):

> *Cumque venisset lector ad locum illum ubi in fine scriptum est: "et ego, indocta et paupercula feminea forma, o plaspheme et derisor spiritus, tibi dico / in illa veritate, qua ego paupercula et indocta forma de lumine sapiencie hec vidi et audivi...".*

> *Plaspheme* is masc. adj., vocative (cf. PL 197, 124 D).

[71] A partial German translation was given by Führkötter, *Das Leben* (note 23) 109-111, but without exact indications either of MS gaps or of her own omissions.

In the conjuration of the priest who represents Abel, at least one line is missing (upper left margin) before the following:

...and flee, crushed by his command. Hear HIM WHO IS [72], saying:

I who am without beginning, but from whom all beginnings proceed, I who am the Ancient of days, say: I am of my own accord the day, I who never came forth from the sun but from whom the sun was
5 lit. I too am reason, that did not take voice from another, but from whom all rationality has breath [73]. ...I contemplate the ⟨abysses?⟩ [74] of my antiquity, which shall never fail, and I have caused those breaths to harmonize in praises, for I have a voice like thunder, with which
10 I move the whole world in the living sound of every creature.

And let that priest and the six others standing there strike the woman gently with their rods: on her head, her back, her breast, her navel, her loins, her knees and her feet [75], and let them say:
15 Now, Satan, and you malignant spirit that exhaust and oppress this human being and this womanly form — by him who lives and who has brought forth and speaks these words through a simple person, unlearned in the way of human instruction, you are commanded, and he himself now commands you, that in his name you depart from
20 this person present, whom you have long ravaged and in whom you still remain. And so through this rod, at the command of the true beginning, namely in the same beginning as ⟨...⟩[76] — you harm her ⟨no⟩ further.

Conjured and overcome, too, by the sacrifice and prayers and help of Abel, in whose name we also strike you.

And again let them strike her as above.
25 Conjured and overcome, too, by the sacrifice and prayers and help of Noah, in whose name we strike you.

And again let them strike her.

Conjured and overcome, too, by the sacrifice and prayers and help of Abraham, in whose name we strike you.
30 And let them strike her as above.

Conjured and overcome, too, by the sacrifice and prayers and help

---

[72] Cf. Exod 3, 14 (the words are not capitalized in **B**).

[73] The end of a fragmentary word (*Adin-* ?) and at least one other line (upper margin, right) are missing before the next words. For further palaeographic details, see the textual notes at the end of section V below.

[74] The word supplied here — ⟨*abissos*⟩ — is wholly conjectural, to give a possible object to the sentence that follows the missing lines.

[75] Here again the text features a heptad, as so often in biblical demonology: compare for instance the seven *daemonia* cast out of Mary Magdalen (Mark 16, 9; Luke 8, 2).

[76] Probably three lines are cut away here (lower margin left).

of Melchisedech, in whose name we strike you.
    And again let them strike her as above.
    Conjured and overcome, too, by the sacrifice and pray⟨ers and
35 help of Jacob, in whose⟩ name we strike you.
    And ⟨let them strike⟩ her ⟨as above.
    Conjured and overcome, too, by the sacrifice and prayers and help
of Aaron, in whose name we strike you.
    And let them strike her as above.
40   Conjured and overcome, too, by the sacrifice and prayers and help
of [77] (?) the supreme priest, the son⟩ of God, to whom all true priests
have sacrificed and still offer sacrifice, in whose name and power we
strike you
    — and again let them strike her —
45 so that, in the same confusion with which, in your first appearance,
you hurtled down from heaven like lead, you may depart confounded
from ⟨this⟩[78] person and not harm her further.

    And may the height that no height has ever touched
    and the depth that no depth has ever fathomed
50   and the width that no width has ever compassed [79]

    free her from your power
    and from your foolish vileness
    and from all your arts,

    so that, confounded, you may flee from her,
55   so that she may neither feel you
    nor know you any more;

    and as you were cut off from heaven,
      so may the Holy Spirit cut you off from her;
    and as you are alien to all felicity,
60   so may you be alien to her;
    and as you never long for God,
      so may you never long to come to her.

    Flee then, flee, flee from her, you fiend, with all malignant aerial
spirits, adjured

[77] The symmetry of the formulae of conjuration allows one to reconstruct with
some safety here, and to infer that probably three lines have been cut away at lower
margin right. Only the precise appellation for Christ, the last «priest» in the ceremony, is irrecoverable; any conjecture here must remain tentative.
    [78] Probably one word (perhaps *isto*) cut away at edge of right margin.
    [79] On earlier medieval transformations of the Pauline phrase (Eph 3, 18), *lati-
tudo et longitudo et sublimitas et profundum*, see the fine discussion by E. Jeauneau,
in: *RTAM* 45 (1978) 118-128.

65   by that force of eternity which created all and which made man,
      and by the benignity of the Saviour's humanity, that freed the self-
same man,
      and by the fiery love that established man as never-failing life.
70 Overcome also
      by the passion that took place on the wood of the holy cross
      and by the resurrection of life
      and by the force that flung the devil from heaven into hell and freed
man from his power —

75 may you, in the same confusion in which in your first appearance you
hurtled down from heaven like lead, depart confounded from this person and not harm her further either in soul or in any limb of her body:
commanded by the almighty one who made her and created her.
AMEN.

80   If the demon is not ⟨yet driven out⟩, then let the second priest, with
the other priests standing beside him, pursue the same *ordo*, until God
helps her.

    The sevenfold conjuration — to channel the seven gifts of the
Spirit to the patient through the seven priests — is followed by a series of triadic incantations, as I indicate by my line-arrangement.
There are six such triads here — or indeed seven, if we count the
triple *fuge*: «Flee then, flee, flee». Possibly the triadic elements correspond also to the triple means — sacrifice, prayers, and help —
used by the priests. The word *ordo* in the final instruction is of particular interest. While it may suggest simply a series of actions ordered in a ritual, I think that for Hildegard, as so often in dramatic
texts, and in her own "Ordo Virtutum", it also had connotations of
drama. As in the "Ordo Virtutum", here too there is a "plot", to
liberate an *Anima* from a *Diabolus*. Where in the prologue of her play
the patriarchs and prophets help to provide an eschatological frame
within which the healing powers, the *Virtutes*, can operate, here the
seven priests have figuratively a twofold role — as patriarchs and
prophets, but also as "Virtutes", gifts of the Holy Spirit. Their mimetic chastising of this "Anima", with their rods, suggests an echo
less of Christian penances than of the twofold function of the
priests' chastising of women in the Roman "Lupercalia": to purify
them — driving the unclean forces away — and to prepare them for
fertility in their marriage-union — in Hildegard, for fertility in virtue, leading to union with God. Significantly, it was the feast of the
"Lupercalia" which was transformed in 494, by Pope Gelasius I, into

the feast of the Purification of Mary [80]. And when the young woman, Sigewize, was brought to Hildegard's convent to be cured, it was
this feast of the Purification (February 2) that Hildegard chose for
beginning the communal prayers and penance on her behalf. In Hildegard's words (**B** fol. 22[rb]):

> *Itaque a purificatione sancte Marie nos et comprovinciales nostri,*
> *utriusque sexus, ieiuniis, orationibus, elemosinis et corporum castigacioni-*
> *bus usque in sabbatum pasche pro ipsa laboravimus.*

On Easter Saturday, during the blessing of the font — another
ceremony of purification and fertility — Sigewize discharged the
foul spirit, «together with faeces, through her private parts» (*per
verecundiam femine cum egestione,* **B** fol. 22[va]) [81], and her recovery
began.

Throughout the episode Hildegard shows notable candour and
modesty. Even Theodoric, in the "Vita", has to admit that Hildegard's scenario, performed in the abbey at Brauweiler, did not
work, but had only a passing effect on the patient. Hildegard herself,
both in the "Vita" and in references in her letters — to her nephew,
Archbishop Arnold of Trier (PL 197, 183 AB), and to the Dean of
Cologne (259 B) — attributes Sigewize's recovery not at all to her
dramatic ceremony (it is not even clear that it was performed again,
on the Rupertsberg), but to the grace that was sought and found
through shared ascetic effort. Indeed to her nephew she stresses that
Sigewize's was a gradual convalescence — *de die in diem* — not a sudden magical release, as from a spell.

To suggest briefly some other facets of Hildegard's nature and
imagination, I should like to add to this text three of the unpublished Berlin letters. I have chosen three that are in many ways distinct in expression and themes from those to be found in the existing
published Hildegard collections. Each of them adds noteworthy details to Hildegard's account of her mode of *visio*: that gift of direct
waking introspective sight into the divine realm with which she had
been blessed — and afflicted — since early childhood [82].

---

[80] Gelasius I, "Adversus Andromachum", in: PL 59, 110-116.

[81] **R** (fol. 327[ra]) has *per verecunda loca* (not *perverenda*, as in PL 197, 126 C).
Both *verecunda* (neut. pl.) and *verecundia* (fem. sg.) were used in Patristic Latin for
the private parts: see A. Souter, Glossary of Later Latin, s.v.

[82] The central "analytic" testimonies are in the autobiographic notes preserved
in the "Vita" (PL 197, 102 ff.), in the "Protestificatio" of "Scivias" (3, 5 ff.), the
prologues of "Liber vite meritorum" (ed. Pitra [note 45] 7-8) and "Liber divinorum

In the first of these Berlin letters (Degering no. 14, cf. note 63 above), one might not at the outset recognize the full uniqueness of Hildegard's *visio*. When she speaks of the spark, or inspiration, of the Holy Spirit, or of seeing God's wonders «in my soul», one might take this to be a familiar spiritual topos. With the next sentences, when she sees human *intentiones* (ways of directing the mind) towards Christ's passion like (*velut*) a vast sky filled with the redness of blood, we become caught up in her particular way of interweaving simile and metaphor, allegory and symbol, statement and experience. At the close of the letter this *velut* has been resolved into identity — she then speaks of «the fiery sky of the Holy Spirit» — and between opening and close it becomes more and more evident that none of the comparisons or metaphors is mere comparison or mere metaphor. They are there not to give a theological message more picturesquely than usual, but quite literally because this is how Hildegard sees what she wants to say. And what she sees within, and sees consciously — never in dream, hallucination or ecstasy, as she often stresses — is not a pure cascade of imagery nor pure matter for meditation. It is the way these two modes constantly blend that is distinctive.

Whoever is touched by a single spark from the Holy Spirit is flooded and filled in such a way that, through this inspiration, he cannot but bring forth new miracles of God's mysteries, ever and ever again, unceasingly. Thus in that vision through which, since infancy, I have seen God's wonders in my soul (as he has granted me by his grace), I have seen the intentions of mankind towards the passion of the son of God like a vast sky filled with the redness of blood. Mingled in that redness was an intense colour as of dawn before rain.

In this sky I saw the intentions of many like flashing stars — those who turned to the Lord's passion with good will, an intention that shone like the day-star that reveals the day. For with that intention they showed forth his passion, yet they did not cast aside helpful concern for their fellow-men.

I saw the intentions of others in the radiance of a star that had a beautiful human form. These, leaving all that was theirs behind, striving totally towards Christ's passion, had their face formed godward. Others again would have tended the passion with loving intention, but because of anguish of heart and sickness of body, and because of the great oppression they had suffered, they could not do so, and I saw their longing and intention in that same sky like a cross that

operum" (PL 197, 741f.), and in the letter to Guibert of Gembloux answering his questions about the nature of her visionary faculty [ed. Dronke, *Women Writers* (note 63) 250-256].

was red, and I heard the voice of blood saying: these are my comrades, I embrace their longing and their mind with great love, and I enfold their anguish in that of my martyrdom. Malignant people crucified me, and malignity of vices afflicts these people, and [yet] they control their nature against their will.

Others gathered up that same passion of Christ with joyous mind, so that their intention was gathered up like grass in all its greenness, and, like trees bursting into greenness before the fruit, they fill mankind with joy. The intentions of yet others breathed a fragrance as of the strong scent of a candescent lily — theirs who took up the Lord's passion with utmost longing, and tended it as best they might with deepest humility, not outflanking anyone in elation of pride.

After this I saw a host of people, like a garden filled with herbs of every kind, aspiring to God inasmuch as they were able; yet some of them, because of a listlessness in their hearts, scarcely thought that the service of Christ could be achieved. These did not climb towards God by any intention, but seemed like useless weeds that choke good herbs.

Then too I heard the sound of a voice, as out of limpid water, saying: this most lovable garden belongs to the omnipotent God — graced with the fairest flowers and the beauty of every greenness, on which he feasts his eyes delectably. But the sound flew from out of the fiery sky of the Holy Spirit, for every intention of the blessed, the elect and holy flows from the Spirit's fountain, as is written: "from his belly living waters flow".

From *Pastor Hermas* Hildegard had learnt a technique of structuring her vision. As so often in Hermas' visions, different states of soul and nuances of attitude are presented as diverse kinds of people. Here Hildegard distinguishes seven kinds. After the third, with the martyred Christ's moving expression of compassion for those whose devotion fails because they themselves are grief-stricken, ill or oppressed [83], the imagery changes from the intense red sky to a teeming, scent-laden garden. Only the last group of people, bored and sceptical, are seen as weeds in that garden.

Hildegard's mixing of metaphors is deliberate, as the last lines of the letter show: the voice she hears comes *velut de pura aqua*; we remember that the sky had been as of dawn before rain (*ante pluviam*), and implicitly the sound of the divine Spirit is the rain that now falls. It falls slaking the garden of human *intentiones*: yet these human strivings themselves constitute a divine garden, fertile and delectable. Thus the Spirit is seen not only as the rain from «where

---

[83] Both the wording and the context — *vocem sanguinis audiebam dicentem: Isti socii mei sunt* — are closer to II Macc 8, 3 than to Gen 4, 10.

Christ's blood streames in the firmament» but as the *fons*, the spring of the garden from which every human *intentio* flows. The Scriptural allusion (John 7, 38) is placed in such a way as to make the Spirit of the spring seem momentarily like an ancient garden-god. Fiery sky, garden, fecundating rain and spring are Hildegard's ways of seeing the interdependence of the divine and human impulses. While her theme here is the ways that minds are drawn to Christ's passion, her approach is not that of the emotional and rhetorical meditation of an Anselm or a Bernard. Instead, she itemises in Hermas' fashion (though not with Hermas' laboriousness). And what gives emotional power to the itemisation is the way what is seen interpenetrates what is thought and felt.

The second letter (Degering no. 36, cf. note 63) begins by further defining the nature of that seeing. It is not as though Hildegard consciously chooses to give her insights a particular artistic form: rather, she records faithfully and directly the words she takes in during her *visio*. Yet these words are not direct, not «naked», but always mean more than themselves. The figurative mode, she claims, has, since the beginning of history, been the one most suited to giving human beings intimations of the divine. She is saying very much what Beatrice was to say to Dante (Par. IV 40-48):

> "This is how one must speak to your imagination,
> for only from the sensible can it grasp
> what later it makes apt for intellection.
> Because of this the Scriptures make concession
> to your mode of knowing, and attribute feet and hands
> to God, and yet intend another meaning.
> So, too, for your sake Holy Church portrays
> Gabriel and Michael with a human semblance,
> and the other who made Tobit whole again».

The remainder of the letter, surprisingly, says nothing more about vision. Hildegard gives advice to her correspondent, an abbess, about how to bring back peace to her unruly convent. Her thoughts become practical, down-to-earth, and shrewd. She touches on all the personalities involved — the chaplain (whom she defends, at least provisionally); the older and younger women in the convent, and the principal teacher (*summa magistra*), well-intentioned but helpless amid the conflicts. On the one hand, there are older nuns (or perhaps canonesses) who are vindictive and who show ill-judged favouritism; on the other, young women (not necessarily all novices or vowed to the monastic life — they could also be aristocratic "boarders" receiving a convent education), who are devoted to vanities, idle chatter, and *singulares amicicias* (a hint, perhaps, of lesbian attachments).

With humorous subtlety Hildegard suggests that the subprioress, chief cause of the disturbances, be deposed and thus made an example — yet the ostensible reason for deposing her should be simply a normal rotation of convent offices (thus giving the woman no pretext for litigation).

Gentle lady, may the Holy Spirit suffuse you, that you may have radiant lowliness, in fear and love of God, as a loyal friend with whom to order all that is yours.

I tell you, it is not my wont, in the vision of my soul, to speak with naked words, but with the words I am taught in the vision — always, moreover, with a certain figurativeness, as is written: "I shall open my mouth in parables, I shall make utterances [hidden] since the [world's] beginning [84]. Indeed since the beginning God has propounded parables and similitudes to men; often men are taught the way to salvation more suitably by these than by naked words.

As for the priest of whom you ask, God has not shown me that he is either a rebel against justice or a useless person, and so I trust in God that he will not take grace away from him. But let the daughters of the cloister strive to shun all vanity (though some people are fettered by it) — they have set it at naught for love of God. In that cloister, besides, there are some women of mature years who are too harsh, lacking mercy when they ought to have it, and also at times capriciously sparing without justice. But some of the young women are vain and cultivate vanity, and thus great turmoil arises among them — the harsh against the vain, the vain against the harsh.

None of these are so completely rebellious against a holy form of life that they could not be curbed by the monastic rule — though their chief teacher cannot stand up to them, she who is neither excessively harsh nor vain, and who would be pleased if they were to live a holy life. But in my vision I see that it is better for her not to resign her governance, lest the restless sisters say: a woman we don't want is now elected, the one we want is deposed — and thus a wicked disobedience and turbulence would arise in the cloister.

Beloved lady, see to it, with God's help, that all uselessness is put right in your cloister — and I trust in God that by his mercy this will come to pass. As for the sister, the subprioress, who troubles the peace of the others by her chaotic behaviour, let her be removed from office, if you please, so as to put fear in the other girls who are disobedient to their teachers. Let it be done in accordance with the custom by which monastic offices are changed around.

Dear friend of God, may God through love and fear of him make

[84] Ps 77, 2 (cf. Matth 13, 35).

you like the red-gleaming dawn that precedes the sun, so that for your community you may [come to] shine like the sun that lights up the whole world [85]. Try hard, also, to banish duplicity in those women who do not walk on true paths, when they speak one thing and have another in mind, so that their judgments are unjust. Such behaviour is like fumes that harm the soil — through this the fruit of virtues parches. And they ally singular friendships with idle talk, and go against what was established by the saints of old; they are like a dark cloud that has no temperate air; the fruit of useful life cannot be hoped for in them.

Gentle lady, all the matters I have mentioned should be looked upon with fear in any community, and should be forbidden as far as God's grace allows. Nonetheless I trust in God that the murkiness and darkness that hedge your foundation may be destroyed and quashed, by efforts already made and still to be made by and in those who are yours. Dearest lady, may the Holy Spirit kindle his fire in you, that in fear and love of God you may happily perfect the care of souls entrusted to you, so that, in eternal bliss, you may be a lucent gem in God.

As this letter is one of the most rich in specific detail in all Hildegard's correspondence, it is regrettable that, lacking the name of the addressee, we can only speculate on the identity of the convent and the precise historical situation. Among the women's communities to whom Hildegard gave advice in other letters, Zwiefalten seems closest in its problems, and could quite possibly be in question here [86]. Expert church historians may be able to take the investigation further. The human interest of the letter, however, lies in what it reveals of Hildegard's reactions in such a situation: her efficiency of personal judgment, incisive but unfanatical, idealistic but with an experienced eye for real shortcomings.

The third letter (Degering no. 42, cf. note 63) is very different again. It is addressed to a widow who (it would appear) had written to Hildegard enquiring about the lot of her husband in the other world, and asking her to prognosticate her own destiny there. That this widow is sent a reply in Latin suggests she was one of the highborn, privileged laity who had received a clerical education. That she asks Hildegard to "see" her husband's fate in her *visio*, and to foretell

[85] Cf. John 1, 9.

[86] See Führkötter, *Briefwechsel* (note 62) 211-214. I do not think the letter is to Hazzecha, abbess of Krauftal (cf. ibid. 207-210), to whom, on the other hand, I believe one of the other Berlin letters is addressed: the long epistle (**B** fols. 41va-42ra) *Domine abbatisse H.* (the initial is not *N.*, as Degering's incipit [note 59] no. 28 suggests). [Cf. *Women Writers* (note 63) 186-8, 257-258.]

hers, suggests that already in her lifetime Hildegard's wider fame may have been largely of that more debased kind — as clairvoyante or fortune-teller — which was to become increasingly the popular image of her in the centuries after her death.

Hildegard's reply is curious. Once more she makes a pronouncement on the nature of her *visio*. At first it seems of a piece with her other statements: in the vision of her soul she sees many of God's *mirabilia*, and the deep and difficult parts of the Scriptures [87]; but her *visio* is not a crystal ball.

And yet, in the very next lines, it seems to become just that. Suddenly Hildegard claims to have seen the exact condition of the dead husband in the otherworld, and to have special knowledge of his hidden thoughts and intentions, ones he had not revealed or carried out in life. So, too, while beginning with a disclaimer of any knowledge of the widow's future fate, she works her way (by a series of unexceptionably pious injunctions) to a hint, at the close of the letter, that she knows this outcome also — knows that both the woman and her husband will at last attain heaven.

> Daughter of the Creator — for it is he who made you — in the love of Christ I tell you that in the vision of my soul I see many miracles of God, and understand the profundities of the Scriptures through the grace of God; but what outcomes, or of what kind, are destined for men is not revealed to me in that vision.
>
> Yet in it I came to know that your husband's soul is in great suffering, but not assigned to perdition, for, though he served his own will rather than God, he nonetheless had in his heart at times a will and desire to do good deeds, which, prevented by death, he did not perform.
>
> Dear lady, I do not presume to ask of God what is to happen to a person, since it is better for them not to know than to know, for the soul's well-being; but I shall gladly pray to the almighty God for you, that he orders all that is yours towards the well-being of your soul and body.
>
> Do not cease to help your husband's soul as much as you can every day for three years — by masses, almsgiving and prayers — so that, through the mercy of Christ's passion, he may be freed from the dire afflictions of his pain. You too must trust in God and commit to him all that is yours, and he will not abandon you but preserve you in eternal bliss.

Here, unusually, the intellectual and imaginative tautness of

---

[87] In Hildegard's idiom, the pl. *scripturae* is almost certainly confined to the Scriptures (not used to mean "writings" in a wider sense).

Hildegard's writing seems to give way to popular concessions. Despite her semblance of denial, in this letter she puts up a pretence of having clairvoyant powers. In Hildegard's visionary trilogy — "Scivias", "Liber vite meritorum", "Liber divinorum operum" — the prophetic element is eschatological only. But in everyday life, was she not tempted now and then to acquiesce in the role of the "Rhenish Sibyl"? Was there not even some degree of complicity in creating, or fostering, that myth?

V

Texts

The conjuration of Sigewize's demon (**B** fol. 21^r, in the margins)

... et iussu illi⟨us⟩ extritus fuge. Audi IPSUM QUI EST, dicentem:

Qui sine initio sum, sed a quo omnia initia procedunt, et qui antiquus dierum sum, dico: Ego per memetipsum dies sum, qui a sole
5 nunquam processi sed de quo sol accensus est. Ego etiam ratio sum, que ab alio non sonuit, sed ex qua omnis rationalitas spirat... ⟨abissos?⟩ antiquitatis mee, que nunquam deficient, considero, ac eadem spiracula in laudibus concinnantia paravi, quia vocem ut tonitruum habeo, cum qua totum orbem terrarum in viventibus sonis
10 omnium creaturarum moveo.

Et tam idem sacerdos quam ceteri sex predicti sacerdotes astantes eam virgis suis moderate percutiant: supra caput, ac supra dorsum, supra pectus, et supra umbilicum, et supra renes, supra genua, supra pedes; et dicant:

15 Nunc autem tu, o Satanas, et maligne spiritus qui hunc hominem et formam mulieris huius fatigas et premis: per illum qui vivit, et qui hec verba per simplicem et humanam doctrinam indoctum hominem protulit et dicit — tibi preceptum est, et ipse nunc tibi precipit, ut in nomine ipsius, de homine isto qui presens est, et quem diu fatiga-

12 eam virgis suis moderate *virgis suis percutiant* B

17 *I construe* humanam doctrinam *as acc. of respect governed by* hominem indoctum; *Hildegard uses* homo *to refer both to herself and Sigewize, and in these contexts (if the testimony of B is reliable) uses masc. and fem. concordance with* homo *indifferently.*

20 sti, et in quo adhuc manes, abcedas; et ideo virga hac, in precepto veri
principii, scilicet in ipso principio quod ⟨... nec⟩ eum ulterius ledas.

Coniuratus et convictus etiam sacrificio ac precibus et adiutorio
Abel, in cuius nomine te quoque percutimus.

Et iterum eam percuciant ut supra.
25 Coniuratus et convictus etiam sacrificio ac precibus et adiutorio
Noe, in cuius nomine te percutimus.

Et iterum eam percuciant.
Coniuratus et convictus etiam sacrificio ac precibus et adiutorio
Abrahe, in cuius nomine te percutimus.

30 Et eam percutiant ut supra.
Coniuratus et convictus etiam sacrificio ac precibus et adiutorio
Melchisedechi, in cuius nomine te percutimus.

Et iterum eam percutiant ut supra.
Coniuratus et convictus etiam sacrificio ac preci⟨bus et adiutorio
35 Jacob, in cuius nomin⟩e te percutimus.

Et eam ⟨percutiant ut supra.
Coniuratus et convictus etiam sacrificio ac precibus et adiutorio
Aaron, in cuius nomine te percutimus.

Et eam percuciant ut supra.
40 Coniuratus et convictus etiam sacrificio ac precibus et adiutorio
(?) summi sacerdotis, filii⟩ dei, cui omnes veri sacerdotes
sacri⟨fi⟩caverunt et sacrificium offerunt, in c⟨uius⟩ nomine et potestate
te percutimus

— et ea⟨m⟩ iterum percuciant —
45 quatinus tu in confusio⟨ne⟩ illa, qua in prima apparitione tu⟨a⟩ sicut
plumbum de celo corruisti, de homine ⟨isto⟩ confusus exeas, nec eam
ulterius ledas.

Sed et altitudo quam nunquam altitudo tetigit,
et profunditas quam nunquam profunditas vallavit,
50 et lat⟨i⟩tudo quam nunquam latitudo comprehendit,

21 nec *is supplied to complete the sense of the final phrase* (*cf.* 46).
22 adiuratio B
29 Abrahe: *corr. from* Abraham B (*by the same hand*)
30 percutiat B (*similarly in 33*)
34-35 precibus ... nomine: *letters cut away, but readings not in doubt.*

liberet eam a fortitudine,
et a stulta nequitia tua,
et ab omnibus artibus tuis,

ita ut tu confusu⟨s⟩ ab ea fugias,
55   sic quod te nec sent⟨i⟩at
nec sciat —

et quemadmodum t⟨u⟩ abscisus es a celo,
    sic abscid⟨at⟩ te spiritus sanctus ab ea;
et sicut tu es alienus ab omni felicitate,
60   sic alienus sis ab ipsa;
et ut deum nunquam desideras,
    sic nunquam desid⟨eres⟩ ad ipsam venire.

Fuge ergo, fuge, fuge ab ipso, diabole, cum omnibus malignis ae-
reis sp⟨i⟩ritibus, adiuratus

65   per vim eternitat⟨is⟩ que omnia creavit et que homi⟨nem⟩ fecit,
et per benignitatem humanitatis salvatoris, que ipsum hominem
liberavit,
et per igneum amorem qui hominem indeficientem vitam con-
stituit.

70 Convictus etiam
per passionem que fuit in ligno sancte crucis,
et per resurrectionem vi⟨te⟩,
et per vim illam que diabolum de celo in infernum proiecit et hominem de potestate ipsius liberavit,

75 ita tu in confusione illa, qua in prima a⟨p⟩paritione tua sicut plumbum
de celo corruisti, de homine isto confusus exeas, nec eam aut in anima
aut in ullis membris corpor⟨is⟩ eius ulterius ledas, iussus ab omnipo-
tente, qui eam fec⟨it⟩ et creavit.
AMEN.

58 Christus *deleted between* te *and* spiritus sanctus B.

65 vim eternitatis: *Hildegard's "Symphonia" in R (fol. 466ʳᵃ) begins with the responsory* O vis eternitatis.

66 hummanitatis B

72 vi⟨te⟩: *I have completed postulating the minimum space cut away at the margin. If, however, as seems possible at 80 below, the margin originally had space for further letters, one might well conjecture e.g.* per resurrectionem vi⟨vificantem⟩.

76 çelo B

80 Si ne⟨cdum expulsus⟩ fuerit, secundus sacerdos cum pre⟨dic⟩tis sacer-
dotibus sibi astantib⟨us⟩ eundem ordinem prosequatur, usque dum
deus illi subveniat.

Letter I (**B** fols. 32rb-33ra)

Quicumque de spiritu sancto una scintilla attangitur, ille sic in-
funditur et impletur quod per inspirationem sancti spiritus nunquam
cessare potest, quin semper et semper nova miracula mysteriorum dei
proferat. Unde in ea visione qua ab infancia mea in anima mea mirabi-
5 lia dei vidi, ut deus per graciam suam michi concessit, vidi intentiones
hominum ad passionem filii dei velut maximum aerem qui ruborem
sanguinis in se habuit, cui rubori admixtus fuit quasi spissus color au-
rore, sicut ante pluviam apparet. In aere namque isto intentiones mul-
torum hominum, velut ful-/ (32va) minantes stelle in aere sunt, vide-
10 bam — illorum scilicet qui cum bona voluntate ad passionem domini
intentionem habebant, que quasi lucifer qui diem ostendit lucebat,
quoniam ipsi cum intentione illa passionem domini demonstrabant,
sed tamen quamque utilem curam quam super homines habebant non
dimittebant.
15   Quorumdam etiam intentiones in candore stelle, pulchram formam hominis habentes, vidi — que, omnia sua relinquentes, toto studio passionem Christi intendendo, faciem formatam coram deo habebant. Quidam vero diligenti intentione passionem domini coluissent,
sed pre dolore cordis et infirmitate corporis, ac pre nimia pressura
20 quam passi sunt, non potuerunt, et horum desiderium et intentionem
in eodem aere velut rubeam crucem videbam, atque vocem sanguinis
audiebam dicentem: Isti socii mei sunt, desideriumque et mentem eorum in magno amore amplector, et dolorem ipsorum dolori martyrii
mei assimilo. Maligni me crucifixerunt, malignitas etiam viciorum
25 istos affligit, ipsique adversus voluntatem suam se constringunt.
    Quidam etiam eandem Christi passionem cum leto animo susce-
perunt, / (32vb) unde et intentio ipsorum in viriditate illa suscipieba-
tur velut quodque gramen, et, velut arbores viriditatem suam ante
fructum emittentes, homines letificant. Quorumdam etiam intentio-
30 nes velut lilium candidum, quod fortem odorem emittit, odorem da-

---

80 Sine (*or* Si ne) B. *My completion* Si ne⟨cdum expulsus⟩ *is tentative only, and
is problematic especially because it presupposes a fairly wide margin space cut away. Yet
even from what survives one can see that the copyist's use of the righthand margin was
irregular, and it may well have been larger than most of the writing would suggest.* —
pre⟨dic⟩tis: p̄ *at margin edge, followed by* tis *corr. (by same hand) from* tes, *in the following line.*

Letter I: De hominum diverso desiderio ad domini passionem *ss. B*

30 dabat *B*

bant — illorum scilicet qui toto desiderio passionem domini suscepe-
runt, et qui eam quantum potuerunt cum summa humilitate, alium in
elatione superbie non precedendo, colebant. Post hec multitudinem
populorum, qui ad deum secundum possibilitatem suam anhelabant,
35 sicut hortum omni genere herbarum plenum videbam, quorum quidam propter tedium quod in cordibus suis habebant, vix expectabant
quod servicium Christi compleretur, et isti nulla intentione ad deum
ascenderunt, sed inutilibus herbis, que bonas herbas suffocant, similes apparebant.
40   Tunc quoque velut de pura aqua sonum vocis sic dicentis audivi:
Hortus iste dulcissimus omnipotentis dei est, ornatus cum pulcherri-
mis floribus et cum pulchritudine omnium viriditatum, in quibus oculos suos delectabiliter pascit. Sonus vero iste de igneo aere spiritus
sancti volavit, quoniam omnis intentio beatorum electorum et /(33ra)
45 sanctorum de fonte spiritus sancti fluit, ut scriptum est: "De ventre
eius fluunt aque vive".

Letter II (**B** fols. 45rb-46ra)

O mitis domina, spiritus sanctus te imbuat ut habere possis cla-
ram humilitatem in timore et amore dei, qua omnia tua velut cum fide-
li amica disponas. Ego tibi dico quod nunquam soleo in visione anime
mee nudis verbis loqui, sed qualibus in ea doceor, et semper etiam ali-
5 qua similitudine, sicut scriptum est: "Aperiam in parabolis os meum,
loquar propositiones ab initio". Deus siquidem ab initio hominibus
proposuit parabolas et similitudines, per quas /(45va) plerumque con-
veniencius quam nudis verbis ad salutem instruuntur.
De sacerdote autem de quo queritis, deus michi non ostendit
10 quod vel rebellis sit iusticie vel inutilis, et ideo in deum confido quod
graciam suam ab ipso non auferat. Filie autem claustri illius ab omni
vanitate (qua nonnulli prepediuntur), quam pro dei amore contempse-
runt, se studiose amoveant. In eodem quoque claustro quedam mature
etatis nimis dure sunt, et absque misericordia ubi eam habere debe-
15 rent, interdum etiam secundum voluntatem suam iniuste parcunt.
Quedam autem iuvenes vane sunt et vanitatem colunt, et ita magnam
inquietudinem invicem habent, scilicet vane contra duras et dure contra vanas. He omnes sancte conversationi intantum omnino rebelles
non sunt, quin regulari discipline constringi possint — licet earum
summa magistra eis resistere non valeat, que nec nimis dura nec nimis
20 vana est, et cui placeret ut in sanctitate viverent. In visione autem video melius esse ut non cesset a regimine suo, ne inquiete sorores dicant: Quam nolumus eligitur, et quam volumus/ (45vb) deponitur, et
ita mala inobediencia et inquietudo in claustro oriatur.

Letter II: Quod per similitudines loqui in spiritu docebatur *ss. B*

21 nolumus] volumus *B*
22 volumus] nolumus *B*

Dilecta domina, da operam, cum dei auxilio, ut omnis inutilitas
25 in claustro tuo emendetur, quod etiam in deo confido per misericordiam ipsius fieri. Soror autem, scilicet subpriorissa, que per inquietos
mores quietem aliarum conturbat, ab officio suo — si tibi placet —
amovenda est, quatinus cetere per hoc extimeant, que magistris inobe-
dientes sunt; et hoc fiat secundum consuetudinem qua officia clau-
30 stri permutari solent.

Cara amica dei, deus faciat te, ex amore suo et timore, ut rutilan-
tem auroram que solem precedit, quatinus congregationi tue velut sol
luceas, qui totum mundum illuminat. Satage etiam duplicitatem amo-
vere ab his que in rectis viis non ambulant, cum unum locuntur et
35 aliud in mente habent, et ideo iudicia earum iniusta sunt. Tales vero
mores sunt quasi nebule terram ledentes, quoniam per eos fructus virtutum arescit; et singulares amicicias ociosis verbis consociant, et ea
que ab antiquis sanctis instituta sunt contradicunt, que et obscure nu-
bi similes sunt, que nullam temperatam /(46ra) auram habet, et ideo in
40 eis fructus utilitatis sperari non potest.

Dulcis domina, hec omnia que predicta sunt in omni congregatio-
ne timenda et prohibenda sunt, quantum per graciam dei possunt. Tamen in deo confido quod obscuritas et tenebrositas que circa tua apparent per labores factos et adhuc faciendos a tuis et in tuis destrui et
45 calcari debeant. Carissima domina, spiritus sanctus ignem suum in te
accendat, quatinus in timore et amore dei curam animarum tibi com-
missarum feliciter perficias, ita ut in eterna beatitudine lucida gemma
in deo sis.

Letter III (**B** fols. 49vb-50ra)

O filia creatoris, quoniam ipse te creavit, in caritate Christi tibi
/(50ra) dico quod in visione anime mee multa miracula dei video, et
profunditates scripturarum per graciam dei intelligo, sed qui vel quales
eventus hominibus venturi sunt in illa michi non revelantur.
5   In eadem autem visione cognovi animam mariti tui in magnis pe-
nis esse, sed non ad perditionem deputatam, quia, licet proprie volun-
tati sue plus quam deo serviret, tamen voluntatem ac desiderium quan-
doque bona operandi in corde suo habebat, que morte preventus ope-
ratus non est.
10   Cara domina, ea que homini futura sunt querere a deo non presu-
mo, cum ipsi ad salutem anime magis prosit ea nescire quam prescire,
sed deum omnipotentem pro te libenter exorabo ut omnia tua ad salutem anime et corporis tui disponat.

41 predicta] predic/dicta B

Letter III: Quod hominum eventus non predixit *ss. B*

10 a deo] adeo B

    Animam quoque mariti tui tribus annis — missis, elemosinis, et
15 orationibus — omni die adiuvare quantum potes non desistas, quatinus a diris penarum afflictionibus per misericordiam passionis Christi
liberetur. Tu etiam in deo confide et omnia tua illi committe, et ipse
te non relinquet ac in eterna beatitudine te conservabit.

7

LA CREAZIONE DEGLI ANIMALI *

Clemente di Alessandria comincia il suo *Protrepticus* con una serie di contrasti, fra i poeti-cantori primordiali dei miti — Amfione, Arione, Orfeo — e il suo vero poeta-cantore, che è Cristo. Per mezzo del loro canto, quei poeti e fondatori pagani mostrarono la loro potenza su sassi, pesci, ed animali; eppure, dice Clemente, essi ingannavano gli uomini e ne facevano schiavi, li spingevano all'idolatria. «Ma il mio cantore non è tale: lui è il solo che abbia mai domato i più nocivi animali — gli umani. Ha domato gli uccelli — cioè, uomini incostanti; i rettili — cioè, i furbi; ha domato i leoni — uomini con passioni scatenate; i porci — gli edonisti; e i lupi — uomini rapaci... Vedi quanta è la potenza del nuovo canto! Ha fatto esseri umani dalle pietre e dalle fiere. È questo che ha dato un ordine di melodia al mondo, ed ha accordato la discordia degli elementi, facendone una sinfonia, affinché tutto l'universo s'armonizzi con lui» [1].

Per Clemente l'apologista, tutto ciò che si affermava falsamente di eroi come Orfeo è compiuto in verità da Cristo. Però, i paralleli fra la concezione pagana e quella cristiana sono così importanti per lui come la disgiunzione fra mito e verità. Il poeta umano-divino manifesta la sua sovranità sugli animali per mezzo del suo canto. Gli animali sono, allo stesso tempo, uomini; dunque il compito di farli entrare nell'armonia divina implica una trasformazione creatrice: nella sua influenza mirabile sugli animali questo poeta si rivela anche come salvatore degli uomini. Quando gli animali-uomini sono coinvolti nella melodia del poeta, allora si realizza una nuova "composizione" — una *sympatheia* cosmica.

Il testo di Clemente suggerisce una certa connaturalità fra l'uomo e gli animali. Si può vederla sotto l'aspetto negativo — gli uomini

---

* *Settimane di studio del Centro italiano di studi sull'alto medioevo* XXXI (Spoleto 1985), pp. 809-842.

[1] *Protrepticus*, I, ed. G. W. Butterworth (Loeb Classics, 1919), pp. 8-12. Per la figurazione di peccati come animali, cfr. anche Clemente, *Stromateis*, V, 8 e M. W. Bloomfield, *The Seven Deadly Sins* (Michigan 1952), pp. 29 e 329 sg. (n. 259).

possono essere bestiali — ma anche sotto quello positivo: uomini e
bestie possono partecipare ugualmente dell'armonia cosmica. Vorrei
esaminare più attentamente alcuni sviluppi di questa nozione di connaturalità fra l'uomo e gli altri animali, in primo luogo nell'esegesi altomedievale di certi momenti della Genesi: l'apparizione delle creature viventi al quinto e al sesto giorno della creazione (*Gen.* I, 20-25),
e Adamo che dà nomi agli animali (*Gen.* II, 19-20). Come vedremo,
c'è un legame profondo (anche se spesso non esplicito) fra quella creazione e nominazione degli animali *in illo tempore* e la creazione
umana di animali dai poeti medievali.

Molti pensieri degli esegeti altomedievali sulla *nominatio* delle
creature possono vedersi nella loro prima formazione negli scritti di
Filone di Alessandria. Filone sottolinea che non c'era niente di ar-
bitrario nell'imposizione di nomi da parte di Adamo: era del tutto
vera e precisa; ogni nome riproduceva l'essenza di ogni animale, quale
esisteva eternamente nella mente di Dio. Dio aveva dato ad Adamo
una prova e una sfida, «affinché per la sua propria capacità l'uomo
potesse attribuire dei nomi mai incongrui o inadatti — nomi che es-
primono chiaramente le qualità delle creature che li portano»[2]. E
Adamo, nella sua perfezione iniziale, superò trionfalmente questa
prova: «i nomi che diede erano pienamente appropriati, perché Adamo indovinò bene i caratteri delle creature che descriveva, con il
risultato che le loro nature furono percepite appena i nomi furono
pronunciati».

Qui Filone adombra un principio che si incontra spesso nel pensiero altomedievale — il principio che Jolivet e Chenu hanno
giustamente chiamato "platonismo grammaticale"[3]. Come dice per
esempio Teodorico di Chartres: «una forma non può esistere senza
nome... Una cosa è un animale perché è chiamata "animale"... È
chiaro dunque che i nomi danno l'essenza alle cose (*nomina res essen-
tiant*)»[4]. Questa frase, usata ripetutamente da Teodorico[5], è collegata
secondo lui all'interpretazione patristica della Genesi, ed anche al
pensiero di Cicerone:

---

[2] Filone, *De opificio mundi*, LII, 149, ed. F. H. Colson e G.H. Whitaker (Loeb
Classics, Philo vol. I, 1929), p. 118.

[3] J. Jolivet, *Quelques cas de «platonisme grammatical» du VIIe au XIIe siècle*, in
Mélanges René Crozet (Poitiers 1966), I, pp. 93-99; M.-D. Chenu, *Un cas de platonisme grammatical au XIIe siècle*, in «Revue des sciences philosophiques et théologiques», LI (1967), pp. 666-668.

[4] *Commentaries on Boethius by Thierry of Chartres and his School*, ed. N.M. Häring (Toronto 1971), pp. 171 sg.

[5] Cfr. l'indice di Häring (*op. cit.*, p. 604), s.v. *essentiare*.

È per questo che i commentatori divini affermano che Adamo impose i nomi attraverso lo Spirito Santo. Anche per questo Cicerone nelle sue *Tuscolane* chiama colui il più felice e più beato fra gli uomini che per primo diede i nomi alle cose [6].

L'imposizione di nomi da parte di Adamo era quindi il suo contributo alla creazione — era l'attività per la quale imitò e partecipò all'attività divina. La stessa intuizione si manifesta singolarmente nell'apocrifa "piccola Genesi", dove gli angeli dicono che, nel corso dei sei giorni della seconda settimana della creazione, essi condussero in ordine tutte le creature viventi ad Adamo. Il primo giorno, per grazia divina, Adamo nominò le fiere; il secondo giorno, gli armenti; il terzo, gli uccelli; il quarto, i rettili, ed il quinto, le creature del mare. Il sesto giorno, Adamo s'accorse della sua solitudine, dunque Dio lo fece dormire e creò Eva dalla sua costa. Quando Adamo si destò, quello stesso giorno, nominò sua moglie. Questo, l'autore pare suggerire, fu il culmine della sua creazione di nomi; con ciò il compito esaemerale di Adamo si fece una *mimesis* perfetta della creazione esaemerale di Dio [7].

Più avanti nello stesso capitolo (III, 28), si legge che, il giorno della caduta di Adamo, gli animali, che avevano usato tutti la stessa lingua, persero la loro facoltà di parlare. Così anche la rottura fra Dio ed Adamo trovò la sua *mimesis* in una rottura fra Adamo e gli animali [8].

Quando Filone si rivolge ad allegorizzare la nominazione degli animali e degli uccelli, l'avvenimento s'interiorizza e diventa microcosmico. Il campo e il cielo sono la mente (νοῦς) dell'uomo; gli animali e gli uccelli sono le passioni umane (un'identificazione che avrebbe potuto influenzare la spiegazione clementina di Orfeo-Cristo); Eva è la propria percezione (αἴσθησις) dei nostri sensi. La descrizione filoniana delle passioni è in gran misura negativa: «selvagge, non domate, le passioni lacerano l'anima; come creature alate, con violenza irresistibile, s'imbattono nell'intelligenza» [9]. La

---

[6] *Op. cit.*, pp. 277 sg. (cfr. Cicerone, *Tusc.* III, v, 10).

[7] *The Book of Jubilees*, III, 1 sgg. (ed. e trad. R.H. Charles, *The Apocrypha and Pseudepigrapha of the Old Testament in English*, II, Oxford 1913, p. 16).

[8] Nell'ottavo secolo, queste tradizioni furono citate, benché con disapprovazione, dal cronografo bizantino Giorgio Sincello, *Chronographia*, I, ed. W. Dindorf (Bonn 1829), pp. 7-8, 14. Cfr. anche X. Muratova, *Adam donne leurs noms aux animaux*, in «Studi Medievali», ser. 3ª, XVIII (1977), pp. 381-382 (n. 54).

[9] Filone, *Legum Allegoriae*, II, 11, ed. cit. (n. 2), p. 230. Filone fa una differenziazione sottile fra la creazione *generica* degli animali (a *Gen.*, I, 24) e la creazione successiva delle singole specie (a *Gen.* II, 19).

nominazione di Adamo è simultaneamente letterale e simbolica: così armonizzò ogni nome con il suo oggetto, e fece del nome un simbolo valido per tutti (σύμβολον ἅπασι) [10]. Allo stesso tempo, attraverso la sua definizione degli animali, Adamo definiva le sue proprie passioni, definiva sé stesso:

> tutto ciò che Adamo chiamò a sé ed accolse come anima vivente, stimandolo quanto la propria anima, diventò nome, non soltanto della cosa chiamata, ma anche di colui che l'aveva chiamata [11].

Vediamo dunque che nella connaturalità della natura umana e quella animale si nasconde un'ambivalenza. Anche la spiegazione filoniana è ambivalente, magari inconsistente. Filone chiama le passioni i nostri avversari (πολέμιοι), ma riconosce inoltre che possono essere serenamente accolte, senza desiderio eccessivo. Ad un certo punto, Filone parla degli uccelli come se fossero arpie che squarciano l'anima; in un altro passo, essi sono «nature raggianti e divine e beate» (λαμπρὰς καὶ θείας καὶ εὐδαίμονας φύσεις) nel cielo della mente umana [12]. Tali cambiamenti di prospettiva s'incontrano anche fra i commentatori altomedievali del mondo latino.

In occidente, alcuni accenni ad un'interpretazione allegorica della creazione degli animali risalgono a sant'Agostino. Il mare, che è il mondo, le cui acque sono amare, produce rettili dotati di anime viventi — cioè i sacramenti, che strisciano nelle onde della tentazione allo scopo di impregnare le nazioni con l'acqua del battesimo. Gli uccelli sono i messaggeri della parola di Dio, che volano in alto fino al firmamento della Scrittura. Anche gli uccelli, benché siano una *marina progenies*, si moltiplicano sulla terra, perché è la terra arida che germoglia nelle virtù, e che produce «l'anima vivente» degli animali, che è l'anima veramente cristiana [13].

Nell'epoca carolingia possiamo già parlare di una *koinê* di letture allegoriche di questo tipo; infatti, le interpretazioni passano spesso da un autore all'altro, alla lettera oppure con leggera parafrasi. Le illustrazioni seguenti, per esempio, possono incontrarsi da Claudio di Torino, Hrabano Mauro, Remigio di Auxerre, e Pseudo-Beda:

> Il quinto giorno furono creati rettili di anime viventi, vale a dire uomini rinnovati nella vita dal battesimo; anche degli uccelli furono

---

[10] II, 15 (*ed. cit.*, p. 234).
[11] II, 18 (ibid., p. 236).
[12] II, 10 (ibid., p. 230).
[13] *Conf.*, XIII, xvii, 20; xx, 26; xxi, 29.

creati, cioè anime sante volando alle altezze superne. In seguito, il sesto giorno, la terra produce un'anima vivente, quando la nostra carne (la terra)... partorisce le gemme vive delle virtù... Poi la terra produce delle bestie — degli uomini potenti nel mondo oppure feroci nella loro superbia; parimenti produce degli armenti — i fedeli che vivono la vita semplice; produce anche dei serpenti innocui: questi sono i santi, vivaci nella loro astuzia, nel discernimento del bene e del male; mentre strisciano, guardano attentamente, quanto è lecito, le cose terrene, allo scopo di comprendere quelle eterne. Non sono i serpenti velenosi, che si attorcigliano ai desideri terreni [14].

—

Lo Pseudo-Beda aggiunge alcuni tratti più insoliti. Secondo lui le acque sono dottori della Chiesa, che generano rettili e uccelli — peccatori e santi. Generano anche le balene — vale a dire, i peccati grandi. Dio li crea, non perché li desidera, ma affinché possa perdonarli. Se però i rettili sono i peccatori, come mai Dio li ha considerati buoni, al pari del resto della creazione? Certo, risponde l'autore, è perché i santi sono messi alla prova da quei rettili. Inoltre, le acque sono per lui il cuore umano, che produce tutti i movimenti del nostro spirito — movimenti striscianti oppure voli verso l'alto; la terra, dunque, è sia la Chiesa, la quale partorisce un'anima che vive in Dio, sia l'uomo esteriore, la carne in cui non si trova niente di volatile, niente di buono [15].

Mentre i due alessandrini — Filone e Clemente — avevano attribuito delle qualità negative agli uccelli come ai rettili e agli animali, i commentatori carolingi vedono gli uccelli soltanto nel loro aspetto più elevato: essere «volatile» vuol dire essere capace dell'ascesa celeste. Così, come vedremo, sono ancora gli uccelli con cui s'identificano nel modo più positivo i poeti: essi sono spesso presentati con la maggiore simpatia fra tutte le creature.

Era normale interpretare l'episodio dell'imposizione dei nomi da parte di Adamo come una dimostrazione della preminenza dell'uomo sugli altri animali. Sant'Agostino cita l'autorità di Pitagora: il primo nominatore umano era il più saggio di tutti gli uomini [16]. Cassiano va più oltre, dicendo che in quel momento Adamo aveva «non solo la pienezza di sapienza, ma anche la grazia della profezia, trasfusa dall'ispirazione divina» [17]. Vediamo dunque con quanta facilità ques-

---

[14] La citazione è di Hrabano Mauro, *Comm. in Gen.*, I, x, in *P.L.*, CVII, col. 468; cfr. Claudio di Torino, in *P.L.*, L, coll. 899-900; Pseudo-Beda, in *P.L.*, XCI, col. 199; Remigio di Auxerre, in *P.L.*, CXXXI, col. 58.

[15] *P.L.*, XCI, coll. 199-200.

[16] *Opus imperfectum contra Julianum*, V, 1, in *P.L.*, XLV, col. 1432.

[17] *Collationes*, VIII, 21, in *P.L.*, XLIX, col. 757.

ta scena poteva essere rivestita di un significato mistico, nel quale il primo Adamo prefigura il secondo. L'interpretazione carolingia comune è che Adamo-Cristo «impose un nome su tutte le creature — cioè, sull'umanità, che, attraverso la rigenerazione, trasmutò in una nuova creazione, perché voleva chiamarla, con il suo proprio nome, cristiana» [18].

Così, per mezzo di allegorie e di figure, è stata costituita una rete di analogie fra il mondo umano e quello degli animali, anche se viene riconosciuto che non si tratta d'altro che di analogie. L'unicità dell'uomo fu dimostrata non solo attraverso l'atto del nominare da parte di Adamo, ma anche attraverso la risoluzione di Dio nella Genesi (I, 25): l'uomo solo era destinato ad esser fatto «ad imaginem et similitudinem nostram; et praesit piscibus maris et volatilibus caeli et bestiis universaeque terrae».

I trattati di Lattanzio e Gregorio di Nissa sulla creazione dell'uomo (quest'ultimo tradotto da Giovanni Scoto Eriugena, con il titolo *De imagine*), contengono un repertorio cristianizzato di motivi stoici e platonici della lode dell'uomo [19]. L'uomo è il solo animale che cammina eretto e che può contemplare il cielo; solo l'uomo ha l'uso delle mani; solo l'uomo ama i suoi figli anche quando non sono più piccoli. Tutti quegli aspetti per cui l'uomo sembra essere fisicamente fragile e senza vantaggi sono stati compensati da una capacità o da un dono che gli permette di primeggiare. La ragione è la sua arma interiore. Non ha bisogno di corna o di unghie, perché ha l'uso del ferro. Eppure Lattanzio, in un'altra opera, il *De ira dei*, ha un passo in cui la connaturalità fra l'uomo e gli altri animali è sottolineata in una misura straordinaria. Qui Lattanzio asserisce che esiste una sola differenza decisiva: citando Cicerone, dice: nessun altro animale ha una conoscenza di Dio [20] —

> Perché le altre qualità che sembrano appartenere all'uomo solo, anche se non siano precisamente le stesse negli altri animali, si può nondimeno vedervi delle qualità somiglianti. Il parlare è proprio dell'uomo, eppure una certa sembianza del parlare si trova anche fra loro. Le loro emissioni possono parere crude dal nostro punto di vista, come forse le nostre lo paiono dal loro; ma per loro, che si capiscono, sono

[18] Remigio di Auxerre, *Comm. in Gen.*, in *P.L.*, CXXXI, col. 63; cfr. Hrabano Mauro, in *P.L.*, CVII, col. 484, e Claudio di Torino, in *P.L.*, L, col. 909.

[19] Cfr. esp. Lattanzio, *De opificio Dei*, II-III, VII-VIII; Gregorio di Nissa, *De hominis opificio*, VII-IX (pp. 215-219 nella traduzione dell'Eriugena, *De imagine*, ed. M. Cappuyns, in «Recherches de théologie ancienne et médiévale», XXXII, 1965, pp. 205-262.

[20] Lattanzio, *De ira Dei*, VII; cfr. Cicerone, *De legibus*, I, viii, 24.

delle parole... Il riso è proprio dell'uomo, eppure vediamo certi cenni di gioia anche fra gli altri animali... Che cosa è così propriamente umano come la ragione e provvedere all'avvenire? Eppure ci sono degli animali che costruiscono parecchie uscite diverse per la loro tana, in caso di pericolo. Altri animali si premuniscono contro l'avvenire...

Poi Lattanzio cita dei versi virgiliani sulle attività delle formiche e delle api [21]. Conclude che è solo alla «giustizia» della religione che nessun altro animale può attingere.

Giovanni Scoto cerca di mostrare l'unità fra l'uomo e gli animali in un modo del tutto diverso. Per lui non si tratta delle loro sembianze di lingua o di pensiero umano, ma della maniera in cui gli animali sono conosciuti, o realizzati, nella coscienza umana. La sua esposizione di questo tema, nel *Periphyseon*, mi pare la più profonda e più originale ch'io abbia incontrato.

L'Eriugena comincia con l'affermazione sorprendente che non solo le anime umane ma le anime di tutti gli animali devono essere immortali: perché, se l'uomo appartiene al genere animale, «come potrebbero morire tutte le specie di quel genere, mentre sopravvive solo la specie assegnata all'uomo?» [22].

Quanto agli aspetti dell'anima sensitiva per cui alcuni animali superano l'uomo — aspetti che i Padri avevano menzionato solo allo scopo di sottolineare il vantaggio incomparabile dell'intelligenza umana — l'Eriugena li utilizza per un argomento ben diverso:

> Qual uomo vede così acutamente come l'aquila o la gazzella?... Il cane di Ulisse riconobbe il suo padrone dopo vent'anni ... Dunque non vedo come tutte queste potenze naturali potrebbero essere presenti nell'anima irrazionale, se essa fosse terra, come dicono i Padri [23].

Non è, aggiunge l'Eriugena, come se volesse distruggere le opinioni dei santi Padri — invece, cerca quali fra le loro opinioni possano essere mantenute più ragionevolmente.

Per la prima volta in questo contesto, Giovanni Scoto introduce l'*anima mundi*, quella vita o anima primordiale (*primordialis vita seu anima*) attraverso la partecipazione alla quale ogni anima ha vita e

---

[21] *Aen.*, IV, 402 sgg.; *Georg.*, IV, 155-157.

[22] *Periphyseon*, III, 39, ed. I.P. Sheldon-Williams e L. Bieler (Dublin 1981), p. 296 (= *De divisione naturae*, in *P.L.*, CXXII, col. 737 C). L'immortalità delle anime degli animali fu affermata nell'apocrifo *Libro dei segreti di Enoch*, LVIII (cfr. R.H. Charles, *op. cit.*, n. 7, II, p. 464) — ma di questo non è stata trovata una versione latina.

[23] *Periphyseon*, ed. cit., p. 298 (*P.L.*, CXXII, coll. 738 C - 739 A).

esistenza — partecipazione che non può cessare neanche quando un'anima particolare non regge più il suo corpo. Se i Padri non estesero questa concezione alle anime di tutti gli animali, l'Eriugena asserisce che questo deve esser stato così solo nel loro insegnamento pubblico, per paura che altrimenti gli uomini comuni si dedicassero ai desideri animaleschi. Fra gli iniziati, sottintende, i Padri avrebbero insegnato l'immortalità di tutte le anime di animali [24].

Nel quarto libro del *Periphyseon* l'Eriugena continua la sua discussione degli animali dopo aver indicato la meta verso la quale si muove la sua argomentazione: questa è la concezione del *reditus*, «il ritorno di tutti gli esseri alla natura che né crea né è stata creata» [25]. Tutto ciò che segue sugli animali è condizionato dalla visione eriugeniana di quella reintegrazione finale. Il legame fra l'uomo e il regno degli animali si rivelerà come un aspetto vitale di quel *reditus*.

L'anima nel mondo, il principio universale della vita che sorge dalla fonte divina, influisce su tutti gli esseri, incluso l'uomo fra gli animali. Brevemente l'Eriugena si permette un'allegoria di tipo filoniano: egli spiega che nel testo greco della Genesi (I, 24) la divisione triplice del sesto giorno è fra «quadrupedi e rettili e fiere». Questa divisione, secondo lui, implica un movimento triplice nell'uomo: quello della percezione sensoriale, che è quadrupedale in quanto si affida ai quattro elementi; quello della natura irrazionale, come l'impeto di ira o di desiderio, caratteristico delle fiere; e in terzo luogo la potenza crescitiva e nutritiva, che penetra l'armonia del corpo silenziosamente, come se fosse un rettile. «Non vedi che l'uomo è in tutti gli animali e che tutti sono in lui, e che l'uomo è al di sopra di tutti?» [26].

L'uomo è animale e non-animale: è stato creato animale insieme con gli altri, e spirituale insieme con gli esseri spirituali. Questo non vuol dire che ha due anime: piuttosto, che ogni creatura — corporea, vitale, sensibile, razionale, e intellettuale — è compresa nell'uomo. Giovanni Scoto aveva ripreso l'idea dello Pseudo-Dionigi che in Dio le affermazioni contrarie possono coincidere; qui estende il concetto dionisiano all'uomo: nell'uomo gli aspetti animaleschi e quelli trascendentali sono veri contemporaneamente.

Poiché ogni creatura è contenuta nell'umana natura, viene affidato all'umanità un ruolo centrale nel *reditus*. Attraverso l'umanità ogni creatura sarà salvata, cioè prenderà parte al ritorno di tutta la natura alla divina causa finale. Questo era il vero significato delle pa-

---

[24] *Periphyseon*, ed. cit., p. 300 (*P.L.*, CXXII, col. 739 B).
[25] *P.L.*, CXXII, col. 743 C (la nuova edizione del quarto libro manca ancora).
[26] *P.L.*, CXXII, col. 752 C.

role di Cristo: «Predicate il Vangelo ad ogni creatura». È anche per
questo che Dio ha creato l'uomo nel genere animale, e ha creato in
lui ogni creatura visibile e invisibile — affinché potesse esserci un
animale in cui l'immagine divina potesse manifestarsi [27].

«Se tutti gli esseri furono creati nell'uomo, e sussistono nell'uomo», conclude il discepolo nel dialogo eriugeniano, questo ci condu-
ce ad un paradosso inaccettabile: esso implicherebbe che le qualità
specifiche dei diversi animali sono tutte presenti nell'uomo — la loro
irrazionalità, per esempio, o la loro capacità di volare. Tali qualità, risponde il maestro, sono di fatto presenti nell'uomo, perché l'uomo le
comprende tutte [28]. Inoltre, per un buon platonista è evidente che la
realtà intelligibile di queste qualità, nell'intelletto umano, supera
quella delle loro manifestazioni fisiche. È per mezzo dell'uomo che
le qualità irrazionali degli animali appartengono alla sfera più alta
delle *notiones*, dove sono conservate incorporee, al di là dei limiti fu-
gaci del corporeo. Nello stesso modo la vera sostanza di ogni uomo
è la nozione dell'umanità che sussiste eternamente nell'intelletto divino, una nozione che non è soltanto una definizione, nel senso logico
di definire, ma che costituisce l'essenza di ogni vita umana individuale [29].

Nel discorso eriugeniano sugli animali intravvediamo due tappe
del processo di *reditus*: come l'uomo è una nozione nell'intelletto divino, così gli animali sono una nozione nella mente umana. L'esistenza umana, dice Giovanni Scoto, può essere capita soprattutto dal fatto che all'uomo è stata concessa una *notio* di tutti gli esseri creati come suoi pari oppure come suoi soggetti. È questa *notio* che Adamo
nominò al momento di nominare gli animali. La nozione degli animali nella mente umana è la loro sostanza; le nozioni umane delle proprietà degli animali e delle loro differenze sono in verità le loro proprietà e differenze. È in questo senso che l'irrazionalità e tutti i tratti
specifici degli animali furono creati nell'uomo [30].

L'Eriugena ci dà non solo una *oratio de dignitate hominis* ma allo
stesso tempo un'immagine più profonda della connaturalità fra l'uomo e gli animali, quale i Padri non avevano mai sognato. Con ciò egli
fornì, per così dire, il fondamento metafisico per una presentazione
degli animali che oltrepassa le possibilità di allegoria e figura. Benché
non risalga direttamente alla sua influenza, possiamo vedere a volte
nei secoli dopo l'Eriugena un grado di identificazione cognitiva fra

---

[27] *P.L.*, CXXII, col. 763 D.
[28] *P.L.*, CXXII, col. 764 C - 765 D.
[29] *P.L.*, CXXII, col. 768 B.
[30] *P.L.*, CXXII, col. 769 A-B.

la sfera umana e quella degli animali che non sarebbe stato possibile in un mondo di cui la prospettiva principale intorno agli animali era la superiorità dell'uomo. Ciò che è nuovo nella creazione letteraria di animali nel decimo e undicesimo secolo è legato ad una riflessione più precisa e dettagliata sulla connaturalità. Le riflessioni di Giovanni Scoto mostrano i primi sintomi (che io sappia) di questo cambiamento di «mentalité».

Cercherò di caratterizzare il vecchio e il nuovo nelle testimonianze letterarie, almeno in un modo rapido e provvisorio, riferendomi ad alcuni testi-chiave.

Le possibilità prima dell'Eriugena si vedono chiaramente nei modi di percezione caratteristici di due opere ben diverse: il *Physiologus* e il *Liber monstrorum*. Il primo, come è noto, era diffusissimo, tanto nella tradizione erudita quanto in quella popolare [31]; esiste in molte lingue e molte versioni dalla tarda antichità in poi. Il secondo non era privo di influenza nel mondo erudito; eppure si tratta di un'opera poco comune. (Fu composta nell'Inghilterra anglosassone, probabilmente verso il 700 nel circolo di Aldelmo di Malmesbury [32]; ne conosciamo solo cinque codici, tutti continentali, del nono e del decimo secolo, e ci sono accenni a quattro altri codici perduti) [33].

Voglio citare degli estratti da tre capitoli del *Physiologus* [34]:

> Il riccio ha la forma di una palla, tutta coperta di spine. Fisiologo dice di lui che ascende alle uve della vite, e le spinge a terra. Poi rotolandosi sulle uve, le fa aderire alle sue spine, e così le porta ai suoi figli, e lascia la vite denudata di frutta.
>
> Quanto a te, o cristiano (*Et tu, christiane*)... allacciati fermamente alla vite spirituale, e così sarai condotto al torchio da vino spirituale, e sarai raccolto nella corte del re divino... Come mai hai lasciato quello spirito maligno (il riccio) ascendere al tuo posto... e ingannarti con le spine della morte, spogliandoti della tua frutta e distribuendola alle potenze ostili? (16).

[31] Cfr. N. Henkel, *Studien zum «Physiologus» im Mittelalter* (Tübingen 1976).

[32] Cfr. M. Lapidge, «*Beowulf*», *Aldhelm, The «Liber Monstrorum» and Wessex*, in «Studi Medievali», ser. 3ª, XXIII (1982), pp. 151-192 (p. 176).

[33] Cfr. *Liber monstrorum de diversis generibus*, ed. C. Bologna (Milano 1977), pp. 167-172. Il testo di Bologna riproduce la vecchia edizione di Haupt (1876), con alcune modificazioni; nelle mie citazioni, seguo l'edizione di F. Porsia, *Liber monstrorum* (Bari 1976), che utilizza quattro dei cinque codici conosciuti.

[34] I passi qui tradotti seguono sostanzialmente il testo di F.J. Carmody, *Physiologus Latinus Versio Y* (Berkeley-Los Angeles 1941); dove il latino di questa versione non è più intelligibile, mi sono riferito al testo greco di D. Offermanns, *Der Physiologus nach den Handschriften G und M* (Meisenheim am Glan 1966): i capitoli XVI, XXI e XLIX del testo latino corrispondono ai capitoli XIV, XLI e II del greco.

C'è un animale sul monte che è chiamato gazzella... Si diletta molto dei monti alti, ma trova il suo cibo nelle vallate. E vede da lontano tutti coloro che si avvicinano, e riconosce se vengono con insidia o con amicizia.

La gazzella ha la sapienza di Dio: si diletta dei profeti, cioè (*hoc est*), i monti alti... Salomone... disse di lei: «Guarda il mio amore, che salta sui monti, che balza sui colli». La gazzella salta sui profeti, balza sui colli, cioè (*hoc est*), gli apostoli. Ha la visione acuta, che significa (*significans*) che il salvatore vede tutte le azioni... da lontano vede coloro che vengono a lui con insidia — quindi conobbe Giuda, che veniva a tradirlo con un bacio; sta anche scritto, «il Signore conosce i suoi»; e Giovanni dice, «Ecco l'agnello di Dio, che toglie i peccati del mondo» (21).

C'è una creatura chiamata... lucertola del sole. Quando essa invecchia, i suoi occhi s'indeboliscono ambedue, essa diventa cieca, e non può più vedere la luce del sole. Cosa farà? Nella bontà della sua natura, cerca un muro esposto all'Oriente, e ne entra una fessura fronteggiando l'Oriente, e poi, quando il sole sorge, i suoi occhi saranno aperti e la lucertola è rinnovata.

Così anche tu (*sic et tu*), uomo, se porti l'abito dell'uomo vecchio, bada di non lasciare indebolire gli occhi del tuo cuore; in quel caso, dovresti cercare il sole intelligibile, il Signore Gesù Cristo, che è chiamato «Oriente» e «Sole di giustizia»... e ti aprirà gli occhi intelligibili del tuo cuore, e avrai un abito nuovo invece del vecchio (49).

La cosa più straordinaria mi pare essere la simbiosi di elementi prevedibili e imprevedibili. I prevedibili sono corrispondenze, che sono spesso segnalate in un modo esplicito: *Et tu, sic et tu, hoc est*, o *significans*. Ma cercare di ridurre tutte le percezioni a corrispondenze sarebbe superficiale. Ci sono molte sorprese, magari una punta di capriccio. La cura del riccio per i suoi figli potrebbe destare l'aspettativa che questa creatura ci sarà rivelata come emblema di pietà, un poco come il pellicano. Invece, Fisiologo ci lascia vedere improvvisamente che le uve sono preziose, e che i figli del riccio sono forze ostili, anzi demoniache. Queste uve hanno delle connotazioni che (benché tradizionali) sono lontane dalla semplicità di qualsiasi *hoc est*. Sono i frutti dell'anima individuale, che crescono sulla vite che (qui solo in un modo implicito) è Cristo. Ma Cristo sulla croce è anche, secondo una figura ben conosciuta tratta da Isaia [35], il *vinaio* che pigia l'uva tutto solo nel torchio. Nella sua Passione, è lui la vite spogliata; quindi trasforma le uve umane in vino, che non è più nutrimento per i ricci, ma una bevanda degna del re divino (che di nuovo è Cristo stesso). Le figure presupposte sono usate con disinvoltura associativa, e con

[35] *Is.* LXIII, 1 sgg.

una concisione che indica quanta agilità intellettuale e immaginativa dobbiamo presupporre nelle comunità paleocristiane che si dilettavano di questi ideogrammi.

Anche quando viene svolta l'immagine della gazzella, non sappiamo ancora se il significato nascosto ci condurrà alla sfera divina o alla demoniaca, oppure all'uomo al crocevia della decisione. Qui i significati principali si rivelano come divini e positivi, però c'è di nuovo un elemento imprevedibile nel passo finale, che adombra tre sensi del «riconoscere»: Cristo penetra l'anima del suo traditore, Cristo conosce ed accoglie i suoi, e alla fine Giovanni riconosce Cristo, e esprime quel riconoscimento nel grido *Ecce agnus dei*. Il mondo della gazzella, che sembrava condurci soltanto a significati allegorici, ci riconduce inaspettatamente ad una percezione diretta. Così ci accorgiamo della piena forza dell'esclamazione di Giovanni, vediamo che l'agnello di Dio non aveva niente a che fare con l'allegoria: era un momento di visione, in cui Giovanni vide simultaneamente l'animale fatto numinoso e incarnato nel suo cugino umano, Gesù [36].

Mentre il riccio significa uno spirito maligno e la gazzella significa Cristo, la lucertola del sole del terzo passo significa l'anima umana, un'anima che l'autore vede come buona di natura, naturalmente capace di volgersi alla luce del sole divino. All'inizio i paragoni potrebbero sembrarci un poco confusi — il legame fra il rinnovamento della visione e quello dell'abito non è immediatamente chiaro (o forse non lo è più per noialtri). L'abito è la carne umana — quindi la proprietà dell'immagine della lucertola che cambia pelle: il corpo rinato, glorificato non deve più vedere *per speculum in aenigmate*. Eppure definire così il significato vuol dire limitarlo troppo: l'immagine del rinnovamento, sia del corpo sia degli occhi del cuore, che avviene mentre si guarda il sole divino e lo si lascia irradiare l'umano, può applicarsi a molti aspetti del mistero cristiano — alle operazioni del battesimo, della penitenza, della grazia, e della redenzione. Ancora l'allegoria non è fissa o rigida: si vivifica di connotazioni imprevedibili.

Physiologus accoglie creature vere e fantastiche senza differenziarle: include la fenice e l'unicorno, la sirena e il centauro, e meglio ancora, il mirmicoleone, con la faccia del leone e il deretano della formica. Era facile per lui dare un significato esemplare alle finzioni, come agli esseri viventi. Il *Liber monstrorum* invece, almeno secondo il mio parere, è del tutto diverso nella sua orientazione. L'autore non fa nessun tentativo di cercare significati, ma oltre a ciò (con la sola ecce-

---

[36] Cfr. W. von den Steinen, *Altchristlich-mittelalterliche Tiersymbolik*, in «Symbolon», IV (1963), pp. 218-243 (p. 220).

zione del suo explicit: *Finit de serpentibus deo gratias amen*) [37], non include una sola allusione cristiana da un capo all'altro del suo libro. Questo mi pare assai insolito in un'opera altomedievale; e perciò mi sorprende che i due curatori recenti del *Liber* non l'abbiano osservato, e che ambedue facciano allusioni frequenti all'atteggiamento cristiano di questo autore. In particolare, essi interpretano i suoi accenni alle finzioni e menzogne dei poeti come un'espressione cristiana di sdegno per la poesia classica.

Ma non bisogna essere cristiano per proclamare che i poeti sono bugiardi — la *Repubblica* di Platone ne dà ampie prove. L'autore anglosassone, lungi dall'essere un bigotto cristiano anticlassico, si è sforzato di farsi razionalista [38]. A questo non riesce completamente — nel senso, per esempio, che mentre distingue fra un piccolo numero di *mirabilia* che possono essere veri e una folla che sono palesemente falsi, non ci dice precisamente dove sta la demarcazione. Neanche allega falsificazioni empiriche quando asserisce, come fa spesso, che i mostri di cui fa l'elenco sono impossibili. Comunque le sue intenzioni — cioè, raccogliere una gamma di materiali, e dare descrizioni neutrali o «cliniche», basate sulle sue fonti letterarie e — a volte pare — su testimonianze dirette, senza alcun ricorso a significati nascosti, e senza il minimo suggerimento che un Dio onnipotente potrebbe creare cose improbabili — queste intenzioni sono chiare. Nel quadro di ciò che ci resta del settimo e ottavo secolo, dimostrano un'individualità eccezionale.

Il punto di vista di questo autore, dunque, non è anticlassico, ma antisuperstizioso. Dappertutto incontriamo le sue espressioni di scet-

---

[37] *Liber monstrorum*, III, 24, ed. F. Porsia (cit. n. 33), p. 286.

[38] Anche Porsia parla del «razionalismo» dell'autore, ma con una sfumatura diversa: «la finalità dell'opera è quella di battere la scienza pagana classica in nome del razionalismo cristiano» (p. 117); «è tutto agostiniano il suo metodo» (p. 109). Quando l'autore del *Libro* allude alla *Philosophorum et poetarum scriptura... quae semper mendacia nutrit* (p. 126), oppure ai mostri che *poetae ac philosophi aurato sermone in suis litteraturis inaniter depingunt* (p. 218), Porsia parla di «polemica anticlassica» (p. 219) e si riferisce allo «spirito del *De civitate Dei*» (p. 129). Ma chi sono i *philosophi* a cui pensava quest'autore? Benché fosse eccezionalmente erudito, egli non dà l'impressione di conoscere scrittori filosofici come Cicerone o Seneca, neanche il *Timeo* latino; mi pare più verosimile che stava pensando a «filosofi» cristiani (S. Agostino stesso aveva usato l'espressione *philosophus* per i sapienti cristiani e per i profeti ebrei, come pure per i pensatori pagani). Temo che l'autore del *Liber monstrorum* abbia considerato come *mendacia*, per esempio, il capitolo di Isidoro *De portentis* (*Etym.*, XI, 3), che conosceva bene; è anche significativo che quando egli adatta la descrizione della vipera (III, 18, p. 278) dal *Physiologus*, lo fa con le parole *de qua scribunt physici*: qui, cioè, i suoi dubbi riguardano una *auctoritas* venerabile del mondo cristiano.

ticismo. Quando prende materiali dal testo sulle Meraviglie dell'Oriente attribuito ad Alessandro, le belve dalla doppia testa presso il Mare Rosso vengono introdotte da *ipsa fabulositas perhibet*, sottolineato da *fingunt*. Anche quando lo scrittore ricorre all'autorità di Virgilio, a proposito dei serpenti e mostri che, secondo l'*Eneide*, erano premonizioni fatali per Cleopatra alla battaglia di Azio, esclama: «Così anche le fallaci favole dei poeti fingono a loro piacere e di proposito (*volu⟨n⟩tarie fingunt*) molte cose che non esistono» [39].

Una volta, la fonte dell'autore non è un testo antico, bensì un dipinto greco che egli stesso ha visto:

> Le favole dei Greci fingono che nel mar Tirreno ci siano... animali terrestri con vari generi di mostri e di belve, che hanno tutti soltanto due piedi, poiché dal petto fino alla coda hanno corpi ricoperti di squame. E da un dipinto di mano greca apprendemmo che, dopo che Scilla, circondata da cani cerulei, aveva spogliato dei marinai la nave di Ulisse, quegli uomini... furono accolti indenni dai dorsi delle belve... E fingono (*fingunt*) che non fecero male a quegli uomini, perché erano desiderosi di accoppiarsi col genere umano... E fra quelle fantasie vane di pittura io vedevo che i bambini, generati in mare da questi uomini e dalle fiere, presumevano di nuotare con delle conchiglie fra le onde, per mungere il latte... [40].

In... fictis cernebam vanitatibus: accanto alla descrizione meticolosa del dipinto c'è il giudizio della sua falsità. Ma il giudizio non rassomiglia a quelli dei primitivi apologeti cristiani. Quest'autore non condanna le favole greche in nome della verità cristiana, ma fa rilevare la loro *intrinseca* mancanza di verità, in un modo che, intuitivamente, è più vicino a Platone che non a qualsiasi Padre della Chiesa.

Le percezioni del *Physiologus* possono essere notevoli per la loro sottigliezza e ricchezza immaginativa; quelle del *Liber monstrorum* spiccano per la loro imparzialità e acume intellettuale. La prima opera accoglie, oppure scopre, *significationes*; la seconda le trascura, magari le respinge. Comunque ambedue dimostrano che appartengono al mondo pre-eriugeniano. Nei loro modi diversi, ambedue queste opere negano la connaturalità. Per entrambi gli autori, il mondo delle creature si definisce come «l'altro». Il Fisiologo costruisce innumerevoli ponti al mondo umano, per mezzo di *hoc est*, o *sic et tu*. L'autore del *Liber* preferisce distruggere i ponti, per mezzo di *fingunt*. Entrambi hanno la coscienza del distacco.

---

[39] *Liber*, III, 23, trad. F. Porsia (p. 285); il testo (p. 284) dà la lezione *volutarie*.
[40] *Liber*, II, 32, trad. F. Porsia (p. 257); ma ho sostituito una mia traduzione, più letterale, per *in eiusdem modi (i.e. picturae) fictis cernebam vanitatibus*.

In alcune poesie originali del decimo e undicesimo secolo vediamo invece degli scrittori che passano oltre le allegorie e figure, e in
un certo senso anche oltre le «finzioni». Ci sono momenti in cui i te-
mi di uccelli ed animali divengono veicoli più diretti di espressione
poetica di quanto non siano stati prima: vanno aldilà di qualsiasi rela-
zione solamente estrinseca fra significante e significato. Questo può
vedersi con Leone di Vercelli, il vescovo-poeta, che, verso il Mille,
fonde parecchie favole di animali in una miscela di riflessione personale e satira politica, ora elegiaca ora esuberante — il suo *Metrum
Leonis* [41]. Poiché lo stato frammentario di questo testo scintillante lascia molti dettagli oscuri o, nel caso migliore, congetturali, mi pare
preferibile prendere le mie illustrazioni da due opere meglio cono-
sciute — dall'*Ecbasis captivi* e dal *Ruodlieb*.

Anche per l'interpretazione di queste due non abbiamo ancora
delle fondamenta completamente solide. Per il *Ruodlieb*, un capolavo-
ro ma anche questo frammentario, stiamo aspettando l'edizione critica e commentata di Benedikt Vollmann. L'estratto che il Vollmann ha
già pubblicato [42] ci lascia vedere quanto contribuirà alla ricostruzione
e spiegazione del testo. Quanto all'*Ecbasis cuiusdam captivi per tropo-
logiam* (è questo il titolo completo) [43], il testo stesso è molto meno
problematico: sono la data e le circostanze della composizione (e
quindi il significato delle molte allusioni) che rimangono incerte. Sono propenso ad accettare gli argomenti sottili di Gustavo Vinay
(1949), e la trama di un'interpretazione politica da lui proposta, che
implica anche la datazione del poema nella prima metà del decimo
secolo, invece dell'undicesimo, come Erdmann e vari eruditi tedeschi
più recenti hanno sostenuto [44]. Eppure la piena certezza dipendereb-

[41] Ed. K. Strecker, *Poetae Latini Medii Aevi*, V, 2 (*M.G.H.*), pp. 483-488.

[42] «*Ruodlieb*», *Fragment XII*, in *Lateinische Dichtungen des X. und XI. Jahrhunderts. Festgabe für Walther Bulst zum 80. Geburtstag* (Heidelberg 1981), pp.
227-248. [Cfr. ora *Ruodlieb. Faksimile-Ausgabe, Bd. II, Erster Teil: Kritischer Text*, a
cura di B.K. Vollmann (Wiesbaden 1985); *Frühe Deutsche Literatur und Lateinische
Literatur in Deutschland 800-1150*, a cura di W. Haug e B.K. Vollmann (Bibliothek
des Mittelalters I, Frankfurt a.M. 1991), pp. 388-511 (testo e traduzione tedesca di
Ruodlieb), pp. 1306-1406 (commento).]

[43] Benché il copista del codice principale (A) abbia scritto TOPOLOGIAM. Per le
mie citazioni, ho utilizzato l'edizione di W. Trillitzsch (Leipzig 1964), che contiene
anche una traduzione tedesca.

[44] G. Vinay, *Contributo alla interpretazione della «Ecbasis Captivi»*, in «Convi-
vium», 1949, pp. 234-252, ha respinto l'argomentazione di C. Erdmann, in «Deutsches Archiv», IV (1941), pp. 382-393. Cfr. anche W. Ross in «Germanisch-
Romanische Monatsschrift», N.F., IV (1954), pp. 266-283 — benché la sua proposta
di datare l'epopea nell'anno 912 fosse già confutata da H.E. Zarncke, in «Sitzb. der

be dal sapere 1) fino a che punto era intenzione del poeta che il suo pubblico identificasse i suoi animali con personaggi particolari della Chiesa o della corte [45]? 2) Se questa era una parte integrante delle sue intenzioni, allora come interpretare il comportamento di questi animali in termini storici? È ben possibile che le fonti per la storia di Lorena, sia nel decimo secolo sia nell'undicesimo, siano troppo scarse per permettere delle risposte definitive, anche dopo uno studio comprensivo.

Sächs. Akad., Phil.-hist. Kl.», XLII (1890), pp. 109-113 — e H. R. Jauss, *Untersuchungen zur mittelalterlichen Tierdichtung* (Tübingen 1959), pp. 56 sgg. Per le opinioni più recenti, cfr. F.P. Knapp, *Das lateinische Tierepos* (Darmstadt 1979), esp. pp. 1-9, e U. Kindermann, in *Die deutsche Literatur des Mittelalters: Verfasser-Lexikon* (2ª ed.), II (1980), coll. 315-321 (che però non conosce l'articolo di Vinay).

Nel 1938 B. Bischoff aveva scoperto alcune *probationes pennae* delle parole *infelix vitulus sudibus quam saepe ligatus* (cfr. *Ecbasis*, 248 e 66), da mani del decimo e dell'undicesimo secolo (cfr. i suoi *Mittelalterliche Studien*, I, Stoccarda 1967, p. 79). H. Thomas, che si è sforzato di mostrare, in una serie di articoli, che la *Ecbasis* sia «eine Trierer Dichtung aus der Zeit Heinrichs IV» (cfr. esp. «Deutsches Archiv», XX, 1964, pp. 130-154), afferma che, a causa della scoperta di Bischoff, «das wichtigste Argument für die bis dahin übliche Datierung ins 10. Jahrhundert fortgefallen war: die Kenntnis der *Ecbasis* durch den Bischof Thietmar von Merseburg». Mentre è possibile «dass der Dichter der *Ecbasis* Teile der Schulsentenz in den Versen 248 und 66 verarbeitet hat» (così Bischoff, loc cit.), non si può escludere l'altra possibilità: se la *Ecbasis* fosse composta nella prima metà del decimo secolo, la *Schulsentenz* potrebbe risalire al poema. È chiaro che la verificazione o falsificazione di questa ipotesi dipenderebbe da una sicura datazione *indipendente* della *Ecbasis*; in ogni caso, le *Federproben* non possono essere utilizzate allo scopo di stabilire un *terminus post quem*.

P. Klopsch, *Carmen de Philomela*, in *Festschrift Karl Langosch* (Darmstadt 1973) pp. 174 sgg., ha mostrato in un modo che mi pare convincente la conoscenza della *Ecbasis* da parte del poeta del *Carmen*, che egli è propenso a datare nel *decimo* secolo; tuttavia, Klopsch concede che la datazione erdmanniana della *Ecbasis* — 1039-1046 — è «vielleicht gerade noch möglich». (La datazione di H. Thomas, dunque, non sarebbe più possibile).

La nota più recente, di A.K. Bate, *Narrative Techniques in the Ecbasis Captivi*, in «Revue Canadienne d'Etudes Néerlandaises», Numéro Spécial, Mai 1983, pp. 3-8, che parla di «Vinay's suggestion that the work was written between 812 and 836» (*sic*, p. 8, n. 25), dimostra purtroppo che l'autore non ha capito ciò che scrisse Vinay.

[45] Mentre il tentativo di L. Gompf di interpretare la *Ecbasis* in una chiave esclusivamente monastica — *Die «Ecbasis cuiusdam captivi» und ihr Publikum*, in «Mittellateinisches Jahrbuch», VIII, 1973, pp. 30-42 — può illuminarne diversi aspetti, le allusioni del poeta al mondo della corte non dovrebbero essere trascurate. L'affermazione di Knapp, *Tierepos* (cit. n. 44), p. 38, «Gompfs Darstellung hat wohl alle Spekulationen, die *Ecbasis* sei eine politische Satire, hinfällig gemacht», è fuori posto, particolarmente in una collana dal titolo «Erträge der Forschung».

Mentre tanto del significato ulteriore — della «tropologia» — del poema rimane enigmatico, si può considerare più facilmente il senso autobiografico suggerito dall'inizio e dalla conclusione. È appunto nel suo aspetto autobiografico che la poesia è più affascinante e la percezione degli animali più individuale.

All'inizio, abbiamo una narrazione doppia della *ecbasis* del poeta, nella sua figura umana come in quella animale. L'inconsueto grecismo *ecbasis* può suggerire un'evasione (dal carcere) [46], oppure un viaggio fuori, una *Ausfahrt* come l'intraprendono gli eroi dei romanzi medievali; ma nel titolo è anche presente il senso tecnico di *ecbasis*, conosciuto da Servio, che significa una digressione poetica. Il poeta presenta l'opera come la sua penitenza, espiando nella sua maturità le frivolezze inquiete della sua gioventù, tentando di recuperare il tempo perduto. Eppure qui si nasconde un'ironia, perché il poeta-protagonista, eroe e vittima, vagabondo e vitellino, è abbozzato con simpatia, anche se si burla di sé stesso: non c'è nessuna condanna schietta dei suoi impulsi giovanili; tutto è equivoco:

Confiteor culpam: mendosam profero cartam.
(Confesso la mia colpa: porgo un libro bugiardo).

Era proprio una colpa offrire un tal racconto favoleggiato, invece di confessioni veraci, come quelle di sant'Agostino? O forse per questo poeta favoleggiare era il modo più individuale e autentico di confessarsi? Anche questo, lo lascia aperto.

In propria persona ricorda la claustrofobia — nel senso più letterale — dei suoi giorni studenteschi:

Un giorno ero seduto nel modo consueto,
guardavo la gente intraprendere le cure comuni,
ammucchiare il frumento nei grandi granai,
mentre degli altri visitavano i campi, e poi le viti dilette,
degli altri ancora trasportavano destramente il raccolto,
non solo ai monaci, che conservano i misteri della Legge,
ma anche ai pellegrini, accattoni e orfani;
vidi tutti gli altri compiere le loro cure,
io solo ero vuoto, rinchiuso nel mio carcere claustrale...
non potevo dire cosa ribolliva nella mia mente silenziosa,
ero come un tronco sterile, al pari di legna bruciata,
e come un vitello misero, tanto spesso legato al palo:

---

[46] Qui possiamo pensare sia al chiostro dell'inizio del poema, sia alla tana del lupo della conclusione. Cfr. M. Wehrli, *Formen mittelalterlicher Erzählung* (Zurigo 1969), p. 118.

proprio come quel vitello, impastoiato dalle redini dei padri,
voglio tessere la sua storia — il filo non è semplice [47].

Come nella lirica d'amore medievale la contemplazione del mondo esteriore può rivelare all'uomo o alla donna innamorata l'intensità della sua inquietudine e vuotezza interna, così questo «campo pieno di gente» (*feeld ful of folk*) [48] diventa uno specchio desolato per il giovane scolaro solitario, contemplativo riluttante. È proprio questo sguardo verso il mondo attivo che detta la sua evasione dal chiostro, un'evasione che in primo luogo procede nella trasformazione poetica: il mondo favoloso si apre per lui, lo studente che è *come* un vitello incatenato diventa quel vitello — nella sua fuga, raggiunge il regno degli animali. Eppure ci accorgiamo ben presto che questa è una metamorfosi del regno umano; a poco a poco si rivela come il mondo interiore del poeta stesso. (Come disse l'Eriugena, tutti gli animali sono nell'uomo). Vediamo come il poeta entra nella sfera immaginata (anche la data misteriosa che sceglie per il suo ingresso, data molto dibattuta dagli eruditi — la luna piena di Pasqua, Aprile 812 — ha la precisione onirica della fiaba):

Il vitello era rinchiuso a casa, afflitto perché il suo collo era legato,
non c'era gioia fuori, c'era la pressione del dolore dentro di lui —
ancora più, gli mancava la compagnia della madre.
Triste, geme assai, sospira di tutto cuore,
alza il volto verso il cielo, e invoca Gesù...
Si preoccupa dell'arte di scappare, per poter saltare dappertutto,
mastica, lecca, e finalmente scioglie le redini;
salta fuori ed esulta, pesta i teneri piedi sulla terra,

---

[47] *Ecbasis*, 50-58, 64-68:
Namque die quadam consueto more sedebam,
Inspexi quosdam generalem sumere curam,
Grandia triticeum cumulare per horrea fructum;
Illos post segetes dilectas visere vites,
Illos collectis sollertes esse vehendis
Non solis monachis, qui servant mistica legis,
Immo peregrinis, mendicis atque pupillis;
Per sibi commissas reliquos discurrere curas,
Me vero vacuo, claustrali carcere septo...
Dicere non poteram, tacita quod mente coquebam.
Ceu truncus sterilis lignis equabar adustis
Ac misero vitulo sudibus quam sepe ligato:
Illi consimilis patrum frenatus habenis,
Cuius et historiam non simplo stamine texam.
[48] William Langland, *Piers Plowman*, Prologo, 17.

sopprime il suo muggito, entra nei prati verdeggianti.
Allora gli è concessa una libertà più sfrenata,
se preferisce salire il sentiero destro o sinistro,
riposarsi o continuare il suo lavoro [49].

Questo mondo di animali è evidentemente cristiano: spesso i
suoi abitanti pregano; più tardi, gli animali meditano sulla Passione
e celebrano la Pasqua. Nell'espressione di Giovanni Scoto, sono animali e non-animali. Da ogni parte ci sono anche degli accenni a significati allegorici, però essi non sono specificati. La madre, la cui pre-
senza manca al vitello, potrebbe ricordarci Sapientia, o Ecclesia, ma
nessuna interpretazione fissa è stata imposta. Cosa significa il sentiero destro del vitello, in confronto all'ozioso sinistro? Ho l'impressione
che l'autore intenda la poesia, piuttosto che la vita monastica — ma
non ce lo dice.

Il vitello nella sua libertà entra in una selva e incontra la guardia
forestale, il lupo che è anche un eremita, affamato dalla sua lunga
ascesi. Accorgendosi del fatto che egli stesso sarà divorato come *victi-
ma paschalis* del lupo, il vitello prega Giove, chiedendo perdono e
promettendo, se sarà liberato, di ringraziare gli dei (*divi*) —

> *His et pro meritis dabitur caper omnibus aris!*

(E per questa protezione un capro sarà sacrificato su ogni altare!)

Cioè, il vitello si risolve ad immolare dei capri, proprio come il
lupo si è deciso ad immolarlo. L'ironia di quel verso — adattato dalla
caricatura prudenziana dei riti dionisiaci nel *Contra Symmachum* [50]
— come delle altre allusioni pagane, serve ad indicare che il lupo, ed
anche gli altri animali introdotti nel corso del poema, sono in un cer-

---

[49] *Ecbasis*, 78-82, 88-94:
  Clauditur ille domi lugens sibi colla ligari;
  Gaudia nulla foris, intus pressura doloris,
  Et quod plus istis, absunt consorcia matris.
  Triste sat ingemuit, cordis suspiria traxit,
  Erigit ad celum facies atque invocat Iesum. ...
  Nititur arte fuge, quo possit currere late,
  Masticat, lingit, tandem sic lora resolvit,
  Prosilit et plaudit, tenero terram pede tundit,
  Mugitum reprimit, vernantia prata revisit.
  Concessa est pecori libertas laxior illi,
  Scandere seu levo malit seu tramite dextro,
  Sumere seu requiem seu continuare laborem.
[50] Prudenzio, *Symm.*, I, 129 (His nunc pro meritis Baccho caper omnibus aris).

to senso aspetti della natura del vitello, oppure del poeta stesso. Come dice il lupo: «Quando disprezzò la sua stalla, errò nella nostra caverna» [51]; e alla fine del poema, il poeta-vitello si accomiata con il verso «Irato, feroce, con denti digiuni» (*Iratus pariter, ieiunis dentibus acer*), che Orazio non aveva applicato a un vitello, bensì a un *vehemens lupus* umano [52].

I personaggi che il vitello incontra — il lupo santarello e crudele, il piccolo riccio vanaglorioso, la lontra, pietosa e intelligente ma alla fine vigliacca, e gli altri che il lupo dipinge nella sua propria favola — la pantera mondana, la volpe ipocrita, ironica e spietata, l'usignolo la cui pietà emotiva oscilla fra eccessi di gioia e di dolore — questi sono gli uomini e le donne [53] del mondo del poeta, e ad un tempo aspetti del suo io interiore. La base poetica è la percezione di connaturalità, l'assimilazione di tipi umani agli animali. Ma questa assimilazione dà origine ad una sottigliezza che si estende oltre i tipi agli individui, perché in tutto il poema i personaggi alternano continuamente le loro *personae* umane e animalesche: il poeta ci lascia vedere le sue creazioni con e senza le loro maschere di animali. Dunque la *tropologia* — tutto ciò che significa il comportamento degli animali in termini umani — non è forzata: il contenuto umano approfondisce quello favoleggiato e ne risulta approfondito. Così, per esempio, il vitello, prigioniero nella tana del lupo, ad un tratto lo abborda umanamente, dicendo:

> Sono un giovanotto imberbe, un vagabondo da Toul,
> confesso il mio peccato — l'errore giovanile mi opprime.
> Sono colpevole per questo: rifiutai di ubbidire al mio professore [54].

Un momento più tardi, quando il riccio e la lontra intravvedono

---

[51] *Ecbasis*, 193 (Dum sprevit stabulum, nostrum divertit ad antrum).

[52] *Ecbasis*, 1228 = Orazio, *Ep.*, II, 2, 29.

[53] Vale la pena di sottolineare che *Vosagina canis* (329) è una cagna, e che per il poeta l'unicorno, che canta *voce puellari* (587), è femminile. Per lui anche *vulpes* e *philomena* sono femminili non soltanto nel senso grammaticale ma come personaggi — la volpe, per esempio, è *regina* (434). Non posso seguire Gompf (cit. n. 45), che, pensando esclusivamente all'ambiente monastico, voleva vedere in tutte queste allusioni degli scherzi omosessuali; le allusioni indicano piuttosto l'apertura del poeta al mondo cortese fuori del monastero.

[54] *Ecbasis*, 124-126:
> Inberbis iuvenis, Tullensis discolus urbis,
> Peccatum fateor, iuvenilis me gravat error.
> Hoc reus existo, nolens parere magistro.

il vitello, il poeta scrive, in un modo rivelatore, «quando mi guardano» (*ut me conspiciunt*, invece di *ut vitulum conspiciunt*) [55].

L'opera diviene più complessa: il poeta aumenta la sua galleria di creature, e fa della sua favola personale, del vitello fuggito, il telaio per un'altra favola, in cui il lupo racconta la storia tradizionale del leone ammalato, ebalorandola liberamente, con la descrizione di tutte le cerimonie pasquali eseguite dagli animali. Dai materiali più eterogenei e refrattari — la doppia favola, i riti pasquali, e la lingua poetica gravata di espressioni oraziane e prudenziane — questo poeta crea una testimonianza personale: ripensa il mondo animale come la sua propria esperienza — di abbazia e corte, scuola e campagna; per lui, esso diventa lo specchio totale in cui il vitello viene a riconoscere la sua natura, e il poeta a trovare la sua vocazione di scrittore.

È spesso stato osservato quante scene del romanzo *Ruodlieb* mettano in evidenza degli animali, e con quanta vivacità questi animali siano presentati; in particolare, è questo il tema di un bel saggio di Max Wehrli, «Ruodlieb und die Tiere» [56]. Però l'evocazione poetica di questi animali è quasi sempre stata interpretata come se si trattasse di dipinti deliziosi senza fine ulteriore: come afferma il Wehrli, «ist nirgends bei den Tierszenen eine symbolische Bedeutung erkennbar; vielmehr scheint die Darstellung genrehaft sich selbst zu genügen» [57]. Vorrei modificare quel giudizio, dopo una considerazione di alcuni momenti nel poema che concernono gli uccelli, momenti che non vedo in nessun modo come autosufficienti: piuttosto, essi tendono continuamente verso i valori e le relazioni umane su cui medita il poeta; sono la sua comprensione e celebrazione della connaturalità fra uccelli e uomini. Qui, come nelle sue rappresentazioni di animali, il poeta ci lascia capire immaginativamente l'idea sulla quale l'Eriugena aveva ragionato — che tutte le qualità degli animali furono create nell'uomo.

Il frammento XI di *Ruodlieb* si apre con un constrato fra due gruppi di uccelli — gracchi e stornelli:

Poi i gracchi mangiano abbastanza e danno cibo alla loro nidiata.
Quando qualcuno offre loro briciole attraverso le aperture della
   gabbia,
presto vi ricorrono, becco aperto,
afferrando avidamente ciò che ciascuno può attingere.

---

[55] Cfr. le fini osservazioni di G. Misch, *Geschichte der Autobiographie* (4 voll. in 8, Francoforte 1949-1969), II, ii, p. 469, e I, i, p. 59.

[56] *Op. cit.* (n. 46), pp. 127-139.

[57] Ibid., p. 135.

Così fra poco tutti si abituano a farlo ben presto.
In seguito, infatti, se lo sportello si apre,
si appollaiano sulle mani e prendono ciò che è dato loro,
e quando sono sazi e lisci per l'esser stati accarezzati,
presto gareggiando entrano nella gabbia spontaneamente,
e lisciandosi le penne col becco, seduti,
sono così lieti che non tacciono tutta la giornata.
Per la figlia della castellana questo diventa un divertimento delizioso,
benché tutto di questo genere sia senza attrattiva per i vecchi.
Niente becchime e niente acqua nella gabbia
degli stornelli: invece si pensava che la fame li obbligasse ad am-
    mansirsi
e a chiedere bocconi attraverso le aperture —
cosa che dapprima i vecchi genitori rifiutano del tutto.
Quando non danno niente alla loro nidiata, i giovani li lasciano
e vengono presto, becco aperto, a coloro che porgono un dito.
Una maestra competente è scelta per la direzione di loro, per insegnare
    loro
a recitare «Pater» e «noster» nel nostro modo,
fino a «qui es in caelis», con «lis, lis lis» triplicato:
che Sorella Stornella insegni loro a ripetere «canite, canite»
— i giovani l'imparano prima dei vecchi [58].

[58] *Ruodlieb*, XI, 1-24:
Tunc sibimet comedunt satis et pullis tribuerunt.
Cum per aperturas in domate quis sibi micas
Prebet, mox illo concurrebant adhiando,
Captantes avide quod quit contingere cuique:
Sic consuefacte sunt post modicum cito cuncte.
Quin post, ostiolum sibi cum fieret patefactum,
In manibus resident, quod eis datur accipiebant,
Dumque fiunt sature, leniendo manuque polite,
Doma sua sponte certatim mox subierunt,
Et componendo rostris pennas, residendo,
Sic gaudendo diem quod non siluere per omnem.
Oblectamentum fit herili deliciosum,
Cum nimis insuave senibus sit tale quid omne.
Pabula nulligena vel limpha stat in domicella
Sturnorum, sed eos duxere fame domitandos,
Ut per aperturas poscant escas sibi dandas —
Quod primo veteres nimium renuere parentes.
Cum pullis non dant, has illi deseruerunt;
Qui digitum prebent, his illi mox adhiabant.
Eligitur sciola super hos doctura magistra
Nostratim fari «Pater» et «noster» recitare,
Usque «qui es in celis» — lis lis lis triplicatis —
Staza soror, «canite, canite» doceat geminare,
Quod pulli discunt, veteres quam discere possent.

Nessun dettaglio, credo, è stato scelto solo per il suo valore descrittivo. Al poeta interessa di esplorare le diverse connotazioni del concetto di «domare». I gracchi, quando li si imbecca, dapprima afferrano il cibo *avide*, ma gradualmente, per mezzo del costume (*consuefacte*), si fanno docili e sottomessi. Se non hanno la cura di dover cercare il loro becchime, diventano così dolci che si lasciano accarezzare, ritornano a casa con allegrezza, pensano a far decoroso il loro aspetto, e hanno una gioia continua, una gioia che si esprime nel loro canto. A poco a poco si acculturano al mondo cortese. Tutte queste tappe sono un'immagine implicita del progresso *umano* nella cortesia; con l'ultimo dettaglio, che la loro gioia e canto continuo incanta la giovane donna aristocratica ma non incanta i vecchi, abbiamo più che mai il senso che, come in Provenza nel secolo successivo, *joi, jovens*, e la lirica sono inseparabili in questo ideale di *cortezia*.

Gli stornelli, invece, non sono così istintivamente adatti alla vita cortese. Sono meno docili, e si avanzeranno per chiedere il becchime solo se hanno fame; per loro la sottomissione non è facile. Ancora a differenza dei gracchi, non pensano spontaneamente alle necessità della loro covata. Eppure anche loro hanno il dono di poter imparare una lingua, magari una preghiera, benché il poeta ci lasci incerti se questa termini con una melisma (*lis lis lis*) o con puro balbettamento. Con *Staza soror* (Sorella Stornella) egli pare quasi anticipare la sensibilità di san Francesco. Fra gli stornelli, il poeta contrasta i giovani e i vecchi: i *veteres... parentes* rifiutano la sottomissione (la frase evoca con premeditazione Adamo ed Eva nella sfera umana); però i giovani possono imparare rapidamente, e divengono felici nell'imparare. Di nuovo *jovens* è sottolineato.

Sono dunque i giovani soprattutto che sono la fonte dell'ottimismo di questo poeta — nel regno degli uccelli e implicitamente in quello umano. Gli esseri che sono giovani e *farouches* (e forse anche avidi e egocentrici) possono essere resi lieti e deliziosi, dilettandosi l'un l'altro e dilettando il mondo; possono diventare sottomessi e rispettosi dei sentimenti altrui.

Non è per caso che un momento più tardi il poeta evoca la danza della giovane coppia aristocratica — il nipote dell'eroe e la fanciulla (*Herilis*) — come i movimenti di due uccelli. E nelle scene successive vediamo come anche loro, così pieni della gioia della giovinezza, imparano a farsi reciprocamente sottomessi e riguardosi. Questo poeta, mentre non dimentica i *veteres... parentes*, è anche convinto che una felicità terrena è possibile, che può essere raggiunta attraverso il progresso nella gentilezza, per mezzo di natura e di cultura; infatti, una gran parte del suo poema si preoccupa di adombrare il fine che più tardi Dante avrebbe chiamato «la felicità di questa vita, che consiste nell'esplicazione delle proprie capacità, raffigurato nel paradiso terrestre» [59]. Il poeta dell'undicesimo secolo evoca quella felicità umana nella sua presentazione di uccelli — la evoca in una maniera simbolica — per mezzo di un simbolismo che rimane sempre implicito e non comporta nessuna allegoria [60].

Mentre gli uccelli possono riassumere la felicità terrena (nel *Ruodlieb* come nella lirica d'amore dell'epoca), possono anche dare un'intimazione del secondo paradiso, il celeste, che, per citare di nuovo la *Monarchia*, è la «felicità della vita eterna, consistente nel godimento della visione di Dio». Per lo Pseudo-Dionigi gli uccelli potevano essere immagini degli angeli; per i commentatori altomedievali della Genesi, come abbiamo visto, gli uccelli erano spesso immagini delle anime umane che hanno il volo più vicino al cielo. La spiegazione più ricca di quell'immagine ch'io conosca si trova fuori della poesia occidentale, nell'epopea mistica, *La lingua degli uccelli (Mantiq uttair)*, del poeta persiano Fariduddin Attar, che scriveva verso il 1200 [61]. Egli dipinge un'assemblea di uccelli, in cui l'upupa incita gli altri ad accompagnarla in un viaggio lungo e pericoloso, per cercare il re leggendario degli uccelli, il Simurgh, che è la fonte inconoscibile di tutta la creazione. Molti uccelli trovano un pretesto per non andare: l'usignolo dice che è troppo vincolato all'amore mortale, l'amore di una rosa; il pappagallo dice che gli basta bere l'acqua della vita; il pavone desidera tornare al paradiso terrestre; l'anatra dice che non vuol lasciare l'acqua. A questi e a tutti gli altri che parlano, l'upupa risponde con *exempla*, per convincerli a rischiare il viaggio malgrado tutto. Finalmente la *queste* è intrapresa, passando attraverso sette vallate (che sono allegorie di sette aspetti dell'esperienza mistica); ma fra

---

[59] *Monarchia*, III, xv, 7.

[60] Per il significato tradizionale dell'uccello nella gabbia, cfr. A. Grabar, *Un thème de l'iconographie chrétienne: l'oiseau dans la cage*, in «Cahiers archéologiques», XVI (1966), pp. 9-16: «Tout compte fait, en ce qui concerne les figurations chrétiennes de l'oiseau en cage, il s'agit partout d'un symbole de l'âme enfermée dans la prison du corps... L'oiseau qui sort de la cage... figure l'âme qui s'élève au-dessus des contraintes du corps» (pp. 15-16). Più vicina al *Ruodlieb* è la concezione rinascimentale descritta da C. Schlumbohm: «Das Frohlocken des Vogels in der Gefangenschaft... ist aus christlicher Sicht Ausdruck der *laetitia spiritualis* oder *coelestis*» (*Rabelais' «Isle Sonante» und das Sinnbild des Vogels im Käfig*, in *Natura loquax*, ed. W. Harms, H. Reinitzer [Mikrokosmos, vol. VII], Francoforte 1981, p. 207).

[61] Per i dettagli seguenti sul poema di Attar, ho utilizzato soprattutto H. Ritter, *Das Meer der Seele* (Leiden 1955), pp. 8-18; ho consultato anche il capitolo dedicato ad Attar in H. Corbin, *Avicenne et le récit visionnaire* (Parigi 1954), I, sez. 18, e la traduzione dell'epopea in prosa inglese, di C.S. Nott: *The Conference of the Birds* (Londra 1954).

i molti uccelli che la cominciano, solo trenta arrivano alla corte reale del Simurgh. Il «climax» del poema dipende da un gioco di parole: il nome divino, Simurgh, è omonimo di *si-murgh*, che significa «trenta uccelli». Dunque, «quando guardano il Simurgh, vedono se stessi, e quando guardano se stessi, vedono il Simurgh, e quando guardano ambedue, vedono solo l'uno, Simurgh».

Alla fine quell'uccello divino esorta gli altri: «Perdetevi in me per ritrovarvi di nuovo in me». Dopo centomila eoni, gli uccelli furono restaurati a se stessi, e entrarono nello stato di «sussistenza dopo la dissoluzione» [62].

Questo è l'equivalente, presso il poeta persiano, di quell'adempimento del *reditus* che Giovanni Scoto aveva descritto. Per Giovanni Scoto, proprio come per Attar, il completamento della connaturalità fra il mondo umano e quello animale si realizza in Dio. L'Eriugena diede all'occidente l'elaborazione più splendida di quel concetto. Comunque, è forse possibile vedere almeno un'anticipazione di esso già agli inizi del pensiero cristiano, nel passo in cui Clemente di Alessandria dipinge Cristo come il vero Orfeo. Per Clemente, il vero Orfeo è colui che doma le creature che sono selvagge per natura, e colui il cui canto raduna e armonizza l'universo. Se il poeta di *Ruodlieb* ci mostra la domazione di ogni genere di creatura, Giovanni Scoto (e, nella sua tradizione, Attar) ci mostra come le creature attingono l'armonia cosmica e vi sono radunate.

[62] Cfr. H. Ritter, *op. cit.* (n. 61), pp. 17-18.

8

HERMES AND THE SIBYLS:
CONTINUATIONS AND CREATIONS *

In 1838 Jacob Grimm, most fecund and penetrating of medievalists, indicated some of the reasons why it was vital to study medieval Latin literature:

> People have been ready to disprize it, without even fully getting to know it. Almost invariably, it has been tolerated only insofar as its poetic art seemed to come nearer to that of classical Latin; yet what should be given prominence are precisely those elements that most distanced it from the classical and led it on to paths of its own... Throughout the Middle Ages the destinies of vernacular diction interact with and confront the influences of the Latin.

The words come from Grimm's prologue to his edition of a group of early medieval Latin poems — epic, romance, beast-fable, lyric, and novella [1]. But his plea for a more steady concern with this literature did not find an institutional echo for another half-century: it was not till 1888 that, for the first time, the University of Munich allowed Ludwig Traube to lecture on the Latin literature of the Middle Ages. It was an auspicious beginning. Today, a century later, Germany has some twenty established Chairs devoted to the subject, and Italy rivals it, with twenty or more.

In England, though it has had outstanding scholars in many areas that feature medieval Latin texts — historical and hagiographic, philosophical and scientific — medieval Latin literature has been far slower to win a fuller formal recognition. It is particularly apt that this should come about in Cambridge, which was the first university in the country to organise any explicit teaching in the field. When

---

* Inaugural Lecture Delivered 9 March 1990 (Cambridge University Press, 1990).

[1] *Lateinische Gedichte des X. und XI. Jh.*, hrsg. von Jac. Grimm und Andr. Schmeller (Göttingen 1838), pp. v-vi. (The "Vorrede", pp. v-liii, is by Grimm).

I came here, still a nervous beginner, this field had already begun to be cultivated by two genial and generous-spirited scholars: Frederick Raby, whose lucidly ordered historical surveys, *Christian Latin Poetry* and *Secular Latin Poetry in the Middle Ages*, showed a command of the entire European range of sources, and of secondary literature spanning from German to Catalan, that was rare in his generation; and Frederick Brittain, who for the first time assembled an anthology, *The Medieval Latin and Romance Lyric*, designed to show that interdependence of Latin and vernacular which Jacob Grimm had perceived. Yet Raby came to medieval Latin poetry from history, Brittain from Romance languages. A formation in medieval Latin literature, such as a number of Continental universities could offer, was unknown in the Cambridge — or the England — of their youth.

Given the long tradition of systematic teaching of medieval history, palaeography, and other cognate disciplines, this earlier neglect is surprising. For the Latin literature written throughout Europe between the late classical period and the humanists is one of the world's major literatures, and one of the most variegated. At the same time, the sheer wealth of what survives, and the relative lateness with which specific studies began, mean that this is still one of the less charted European literatures, one where an almost excessive number of discoveries is yet to be made, and where heights of individual artistic achievement remain to be recognised and assessed in nearly every genre, in poetry, drama and prose. Ideally, my preferred method for illustrating this would be to look at one or two such high achievements with you in detail, suggesting approaches to interpretation and criticism. Yet this would also involve confronting many textual minutiae, which can be laborious, however exciting the insights to which they may lead. So I have chosen to focus rather on a wider question, of imaginative or thematic history. Here one can present a certain amount of evidence without becoming too enmeshed in philological detail, and still show something of the incomparable contribution that studying medieval Latin writings can make to the comprehending of Europe's past.

Outstanding among the pre-Christian personae who captured the imagination of the Christian Middle Ages were Hermes Trismegistus ("thrice-greatest Hermes") — a legendary sage of vast antiquity and superhuman wisdom — and the Sibyls: divinely inspired seeresses who had recorded truthful prophecies since before the fall of Troy. To introduce the medieval Hermes and the medieval Sibyls, let me begin with a place where some of their utterances were linked with particularly memorable visual images: the pavement of the Duomo at Siena.

The marble pavement shows ten Sibyls — two rows of five — portrayed by several artists in the years 1482-3. The Delphic Sibyl, the first on the right on entering the Duomo, is "she of whom Chrysippus wrote in his book on divination". She has transformed the renowned Delphic precept — Γνῶθι σαυτόν, "know yourself" — into: "know your God himself, who is the Son of God". Three Sibyls (the Tiburtine, Erythraean, and Cumaean) prophesy the Nativity — the Cumaean (Figure 1), "whom Vergil mentioned in the *Fourth Eclogue*", with the Vergilian verses which, since the time of Emperor Constantine, had often been applied to the coming of Christ to earth:

The last era of the Cumaean prophecy has come,
the great sequence of ages is born anew;
now the Virgin returns, the golden age returns,
now the firstborn is sent down from high heaven[2].

In her right hand the Sibyl of Cumae holds the golden bough, that she showed to Charon, to take Aeneas across the Styx; under her left arm she tucks the three volumes of her collected works which she sold to King Tarquin for the price of nine; the six that she destroyed lie at her feet.

The Persian Sibyl is depicted foretelling Christ's miracle of the loaves and fishes. Three other Sibyls — the Samian, Hellespontic, and Libyan — predict moments of Christ's passion. The dark-skinned Libyan Sibyl (Figure 2), veiled and garlanded, who was "mentioned by Euripides", holds a book open at the words: "Receiving blows, he shall be silent, he shall offer his innocent back to the scourge". Her tablet says: "He shall come into iniquitous hands; with their polluted hands they will slap God; he, wretched and ignominious, will offer the wretched hope".

The Cimmerian Sibyl [3] foretells the resurrection: "After a three-days' sleep he shall end death's fateful power". Finally one Sibyl, the Phrygian (Figure 3), "she who made her vaticination at Ancyra", has a book whose open pages proclaim "I alone am God, there is no other God", and a tablet that prophesies Doomsday. Below the tablet three naked figures — a woman, a suppliant man, and perhaps a child — peer out of their grave, waiting to be judged.

Five years after the Sibylline images were completed, the artist

---

[2] *Ecl.* 4, 4-7.

[3] The artist has inscribed *Cumaea* instead of *Cimmeria* (cf. the variant *cimmeam* for *cimmeriam* at Lactantius, *Epit.* 5, 1).

Giovanni di Stefano, who had been responsible for at least two of these, created the more ambitious and mysterious picture (Figure 4) of "Hermes Mercurius Trismegistus, contemporary of Moses", which is set in a key place in the larger design: it is the first image to meet the eye as one passes through the main portal of the cathedral. Hermes is credited with knowledge of the divine Father and Son: the tablet he holds in his left hand says: "God the Creator of all made a visible God as his companion; he made him the first and only one, delighted in him, and greatly loved his own Son, who is called the holy Word". Cicero had told that a Hermes who was worshipped by a people in Arcadia gave the Egyptians their *leges et litteras* [4]. It is these that Hermes is here offering with his right hand: "You Egyptians, take the letters and the laws".

The identity of the two figures whom he addresses has been much debated. Does the one in Oriental robes represent the native Egyptians, the other, in classical garb, the Greeks in Egypt? [5] Or is the turbaned figure, as Frances Yates suggested, none other than Moses, Hermes' alleged contemporary? [6] If this is right, the notion that Hermes was the giver, the instructor of Moses, would be an extreme instance, not just of ecumenicism, but of exalting pagan wisdom over biblical. And it is at least possible that this was meant. In the Acts of the Apostles (7, 22), Stephen speaks of Moses "nurtured by all the wisdom of the Egyptians", and this thought could well underlie the Siena image. So, too, in the years of its execution, Marsilio Ficino was celebrating Hermes not only as the fount of inspiration of Pythagoras and Plato, but as a sage even greater than the Old Testament prophets.

At all events, the central meaning in Siena is clear. Out of every region of the known world, ten pagan women, of inspired wisdom, bring their prophetic intuitions of Christian history, from the birth of Christ to the Judgement, while the most ancient and commanding of pagan philosophers reveals to mankind, on the one hand letters and laws, and on the other the first principles of Christian theology — Father and Logos, invisible and visible God. The pictures proclaim the universality of that double revelation in space and in time.

When we turn to the traditions that culminate in Siena, our first impression may well be, overwhelmingly, of continuities rather than creations. The names of the ten Sibyls, for instance, and every

---

[4] N.D. 3, 22, 56 (cit. Lactantius, *Inst.* 1, 6, 2).
[5] Cf. E. Iversen, *The Myth of Egypt...* (Copenhagen 1961), pp. 61, 153.
[6] *Giordano Bruno and the Hermetic Tradition* (London 1964), p. 42.

historical-biographical detail inscribed on their portraits, stem from a single passage in an early fourth-century work, *The Divine Institutions*, by the African Church Father Lactantius. Nor was Lactantius inventing these details: he was citing a lost work *On Things Divine* by the Roman polymath Varro, from the first century B.C. [7] For fifteen centuries these names and this information were preserved unchanged.

With the utterances ascribed to the Sibyls in Siena, the matter is more complicated. Those of seven of the Sibyls can likewise be found in diverse parts of Lactantius' book. Here his citations come from a collection of *Sibylline Oracles*, composed in Greek hexameters [8]. These *Oracles* were widely held to be holy and venerably old. After all, the Erythraean Sibyl had prophesied the fall of Troy, and the Persian Sibyl was believed to be more ancient still. Yet today we know that even the oldest parts of the extant *Oracles* go back only to the second century B.C.; later they were continually reworked, added to and interpolated, by Jews and early Christians alike, in the service of their theologies. The last additions to the Greek text (which include prophecies of Islamic conquests) were made long after Lactantius, in the seventh century A.D.

Similarly with the writings ascribed to Hermes. These were developed under the early Empire, by Greek-speaking Egyptians, who diffused them as works far older than Plato's (when in fact they drew on Plato freely, and were influenced by the more mystical aspects of the Platonism of their own day). Hermes' proclamation in Siena is adapted from the *Asclepius*, the Hermetic work best known in the Latin West [9]. It is a dialogue in which Hermes, the protagonist, re-

---

[7] *Inst.* 1, 6, 8-12.

[8] Delphica: *SO* 8, 329, *Inst.* 4, 6, 5; Cimmeria: *SO* 8, 312-14, *Inst.* 4, 19, 10; Persica: *SO* 8, 275-8, *Inst.* 4, 15, 24; Lybica (book): *SO* 8, 290-2 (*om.* 291), *Inst.* 4, 18, 15-17; (tablet) *SO* 8, 287-9 and 257, *Inst.* ibid. and 4, 16, 17; Hellespontica: *SO* 8, 303-6, *Inst.* 4, 18, 19 and 4, 19, 5; Phrygia (book): *SO* 8, 377, *Inst.* 1, 6, 16; (tablet) *SO* 8, 239-42 (*om.* 240) and 4, 41-6 (*om.* 44), *Inst.* 7, 16, 11; 20, 3; 23, 4; Samia: *SO* 6, 21-5, *Inst.* 4, 18, 20. In the *Institutions* the passages from the *Oracles* are cited in Greek, though Latin paraphrases were added in some early MSS. The lines drawn from *SO* 8 are translated very differently in the Latin rhythmic prose version of this book in MS Karlsruhe Aug. 182, s. IX in., fols. 33v-36v. Another Latin version of some of the words, based on Lactantius, can be found in Augustine, *Civ. Dei* 18, 23 (CC 48, 615).

[9] *Asclepius* 8 (*Corpus Hermeticum*, ed. Nock-Festugière, 2, 304 f). In the Siena inscription, *secundum* has become *secum*, and the wording is closer to Lactantius (*Inst.* 4, 6, 4, citing the Greek, and *Epit.* 37, 4, a Latin paraphrase) than to the extant Latin *Asclepius*. The Greek passage from *Poimandres* 12 (Nock-Festugière 1, 10),

veals his awesome grasp of the invisible chains that bind the cosmos. The words of the Erythraean and Tiburtine Sibyls in Siena, on the other hand, seem to come from no late-antique text, but from the most modern contribution to Sibylline studies, in the artists' own time — from a book by the Dominican Filippo Barbieri, published in Rome in 1481 [10].

What are the secrets behind this amazing continuity of motifs — from Varro, who dedicated his book to Julius Caesar, to the artists in Siena fifteen hundred years later? Do the ostensibly pagan Hermes and Sibyls survive so long merely because Lactantius and others had christianised them enough to make them innocuous? On the contrary, as I shall try to show, in medieval Latin poetry and thought the rôles of Hermes and the Sibyls could be freshly perceived and audaciously recreated, in ways that Lactantius could not have foreseen. Their *fortuna* is something rich and strange — no simple continuity.

But first let us pause briefly with Lactantius himself. No one before him, to my knowledge, brought Hermes and the Sibyls together as prime witnesses to Christian beliefs. Nor was anyone after him so obsessed with these mystical "pagans" — whom Lactantius cites far oftener and more extensively than he ever cites the Bible. What impelled him?

He had been trained as a rhetorician in Africa in the late third century, but Emperor Diocletian had summoned him to teach in Nicomedia, the new imperial capital in the East. In February 303, when Diocletian ordered the persecution of Christians — only two years before his abdication and death — Lactantius, who was a convert, had to relinquish his Chair. He lived and wrote in poverty for fourteen years, till another Emperor, Constantine, called him to Trier as tutor to his son.

---

often claimed as the source for Siena (e.g. by F. Ohly, *Schriften zur ma. Bedeutungsforschung,* Darmstadt 1977, p. 206), is only loosely similar.

[10] *Discordantiae nonnullae inter SS. Hieronymum et Augustinum:* cf. E. Mâle, *Quomodo Sibyllas recentiores artifices repraesentaverint* (Paris 1899), pp. 29-47. Note, however, that the prophecies Barbieri ascribes to the Erythraean and Tiburtine Sibyls were already current earlier: cf. M. Hélin, "Un texte inédit sur l'iconographie des Sibylles", *Revue Belge de philol. et d'hist.* 15 (1936) 349-66, at pp. 360, 36 f and 362, 17f; J. López Yepes, "Una 'Representación de las Sibilas'...", *Rev. Arch. Bibl. Mus.* 80 (1977) 545-67, esp. p. 560. But López's text is probably not, as he claims, a Sibyl-*play* ("*Ordo Sibillarum*", p. 562) — rather a set of *tituli* for a painting or monument. (The same holds of his "*Planctus Passionis*", ibid. p. 561). For the Erythraean Sibyl's words cf. also O. Holder-Egger, "Italienische Prophetieen des 13. Jhdts. I", *Neues Archiv* 15 (1890) 159.

Lactantius wrote in order to convert others, but his spirit was ecumenical. He longed to harmonise the speculations of the pagan past, the Jewish past, and his new-found Christian present. Yet there was something more personal, more moving too, about this highly-placed professor, suddenly dismissed and pauperised because of his convictions. Lactantius wrote, he says,

> in order to confirm what I say not from our [Christian and bibli-cal] writings but especially from those of others, in order to show that not only among us, but among those very people who persecute us, the truth... is kept safely sealed [11].

In the Hermetic and Sibylline texts (whose great age and integrity he never came to doubt), Lactantius found a conception of divinity of a severe grandeur that was alien to the polytheism of the world around him. He was convinced that Hermes and the Sibyls, followed in this by the greatest pagan poets and philosophers, recognised one God, one Spirit and ruler of all things. Hermes, whose testimony is "godlike" (*simile divino*), who, "even if he was human, was the most ancient and most learned in every kind of wisdom", called God *dominus* and *pater*, as Christians were to do; but for Hermes also "he is himself of himself and through himself", he is "the one who is, the nameless one" (ὁ ὢν ἀνώνυμος). So too a Sibyl called God "self-begotten", "unbegotten", and "uncreated" (αὐτογενής, ἀγέν-ητος, ἀποίητος); the Erythraean Sibyl, like Hermes, recognised the Logos as the Son of God; both saw the human being as made in the divine image.

With the more specific Sibylline prophecies of Christ's life and death, Lactantius does confront the question, could these be Christian forgeries, "counterfeited and composed by people of ours"? —

> Certainly (he replies) no one will think this who has read Cicero, Varro and the ancients, who mention the Erythraean Sibyl and the others from whose books we give these examples: those Roman authors died before Christ was born. Indeed I do not doubt that in former times these songs were held to be ravings, since no one understood them then... The Erythraean Sibyl herself says:

> > They will call the Sibyl insane and mendacious; but when all this comes to pass,

[11] *Inst.* 7, 25, 1. The Lactantian citations below are from *Inst.* 1, 6, 4; *Epit.* 4, 4; *Inst.* 1, 7, 13; 4, 15, 26-9. With the last passage compare Constantine's "Address to the assembly of the saints" 19, 1-3, ed. A. Kurfess, *Sibyllinische Weissagungen* (Munich 1951), pp. 210-12.

then you'll remember me, and no one then will call me
mad — I shall be called the great God's prophet.

We must not think too harshly of Lactantius' critical naiveness.
He could not order microfilms of the oldest Hermetic and Sibylline
manuscripts, from Alexandria or Rome, to check whether these already contained the archetypes of the Christian unconscious. And
even if he had a manuscript that looked very ancient, there was no
palaeographic handbook to help him decide whether it had been copied B.C. or A.D. Yet however recent his manuscripts, Lactantius
would also have known that a priestly caste could preserve revered
texts orally unchanged over centuries — even (as we know to be the
case with Vedic hymns) over millennia. We can see that Lactantius
was filled with just such reverence for his Sibyllina and Hermetica:
"These fragments I have shored against my ruins". Lactantius (like
Eliot) passionately wanted to save something of value from the
speculative tradition with which he had grown up — and this passion
will both have spurred his writing and inclined his judgement.

The way medieval authors perceived Hermes and the Sibyls was
influenced by Augustine even more than by Lactantius. (As a crude
quantitative indicator, *The City of God* is transmitted in some 400
manuscripts, Lactantius' *Institutions* in some 150). Augustine's attitude varies and is at times ambiguous, yet essentially he shows mocking hostility to Hermes but gives a measure of welcome to Sibyls.
Thus in an early work, *Contra Faustum*, he writes:

> If the Sibyl or Sibyls, Orpheus, and some Hermes or whoever
> (*nescio quis Hermes*), and other pagan *vates*... are alleged to have fore-
> told, or told, things true about the Son of God or the Father, this can
> indeed be of help for refuting pagan vanities, but is no reason for our
> embracing these authorities [12].

In *The City of God* Augustine, denouncing Hermes for his idolatry, also shows anger at claims such as Lactantius had made: Hermes
is neither as old nor as wise as Lactantius thought:

> Let no pagan people boast that their wisdom is more ancient than
> that of our patriarchs and prophets — not even the Egyptians... At
> the time of Moses' birth there was a great astrologer, Atlas, brother

[12] PL 42, 290. The Augustine citations below are from *Civ.
Dei* 18, 39 (CC 48, 634f); 18, 22 f (ibid. 613 f).

of Prometheus, maternal grandfather of the elder Hermes, whose grandson was Trismegistus.

To sustain his claim of the priority of Hebrew wisdom, Augustine here adopts a Patristic legendary chronology [13] that would have done a heathen mythographer proud.

Unlike Hermes, in Augustine's view, the Erythraean Sibyl speaks with such force against idolatry that "she seems to be among those who belong to the City of God". She is the one Sibyl about whom Augustine has no reservations. She was the contemporary of Romulus and of Hosea, eight centuries before Christ, but "wrote certain things that manifestly refer to Christ". Augustine's great bequest to medieval Sibylline traditions was his citation in *The City of God* (XVIII 23) of this Sibyl's poem about Judgement, *Iudicii signum*, from Book VIII of the *Oracles*. He had himself seen the original Greek lines, and the "Christ" acrostic — ΙΗΣΟΥΣ ΧΡΕΙΣΤΟΣ ΘΕΟΥ ΥΙΟΣ ΣΩΤΗΡ — that binds them. His Latin version cannot quite reproduce the full acrostic — nor can I in English, though I've managed JESUS in the first five verses and SOTER in the last. I shall cite these ten, to give at least an impression of this text:

Judgement's sign: the earth shall drip with sweat;
Everlastingly the King shall come from heaven, who
Shall be present to judge bodies and the world.
Unfaithful and faithful shall thus behold God
Sublime among the saints, at time's utmost limit...

Soon shall the trumpet send its mournful sound down from
On high, groaning at the outrage and the many pains.
The gaping earth shall reveal Tartarus' chaos.
Every king shall be assembled before the Lord; a
River of fire and sulphur shall fall from heaven.

From the late ninth century on we have a melody for the verses. It is notated in some fifty liturgical manuscripts all over Europe — from Limoges to Cordova to Beneventum.

Did the singer in the ninth or tenth century enact the Sibyl's rôle, or only sing it? Was the music performed by "a choirboy in womanly dress, wearing a robe with sleeves slit to the shoulders, richly embroidered in Oriental taste"? Did he "arrive at the cathedral... finely painted and mounted on a well-caparisoned horse, with a great retinue of children and drummers, psalteries, trumpets, tambourines

[13] Cf. Eusebius-Jerome, *Chronicon* 2, PG 19, 369; 374; 384.

and rebecs"? These are quotations from two much later descriptions of the performing of the Sibyl's song [14]. It is tempting to suppose that similar vitality of performance already existed in the earliest period, though about this we lack specific documentation.

The Sibyl's song also reached the Middle Ages by routes other than *The City of God*. At least two poets in seventh- or early eighth-century England, for instance, tried their hand at a fresh Latin translation from the Greek [15]. But much more influential than their work was an ugly pseudo-Augustinian sermon, *Against Jews, Pagans, and Arians*, that again included Augustine's text of the song. A part of this sermon, which focussed on the "blind" Jews who denied the Messiah's birth, was sometimes chanted as a lesson in the Christmas season [16]. The homilist refutes the Jews from their own Scriptures, summoning Old Testament prophets to repeat the utterances which Christians took to be foreshadowings of Christ. Isaiah says his piece — "Behold a Virgin shall conceive and shall bring forth a son" — and other prophets theirs. At the climax, "so that the foreheads of

---

[14] P. Aebischer, "Le 'Cant de la Sibil-la'", in his *Neuf études sur le théâtre médiéval* (Geneva 1972), pp. 17 f.

[15] One ("Iudicio tellus sudabit maesta propinquo") was edited by W. Bulst, *Zeitschrift für deutsches Altertum* 75 (1938) 105 f. The other, in MS Corpus Christi Cambridge 173, fol. 83v (II 27v), is unpublished. More than half the 25 verses (the last = *SO* 8, 241) are partly or wholly obliterated. The more fully legible ones at the opening and close are (slightly increasing those given in M. R. James, *Catalogue* 1, 400 f):

    83va Iudicii signum: sudavit rufada tellus
        et saecli veniet qui cuncta lavabit se coram
        celsus iudex orbemque probabit;   [verse incomplete, no gap MS]
        una deum cernent homines fidi atque infidi./
    83vb ....
        longe aberunt ⟨.....⟩ visenturque aedita nudi,
        ipsaque planities sternet montes, mare, campos,
        ventus tunc frustravit, spectavit navigia namque
        spumantes flu⟨v⟩ios ignis fontesque cremabit,
        salpix luctifera caelo tunc voce sonabit,
        adfore iam monstratur, erumnasque adfore saecli,
        loetiferumque chaus monstravit terra dehiscens.

The very rare *salpix* is a favourite word of Aldhelm's (R. Ehwald, *Aldhelmi Opera*, MGH, p. 697, lists 10 examples); so too Aldhelm uses *letifer* 15 times (ibid. p. 638). This version, like Bulst's, probably stems from the milieu of the disciples of Theodore and Hadrian.

[16] The lesson is ed. K. Young, *The Drama of the Medieval Church* (Oxford 1933) 2, 126-31, who also assembles the principal *Ordo prophetarum* texts, ibid. 2, 138-90, 458-62; the complete sermon is in *Opera Quodvultdeo tributa*, ed. R. Braun (CC 60, 225-58).

both Jews and pagans may be smashed by a single stone", the preacher adduces the Sibyl, who sings her prophecy, *Iudicii signum* (in some manuscripts of the lesson the melody has been inserted).

From the late eleventh century to the fourteenth, a Latin "play of the prophets" (*Ordo prophetarum*), deriving from this sermon, is known to have been performed at eight centres in northern Europe, and here again the climax was always the Sibyl's song [17]. In the play-texts, however, the hate-filled tone of the old sermon has gone. The playwrights' emphasis is far more on the marvel that long ago some divinely gifted Jews and pagans *had* seen, or foreseen, so much that Christians believe.

This is the way, too, that brilliant twelfth-century writers such as Peter Abelard and Thierry of Chartres approach the Hermetic and Sibylline texts. Augustine had been choosy, and seldom wholly at ease, about accepting any pagan premonitions of Christian beliefs. Lactantius had craved with all his heart to accept them — yet his acceptance included an element of political strategy, to win more converts to the Christian cause. Abelard and Thierry, by contrast, appropriate pagan texts so uninhibitedly that one can see why Abelard's enemy St Bernard, complaining to the Pope about the philosopher's attitude to Plato, wrote: "While Abelard sweats away to make Plato a Christian, he just proves himself a pagan" [18].

What moves Abelard most about the Sibyls is that these inspired teachers were women. Here Abelard reveals himself a full-blooded feminist (even if at other moments in his life and writing his feminism had some serious lapses). In his third letter to Heloise, he warmly praises womankind for some twenty-five pages. His thought moves from Mary Magdalen, "the apostle of the apostles" (*apostola apostolorum*), and Elizabeth and Anna, "the prophets of the prophets", to the first and greatest women who were blessed with exceptional gifts:

> If we extend this grace of prophecy to the pagans, let the *vates*, the Sibyl, come into our midst and tell what was revealed to her about Christ. If we compare all the male prophets, even Isaiah himself, with her... we shall see that in this grace a woman far surpasses men [19].

[17] *Pace* Aebischer (cit. n. 14, p. 20), even if only "un ou quelques vers" of the Sibyl's song are copied in play-texts, we should not assume that a mere fragment was sung: the verses copied are a cue for the complete song, so well known that it did not need writing out in full.

[18] *Sancti Bernardi Opera* 8, ed. J. Leclercq, H. Rochais (Rome 1977), p. 26.

[19] Ed. J. T. Muckle, *Mediaeval Studies* 17 (1955) 271 f. (On the authenticity of

Since she foretold even Christ's descent into the underworld, "she seems to surpass not only the prophets but the evangelists themselves, who wrote very little about that descent".

In the diverse redactions of his *Theologia*, Abelard assembled testimonies to the concept of the Trinity first from Hebrew prophets and then from pagan philosophers. In the last and fullest version of his book, he argues for the salvation in the Christian heaven of pagan sages who had lived long before Christ's birth. If someone were to object that they can't be saved without having believed in Christ, Abelard rejoins — how could one prove that they did not? For they saw that Christ was prophesied by a pagan woman, the Sibyl, far more clearly than by almost any Hebrew prophet.

When Abelard turns to the pagan philosophers who bear witness to Christian thought, he chooses to begin with Hermes:

> First let that most ancient and renowned among philosophers, Hermes, come forward, whom for his excellence they have even called a god.

(Note how different this moment of euhemerism is from the conventional hostile kind common among early Church Fathers: far from trying to dethrone Hermes by saying "he was only human", Abelard comes closer to the impulse of the authentic Euhemerus: "*this* is how he came to be thought of as divine").

Wherever the language of Hermes' utterances is not fully compatible with Christian formulations — as when he speaks of God *fashioning* his Son — Abelard blithely explains and harmonises, showing that the discrepancy is only verbal. After a long discussion of the world-soul, in which Abelard sees allusions to the Holy Spirit in Plato, Pythagoras, Cicero, Vergil and other pagans, "by way of a most beautiful imagery filled with hidden meaning", he suddenly becomes aware that all his witnesses so far have been men:

> But lest one of the sexes seem to be lacking... among those who outstrip the rest of mankind in wisdom, let the famous Sibyl also be brought on.

the letters, which has been challenged in various ways, see esp. the judicious assessment by D. Luscombe, "From Paris to the Paraclete: The Correspondence of Abelard and Heloise", *Proc. Brit. Acad.* 74 (1988) 247-83). The other Abelard passages below are from *Theologia "Scholarium"*, ed. E. M. Buytaert, C. J. Mews (CC CM 13, 363-400). When Abelard cites Hermes (p. 363) or the Sibyl (p. 398, and Muckle p. 271) from "Augustinus contra quinque haereses", this is the pseudo-Augustinian work ed. R. Braun (cit. n. 16) pp. 259-301.

Just before this, Abelard had cited St Augustine's dramatic contrast, in his *Confessions*, between Platonic books and Christian ones: for Augustine, however much these books may share intellectually, no Platonic book knows of Christ's incarnation or of his sacrificial death. Augustine hammered this in like a refrain: *Non ibi legi... non habent illi libri... non est ibi* — I did not read it there... those books don't have it... it is not there [20].

Abelard, by bringing in the Sibyl precisely at this moment, counters Augustine in a unique way. If the Platonists did not have this revelation, if even Vergil "perhaps was not conscious of what the Holy Spirit spoke in the Sibyl or in himself", there was a woman who knew still more: for, "in her prophesying, the Sibyl omitted neither the divinity nor the humanity of the Logos". With the Sibyl's oracles Abelard could answer Augustine positively: "I have read it there... those books do have it... it is there".

Thierry of Chartres, Abelard's contemporary, says little about Sibyls, but Hermes is one of his heroes. The reason I mention Thierry here is that in his *Treatise on the Six Works of Creation* [21], to evoke the profoundest aspects of cosmology, he summons both biblical and pagan authorities, as Abelard does, but reversing Abelard's order. For Thierry the Old Testament prophets do not have priority: in his individual variation on an *Ordo prophetarum*, Hermes is the first to affirm the Spirit which inheres in and governs the material universe; he is followed in this by Plato and Vergil. Only then are three biblical figures — Moses, David, and Solomon — introduced, to corroborate the insights of the three pagans. All of them truly perceived that divine power which Christians call "the Holy Spirit". With Thierry we come intellectually closest to Siena, to the Hermes who dominates the entrance to the cathedral.

So far I have chiefly stressed continuities in the Hermetic and Sibylline traditions; now I should like to illustrate some new creations. In diverse centuries we can observe medieval authors not just preserving the ancient traditions but inventing them. I do not mean simply rewriting Sibylline oracles, in order to make them "prophesy" events of the rewriter's time — though this was much in favour again from the tenth century onwards. I am thinking rather of a real imaginative renewal, where texts are freshly fabricated and attributed once again to Hermes, or to a Sibyl who flourished long before Christ (or even before the fall of Troy). I shall try briefly to evoke

[20] *Conf.* 7, 9, 13 f.
[21] Ed. N. M. Häring, *Commentaries on Boethius by Thierry of Chartres and his School* (Toronto 1971), pp. 553-75, at pp. 566 f.

two notable creations of this kind: a Sibylline text and a Hermetic one [22].

The first, a *Prophetia Sibyllae magae* in 136 verses, has been accessible since 1951, but has remained little known and little loved. Its editor indeed called it a "barbaric poem", and censured its "loose sequence of thought" [23]. Mindful of Jacob Grimm, I would suggest that "barbaric" be replaced simply by "unclassical". The poet's versification, though based on Roman hexameter composition, constantly transgresses the Roman norms. His (or her) verses are often hypermetric, often short; a few pentameters are interspersed here and there. There is an exceptional amount of lengthening of short syllables (not just at caesurae), and frequent hiatus. Yet I cannot see why the many departures from ancient prosody should necessarily be viewed as poetic blemishes. For me they are, in the first instance, precious pointers to where and when the *Prophetia* was composed. This, I suggest, was most probably seventh-century Spain — the only time and place I know where the surviving Latin hexameter verse shows numerous close parallels to this particular range of developments [24].

---

[22] The extracts cited from these two texts are edited afresh in the Appendix. For much of the translation from *Mundus origo*, I am indebted to Ursula Dronke.

[23] B. Bischoff (cit. App. p. 243), pp. 171, 168.

[24] This will be documented in detail in a new edition with extensive discussion of the poem, *Mundus origo mea est...*, that I am preparing for *Studi medievali*. Here I would only signal a few seventh-century Spanish Latin compositions that display notable metrical analogues to the Sibylline poem: "Pulcrifico radians mentis et vite febo" (ps-Fructuosus, s. VII², ed. M. C. Díaz y Díaz, *Hispania Sacra* 4 (1951) 142); "Crux alma gerit sanctorum corpora fratrum" (? Braulio, s. VII¹, ed. J. Vives, *Inscripciones cristianas*, Barcelona 1942, no. 272); and Vives nos. 281, 285-7, 313 f, 350. Even so outstandingly crafted a poem as the *Epitaphion Antoninae* (s. VII¹, ed. Díaz, *Anecdota Wisigothica* 1, Salamanca 1958, 47 f) contains metrical licences that cannot be explained in terms of *productio ob caesuram* or other traditionally recognised freedoms: e.g. 5 carā consortia plango 7 Nempe tuā merita 26 infestā vivis 28 nec parcīs ullis 29 Faucibŭs mortificis.

With all their metrical liberties, these Spanish Latin poets still show a degree of commitment to quantitative verse that suffices to demarcate them from the contemporary and slightly later writers of "rhythmic" or "Langobard" hexameters (and occasionally pentameters), who are discussed by W. Meyer, *Ges. Abh. zur mlat. Rythmik* (Berlin 1905-36) 1, 229-35; 3, 189-204; D. Norberg, *Introduction à l'étude de la versification latine médiévale* (Stockholm 1958) pp. 101-5; P. Klopsch, *Einführung in die mlat. Verslehre* (Darmstadt 1972) pp. 19-27.

Bischoff (cit. App., at p. 170) suggested that *Mundus origo* could "hardly be later than the fifth century", because of the poet's "pronounced Monarchianism". Yet it should be noted that among the three apparently Monarchian passages in the poem at least one is corrupt: at 20, *proprius* should read *propius* (cf. App. *ad loc.*), and this excludes a Monarchian sense. At 29 — if the text *Et proles ipsē pater* is cor-

As for the sequence of thought, I would see it not as loose but as calculatedly mysterious: the poet vividly conjures up the very quality and movement of Sibylline discourse, while remaining artistically in control. To show this fully will require a detailed commentary, including specific comparisons and contrasts with the poetry of the Greek *Oracles*. Today I can only signal a few of the moments I find most arresting. The *Prophetia* begins:

> The universe is my origin, my soul I have drawn from a star,
> My virgin body God has set trembling in every limb.
> ⟨I shall tell whatever God puts in my mouth,⟩
> if my abundant faith has had true insight into hallowed matter.
> Many a song my own singings have uttered within myself;
> the songs which I write, those God knows...
>
> In the beginning without end was God, originator of all,
> and he separated chaos away from friendly Night
> and ordered Day to stand out, and Night and Day
> to take turns with their luminaries and be moved with the stars,
> and by these the ages of the world should be renewed in their round.
> He poured a deluge over the earth, and a heavenly gift [25].
> And then, after God had tamed the waters with banks,
> the firstborn, born of his own name, from heavenly place
> descended to earth, human, as the child of a chaste virgin,
> wearing on royal neck a never-ending crown,
> and the Father himself approached closer to himself in that birth...

The Sibyl is pervaded by God's presence, and speaks what he bids her speak. Yet two elements here are not found in the Greek *Oracles*: the Platonic motif, that her soul comes from a star, and the stress on the active rôle of the Sibyl herself. She is no mere vehicle of divine utterance: she strives to rehearse the divine song that wells up within her.

This song is at first a cosmogony. It begins with another Platonic notion — the universe pre-exists as thought in the divine mind — and hints at a cosmic cycle, a renewal of the ages (a Stoic conception that is far from the book of Genesis). So too this Sibyl omits all men-

---

rect — and at 63, *Qui pater ipse sibi*, there are indeed Monarchian phrasings, but these must reflect expressions such as αὐτοπάτωρ in the poet's (direct or indirect) Greek sources (cf. Kurfess, cit. n. 11, p. 252). Moreover, Monarchian writings that originated in Spain were utilised there well after the fifth century, and continued to be preserved in Ireland from the seventh century till the ninth: cf. D. Dumville, *Proc. of the Royal I.A. 73C*, 8 (1973) 323-5.

[25] I.e. the rainbow (cf. Gen. 9, 13-17).

tion of the Fall: in two verses she moves from an allusion to the
Flood direct to Christ's incarnation. Soon afterwards she adapts and
unites two "Sibylline" verses from Vergil, one from the *Fourth Eclogue*, the other from *Aeneid* VI [26]:

> He shall rule an earth made peaceful by his father's virtues,
> afterwards mounting back to the heavens, his father's golden roofs.

Here we move into that world of Cumaean song where the
Christ-child is seen in terms of Vergil's world-ruler, and Christ's
ascension in terms of a return to the *aurea tecta*. These golden roofs
belong not only to the Christian heaven, but to that cavernous temple where Aeneas and his men encountered the Sibyl, who revealed
their destiny. The connotations suggest that Christ, the "true Apollo", is inspiring this Sibyl and enabling her likewise to warn human
beings, to foretell their fate.

This the *Sibylla maga* does as she turns to address "mortal man",
reminding him of the day of Judgement that looms ahead. She feels
herself to be among the guilty who will be judged: "I expect fire, and
fire will not be satisfied with fire". Her prophecy, gloomy and menacing at first, culminates in the vision of a luminous heaven where God
speaks to his assembled saints. The individuality of the Latin poet
is seen in the many beautiful details with which the Creator now
recalls his thoughtfulness in the art of creating:

> "Indeed it is I who made the framework of the sky, who made the
>   stars,
> ordered the world to shine with twofold light,
> poured out lands and seas and poured forth souls...
> who formed the shining skin from gluey mud...
> willed the grass to grow green in the furrows on the dry earth,
> closed the ends of the frail stalks with spiky seed,
> painted the earth with flowers of various bud,
> took thought for the sweet souls of bees and for their dwellings..."

Nonetheless, even if hope remains for mankind, the divine address evoked by the Sibyl ends on a melancholy note:

> "But I — why have I redeemed all with my blood,
> if they have exchanged the kingdom for an earthly seat of men?
> Their greed was greater than their dread of darkness.
> Man will not seek me in time, so that his soul may be mine".

---

[26] *Ecl.* 4, 17; *Aen.* 6, 13 (both noted by Bischoff *ad loc.*).

This leads the Sibyl to conclude by urging her audience to "the short path to life", in action, words, and diet ("to set out whatever simple food nature has"). As she takes her leave, she returns to the Platonic image of her opening verse: even as it is still possible for the whole human race to pay its debt, so is it possible for her not to be consumed by fire but to return to the star from which she drew her being:

> Now I, a mortal, have uttered the songs that I knew,
> which neither the sacred day nor the avenging hour has destroyed.
> If I am worthy, may he seize me and set my soul on the star.
> The brief life of man when ended is melted with the years.

This seventh-century Latin poem is not translated or adapted from any of the *Oracles* in the Greek collection: it is a fresh creation. The Greek texts are repetitious and turgid by comparison, their composition is helter-skelter — which is one reason why they could so easily be altered or interpolated with impunity. The Latin poem, far shorter than most of the Greek *Oracles*, is succinctly and compellingly organised: it spans from cosmogony to Judgement, from the creation of the world to its destruction, with a unifying imaginative vision.

There are several Hermetic texts freshly fabricated in the twelfth century; the most enigmatic and most captivating is the *Book of the Twenty-four Philosophers (Liber XXIV Philosophorum)*, composed, it would seem, in France around 1150. The text still bristles with problems; there is no critical edition [27]. In all, twenty

---

[27] The recent text by F. Hudry, *Le Livre des XXIV Philosophes* (Grenoble 1989), is unfortunately eccentric and often garbled. The editor bases it on MS Laon 412, which she holds to be much the oldest, setting it ca. 1220-30. Yet M.-Th. d'Alverny dates this MS "s. XIII ex." (*Arch. d'hist. doctr.* 28, 1961, 300). It is one of the nine MSS that d'Alverny assigns to s. XIII (*Catal. Trans. et Comm.*, Washington 1960 ff, 1, 151-4; 3, 425 f); its obscurer readings in my view have no privileged status, but should be corrected from other MSS to restore grammar and sense. For a complete text of the sayings and the first commentary one must still turn to Baeumker's edition (cit. App.), which, despite "lectures erronées et des choix de variantes assez arbitraires" (d'Alverny, *Arch. d'hist. doctr.* 17, 1949, 231), yields sense more steadily than Hudry's. The second commentary remains unpublished (for one extract, cf. P. Dronke, *Fabula* (Leiden-Cologne 1974), p. 145). Hudry's claim that the *Liber* "serait directement issu du *De philosophia* d'Aristote" (p. 52) is likewise unreliable. Among the testimonies to Aristotle's lost work, only one (Cicero, *N.D.* 1, 13, 33 — *menti tribuit omnem divinitatem*) has a certain analogue in the *Liber*: yet there the wording — *Deus est mens oracionem generans...* — implies a notion of the Logos which is alien to Aristotle. It is also improbable that the *De philosophia* sur-

manuscripts of the *Liber* have been found, of which the nine oldest go back to the thirteenth century [28]. No earlier manuscript survives, though the work is quoted in various twelfth-century sources. In half the extant manuscripts the *Liber* is attributed to Hermes, Mercurius, or Trismegistus, or any combination of these names.

The prologue explains:

> When the twenty-four philosophers were assembled, it only remained for them to enquire: what is God? By general consent they adjourned and decided on a time for meeting again, so that they should not bestow each his own arbitrary appellations on God by way of definition, [but] that they might take out of their own definitions something about God that was certain and agreed by them all.

There follow twenty-four oracular, deliberately paradoxical sayings, to which explanations are subjoined in the majority of manuscripts. The first philosopher says:

> God is the monad begetting the monad, reflecting a single ardour back into himself.

The dictum of the next is the most celebrated and most often adapted by later authors, from Jean de Meun and Rabelais to Pascal [29]:

> God is the infinite sphere whose centre is everywhere, whose circumference is nowhere.

Insofar as there is imagery among these speculative paradoxes, it tends to the abstract and the mathematical. The God whom these sages try to define is that "Dieu... des Philosophes et des savants" whom Pascal in his *Mémorial* strove to reject, in order to affirm the very different "Dieu d'Abraham, Dieu d'Isaac, Dieu de Jacob... Dieu

vived into the Middle Ages: Hudry claims it was still read by Augustine (p. 50), and even by Albertus Magnus (p. 62)!

[28] This is the number of MSS described by d'Alverny (*Catal.* cit. n. 27). Hudry (p. 15) writes of 22 MSS, but does not mention any beyond those in d'Alverny. The original form of the *Liber* remains an open question: among the nine early MSS three give only the *logoi* of the philosophers; two include a prologue and an exposition of the *logoi*, and four add to these a second, fuller commentary. It seems likeliest that the work began simply as a series of twenty-four *logoi*, perhaps with prologue — but we cannot be wholly certain.

[29] Jean de Meun, *Roman de la Rose* (ed. Langlois) 19129-32; Rabelais, *Le tiers livre* ch. 13 (*Oeuvres complètes*, ed. Boulenger-Scheler, p. 371); Pascal, *Pensées* 84 (*Oeuvres complètes*, ed. Chevalier, p. 1105).

de Jésus-Christ" [30]. The God of the *Liber*, we might also say, is that unfathomable divinity whom Lactantius had sought in his Hermetic and Sibylline texts, the texts he believed to be the most archaic and grandest, those most free of the caprices of anthropomorphism.

The image of the sphere is taken up in another of the dicta: "God is the sphere that has as many circumferences as it has points". It recurs, too, in the exposition of a different image, that of nothingness. Under the utterance, "God is the opposition of nothingness through the mediation of being", comes the explanation:

> This definition allows God to be imagined as a sphere at whose centre nothingness is imprisoned [31]. And the divine sphere continuously activates the divine handiwork, in which it eternally detains that nothingness in being, and from which, by the exuberance of its goodness, it called into being the object which is as it were near the centre.

The only other visual image in the work is that of light and dark:

> God is the dark left in the soul after all light.

> God is the light that does not grow bright by diffraction: only godlikeness (*deiformitas*) passes through the object.

This inaccessible deity that is "known by the mind only through ignorance", this "beginning without beginning, process without variation, end without end", is only once imagined in the relation of love, and that too becomes charged with paradox. The eighth philosopher says:

> God is the love which, the more it is held fast, the more it hides.

And in the explanation we read:

> In the first cause, the source of life is the source of all life. So there it is itself the fountain of love... It is itself the love of the creature, inasmuch as the creature is ordered by it; the more you unite yourself to it, the more will you be exalted and it be lifted up higher still. And that is its way of hiding.

---

[30] *Oeuvres complètes*, p. 554.
[31] This conception of nothingness derives from Eriugena's *Periphyseon*: cf. P. Dronke, *The Medieval Poet and his World* (Rome 1984), p. 49.

How did such a work come to be composed in the mid-twelfth century, and to be given out under the name of Hermes? A number of Latin works from this time and after apply to metaphysics and theology something akin to a geometrical method, beginning a discussion with axioms, definitions or rules [32]. Boethius had attempted it in his brief essay *On Hebdomads,* and this was expounded in the earlier twelfth century by the leading Chartres philosopher Gilbert of Poitiers. At the same time Euclid's *Elements* became available in two Latin versions, and two Neoplatonic works were translated which used metaphysical propositions that resembled axioms and a method that resembled the Euclidian: the *De causis* (based on Proclus, but thought to be a work of Aristotle's), and Proclus' own *Elementatio physica,* translated ca. 1160 in Sicily. From then till the end of the century writing deductive or axiomatic works about God became a fashion, especially among the Porretani — that is, the disciples of Gilbert of Poitiers. The most remarkable of these was the poet-philosopher Alan of Lille. Alan is also the first to quote from the Hermetic *Liber,* in a youthful *Discourse on the Intelligible Sphere* [33], from the 1160s (the period in which he wrote his epic *The Complaint of Nature*); he cites it more extensively in the next decade, in his own "geometrical" work, his *Rules of Heavenly Law.* If, as Marie-Thérèse d'Alverny has plausibly proposed, the Hermetic book itself stems from the Porretan milieu, could it have been perpetrated by Alan of Lille? This seems to me unlikely: for when Alan cites the *Liber,* his wording is never identical with the original, and his earliest citation from it he attributes to none other than Cicero! [34] Yet that may be a deliberate mystification. Alan, as a prominent Porretanus, may well have known who composed the mysterious book, and indeed we can see that one of his contemporaries assumed that Alan had been a party to the secret. For in one of the earliest manuscripts of Alan's own *Rules of Heavenly Law,* still copied in his lifetime, the heading says: "This author is called Mercurius Alanus Porretanus Trismegistus" [35]! The caption is too early to have been garbled through ignorance. In my view it is more likely to have been a *jeu d'esprit.* The suspicion that the newly "discovered" Hermetica were

---

[32] Cf. the illuminating account by C. H. Lohr in *Pseudo-Aristotle in the Middle Ages,* ed. J. Kraye et al. (London 1986), pp. 53-62.

[33] Ed. M.-Th. d'Alverny, *Alain de Lille: Textes inédits* (Paris 1965), pp. 163-80, 295-306.

[34] Ibid. p. 297.

[35] *Regulae caelestis iuris,* ed. N. M. Häring, *Arch. d'hist. doctr.* 48 (1981) 97-226, at p. 105.

not of immense antiquity but originated in the circle of the Porretani
will have led this copyist to tease his readers by conflating the names
of Hermes with that of the most famous living Porretanus. The import of the heading is I think not unlike that of one I saw in a recent
issue of *Le Monde* (2.11.89), where an article on a British film-maker
was headed "Peter Méphisto Greenaway".

The idea of a symposium of oracular sentences about God, ficti-
tiously ascribed to renowned authors or sages, can be traced much
earlier in the Greek world. I would suggest that behind the *Liber*, at
least indirectly, there lies a late-antique Greek text, ΠΡΟΦΗΤΕΙΑΙ
ΤΩΝ ΕΠΤΑ ΣΟΦΩΝ, a Christian "Seven Sages" fantasy, that combines the more abstract, Hermetic type of divine sayings with the
Sibylline type, which are often more specific in their allusions to
Christ. In this "Seven Sages" text [36], the first to appear is Apollo.
He is asked who will inherit his temple in Athens, and in answer
foretells the birth of the divine Logos from the maiden Mary. Several
of the other sages are given oracular sayings not unlike those in the
Liber. Thus Bias says: "He is intelligible light out of intelligible
light"; Thucydides: "Through him his own Logos is made being";
and Menander: "Whether God is or is not, honour and apprehend
him as being". The seventh sage here is Plato, whose words unite the
Sibylline and Hermetic modes:

The old is young and the young is old;
the Father is the Son and the Son the Father;
the one is three and the three one;
the fleshless is made flesh;
earth has begotten heaven's creator.

To ascertain the intentions behind such fabulation, from late
Antiquity to the world of Alan of Lille, since we have no outright
testimonies, no "confessions of a fabulator", only very tentative and
partial suggestions can be made. In general terms, we can accept Um-
berto Eco's insight, that "people in the Middle Ages falsified so as
to reconfirm the trust in something (in an author, an institution, a
current of thought, a theological truth), and so as to uphold an 'order', whereas people today falsify so as to create distrust and disorder" [37]. At one end of the spectrum we can reckon, in the Middle
Ages, with a wholly serious intent: the author's self-effacement in

[36] Ed. B. Snell, *Die Sieben Weisen* (Munich ³1952), pp. 158-60. A similar text,
ibid. pp. 160-6, includes "Don Trismegistus" among the Seven Sages.
[37] *Fälschungen im Mittelalter* (MGH Schriften 33, Hannover 1988), 1, 82.

the service\ of a truth that he believes will be so much more widely acknowledged if it seems to emanate from a venerable source, such as Hermes or a Sibyl. Behind the self-effacement may lurk resignation or irony — as the author realises how much more works of the *antiqui* are prized than those of the *moderni*; or again, when it is a matter of particularly daring speculations, there may be an inbred fear of persecution: it feels safer then to shelter behind an imposing name. On other occasions we cannot exclude an element of games-playing with the world of learning. Most scholars today, for instance, think it likeliest that the treatise *Institutio Traiani*, which John of Salisbury adduces many times and attributes to Plutarch, is a *fictio auctoris* (Peter von Moos's expression), "deriving partly or wholly from John's power of imagination and of combining reminiscences" [38]. And if some scholars still maintain that Wolfram von Eschenbach, writing his *Parzival*, really worked with an otherwise unheard-of Provençal romance by one Kyot, who — Wolfram insists — told the story of the Grail far more accurately than Chrétien de Troyes, I think no one would any longer accept the German poet's further claim, that Kyot learnt the mysteries of the Grail from a pagan book written in Arabic, by Flegetanis, a scientist (*fisîôn*) whose father worshipped a calf and whose mother was descended from Solomon [39].

Above all, with works such as the *Prophetia Sibyllae magae* and the *Liber XXIV Philosophorum*, we must reckon with a sheer creative passion to further a corpus of texts that was admired and honoured. It was possible not just to create a fresh Sibylline work in the seventh century, or a fresh Hermetic one in the twelfth, but in doing so to attain new heights in these two genres. Such authors go far beyond the familiar ranges of *imitatio*: they achieve keen originality even while pretending to none.

We have become accustomed to studying the survival of Antiquity. Yet medieval Latin literature can also show us how much more Antiquity could do than just survive. With Abelard and Thierry of Chartres we see not merely the continuation of late-antique conceptions — no simple *Nachleben* or after-life, as if of ghosts — but something more exhilarating: their advance into new conceptions, and at times into greater ones. Abelard's use of Hermetic and Sibylline testimonies is more profound than that of Lactantius, Thierry's approach to Hermes more magnanimous than Augustine's. Thierry's brother, Bernard of Chartres, is celebrated for saying: "We are like

---

[38] Ibid. 1, 739; 778.
[39] *Parzival* 453, 11-33; 827, 1-5.

ULTIMA CVMÆI VENIT IAM
CARMINIS AETAS MAGNVS
ABINTEGRO SAECLORVM
NASCITVR ORDO IAM RE
DIT ET VIRCO REDEVNT
SATVRNIA REGNA IAM
NOVA PROGENIES CÆLO
DEMITTITVR ALTO

SIBYLLA CVMANA CVIVS MEMINIT VIRGILIVS EGLOG IV

Fig. 1. The Cumaean Sibyl (Giovanni di Stefano, 1482)

Fig. 2. The Libyan Sibyl (Guidoccio Cozzarelli, 1483)

Fig. 3. The Phrygian Sibyl (Benvenuto di Giovanni, 1483)

Fig. 4. Hermes Mercurius Tri<s>megistus, contemporary of Moses (Giovanni di Stefano, 1488)

the dwarfs perched on the shoulders of the giants, and so we can see further than they". But here it is rather the new *giants* who are perched on the shoulders of the old ones, and they see not just further but differently.

It can be similar with the new creations of the medieval Latin world. No ancient Sibylline text can match the imaginative fullness and control of the seventh-century *Prophetia,* no ancient Hermetic text combines gnomic and mysterious statement with the succinct force of the *Book of the Twenty-four Philosophers.* These texts represent not the after-life of Antiquity but its *Vita Nuova.*

In order to see both the new giants and the old aright, in order to trace both the continuity of ancient thought and imagination and their creative renewals, the discipline of medieval Latin literature is a necessity.

APPENDIX

⟨i⟩ From *Mundus origo mea est*

    Mundus origo mea est, animam de sidere traxi,
      Intactum corpus concutit omne deus.
    ⟨Narrabo quodcumque deus mihi spirat in ore, ⟩[1]
      Si bene devotum senserit ampla fides.
5   Multum mea mecum dixerunt carmina carmen;
      Carmina quae scribo, noverit illa deus...

10   Principio sine fine deus, deus omnibus auctor,
      Remotumque cahos noctis discrevit amicae
    Et iussit stare diem noctemque diemque
    Luminibus mutare vices astrisque moveri,
    Et rerum quibus reparentur [2] saecula gyro [3].
15   Diluvium terris fudit donumque [4] supernum.
    Ast deus postquam ripis conpescuit aquas,
    Primus ab aetherio proprio de nomine natus
    Ad terras descendit homo, intactae virginis infans,
    Purporea cervice gestans sine fine coronam,
20   Et pater ipse sibi propius [5] accessit in ortu...

31   Pacatumque [6] reget patriis virtutibus orbem,
    Postea caelos repetens et patris aurea tecta...

84   "En ego sum qui machinam caeli [7], qui sidera feci,
    Qui gemino mundum nitere lumine iussi,
    Qui terras mariaque fundi animasque profundi...
90   Qui cutem nitidam limo glutinante formavi...
    Arida qui volui sulcis viridescere gramen,
    Qui culmos fragiles spicato [8] semine clausi,
    Qui floribus terram variato germine pinxi,
    Qui dulces animas apium domosque [9] providi...
110   En ego, cur meo redemi sanguine cunctos,
    Si de sede regnum hominum terrena mutarunt?
    Cupiditas maior quam de tenebris *erat horror* [10].

---

1 *versum supplevi; nulla lacuna* VP   2 repararentur OP reparentur *ex* repararentur *corr.* V   3 gyros VP gyrus O   4 dorsumque VOP *em.* Bi   5 proprius
VOPBi   6 Pacatumque *ex* Paccatumque *corr.* V   7 caeli *stat etiam in* O (*sed
contra Bi: cf. p. 170 n 23*)   8 spicatos P   9 domosque VP -usque O   10 erat
horror *scripsi* honor erat VOP horror erat *corr.* Bi

Ut mea sit anima, ipse me non tempore quaeret.".....

133   En ego [11] mortalis quae scivi carmina dixi,
          Quę nec sacra dies nec ultrix *hora* cecidi⟨t⟩ [12].
          Digna si sum, rapiat animamque in sidere condat.
          Vita brevis hominis finita solvitur annis [13].

V Valenciennes 404 (386), fol. 62v-65r, s. IX   **O** Oxford Bodl. Auct.
T.II.23, fol. 90r-93r, s. IX (to v. 123 only) **P** Prague Univ. Libr. XIII.G.18,
fol. 238r-239r, s. XV   **Bi** B. Bischoff, "Die lat. Übersetzungen und Bearbeitungen aus den Oracula Sibyllina" (1951), repr. in *Mittelalterliche Studien*
I (Stuttgart 1966) 150-71, text pp. 164-8   I follow the spelling of **V**, but distinguish the letters u/v; punctuation is my own.

11 En ego] *littera erasa post E* V   12 colla cecidi VP colla caecidi Bi (*ultrix hora:
cf. Sil. It. 5, 655*)   13 EXPLICIT PROPHETIA SIBILLAE MAGAE *post 136* V

     In several of the verses above, a simple change could give a "correct"
hexameter: e.g. at 5, reading *Multum dixerunt mea mecum carmina carmen*,
at 16, reading *Ast dominus*, or at 19, reading *cervice gerens*. Yet such changes
are too uncertain to warrant a place in the text. I am most grateful to
Giovanni Orlandi for his helpful suggestions in this regard.

(ii) From the *Liber XXIV Philosophorum*

     Congregatis 24 philosophis, solum eis in questione remansit: quid est
deus? Qui, communi consilio, datis induciis et tempore iterum [1] convenien-
di statuto, ne [2] singuli de deo proprias proponerent impositiones [3] sub
diffinitione, ut ex propriis diffinitionibus exceptum [4] certum aliquid de deo
communi consensu [5] statuerent [6], ⟨sic dixerunt⟩:
  I   Deus est monas monadem gignens, in se unum [7] reflectens
       ardorem.
  II   Deus est spera infinita, cuius centrum est ubique, circumferencia
       nusquam.
  VII Deus est principium sine principio, processus sine variatione, finis
       sine fine.
  VIII Deus est amor qui, plus habitus, *magis latet* [8].
       ...*In* [9] prima causa [10] id a quo vita [11] est ipsum a quo vita tota.

1 verum O   2 ne] *sic* S ut OCBa   3 impositiones] *sic* SO (*cf.* OLD, *s.v. im-
positio, 2*) propositiones CBa   4 excerptum CBa certum *om.* Ba   5 assensu
OC   6 sic dixerunt *supplevi e cod. Vat. Lat. 3060 cit. Ba* Quorum unus sic
proposuit (*e cod. Laudin. 412*) Ba   7 unum] *sic* SOCF suum Ba   8 magis
latet] *sic* C plus placet SOFBa   9 en S ex O   10 causa prima C   11 vita
tota et O vita est ipsum a quo *om.* C

Igitur id ipsum est fons amoris in illo [12]... Tunc est id ipsum amor creature, prout ordinata est creatura ab ipso; cui [13] quanto magis te [14] unificaveris, tanto exaltaberis et tanto elevabitur [15]. Et hoc eius latere [16].

XIV Deus est opposicio nichil mediacione entis.

Hec diffinitio ymaginari facit deum [17] esse speram, in cuius centro nichil incarceratur. Et est continue agens spera divina opus divinum, quo detinet nichil in suo esse eternaliter. A quo per exhuberanciam sue bonitatis vocavit in esse rem que est quasi circa centrum [18]...

XVIII Deus et spera cuius tot sunt [19] circumferencie quot sunt [20] puncta.

XXI Deus est tenebra in anima post omnem lucem relicta [21].

XXIII Deus est qui sola ignorantia mente [22] cognoscitur [23].

XXIV Deus est lux que fraccione non clarescit, transit sed sola deiformitas in re [24].

S Seville Colombina 7-2-26, fol. 43v-47r, s. XIII (with both commentaries) O Oxford Bodl. Digby 67, fol. 89r-92v, s. XIII (with both commentaries) C Cambridge UL Ii.i.29, fol. 84r-86v (= old foliation 82r-84v), s. XIV (with first commentary) F Cambridge Fitzw. McClean 169, fol. 262v-263v, s. XV (sentences only) Ba C. Baeumker, "Das pseudo-hermetische 'Buch der vierundzwanzig Meister'", *Gesammelte Aufsätze und Vorträge* (Münster 1927) pp. 194-214, text pp. 207-14 I follow the spelling of S, but distinguish the letters u/v; punctuation is my own.

12 et in illo SO   13 cui *om.* O   14 te *om.* OBa   15 elevabit C elevaberis Ba   16 et hoc eius latere] *sic* S ex hoc eius latere O et hoc eius latere est C Et hoc est eius placere Ba   17 ymaginati S facit ymaginari deum C f.D.i. Ba   18 quasi centrum O   19 sunt tot S   20 sunt *om.* C   21 relicta *om.* S (*an recte?*)   22 mente *om.* F   *23 Haec est sententia XXIII in SOCF,* XXIV *in Ba*   24 Deus... re *om.* SOCBa (*non recte, ut mihi videtur, quia commentum in Ba p. 214, 10-19, pertinet ad hanc sententiam*).

III

HELOISE WITH AND WITHOUT ABELARD

9

ABELARD AND HELOISE IN MEDIEVAL TESTIMONIES *

It gives me deep pleasure to begin by commemorating W. P. Ker, in whose honour this series of lectures was devised. He remains perhaps the most inspiring critic of medieval literature whom these islands have produced. His writings combined a European breadth of learning with meticulous detailed insight; his style was both evocative and precise; he has made several generations long to read the medieval works that he discussed. These qualities continue to make Ker's work vital to younger literary scholars. For me they represent as it were the Platonic idea — real, even if unattainable — of an approach I should like to be able to bring to literary questions, such as those on which I wish to focus today.

Is the correspondence of Abelard and Heloise authentic, or a forgery? The problem arises because of a collection of eight letters, which survives as a collection in nine manuscripts, and which in its proportions and structure is unparalleled in medieval letter-writing. It begins with Abelard's autobiographic letter, known as the *Historia Calamitatum*, ostensibly written to console an unnamed friend. This recounts Abelard's personal triumphs and rebuffs in the schools; his seduction of Heloise, which turned from a calculating manoeuvre into ardent mutual love; his marriage to Heloise, despite her fierce protestations that she wanted to stay free, and wanted him to stay free; it tells of Abelard's castration, when her relatives thought he had betrayed the marriage by sending Heloise to shelter in a convent; Heloise's enforced taking of the veil as nun; Abelard's further misfortunes as monk, theologian, and abbot. After this come the four so-called "personal" letters: the passionate, imploring letters of Heloise, and Abelard's attempts to meet her entreaties by spiritual consolation and encouragement. Yet more than three quarters of the collection in bulk consists of the three final letters, which are con-

* The twenty-sixth W.P. Ker Memorial Lecture, University of Glasgow Press, 1976.

cerned with spiritual direction, where Heloise asks Abelard's advice on matters pertaining to her monastic community, and he replies with a discussion of woman's rôle in the religious life and with a Rule for the sisters in the community he himself had founded.

Such in brief is the correspondence the genuineness of which has been challenged and debated since the late eighteenth century. The moves in this debate — at least as far as 1973 — have recently been retold, and dissected, with astringent irony, by the Swiss scholar Peter von Moos [1]. I shall not — let me reassure you at once — reopen the debate with a new theory, and indeed shall say only a little about the debate itself. Yet perhaps before we look at the medieval testimonies concerning Abelard and Heloise, it is as well to signal certain features of the modern testimonies.

In the modern debate about the letters, there was a lull of over a decade. Etienne Gilson, in a famous book, *Héloïse et Abélard* (first published in 1938), was able to show that most — even if not all — of the older arguments against the letters' authenticity were without foundation. In 1953, however, the skirmishes were reopened, by the Basilian monk Joseph Muckle, to whom we owe what is still the only

---

[1] *Mittelalterforschung und Ideologiekritik. Der Gelehrtenstreit um Heloise* (Munich, 1974). In addition to the works discussed in von Moos's book, the following recent studies are relevant to the argument of the present essay: *Pierre Abélard — Pierre le Vénérable* (Colloques internationaux du CNRS No. 546, Paris, 1975): esp. the contributions of Mary M. McLaughlin, "Peter Abelard and the Dignity of Women" (pp. 287-334), N. M. Häring, "Abelard Yesterday and Today" (pp. 341-403), A. Vernet, "La tradition manuscrite et la diffusion des ouvrages d'Abélard" (pp. 405-8), J. Monfrin, "Le problème de l'authenticité de la correspondance d'Abélard et d'Héloïse" (pp. 409-24), P. von Moos, "Le silence d'Héloïse et les idéologies modernes" (pp. 425-68), and J.F. Benton, "Fraud, Fiction and Borrowing in the Correspondence of Abelard and Heloise" (pp. 469-512). This symposium will be cited as *Colloque* in the notes below. Further, cf. E. Baumgartner, "De Lucrèce à Héloïse", *Romania* 95 (1974), 433-42; J.F. Benton, "Philology's Search for Abelard", *Speculum* 50 (1975), 199-217; M.T. Beonio-Brocchieri, *Introduzione a Abelardo* (Bari, 1974); L. Engels, "Abélard écrivain", *Peter Abelard*, ed. E. M. Buytaert (Mediaevalia Lovaniensia Series I/Studia II, Leuven-The Hague, 1974), pp. 12-37; H. Fromm, "Gottfried von Strassburg und Abaelard", *Festschrift für Ingeborg Schröbler* (Tübingen, 1973), pp. 196-216; H. Kolb, "Peter von Moos, Mittelalterforschung...", *Euphorion* 68 (1974), 286-95; P. von Moos, "Palatini quaestio quasi peregrini", *Mittellateinisches Jahrbuch* 9 (1974), 124-58; *id.*, "Die Bekehrung Heloises", *ibid.*, 11 (1976), 95-125; *id.*, "Cornelia und Heloise", *Latomus* 34 (1975), 1024-59; *id.*, "Lucan und Abelard", *Hommages à André Boutemy* (Collection Latomus, Brussels, 1976), pp. 413-43; B. Radice, *The Letters of Abelard and Heloise* (Harmondsworth, 1974); E. Ruhe, *De amasio ad amasiam* (Munich, 1975), esp. pp. 50-60. Other works are cited and discussed in notes below. I have been able to take into account only those writings that were accessible to me by March 1976.

complete critical edition of the eight letters in the collection [2]. There also exist a number of letters by both Abelard and Heloise to each other which stand outside this collection [3]; these have never been critically edited at all, and their authenticity has never, as far as I know, been questioned.

The letters outside the celebrated and controversial collection are throughout religious in their orientation. It is clearly the irreligious element in the collection — above all in the two first letters of Heloise that we find there — which has made modern scholars uneasy about genuineness. I quote from Muckle's introduction:

> [Heloise] had written that the status of concubine appeared to her sweeter than that of wife; that she would prefer to be Abelard's mistress than the wife of Augustus with the world as a dowry.
>
> One would expect that Abelard would have chided her and tried to set her right in regard to such extravagant and sinful dispositions... One might expect some word of disapproval of such impassioned and sinful protestations of love [4].

One might indeed, if Abelard had been Father Muckle. I say that not in order to make fun of this learned editor, but simply to underline the fact that his suppressed premise here is not scholarly but subjective: his criterion of what is possible or likely in the relations between Abelard and Heloise is, "What would *I* have done in Abelard's place?" (And he does not seem to realise that this is the criterion underlying his arguments). To cite him once more:

> ... her letters picture Heloise as leading a double life: that of a religious superior bound by vows, and as a woman of sensual mind, serving Abelard and not God, or as she herself puts it, being such a

---

[2] *Mediaeval Studies* 12 (1950), 163-213 (Abelard's Letter of Consolation to a Friend); 15 (1953), 47-94 (The Personal Letters Between Abelard and Heloise); 17 (1955), 240-81 (The Letter of Heloise on Religious Life and Abelard's First Reply); 18 (1956), 241-92 (Abelard's Rule for Religious Women, ed. T.P. McLaughlin). Below, however, I cite the *Historia* and the first two letters of Heloise from the text of J. Monfrin, *Historia Calamitatum* (3rd ed., Paris, 1967), because his line-numbering makes it possible to give more precise references for citations.

[3] Viz. Abelard's *Fidei confessio ad Heloisam* (*Patrologia Latina* 178, 375-8); his Epistles to Heloise accompanying the collection of *Sermones* (*ibid.*, 379-80), the *Expositio in Hexaemeron* (*ibid.* 731-2), and the collection of *Hymni et Sequentiae* (*ibid.* 1771-4); from Heloise to Abelard we have the Epistle introducing the *Problemata* (*ibid.* 677-8), and the forty-two *Problemata* themselves (*ibid.* 678-730), with Abelard's answers.

[4] *Mediaeval Studies*, 15 (1953), 59.

hypocrite as to fool even Abelard himself. On the other hand, Heloise enjoyed a good reputation among the religious leaders of the time from the Pope down... which was that of a sincere, able and holy religious and a worthy abbess.

In view of the evidence, I am inclined to think that the first two letters of Heloise, at any rate, were worked over and perhaps expanded to some extent [5].

But what *is* the evidence? It is the explicit affirmation, in one of the letters attributed to Heloise, that her outwardly blameless and exemplary religious life was a façade she maintained for Abelard's sake, but that she had undergone no inner conversion and felt no vocation for the spiritual life. As the Latin text has it:

> Diu te, sicut et multos, simulatio mea fefellit, ut religioni deputares ypochrisim [6].

That is, "For a long time my façade has deceived you, as it has deceived many people — so that you might take my dissembling for religious experience". Clearly it was on the basis of Heloise's outward behaviour that the religious leaders of her day, and Abelard himself, judged her to have become a deeply pious nun. It is only a modern conviction that it would have been impossible to sustain such a façade which makes Muckle think that this analysis — and the many paragraphs in the Heloise letters which amplify and support it — cannot be authentic. But that is subjectivism, not evidence.

Where Muckle and Misch [7] and others have thought the letters contained elements too sensual and sinful to be entirely true, it is paradoxical that other recent scholars — especially D. W. Robertson and Peter von Moos [8] — have thought the letters too exemplary to be entirely true. According to this view, the sensuality is there, but the letters are organised in such a way as to show how it was overcome: the letters have been shaped in a literary way, to present a story of conversion. Through grace and through the spiritual advice of

---

[5] *Ibid.*, p. 67.

[6] Ed. Monfrin, p. 123, ll. 244-5.

[7] G. Misch, *Geschichte der Autobiographie* III i (Frankfurt a.M., 1959), pp. 523-719.

[8] D.W. Robertson, Jr., *Abelard and Heloise* (New York, 1972). I am particularly grateful to Professor Robertson for sending me a copy of his book at a time when it was not yet obtainable in England. Peter von Moos has argued the "exemplary" nature of the correspondence in *Colloque*, pp. 425-68, and from another standpoint in *Mlat. Jb.*, 9 (1974), 124-58.

Abelard, Heloise overcomes her sensual longings and her blasphemous protests against divine injustice, and is converted within: she becomes the submissive, exemplary nun that Abelard wanted her to be.

The evidence here turns on a crucial passage at the opening of the third letter attributed to Heloise. After the two passionate and unrepentant letters, each followed in the collection by a reply in which Abelard urges her to pray and to direct her love towards God, the third letter ascribed to her begins with her addressing Abelard:

> To him who in a special way is hers, she who is uniquely his.
> Lest perchance you can accuse me of disobedience in any way, I have set the curb of your command even upon my words of measureless pain, so that at least in writing I may moderate what is difficult, if not impossible, to suppress when speaking with you [9]. For nothing is less under our control than our own mind... If only my aching mind were as ready to obey as the hand that writes! And yet you can give me some remedy for my pain, even if you cannot wholly take it away. As one nail drives out another, so a new thought can shut out the old, when the mind, intent on something else, is forced to let go or interrupt its remembering of the past...
> Therefore all of us here, handmaidens of Christ, and your daughters in Christ, beseech you now as our spiritual father for two things which we find extremely important... [10]

The rest of this letter, and all further correspondence attributed to Heloise, shows her writing in the name of her community, on matters concerning the monastic life. No other emotional utterance is recorded. This then is the only explicit passage in the collection from which a spiritual conversion might be inferred. The question is, would it be a legitimate inference?

Overtly at least, Heloise does not say here that she repents: she says she can obey Abelard to the extent of controlling her words, but not her thoughts. And then she changes the subject, and writes of less inflammable matters. Peter von Moos comments:

> One can suppose that this worthy programme in fact... calmed the tempest (in her soul)... By the very intention of hiding her grief and waiting for other remedies, she could be indicating discreetly that she has embarked on the virtuous path opened by Abelard [11].

[9] The Latin has simply "in sermone", but the meaning "in speaking with you" seems to me to be implied by the formulation at the opening of the sentence: "Ne me forte in aliquo de inobedientia causari queas".

[10] *Mediaeval Studies*, 17 (1955), pp. 241-2.

[11] *Colloque*, pp. 454, 456 (cf. *id., Mlat. Jb.*, 11, 112 and 114-15). Monfrin (*Col-

Indeed one can suppose that Heloise's passion was calmed by her religious activities; one can also suppose that it was not. At the opening of this letter she *could* be discreetly indicating her inner conversion, yet this is not the necessary, or even perhaps the most obvious, way of interpreting her words. Von Moos's interpretation depends, once more, not on textual analysis but on a tacit subjective assumption about what was emotionally possible or likely in such a situation.

Von Moos, like the other scholars who believe that the letters as a whole form a literary *exemplum* of conversion, sees the collection as a carefully planned, unified composition [12]. But this to me entails a strange paradox. If the collection contained genuine private letters between the real Abelard and the real Heloise, then I could see how the question of her inner conversion might not have needed to be spelt out blatantly, and could have been left in the sphere of discreet indications and suppositions. If, on the other hand, the letters are shaped as a coherent and exemplary tale of conversion, is it not strange that this conversion, the *raison d'être* of the work, is never made explicit? In medieval hagiography there are countless stories of a woman's conversion from sensuality to saintliness. Yet I know of none, and can imagine none, where we could be left in the faintest doubt by the end of the work as to whether the heroine was really converted or not. That would defeat the whole purpose of the genre. The fact that there can be even a meaningful discussion about whether or not the Heloise of the letters ever assented inwardly to religious life, for me rules out the possibility that the letters belong to the literary genre of conversion-stories.

The most recent grounds for doubting the authenticity of the Abelard and Heloise letters have been advanced by an acute and erudite historian, John Benton. While Benton believes, like other scholars I have mentioned, that one goal of the correspondence "is to tell the story of two instances of spiritual conversion: first Abelard... then Heloise", he also claims there was "a second major goal which the compiler or authors of the correspondence had in mind, and that was to provide a Rule for the Paraclet" [13]. To prove the Rule in the correspondence fraudulent, Benton tries to show that it does not ac-

---

loque, p. 420) likewise claims that "Les lettres II à IV montrent l'acheminement vers la conversion d'Héloïse", though he qualifies with the words "conversion difficile... incomplète peut-être".

[12] *Mlat. Jb.,* 9, 156 ("jedenfalls eindeutig kom-poniert"); *ibid.* 11, 110 ("ein strukturiertes Ganzes").

[13] *Colloque,* p. 473.

cord with what we know independently concerning Heloise's convent and its Rule. Again, he alleges discrepancies between passages in the *Historia Calamitatum* and other, independent evidence that we have about Abelard's life. This leads him to a complex theory of multiple authorship for the correspondence: it is a conspiracy theory, uncovered rather in the manner of Sherlock Holmes. It has been lucidly summarised by a recent scholar as follows: in the late thirteenth century, a forger compiled Epistle VIII

> in order to introduce male dominance in the convent and a laxer Rule which would permit the eating of meat. (Forger) A commissioned a second forger (B), perhaps a member of the university of Paris, to add documents which would authenticate his own work. B forged the *Historia* and the personal letters, drawing on a twelfth-century work of fiction based on Abelard's life and written as a literary exercise by another unknown (C)... A may also have had help from a more literary D [14].

Benton's doubts concerning the genuineness of the monastic Rule contained in Epistle VIII will have to be tested further by expert monastic historians [15]. I would, however, underline the fact that this Rule survives complete in only one of the nine manuscripts containing the correspondence; it is abbreviated in two others, and missing in all the rest [16]. Thus for instance it is missing, except for its accompanying covering letter, in the manuscript Petrarch owned, which may well be the earliest of our extant copies of the collec-

---

[14] B. Radice, *op. cit.*, (n. 1), p. 48 n. 2 (Dr. Radice refers to the *Regula* as *Ep.* VII not VIII, because she departs from the tradition of numbering the *Historia Calamitatum* as *Ep.* I).

[15] The crucial questions here, as Monfrin and Miethke indicated in the discussion of Benton's paper (*Colloque*, pp. 507-8), are:
(1) How certain is it that the *Institutiones*, with which Benton compares the *Regula*, were the Rule actually followed at the Paraclete in its earliest period?
(2) How far is it legitimate to compare an *idea* of a Rule, such as that described in *Ep.* VIII, with a normative document such as the *Institutiones*, which shows that "cette fondation s'insère dans des structures préexistantes"? I should perhaps add that I was very much impressed by Mary McLaughlin's analysis of the *Regula* (*Colloque, art. cit.*), and found her attempt to show its congruence with the whole of Abelard's thought about women (in his acknowledged genuine writings) both compelling and historically plausible.

[16] A useful summary of the MS situation regarding the *Regula* is given by T. P. McLaughlin, *Mediaeval Studies*, 18 (1956), 241: the MS T presents the only complete text; CE "contain numerous and long lacunae"; ABRH contain "only the introduction to this letter".

tion [17]; it is entirely missing in Jean de Meun's French version of the correspondence, which is based on a Latin manuscript perhaps older than any we now possess [18]. This suggests to me that the questions concerning the Rule in Epistle VIII may be quite distinct from those concerning the rest of the correspondence.

What of Benton's points against the veracity of the *Historia Calamitatum*? It is significant that Benton himself concedes at the outset that "No one of the possible errors or discrepancies which follow is in itself determinative" [19]. Some of the alleged errors seem to me to be based on misunderstandings of the text of the *Historia* [20],

---

[17] J. Leclercq, *Revue du Moyen Age Latin*, 1 (1945), 391, writes of this MS (B.N. lat. 2923): "écrit probablement dans le midi de la France vers le milieu du XIIIᵉ siècle"; but J. Monfrin (*ed. cit.*, p. 19) says "plus probablement vers la fin du siècle", and E. Pellegrin, *La Bibliothèque des Visconti et des Sforza* (Paris, 1955), p. 87, suggests "début du XIVᵉ siècle".

[18] One remarkable, and hitherto wholly neglected, example of the interest of the Latin text that Jean had before him occurs at the opening of Heloise's first letter. The edited text reads (Muckle, *Med. Studies*, 15, 1953, 68; Monfrin, p. 111):

> Missam ad amicum pro consolatione epistolam, dilectissime, vestram ad me forte quidam nuper attulit.

Yet from Muckle's apparatus we learn that one MS (F) omits *vestram*, and that no fewer than four MSS (BDRY) read *quidem*, not *quidam*. If we turn to Jean's translation, the MS (J) reads:

> Tres chiers amis, *voz* homs m'a nouvellement monstré vostre epistre que vous envoyastes à *nostre* ami pour confort. (Italics mine).

Neither Muckle nor Monfrin mentions these significant readings, even though Monfrin (*ed. cit.*, p. 30) claimed, "nous avons indiqué les leçons de *J* chaque fois qu'elles nous paraissaient donner une information sur l'état du texte latin". F. Beggiato, in his edition of Jean de Meun's version (*Cultura Neolatina*, 32, 1972, 219), records these readings in his apparatus, but in his text emends to *uns homs* and *vostre ami*, in order to bring the French text into line with Muckle's and Monfrin's Latin. But should we not entertain the possibility that Jean's version was a correct reading of the Latin text he was using, and that in this text Heloise in fact said to Abelard "Your man has lately brought me the letter which you sent to our friend to comfort him"? (That is, Jean's Latin MS may have read *amicum nostrum* and *vester*, and quite possibly *quidem* — or it could have read *vestrum quidam* — but it could not have read *forte quidam*). If Heloise began by saying that a man sent by Abelard had brought her a copy of the letter which her husband had in the first place written to console a mutual friend (*nostre ami*), then the whole notion that Heloise saw this letter *by chance* — so often singled out as an artificial and implausible literary device for linking her first Epistle to the *Historia* — would become baseless. One might even be tempted then to speculate whether this *amicus* — today almost universally regarded as a literary fiction — might not be identical with the author of the Orléans poems discussed below.

[19] *Colloque*, p. 484.

[20] Cf. the "charge of tritheism" (*Colloque*, p. 484), and Jolivet's acute observa-

others presuppose granting as certain a number of points — such as re-dating a vital letter of Roscelin's — which are themselves highly conjectural [21]. If any of the supposed errors in the *Historia* should turn out to be fully demonstrable, it will be necessary to revert to the further question: is such an error due to a redactor or an interpolator? To one, or several? Or must we envisage an outright forgery? It is a long way from suggesting "possible errors or discrepancies" in the *Historia Calamitatum* to Benton's inference that "the story of Abelard's adversities is an imaginative work of fiction" [22]; it is even more speculative to build on this inference the further one, that "the letters which follow and respond to (the *Historia*) cannot be genuine" [23].

Meanwhile I would make only one observation of a literary, rather than historical, nature: when Benton is dealing with those parts of the correspondence which concern Heloise and her love for Abelard, he becomes as subjective as any of his predecessors. Where he is not discussing matters which turn on factual evidence, such as the reliability of cartularies or monastic Rules, he too relies on what he imagines — without evidence — to be emotionally possible or appropriate for the situation of the famous pair. Thus he claims:

> Since the arguments against marriage in the *Historia Calamitatum* were probably taken by a man from a treatise by Abelard, and her letters in the correspondence may have been composed by a thirteenth-century author who wanted to put women in their place, we need not imagine [Heloise] as so submissive or as so tortured by sensuality as she appears in the correspondence... we are now free to see these two great figures (Abelard and Heloise) in more positive terms [24].

But without the support of literary evidence, the notion that Heloise's letters were written "to put women in their place" is fantasy. To be told how we need not imagine Heloise is hardly valuable without a stringent discussion of how the texts lead us to imagine

tions in the discussion, p. 510; or Benton's notion that the Saint Denis episode in the *Historia* "is flatly contradicted" by a genuine letter of Abelard's (p. 489), and Monfrin's rejoinder (p. 507).

[21] Benton believes that "this letter must be dated before the Council of Soissons" (p. 487), i.e. before 1121; Gilson, *Héloïse et Abélard* (3rd ed., Paris, 1964) suggests about a decade later, "lorsqu'il s'attarda près d'Héloïse lors de son retour au Paraclet" (p. 63 n. 2).

[22] *Colloque*, p. 483.

[23] *Loc. cit.*

[24] *Ibid.*, p. 501.

her. From these sentences it is clear only that for Benton "more positive" means "less sensual", and that he has allowed this value-judgement to replace stylistic argument.

A more openly moralistic series of value-judgements pervades D. W. Robertson's recent book *Abelard and Heloise*. To him the love of these two is a "sordid affair" [25], and he is convinced that it must have been so viewed by everyone in the Middle Ages. "Medieval readers", he says, "were not sentimental" [26]: that is, they could not have seen the "sordid affair" in a romantic or tragic perspective, and it is an anachronism to suppose they could have done so. On the contrary, Robertson says of Abelard (whom he imagines as a thoroughgoing homilist in his later life, writing the *roman à lettres* as an exemplary tale of conversion):

> it is obvious that Abelard does not here present [Heloise] in a very good light, but makes her instead ridiculous [27].

The collection was planned — Robertson believes — to show how Heloise vanquished her "ridiculous" human love, thereby growing "from a vain and amusingly unreasonable young girl into a mature and respected abbess" [28].

Professor Robertson deserves credit for making these premises fully explicit, and for making explicit also his claim that these, his subjective assumptions, were universally held by "medieval readers". Here at least is a claim we can test. Insofar as we have early medieval testimonies regarding the love of Abelard and Heloise, what kinds of thoughts and feelings do these testimonies reveal? What was emotionally and expressively possible for contemporaries of Abelard and Heloise, and for the generations that followed them, when they thought about that love? To determine this, which is the main purpose of my study, we have available a considerable amount of evidence; much of it has been neglected, some has remained unknown [29]. I should like briefly to interpret the principal early tes-

---

[25] Robertson, p. xiii.
[26] *Ibid.*, p. 58.
[27] *Ibid.*, p. 54.
[28] *Ibid.*, p. 97.
[29] It is remarkable, for instance, that in her book of close on 700 pages about *Héloïse dans l'histoire et dans la légende* (Paris, 1933), Charlotte Charrier could begin the section on Heloise in the Middle Ages with the heading "Indifférence du moyen âge pour les aventures d'Héloïse et d'Abélard", and could go on to say "Le moyen âge s'est très peu occupé de l'histoire d'Héloïse et d'Abélard" (p. 368).

timonies and analyse their implications. This will clearly not of itself
bring us to a decision on the authenticity of the collection of letters;
yet in one way it will help prepare the ground for such a decision.
The relationship portrayed in the letters need no longer be labelled
authentic or fictitious because of modern *a priori* assumptions as to
what attitudes were possible in the twelfth century: we can begin
afresh, from medieval assumptions and medieval attitudes for which
we have concrete evidence.

My first testimony is one that comes from Abelard himself. In
the last years of his life, Abelard composed a poem of advice for his
son, Peter Astralabe, the child he had had by Heloise. It is basically
a collection of *sententiae*, like the *Disticha Catonis* in Latin or the
gnomic verses in Old English and Old Norse. Yet among the more
general didactic verses it contains some keenly individual ones, such
as these:

> Religious worship varies with so many disparate sects
> that the true path of life is hardly clear.
> Because the world believes so many conflicting doctrines,
> each makes his own, by way of his own background.
> In the last resort, no one dares rely on reason in this,
> since what he longs to achieve is some kind of inner peace.
> A man can sin only through contempt for God —
> only contempt can here make culpable.
> It isn't contempt if one doesn't know how to act,
> unless such ignorance is due to one's own fault.
> Sins can leave you more easily than you them,
> if, when the power to do wrong is past, you repent.
> Yet there are those whose past sins still so allure them
> that they can never feel truly penitent.
> Rather, the sweetness of that bliss remains so great
> that no sense of atoning for it has force.
> This is the burden of complaint of our Heloise,
> whereby she often says to me, as to herself,
> "If I can not be saved without repenting
> of what I used to commit, there is no hope for me.
> The joys of what we did are still so sweet
> that, after delight beyond measure, even remembering brings relief".
> For one who tells the truth there is no strain in telling —
> it is feigning that's the effort, before one speaks [30].

If these verses are, as I believe, genuinely by Abelard, they

---

[30] I give a new edition of the Latin text of these verses, with documentation,
below pp. 279-80.

would show us that Abelard at least continued to think that Heloise remained unrepentant; they would make the case of scholars who see the letters as the story of Heloise's conversion very shaky indeed. The chief reason I believe these verses authentic is that they reveal a train of thought which is entirely Abelardian. An interpolator familiar with Abelard's writings might easily have composed one or other of the distichs here; it would have been far harder to recapture and imitate the exceptional processes and movement of Abelard's thought. In a poem where many distichs are only loosely related or are entirely self-contained, the thought here passes from a rational relativism, such as Abelard formulates by way of his *Philosophus* in the *Dialogue between a Philosopher, a Jew, and a Christian* [31], to the conviction that intention alone determines the moral quality of human action, the conviction central to the argument of Abelard's *Ethics* [32]; from the ethics of intention we move to the intention of repentance (or its absence), on to Heloise's intention, which is cited in words very close to those in Heloise's second letter in the collection [33]. From there to the notion that telling the truth is easy, lying difficult — which at least by implication assesses the truthfulness of Heloise in her complaints. After this, the impersonal didactic advice resumes.

    Nonetheless, I have no independent external evidence that these verses are by Abelard. John Benton is inclined to doubt their

---

[31] *Dialogus inter Philosophum, Iudaeum et Christianum* (ed. R. Thomas, Stuttgart-Bad Cannstatt, 1970) ll. 92ff. (*P.L.* 178, 1614f.).

[32] Cf. Peter Abelard's *Ethics* (ed. and tr. D.E. Luscombe, Oxford, 1971), esp. pp. xxxii-xxxvi.

[33] Compare the verses:

    Sunt quos delectant adeo peccata peracta
        Ut nunquam vere peniteant super hiis,
    Ymo voluptatis dulcedo tanta sit huius,
        Ne gravet ulla satisfactio propter eam.
    Est nostre super hoc Heloyse crebra querela,
        Qua mihi que secum dicere sepe solet:
    "Si, nisi peniteat me commisisse priora,
        Salvari nequeam, spes mihi nulla manet.
    Dulcia sunt adeo commissi gaudia nostri
        Ut memorata iuvent que placuere nimis".

And the lines in the letter:

        Quomodo etiam penitentia peccatorum dicitur, quantacumque sit corporis afflictio, si mens adhuc ipsam peccandi retinet voluntatem et pristinis estuat desideriis?... In tantum vero ille quas pariter exercuimus amantium voluptates dulces mihi fuerunt ut nec displicere mihi nec vix a memoria labi possint. (Ed. Monfrin pp. 121-2, ll. 173-6, 193-5).

authenticity [34], and indeed such a doubt cannot be dismissed out of hand. Unfortunately we have neither a critical edition of the *Carmen ad Astralabium* nor a complete recension of the manuscripts; in gnomic verse it is notoriously easy to add and to interpolate; and many passages in the various manuscripts of the *Carmen* which are known to me [35] do appear to be repetitious or misplaced.

Yet even if the crucial passage should turn out to be an interpolator's work, its implications for our enquiry are profound. Someone in the twelfth or early thirteenth century who, if he was not Abelard, was intimately familiar with Abelard's thought and writings, envisaged Heloise as continuing unrepentant. We can no longer say that this is an unmedieval, romantic and modern notion, and rule it out on *a priori* grounds. Moreover, how do we then account for the verbal correspondences with Heloise's second letter? If that letter was forged, did the forger just happen to have access to a manuscript of the *Carmen* which contains this interpolation? In the same paragraph of the letter, there is another very close verbal correspondence to a poem of Abelard's, which no one has yet suggested could be by a forger: the *planctus* of Israel over the death of Samson. As in Abelard's *planctus*, the writer of the letter, arguing that women always, wittingly or unwittingly, cause the downfall of great men, claims that Samson committed suicide through a sense of failure and sheer grief — a notion completely at variance with traditional theological interpretations of Samson [36]. Abelard's Samson *planctus* survives in a unique twelfth-century manuscript [37]. If we assume that

[34] "Philology's Search for Abelard", pp. 202-3.

[35] See below, p. 280.The largest list of MSS to date is that given in H. Walther, *Initia carminum*, 1646 (cf. also his *Ergänzungen und Berichtigungen*, Göttingen, 1969, s.v. 1646. Notwithstanding Walther's explicit mention of twelve MSS, N. M. Häring (*Colloque*, p. 377), discussing the MS tradition of the *Carmen*, knows only of six. His reference to a further MS, not noted in Walther, "Bodley 8622", turns out to be to a transcription made ca. 1626, by Richard James, of the text in Cotton Vitellius C VIII: see *Catalogi* I (ed. H. O. Coxe, Oxford, 1853) 888, no. 30. A. Vernet (*Colloque*, p. 407), who writes "ainsi le manuscrit du poème à son fils Astrolabe est du début du XIIIe siècle", appears to believe that the *Carmen* survives in a unique manuscript.

[36] I give a text and translation of this *planctus* in *Poetic Individuality in the Middle Ages* (Oxford, 1970 [2nd ed., London 1986]), pp. 121-3, and of the corresponding passage in the letter *ibid.*, pp. 138-9; for the ways in which both the *planctus* and the letter depart from "The traditional figure of Samson", see the section of that title (*ibid.*, pp. 123-32) and the following section on "The individuality of Abelard" (pp. 132ff.).

[37] The information given by N. M. Häring about the *planctus* MS (*Colloque*, pp. 375-6) contains several errors: whereas the six *planctus* are preserved as a cycle

Heloise's second letter is forged, shall we also assume, then, that the forger had access to this *planctus* manuscript and copied phrases from it, as well as from the interpolated *Carmen ad Astralabium*? Was one of the counterfeiting villains — A, B, C, or D — a collector of manuscripts of the rarest Abelardiana? Or is this stretching credibility beyond reasonable bounds?

My next testimony is from a poem, difficult because filled with topical allusions, which in the earlier of its two surviving manuscripts is entitled *Metamorphosis Golye episcopi* [38]. I think all scholars who have discussed this poem agree that it was written around the year of Abelard's death (1142—or, as some believe, 1143), that it is by a partisan of Abelard's, that the poet alludes to Abelard by the name Palatinus (Abelard was born at a place known as Palatium, or Le Pallet, near Nantes in Brittany), and that the poet champions Abelard against the cowled monks, headed by Saint Bernard, who had had the philosopher officially silenced by a church condemnation at Sens in 1140.

About the meaning of the poem there is less agreement, and much remains enigmatic. It is cast in the form of dream-vision, whose central allegory derives from Martianus Capella: in a palace presented as an epitome of the whole cosmos, the wedding of Mercury and Philology is celebrated. The gods and goddesses, the Muses and the Graces are present, as in Martianus, and here too Silenus and his satyrs make the occasion riotous. What is distinctive at this wedding is the continuing conflict between Aphrodite and Pallas Athene, between love and learning, which shows its effects among

---

only in the MS Vat. Reg. lat. 288, one of them, "Dolorum solatium", survives also in the MSS Paris B.N. n. acq. lat. 3126 and Oxford Bodley 79 (cf. *Poetic Individuality*, p. 231). Häring does not know of these, but suggests that there is "a version preserved in Florence" of the whole cycle of *planctus*, in Laur. Aedil. eccl. 197: this MS in fact contains none of Abelard's *planctus* but it contains a copy of an eleventh-century sequence, "Parce continuis", which some scholars have attributed to Abelard, though I have tried to show (*Medieval Latin and the Rise of European Love-Lyric*, 2nd ed., I x-xi, II 347) that this cannot be correct.

[38] See the edition by R. B. C. Huygens, *Studi medievali*, 3a serie, 3 (1962), 764-72. There is another song, *Plange planctu nimio*, which laments Abelard's condemnation at the Council of Sens in 1140, and which must have been composed almost immediately after the event (as the words *quia ruit hodie / magister prudentie / salutaris* imply). It has been printed from a twelfth-century MS (Savignano 45) by F. J. Worstbrock, in *Archiv für Kulturgeschichte* 50 (1968), 291-3. The song has a special interest in that the poet adapts the form of Abelard's own *Planctus David super Saul et Ionatha* (ed. P. Dronke, *Poetic Individuality in the Middle Ages*, pp. 203-9, with transcription of the melody by I. Bent). This anonymous *planctus*, however, contains no allusion to Heloise.

mortals and gods alike. For the wedding-guests include mortals —
philosophers, poets and sages, ancient and modern. Some are shown
as still wholly absorbed in their knowledge or their disputations;
others, at least of the ancients mentioned, think of Aphrodite more
than of Athene:

> Mournful Ovid brought with him his Gothic lass,
> Propertius brought his Cynthia, Tibullus Delia,
> Cicero brought Terentia, Catullus Lesbia —
> the sages had assembled here, none without her who was his own.

> Each beloved is a flame and spark for her man —
> the glow of Calpurnia sets Pliny ablaze,
> Prudentilla makes Apuleïus flame with love,
> each girl holds her man in her embrace.

When the company has been surveyed, one great man is found
to be missing:

> The bride then asks, where is her Palatine,
> he whose spirit showed itself totally divine?
> She asks why, like an exile, he has now withdrawn,
> he whom she had cherished at her breasts.

> Against this philosopher many learned men cry out:
> the cowled chief of the cowled populace —
> all like onions sheathed in their triple tunics —
> it was he who enforced silence on so great a sage [39].

---

[39] Sts. 45-6, 54-5 (*ed. cit.*, pp. 770-1; for the first line cited I adopt the emendation of S. T. Collins, which Huygens cites *ad loc.*):

> Secum suam duxerat Getam Naso pullus,
> Cynthiam Propercius, Delyam Tibullus,
> Tullius Terenciam, Lesbiam Catullus,
> vates huc convenerant, sine sua nullus.

> Queque suo suus est ardor et favilla,
> Plinium Calpurnie succendit scintilla,
> urit Apuleium sua Prudentilla,
> hunc et hunc amplexibus tenet hec et illa...

> Nupta querit ubi sit suus Palatinus,
> cuius totus extitit spiritus divinus,
> querit cur se subtrahat quasi peregrinus,
> quem ad sua ubera foverat et sinus.

> Clamant a philosopho plures educati:
> cucullatus populi Primas cucullati
> et ut cepe tunicis tribus tunicati,
> imponi silencium fecit tanto vati.

The poet cries out against those superstitious, mindless monks, and then, as the poem closes, the assembly of gods issues a decree: "Let that cowled herd be shamed, and driven out of Philosophy's schools — Amen!"

This daring close makes the poem's title clear: Bishop Golias is the subversive mock-bishop of the Feast of Fools, who while the feast lasts can sanction even outrageous criticism of the church's establishment. His "metamorphosis" is both the way he would like to see the world changed and his own raptness as dreamer — the visionary state in which (so he would have us believe) true insight is possible. A Carolingian letter to a (genuine) bishop speaks of his consecration as turning him "by a certain wondrous metamorphosis (*quadam mirabili metamorphosi*) into another man... introducing him into the powers of God, the treasures of wisdom and knowledge, cognizant of divinity" [40].

In terms of the poem's allegory, the bride who misses Abelard, her Palatinus, is Philologia; but I cannot agree with the recent claim that she has nothing to do with Heloise [41]. The theme of Aphrodite's and Pallas Athene's conflict, and the picture of the ancient poets and sages who are joyfully embraced by the women whom they loved on earth, ensure that no one in the poem's first audience would forget — if they needed reminding — that *this* philosopher had a mortal *nupta*, as well as being espoused to wisdom. Obliquely, but I think unmistakably, the poet conveys the sense of loss, felt not only by Philologia on behalf of the learned world but by Abelard's own *nupta*. He conveys it compassionately and with affection. In a poem as full of satire as this one it would have been easy for the poet to treat Abelard's love-affair satirically; yet he does not do so. Again, had the poet been concerned to stress only Abelard's intellectual greatness, he would undoubtedly have avoided a wording susceptible of an erotic meaning. Yet he does not avoid it. He relies on both the intellectual connotations and the erotic, and thereby makes his strophe on Abelard the most serious and the tenderest in his high-spirited poem.

Another poetic testimony to Abelard and Heloise is difficult, like the *Metamorphosis Golye*, but it is also more explicit in its details, and probably a decade or two earlier in its composition. It con-

---

[40] MGH *Epistolae Karolini Aevi*, III 635.

[41] J. F. Benton, "Philology's Search for Abelard" (*cit. supra*, n. 1); cf. also P. von Moos, *Mlat. Jb.*, 11 (1976), 120 n. 44. There is a fine discussion of the poem in W. Wetherbee's *Platonism and Poetry in the Twelfth Century* (Princeton, 1972), pp. 128-34.

sists of two short poems in the midst of some verses copied on the final pages of a medical and exegetic manuscript at Orléans, copied carelessly and defectively by a hand of the late twelfth or early thirteenth century [42]:

> Peter set out for Paris when his mother had taken the veil. Nor will the cruel man's beloved come back other than veiled: the mother spontaneously takes the veil, the beloved friend unwillingly.
>
> It was appropriate for an old woman who is cold in body, it is destructive for a tender, not at all venerable girl — she whose face had set her above many, whose philosophy had set her above all other girls, she through whom alone Gaul has worth.
>
> Yet her cruel friend endured abandoning her — if anyone calls him "friend" not because he loves, but is loved: he ordered her whom he had abandoned to be veiled. She obeyed, nor could she have left unfulfilled for her husband whatever love can fulfil.

*

> Two jewels, Gaul, adorned you once: Mathias the consul and Peter the philosopher. The one was the glory of chivalry, the other, the light of the clergy; a single wound bereft you of both jewels. Envious fate deprived both these exalted men of their genital parts; an unlike cause made them alike in the wound. The consul was undone by a just charge of adultery; the philosopher fell by a supreme betrayal.
>
> The shameful wound attached the philosopher to monks, and took study away from you, Philosophy. A woman destroyed Adam, Samson, Solomon — Peter, alas, has been added, destroyed by a like fall. This was the public downfall of the highest men... Only the wife of Peter is free of guilt: there was no consent on her part, to make her culpable.

Abelard (or the author of the *Historia Calamitatum*) relates how his mother took the veil and how she begged him to return from Paris to Brittany for that occasion. And few readers of the *Historia Calamitatum* will forget the harrowing moment at which Abelard, not trusting Heloise's loyalty, compelled her to take the veil at Argenteuil even before his own entry into monastic life at Saint-Denis. Heloise, says the *Historia Calamitatum*, "was veiled first, spontaneously, at my command" — *prius ad imperium nostrum sponte velata*. This is what the first Orléans poem corroborates (*paruit illa, Nec quid*

---

[42] I give an edition of these poems (*infra* pp. 280-284), together with some notes on the MS and with full documentation for the parallels and identifications suggested in the course of the essay.

amor possit non implevisse): Heloise obeyed Abelard spontaneously, however unwilling she was to become a nun. The *Historia* does not make the contrast which this poet makes between the two ceremonies of veiling, of the old woman and the young, the one choosing freely, the other agreeing against her heart, nor does the *Historia* express the fierce compassion for Heloise which this poet shows. The poet sees the full cruelty of Abelard's command to Heloise, and admires the unflinching absoluteness of her love. The poet, that is, is one of those romantics who, scholars tell us, could not have existed in the Middle Ages. Because he sees Heloise as a heroine of love, this poet is an anachronism — at least according to a widely held modern view. Yet we cannot conjure him out of existence.

Not only the events alluded to in this poem, but a number of expressions, have correspondences in the *Historia Calamitatum*. There too we learn that "many people" (*plurimi*) thought Abelard was inflicting an intolerable burden on Heloise; there too Heloise is described as commendable in her looks and unique in her learning, most renowned for this in the whole kingdom of France. Before evaluating these correspondences, let us turn to the second poem, which may well be by the same author. Here too we see a poetic technique of balance and contrast: in the first poem, between Abelard's mother Lucia and Heloise; in the second, between Abelard himself and "Mathias consul". I have been able to identify this Mathias with probability even if not complete certainty: "Mathias consul" is mentioned in records of the time as Count of Nantes, the town beside which Abelard was born, and as the son of Duke Hoel, who was the overlord of Abelard's family. The Breton chronicles set his death variously in 1103/4 or 1101; they also portray him as something of a scapegrace, who violated and plundered the cemetery of Nantes: they see his early death as God's punishment for this wicked deed. On the other hand, I know of no independent evidence of his castration.

If this identification of "Mathias consul" is correct, it has important consequences for the dating of the poem. It must have been written by a man or woman who knew the personalities — and the gossip — of Abelard's native region, and at a time when the poet's first audience would still have known who "Mathias consul" was and what the local scandals about him had been. Though he admires Mathias for his valour, the poet sees his punishment as fair; he admires Abelard more, however, and hence calls the vengeance that was taken on Abelard betrayal, *prodicio* — the word used for it repeatedly in the *Historia Calamitatum* and the *Letters*. Yet once more his deepest sympathy is for Heloise. In the second letter ascribed to her she lists the *exempla* of the great men whom women destroyed —

Adam, Samson, Solomon. So far this is a well-known topos. It be-comes unusual when she adds Abelard to the list; it becomes unique when she says that, though she caused Abelard's downfall, she was innocent, because she had never consented to the ill-fated marriage on which Abelard insisted, and which precipitated the tragedy.

The last two lines of the poem, with their present tenses, indi-cate that it was written at least before Heloise's death in 1163; the allusions to "Mathias consul" suggest it was well before that date. So, too, the first poem gives the impression of a reaction arising out of recent events — I should be surprised if it was written much more than a decade after the veiling of Heloise in 1118. How, then, do we account for the numerous affinities between these poems and the collection of letters? The easiest assumption, if the letters are at least substantially genuine, would be that the poet knew Abelard and Heloise personally and shared some of their thoughts with them. If the *Historia Calamitatum* and Heloise's letters are forged, on the other hand, the problem is more difficult, for we cannot find these details from the poems in any other extant sources. Should we not then have to assume that one of those villainous forgers — A, B, C, or D — had acquired, for source-material, not only the interpolated *Carmen ad Astralabium* and the unique manuscript of Abelard's cycle of *planctus*, but the equally unique Orléans manuscript — or perhaps its lost archetype? [43] Once more, the moment we try to envisage this possibility in terms of the extant texts and their transmission, we are led, it seems fatally, to a series of wild improbabilities.

From the twelfth century I would still mention briefly two fur-ther testimonies. There is a pair of epitaphs for Heloise and Abelard in a poetic miscellany copied, by a twelfth-century hand, probably at Schaffhausen; the nature of the copyist's errors make clear it is no autograph. Another epitaph, for Heloise, is preserved in a later manuscript, but almost certainly belongs with the Schaffhausen ones [44].

---

[43] The hypothetical alternative, that the author(s) of the Orléans poems drew on a forged Abelard-Heloise correspondence, can be dismissed as far-fetched — the chronology would in that case imply that the correspondence was forged and circu-lated while its protagonists were still alive. If this had been the case with someone of Abelard's fame, is it conceivable that all contemporaries would have passed the existence of such a forgery over in silence?

[44] I give a text of all three epitaphs below, pp. 284-285. Benton ("Philology's Search", p. 201) challenged the date of composition of the epitaph for Heloise be-cause of the lateness of the MS. He does not seem to have noticed how close it is in style and conception to the Schaffhausen ones, nor observed the indications of the MS tradition: namely that this later MS contains on the same page a text of

Epitaphs normally tend to speak hyperbolically of the dead —
but these are not conventional epitaphs. Whilst many composed for
great ladies might speak of their subject as "the beauty and glory of
womankind" (*feminei sexus decor et decus*), or praise their radiance
and excellence (*fulgore, valore*), what is unusual here is the sense of
two lovers perfectly matched: "she was the equal of her Peter in feeling, deeds, and intellectual skill" (*Illa suo Petro par sensu, moribus,
arte*). The second epitaph is said by the copyist — somewhat improb-
ably — to be Abelard's own composition. What is remarkable in it
is the poet's sense of the unity of human and divine love, of the consummation of the human in the divine:

> Una fuere caro tumulus quos continet unus,
>> Nec minus amborum spiritus unus erat.
>> Nunc quoque communem dat bene terra thorum.

One flesh, one tomb, one spirit, one bed of earth: all these figure
the oneness of the lovers in Christ (*utrosque tuos, Christe*). So, too,
in the third epitaph, Abelard and Heloise will remain united for ever,
the oneness of their bed and of their tomb, and the oneness of their
monastic life, leading to eternal oneness in their home beyond the
stars:

> Unus nunc tumulus sicut et ante thorus,
> Unum propositum viteque professio sacre,
>> Una perennis eis sit super astra domus.

The sexual love of Abelard and Heloise is neither condemned
nor ignored: the poet affirms the earthly aspect of their love, for to
him it is out of the earthliness that the heavenly fulfilment grows.

What may seem more astonishing is that a very similar affirmation can be found at the close of the famous letter in which Peter
the Venerable, abbot of Cluny and prince of the Church, who pro-
tected and gave shelter to the fugitive Abelard in his final years,
writes to console Heloise at Abelard's death. Though the letter is
often alluded to and often cited, I do not think the full significance
of its last sentences has been recognised. There Peter the Venerable
writes:

> My illustrious and dearest sister in God: this man to whom you

some of the Schaffhausen lines, more accurate than the twelfth-century MS, which
can be corrected with the help of the later one.

cleaved, after the sexual oneness, with the stronger and finer bond of divine love, he with whom and under whom you have long served God — I tell you, God is now cherishing him in his lap, in place of you, or like a replica of you. And at the second coming, at the sound of the archangel and the trumpet heralding God descending from the heavens, God will restore him to you through his grace, having preserved him for you [45].

The great abbot of Cluny does not shun a language rich in erotic connotations. At this solemn moment he uses sexual expressions consciously and daringly: in the compass of a single sentence, the words *carnalis copula, vinculum, adherere, gremium, confovere* all serve to establish a perspective which is both human and divine, and which brings with it a profound optimism: the lovers Abelard and Heloise will be reunited in heaven as lovers. The heavenly bond of *caritas* is stronger and finer (*validior, melior*) than the physical bond (*carnalis copula*) — yet Peter feels no need to disparage that bond. Not a word about their being washed clean of the foulness of earthly lust: there is not a phrase in Peter's letter such as the twentieth-century moralistic scholars delight in using, and delight in thinking makes them more truly medieval in outlook than the rest of us.

From the early thirteenth century we have a testimony of the extent to which the two lovers had become a romantic legend. The context of this testimony, in the oldest manuscript of the Chronicle of Tours, is a surprising one, for the entry begins with a hostile description of Abelard. Abelard is seen as having perturbed the church by the profane novelty of his teachings, and as having evaded the Council at Sens, to appeal to Rome, because he was afraid of justice. But when the chronicler turns to Heloise he has nothing but praises — for her religion, her learning, her loyalty to her dead husband's memory, The climax is his picture of Heloise in her last sickness bidding her nuns to place her in Abelard's tomb when she dies. As the tomb is opened, the dead Abelard stretches out his arms and enfolds her in his embrace [46]. We might be in the mid-nineteenth

---

[45] Letter 115, ed. G. Constable, *The Letters of Peter the Venerable* (2 vols., Cambridge, Mass., 1967) I, 307-8:

> Hunc ergo venerabilis et carissima in domino soror, cui post carnalem copulam tanto validiore, quanto meliore divinae caritatis vinculo adhesisti, cum quo et sub quo diu domino deservisti, hunc inquam loco tui, vel ut te alteram in gremio suo confovet, et in adventu domini, in voce archangeli, et in tuba dei descendentis de caelo, tibi per ipsius gratiam restituendum reservat.

[46] I print the Tours Chronicle's testimony concerning Abelard and Heloise below, pp. 285-286.

century, in the macabre-sentimental realm of Théophile Gautier's *La morte amoureuse* — yet it is important to recognise that this too was an emotional and expressive possibility already within two generations of Heloise's death. Perhaps this should serve as a warning against accepting the letters as genuine too quickly and too uncritically: clearly it was possible to create romantic fictions around historical figures. And yet the lines in the Tours Chronicle are not really comparable with the letters, either in scale or in imaginative seriousness.

A similar spirit imbues the song *Requiescat a labore*, which purports to be a dirge for Abelard sung by Heloise and the nuns at the Paraclete convent (in the last strophe, if the plural forms are correctly recorded, we should have to imagine the sisters commemorating both Abelard and Heloise) [47]. The phrase "tragic love" (*doloroso... amore*),

---

[47] Ed. E. Du Méril, *Poésies populaires latines antérieures au XIIᵉ siècle* (Paris, 1843) pp. 176-7 (I have introduced minor modifications of spelling and punctuation):

Requiescat a labore
doloroso et amore!
  Unionem caelitum
    flagitavit:
    iam intravit
  Salvatoris aditum.

In obscura tumbae cella
alma micat iusto stella:
  instar ipse siderum
    refulgebit,
    dum videbit
  in fulgore Dominum.

Salve, victor sub corona,
sponse in nitente zona!
  millibus cum lacrymis
    quem salutat,
    tua nutat
  vidua in tenebris.

In aeterna mihi iunctum
amo dignior defunctum
  beatorum socium:
    mors piavit,
    quae sanavit
  insanatum animum.

Tecum fata sum perpessa:
tecum dormiam defessa
  et in Sion veniam!

the image in the third stanza of Abelard greeted by a thousand tears as his widow droops in darkness, and in stanza 5 the heroine's own cry of longing for death, all seem like an elaboration of the fantasy and emotional indulgence of the chronicler from Tours. The date and provenance of the song, however, remain uncertain. Despite a recent assurance that Helen Waddell found positive evidence that "it was written in the twelfth century" [48] — the manuscript unfortunately

Solve crucem,
duc ad lucem
degravatam animam.

Sanctae animae, favete!
Consolare, Paraclete!
Audin? sonat gaudia
cantilena
et amoena
angelorum cythara.

*

Requiescant a labore
doloroso et amore!
Unionem caelitum
flagitabant:
iam intrabant
Salvatoris aditum.

[48] Cf. M. Blackett, *The Mark of the Maker: A Portrait of Helen Waddell* (1973), p. 57 (citing a letter of Helen Waddell's to George Saintsbury, from Paris, 1924): "I am back at B.N. to find out if... *Requiescat a labore...* is genuine, or at least twelfth century, and not a sentimental forgery. It seems too good to be true". (In a later letter she records her delight at finding it was written in the twelfth century).
I am most grateful to John Benton for drawing my attention to this book. A recent letter to Miss Blackett, asking if she could elucidate her parenthetic comment, has brought no reply. It is curious that Hauréau, in his handwritten index of incipits, now photographically printed, listed the song, yet without any MS references, such as he normally gives, in particular for Parisian MSS. Cf. B. Hauréau, *Initia* V (Turnhout, 1973), R 23, s.v. *Requiescat a labore*, where the references are only to A. A. L. Follen, *Alte christliche Lieder* (Eberfeld, 1819), p. 129, and to Du Méril; in the *Appendix* to Hauréau, the *schedarium* of J. A. Schmeller and Wilhelm Meyer, II (Turnhout, 1974), 363, a reference to Du Méril is supplemented by one to H. A. Daniel, *Thesaurus Hymnologicus* IV, 350. These three references are once more the only ones to appear in U. Chevalier's *Repertorium Hymnologicum* (17318); in his *Addenda* (V 17318) Chevalier adds a reference to H. Stadelmann, *Altchristliche Hymnen und Lieder* (Augsburg, 1855).
At all events, the recent claim of J. Szövérffy, *Peter Abelard's Hymnarius Paraclitensis* (Albany-Brookline, 1975) I 11, n. 9, that "'Requiescat a labore'... is a falsification, probably by M. Carriere [*Abälard und Heloise...* Giessen, 1853]", cannot be

has never been specified and perhaps is lost — I am still not wholly satisfied that it is a medieval song, rather than a later *imitatio*. The consistent use of double rhyme in this song — in marked contrast with Abelard, who steadily avoids double rhyme, both in his cycle of *planctus* and in the 133 hymns he wrote for Heloise and her convent — makes it extremely unlikely that we can link the song with the earliest period of the Paraclete, let alone with Heloise herself. At the same time, I can see nothing in the form or language that precludes a date from the later twelfth century onwards.

From romantic legend let us now turn to real life. Two years ago a young German scholar, Ewald Könsgen, published a remarkable discovery: a collection of more than a hundred excerpts from Latin love-letters between a man and a woman, which range from a line or two to several pages; many are in rhymed prose, some are in verse [49]. Though they were copied only in the 1470s, I would accept Köns-gen's arguments dating the composition of the letters to the early twelfth century and locating them in the region of Troyes. I also endorse his perceptive demonstration that the extracts are from genuine letters and not from a rhetorical *ars dictandi*: the stylistic differences between the man's letters and the woman's, he shows, are both so numerous and so unobtrusive that an inventor of model letters could hardly have differentiated them deliberately in such a way [50]. But as to the possibility so temptingly raised by the sub-title of Könsgen's book — *Briefe Abaelards und Heloise?* — I must respond to his question-mark with scepticism. We know that Abelard and Heloise, during their time as lovers, did write each other love-letters [51]; the time and place of the newly-found letters would fit; their range of thoughts and emotions is at times quite close to those in the Abelard-Heloise collection. To signal swiftly some of the most relevant parallels: the man is the girl's *magister*; she loves him and admires him, as a great philosopher and poet: "nurtured in the home of philosophy, you have drained the fount of poetry" [52]. Yet she also

---

correct, as the existence of Du Méril's and Follen's texts — 1843 and 1819 respectively — proves.

[49] *Epistolae Duorum Amantium*, ed. E. Könsgen (Mittellateinische Studien und Texte VIII, Leiden-Köln, 1974).

[50] *Ibid.*, pp. 80-85.

[51] Heloise (ed. Monfrin, p. 117, ll. 269-70):
> Cum me ad turpes olim voluptates expeteres, crebris me epistolis visita-bas, frequenti carmine tuam in ore omnium Heloysam ponebas...

Cf. also *Hist. Cal.*, ll. 296-9.

[52] *Epistolae*, 112 (p. 61): *Iam philosophie laribus nutritus poeticum fontem ebibisti.* Cf. Könsgen's Boethian parallels *ad loc.*

sees him as hounded by the *invidia* of his colleagues and rivals, who are lesser men. She claims, like the Heloise of the letters, that while some people love for wealth or for voluptuousness, her love is both pure and grounded in objective truth: for he is the most outstanding of men; the arrogance of the French must yield before him [53]. In his reply he sees her not only as beautiful and gracious, but as "the only disciple of philosophy among all the girls of our time" (*soli inter omnes etatis nostre puellas philosophie discipule*) [54].

The parallels are extremely suggestive — yet the difficulty is, one can find such parallels elsewhere too, in other letter-collections between men and women of this period. For all their individual touches, these letters take their place within a specific tradition, one that we can follow at Regensburg in Bavaria and Le Ronceray on the Loire in the late eleventh century, and again in Bavaria, at Tegernsee, in the early twelfth [55]. From all these places we still have groups of amatory letters between learned young women and the *magistri* who taught them, letters in verse or in rhymed prose, which are "real" letters, however much they may be stylised, in that they stylise a range

---

[53] *Epistolae*, 49 (pp. 25-7):

Rose immarcessibili beatitudinis flore vernanti illa, que te super omnes homines diligit, florendo crescere et crescendo florere. Nosti, o maxima pars anime mee, multos multis se ex causis diligere, sed nullam eorum tam firmam fore amiciciam quam, que ex probitate atque virtute et ex intima dilectione proveniat. Nam qui ob divicias vel voluptates sese diligere videntur, eorum nullomodo diuturnam arbitror amiciciam, cum res ipse, propter quas diligunt, nullam videantur diuturnitatem habere. Quo fit, diviciis vel voluptate deficientibus eorum eciam deficiat simul et dilectio, qui non propter se res, sed se propter res dilexerunt.

Sed mea dilectio pacto longe tibi alio sociata est. ...Magistro inquam tanto, magistro virtutibus, magistro moribus, cui iure cedit francigena cervicositas et simul assurgit tocius mundi superciliositas; quilibet compositus, qui sibi videtur sciolus, suo prorsus iudicio fiet elinguis et mutus.

The implication in *cui iure cedit francigena cervicositas* may be, as Könsgen (p. 91) suggests, that this *Magister* does not himself belong to the *francigenae*, but has, as an "outsider", established himself in their midst.

[54] *Epistolae*, 50 (p. 28).

[55] I have edited the Regensburg and Tegernsee letters in *Medieval Latin and the Rise of European Love-Lyric* (2nd ed., Oxford, 1968) II, 422-47, 472-82; cf. the discussion *ibid.*, I, 213ff., 221-32. The most interesting of the Le Ronceray verse love-letters were edited by W. Bulst, "Liebesbriefgedichte Marbods", *Liber Floridus* (Festschrift Paul Lehmann, St. Ottilien, 1950), pp. 287-301. On the Regensburg verses cf. also Anke Ebel, *Clm 17142: Eine Schäftlarner Miscellaneen-Hs. des 12. Jahrhunderts* (Munich, 1970); I have suggested elsewhere, however (*Studi medievali*, 3ª serie, 12, 1971, 847, n. 37), why I do not find Dr. Ebel's slightly later dating of these verses (1106) plausible.

of genuine relationships. In language the Troyes collection is nearest, I think, to the letters from Tegernsee; it is stylistically much further from the Abelard-Heloise collection, and from the writings of Abelard and Heloise which we know outside that collection. Humanly, it shows the pattern we can perceive so often in Regensburg, Le Ronceray, and Tegernsee, of a young girl hesitantly in love with, and still somewhat overawed by, her older *magister* — the first man she will have come to know at all intimately, and the first with whom she is able to extend her range of expression, finding new emotions by articulating them, by "experimenting" both with her pen and with her thoughts and feelings.

What Könsgen's discovery and fine edition have shown is at least this: that it was possible, in the early twelfth century, for a situation of two lovers not unlike Abelard and Heloise as they must have been before the tragedy, to be given an expression that is both literary and authentic. For the rhetoric and literary art in such letters in no way precludes their authenticity: the education of such a man and woman will have made the seemingly artificial modes of expression "second nature".

Among all the direct allusions to the love of Abelard and Heloise in the twelfth century, I know of only two that contain an element of moral condemnation. Yet this condemnation there takes the form not of homiletic earnestness but of ribald mockery [56]. The allusions occur in two letters addressed to Abelard after his castration, by Fulco, Prior of Deuil, and by Roscelin. The personal enmity between Abelard and Roscelin, who had been his teacher, is well known; we do not know what lay behind Fulco's hostility. In fact, with the notable exception of Georg Misch [57], scholars have read Fulco's letter so carelessly that they have taken it for a well-disposed and

[56] I leave out of account Rodulfus Tortarius (ed. M. B. Ogle and D. M. Schullian, Rome, 1933), whose *Epistola* VI (*ibid.*, pp. 289ff.) cannot in my view be sensibly related to Abelard and Heloise. This Epistle is a *fabliau*, set in Antiquity, in which a self-mutilated eunuch guards Flora, a wanton woman who has two captains as her lovers. I had thought Cuissard's notion (*Documents inédits sur Abélard*, Orléans, 1880, pp. 29-31), that this verse *fabliau* refers under plain cover to Abelard and Heloise, too fanciful to require discussion; but the assertion was repeated by Mlle. Charrier (*Héloïse*, p. 54): "Syncopus ne saurait désigner qu'Abélard et la belle Flora n'est autre qu'Héloïse" — once more without any attempt at substantiation. On the principle "ne saurait que", it would seem that every mention of a eunuch in medieval imaginative literature must be interpreted as an allusion to Abelard.

On the fragment of what was probably a satiric presentation of Abelard's wooing of Heloise, see the note on p. 283 below.

[57] *Geschichte der Autobiographie*, III i, p. 568.

serious attempt to console Abelard for his calamities. Yet it is not difficult to perceive the gleam of malice in this parody of a *Consolatio*: for Fulco, Abelard is neither the dedicated seeker after truth nor the man who, in the *Historia Calamitatum*, claims that Heloise was his first and only love. Fulco sees him as a debauchee and a mercenary charlatan:

> For the thing that caused your fall, as people say, was the love of women, and the snares of lust by which women capture their whoremongers — but I think I had better pass this over, rather than say anything that might be unseemly for a monk of our order and rule to say...
>
> Whatever money you could gain, over and above your daily food and needs, selling your knowledge by speechifying, I heard tell that you never ceased to fling it away down the wasteful whirlpool of harlotry. It was the greedy rapacity of prostitutes that snatched away all you had... [58]

Note the hypocrisy with which Fulco claims that he will not speak foully, and then proceeds to do so after all, and note his cunning disclaimers — "as people say", or "as I heard tell". Towards the close of this letter (which incidentally contains allusions to the Pope and his court at Rome so scandalous that they were expurgated in the *Patrologia Latina*) [59], Fulco, pretending to see Abelard's castration as tragic, makes it instead into a cruel farce. The whole city, he says, lamented Abelard's misfortune: bishop, canons, clergy and citizens. We might be taken in by this show of compassion — as most modern scholars have been — but I think the next sentence gives the game away:

> How shall I relate the lament of all the women, whose faces streamed with womanly tears as they heard the news, because of you,

[58] *P.L.* 178, 372-3:

Nam illud quod sic te, ut aiunt, praecipitem dedit, singularum scilicet feminarum amorem, et laqueos libidinis earum, quibus suos capiunt scortatores, melius mihi videor praeterire, quam aliquid dicere quod ordini nostro et regulae nostrae religionis non concordet...

Quicquid vere scientiae tuae venditione perorando praeter quotidianum victum et usum necessarium, sicut relatione didici, acquirere poteras, in voraginem fornicariae consumptionis demergere non cessabas. Avara meretricum rapacitas cuncta tibi rapuerat...

[59] For the text of the remainder of the letter, and its dating before the close of 1118, see D. Van den Eynde, "Détails biographiques sur Pierre Abélard", *Antonianum* 38 (1963), 217-20.

their cavalier, whom they had lost — weeping as if each one of them had found their husband or their lover killed in battle? [60]

The lamentations of scholars and populace, which are described in the *Historia Calamitatum* in bitter, pathétique language [61], are here treated as the stuff of *fabliau*: the cock of the roost has been caponised.

Roscelin's letter contains even more unseemly moments: he answers a previous attack that Abelard had made on him as if he were taking part in a literary exchange of abuse, a "flyting" or *tenso*. Abelard, says Roscelin, can no longer prick with his tail, which has been cut off; so now he should fear divine justice, lest he lose his pricking tongue as well. Roscelin describes Abelard's betrayal of Heloise's uncle, and the seduction of Heloise, with merciless invective: at this stage he labours the notion of Heloise as a poor, wronged, innocent young girl. Yet soon after, for the sake of a new attack, Roscelin makes a transition as hypocritical as Fulco's. Now he presents Heloise as a prostitute, for whose sake Abelard makes money by his false and unauthorised teaching, and Roscelin's language takes on a viciousness that is hardly matched even in *fabliaux*:

> You don't even *send* the money to your whore, to pay for your debauchery, you still take it to her yourself. While you could enjoy her, you paid in advance; now you sin even more, rewarding her for the past debauches rather than buying future pleasures [62].

Medieval *fabliaux* tend to conclude with a *moralitas* (often ironic or frivolous). Here, too, we see it is the scurrilous mockers, Fulco and Roscelin, who present themselves as moralists. Yet these two men, who show moral indignation about Abelard and Heloise, have not, perhaps, the greatest integrity among the witnesses we have consi-

---

[60] *P.L.* 178, 374:

Quid singularum feminarum referam planctum, quae sic, hoc audito, lacrimis, more femineo, ora rigarunt, propter te militem suum, quem amiserant, ac si singulae virum suum aut amicum sorte belli reperissent exstinctum?

[61] *Hist. Cal.* (ed. Monfrin), ll. 592ff.

[62] Ed. J. Reiners, *Der Nominalismus in der Frühscholastik* (Münster, 1910), pp. 62ff.:

Atque collecto falsitatis quam doces pretio scorto tuo in stupri praemium nequaquam transmittis sed ipse deportas, et qui dum poteras in pretio expectatae voluptatis dabas, modo das in praemium, plus utique remunerando stuprum praeteritum peccans, quam emendo futurum.

dered, nor are they the most typical of their age — or indeed the most attractive.

We might suppose that there would be an element of satire or fabliau in Jean de Meun's allusions to the love of Abelard and Heloise — Jean de Meun, who continues to be known far more for his *gauloiseries* than for the humane imaginative breadth of his world-picture. Yet any expectation of humour from Jean in this context would be disappointed. When Jean translates the Abelard-Heloise letters [63], all the headings, which are his own, and his many personal interjections and exclamations, show his compassionate understanding of the love of Abelard and Heloise; more, they show that admiration for Heloise which Jean also expressed by way of one of his characters in the *Roman de la Rose*, saying: "I do not believe, by my soul, that there's ever been such a woman since" [64].

In Jean's translation he repeatedly calls her "la saige Heloys" (the same word as François Villon later used for her) [65], "la belle Heloys", "la bonne Heloys". When, in the *Historia Calamitatum*, Heloise denies that she is married to Abelard, swearing that this is a false rumour, Jean adds the exclamation, "And this is what the beautiful girl did, to preserve Abelard's honour!" (*Et ce faisoit la belle pour son honnour garder*) [66]. But the most arresting notes and interjections of Jean de Meun's occur in Heloise's two letters. In the first, where Heloise makes the impassioned protestations that begin "God knows, I never desired anything but you", Jean emphasises the passage by his heading:

Here the wise Heloise speaks and resorts to argument, and shows

---

[63] Jean's translation of the *Historia Calamitatum* was published by Charlotte Charrier (Paris, 1934), his translation of Heloise's first letter by F. Beggiato, *art. cit.* (n. 18). The remainder of Jean's version is still unpublished, though various scholars have announced their intention to publish a complete edition. The medieval French translation of the letter of Peter the Venerable to Heloise, from the same MS, has recently been edited by M. Zink (*Colloque*, pp. 29-37), but this translation is not by Jean de Meun (see Appendix B below).

[64] *Roman de la Rose* (ed. F. Lecoy), ll. 8795-6:
Mes je ne croi mie, par m'ame,
c'onques puis fust nule tel fame.

[65] Does this really imply, as Mlle. Charrier argued (*Héloïse*, pp. 388-91), that Villon had read the letters in Jean's version? I think more evidence than the expression *la tres sage Heloys* in the *Ballade des dames du temps jadis* would be needed for us to be certain of this.

[66] *Jean de Meun. Traduction de la première épître* (ed. Charrier), p. 101.

Abelard that it was true love and loyal with which she loved him, and she says: *Donque encore, Dieu le scet, ne desirai fors que toy...*[67]

From the second letter, which is still unpublished, I would signal four moments [68]. The first is again a heading, where Jean emphasises that one of Heloise's great *planctus* is about to begin: "Now Heloise laments as I shall unfold..." (*Or se complaint Heloys si com je movray*). A little later, between two exclamations of Heloise — "Oh wretched that I am, I who was born to be the cause of so great a misdeed", and "Oh greatest and known destruction: it is through women that the greatest men are destroyed", Jean inserts a gloss which, like the note signalling Heloise's *planctus*, indicates his awareness of rhetorical form as well as content in the letters: *Or argue Heloys contre li mesmes* — "Now Heloise is arguing against herself". In two other passages Jean inserts his own comment: *Encore l'amoit elle comme forsenee!* — "Still she loved Abelard like one beside herself!" Again, when Heloise begs Abelard to cease praising her for her presumed sanctity, Jean adds in parenthesis: *Nota, oncquez femme ne parla plus saigement* — "Note: never did a woman speak more wisely". In short, Jean's sympathetic understanding of Heloise, of the quality of her love as of her writing, is beyond question. The scholars who see Jean predominantly as an ironist are one-sided: Jean's magnanimity can comprehend the serious, even tragic, aspect of these letters.

Finally, I cannot resist offering a glimpse of another unpublished work, called "the letters of abbess Heloise of the Paraclete" (*les epistres de l'abesse Heloys du Paraclit*), a work that is certainly forged. It survives in a unique manuscript of about 1500, splendidly illuminated [69], where the text contains a number of fragmentary and garbled passages — a manuscript, that is, which cannot be an autograph. The work belongs in my view to the fifteenth century, but perhaps still to the fourteenth. Here Heloise is presented as a *dame*

---

[67] Ed. F. Beggiato, p. 224:
   Ci parle et descent à son propos la saige Helois et monstre à Abaielart que c'estoit vraye amour et loiaulx dont elle l'amoit et dist:
   Donque encore, Dieu le scet, ne desirai fors que toy...
[68] The texts are given below, pp. 286f.
[69] A good description is given in G. F. Warner and J. P. Gilson, *Catalogue of Western MSS in the Old Royal and King's Collections* II (1921), 203-4; see also G. F. Warner, *Illuminated MSS in the British Museum*, Third Series (1901); P. Champion (ed.), *Charles d'Orléans, Poésies* I (Paris, 1923), x-xii.

galante, a mistress of the art of love [70]. I cite the opening:

> All those who want to understand this book should know that when Master Peter Abelard had held sway a long time and practised his arts, his conscience caught up with him. He founded an abbey near the Seine in the region of Champagne, known as the abbey of the Paraclete.
>
> In this abbey a nun was elected abbess whose name was Heloise. This Heloise was well versed in the knowledge of the seven arts, and in accordance with the nature of the seven arts she had seven graces: namely, the avoidance of bad speech, the shunning of bad hearing, of bad sight and bad behaviour, the living without covetousness and without sinful touch; above all else she hated wantonness.
>
> Because of this, all who want to be tried in the art of love and to keep and maintain it must praise abbess Heloise, who teaches a disciple of hers, whose name is Gaultier.

Why is Heloise's disciple here called Gaultier? I think because Gaultier had been the name of the disciple who was instructed in one of the most famous medieval arts of love, the *De amore* of Andreas Capellanus. It is the name of Gaultier, not Andreas, which features in the Bishop of Paris's condemnation of that book in 1277 [71].

Heloise's interest in love, in the hundred pages of manuscript in which she proceeds to instruct Gaultier, is suspiciously similar to that of Andreas Capellanus; she shares many of Andreas' preoccupations and values. Like him, she believes that love is a source of virtue and can make even base-born people noble, and yet — again like him — she returns often to the problem that class-distinctions do exist and are likely to remain, and that the poor have far less chance of loving illustriously than the well-born and the rich. She offers her views on everything from moral qualities to the use of cosmetics. The general tone is shrewd and worldly; the style, repetitive and long-winded. And yet there are moments where even this fictitious Heloise seems to echo something of the uncompromising idealism of some of the earliest testimonies to the historical Heloise, something of their hope against hope that human and divine love can ultimately harmonise:

[70] I edit a substantial extract below, pp. 287f. The passages cited in English correspond to paragraphs 1-3 and 10-11.

[71] Cf. M. Grabmann, "Das Werk de Amore des Andreas Capellanus und das Verurteilungsdekret des Bischofs Stephan Tempier von Paris vom 7. März 1277", *Speculum* 7 (1932), 75-9. There are numerous editions of the *De amore*; that of E. Trojel (Copenhagen, 1892, several times reprinted) offers a critical apparatus as well as text.

For, the loving lover should have a greater reward for his intent than he who is reluctant to fulfil his love. And this rule comes through the grace of our Lord God the Father, who leaves the accomplishment of all good and the avoidance of all harm to everyone's freedom, and gives recompense inasmuch as they have done good or ill...

And because of this I beseech God, said abbess Heloise, that he give all true lovers the just reward for their merits, according as they have deserved by the unfaltering judgement of love.

To return to the earlier testimonies by way of conclusion. What they show us, I suggest, is that there is no *a priori* reason against taking the Abelard-Heloise letters at their face value. To say this does not of course eliminate the more detailed questions: to what extent has the collection — which is clearly not just a group of randomly assembled letters — been edited as well as collected, and who was responsible for that editing? [72] But whatever historical aspects of the letters may still be debated, we have no reason to doubt their authenticity on the ground that they express thoughts and emotions incompatible with what we know of twelfth-century thought and emotion. All the attitudes revealed in the letters can be paralleled in early testimonies outside the letters. The two contemporaries — Fulco and Roscelin — who mocked and caricatured the tragedy, under the pretext of moral indignation, did so not because this was the only medieval way of regarding it, or even the most obvious way. Rather, it seems they were motivated by a personal dislike of Abelard. By contrast, the majority of contemporaries of whom we have evidence, and the generations immediately following, up to the time of Jean de Meun, were convinced of the uniqueness and stature of Abelard's and Heloise's love, and regarded their tragedy with wonderment and compassion. And no one in the twelfth or thirteenth century, to my knowledge, ever suggests that Heloise came to see the error of her ways in loving Abelard. Of what many of our modern judges so confidently affirm, the medieval evidence shows no trace.

[72] On this point, see the judicious comments of Monfrin, *Colloque*, pp. 409-24, esp. p. 424:

Personne ne considère que le recueil représente la mise bout à bout de lettres originales. Il s'agit d'un dossier organisé. Il paraît établi d'autre part que ce dossier, aussi haut que l'on peut remonter, vient du Paraclet.

Since these pages went to press, the problems of the critical evaluation of medieval letters, and especially of the formation of collections, have been finely discussed in a wider context by Giles Constable, *Letters and Letter-Collections* (Typologie des sources du moyen âge occidental, Fasc. 17, Turnhout, 1976), ch. III.

APPENDIX A
Texts newly edited

I From the *Carmen ad Astralabium*

Berlin, Deutsche Staatsbibliothek (Preussischer Kulturbesitz) Lat. oct. 172, s. XIII, fols. 6v-7r
Madrid, Biblioteca Nacional Bb 78, s. XIII, fols. 116rb-va
Paris, Bibliothèque Nationale n.a.lat. 561, s. XIII, fols. 42r-v

> Tot fidei cultus sectis divisus habetur
>   Ut que sit vite semita vix pateat.
> Quod tot habet fidei contraria dogmata mundus,
>   Quisque facit generis traditione sui.
> 5 Denique nullus in hiis rationem consulere audet,
>   Dum quacumque sibi vivere pace cupit.
> Contempnendo deum peccat solummodo quisque,
>   Nec nisi contemptus hic facit esse reum.
> Non est contemptor qui nescit quid sit agendum,
> 10 Si non hoc culpa nesciat *ip*se sua.
> Te peccata magis quam tu peccata relinqunt,
>   Si, cum non possis ledere, peniteas.
> Sunt quos delectant adeo peccata peracta
>   Ut nunquam vere peniteant super hiis,
> 15 Ymo voluptatis dulcedo tanta sit huius,
>   Ne gravet ulla satisfa⟨c⟩tio propter eam.
> Est nostre super hoc Heloyse crebra querela,
>   Qua mihi qu*e* secum dicere sepe solet:

1 fidei sectis mundus d.h. M   fidei sectus divisus mundus h. P
3 Nam M   4 facta que sunt g.t.s. M   5 ratione M   6 studet P
8 et sibi contemptus hunc M   Nil nisi contemptus hunc P
9 Between 9 and 10, M inserts:
   nam leve corrigitur qui se delinquere nescit.
   Plaga tamen minor est, sed medicina gravis.
10 esse sua B   11 tu relinquas peccata relinqunt M   tu p. relinquent P
13 obletant adeo in tantum peccata parata M   oblectant a.p. peracta P
14 peniteat super hoc M   15 voluntatis M   16 eos u.s.p. ea M
17 super hoc scilicet mentis Elise M (P has an interlinear gloss, *miserie*, above
   Eloyse, in a contemorary hand; other explanatory glosses are written above ll.
   14-16, 20, 22, 23)
18 Qua mihi qua secum B   quam michi quam secum dicere solet M   Que
   michi que secum d.s.s. P

"Si, nisi peniteat *me* commisisse priora,
20   Salvari nequeam, spes mihi nulla manet.
Dulcia sunt adeo commissi gaudia nostri
    Ut memorata iuvent que placuere nimis".
Qui dicit verum non hoc dicendo laborat:
    Fingere falsa prius nititur, inde loqui.

19 Si nisi p.c. sepe priora B   Si non p. me comisise p. M   Sine p.m.c.p. P (Si, nisi P: *Hauréau*)
20 *sic* BMP (foret P: *Hauréau*)
21 Dulcia adeo c.g.n. P (Dulcia sunt P: *Hauréau*)
22 ut vetera memorata iuvent que placuere (*om.* nimis) M
24 nitimur MP

For the text of these lines I have used the Berlin MS as a base, correcting with the help of the Madrid and Paris ones. All three are MSS of the long version of the *Carmen ad Astralabium*, with over a thousand lines, which was printed from the Paris MS by Hauréau (*Notices et extraits des mss. de la Bibl. Nat.* XXXIV 2, pp. 153-87). These three are the only MSS at present known to me which contain all of the 24 lines given above. [On these and the other MSS, and on the two briefer recensions of the *Carmen*, cf. now J.M.A. Rubingh-Bosscher, *Peter Abelard. Carmen ad Astralabium. A Critical Edition*, Groningen 1987, pp. 19-92].

II-III   Two poems about Abelard and Heloise

Orléans, Bibliothèque municipale 284 (238), s. XII/XIII, p. 183

Parisius Petrus est velata matre profectus,
Nec nisi velata crudelis a⟨mica⟩ redi⟨b⟩it:
Sponte pa*re*ns, invita quidem velatur amica.
Conveniens erat hoc anui que corpore fr*i*get,
5   Damnosum tenere minus or⟨r⟩endeque puelle,
Quam facies multis, quam philosophia puellis
Pretulerat cunctis, qua sola Gallia pollet.
Deseruis⟨s⟩e tamen tulit hanc crudelis amicus —
Siquis non quod amet sed ametur dicat "amicus":
10   Desertam ius⟨s⟩it velari. Paruit illa,
Nec quid amor pos⟨s⟩it non implevisse mari⟨to⟩.

1 Cf. *Hist. Cal.* (ed. Monfrin) ll. 155ff.
2 Cf. *Hist. Cal.* ll. 625ff.
3 parans MS   4 frīget MS
5ff. Cf. *Hist. Cal.* ll. 629ff. (also ll. 284-8)
10 us MS   11 marī MS

Ornavere due te quondam, Gallia, gemme:
  Mathias consul philosophusque Petrus.
Milicie decus hic, cleri lux extitit ille,
  Plaga tibi gem⟨m⟩as abstulit una duas.
5   Invida sors summos privat genitalibus ambo,
  Dispar causa pares vulnere fecit eos.
Consul adulterii damnatur crimine iusto,
  Phil⟨os⟩ophus summa prodicione ruit.
Phil⟨os⟩ophum monachis adiuncsit plaga pudenda
10   Et studium demsit, philosophia, tibi.
Ada⟨m⟩, Samsonem, Salomonem perdidit uxor:
  Ad⟨d⟩itus i o Petrus — clade ruit simili.
Publica summorum clades fuit ista virorum,
  ....
15   Sola tamen Petri coniux est criminis expers,
  Consensus nullus quam facit esse ream.

2 Mathias consul: cf. *Recueil des historiens des Gaules et de la France* XII (Paris, 1877), p. 562 (Ex Chronico Kemperlegiensis, Monasterii Sanctae Crucis): MCIII. Matthias Nannetensis Consul, Hoëlis Consulis filius, moritur.
Ibid., XII, p. 559 (Ex Chronico Britannico Altero):
MCIV. Obiit Matthias Nannetensis, Hoëli Comitis [Cornugalliae] filius. Hic vero hoc eodem anno cimiterium beatorum Petri et Pauli violare, consilio suorum Baronum, praesumpserat, res Canonicorum Nannetensis Ecclesiae iniuste diripiendo. Unde manifestissime apparet divina ultione ipsum suosque coadiutores ipso anno morti esse datos.
Cf. similar account *ibid.*, XII, p. 566 (Ex Chronico Briocensi), where Mathias's death is given as MCI.
3 extititit MS
5 summis MS
8 Cf. *Hist. Cal.*, ll. 424; 591; 604-5; Heloise, *Ep.* I (ed. Monfrin, *ibid.* p. 111), l. 17.
9-10 Cf. *Hist. Cal.*, ll. 623-5; 668-75.
10 deuisit MS
11-12 Cf. Heloise, *Ep.* II (ed. Monfrin, *Hist. Cal.*, pp. 120-1) ll. 133ff (= *Ep.* IV, *P.L.* 178, 195CD).
13 cladis MS At the end of this line MS contains an insertion-sign for the missing pentameter; there is a corresponding sign in the margin, but the pentameter was not written in.
15-16 Cf. Heloise, *Ep.* II (ed. Monfrin, p. 121) ll. 153ff. (= *Ep.* IV, *P.L.* 178, 195D-196A); *Ep.* I (ed. Monfrin, p. 116) ll. 211ff. (= *Ep.* II, *P.L.* 178, 186A).

The last two pages of this MS (pp. 183-4) contain a miscellany of verses, both metrical and rhythmic, which were first signalled in 1880 by Ch. Cuissard, *Documents inédits sur Abélard*, pp. 33-47. Cuissard unfortunately took this miscellany to be a single poem, in three parts, and to be concerned entirely with Abelard and Heloise. He also attemped a transcription, in which, because of numerous misreadings and an inadequate notion of prosody, many verses ended up neither metrical nor rhythmic. The first poem printed above, for instance, begins thus in Cuissard's text:

> Felix qui summa potuit diligere (?)
> Parisius Petrus velata matre profectus.
> Necnon velata rediit crudelia (?)
> Sponte parans in vita quod velatur amica.
> Conveniens erat his annus quoque corpore...

The line *Felix qui potuit summa diligere* (*sic* MS) in fact belongs to the preceding *rhythmus*, and indicates Cuissard's inability to distinguish the various pieces in the miscellany. I append a brief note itemising these, together with the essential corrections to Cuissard. —

1. A leonine distich, not noticed by Cuissard:
> Celum, ter⟨r⟩a, cahos — disti⟨n⟩cgtio trina locorum —
> Excipiunt animas pro iudiciis meritorum.

2. (Cuissard ll. 1-31) Mundus deciduus et homo fragilis

This mortality-lyric survives in two versions: with the above incipit it occurs in four MSS (cf. M.-Th. d'Alverny, *Alain de Lille: Textes inédits*, Paris, 1965, pp. 40-1); a variant version, inc. "Cur mundus militat sub vana gloria", occurs in over forty MSS (cf. H. Walther, *Initia Carminum* 3934; *Nachträge* 3934); a convenient text of the former can be found in *Analecta Hymnica* XXXIII no. 244, of the latter in *The Oxford Book of Medieval Latin Verse* (ed. F.J.E. Raby), no. 284. The relation between the two versions remains problematic. Neither has any connection with Abelard and Heloise, as Cuissard claimed. The principal misreadings in his text are:

1 decidivus (deciduus MS)   3 atque est (ut aqua MS)

20 superant (suptraunt MS — i.e. subtrahunt)

19,21 Cuissard ignores the MS indications reversing the order of *sunt eius gaudia* (19) and *hoc* (*sic* MS) *mundi gloria* (21)

22 Que est omnino velut massa pulveris (o essca vermium o masa pulveris MS)

25 magni penditur (magnis pænditur MS)

28 potest (potes MS, t *expunged*)

30 sic fecere (cor sit in etere MS)

31 summa potuit (potuit summa MS — Cuissard ignores the reversal-signs)

3. Parisius Petrus est velata matre profectus (Cuissard ll. 32-42)

4. Ornavere due te quondam, Gallia, gemme (Cuissard ll. 43-57)

As the MS readings for these two poems are given in full above, it is not necessary to elaborate on Cuissard's transcription.

5. Fragments and epigrams. Each set of verses is marked as separate in the MS. The following lines in Cuissard should be corrected:

(*a*) 58-9: 58 ex edicto (ex condicto MS — for the expression, cf. Calcidius, *Tim.* 17a; Abelard, *Dialogus*, ed. R. Thomas, ll. 64-5)   59 Et triplici captum strue ligemus unum (*sic* MS and Cuissard — for sense and metre, corr. *fune ligemus eum*?) It is conceivable, but by no means necessary, that these verses formed part of a description of Abelard's castration.

(*b*) 60-63: these verses should read:

> Aut me cecatum furor excusa*b*it amoris   (excusavit MS)
> Aut reus immense proditionis ero.
> Omnia preter te mihi tradidit hospes supellex:
> Nil volo preter te, nec Iosep⟨h⟩ alter ero!

They appear to have formed part of a satiric presentation of Abelard's courtship of Heloise (compare the fabliau elements in the letters of Fulco and Roscelin discussed above, pp. 272-275): in the MS Zürich Zentralbibliothek C 58/275, s. XII, fol. 5vb, in the column opposite the two Abelard epitaphs printed below (V-VI), we find three of these lines with the following heading:

Petrus de hospite suo, qui sibi omnia commendabat.

Aut me cecatum furor excusabit amoris,
    Aut reus immense prodicionis ero.
    Omnia preter te nec Ioseph alter ero.

The omission of an essential hexameter in this MS (which is slightly older than the Orléans one, and stems from Schaffhausen, far from the regions where Abelard and Heloise lived out their lives) again indicates how old the material preserved in the Orléans verses must be. (The Zürich lines were printed by J. Werner, *Beiträge* p. 25 — see below p. 284).

(c) 64-6: 64 should read:
Re⟨m⟩ mona⟨c⟩hi, Roberte, tenes, si nomen ab⟨h⟩orres?
65... gravidi (Aut vero gaudes MS). These verses clearly cannot refer to Abelard.

(d) 67-9: 68 namque (cumque MS)   69 Ob cariem, summo (Obtarem, si modo MS). The sentence remains incomplete. *Petrum* in 68 clearly equals *papam*, and cannot refer to Abelard.

(e) 70-1: correctly transcribed in Cuissard. This satiric epigram would not seem to be relevant to Abelard.

(f) 72-5: these verses (which certainly refer to Abelard) should read:
Si tibi non esset mundi conten⟨p⟩tus habendus,
    Petre, quid es monachus? es quia philosophus.
Co⟨n⟩stat philosophos hoc conten⟨p⟩sis⟨s⟩e priores,
    Quod prius am⟨m⟩onuit ipsa Sofia suos.   (phofia MS)

On the *contemptus mundi* of the *philosophos... priores*, see esp. *Hist. Cal.* ll. 1051ff., where they are likewise called *priores philosophos*.

6. (MS p. 184, Cuissard ll. 76-87) Nec catus in nitida servari pelle valebit
The following points especially need correction:
78   Velle (SePe MS — i.e. S⟨a⟩epe)
83   Agnus velut (Agnus hic est MS)
85   caris pellibus (caris est pellibus MS — but the silent correction is of course necessary)
86   he quoque protegerent nec quod decorarent (his que protegerent non que decorarent MS)
87   sunt (sint MS)

Ll. 76-7 occur also in the *Carmen ad Astralabium*, as Cuissard pointed out; but they may well have been a traditional *sententia*; they lend no support to seeing these verses as addressed specifically to Heloise.

I am grateful to Professor John Benton, of the California Institute of Technology, for providing me with photographs of the Orléans pages, and for inviting me in 1974 to work on the text of these poems, about which he is himself preparing a historical study. On the other hand I must take sole responsibility for the historical identifications and parallels advanced in this essay, as well as for the critical texts, translations and notes, and for the corrections to Cuissard proposed above. [At the invitation of John Benton and Marie-Thérèse d'Alverny, I have published a complete edition of the poetry on pp. 183-184 of the Orléans MS in *AHDLMA* XLIX (1982) 277-81].

IV-VI   Three epitaphs for Heloise and Abelard

Bern, Bürgerbibliothek 211, s. XV, fols. 160v-161r
Zürich, Zentralbibliothek C 58/275, s. XII, fol. 5va

The first of these three texts (IV) was edited in *Medieval Latin and the Rise of European Love-Lyric* (2nd ed., Oxford, 1968) II, pp. 469-71; there in the discussion I cited the other two on the basis of J. Werner's *Beiträge zur Kunde der lateinischen Literatur des Mittelalters* (2nd ed., Aarau, 1905), p. 24, suggesting some tentative modifications. The texts of V and VI, on the other hand, are here edited from a photograph of the Zürich MS (Z), which was kindly obtained for me by Professor Brian Vickers.

IV (only in B)

Epytaphium Heloyse

Feminei sex⟨us⟩ decor et decus hec Heloyssa
  Mole sub hac lapidum clauditur, ante dies.
Illa suo Petro par sensu, moribus, arte,
  Scripturas omnes noverat absque *pare*.
5   Os, virtus, formam, famam, fulgore, valore,
  Que sunt rara satis, perpetuavit ei.
Iunius implevit septemque decemque Kalendas,
  Hoc facto cursu tempore dixit ⟨ave⟩.

4 fere MS   7 kalandas MS

V (only in Z)

Epitaphium Petri Baiolardi a semet conpositum

"Servi animam servans, ancillis redde cadaver!" —
  Hanc tibi fundo, deus, nocte dieque precem.
Una fuere caro tumulus quos continet unus,
  Nec minus amborum spiritus unus erat.
5   Nunc quoque communem dat bene terra thorum.
Habaelardus hic est; hec illius est Heloysa:
  Imo utrosque tuos, Christe, fuisse scias. Amen.

1-2 Cf. Abelard, *Ep.* II (ed. Muckle, *Med. Studies* 15, 1953, 76-7; = *Ep.* III, *P.L.* 178, 191C-192C), the last three paragraphs, esp. the lines:
  cadaver, obsecro, nostrum ubicumque vel sepultum vel expositum ia-
  cuerit, ad coemeterium vestrum deferri faciatis ubi filiae vestrae, immo in

Christo sorores, sepulcrum nostrum saepius videntes, ad preces pro me Domino fundendas amplius invitentur.

4 unus: thus originally MS, but corrected to *intus*, with a second *intus* superscript MS
6 Heloysa: *id est amica* superscript MS

VI (title only in B, where it is followed by ll. 1,4; all seven lines in Z)

Aliud quod est insculptum in libro quem ymago sua supra tumulum tenet

Est satis in titulo: Petrus hic iacet Habaelardus,
   Dilectumque tenens huic Heloisa latus.
V⟨ersibus hic⟩ studium coniunxit philosophie,
   Huic soli patuit scibile quicquid erat.
5   Unus nunc tumulus, sicut et ante thorus,
   Unum propositum viteque professio sacre,
   Una perennis eis sit super astra domus. Amen.

1 titulo: corr. from *tumulo* B
3 Z has the letter *V* followed by 9 or 10 blank spaces before *studium* (not 4 spaces, as one might infer from Werner's 4 dots). I owe the suggestion for completion, V⟨ersibus hic⟩, to Edouard Jeauneau; while of course conjectural, it gives a satisfying syntactic structure to the first two couplets (*hic... huic... hic... huic*).
4 *sic* B, patuit quicquid risibile fuit. Z
  In B the *Epytaphium Heloyse* is followed by:
              Aliud
  Hoc tumulo abbatissa   iacet prudens Heloyssa.
  Paraclitum statuit,   cum paraclito requiescit.
  Gaudia sanctorum   sua sunt super alta polorum.
  Nos meritis   precibusque suis   exaltet ab imis.
  Histoire littéraire de la France (XII 646) suggested a late dating for these verses, at least a century after Heloise's death; but the nature of the rhyming — in which three leonine verses are followed by one of the type known as *trinini salientes* — almost certainly indicates twelfth-century composition.

VII   From the Chronicle of Tours (before 1227)

Berlin, Deutsche Staatsbibliothek Phill. 1852, s. XIII, fols. 204va-205ra

Anno domini M°C°XL°, et Corradi imperatoris III° et Ludovici regis III°, obiit magister Hugo, Sancti Victoris canonicus, in peritia septem liberalium artium nulli (204vb) secundus, qui etiam librum de sacramentis, duobus voluminibus comprehensum, composuit.

Tunc Senonis, presente rege Ludovico, episcoporum et abbatum factus est conventus contra magistrum Petrum Abaielardum, qui quadam prophana verborum et sensuum novitate ecclesiam perturbarat. Qui ab eis interpellatus et de iusticia veritus, ad apostolice sedis audientiam appellavit, et sic evadens, non multo post Cabiloni apud Sanctum Marcellum obiit.

Construxerat enim cenobium in territorio Trecacensi, in prato quodam ubi legere solitus fuerat, quod Paraclitum nominavit; in quo sanctimoniales plurimas congregavit, et quandam religiosam feminam, quondam uxorem suam, litteris Latinis et Hebraicis eruditam, eis abbatissam prefecit. Que, vere ipsius amica, magnam ei post mortem in assiduis precibus fidem servavit, corpusque eius de loco ubi obierat transtulit ad predictum cenobium. In cuius tumulo hoc epytaphium est insertum:

Est satis in titulo: Petrus hic iacet Abaïlardus,
Cui soli patuit scibile quicquid erat.

Hec namque, sicut dicitur, in egritudine ultima posita, precepit ut mortua infra mariti tumulum poneretur. (205ra) Et sic, eadem defuncta ad tumulum apertum deportata, maritus eius, qui multis diebus ante eam defunctus fuerat, elevatis brachiis illam recepit, et ita eam amplexatus brachia sua strinxit.

Anno domini M°C°XLI°, et Corradi imperatoris IIII° et Ludovici regis IIII°, Rogerus de Sicilia, post occupationem Calabrie et Apulie principatu⟨u⟩m, Innocentium papam bello cepit...

Through the kindness of the Deutsche Staatsbibliothek, who presented me with photographs of these pages, I have been able to print above, for the first time, the complete entry concerning Abelard and Heloise in the Berlin MS of the *Chronicon Turonense*, an entry of which d'Amboise and Duchesne printed an excerpt in 1616. This excerpt, reproduced in *P.L.* 178, 91-2, has often been alluded to by later scholars — cf. most recently E. McLeod, *Héloïse* (2nd ed., 1971), p. 290; on the sources for the phrase *litteris Latinis et Hebraicis eruditam*, cf. *ibid.*, pp. 16-18, 182-3, 255-6. [The anecdote of the "two lovers" in Gregory of Tours (*Hist. Franc.* I 47, and *In gloria conf.* 31), mentioned in connection with this episode by Peter von Moos, differs from it not only in minor details (e.g. the woman dies first, and speaks again during her own burial), but also in two essential aspects: 1) these "lovers" never consummate their marriage; 2) while their graves move next to each other, he and she do not unite or embrace in one grave — that is, in death as in life they lie side by side *without* any physical contact. If the author of the Abelard-Heloise legend had that of Gregory of Tours in mind, he has radically transformed it, so as to exalt, and not deny, a sensual bond].

VIII   From Jean de Meun's translation of Heloise's second letter

Paris, Bibliothèque Nationale, fr. 920, s. XIV ex., pp. 82, 84, 89, 90

(i) *Or se complaint Heloys si com je movray:*
    Mes se je t'avoye perdu, que me remaindroit il à esperir, ou quelle cause avroi ge de remanoir en ceste vie...?

à esperit: sic MS; corr. *à esperer* (Lat. *sperandum*)?
(Latin: Monfrin, p. 119, ll. 67-8)

(ii) O moy chetive, qui fu engendree à estre cause de si grant felonnie!
Or argue Heloys contre li mesmes:

O souveraine et acoustumee destruction: par femmes sont les souverains hommes destruiz...

(Latin: Monfrin, p. 120, ll. 122-3)

(iii) *Encore l'amoit elle comme forsenee!* Mes dieu le scet, que en tout l'estat de ma vie je redoute encore plus à courrocier toy que dieu, et plus desire plaire à toy que à dieu.

(Latin: Monfrin, p. 123, ll. 239-40)
The same phrase is inserted earlier (p. 88), in the midst of Heloise's discussion of divine grace (Monfrin, p. 122, ll. 211-14):

> la grace de dieu par nostre seigneur Jesucrist — *Encore l'amoit elle comme forcenee* — Li miens treschiers amis, ceste grace est venue au-devant et est donnant à toy medicine contre ces aguillons.

It seems to me at least possible that this insertion of the exclamation is due to a copyist rather than to Jean himself.

(iv) Je te pri que tu te taises — *Nota, oncquez femme ne parla plus saigement* — de ma loenge, que tu n'enqu*ue*res la laide reprehencion de flaterie et le blasme de mençonge...

enquieres: sic MS
(Latin: Monfrin, p. 123, ll. 201-2)

IX   From *Les epistres de l'abesse Heloys du Paraclit*

London, British Library, Royal 16 F. II, ca. 1500, fols. 137v-187v

1   Tous ceulx qui ce livre veullent entendre doivent savoir que quant maistre Pierre Abaielart eut longuement regné et usé de ses arts, sa conscience le reprist. Il fonda une abbaye pres de Sayne en la terre de Champaigne, que l'en appelle l'abbaye du Paraclit.

2   En celle abbaye du Paraclit fut une nonain eslue abbesse laquelle eut nom Heloys. Icelle Heloys fut bien introduite en la science des sept arts, et selon l'estat des sept arts elle eut sept graces. C'est assavoir: mauvaises parolles eschiever, mauvaises ouÿes fuyr, mauvais voyemens, mauvais contenemens, vivre sans rapine et sans mauvais attouchemens; sur toutes riens elle hayoit luxure.

3   Et pour ce toutes gens qui veulent estre esprouvez en l'art d'amours et la garder et maintenir doyvent louer l'abbesse Heloys, qui enseigne ung sien disciple, qui Gaultier ot nom. Premierement elle lui demonstre, se il la veult croire, comment il se pourra maintenir et gouverner entre les vrays amans, et soy bien garder sans estre blecié des darts d'amours...

4   Qui veult amour vrayement demener, vrayement doit amer et foy doit tenir et garder et loyaulté avoir en soy. Premierement nous devons savoir que amour est passion de souffrir. Car aincois que amour soit vrayement parfaicte, il couvient qu'elle soit pesee en droit poiz des cuers des deux amans...

5   L'abbesse Heloys monstre à son disciple par certaines raisons comment

povres amans ne se peuent si bien ordonner à servir amours comme les nobles et les riches. Car les povres amans n'ont dont ilz puissent nourrir droit-
turierement leurs amours...

6   L'abbesse Heloys demonstre et si enseigne à son disciple, qu'il garde
que le malice de folle femme ne le deçoive. Car la nature de fole feme est
telle, et a les parolles si plaines de grant doulceur que puis que la femme
a l'omme enlacié, à paine se peut deslacier de ses las.

7   La proesse des bonnes meurs acquiert amour vraye et lui donne le
resplendissement de vrayement amer... Et aucune fois avient que l'amant
qui n'est pas né de noble lignaige a plus de grace et de proesse en soy que
celuy qui est extrait de noble lieu. Et par ceste raison seulle prouesse
d'amour est digne de louenge...

8   L'abbesse Heloys du Paraclit cy enseigne et demonstre à son disciple
que aucune dame si est nee du peuple, aucune si est plus noble, et aucune
si est mains noble. Aussi est il entre les hommes...

9   L'abbesse Heloys demonstre et enseigne à son disciple que amour fait
les couars hardis, les rudes courtois, les avaricieux moult larges, et les bas
met en noblece tres hault...

10   Car l'amant qui ayme si doit avoir greigneur guerredon de sa voulenté
que celui qui est contraire à acomplir ses amours. Et ceste regle vient par
la grace de nostre seigneur dieu le pere, qui seuffre que tous biens soyent
fais et tous maulx soyent laissiez à la franchise de toutes gens, et en donne
les loyerz selon ce qu'ilz ont fait de bien ou de maulx...

11   Et pour ce prie je dieu, dit l'abesse Heloys, qu'il donne à tous vrais
amans le digne loyer de leurs desertes, selon ce qu'ilz ont desservy par le
droit jugement d'amours.

8 qui MS
Paragraphs 1-3 are from fols. 137r-v; 4 is from 138r; 5 is from 139r; 6 is from 139r-v;
7 is from 139v-140r; 8 is from 140v; 9 is from 144v; 10 is from 158v-159r; 11 is from
161r.

APPENDIX B

A note on Abelard and Heloise and the early humanists

Till 1974 the sole surviving manuscript of Jean de Meun's translation
of the letters of Abelard and Heloise (Paris B.N. fr. 920) was held to be a
copy from the early fourteenth century. This assumption has now been
shown false in an important article by Carla Bozzolo [1]: she found not only
that the watermarks of the paper pointed to the last decade of the fourteenth century, but that she could identify the handwriting of the copyist:

[1] "L'humaniste Gontier Col et la traduction française des *Lettres* d'Abélard et
Héloïse", *Romania* 95 (1974), 199-215.

it was the hand of the French humanist Gontier Col. Yet the manuscript
is also a testimony to humanist interests in a more profound sense than that
of copying. As Dr. Bozzolo shows, it consists of two parts that are quite distinct in language and style. The first part begins with the *Historia Calamitatum* and concludes with letter VII of the correspondence. This translation
stems from the thirteenth century, and there is no reason why it should not
be identified with the version which Jean de Meun claims that he made.
But the second part consists of three further documents, which are not
found united anywhere else in the manuscript tradition: Abelard's simple
and moving "confession of faith" to Heloise; a second, public apologia of
Abelard's, clearing his name of heretical beliefs he had been accused of
teaching; and finally, Peter the Venerable's compassionate letter to Heloise,
which could be seen both as a tender tribute to her and as a resplendent
funeral-oration for Abelard [2]. According to Dr. Bozzolo, these three pieces
were translated not by Jean de Meun but by a late fourteenth-century humanist, and it was possibly Gontier Col who, by bringing together the two
sets of translations, completed the collection of letters in his own way.

Petrarch's keen interest in the Abelard-Heloise letters has long been
known to scholars, yet it has always been regarded as an isolated phenomenon. Now, thanks to Carla Bozzolo's research, we see that humanist interest
in Abelard and Heloise can be far more widely documented [3]. In 1395
Coluccio Salutati writes to his friend the French humanist Jean de Mon-
treuil, whom he had previously asked for a copy of the Abelard-Heloise letters, saying: "I rejoice at having renewed Abelard's name, which was
unknown in France, for you and perhaps for many others also". Yet Salutati's words were provocative rather than accurate: Abelard had *not* remained
wholly unknown in France. Roberto de' Bardi, chancellor of the University
of Paris and friend of Petrarch, possessed a copy of the letters, and another
Frenchman, Jean de Hesdin, had challenged Petrarch's claim that there
were no eloquent writers or poets outside Italy by producing Abelard as
France's answer to the Italians. Salutati likewise praises Abelard for his *elo-
quentia*: one has the sense that the letters were being viewed in terms of
the continuity of the classical tradition. In the early years of the fifteenth
century a French bibliophile, Nicolas de Baye, collected five Abelard
manuscripts, including two of the correspondence; the letters are on two occasions denounced for their inflammable content by another famous chancellor of Paris University, Jean Gerson; and Christine de Pisan in one of
her letters paraphrases Heloise's ardent words, that she would rather be
Abelard's *meretrix* than Empress of the whole world.

The fact that, although she was writing in French, Christine uses
Heloise's own Latin expression *meretrix* here, suggests to me that she had

---

[2] The *fidei confessio ad Heloisam* is in *P.L.*, 178, 375-8, the public *apologia seu
fidei confessio, ibid.*, 105-8; on Peter the Venerable's letter, see P. von Moos, *Consolatio* I (Munich, 1971), esp. pp. 277-8, and above, pp. 266-7.

[3] The remainder of this paragraph is a brief summary of Dr. Bozzolo's
evidence.

in mind not only the *Roman de la Rose* [4] — there the word is *putain* — but also Heloise's Latin original.

Despite these testimonies, many of them previously ignored, of French and Italian humanists' concern with Abelard and Heloise, the one humanist whose reactions to the letters we can still trace in detail is and remains Petrarch. Petrarch owned what may well be the earliest of our extant manuscripts of the correspondence — some experts date its handwriting to the mid-thirteenth century [5] — and his sensitive annotations of the text were published in full by Nolhac [6]. Petrarch's reading of Abelard and Heloise spurred him to set down some of his own most secret thoughts and emotions.

His notes are most frequent in the first letter of Heloise. Beside her protestation that Abelard was the one-and-only possessor of her body and spirit, and that she never sought for anything in him save him alone, Petrarch writes: "You, Heloise, act with the utmost sweetness and gentleness in everything" (*Valde predulciter ac blande per totum agis, Heloysa*). When she says of Abelard, "What king or philosopher could equal your fame? What region, city or town did not burn to see you?", Petrarch in his note shows a humorous sympathy, writing: "Here she tells of Peter's fame — if love does not make her testimony suspect" (*si modo testimonium non suspectum amor facit*). When Heloise claims that the love-songs Abelard composed for her made her both famous and envied by other women, Petrarch writes: "How like a woman!" (*Muliebriter*). When she protests to Abelard, "Now most of all, if my spirit is not with you it is nowhere — without you it cannot exist anywhere", Petrarch's note commends both the ardent words and the eloquence of expression: *amicissime et eleganter* — most lovingly written, and elegantly too.

The other larger group of Petrarch's notes occurs in Abelard's second letter to Heloise (*Ep.* V). Here on three occasions Petrarch addresses Abelard himself: the triple vocative, *Petre*, suggests a dialogue between the two minds across the centuries. When Abelard tries to persuade Heloise that God was justified in taking vengeance on them after their marriage, even though he had not done so before, while they lived as lovers, Petrarch writes: "You say this, Peter, either in anger or in great self-torment" (*Vel iratus, vel valde compunctus es, Petre*). As Abelard attempts to justify the ill-starred marriage with Heloise by saying that it was this marriage which, even against her will, took her providentially away from the world, dedicating her to God, Petrarch comments: "So, if I am not wrong, it was most mercifully meant, Peter, that your Heloise should be drawn after you, even though unwilling, by that same bond by which she was bound willingly to you before".

But perhaps Petrarch's greatest tribute to Abelard is the one he

---

[4] Thus Carla Bozzolo, *art. cit.*, p. 213.

[5] See above, n. 17.

[6] P. de Nolhac, *Pétrarque et l'humanisme* (2nd ed., Paris, 1907) II, pp. 220-2.

makes in *De vita solitaria*, speaking of Abelard's withdrawal into solitude and contemplation in the wilderness near Troyes, where nonetheless students from all over Europe flocked to him. In his quest for contemplative serenity Petrarch sees Abelard as not only akin to the glorious writers of antiquity but as a near-contemporary: he writes: "Let me add to so many of the ancients one more recent name... I hear that some thought his orthodoxy suspect, but certainly he was a man of no small genius: Peter Abelard". A moment later, when Petrarch says that even in solitude Abelard did not find the peace he longed for [7], we can surmise how deep Petrarch's empathy for his predecessor must have been. This man who was a legend as poet and philosopher, and as the lover of a sublime woman, but who also thirsted to attain the heights of the contemplative life, whose passion for Heloise could therefore never have been free of spiritual conflict, the thinker whose letters are steeped in Cicero and Seneca, the author of the remarkable self-analysis which is the *Historia Calamitatum* — is it not likely that Petrarch perceived the resemblances in all these features, and that the *Historia* was not simply one aspect of Petrarch's reading but one of the creative elements in his own self-analysis and self-presentation in the *Secretum* [8]?

I should like to suggest that there may have been one other illustrious reader of the Abelard-Heloise letters at this time: Petrarch's friend Giovanni Boccaccio. That Boccaccio *could* have looked at Petrarch's manuscript of the letters is beyond question; that he did so seems to me probable because of certain unusual features in the portrayal of his heroine in the *Fiammetta*. When Fiammetta, in the depths of grieving for the loss of her lover Panfilo, says:

> Certo, io intesi più volte di molte essere oppinione, me di tanta amicizia essere congiunta con Dominedio, che niuna grazia a lui da me dimandata, negata sarebbe; e più volte ancora dalle sante persone per santa fui visitata, non conoscendo esse quel che nell'animo nascondea il tristo viso, e quanto li miei disiderii fossero lontani alle mie parole. O ingannevole mondo, quanto possono in te gl'infinti visi più che li giusti animi, se l'opere sono occulte! Io, più peccatrice che altra, dolente per li miei disonesti amori, però che quelli velo sotto oneste parole, sono reputata santa; ma conoscelo Iddio, che, se senza pericolo

---

[7] Francesco Petrarca, *Prose*, ed. G. Martellotti *et al.* (Milan-Naples, 1955), p. 528:

> Iungam tot veteribus recentiorem unum... apud quosdam ut audio suspecte fidei at profecto non humilis ingenii, Petrum illum cui Abelardi cognomen est... solitudinis trecensis abdita penetravit... sine requie tamen optata...

There is a further allusion to Abelard in Petrarch's *Invectiva contra eum qui maledixit Italie* (ed. A. Bufano, *Opere latine di Francesco Petrarca*, Turin, 1975, p. 1190).

[8] For the *Secretum* we now have the advantage of an admirable detailed commentary: F. Rico, *Vida u Obra de Petrarca I: Lectura del Secretum* (Padua, 1974).

essere potesse, io con vera voce di me sgannerei ogni ingannata persona, né celerei la cagione che trista mi tiene; ma non si puote [9].

Indeed I often perceived it was the opinion of many women that
I was united with God in so great a friendship that no grace asked of
him by me would be denied; more often still I was visited by holy people as if I were a saint, people not knowing what my sad looks concealed within my mind, nor how far my desires were from what I
spoke. Oh easily deceived world, how much more feigned looks prevail
in you than upright minds, provided the deeds are hidden! I, more sinful than other women, aching for my dishonourable delights of love,
because I veil them beneath honourable words, am thought a saint;
but God knows that, if it could be done without danger, I'd tell the
truth about myself and disabuse all who have been deceived, nor
would I hide the cause which keeps me in sorrow; but this cannot be.

I can recall no parallel to these thoughts in the romances or the
artes amandi, or in the ancient authors (such as Seneca and Boethius)
whom Boccaccio is known to have used while composing the *Fiammetta*. Is not the truly striking parallel that of Heloise rejecting
Abelard's imputation of sanctity to her? Already in the *Historia
Calamitatum* Abelard writes: "God granted so great a grace in the
eyes of all to my sister Heloise, who had charge of the other nuns,
that bishops loved her as a daughter, abbots as a sister, the laity as
a mother; and all alike marvelled at her piety, her prudence, and the
incomparable gentleness of her patience in everything. The more
rarely she let herself be seen, that she might devote herself more
purely to holy meditations and prayers within her cell, the more ar-

---

[9] I cite from the edition of C. Salinari and N. Sapegno, *Decameron, Filocolo,
Ameto, Fiammetta* (Milan-Naples, 1952), p. 1156. Francisco Rico has kindly pointed
out to me that Gianfranco Contini alluded to the letters of Heloise in connection
with Boccaccio's *Vita di Dante* (*Letteratura italiana delle origini*, Florence, 1970, p.
803), "circa l'independenza necessaria all'intelletuale". Contini does not, however,
suggest a direct relationship, and the *tesi* he has in mind does not in fact occur "in
una delle lettere di Eloisa", but in the report of her which Abelard gives in the
Historia Calamitatum: "Dehortatio supradicte puelle a nuptiis" (ed. Monfrin, pp.
75-9).
    The question of when Boccaccio first met Petrarch remains problematic (cf. V.
Branca, *Tutte le opere di Giovanni Boccaccio* I, Verona, 1967, pp. 48-50): did he meet
Petrarch in Naples in 1341, or not before Florence in 1350? This later date comes
after the presumed period of composition of *Fiammetta*, "forse fra il 1343 e il 1344"
(*ibid.*, p. 66), though as Branca admits (*loc. cit.*) for this we have "nessun dato preci-
so, ma solo indizi vaghi".

dently the outer world demanded her presence and her spiritual advice [10]".

In the next letter Abelard writes, asking Heloise to pray for him: "...let me come to you alone, whose sanctity undoubtedly has the greatest influence in the eyes of God (*cuius apud deum sanctitatem plurimum non ambigo posse*), and who are bound to do all you can for me...[11]".

But then, in a renowned passage in her second letter, Heloise tells Abelard why his notion of her piety and sanctity — the notion shared by the outer world — is false:

> In tantum vero ille quas pariter exercuimus amantium voluptates dulces mihi fuerunt ut nec displicere mihi nec vix a memoria labi possint... que cum ingemiscere debeam de commissis, suspiro potius de amissis...
>
> Castam me predicant, qui non deprehendunt ypocritam; munditiam carnis conferunt in virtutem, cum non sit corporis sed animi virtus. Aliquid laudis apud homines habens, nichil apud Deum mereor, qui cordis et renum probator est et in abscondito videt. Religiosa hoc tempore iudicor in quo iam parva pars religionis non est ypochrisis, ubi ille maximis extollitur laudibus qui humanum non offendit iudicium...
>
> In omni autem (Deus scit) vite mee statu, te magis adhuc offendere quam Deum vereor... Diu te, sicut et multos, simulatio mea fefellit, ut religioni deputares ypochrisim: et ideo, nostris te maxime commendans orationibus, quod a te expecto a me postulas... Nulla quicquid meriti apud Deum optinent, que reprobis eque ut electis communia sunt: hec autem ea sunt que exterius aguntur, que nulli sanctorum tam studiose peragunt quam ypochrite [12].

The lovers' blisses that we enjoyed together were so sweet to me, they could never cause me to feel regret — I can scarcely even stop thinking about them... I, who should be moaning with sorrow for what I committed, am instead sighing for what I have lost...

They proclaim me chaste, not perceiving my hypocrisy; they see physical abstinence as a virtue, though virtue is a matter not of the body but the mind. Having some praise in the outer world, I deserve none in the eyes of God, who is "the scrutiniser of the heart and loins" and who "sees in the hidden depths". I am thought to be pious at a time such as this, when there's little piety that is not hypocrisy, when one is singled out for the highest praise if one doesn't offend human judgement...

---

[10] *Hist. Cal.* (ed. Monfrin), ll. 1331-40.
[11] Ed. J. T. Muckle, *Mediaeval Studies*, 15 (1953), 75.
[12] Ed. Monfrin (*Hist. Cal.*, pp. 122-3), ll. 193ff.

In every aspect of life — God knows — I am still more afraid of offending you than God... For a long time my dissembling has deceived you, as it has deceived many people, that you might take my hypocrisy for religious experience, and so, commending yourself to my prayers, you ask of me that intercession with God which I expect from you... The things that reprobates and saints alike share can win no favour in the eyes of God — that is, the things done outwardly: not even saints perform these as studiously as hypocrites do.

The parallel is the more remarkable in that nothing in Boccaccio's characterisation of Fiammetta up to this point in the romance could have led us to suppose she might be taken for a saint. This would seem to make the edges of the borrowing clear. Dante's Francesca, I have argued elsewhere [13], owes some aspects of her defence of love to the Heloise portrayed in the *Roman de la Rose*; Boccaccio's Fiammetta may well be the first heroine in western literature to owe some of her relentless self-explication — her anguished exposure of her own outwardly pious demeanour, her realisation that the outer world is easily deluded in matters of sanctity and piety, and her sense of being unable to pray to God effectively — to the Heloise of the Latin letters *.

[13] "Francesca and Heloise", *Comparative Literature*, 26 (1975), 113-35.

* Among the friends and colleagues who kindly read this study in typescript, I owe special thanks to Peter von Moos and Francisco Rico for their stimulating and valuable comments. [The points at which I interpret the Abelard-Heloise *Letters* differently from von Moos are discussed more fully in my *Women Writers of the Middle Ages* (Cambridge 1984), Ch. 5].

10

HELOISE'S *PROBLEMATA* AND *LETTERS:*
SOME QUESTIONS OF FORM AND CONTENT *

While the letters of Heloise have been a focus of much discussion in recent years [1], the *Problemata* have been neglected. The genuineness of Heloise's letters continues to be challenged; that of the *Problemata* had been neither challenged nor investigated. At first view, the evidence for the authenticity of the *Problemata* might seem slender compared with that for the more famous *Epistolae.* Only one manuscript is known: Paris B. N. lat. 14511, from Saint-Victor. The second part of this composite manuscript, copied probably in Paris in a hand datable towards 1400, contains both the *Problemata* (fols. 18r-44v) and Abelard's letter *de studio literarum,* addressed to the community at the Paraclete (fols. 44v-50v). The memory of Abelard and Heloise was kept alive at Saint-Victor — their names occur in the necrology there — and the unique text of the *Problemata,* though copied so late, is a relatively good one. It was corrected from an exemplar in many places, by a hand contemporary with that of the copy-

---

* *Petrus Abaelardus (1079-1142). Person, Werk und Wirkung,* ed. R. Thomas et al. (Trierer Theologische Studien 38, Trier 1980), pp. 53-73.

[1] In addition to the books and articles signalled in my *Abelard and Heloise in Medieval Testimonies* (Glasgow 1976), esp. p. 32 n. 1 [*supra* p. 248 n. 1], the following — mainly very recent — studies deserve mention: J. F. Benton and F. Prosperetti Ercoli, "The Style of the *Historia Calamitatum*", *Viator* VI (1975) 59-86; G. Constable, *Letters and Letter-Collections* (Typologie des sources du Moyen Age occidental 17, Turnhout 1976); J. Jolivet, "Abélard entre chien et loup", *Cahiers de civilisation médiévale* XX (1977) 307-22; U. Kindermann, "Abaelards Liebesbriefe", *Euphorion* LXX (1976) 287-95; J. Leclercq, "Modern Psychology and the Interpretation of Medieval Texts", *Speculum* XLVIII (1973) 476-90; D. E. Luscombe, *Peter Abelard* (Historical Assn., London 1979); J. Miethke, "Abaelards Stellung zur Kirchenreform", *Francia* I (1972) 158-92; H. Silvestre, "Réflexions sur la thèse de J. F. Benton...", *Recherches de théologie ancienne et médiévale* XLIV (1977) 211-16; S. Vanni Rovighi, "Un dibattito sull'autenticità..." *Aevum* L (1976) 357-9; E. B. Vitz, "Type et individu dans l'"autobiographie' médiévale", *Poétique* XXIV (1975) 426-45: P. Zerbi, "Un recente dibattito...", *Studi di letteratura e di storia in memoria di Antonio Di Pietro* (Milano 1977), pp. 3-43.

ist [2]. The links between the *Problemata* and the letters, moreover, are so far-reaching that the questions of authenticity concerning the two works can hardly be considered separately. These are not questions I wish to re-open today. Nor shall I speculate here on the extent to which either work as it survives was revised or edited for publication, or on whether Heloise herself may have undertaken such revision or editing. I shall accept, at least as a working hypothesis, the conclusions of Van den Eynde in his valuable study "Chronologie des écrits d'Abélard à Héloïse" [3]. There he showed that the *Problemata* are "the continuation and complement" of the correspondence, and that Heloise's prefatory epistle to the *Problemata* makes a number of explicit links with her third letter to Abelard. Both the letters and the *Problemata* would appear to be datable to the years 1132-1135.

Although a vast amount has been written on Heloise's letters, a number of important questions have been ignored. First, there has been no detailed discussion of the style of the letters, no attempt to characterize the principal features of that style or ascertain its possible sources. Second, notwithstanding some fine work by Peter von Moos [4], the structure of Heloise's letters still requires more careful consideration. The same holds true, even more, for both the style and structure of the neglected *Problemata*. A third range of questions concerns the description and evaluation of the links between the *Epistolae* and *Problemata*. A fourth — perhaps from the vantage of literary and intellectual history the most important — concerns individuality of expression and content in both these works. For Heloise should be considered not only in relation to Abelard, as has always been customary, but also in relation to other medieval women writers, to see precisely in what ways a womanly awareness comes to be expressed — and to be called in question — in her writings, and how her self-understanding compares with that of other medieval women who have left us written testimonies. This last problem is one

---

[2] For the palaeographical details, and for photographs of the *Problemata*, I am deeply indebted to Marie-Thérèse d'Alverny. The text of the *Problemata* (= P.L. 178, 677-730) is here cited from the MS throughout. Heloise's first two letters to Abelard (*Epp.* I, II) are cited from J. Monfrin's edition of the *Historia Calamitatum* (Paris [3]1967), pp. 111-24; this text has the advantage of lineation. Her third letter (*Ep.* III) is cited from J. T. Muckle's edition, *Mediaeval Studies* XVII (1955), 241-57. These three letters correspond to *Epp.* II, IV, VI in P. L. 178, cols. 181-8, 191-8, 213-26 respectively.

[3] *Antonianum* XXXVII (1962) 337-49, esp. pp. 340-2, 349.

[4] Especially in the essays "Palatini quaestio quasi peregrini", *Mittellateinisches Jahrbuch* IX (1973) 124-58, and "Die Bekehrung Heloises", ibid. XI (1976) 95-125.

that I shall return to in detail, in the course of a forthcoming book on women writers from the third century to the thirteenth. [*Women Writers of the Middle Ages* (Cambridge 1984), Ch. 5]. For the present, I can only adumbrate swiftly some of the work that needs to be done regarding Heloise, in each of the four topics mentioned. The suggestions advanced are necessarily provisional; they are to indicate, above all, how much remains open and how rewarding fuller investigations could be.

It was suggested already in 1910 that Heloise in her letters made use of deliberate rhythmic cadences or *cursus* [5] — but surprisingly, this suggestion has never been verified or seriously studied. Since the appearance of Tore Janson's *Prose Rhythm in Medieval Latin* (1975) [6], however, medievalists have at their disposal a precise notation for describing all varieties of Latin prose rhythm, and a statistical technique sophisticated enough to characterize the rhythmic patterns in each author and sensitive enough to determine in every instance whether the rhythms are chosen or are such as could be fortuitous. Janson, moreover, has given us precious detailed information concerning rhythm in the prose of nearly sixty authors from the ninth century to the early thirteenth. He has not looked at Abelard and Heloise themselves, but has set out evidence that enables us to compare their prose rhythms in detail with those of authors such as Hildebert, John of Salisbury, Peter the Venerable, or Peter of Blois [7]. It seemed to me best to begin a stylistic study by investigating the question of *cursus* in Heloise and Abelard, using Janson's methods and techniques. I chose to test the rhythms in a sample consisting of the first 200 sentence-endings in Abelard's letters to Heloise, and another of the first 200 in Heloise's letters to Abelard. In compiling these samples, I naturally excluded the opening salutations, and any sentences that were quoted from other sources. I included sentences ending with a question-mark or exclamation-mark only if they contained a finite verb [8].

---

[5] G. Constable (ed.), *The Letters of Peter the Venerable* (2 vols., Cambridge Mass. 1967) II 34, citing A. C. Clark, *The Cursus in Medieval and Vulgar Latin* (Oxford 1910), pp. 19-20.

[6] *Prose Rhythm in Medieval Latin from the 9th to the 13th Century* (Studia Latina Stockholmiensia XX).

[7] See especially Janson's Tables A 38, 40, 43, 45 (pp. 113-14).

[8] For Heloise, the sample takes in the whole of her *Epp.* I-II, together with the first 33 sentences of *Ep.* III; for Abelard, it takes in the whole of his first Epistle to Heloise, and 138 sentences from the second: in the ed. of J. T. Muckle (*Mediaeval Studies* XV, 1953), pp. 68-77, 82-91.

After completing the analysis of all sentence-endings in the two samples, I followed Janson in applying the statistical method known as the χ^2 test to the most frequently recurring types of cadence [9]. By means of this test it is possible to establish with certainty which types of cadence are actually favoured by the authors, and to demarcate these from the cadences that are fortuitous, or rather, that cannot be proved more than fortuitous.

From these tests results emerged that were more decisive and more startling than I could have surmised simply from attentive reading of the letters. While both Abelard and Heloise employed a relatively high proportion of rhythmic *cursus*, only two cadences — *cursus velox* and *cursus tardus* — were definitely favoured by them. The χ^2 test for these was abundantly positive, establishing that Abelard's and Heloise's use of these two cadences was intentional [10]. On the other hand — and this is unusual in the light of Janson's results for his group of authors — although the third most frequent cadence in both Abelard's letters and Heloise's was the *cursus planus*, in neither of them did it occur often enough to give a high value in the χ^2 test [11]. That is, their use of the *planus* cadence — which is in fact one of the commoner "natural" cadences in Latin — is not demonstrably present because of deliberate preference; the actual percentage of instances in the samples, however, makes this likely nonetheless. The same holds of the so-called *cursus trispondiacus* (p 4p): while this also occurred relatively often in Abelard's sample and in Heloise's, it did not give a conclusively high value in the χ^2 test.

It is remarkable that, while Abelard in his sample of 200 sentence-endings has 28 examples of pure *cursus velox* and 23 of pure *cursus tardus*, Heloise has 27 of pure *velox* but as many as 31 of pure *tardus*. Such a preponderance of *tardus* over *velox* is extremely unusual in medieval Latin rhythmic prose. If to the examples of pure *tardus* and *velox* in Heloise we add those variant forms that were recognized by medieval theorists, Heloise has no fewer than 51 exam-

---

[9] See the fine discussion of the method by Janson, op. cit. (n. 6) pp. 20 ff.

[10] In Janson's notation, the strict form of *cursus velox* (*hóminem recepístis*) is written pp 4p — that is, the second-last word is proparoxytone, the last a four-syllabled paroxytone. Similarly, the strict form of *cursus tardus* (*íre tentáverit*) is written p 4pp, and that of *planus* (*íllum dedúxit*) is written p 3p.
In Heloise's sample, a χ^2 test for pp 4p yields 12.96 (pp 4p: 12.05; all others: 0.91); and a test for p 4pp yields 15.28 (p 4pp: 14.06; all others: 1.22). The corresponding χ^2 tests for Abelard yield, respectively, 12.17 (pp 4p: 11.26; all others: 0.91), and 13.85 (p 4pp: 13.09; all others: 0.76).

[11] In Heloise's sample, a χ^2 test for p 3p yields 0.25 (p 3p: 0.23; all others: 0.02); in Abelard's, 2.76 (p 3p: 2.57; all others: 0.19).

ples of *cursus tardus* in her sample of 200 sentence-endings, as against 32 of *velox*. That is, where 16% of her cadences are of the *velox* type, 25.5% are of the *tardus* type. In Abelard, *tardus* with the admitted variants rises to 18% [12].

I do not know if Heloise's keen adherence to *tardus* cadences, exceptional as it is, is sufficiently distinct from Abelard's practice to differentiate her prose style decisively from his. The individuality of her prose, I would suggest, can be perceived rather in her conjunction of these patterns of rhythmic cadence with passages of sustained *Kunstprosa*, rich in rhymes and homoioteleuta. Such passages can occur at times, too, in Abelard's letters, at certain moments expressing deep emotion, urgent admonition, or prayer [13]. Yet they are distinctly rarer and briefer than in the letters of Heloise. She has extended passages in which rhyme, assonance and parallelism have been sensitively interwoven, the cadences that depend on rhythm and those that depend on rhyme being artistically harmonized. Moreover, such examples of highly-wrought diction occur not only in her two renowned impassioned letters to Abelard — where we might expect Heloise to use every resource of persuasion she knew in order to regain Abelard's personal commitment to her; they occur likewise in the far calmer letters: the third to Abelard, and the epistle with which the *Problemata* begin, as well as in Heloise's solemn, measured letter of reply to Peter the Venerable. (See Examples 1-4 in the Appendix below).

This very unusual combination of features — the practice of a *cursus* that favours *tardus* much more than *velox*, and the frequent conjunction of the *tardus* and *velox* cadences with elaborate rhyme, both within sentences and at sentence-endings — all this enables us to make some precise inferences about the sources of Heloise's epistolary style.

[12] See the tables in the Appendix below. On the variants explicitly mentioned in medieval theoretical texts, see Janson pp. 28-29. To those specified there must be added the variant pp 3 pp for *tardus*, which occurs as a demonstrably desired cadence in authors as diverse as Alvarus of Cordova, Anastasius Bibliothecarius, Liutprand, Peter Damiani, Pope Gregory VII, Berengarius of Tours, Alphanus of Salerno, and Pope Paschalis II. These examples (deduced from Janson's tables, pp. 109-15) suggest to me that this variant of *tardus* came to be favoured particularly in Italy in the later eleventh century. For *planus* I have also included the variant pp 2, since Janson's tables show it to be a desired cadence in numerous authors throughout Europe from the ninth century onwards.

[13] Cf. for instance, in Abelard's second letter to Heloise, the passage *Vide soror... intuere* (ed. Muckle, *Mediaeval Studies* XV 92, lines 1-7; P.L. 178, 209 D), or *Puni, obsecro... rogat Propheta* (ibid. XV 93, the last five lines; P.L. 178, 212 B).

Among the authors whose prose cadences Janson has analysed there are a certain number who favour *tardus* cadences more than *velox*, yet nearly always such authors favour the simpler *cursus planus* considerably more than either *tardus* or *velox*. This is true for instance of Hincmar of Reims in the ninth century, or of Liutprand of Cremona in the tenth [14]. The only notable earlier author who favours *tardus* more than *velox*, and who does not favour *planus* at all, is Gerbert of Reims [15]. Yet Gerbert's letters do not show a particularly high proportion of desired rhythmic cadences among his sentence-endings as a whole, and besides, there are no traces of sustained deliberate rhyme. Conversely, Rather of Verona's letters show abundant use of rhymed prose, but no steady evidence of *cursus* [16].

In the twelfth century, all the leading writers whose prose rhythms Janson has investigated — Hildebert, John of Salisbury, Bernard Silvestris, Peter the Venerable, Peter of Blois — show a decisive (indeed often massive) preponderance of *cursus velox* over *cursus tardus* [17]. All of these writers also specifically favour *cursus planus*, though they do not use it anything like as often as *velox*. Rhythmically, therefore, the difference between Abelard and Heloise on the one hand and the major stylists of the twelfth-century French and Anglo-Norman world on the other is profound. Moreover, none of these stylists displays an artistry comparable to Heloise's in her elaborate use of rhyme.

Only one author among those studied by Janson exhibits a pattern of cadences that is closely comparable to Abelard and Heloise: it is the Italian Adalbertus Samaritanus, in his treatise on letter-writing, the *Praecepta dictaminum* [18]. This treatise, which Franz-Josef Schmale in his fine edition argues was a complete innovation in rhetorical teaching, began to circulate about 1115 and reached northern France shortly thereafter [19]. Already in the 1130s there is evidence

---

[14] Janson, Tables A 1, A 3 (p. 109).

[15] Ibid. Table A 15 (p. 110).

[16] Cf. F. Weigle, "Die Briefe Rathers von Verona", *Deutsches Archiv für Erforschung des Mittelalters* I (1937) 147-94. Weigle is correct in what he says of Rather, though his assumption that regular *cursus* was not yet possible in the tenth century — in support of which he cites some distinguished older scholars, including Wilhelm Meyer and Eduard Norden — has obviously been disproved since he wrote.

[17] See the Tables cited in n. 7; for Bernard Silvestris, see Table A 42 (p. 113), and the observations in my edition of Bernard's *Cosmographia* (Leiden 1978), pp. 58-63.

[18] Ed. F.-J. Schmale, MGH, Quellen zur Geistesgeschichte des Mittelalters III (Weimar 1961).

[19] Ed. cit. pp. 1-20; for another view, presenting Alberic of Monte Cassino as

of its having been known and used, for instance, at Sens [20]. Adalbertus, in the course of his brief treatise (191 sentences), has 44 examples of strict *cursus tardus*, as against 18 of *velox* and 23 of *planus* [21]. I do not know where such proportions can be paralleled except in the letters of Abelard and Heloise [22]. Moreover, Adalbertus' model letters, which constitute the main part of his treatise, are all marked by their pervasive *Kunstprosa*, with regular — at times almost excessive — employment of rhyme. (See Example 5 in the Appendix) [23].

Stylistically, the coincidence is too great to be mere coincidence. Should one infer, then, that Abelard, and more pronouncedly Heloise, learnt from Adalbertus' treatise and modelled their epistolary style on his? It is tempting to conclude this, yet it may also be too simple. Certainly Adalbertus, by virtue of his choice of cadences, occupies a unique place in the tradition of the *ars dictandi*, whether or not we follow Schmale in seeing him as the actual inventor of this *ars*. Neither of Adalbertus' best-known Italian contemporaries among the rhetoricians, Hugh of Bologna or the slightly older Alberic of Monte Cassino, uses any form whatever of deliberate *cursus* (this fact, again, was established by Janson), whereas later French teachers

---

the first major teacher of *ars dictaminis*, see H. Bloch, *Settimane di studio del Centro italiano di studi sull'alto medievo* XIX (1972) 587-99. The ultimate origins of this *ars*, and the question, what methods of teaching letter-writing existed in the schools of eleventh-century France, remain problematic, and would repay detailed investigation.

[20] G. Constable, *The Letters* (cit. n. 5) II 32.

[21] See the table (based on Janson) in the Appendix below. With the variants included, the figures for Adalbertus become: *tardus* 64, *velox* 22, *planus* 36.

[22] It would be valuable to make a detailed study of the *Epistolae duorum amantium* (ed. E. Könsgen, Leiden-Köln 1974) with these stylistic considerations in mind.

[23] It is perhaps worth signalling the dominance of *tardus* cadences in two passages, from Heloise and Adalbertus (Appendix, Exx. 1 and 5), which I chose not in order to illustrate *cursus* but rather to show the more extravagant uses of rhymed prose in the service of emotional utterance. In the passage from Heloise, four of the six sentences end in a *tardus* cadence, in that from Adalbertus, five out of the seven. This passage shows how the *dictator* imagines artistically persuasive renderings of the themes of abandonment, sorrow, and appeal for support — here the expressive techniques are of special relevance to the letters of Heloise. It should be noted, however, that this particular letter in the *Praecepta* is intended for a student, who is asking his parents for financial — not moral — support ! The student, presumably a young Italian, goes on to speak of himself as exiled in France — among *alias gentes et feras nationes* — in much the same tone as Abelard was to use of Saint-Gildas: *Terra quippe barbara... et gens terre illius inhumana atque incomposita* (*Hist. Cal.*, ed. Monfrin, ll. 1243-7).

of letter-writing, such as Bernard of Meung, overwhelmingly favour *cursus velox* rather than *cursus tardus* [24]: in this they remain absolutely within the French and Anglo-Norman tradition of prose rhythm that spans the century from Hildebert to Peter of Blois. However, according to Schmale's researches, Adalbertus' treatise was almost at once drawn upon heavily by several other *dictatores* [25]. Until the whole group of early twelfth-century *artes* is edited and their interrelationships are fully clarified, a definitive judgment will not be possible. Yet the evidence indicates that both Abelard and Heloise must have known either Adalbertus' *ars* itself or one that was very close to it, and that they were stylistically influenced by such an *ars*, though Heloise imitated the features more consciously and extensively than Abelard. That is, not only is Heloise's writing a product of high artistic nurture, but we can see how it was enhanced by one of the most modern and most unusual stylistic currents of her day. In style she — and to a lesser extent Abelard — belongs to a specific *nouvelle vague* in letter-writing. This wave was soon to ebb again both in Italy and France, yet its crest brought with it such innovations, not only in the sheer technique of combining certain cadences and rhyme, but also in extending and refining the artistry of persuasion, that however much we may feel that the human content of Heloise's letters surpasses what can be found in treatises, we must nonetheless reckon with a treatise showing her certain expressive techniques, and thereby liberating her powers of self-expression.

The rhetorical structure of Heloise's letters raises complex and fascinating questions. Today I can give only a few indications of the kind of analysis that seems to me worth pursuing.

In her first letter to Abelard, after a prelude recalling details from the *Historia calamitatum* and the effect that reading these had on her, Heloise tries to persuade Abelard of his unique obligation to her and her community at the Paraclete:

> Huius quippe loci   tu post deum   solus es fundator,
> solus   huius oratorii   constructor,
> solus   huius congregationis   edifficator [26].

[24] The relevant tables in Janson for Hugh of Bologna, Alberic, and Bernard of Meung are, respectively, A 48, 27, 49. Tables A 47-49 offer a striking *aperçu* of the stylistic differences between Adalbertus and Bernard of Meung (18 strict *velox* as against 394, 44 strict *tardus* as against 2), and of how much both teachers differ statistically from Hugh of Bologna, who, like Alberic, favours no rhythmic cadences at all.

[25] Ed. cit. pp. 17-20.

[26] Ed. Monfrin, ll. 76-78 (p. 13); here and below, the line-arrangement of the text, and some modifications of punctuation, are my own.

The repeated *solus* recurs soon afterwards, introducing a leitmotif of both the letters and the *Problemata*: this is the motif of Heloise's total obedience to Abelard, to his *iussus*. Abelard commanded her into marriage, just as later he commanded her into monastic life. She obeys his commands, then and now, unconditionally, however great the cost to herself:

> ...qui solus es   in causa dolendi,
> solus sis   in gratia consolandi.
> Solus quippe es   qui me contristare
>   seu consolari   valeas,
> et solus es   qui plurimum id mihi debeas,
> et nunc maxime, cum universa que iusseris in tantum impleverim
> ut, cum te in aliquo offendere non possem,
> me ipsam pro iussu tuo perdere sustinerem [27].

Iubere, iussio, iussus and their cognates recur throughout Heloise's letters to Abelard — as do *obedire, obedientia* and related words; and they are inseparable from the refrain-like *solus*: that Heloise has done everything at Abelard's command is also the reason for the bond she claims with him alone. The thought may even carry over, by *annominatio*, into the theme of consolation: for Abelard to console her (*con-solari*) is for him to share — and thus alleviate — her solitude. For, as Isidore explains (*Etym.* X 38), a *consolator* is one who devotes himself *soli... cui loquitur, et solitudinem levat.*

At the close of Heloise's third letter (which had opened with renewed resolves to obey Abelard's *iussio*, to curb her expressions of immoderate grief, and to seek from him only such consolation as a spiritual director can give), the tripartite sentence expressing Abelard's unique role, which had opened the first "movement" of the first letter, recurs, transformed. In the last paragraph Heloise writes:

> Tu quippe   post deum   huius loci fundator,
> tu   per deum   nostre congregationis es plantator,
> tu   cum deo   nostre sis religionis institutor [28].

Only the first line in this triad closely resembles its counterpart in

---

[27] Ibid. 11. 132-8 (p. 114).

[28] Ed. Muckle, *Mediaeval Studies* XVII 253. H. Silvestre, art. cit. (n. 1) p. 215, who fails to see the rhetorical design here, imagines that this passage helps to show the inauthenticity of the letters: "On observe également des insistances suspectes... On y souligne vraiment trop le rôle de *fundator,* de *plantator,* d'*institutor* du Maître..."

the opening letter; in the other two, Heloise's further obedience to Abelard's thoughts and wishes is made clear. Instead of the repeated utterances "only you, only you can help me", she now goes on to say "you through God", "you with God"; and the last line here, with its invitation *nostre sis religionis institutor*, transmutes the earlier, more self-bound expression *solus sis in gratia consolandi*: there Heloise had made no mention of religion or of God.

There is an element of circular form in the relation between the opening of the first letter and the close of the third; at the same time, the nuances are different: they suggest Heloise's attempt to overcome her personal grief by thinking more deeply of the spiritual life of her community, in obedience to Abelard's command.

I would suggest a similar element of circular form in the *Problemata*. Here the opening [29] takes up the motif of Heloise obeying Abelard's command, in the sense that had been clarified in the third letter. Abelard has enjoined her and her nuns to study Scripture intensively; they do so, *tuam in hoc quoque quoad possumus implentes obedienciam* — obeying in this too, as best we can; just as previously Heloise had obeyed, as best she might, in curbing her grieving protests — at least in word, and, if she could, even in thought [30]. And just as in the letters — near the opening of the first and at the close of the third — Heloise stressed that this obedience of hers implied an obligation for him, so again the *Problemata* begin by stressing not only Heloise's submission but Abelard's corresponding debt: *quid debeas recorderis / et debitum solvere non pigriteris* [31]. In this instance, the "debt" is to answer the questions that have arisen out of the women's scriptural reading. But I think it is also significant that the last of these forty-two questions returns yet again to the theme of command and obedience. It reads:

[29] See the extract edited in the Appendix below.

[30] *Ep.* III (ed. Muckle, XVII 241):
Revocabo itaque manum a scripto
in quibus linguam a verbis temperare non valeo.
Utinam sic animus dolentis
parere promptus sit
quemadmodum dextra scribentis!

[31] Compare *Ep.* I (ed. Monfrin), ll. 111-13:
...debito pensa, ut quod devotis communiter debes feminis, unice tue devotius solvas.

J. Leclercq, art. cit. (n. 1) p. 483, points out that the text of St Paul which underlies this passage (and, we might add, that in the *Problemata*) is *1 Cor* VII 3: *Uxori vir debitum reddat... et uxor viro.* He makes the admirable comment: "The invitation has a barely concealed nuptial symbolism raised to the level of devotion".

(fol. 41ra) Utrum aliquis in eo quod facit a domino sibi concessum vel etiam iussum peccare possit querimus.

We ask whether anyone could sin in something that she does which has been conceded or even commanded by her lord.

The word *dominus* is ambiguous here: whilst it may refer to God, it can clearly also refer to Abelard, as it does, for instance, at the close of Heloise's third letter: *Tibi nunc, domine, dum vivis, incumbit..*.[32] (On you, my lord, it is incumbent, as long as you live...). And it is hard to read this final *Problema* without perceiving an echo of the anguished reproach Heloise had made Abelard in her second letter: in every aspect of her life, she had said, she fears to offend Abelard more than God, longs to please him more than to please God, because *Tua me ad religionis habitum iussio, / non divina traxit dilectio*[33] — it was your command, not love of God, that drew me into the religious life.

It would seem that the preoccupation which prompted the final *Problema* lies not so much in the theological issues about what is sinful, pardonable or good in the sexual pleasures of marriage, which Abelard, drawing on Paul and Augustine, discusses in his reply. Rather, the question implied the greater, existential difficulty: what is the standard of integrity for one who lives a life she has not chosen, that has been imposed on her as a command by her *dominus*, her husband? The motif of the command takes us back not only to the beginning of the *Problemata*, closing this circle of obedience, question, and appeal to Abelard to pay his debt as counsellor; in a sense it also leads back into the first circle of three letters, where the meaning of that *iussio* was reflected on in rending human terms.

At the same time, it is important to stress that, in the *Problemata* as in the letters, the questionings and probings are given a highly conscious literary formation. Heloise, having formally learnt and mastered a particular range of rhetorical techniques, in both *Epistolae* and *Problemata* summons up every resource she has — stylistic, intellectual, and emotional — to express herself in a manner that she deems worthy of her. She writes not only for Abelard privately: such expressions as *noverunt omnes* suggest she is aware, at least implicitly, of writing for the world, for posterity. In her second letter, where the deliberate rhetorical organization is perhaps easiest to perceive at a swift glance, she is writing, we might say, her counterpart to the

[32] Ed. Muckle, XVII 253.
[33] Ed. Monfrin, 11. 241-2 (p. 123); cf. *Ep.* 1, 11. 238-9 (p. 116): *non religionis devotio, sed tua tantum pertraxit iussio.*

Heroides. Yet not in the playfully feigned fashion of the young woman Constantia in the previous generation, composing an *Heroides* epistle for Baudri of Bourgueil [34], but with an art of incomparable seriousness.

To indicate the rhetorical structure of such a letter may seem an overclinical procedure to readers who are more concerned with emotional response; yet I believe it is vital to set that response in its right *literary* context, stylistically and intellectually. For, in Curtius' striking phrase, "Das schönste Obst reift an Spalieren [35]".

Heloise at all events shows her awareness of the *Spalieren* [36]: at the opening of her second letter she stresses that, in terms of *ars dictandi*, Abelard had committed a *soloecismus*: transgressing the norms of letter-writing and indeed of nature itself (*preter consuetudinem*

---

[34] Ed. P. Abrahams, *Les œuvres poètiques de Baudri de Bourgueil* (Paris 1926), pp. 344-9; cf. my *Medieval Latin and the Rise of European Love-Lyric* (2 vols., Oxford [2]1968), esp. I 217. A new edition of Baudri's poetry by K. Hilbert, *Baldricus Burgulianus. Carmina* (Editiones Heidelbergenses 19) has been announced for 1979. [Ed. K. Hilbert, pp. 271-6].

[35] Ernst Robert Curtius, *Europäische Literatur und Lateinisches Mittelalter* (Bern [2]1954), p. 204.

[36] The following schematic articulation of the letter, with line-references to Monfrin's text, may help clarify the discussion below:

   1 *Salutatio*
   2 The manner of Abelard's *salutatio* in his letter (*contra ordinem*)
  11 The matter of Abelard's letter (*desolatio*)
I. 26 Imprecation 1 (*Parce...*)
      [*auctoritates:* Matthew, Seneca]
  48 Catachresis 1 (*Mortis tue mentio mors*)
  54 Imprecation 2 (*Parce...*)
      [*auctoritas:* Lucan]
  72 Catachresis 2 (*crudelem mihi per omnia deum!*)
II. 81 *Planctus* 1 (*O me miserarum miserrimam...*)
     [97 justification of *planctus*]
 122 *Planctus* 2 (*O me miseram...*)
     [124 justification of *planctus*: Proverbs, Ecclesiastes]
III. Self-analysis:
 153 *Penitentia*
 193 *Voluptates*
 221 *Hypocrisis*
IV. *Recusatio*:
 247 *Noli...Noli...Noli...Noli...*
     [*auctoritates:* Isaiah, Ezekiel, Ecclesiastes]
 261 *Quiesce...Nemo...Nulla...*
     [*auctoritates*: Jeremiah, Proverbs, Ecclesiasticus]
 282 *Nolo...Non...Non...*
     [*auctoritates*: Corinthians, Timothy, Jerome]

epistolarum, immo contra ipsum ordinem naturalem rerum), he had
written to her placing her name before his in the *salutatio* of his Epistle. As he had transgressed in the manner of his reply, so too in the
matter. Instead of giving her the solace she had implored, he had
written in such a way as to foment her grief: his letter was *desolatio*,
not *consolatio*. In this prelude, Heloise elaborates the contrasts between what is and what should have been in sentences laden with an-
tithetical and anaphoric expressions. The reversals of the *rectus...
ordo* (7) on the plane of rhetoric foreshadow the human reversals, in
the *ordo naturalis rerum*, which become the theme of her lament.

The principal part of the letter can perhaps be helpfully analysed in terms of four "movements". The first of these consists of two
groups of imprecations (beginning at lines 26 and 54 in Monfrin's
text), each introduced by the refrain *Parce...parce...* Each is but-
tressed by *auctoritates* (Matthew and Seneca in the first group, Lucan
in the second); each comes to its climax in a memorable figure of
catachresis: the first with the words

> Mortis tue mentio mors quedam nobis est

(the mention of your death is a kind of death to us), the second with
the exclamation

> O si fas sit dici, crudelem mihi per omnia deum!

(oh if it were lawful to be spoken, God cruel to me in all things), and
the oxymora that follow from it (*o inclementem clementiam! o infor-
tunatam fortunam!...*).

The next movement I would see as a lyrical *planctus*, again in
two parts, each introduced by a refrain-like phrase: *O me miserarum
miserrimam* (81), *O me miseram* (122). So, too, in each half of this
planctus the grounds for lamentation are adduced and justified: in
the first, which includes the lament against Fortuna (see Appendix,
Ex. 1), it is that the whole course of justice has been overthrown;
in the second, that women always cause the downfall of great men.
(Here a range of biblical *auctoritates* is cited in support).

The third movement in the letter, I would suggest, consists essentially of a self-portrait. It has three principal motifs, that are
linked by the notion of repentance: the first (beginning at 153) is
self-defence: her misery, Heloise argues, is a penance she gladly accepts for Abelard's sake; Job, Gregory and Ambrose are adduced as
authorities to characterize true, religious penitence. The next motif
(193) is an introspective reverie: hers is no true penitence, she has not

received divine grace, she dreams only of the voluptuousness she has lost. This leads into the third motif, of self-analysis: she expounds the nature of her hypocrisy in living the religious life, a life that was never her own choice but Abelard's *iussio*.

The final movement (starting at 247) is a series of negatives, an elaborate figure of *recusatio*. With four sentences that begin with the imperative, *Noli*, Heloise rejects Abelard's view of her as pious and acquiescent, as one who can help him by her prayers; she enlists quotations from Isaiah, Ezekiel and Solomon in support of her claim. A second group of sentences of negation, beginning *Quiesce... Nemo... Nulla...* is supported by four other scriptural passages; finally, in the conclusion of the epistle, there are three sentences beginning *Nolo... Non... Non...*, and three further *auctoritates*: Corinthians, Timothy, and Jerome. It would be trifling to insist that this final movement comprises ten negations, counterpointed by ten authorities; I mention it only to underline that even the lacerating self-portrayal in this letter has been shaped with symmetries that may extend to the minutest details; that the personal content is inseparable from the range of learned reference and the pervasive rhetorical art.

Outwardly at least, the *Problemata* seem far less personal than the three earlier letters, yet there are numerous links between the two works, reflecting some of the same preoccupations. To indicate very briefly one or two of these: the citation of Jerome in the introduction — *Ama scienciam scripturarum et carnis vicia non amabis* — must relate directly to the way that Heloise, through the study of Scripture, is trying to obey Abelard's command, to efface her delight in voluptuous memories and her sighs for the life she has lost; for, as she herself comments in her third letter, speaking of the irrelevance of parts of the Benedictine rule to a community such as hers, it is not the temptations of over-eating or drunkenness that present danger to her and her young women. The *vicia carnis*, it is clear, are sexual ones, and ones that now lie in thought and desire, not in reality — for, like Abelard, Heloise is convinced that guilt lies in intentions, not in acts. The lines from Jerome suggest it is the indulgence in sensual reveries, such as Heloise describes in her second letter, that she hopes to tame by devoting herself to scriptural study, to obey Abelard as best she can in trying to make the spiritual life an inner reality for herself.

The fear that she has not yet achieved this fully may lie behind the second question, where she returns to a problem that had concerned her in her third letter: the meaning of the passage in James' Epistle that seems to say, whoever offends in one point of the law becomes guilty in all. Conversely she asks (Problem 14), why do the

Beatitudes in the Sermon on the Mount sound as if each one alone were enough to make blessed? Here Abelard, expounding "blessed are the pure in heart" in his reply, dwells especially on those who, in marriage, enjoy physical voluptuousness: they can be *mundi corde, et non corpore*, and hence they can be blessed, "even in yielding to much voluptuousness and sensual desire".

˙ The question of the nature of true penitence — brooded over with anguish in Heloise's second letter — is taken up once more in her eleventh *Problema*: why should there be more joy in heaven over one sinner who repents than over the ninety-nine just who do not need to? Is it not better and more perfect to avoid sin than to sin and make amends? Abelard, answering that the repentance is not worth more as such, but that the joy is greater because of all the anxiety and grief that had preceded, assuredly still has Heloise's earlier letter in mind.

Many of the *Problemata* are purely exegetical and appear to have no personal connotations. Close reading suggests that Heloise must have dispatched the problems in groups, for some (such as 10-12, or 25-26) can be seen to belong together by way of verbal links, and certain larger groups (such as 14-20, or 30-39) are linked both by verbal cross-references and by arising out of the same series of biblical chapters (Matthew V-VII, or 1 Kings I-II); these texts will have been the object of intensive study at the Paraclete. It is possible to conjecture personal reverberations in a number of other *Problemata*, such as those concerning Anna, *mulier nimis infelix* (31-34), or the woman taken in adultery (8), yet it could also be over-speculative, or even falsifying, to try to make explicit here certain analogies that are, if anything, oblique and not insistent. One other *Problema*, however, should at least be mentioned: when Heloise asks Abelard to elucidate the biblical "do as you would be done by" (20), the problem she puts to him is:

> Si quis enim vult ut in malo sibi quisquam consenciat, numquid debet illi prebere consensum iure consimili [37]?

It would be difficult to read this question — that arises so unpredictably out of the biblical phrase — without recalling Heloise's consent, against her conscience, to Abelard's insistence on marriage, or the words in her first letter: *Que plurimum nocens, plurimum, ut nosti, sum innocens* [38].

---

[37] B. N. lat. 14511, fol. 33va (= P. L. 178, 708 B, with the reading *in re consimili*).

[38] Ed. Monfrin, ll. 211-12 (p. 116).

Just as, in her third letter, Heloise seeks a rule for the Paraclete that is specifically apt for herself and her community, so too, I submit, in the other letters and in the *Problemata* one of her principal concerns is to find a way of life and an ethic that is authentic for her, no mere extrinsic imposition, law or command. As she realizes that much of the Benedictine Rule is inept to guide the lives of women — for it was not set down with that in mind — so too is she aware that her own life — and her destiny, as it was shaped by Abelard's commands — is unique, and needs to be sustained by a guidance that cannot be found ready-made, whether in Scripture or *auctoritates*. In her quest for an integrity that is her integrity, a rule that can become her inner rule, she has much in common with certain other sensitive medieval women who have left us some record of their comparable endeavour. I should like to conclude with three brief illustrations of this point.

In 843, Duchess Dhuoda, living at Uzès in Provence, in enforced separation from her husband and children, completed the *Liber manualis* that she wrote for her sixteen-year-old son William. Historians and philologists have scarcely noticed that, if one listens attentively to the often ungainly, often uncertain Latin of Dhuoda's prose and verse, one of the most cherishable and most distinctive voices in medieval literature can still be heard. Gradually it becomes clear how little of what Dhuoda set down for her son can be seen in terms of conventional wisdom, of *sententiae*: there emerges a woman wholly individual in her empathy of thought and feeling. —

> I urge you, William, my handsome, lovable son, amid the wordly preoccupation of your life, not to be slow in acquiring many books where, through most holy teachers, you should discover and learn something about God the creator — more things and greater than are written here... What more shall I say? Your Dhuoda is always there to encourage you, my son, and when I am gone, which will come to pass, you'll have the little book of moral teaching here as a memorial: you will be able to look at me still, as into a mirror, reading me with your mind and your body and praying to God; you will find there too, in full, what tasks you owe me. My son, you will have teachers who will give you more lessons, and more valuable ones, yet not in the same way, with the heart burning within, as I with mine, my first-born one [39].

In the verse prologue, likewise, Dhuoda shows she is aware of

---

[39] Dhuoda, *Manuel pour mon fils* (ed. P. Riché, SC 225, Paris 1975), pp. 114-16.

the uniqueness of what she can give: she prays for God's grace to bestow on William

> peace and security of body and mind, that he may flourish in the world, and have children, and hold what is here in such a way as not to lose what is beyond... Let him be generous and prudent, merciful and brave, let measure never desert him; he will never have anyone like me (to tell him this), I who, though unworthy, am also his mother... [40]

In the abstract we might say that Dhuoda's aim in her book for William was to work out for him a "Ritterliches Tugendsystem", ideals that were inseparably chivalric and Christian. Long before Walther von der Vogelweide despaired of bringing "possessions and honour in the world, and God's grace, together in a single heart" —

> jâ leider desn mac niht gesîn,
> daz guot und weltlich êre
> und gotes hulde mêre
> zesamene in ein herze komen [41] —

and even longer before Curtius and other scholars debated whether a "chivalric system of virtues" was theoretically possible in the twelfth century [42], Duchess Dhuoda had shown her son that it was existentially possible. With her loving heart she tried to outline for William the particular harmony that he might achieve between his *mundanae curae* and the grace of God. The precepts of the clerical world, she knows, might be more learned or worthier in themselves than anything she could offer; but could they ever mean as much to

---

[40] Ibid. p. 76:

Pax et securitas	corporis et mente,
In quo in saeculo	vigeat cum prole,
Ita tenens ista	careat ne illa...
Largus et prudens,	pius et fortis,
Temperantiam necne	deserat unquam.
Mis michi similem	non habebit unquam,
Quanquam indigna	genitrixque sua.

The phrase *pax et securitas* is from 1 *Thess.* V 3, where the context evokes the sense of sudden doom (*tunc repentinus eis superveniet interitus*) and the momentousness of the second Coming.

[41] Walther von der Vogelweide, *Die Gedichte*, ed. Lachmann-Kraus-Kuhn (Berlin [13]1965), 8, 19-22.

[42] The principal essays in the debate have been assembled by G. Eifler: *Ritterliches Tugendsystem* (Wege der Forschung LVI, Darmstadt 1970).

her son, could they ever be as sensitively adapted to his specific situation in life?

The same quest for a moral ideal congruent with a unique situation can be perceived, I think, in the testimonies concerning an English contemporary of Heloise's, Christina of Markyate — testimonies that, though not written down by Christina herself, are nonetheless essentially autobiographical [43]. Her life was recorded in loving and vivacious detail, by a monk of St. Albans around the mid-twelfth century, while Christina (born c. 1096-98) was still alive and near at hand. The fullness of the later part of the surviving narrative — though unfortunately it is both fragmentary and incomplete — makes clear that the biographer was obtaining his information from Christina's lips, and was still able to question her regularly about details. While he occasionally allowed himself to veer towards the conventions of hagiography, such moments contrast so patently with all else in his account that it makes the authenticity of the remainder the more evident.

One might feel that the first tempests in Christina's life — her resolve, against all brutality from parents and relatives, to remain a virgin and not consummate the marriage that had been forced on her — could be a mere ascetic commonplace. Hence it is the more surprising that, when she had escaped her husband, so as to live a hermit's life, Christina admits to feeling a passionate sexual attraction to the cleric whom the Bishop of York had appointed as her protector and chaperon. This man, who desired Christina equally, is never named — presumably he was still living, and perhaps prominent, at the time the *Life* was being written. Yet after the unhappiness of sexual loathing for her husband Burthred, and of guilty, unsatisfied longing for her unnamed protector, Christina found a very different — and it would seem radiant — relationship with another man, Abbot Geoffrey of St. Albans. It was a refined, half-spiritualized eroticism that became Christina's inner *regula*.

The more startling aspects of her relationship with Geoffrey emerge clearly from the *Vita* — I know of nothing quite like them in the realms of Christian *amicitia* or of real or imagined *hôhe minne*. One might say that Christina became Abbot Geoffrey's spiritual director, with almost telepathic insight into his secret thoughts and plans and movements. At times she seems to show a tyrannical possessiveness towards him, as when she is able on three occasions to

---

[43] *The Life of Christina of Markyate*, ed. and tr. by C. H. Talbot (Oxford 1959). Cf. most recently C. J. Holdsworth, "Christina of Markyate", in *Medieval Women*, ed. D. Baker (Oxford 1978), pp. 185-204.

prevent him from making an eagerly anticipated — and indeed officially demanded — journey to Rome. Geoffrey appears at first as an autocratic, wordly-wise figure, engrossed in financial-political intrigues for his great abbey — the medieval equivalent of an overweening College President or Vice-Chancellor. Yet by Christina's "amour rédempteur" this man is transformed: he becomes inwardly ennobled, made capable of spiritual progress through her tenderness for him. Throughout, they both openly persist in extravagant expressions of endearment and companionship — he is her *dilectus*, her *familiarissimus* — though fully aware of the slanderous murmurs of the world around them.

To illustrate at least one aspect of their relationship: the second time Geoffrey was to be sent as ambassador to Rome, and he was looking forward to seeing his Roman friends again (*familiares suos revisere cupiebat* [44]), Christina,

> stifling her sighs, said: Go with the Lord, for I am certain that, whether you go or stay, in you the divine will shall be fulfilled. For in my prayers I saw a certain enclosure, made of radiant white woodwork... lacking door and windows, like a cloister, but round. The grass within that little meadow was greener than all common grasses; delighting in it, I saw you, the cause of my anxiety, standing joyfully enough within that walled meadow, with a kind of embraceable sweetness (*quadam amplectenda dulcedine*). And when I was still anxious, lest you should have no way of slipping out, by digging or by any other art, I was told: the walled meadow that you see has only one keyholder — God [45].

Geoffrey was suddenly, inexplicably, called back from his embassy, and the biographer adds:

> Christina won, in that she knew how to love more victoriously (*victoriosius diligere novit*); she knew how to love more victoriously in that she strove to obtain the outcome of all causes from God.

Christina's love for God, and her blissful "imprisoning" of her beloved Geoffrey, seem to have been totally integrated, or blended, in her thought.

The ideal of emotional openness and tender sensibility, rising

---

[44] *The Life*, p. 162.

[45] Ibid., p. 164. My translation (here and in the lines below) differs from that of Talbot in a number of ways, that relate especially to the visual details and the nuances of emotion.

into spirituality, to which Saint Christina and Abbot Geoffrey aspired together, is never spelt out explicitly; yet it seems to me an unmistakable instance, like that of Heloise and Abelard, or of Dhuoda and William, of the ethical ideal that is sought existentially, in terms of a relationship which is recognized and affirmed as unique. The ideal is seen as genuine inasmuch as it fits that relationship.

My final example is from a group of texts that have recently become famous; they are exceptional in that here, from Latin records, we can reconstruct with almost verbal certainty the words and thoughts of a number of unlettered medieval men and women: I am referring to the interrogations of those suspected of Cathar sympathies, or of being themselves Cathars, in the region of Montaillou. Notwithstanding the brilliance of Le Roy Ladurie's discussion in his book *Montaillou* [46], and the fact that the complete records were published by Duvernoy in 1965 [47], the texts are still capable of yielding far more than historians have realized: we can elicit from them not only some striking sentences and replies to interrogations, but at times we can retrace the whole texture, movement and individuality of a particular person's thoughts.

A peasant-girl, Grazida Lizier, born at Montaillou in 1297/98, was seduced by the promiscuous Pierre Clergue, rector of the local church, when she was fourteen or fifteen. Later, he arranged for her to be married, but continued to enjoy her. In Grazida's statements, taken down when she was twenty-one, we can perceive her moving search for a standard of integrity — an ideal, against huge odds — in this potentially sordid situation [48]:

> Yes, my husband knew that the priest Pierre made love with me; he told me to take care it should be with no other man. Pierre and I never made love when my husband was in the house, only when he was out. I didn't know Pierre was a cousin of my mother, Fabrissa — no one had ever told me, I didn't know my mother was even related to him. No, had I known she was related to Pierre — she was illegitimate — I wouldn't have allowed him near me. I did not think I was sinning with him, for our love-making gave joy to us both.
>
> At the time we gave joy to each other mutually, I did not think

[46] E. Le Roy Ladurie, *Montaillou, village occitan de 1294 à 1324* (Paris 1975).

[47] *Le registre d'inquisition de Jacques Fournier*, ed. J. Duvernoy (3 vols., Bibliothèque méridionale XLI, Toulouse 1965).

[48] The complete Latin text of Grazida's testimonies is in Duvernoy, *Le registre*, I 302-6. I have turned the sentences back from indirect to direct speech, but otherwise have translated literally. [A critical text is given in my *Women Writers of the Middle Ages* (Cambridge 1984), pp. 265-78; discussion ibid. pp. 203-10].

I was sinning — nor does it seem so to me now. But today there'd be no joy in it for me — so, if I were to make love with him now, I believe it would be a sin.

... I don't know, but I've heard it said there is a paradise, and I believe it; I've also heard it said there is a hell, but that I don't believe, though I won't urge it is untrue. I believe there is a paradise, for it is something good, as I have heard; I don't believe in hell (though I don't argue against it), for that is something evil. I've often heard that we shall rise again after death — I don't believe that, though I don't discredit it.

I still believe it is no sin when love-making brings joy to both partners. I have believed that ever since Pierre first knew me. No one taught me this idea, except myself. I haven't taught it to others — no one has ever asked me about it.

I believe God made everything that is good for mankind and useful for the created world — such as human beings, the animals we eat or use, cattle, sheep, goats, horses, mules, the fruits of the earth and of trees, things we can eat; but I don't think God made wolves, flies, mosquitoes, or such things as are harmful to men, nor do I think he made the devil, for that is something evil, and God made nothing evil.

Augustine's and Boethius' doctrine, that evil has no existence of its own but is *privatio boni*, has clearly entered the unlettered world, and become a key notion in Grazida's conception of things. As is well known, the concept of evil as *privatio boni* is quite alien to the mainstream of Catharist teaching, which affirms evil as an actual principle in the corporeal world [49]. What is more remarkable, I think — and was overlooked by Le Roy Ladurie — is how much, even though Grazida was led towards some of her ideas by Pierre Clergue, her own thoughts diverge from his. Where Pierre, as Grazida reports, had a cynical nihilistic attitude — sex is as sinful in marriage as outside it, so it makes no difference who your partner is (*tantum valebat una mulier sicut alia, et tantum peccatum erat cum una et cum alia*), and it's not really "sin" at all, as long as the man gives his partner pleasure (*solummodo quod ei placeat, peccatum non erat*) — she herself was deeply concerned with the quality of *shared* joy, which alone, she thought, could free love from all taint. At the same time she was troubled by the thought of having, unwittingly, lain with a kinsman: "I never believed, as Pierre did, that it made no difference who the woman was..."

Most astonishing is the conviction that springs from Grazida's self-understanding. "Asked if she still believes that love-making is no

[49] Cf. for instance A. Borst, *Die Katharer* (Stuttgart 1953), pp. 145-56.

sin if it brings joy to both lovers, she answered: it is not, in her belief... Asked who had taught her such things, she said, no one but herself (*nullus sed ipsamet* [50])". Grazida affirms the primacy of the individual conscience. She, too, belongs with those women who cultivated and made articulate a *conscientia* that was no prefabricated series of moral imperatives, but rather was a developed inner cognizance, truthful and hence authentic for her who gave it expression. It is in relation to this tradition — that can include Dhuoda the duchess and Grazida the peasant-girl, as well as the great women saints and mystics of the twelfth and thirteenth centuries — that I should like to consider more fully the utterances that Heloise has left us, both in her *Epistolae* and her *Problemata*.

[50] Ed. Duvernoy, *Le registre*, I 304. The MS (Vat. lat. 4030, fol. 57ra) reads: *Interrogata quis docuit eam predicta, dixit quod nullus sed ipsamet* (not *quis docuit errorem predictam*, as Duvernoy prints).

APPENDIX

I. *Illustrations of rhymed prose*

The text of Ex. 3 is based on the unique MS; that of Exx. 1, 2, 4, and 5 on the following printed editions, though with my own line-arrangement and punctuation: 1 J. Monfrin (*Historia Calamitatum*), pp. 119-20; 2 J. T. Muckle, *Mediaeval Studies* XVII 241; 4 G. Constable, *The Letters of Peter the Venerable* I 400; 5 F.-J. Schmale (MGH, 1961), pp. 66-68.

1. Heloise, *Ep.* II, the *planctus* against Fortuna:

> Quam mihi nobilium
> potentium   feminarum
> Fortuna umquam preponere
> potuit, aut equare?
> Quam denique adeo deiecit
> et dolore conficere potuit?
> Quam in te mihi   gloriam   contulit?
> Quam in te mihi   ruinam   intulit?
> Quam mihi vehemens in utramque partem extitit,
> ut nec in bonis   nec in malis   modum habuerit?
> Que, ut me miserrimam omnium faceret,
> omnibus ante beatiorem effecerat,
> ut, cum quanta perdidi pensarem,
> tanto me maiora   consumerent   lamenta
> quanto me maiora   oppresserant   damna,
> et tanto maior amissorum   succederet   dolor
> quanto maior possessorum   precesserat   amor,
> et summe voluptatis   gaudia
> summa meroris   terminaret tristicia!

2. Heloise, *Ep.* III, opening:

> Suo specialiter
> sua singulariter.
> Ne me forte in aliquo de inobedientia causari queas,
> verbis   etiam immoderati doloris
> tue frenum impositum est iussionis,
> ut ab his me saltem
> in scribendo temperem,
> a quibus in sermone
>   non tam difficile

quam impossibile
est providere.
 Nihil enim minus
in nostra est potestate
 quam animus,
eique magis obedire
cogimur quam imperare
  possimus.

3. Heloise, *Problemata*, from the opening epistle (B. N. lat. 14511, fol. 18rb-va):

Quorsum autem ista, dilecte multis,
  sed dilettissime nobis?
Non sunt hec documenta,
  sed monita,
ut ex hiis quid debeas recorderis
et debitum solvere non pigriteris.
Ancillas Christi,
spiritales filias tuas,
in oratorio proprio congregasti,
  ac divino
mancipatas obsequio
divinis nos intendere verbis
ac sacris leccionibus operam dare
plurimum semper exortari consuevisti...
Quibus quidem [1] monitis
tam ego quam sorores nostre
  plurimum incitate,
tuam in hoc quoque
quoad possumus implentes obedienciam,
     dum huic operam
studio damus, eo videlicet amore
  literarum correpte [2]
de quo predictus dottor quodam loco meminit —
"Ama scienciam scripturarum et carnis vicia non amabis" —
multis questionibus perturbate,
pigriores efficimur in leccione,
et quod in sacris verbis magis ignoramus
minus diligere cogimur,
dum infructuosum laborem sentimus
     cui operam damus.
Proinde questiunculas quasdam
 discipule dottori,

[1] *qui* superscript in corrector's hand.
[2] *correpte* corr. from *corrette*.

filie   patri   destinantes,
supplicando   rogamus [3],
rogando   supplicamus
quatinus hiis solvendis
intendere non dedigneris,
   cuius ortatu
   immo et iussu
hoc precipue studium aggresse sumus.

4. Heloise, Letter to Peter the Venerable, opening:

Visitante   nos dei misericordia,
dignationis vestre   nos visitavit gratia.
   Gratulamur,
pater benignissime,
et quod ad parvitatem nostram magnitudo vestra descenderit,
   gloriamur.
Est siquidem vestra visitatio
magna magnis quibuslibet gloriatio.
Norunt alii quantum eis utilitatis
vestre contulerit presentia sublimitatis.
Ego certe non dicam enarrare dictu,
sed nec ipso valeo comprehendere cogitatu,
quam utilis, quam iocundus
vester michi fuerit adventus.

5. Adalbertus Samaritanus, *Praecepta dictaminum*, from Ep. 16:

Nullam post hanc consolationem
   paternam   vel maternam   suscepi,
nullam legationem,
   ut debui,   accepi...
Quo magis ammiror, cur natum paterna sprevit affectio,
et quid genitricis sui geniti sic est oblita dilectio.
Cum igitur causam opinari non valeo,
                           sedens mereo,
cogitationum validis procellis illidor,
immensis mestitie fluctibus quattior...
Hinc est cordi   innata mestitia,
hinc imo pectori   longa suspiria.
Interea loci dum sic coartor,
dum vehementer angustior,
cedit nostris partibus quidam, qui mihi notus affuit,
qui vos vivere et valere   constanter asseruit.

---

[3] *sup^do* expunged after *rogamus*.

Hinc est menti natum   inopinabile gaudium,
sed non minore   cum indignatione   confusum...
Relictus ergo a vobis, quos appellem,
quos invocem,   quos implorem,   quos obsecrem?

II. *Patterns of rhythmic cadence*

(a) Samples from Heloise, Abelard, and Adalbertus Samaritanus

(The format of these tables is derived from Janson, and figures for Adalbertus are based on Janson's Table A 47)

	Heloise	Abelard	Adalbertus
6p	0	6	0
6pp	1	2	3
1 5p	2	1	2
p 5p	2	3	3
pp 5p	3	1	7
1 5pp	2	1	2
p 5pp	5	4	0
pp 5pp	1	1	1
1 4p	3	10	4
p 4p	14	17	4
pp 4p	27	28	18
1 4pp	2	3	4
p 4pp	31	23	44
pp 4pp	2	3	6
pp 1 3p	3	4	4
other 1 3p	7	3	1
p 3p	17	20	23
pp 3p	7	9	7
p 1 3pp	9	9	10
other 1 3pp	3	6	0
p 3pp	14	10	20
pp 3pp	11	4	10
pp 1 1 2	0	0	0
p 1 2	6	2	5
other 1 2	2	2	0
pp 2 2	2	0	0
other p 2	8	12	2
pp 2	11	9	8
1	5	7	2
Sum	200	200	190

(b) A comparison of χ^2 values for Heloise, Abelard, and Adalbertus

	Types of cadence	Observed frequency	Expected frequency	$\dfrac{(O-E)^2}{E}$
Heloise	pp 4p	27	14	12.05
	p 4pp	31	16	14.06
	p 3p	17	15	0.23
	All others	125	155	5.81
Sum		200	200	32.15
Abelard	pp 4p	28	15	11.26
	p 4pp	23	11	13.09
	p 3p	20	14	2.57
	All others	129	160	6.01
Sum		200	200	32.93
Adalbertus	pp 4p	18	8	12.50
	p 4pp	44	28	9.14
	p 3p	23	18	1.39
	All others	105	136	7.07
Sum		190	190	30.10

(c) Percentages of *velox, tardus,* and *planus*

(*Velox:* pp 4p, with the variants pp 1 3p and pp 2 2; *tardus:* p 4pp, with the variants p 1 3pp and pp 3pp; *planus:* p 3p, with the variants p 1 2 and pp 2; percentages are rounded to the nearest half-percent)

	Heloise	Abelard	Adalbertus
velox	16	16	11.5
tardus	25.5	18	33.5
planus	17	15.5	19

These figures may be contrasted with the equivalent for the letters of Peter the Venerable and John of Salisbury, and for the prose in Bernard Silvestris' *Cosmographia* (calculated from Janson's Tables, p. 113):

	Peter	John	Bernard
velox	29	36.5	79
tardus	10.5	15.5	4
planus	30.5	16.5	14

In discussion, John Benton and David Luscombe asked me to append, for purposes of comparison, some statistics for the *Historia Calamitatum* and for Heloise's portions of the *Problemata*. The percentages for a sample based on the first 200 sentences of the *Historia Calamitatum* (accepting

Monfrin's punctuation throughout the sample, and excluding all sentences that feature either quotations or reports of others' words) were as follows:

velox: 9.5   tardus: 19   planus: 17.5

The χ^2 values for the three "strict" forms were as follows:

pp 4p: 0.27; p 4pp: 6.25; p 3p: 0.64; all others: 1.44; total: 8.60

The incidence of *velox* in this sample was unexpectedly low; the preponderance of *tardus*, however, not only over *velox* but also over *planus*, is noteworthy.

The *Problemata* contain too few sentences by Heloise, free of quotations from Scripture or other sources, for an appropriate sample to be gathered or tested. It is interesting to observe, however, that in Heloise's prefatory epistle, which introduces the 42 Problems, no fewer than 5 of her 10 sentences* end in a strict *tardus* cadence (p 4pp): *magístram prepóneret: mancipásti obséquio* (where Migne punctuates with semicolon); *placére studúerit; vidéntis appósitum: solvéndas dirígimus*. The epistle thus shows Heloise's characteristic fondness for this particular cadence.

I believe it would be imprudent to use statistics of the nature of those given above for discussing questions of authenticity. Only dramatic differences in proportion among the chief rhythms in the *Historia Calamitatum* sample and that from Abelard's letters to Heloise, for instance, might have led one to suspect the work of diverse hands, or of interpolators. Conversely, the relative consistency of the results (especially the steady preponderance of *tardus* over *velox*, so unusual in its time and place) cannot be used as positive evidence — unless one could be sure that no similar proportions might be found in any thirteenth-century authors, or in twelfth-century authors who have not yet been investigated **.

---

* On what is accepted as a sentence, see the observations above, p. 297.

** I am grateful to Swasti Mitter for clarifying aspects of the χ^2 testing procedure for me, and for checking the statistical parts of this paper.

11

HELOISE, ABELARD, AND SOME RECENT DISCUSSIONS

Among discussions of the letters of Abelard and Heloise in the last decade, David Luscombe's British Academy Lecture, "From Paris to the Paraclete: The Correspondence of Abelard and Heloise", is the most authoritative and most comprehensive [1]. It begins with a meticulous account of how the *Historia calamitatum* and the subsequent letters relate to, and are not contradicted by, the range of other contemporary evidence that we have concerning Abelard and Heloise. Then Luscombe proceeds to show some of the links of thought and purpose that bind the Abelard-Heloise correspondence not only to the work known as *Problemata Heloissae* but also to the many later writings that Abelard sent Heloise and her community at the Paraclete. Luscombe concludes:

> this additional correspondence between Heloise and Abelard — the letters accompanying and prefacing the books of hymns and sequences, the Biblical problems, the *Hexameron* commentary and the sermons — is closely connected to their collected correspondence — the eight letters which begin with the *Historia* and conclude with the

[1] *Proceedings of the British Academy* LXXIV (1988, publ. 1989) 247-83. The other principal studies discussed below are, first, the three in *Fälschungen im Mittelalter*, Teil V (MGH, Schriften, Bd. 32, V, Hannover 1988): J.F. Benton, "The Correspondence of Abelard and Heloise", pp. 95-120; H. Silvestre, "Die Liebesgeschichte zwischen Abaelard und Heloise", pp. 121-65; D. Fraioli, "Against the Authenticity of the *Historia calamitatum*", pp. 167-200; then, T. Janson, "Schools of Cursus in the Twelfth Century and the *Letters* of Heloise and Abelard", *Retorica e poetica tra i secoli XII e XIV*, ed. C. Leonardi, E. Menestò (Scandicci [Firenze] 1988), pp. 171-200. For other recent studies relating to the *Letters*, see my *Women Writers of the Middle Ages* (Cambridge 1984), p. 326, and the notes in Luscombe 1989. There are particularly perceptive interpretations of aspects of the *Letters* in L. Georgianna, "Any Corner of Heaven: Heloise's Critique of Monasticism", *MS* XLIX (1987) 221-53; C. Brooke, *The Medieval Idea of Marriage* (Oxford 1989), esp. pp. 90-118; and H.C.R. Laurie, *The Making of Romance. Three Studies* (Genève 1991), Ch. 3.

Rule for the abbey. Both this correspondence and the collected correspondence must be considered together and cannot be considered apart, for they constitute in their entirety a single achievement, that of providing the abbey in effect with a corporate strategic and operational plan... The making of the collected correspondence cannot be reasonably detached from this wider, distinct activity on behalf of the abbey of the Paraclete [2].

This perception of the long-lasting intellectual exchanges between Abelard and Heloise in her community, and of their collaboration in a corpus of writings that includes the famous correspondence but extends beyond it, seems to me both valid and methodologically important. Future discussion of the authenticity of "the personal letters between Abelard and Heloise" (to cite the title chosen by their editor, J.T. Muckle) [3], if it is to make a serious contribution, must take careful cognizance of this entire corpus.

That, unhappily, is not the case in the three essays on the correspondence which appear in the fifth of the imposing tomes of the Monumenta Germaniae Historica: *Fälschungen im Mittelalter* (1988). These essays (published just in time for Luscombe to have been able to make brief comments on them) are filled with notions that might seem persuasive as long as they are kept atomistic and not tested against a more complete reading of the Abelard-Heloise corpus. The arguments and conclusions of the three scholars involved, moreover, are entirely incompatible with one another. In the first essay John Benton, after apologising for an earlier study, "The Style of the *Historia Calamitatum*", which he had written with F.P. Ercoli — "All of the percentage-based conjectures about the *Historia* in that article

---

[2] Luscombe 1989, p. 270.

[3] *MS* XV (1953) 47-94 (*Letters* I-IV in Muckle's numbering); the next two letters (Muckle V-VI) are edited *ibid.* XVII (1955) 240-81. In Muckle's edition, Heloise's three letters are numbered I, III, and V, and Abelard's replies are II, IV, and VI. However, for the present essay I shall refer chiefly to the numbering in Migne, P.L. 178, where "I" designates the *Historia calamitatum*: thus Heloise's letters are numbered II, IV, and VI, and Abelard's replies become III, V, and VII. This is the numbering followed by Benton as well as Beggiato, who are cited below.

In what follows I speak, as in my earlier studies, of the letters of Abelard and the letters of Heloise. This is not to beg the questions concerning authenticity, but to avoid clumsy circumlocutions. While I do try to show that the recent arguments against the authenticity of the *Letters* are flawed, those who wish can translate all my allusions in a way that accommodates scepticism — "the letters ascribed to Abelard", "the letters ascribed to Heloise", "Abelard's alleged account", "Heloise's alleged statement"... — or else mentally put "Abelard" and "Heloise" in inverted commas throughout.

are erroneous" — marshals statistics anew in order to claim that Abelard wrote, *inter alia*, the letters "supposedly written by Heloise" (V 98). In the next essay Hubert Silvestre argues in favour of a different, earlier thesis of Benton's, which Benton had meanwhile abandoned: namely that the whole correspondence was fabricated — both the Latin and the French version — by Jean de Meun in the late thirteenth century, and/or by one of his friends. Finally, Deborah Fraioli, who begins by trying to interpret the *Historia calamitatum* as a satire directed against Abelard, goes on to claim that the whole collected correspondence presents both Abelard and Heloise as "ridiculous caricatures", and hence cannot possibly have been written by them, but must be by an anonymous forger, of unspecified date, who — unlike Jean de Meun — was relentlessly hostile to them.

These three essays, so diverse in their theses, have one thing in common: they are stronger in ingenuity than in logical rigour. Rather than discuss their multifarious assertions in detail, I shall focus on only a few salient features in each and indicate why these display insufficient stringency of method and argument.

On the basis of a computer-aided frequency count of 24 words in the correspondence (*a/ab, ad, amplius, autem, cum, de, diligenter, est, et, etiam...*), Benton shows that "When one compares the letters of 'Heloise' [quotation-marks his] (Two, Four and Six) with [Abelard's] letters Three, Five and Seven, only one word (*etiam*) differs by as much as one standard deviation. That is to say, on the basis of the frequencies I have analyzed so far, the style of the two sets of letters is virtually identical" (V 101 f).

If one were to consider other instances of the writings of a master and disciple in the twelfth and thirteenth centuries, and were to test their word-frequencies for 24 such words in a similar way, I strongly suspect there would be other cases where, on these premises, the style of master and disciple would emerge as "virtually identical". Should one, in any such case, propose that the two were a single person? I think the reasoning behind Benton's use of evidence shows a confusion between a necessary condition for identity and a sufficient one.

Any rigorous criterion of proof in these circumstances would demand:

1) an investigation (on the basis of a fair range of authors) of which frequently-used words are statistically *significant* for establishing distinct or identical authorship;

2) detailed data of the comparative frequencies of these words in the writings of *other* masters and their disciples, as well as of authors who are closely linked by belonging to the same school;

3) a discussion of the literary conditions under which we can distinguish close affinity from identity;

4) a discussion of the statistical conditions — where are similar frequencies similar enough to suggest not close affinity but identity?

That I have used the words "master" and "disciple" — which indeed are suggested, for the beginning of Abelard's relation with Heloise, by the account in the *Historia calamitatum* — does not mean that I agree with Benton's underlying assumption, that Heloise (if she wrote at all) must have been merely a passive recipient of Abelard's ways of expression. Compare for instance Benton's turns of phrase: "if Heloise had enough intellectual contact with Abelard to be able to write in his style, using his pattern of *cursus* and his favourite quotations", or again, "if the adolescent Heloise learned to imitate the style of her mature teacher" (V 108). As I have tried to show elsewhere [4], there is evidence that stylistically Heloise was as much a giver as a receiver.

In the case of Hubert Silvestre, the hypothesis to which his discussion leads is identical with that expressed in his Belgian Academy essay, three years earlier, of which the German contribution to the *Fälschungen* volume is an extended version. From a perfectly factual and correct observation of the import of Jean de Meun's verses about Heloise in the *Roman de la Rose* —

> aux yeux de l'Héloïse de Jean de Meun, c'est le mariage qui a été et pour elle et pour Abélard la source de tous les maux: fussent-ils restés amants que leur bonheur eût été assuré —

Silvestre continues:

> Cette insistance significative sur les avantages de l'union libre fait admettre comme des plus vraisemblable l'hypothèse que le dossier Abélard-Héloïse a été conçu et mis en oeuvre par Jean de Meun — ou l'un de ses amis partageant son état d'esprit — pour défendre et cautionner une thèse hétérodoxe qui lui tenait particulièrement à coeur: le droit pour le clerc majeur de se soustraire aux obligations morales de continence que lui imposait son état et donc le privilège reconnu pour lui d'entretenir une concubine [5].

It is generally agreed that Jean de Meun, who states in the Pro-

---

[4] Dronke 1984 (cit. n. 1), esp. pp. 111 f.

[5] "L'idylle d'Abélard et Héloïse: la part du roman", *Académie Royale de Belgique, Bulletin de la classe des lettres et des sciences morales et politiques*, 5e sér. LXXI (1985) 157-200, at p. 197; cf. *Fälschungen* V 162 f.

logue to his version of Boethius that his translations from the Latin included "les Epistres Pierres Abaelart et Heloys sa fame" [6], is the author of the extant (thirteenth-century) French version of *Letters* I-VII. The hypothesis that he, or one of his intimates, also concocted the Latin original, comes up against the grave difficulty, how to account for the *divergences* between the Latin and French texts. These Silvestre has not discussed. Admittedly the vernacular version has been transmitted imperfectly, in a single codex. There are many instances where the French has been copied badly, and some at least where it would seem that the translator had before him a Latin text rather different from that preserved in the extant manuscripts. (I have discussed one remarkable example of this above, p. 254, n. 17). But there are other instances where, to all appearances, the French translator had before him the Latin text familiar to us, but did not fully understand it or fully attend to its meaning. If this can be substantiated on even a few occasions, it can hardly be reconciled with the idea that the Latin and French stem from a single author or from his immediate entourage. I shall consider in some detail four examples of such discrepancies from Heloise's first letter to Abelard.

1) When Heloise writes of "the famous argument of the philosopher Aspasia, which she had with Xenophon and his wife, found in Aeschines Socraticus" (*inductio illa Aspasie philosophe apud Socraticum Eschinem cum Xenofonte et uxore eius habita*) [7], there are no significant variants in the Latin manuscripts, but the French translator makes a curious and revealing mistake. The word *apud* is here clearly meant to indicate a literary source — as Petrarch recognised in his marginal note in the manuscript of the *Letters* that he owned (B.N. lat. 2923), where he specifies that the passage from Aeschines Socraticus could be found in Latin in Cicero's *De inventione* [8]. But the translator — let us say Jean de Meun — learned yet not quite as learned as Petrarch or Heloise, took this *apud* to refer not to a literary citation but to a house. The French text speaks of "the argument that the philosopher Aspasia brought against Xenophon and his wife in the house of Aeschines, who was a disciple of Socrates": *l'argument que Aspasse la philosophe fist contre Jenophon et sa femme en l'ostel [l]Eschines, qui desciple fu Socrates* [9].

---

[6] *Li Livres de Confort de Philosophie*, ed. V.L. Dedeck-Héry, *MS* XIV (1952) 165-275, at p. 168.

[7] *MS* XV 71 (= Abélard, *Historia calamitatum*, ed. J. Monfrin, Paris ³1967, p. 115). Here and below I follow Monfrin's (unnormalised) spelling, but refer to Muckle's more complete *apparatus criticus* when alluding to variants.

[8] Cf. *MS* XV 71, n. 91.

[9] B.N. fr. 920, s. XIV ex. (= J), p. 66. For citations of the French, I have relied

2) Similarly, when Heloise protests that Abelard had compelled her to take monastic vows even before he himself took his, she exclaims: "I would as readily, God knows, without the least hesitation, have gone ahead of you or followed you, at your bidding, hastening to Vulcan's regions" (*Eque autem — deus scit — ad Vulcania loca te properantem precedere vel sequi pro iussu tuo minime dubitarem*) [10]. Her classicising expression, *ad Vulcania loca*, designates the fires of hell. Again the variants in the Latin manuscripts are only very minor ones, and do not affect these crucial words. Their allusion and precise implication seem to have escaped the translator, who wrote: "For, God knows, even if [*lit.* it being the case that] you hastened to leap into a fire, I would not hesitate to go before or to follow you at your command": *Car, Dieu le scet, ce que tu te hastasses de saillir en un feu, je ne doubtasse pas à aler avant ou à toy suivre à ton commandement*" [11]. By putting *saillir en un feu* for *ad Vulcania loca*, the translator shows he took the Latin to mean an example of impulsive, painful or foolish, earthly behaviour, and not the course to damnation in the otherworld. He has misunderstood, and thereby trivialised, the force of Heloise's outcry.

3) A more subtle and far-reaching departure from the Latin occurs in the passage where Heloise reminds Abelard that, in his letter to a friend (the *Historia calamitatum*), "you did not disdain to expound some of the reasons by which I tried to dissuade you from our marriage and ill-starred wedding, though you kept silent about most of the reasons why I preferred love to marriage, freedom to a chain". The Latin of these lines —

rationes nonnullas quibus te a coniugio nostro et infaustis thalamis

on my microfilm of the manuscript, collating this with the edition by F. Beggiato, *Le lettere di Abelardo ed Eloisa nella traduzione di Jean de Meun* (2 vols., Modena 1977). This appeared the year after my own *Abelard and Heloise in Medieval Testimonies* (= *supra*, pp. 247-94), in which I edited some key sentences from J (*supra*, p. 286f). Beggiato's edition was criticised, with some justice but also with much exaggeration, by E. Hicks, *Romania* CIII (1982) 384-97. Hicks's own knowledge of the transmission of the *Letters* reveals itself as inadequate, when he writes, e.g., "En effet, aucun manuscrit [latin] connu ne remonte à l'époque de la traduction" (p. 392). On the disparity between the French and Latin analysed above, cf. also Beggiato II 134, n. 16. In this passage, J has *leschines*, Beggiato (I 85) rightly suggests deleting the initial *l*. He reads the name *Jenophon* (*sic* J) as *Xenophon*, without comment.

[10] *MS* XV 72 (= Monfrin p. 116).
[11] J p. 69 (two words deleted between *aler* and *avant*).

*revocare conabar exponere non es dedignatus, sed plerisque tacitis quibus
amorem coniugio, libertatem vinculo preferebam* [12] —

presents no textual problems and no variants (except *infaustisque* for
et infaustis). But the French version, as Fabrizio Beggiato noted, has
a rather different import from the Latin. While the first half of the
passage cited is identical in sense, in the second (beginning *sed
plerisque tacitis*) the thought becomes: "But let it be that I keep silent
about several reasons by which I would prize love more than marriage and freedom more than bond": *Mes ja soit ce que je en taise
pluseurs par quoy je priseroie mielx amour que mariaige et franchise que
lien (leu J)* [13].

The French translator does not appear to have noted the precise
force of the ablative absolute construction *sed plerisque tacitis...*
Working perhaps too hastily, he took this to mean that Heloise herself kept and keeps silent about some of her reasons for favouring
free love. The changes of subject, tense and mood from the Latin effect changes of meaning. Heloise in the Latin refers to Abelard's
report of what she had said then; her point is that Abelard had told
the friend some of her arguments but by no means all. And her verb
preferebam is definite, not conditional. The text permits no doubt
that, at the time, Heloise had told Abelard himself her full reasons:
it was the recipient of Abelard's *Historia* who was given only a selective account. In the French, by contrast, it is as if Heloise, at the
time of writing to Abelard, were claiming that she still has several
reasons which she is keeping from him, and as if she were referring
to a general or hypothetical state of affairs ("by which I *would* prize
love more than marriage...") rather than to her specific situation in
the past.

4) Lastly, let us consider the renowned paradox by which
Heloise sums up her fate. She believes that, by finally assenting to
the marriage, she had greatly harmed Abelard, and at the same time
she knows she is blameless, because her intention towards Abelard
had always been wholly selfless —

Que plurimum nocens, plurimum, ut nosti, sum innocens [14].

I who, most nocent, am, as you know, most innocent.

---

[12] *MS* XV 71 (= Monfrin p. 114).
[13] J p. 65; cf. Beggiato II 134, n. 14, I 84 and II 65 (for the emendation *lien*).
In J, *Mes* begins a new sentence (*mes* Beggiato).
[14] *MS* XV 72 (= Monfrin p. 116).

The French translator has:

> *qui fu⟨i⟩ trop nuissans à pluseurs, et suis tres innocent si comme tu as sceü* [15].

I who was too harmful to several people, and am very innocent, as you have come to know.

The translator has not seen the force of the punning parallel and antithesis, *plurimum nocens / plurimum innocens*; and he has translated the first adverb *plurimum* ("greatly", "most") as if reading *pluribus* ("to many people").

If the Latin and French texts stem, as I am convinced, from different periods and different authors and milieux, it is possible to suppose one of two things:

a) that, even though the extant manuscripts are unanimous in the way they preserve the Latin phrase (only the initial *que* has the variants *quod*, *quam* and *et*), a lost manuscript, used by the French translator, read "Que pluribus nocens, plurimum, ut nosti, sum innocens";

b) that the translator, working over-hurriedly, read the first *plurimum* — which may well have been abbreviated in the copy he had before him — as if it were *pluribus*.

The second seems to me the likelier alternative. If Silvestre were right, on the other hand, and the Latin and French texts stemmed from the same author, Jean de Meun, or both originated in his intimate circle, then the divergence would be hard to account for. That is, one would probably be compelled to claim that the original Latin text read *pluribus* — corresponding to *à pluseurs* — and that a Latin copyist, a blundering genius, had substituted a second *plurimum* and thereby, accidentally, had created Heloise's memorable phrase. All the Latin copyists of whom we know (the argument would have to run) then became so enamoured of this *felix culpa* of the early scribe that they followed him (or her) to a man (or to a woman).

These four examples of discrepancies between the Latin and French texts are illustrations only. My point, however, is that, logically, *all* discrepancies between the Latin and the French would have to be accounted for convincingly before Silvestre's Jean de Meun hypothesis could be seriously entertained.

In the third essay about the correspondence, in the Monumenta volume, Deborah Fraioli sees Heloise's reasons against marriage, as

[15] J p. 67 (*qui fu* J, *Qui fu⟨i⟩* Beggiato I 87).

Abelard reports them in his letter to a friend, "as an argument against the authenticity of the *Historia calamitatum*". It has long been recognised that, while in her arguments Heloise draws on what St Jerome says in his *Adversus Iovinianum*, she uses Jerome's type of dissuasions from marriage with a very different intent: not, like the saint, in order to extol virginity, but in order to extol free love. Or better, as Gilson finely observed, she extends Cicero's ideal of perfect *amicitia* between two men, in which each friend loves the other freely for what he is, and not on account of any claim or for the sake of any advantage, to an ideal of love between a man and a woman [16]. To Gilson (as to me), Heloise's exposition of "la morale de l'amour pur", both in the reported arguments in the *Historia* and directly in her letters (*Nichil umquam... in te nisi te requisivi: te pure, non tua, concupiscens*) [17], seems a dignified, serious and fruitful "misapplication" of Jerome's thoughts. Fraioli, on the other hand, calls it a "ludicrous misapplication". She claims it is "designed to ridicule the incontinence of Abelard and Heloise". This leads her to the assertion

> that the *Historia calamitatum* and the accompanying letters are a literary forgery and an anti-Abelardian satire written by a third party... designed to cast Abelard humorously in the worst possible light (V 169).

Later in her essay she goes even further, contending that in the correspondence

> both Abelard and Heloise become ludicrous caricatures of pride, ignorance, impertinence, and lust, so much so that the possibility of their having anything to do with the authorship of these texts becomes too remote, in my opinion, to be entertained even as a possibility (V 185).

One could simply point out that this represents a somewhat idiosyncratic subjective response to the *Letters*, and that other readers — even those fully aware of the tone and meaning of the *Adversus Iovinianum* — have not seen the protagonists in the correspondence as "ludicrous caricatures". But perhaps it should be added that words such as "ludicrous", "ridicule", "satire", and "humorously" in Fraioli's discussion are not quite what they seem. In a passage between the two I have just cited, Fraioli speaks of "Heloise in her infamous

---

[16] E. Gilson, *Héloïse et Abélard* (Paris ³1964), Ch. IV.
[17] *MS* XV 70 (= Monfrin p. 114).

statements advocating free love" (V 179). With this word, "infamous", the mask of scholarly concern with the correct interpretation of a text is dropped. Advocating free love, it seems, is something for which Fraioli feels violent personal disapproval. For the most part she keeps this concealed, by talking of humour, satire and ridicule rather than of infamy. But the implications (which become more than implicit with that word "infamous") are unmistakeable. In effect Fraioli is saying: If anyone in the Middle Ages advocates what I disapprove of, she can't have been serious, it must have been meant as a joke or a caricature. This advocate mut *really* have thought about free love just as St Jerome and I and all right-thinking people do. It is a disingenuous attempt to claim wider validity for one's personal prejudice, letting it colour, rather than elucidate, the texts of one's choice.

The other crucial difficulty that faces any reading of the correspondence such as Silvestre's or Fraioli's is that a very substantial portion of it — about five sixths in all — is unexceptionably virtuous and pious. Abelard's first two letters to Heloise would be hard to read as anything but ardent spiritual exhortations. Heloise's third letter to Abelard contains nothing that is at all unseemly for a respected abbess to express. No one has yet suggested that the two very long answers that Abelard gave to this letter — *De origine sanctimonialium* and *Regula sanctimonialium* — are anything other than what they seem: the serious reflections of a spiritual director. Admittedly the *Regula* does not feature in the French version of the *Letters* ascribed to Jean de Meun. But if we allowed, even as a hypothesis, a forger who was like Silvestre's advocate of concubinage, or like Fraioli's anti-Abelardian, anti-Heloisan satirist, we should have to ask, how could such a man have also wished to fabricate on such a scale so much that is solemn and devout? And to what end? It might seem easier to suppose that in the solemn passages he was making use of authentic materials, and that he himself introduced only the "profanities" — the arguments against marriage, and Heloise's first two letters, with their impassioned expressions of sensual longing. Yet this would be extremely difficult to make plausible in terms of textual transmission, since there is no sign that there ever existed a manuscript in which the "profanities" were lacking. In short, another serious weakness in the arguments of both Silvestre and Fraioli is that they treat the letters monolithically, rather than taking cognizance of their diverse facets and intentions, as any accurate detailed reading must.

The question of accurate reading again arises when Fraioli says of the comedy, *Babio* (composed in England ca. 1150, according to the latest researches) [18], that it "bears striking similarities to the *Historia calamitatum*" (V 187). Since this is not the first time such a claim has been made, it may be helpful to recall the main features of this comedy's plot. An elderly miser, Babio ("the simpleton"), is infatuated with his stepdaughter, Viola [19]. She detests him, and out-wits him so as to marry the young man of her choice. Meanwhile Ba-bio's wife, Petula ("the wanton one"), has a love-affair with their steward, Fodius ("the digger"). Babio twice tries to catch them *in flagrante* by returning home unexpectedly at night. The second time Fodius, with Petula's complicity, pretends to mistake Babio, in the darkness, for a robber, and castrates him. Babio becomes a monk, leaving his wife to his steward to enjoy.

If Abelard, with Heloise's help, had castrated Fulbert, one just *might* be tempted to see a certain parallel between this plot and the events recounted in the *Historia calamitatum* [20]. As it is, the "striking similarities" remind me rather of those that Fluellen saw between Harry of Monmouth and "Alexander the pig" of Macedon (*Henry the Fifth*, IV 7):

> ... the situation, looke you, is both alike. There is a river in *Macedon*, & there is moreover a River at *Monmouth*... tis alike as my fingers is to my fingers, and there is Salmons in both.

On the question of the attribution of the Abelard-Heloise let-ters, the most valuable recent discussion, along with Luscombe's, seems to me to be that of Tore Janson [21], who attempts to show what an analysis of prose rhythm in the correspondence can contribute towards a solution. Janson's study brings two noteworthy results. The

---

[18] See the fine edition by A. Dessì Fulgheri, in *Commedie latine del XII e XIII secolo*, vol. II (Genova 1980), pp. 129-301.

[19] It is, I believe, certain from *Babio* 207 (*non genus ut genitrix*, "the daughter isn't like the mother") that Viola is the daughter of Babio's wife, Petula.

[20] While attempts to see resemblances between the plot and characters in *Babio* and in the *Historia calamitatum* seem to me hopelessly far-fetched, it is nonethe-less possible that, in mid-twelfth-century England, *any* comic mention of a man who becomes a monk because he's been castrated could have brought to mind, at least for some of the audience, Abelard's *moniage* a generation earlier. The mental link, castration — monastery, still surfaces for instance in Villon's *Ballade* (*Le Testament* 338 f): *Pour qui chastré fut et puis moyne / Pierre Esbaillart a Saint Denys.*

[21] Janson 1988 (see n 1 above). Page-references in what follows, unless other-wise stated, are to this article. References to "Janson 1975" are to his book, *Prose Rhythm in Medieval Latin from the 9th to the 13th Century* (Studia Latina Stockhol-miensia XX). A brief explanation of Janson's notation for cadences is given above, p. 298 n. 10; for further details, see *Prose Rhythm* pp. 13-15.

first follows from his table showing the most frequent cadences in Abelard's letters to Heloise (p. 183):

> Clearly, we have an author who uses prose rhythm. He favors *tardus* more than *planus*: that fact alone makes it incredible that the text is written later than around the middle of the 12th century.

That is, on the basis of the frequencies of the diverse cadences one can rule out the possibility of a thirteenth-century forgery: "I regard it as quite improbable that a medieval author would succeed in imitating the prose rhythm of an earlier age in a long text... he would have to get the proportions between cadences correct... I believe a credible forgery could not be done" (p. 184).

The other result is expressed as follows:

> In view of the very great similarities in prose rhythms between the letters to Heloise and those to Abelard, I personally regard it as probable that one of the two gave all the letters their final shape. With attention still confined to prose rhythm, facts can be adduced to support either candidate. The prose rhythm in the letters is extremely close to that in the *Sermones* by Abelard, which of course points to him. On the other hand, it is somewhat difficult to explain why Abelard should have bothered to spend more efforts on prose rhythm in editing the letters to and from Heloise than he spent on that in any other work, including the closely connected *Historia calamitatum*. Heloise, on the other hand, may well have been slightly more careful than her teacher in this matter. I suspend judgment on this problem, but I propose that one of them edited the whole collection (or conceivably wrote it all) rather than that each of them wrote quite independently (pp. 195f).

I have quoted this careful and nuanced statement in full because it is rather different from John Benton's paraphrase of it (*Fälschungen* V 101), where he speaks of "Janson's conclusion that there was a single author" (*sic*). I should like to return to the question, how great in fact are the similarities in prose rhythm between the letters to Heloise and those to Abelard, and to indicate, while fully accepting Janson's data, that some qualifications may be needed when it comes to their interpretation.

Whereas in Abelard's letters to Heloise, in Janson's words, "the main forms of *velox, tardus* and *planus* come first, in that order" (p. 183), I would suggest that it is perhaps significant that, in Heloise's letters to Abelard, the order is *tardus, velox, planus*. This emerges from my 1980 tables (p. 320 above), based on two samples of 200 sentences each — tables that Janson himself adopts and reproduces in his recent study (p. 198, Tables 1 and 2) [22]. To summarize their evidence for the main forms of *velox, tardus* and *planus*:

Table 1

	Abelard to Heloise		Heloise to Abelard	
		(%)		(%)
Main *velox* (pp 4p)	28	14.0	27	13.5
Main *tardus* (p 4pp)	23	11.5	31	15.5
Main *planus* (p 3p)	20	10.0	17	8.5

From Janson's more comprehensive Table 11 (p. 193), which analyses the cadences in the first three letters of Abelard to Heloise (434 sentences) and in the entire letters of Heloise to Abelard (276 sentences), we can derive a fuller comparison of the proportions of *velox, tardus* and *planus* in the two groups of letters. Here I give the percentages reflecting Janson's figures for *velox, tardus* and *planus* as they occur in these letters.

Table 2

	Abelard to Heloise	Heloise to Abelard
Velox (pp 4p, pp 1 3p)	16.0	14.0
Tardus (p 4pp, p 1 3pp)	16.0	19.0
Planus (p 3p, pp 2, p 1 2)	16.5	18.0

[22] One group of misprints has unfortunately crept into Janson's tables (pp. 198-200). There the figure for strict *tardus* (p 4pp) in Table 2 (Heloise to Abelard) should read "31", not "59": otherwise the sum total of her sample would be 228 cadences, not 200 (cf. *supra* p. 320). The "59" instances of p 4pp listed here in fact belong to the next column, Table 3, the sample of 245 cadences from Guibert of Nogent, in place of the erroneous "36" (see Janson's extract from this table on p. 180 of his article). Similarly, the 20 instances of p 4pp listed in column 4 belong to column 5 (Roscelin), whilst the 33 listed in column 5 belong to column 6 (Abelard): these are the 33 examples of strict *tardus* in Abelard's third letter to Heloise (Muckle VI, Migne VII), which, added to the 23 from his earlier letters (cf. p. 198, Table 1), give the total 56 examples of p 4pp that are cited correctly in Janson's tables on pp. 191 and 193.

That is, on these figures Abelard uses the same percentage of *velox* and *tardus* cadences, but Heloise uses 19 percent of *tardus* and only 14 percent of *velox* ones.

There is, however, one other variant of *tardus*, pp 3pp in Janson's notation, which he left out of account in his Table 11. This variant of *tardus* was favoured by a number of authors especially in the Italian tradition — Anastasius Bibliotecarius, Liutprand, Gregory VII, Alphanus of Salerno — though also by Berengarius of Tours in northern France (cf. Janson 1975, pp. 109-112, Tables 2, 3, 17, 20, and 28). These are all authors who, like the Abelard and Heloise of the *Letters*, likewise favour a high proportion of strict (p 4pp) *tardus* cadences. In Janson's two larger samples of letters, pp 3pp occurs 8 times among the 434 cadences of Abelard, and 12 times among the 276 cadences of Heloise. Thus if these instances are added to the *tardus* cadences listed in Janson's Table 11 (1988, p. 193), the percentage of *tardus* for Abelard rises to 17.5 (i.e. 77 cadences out of 434), and that of Heloise rises to no less than 23 (i.e. 64 cadences out of 276). To sum up the revised percentages:

Table 3

	Abelard to Heloise	Heloise to Abelard
All *velox*	16.0	14.0
All *tardus*	17.5	23.0
All *planus*	16.5	18.0

In short, while I still feel a touch of the uncertainty I expressed in 1980 (see above, p. 299), about whether one can distinguish Heloise's prose style from Abelard's on grounds of cadences alone, I would feel even more uneasy about any claim that there is no real distinction in cadences between the letters ascribed to her and those ascribed to him. On her side the preference for *tardus* over *velox* (23 percent to 14, if we include all admitted variant forms) appears to be so much greater than his (17.5 percent to 16) that it would be imprudent to brush this datum aside as negligible.

The other indication of a difference between Heloise's prose and Abelard's is again delicate to assess: it is that she combines a greater fondness for *tardus* cadences with a more extensive use of rhyme than Abelard's. It was this combination of the predominance of *tardus* cadences and rhyme that led me in 1980 to suggest that Heloise had learnt some aspects of her prose style from an Italian rather than a northern French tradition of prose composition. This suggestion has now been challenged by Janson (1988). Here, on reflection, I think both my own earlier statements and his recent ones need some modification.

Janson gives a helpful sketch of the varieties of *cursus* in eleventh- and early twelfth-century Italy and France, yet there are also aspects of the evidence that I would not interpret quite as he does. After distinguishing in Italy a tradition with a preference for *tardus* (epitomised by Gregory VII) and another with a preference for *velox* (epitomised by Peter Damiani), Janson goes on to speak of a number of authors in France towards 1100 "who combine the preferences of both schools". He mentions Hildebert and Ivo of Chartres, commenting (p. 181):

> Their general usage is very similar to that of their contemporary Guibert of Nogent, including his tendency to favor the *tardus* over the *planus*. But they have added a clear preference for the *cursus trispondiacus* [i.e. p 4p], which is otherwise almost always absent from the usage of the authors in the tradition from Northern Italy.

When he turns to Abelard, Janson says that Abelard too "has no aversion against the *trispondiacus*, but rather seems to favor it" (p. 183).

Two qualifications are essential here. One is that Hildebert and Ivo both use more than twice as many *velox* cadences as *tardus* ones. This at once distances them considerably from the practice of Abelard and Heloise. In Janson's own Hildebert sample (1975, p. 113, Table 38), there are 95 main *velox* (and 75 *trispondiacus*) to 36 main *tardus*; in Ivo's (1988, p. 198, Table 4), there are 45 main *velox* (and 55 *trispondiacus*) to 20 main *tardus*.

The other is that while in my two samples, each of 200 sentences, from Abelard and Heloise, which Janson reprints, Abelard's letters have 17 instances of *trispondiacus* and Heloise's 14, nonetheless a χ^2 test for both gives a result far too weak to show that this cadence is other than fortuitous. The tests give χ^2 values of 3 and 2.6 respectively. Even more remarkably, in Janson's own sample of 303 sentences from the *Historia calamitatum* (p. 191, Table 8), while there are no fewer than 43 instances of *trispondiacus* (i.e. 14 percent) — it is the most frequent single cadence in the whole sample — the χ^2 test gives the value 0: that is, the observed frequency exactly matches the expected frequency. (These three tests are set out more fully in the Appendix below). This is because *trispondiacus* is one of the more "natural" cadences in Latin prose. While with certain authors such as Hildebert it can be demonstrated that they favour *trispondiacus,* in others it can occur quite frequently without one's being able to determine that it was a chosen manner.

In 1980, after remarking that, among authors so far studied in detail for their prose rhythm, only the Italian Adalbertus Samaritanus, in his *Praecepta dictaminum* (ca. 1115), seemed to show a combination of predominant *tardus* and frequent rhyme comparable to Heloise's, I suggested that in her prose artistry she could have been influenced by his, or closely related Italian, rather than northern French, techniques of *dictamen* (see above, p. 302). Janson comments:

> It is certainly possible that Abelard and Heloise might have read Adalbertus' treatise, and learnt something from it. However, for someone who lived in Northern France in the early decades of the 12th century, there were other sources of inspiration that were closer at hand. Hildebert of Lavardin lived until 1134, and his letters became stylistical models for subsequent generations. There were also other famous men of letters, like Hugh of Fleury, who used *cursus* and rhymed prose to a remarkable extent.

As for the predilection for *tardus*:

> this peculiarity is found not only in the older Roman tradition, with which Adalbertus is connected, but also in many writers of the French tradition. And the letters to Heloise as well as those to Abelard show a feature found abundantly in the French tradition but not in Adalbertus: the *cursus trispondiacus* (p. 186).

Yet I find it difficult to see Hildebert as a source of inspiration for the prose style of Heloise (or Abelard), because his prose shows a massive preponderance of *velox* and *trispondiacus* over *tardus*. In the case of Hugh of Fleury there is admittedly rhyme as well as *cursus* — but the proportions of cadences are again very different from those in the Abelard-Heloise correspondence. Since Janson has not provided a table for Hugh, I have analysed a sample of 200 cadences from his prose in the Appendix below, juxtaposing the results with my sample of 200 from Heloise. The proportion of the main *velox* cadence, for instance, in Hugh (53 among the 200) is so different from Heloise's (27) that a relation, or even affinity, between their prose styles would be hard to make plausible. And while it is true that there happen to be more instances of *trispondiacus* in my Abelard and Heloise samples than in Adalbertus, there is, as we saw, no evidence that in them these cadences are more than fortuitous. There is no question of any resemblance here to Hildebert or Ivo, for whom *trispondiacus* had been, along with *velox*, the most favoured cadence.

Another objection of Janson's, however, seems to me to have greater force:

> In Adalbertus' treatise, there are no written instructions about prose rhythm, as was found in later *artes dictandi*: no such instructions are found until about 1180... prose rhythm was always originally learnt from a teacher, not discovered in texts. Naturally, once the basic principles had been mastered, one might be influenced by the usage of others to adjust one's own practice to some extent. I have not seen any case in which one has reason to suspect more than a moderate influence of this kind. I find it hard to believe that Abelard would have become so impressed by the rather short textbook of Adalbertus that he changed a long established writing habit (pp. 186 f).

I would agree that it is not necessary to suppose, as I had suggested, that Heloise (or Abelard) learnt their particular prose rhythms from an Italian treatise such as that of Adalbertus — or indeed from any treatise. But what still seems to me probable, especially with Heloise, is that, already inclined by her literary schooling to write in a style that most favoured *tardus*, she received a further stimulus, to combine this prominence of *tardus* cadences with frequent rhymes, which is far more unusual. Still the only place known to me from the printed sources where precisely this combination can be found is in the model letters in Adalbertus' *Praecepta*, a work that had reached northern France only about a decade before Heloise (presumably) wrote her letters to Abelard. Perhaps Heloise needed no external promptings to enhance her *tardus*-dominated cadences with rhymes; yet it seems to me to have been a new and exceptional — as well as shortlived — technique, first attested in an Italian *dictator*, that Heloise, already a finely trained stylist, either assimilated or (perhaps less probably) paralleled spontaneously.

I also wish to correct my earlier suggestions in another point. What Janson's valuable assemblage of evidence indicates is that, apart from the question of rhyme, both Heloise's practice of *cursus* and Abelard's can be seen in relation to a specific current of prose rhythm which is traceable in France from the time of Odilo of Cluny (✝ 1049) to Guibert of Nogent (1053-1124), and which includes the epistolary prose of Abelard's teacher Roscelin (ca. 1050-ca. 1125). In this current (unlike the principal one in northern France, in which *velox* predominates massively), *tardus* is strongly favoured — nearly always more so than *velox* and always more so than *planus*. I give a table comparing Abelard (both in the *Historia calamitatum* and the *Letters*) with Odilo, Roscelin and Guibert, in respect of their percentages of the main forms of *velox, tardus* and *planus:* [23]

Table 4

	Odilo	Roscelin	Guibert	Abelard Hist. cal.	Abelard to Heloise	Heloise to Abelard
Main *velox*	13.5	9.5	15.0	9.5	14.0	13.5
Main *tardus*	24.5	19.0	24.0	12.0	11.5	15.5
Main *planus*	14.0	15.0	23.5	7.5	10.0	8.5

That Abelard, insofar as he inclined to rhythmic prose (which he did not at all in his technical writings), derived certain tendencies of cadence from Roscelin or someone similar among his early teachers, is likely enough. So too Heloise, who received her schooling in the Benedictine convent at Argenteuil, may well have had her attention drawn to the rhythmic style of a renowned Benedictine abbot such as Odilo. However, if their *pattern* of cadences could, after all, be accounted for without reference to Adalbertus or Italy, it is not quite so easy to explain how Heloise came to combine her rhythmic pattern with frequent rhyme. It may have been through sheer creative inspiration — yet there is also the distinct possibility that she, who *per habundantiam litterarum erat suprema* [24], came in contact, towards 1130, with some of those very recent and very unusual Italian model letters that were equally rich in *tardus* cadences and in rhymes. When she summoned the full force of her eloquence to persuade Abelard not to neglect her and her community, she may well — instinctively rather than programmatically — have availed herself of their example. And inasmuch as Abelard too, in his letters answering her, combined a rhythm that inclined to *tardus* with a measure of rhyming, he may well have been writing under her influence, rather than she under his.

[23] The sources for these percentages are as follows. Odilo: Janson 1975, p. 111, Table 19; Roscelin: Janson 1988, p. 198, Table 5; Guibert: *ibid.* p. 198, Table 3; Abelard, *Hist. cal.*: *ibid.* p. 199, Table 8; Abelard to Heloise: *ibid.*, p. 198, Table 1; Heloise to Abelard: *ibid.* p. 198, Table 2. For Roscelin, Guibert, and Heloise to Abelard the misprints in the figures for the main *tardus* cadence (see n 22 above) have been corrected: thus Roscelin has 20 instances of p 4pp (out of 106), Guibert 59 (out of 245), and Heloise 31 (out of 200).

[24] *Hist. cal.*, ed. Monfrin, p. 71. [Since these pages were written, a forthcoming new edition of *La vie et les epistres Pierres Abaelart et Heloys sa fame*, by E. Hicks, has been announced by Editions Slatkine, Geneva; Colette Jeudy (Institut de recherche et d'histoire des textes) has promised an account of a further Latin MS — still privately owned — of the Abelard-Heloise correspondence, to appear in *Latomus*.]

APPENDIX

I *The use of* trispondiacus *(p 4p): three χ^2 tests*

Abelard to Heloise (sample of 200 sentences, given above, p. 320):

	Observed frequency	Expected frequency	$\dfrac{(O-E)^2}{E}$
p 4p	17	24	2.04
All others	183	176	0.96
			3.00

Heloise to Abelard (sample of 200 sentences, given above p. 320):

p 4p	14	21	2.33
All others	186	179	0.27
			2.60

Abelard, *Hist. cal.* (sample of 303 sentences, given by Janson p. 199, Table 8):

p 4p	43	43	0.00
All others	260	260	0.00
			0.00

II *A comparison of cadences in Heloise and Hugh of Fleury*

	Heloise	Hugh
6p	0	2
6pp	1	0
1 5p	2	1
p 5p	2	2
pp 5p	3	0
1 5pp	2	3
p 5pp	5	2
pp 5pp	1	1
1 4p	3	5
p 4p	14	5
pp 4p	27	53
1 4pp	2	0
p 4pp	31	29
pp 4pp	2	3

pp 1 3p	3	10
other 1 3p	7	2
p 3p	17	30
pp 3p	7	7
p 1 3pp	9	4
other 1 3pp	3	0
p 3pp	14	1
pp 3pp	11	0
pp 1 1 2	0	0
p 1 2	6	4
other 1 2	2	0
pp 2 2	2	2
other p 2	8	3
pp 2	11	19
1	5	12
Sum total	200	200

Heloise's sample comprises the sentence-endings in her first two letters (ed. Monfrin) and the first 33 sentences in her third letter (ed. Muckle). The sample from Hugh of Fleury is drawn from his *Tractatus de regia potestate et sacerdotali dignitate*, ed. E. Sackur, MGH *Libelli de lite* II 465-94: it comprises all sentences from the opening of the Prologue (p. 466 Inc. *Henrico Anglorum regi gloriosissimo*), to the first sentence of I 11 (p. 478 Expl. *aliquo pacto communicet*), including the eleven chapter-headings but excluding sentences that end in quoted words.

IV

THE MEDIEVAL *PLANCTUS*

12

THE LAMENT OF JEPHTHA'S DAUGHTER:
THEMES, TRADITIONS, ORIGINALITY *

> Siate fedeli, e a ciò far non bieci,
> come Jeptè alla sua prima mancia;
>   cui più si convenìa dicer «Mal feci»,
> che, servando, far peggio; e così stolto
> ritrovar puoi il gran duca de' Greci,
>   onde pianse Ifigenia il suo bel volto,
> e fe' pianger di sé i folli e i savi
> ch'udir parlar di così fatto colto.
>
> Dante, *Paradiso*, V, 65-72

I

The Pseudo-Philo

In the first century A. D., an author known today as the pseudo-Philo composed a lament for Jephtha's daughter, which she sings before she goes to her death, the victim of her father's vow. In the language it uses and the emotions it portrays, this lament stands in sharp contrast to everything else in the pseudo-Philo's book, the compilation called *Liber Antiquitatum Biblicarum* [1].

This work as it survives, in a fragmentary Latin translation from the Greek [2], made perhaps in the fourth century, is basically a

---

* Written with Margaret Alexiou. *Studi medievali*, 3ª serie, XII (1971), 819-863. The article was conceived and written jointly, but Margaret Alexiou is primarily responsible for the Byzantine and modern Greek material, Peter Dronke for the Latin and Provençal.

[1] Ed. Guido Kisch, *Pseudo-Philo's Liber Antiquitatum Biblicarum*, Notre Dame, 1949; transl. M. R. James, *The Biblical Antiquities of Philo*, London-New York, 1917. Peter Dronke is indebted to Bernhard Bischoff for first drawing his attention to the Jephtha episode, and to L. P. Wilkinson and Anthony Bulloch for some valuable suggestions on the text of the lament.

[2] It is generally agreed that behind the lost Greek version lay a Hebrew origi-

chronicle, extending from Adam to the death of Saul. Throughout, the author aims to supplement the biblical material. He does this, especially at first, by adding long and fanciful genealogies; he elaborates the biblical narrative by additional episodes that seem to him in keeping with what the Bible tells; or again, he amplifies the biblical accounts themselves by attributing speeches to the characters in episodes that the Bible had told succinctly, in indirect speech. There is very little in the entire text that reflects a lyrical impulse. The few relevant passages are the following. At II, 10 there is a brief "song" of Lamech: this is little more than a citation, with two additional phrases, of his words in *Genesis*, IV, 23-4. At IX, 2, the Israelites are given three sentences of lamentation at Pharaoh's plan to slay their male children. The hymn ascribed to Debbora and Barach (XXXII, 1-17) is as long as that in *Judges* V, 2-32, but very different in content — it dwells chiefly on earlier episodes in Israel's history — and is considerably less lyrical than the biblical hymn (at least as far as the Latin text can intimate). The hymn of Anna (LI, 3-6) is essentially a paraphrase of her biblical hymn (*I Samuel*, II, 1-10). Near the close of the extant part of the work David is given a short psalm to sing as he is anointed by Samuel (LIX, 4), and another which is said to be the song he sang to make Saul's evil spirit depart (LX, 2-3): only this last has a certain grandeur and originality of conception. But it is the grandeur of a cosmogony, inspired by the opening of *Genesis* as well as apocryphal accounts — it is not concerned with human emotions.

By contrast, the only other substantial innovation in the whole treatise, the lament of Jephtha's daughter, dwells passionately on human emotions and is rich in dramatic potential. The author is emotionally involved in the episode in a way the biblical author had not been: when Jephtha makes his terrible vow, the pseudo-Philo shows his own commitment by the words he adds (XXXIX, 11): God is furious with Jephtha — his was a thoughtless, even insolent, vow — and God determines to punish him. He will grant Israel victory in battle, but for Israel's, not for Jephtha's, sake:

Et iratus est Dominus ira et dixit: Ecce devovit Ieptan ut offerat mihi omne quod primum obviaverit ei. Ecce nunc si canis primum ob-

---

nal (James, pp. 28-29; Kisch, pp. 16-18). Kisch goes so far as to say (p. 18), "The spirit of rabbinic Judaism and its typical ancient literature permeates the work in its entirety; and the author's own inventions are woven into it". At the same time, as will emerge in this discussion, the nature of the lament of Jephtha's daughter indicates a link with Hellenistic Greek traditions.

viaverit Iepte, numquid canis offeretur mihi? Et nunc fiat Iepte oracio eius in primogenitum fructum ventris sui, et peticio eius in unigenita ipsius. Ego autem liberans liberabo populum meum in eo tempore, non pro eo sed pro oracione quam oravit Israel.

The daughter, anonymous in the Bible, is here given the name Seila, "she who was demanded". Jephtha stresses the meaning of her name as he tells her she must be sacrificed. Her answering speech is fuller than in the Book of Judges, and reveals her character more acutely: she is bolder and more decisive than in her biblical lines, she rejoices in the thought of an heroic, exemplary death. She recalls the way Isaac had been demanded for sacrifice, and hopes only that her death will be acceptable to God — for hers is spontaneous (whereas Isaac's had been a divine command). At the same time her reply foreshadows the full lyrical *planctus* that is to follow: she sees her proposed time of lamentation as establishing a bond with nature, an elemental unity of sorrow in which not only her girl-friends but the trees and the beasts will share (XL, 2-3):

> Et dixit ei Seila filia eius: Et quis est qui contristetur moriens, videns populum liberatum? Aut immemor es que facta sunt in diebus patrum nostrorum, quando pater filium imponebat in holocaustum, et non contradixit ei, sed epulans consensit illi, et erat qui offerebatur paratus, et qui offerebat gaudens. Et nunc omnia que orasti non destruas, fac autem unam peticionem quam peto a te antequam moriar. Et postulationem minimam exoro, priusquam reddam animam meam, ut vadam in montes et maneam in collibus et ambulem in petris, ego et convirgines mee, et effundam in eis lacrimas meas et referam tristicias iuventutis mee. Plorabunt me ligna campi, et plangent me bestie campestres, quia non sum tristis in hoc quod moriar, nec dolet mihi quod reddo animam meam, sed quoniam in oracione preoccupatus est pater meus, et spontaneam me obtuli in sacrificium, timeo ne non sit acceptabilis mors mea, aut in vano perdam animam meam. Hec referam montibus, et post revertar.

Once more the author declares his involvement, through the judgement he ascribes to God (XL, 4): "I have seen her to be wiser than her father, more true in feeling than all who now are wise. And now let her soul be preserved as she demanded, and her death will for all ages be precious in my sight".

Now the pseudo-Philo sets down the lament Seila made on the mountain, before her death (XL, 5-7):

> Audite montes trenum meum,
> et intendite colles lacrimas oculorum meorum,

et testes estote petre in planctu anime mee.
Ecce quomodo accusor,
5   sed non in vano recipiatur anima mea.
Proficiscantur verba mea in celos,
et scribantur lacrime mee ante conspectum firmamenti,
ut pater non expugnet filiam quam devovit sacrificare,
et ut princeps illius unigenitam audiat in sacrificio promissam.

10   Ego autem non sum saturata thalamo meo,
nec repleta sum coronis nuptiarum mearum.
Non enim vestita sum in splendore secundum ingenui*tate*m meam,
et non sum usa mos*ch*i odoris mei,
nec fronduit anima mea, oleo unctionis quod preparatum est mihi.

15   O mater, in vano peperisti unigenitam tuam,
quoniam factus est infernus thalamus meus,
et *unguenta* mea super terram
et confectio omnis olei quam preparasti mihi effundetur,
et albam quam nevit mater mea, tinea comedet eam,
20   et flores corone quam intexuit nutrix mea in tempore marcescent,
et stratoriam quam texuit ingenium meum de iacinctino
et purpuram meam vermis corrum*pet*.
Et referentes me convirgines mee
in gemitum per dies plangant me.

25   Inclinate arbores ramos vestros, et plangite iuventutem meam.
Venite fere silve, et conculcate supra virgini*tatem* mea*m*,
quoniam abscisi sunt anni mei,
et tempus vite mee in tenebris inveterabit [3].

[3] Text after Kisch, ed. cit., pp. 221-2, with my own divisions into lines and sections, and the following changes. I adopt from Sichardus' *editio princeps* (1527) the readings 4 *accusor* (*accusamur* MSS and Kisch, but note the singulars throughout), and 26 *virginitatem meam* (*virgines meas* MSS and Kisch): both of these may go back to his "exemplar pervetustum", the lost MS from Lorsch. At 13 Sichardus has *Moysi* (along with four MSS), and suggests emending to *moscho*; Kisch retains *Moysi* without comment. I have emended to *moschi* (in apposition to *odoris mei* — for late Latin *utor* with genitive cf. Hofmann-Szantyr, p. 83); the remaining MSS have *Non sum usa preciosi odoramenti mei*. At 12 my emendation *ingenuitatem* has some basis in two MSS (which read *sedens in ingenuitate mea*); Kisch prints the Admont MS *secundum ingenuam meam*. At 17, all MSS and Kisch have *genua* (ed. princ. *genuam*). At 22, most MSS and Kisch have *corrumpat*, but one MS and the ed. princ. support *corrumpet*. Some of the more unusual wordings in the Latin text may reflect the Greek from which the translator worked: e.g. 4 *accusor* (or *accusamur*) may reflect Gk. κατηγορεῖν; 9 *princeps* (where one might expect *Dominus*) may simply be rendering Gk. κύριος; 23 *convirgines* (not recorded in *TLL*) must have been formed on the basis of Gk. συμπάρθενοι. [On this lament, see more recently P.M. Bogaert, in *Revue Théologique de Louvain*, III (1972), 334-344; M. Philonenko, in *Les syncrétismes dans les religions grecque et romaine*, Paris, 1973, pp. 165-177; and the ed. of D.J. Harring-

The text presents some difficulties, which an interpretative translation may signal, if not resolve:

> You mountains, hear my lamentation,
> and you hills, watch the tears of my eyes;
> witness, you rocks, the lament of my soul.
> See how I am singled out —
> 5   but let my soul not be taken away in vain!
> Let my words mount to the heavens,
> let my tears be written in the sight of the firmament,
> that the father may not overrule the daughter he has vowed to sacrifice,
> and that his Lord hear, an only daughter has been promised in sacrifice.
>
> 10   But my hunger for my bridal bed has not been quenched,
> nor am I sated with wedding-garlands.
> I have not been dressed in splendour, as befits my birth,
> nor have I used my perfume of musk,
> nor has my soul put forth its leaves, though the oil to anoint my body was prepared.
>
> 15   Oh mother, it was in vain you bore your only daughter,
> for hell has become my bridal bed,
> and my unguents will be spilt on the earth
> and all the oil you blended for me wasted,
> and the white dress my mother sewed, the moth will eat it,
> 20   and the flowers in the garland my nurse plaited will wither in time,
> and the hyacinth coverlet I wove with my own skill,
> and my purple robe, worms will ruin.
> And my maiden friends, when they tell of me,
> shall weep and groan for me through the days.
>
> 25   You trees, incline your boughs and lament my youth.
> Come, forest beasts, and tread on my virginity,
> for my years have been cut away,
> and the spring of my life will grow old in darkness.

Even through the somewhat ungainly, at times obscure, Latin in which this *planctus* survives we can glimpse a lyrical lament, passionate and beautiful. Artistically, it would seem to have the virtues and the flaws implied by the two senses of "pathétique": it is over-emphatic in its emotional insistence, at the same time it is genuinely moving, it has more of a heroine's dignity than of sentimentality. For

---

ton and J. Cazeaux, *Pseudo-Philon: Les Antiquités Bibliques* (SC 229-230), Paris, 1976. Philonenko's parallel in his essay (p. 175), between *Iph. A.* 1211-15 and the opening of Seila's lament, is, however, too tenuous to support his claim that Pseudo-Philo had read Euripides' play.]

the medieval Latinist the most immediate interest of this lament lies undoubtedly in its relation to Peter Abelard's *Planctus virginum Israel super filia Iepte Galadite*, the greatest *planctus* composed in the twelfth century. This relation, and the question of what other traditions of laments of a young girl dying Abelard might have known, will be discussed later. First, however, we must ask, what lies behind the pseudo-Philo's individual treatment of the anonymous biblical figure? What impelled him to compose a *planctus* so strikingly unlike anything else in his long and edifying chronicle? What traditions could he have known?

The division of Seila's *planctus* into four sections may help to clarify the articulation of thought. The first is dominated by a series of invocations: the natural world (*montes, colles, petre* — all echoed from her speech to her father) and even the heavens (*celi, firmamentum*) are summoned by Seila to witness both her grief and her heroism [4]. The second section is a series of negatives, stressing the beauty of the young life that is going to waste. It is filled with the imagery of marriage — bridal bed, garlands, wedding-dress, perfume and oil — all these will be denied through her early death, and even her soul will wither without having spread its leaves.

In the third section all these images are given a new modulation, governed by the conceit that is the pivotal point of the lament: *quoniam factus est infernus thalamus meus*. Death is a different kind of marriage, a grim parody of a marriage; all the delightful and sensual accompaniments of the bride will die with her — they will share, that is, in the fatal, underworld wedding.

The fourth section returns to the invocations of the opening (and more particularly to those foreshadowed in Seila's earlier speech). The trees and animals — unlike the objects associated with the wedding-ceremony — are still alive, and they can share the heroine's sorrow, whether by a gesture of lament, or by the more brutal gesture associated with the animals (*conculcate*), which nonetheless is an expression of Seila's desire: she had longed for her virginity to be destroyed.

For all these elements — the invocations to nature and the heavens, the series of negations relating to the wedding, the dark

---

[4] There is a vast range of parallels to such invocations in Greek tradition, Anthony Bulloch has pointed out to us one particularly early and striking example:

ἄστρα τε καὶ ποταμοὶ καὶ κύματα πόντου

from Pindar's *Threni* (fr. 136, ed. B. Snell , 3rd Teubner ed., Leipzig, 1964). In the course of the present article, however, we shall mention only a few such invocations, which are directly relevant to the discussion of bridal laments.

parallels between marriage and death, the share of nature in the human sorrow — abundant analogues can be found: in a long, unbroken Greek tradition of laments over young girls, or laments put in the mouths of the young girls themselves.

II

The Greek tradition

1) *Greek drama*

In the two ancient tragedies in which a young heroine dies as sacrificial victim, the *Antigone* and the *Iphigenia in Aulis*, Sophocles and Euripides show themselves aware of the parallels and antinomies, wedding-and-funeral, love-and-death. The imagery used to express the sacrifice in each play dwells both on the negatives — she will have no marriage, no bridal garlands, no nuptial music — and on the macabre analogy: she *will* be a bride in the otherworld, a bride of Hades or Acheron.

Soon after the entry of Antigone's fiancé Haemon, his father Creon says to him (653-4):

> μέθες
> τὴν παῖδ' ἐν "Αιδου τήνδε νυμφεύειν τινί.
> Cast off
> the girl, let her marry someone in Hades.

In her farewell scene, Antigone herself makes continual allusion to both the negations and the analogy (814-16, 877-82, 891, 917-20):

> οὔθ ὑμεναίων ἔγκληρον, οὔτ' ἐπινύμφειός
> πώ μέ τις ὕμνος ὕμνησεν, ἀλλ' 'Αχέροντι νυμφεύσω.
>
> ἄκλαυτος, ἄφιλος, ἀνυμέναιος ταλαίφρων ἄγομαι
> τὰν πυμάταν ὁδόν· οὐκέτι μοι τόδε
> λαμπάδος ἱερὸν ὄμμα
> θέμις ὁρᾶν ταλαίνα·
> τὸν δ' ἐμὸν πότμον ἀδάκρυτον
> οὐδεὶς φίλων στενάζει.
>
> ὦ τύμβος, ὦ νυμφεῖον...
>
> ἄλεκτρον, ἀνυμέναιον, οὔτε του γάμου
> μέρος λαχοῦσαν οὔτε παιδείου τροφῆς,
> ἀλλ' ὧδ' ἔρημος πρὸς φίλων ἡ δύσμορος
> ζῶσ' εἰς θανόντων ἔρχομαι κατασκαφάς.

I have not shared in the wedding-song,

nor has any bridal hymn yet been sung for me: it is Acheron I'll wed!

Unwept, unloved, unwedded, wretched I'll walk
the final road; no longer
shall I see the holy
eye of the sun;
my tearless fate
no friend will bewail.

Oh tomb, oh bridal chamber...

Without a bridal bed, without a marriage-song, having achieved
neither wedding nor the tending of a child,
thus destitute of friends, ill-starred,
I go alive into the caverns of the dead.

Then the chorus parallels Antigone's destiny with that of Danae
(944-6):

ἔτλα καὶ Δανάας οὐράνιον φῶς
ἀλλάξαι δέμας ἐν χαλκοδέτοις αὐλαῖς·
κρυπτομένα δ᾽ ἐν τυμβήρει θαλάμῳ κατεζεύχθη.

Danae's body endured to leave the heavenly light
for her brass-built chamber:
hiding in that tomb, it became her bridal bower.

Finally in the messenger's speech, relating the tragic love-death of
Haemon and Antigone, these images re-emerge in their finest conjunction through opposition (1204-5, 1240-1):

αὖθις πρὸς λιθόστρωτον κόρης
νυμφεῖον "Αιδου κοῖλον εἰσεβαίνομεν...

κεῖται δὲ νεκρὸς περὶ νεκρῷ, τὰ νυμφικὰ
τέλη λαχὼν δείλαιος εἰν "Αιδου δόμοις.

Again we made our way to the girl's stony dwelling,
the hollow bridal bower of Hades...
Haemon lies, dead on the dead one, finding the consummation
of his marriage, wretchedly, in the halls of Hades.

Thus we see that, beyond the parallel of situation — the sacrificial death of a young heroine — a range of expressions and images
in Sophocles' play are comparable to those in Seila's lament, and
could already in the fifth century B. C. show themselves as recognis-
able threads in a poetic fabric. So too in the *Iphigenia in Aulis*, where
the contrast between Agamemnon's pretext — Iphigenia's marriage
to Achilles — and the reality — her fate as sacrificial victim, the

price, like Seila, of a military success — is crucial to the dramatic structure.

Near the opening of Euripides' play the messenger bringing Iphigenia and Clytemnestra to Aulis alludes to all the preparations for the mysterious marriage (433-9):

'Αρτέμιδι προτελίζουσι τὴν νεάνιδα,
Αὐλίδος ἀνάσσῃ. τίς νιν ἄξεταί ποτε;
ἀλλ' εἶα, τἀπὶ τοισίδ' ἐξάρχου κανᾶ,
στεφανοῦσθε κρᾶτα· καὶ σύ, Μενέλεως ἄναξ,
ὑμέναιον εὐτρέπιζε καὶ κατὰ στέγας
λωτὸς βοάσθω καὶ ποδῶν ἔστω κτύπος·
φῶς γὰρ τόδ' ἥκει μακάριον τῇ παρθένῳ.

They are giving the girl with her wedding-offering to Artemis,
queen of Aulis. But who shall the bridegroom be?
Come then, let us prepare the baskets for the sacrifice,
garland our heads, and you, lord Menelaus,
begin the bridal hymn; let the flute and the din
of dancing feet echo throughout the tents,
so that a blissful daylight greets the maiden.

In the first line cited, a tragic second meaning is implicit, which casts its shadow over all the details that follow. A moment later Agamemnon in his soliloquy gives these lines their explicit grim perspective (460-1):

τὴν δ' αὖ τάλαιναν παρθένον — τί παρθένον;
"Αιδης νιν ὡς ἔοικε νυμφεύσει τάχα —

And as for the wretched maiden — why do I call her that?
Hades, it seems, will be her bridegroom soon.

When at the close Iphigenia has determined to go nobly into her death, she, like the messenger in *Antigone*, brings this language of wedding and sacrifice to its culmination in a fusion of opposites (1397-9):

δίδωμι σῶμα τοὐμὸν 'Ελλάδι.
θύετ', ἐκπορθεῖτε Τροίαν. ταῦτα γὰρ μνημεῖά μου
διὰ μακροῦ, καὶ παῖδες οὗτοι καὶ γάμοι καὶ δόξ' ἐμή.

I give my body to Hellas.
Sacrifice it, ravage Troy! For this is my memorial
through the ages — this my children, this my marriage and my glory.

Finally, the theme of death as marriage and marriage as death is sustained implicitly throughout Cassandra's scene in Euripides'

Trojan Women. After the opening lament for the fall of Troy, Talthybius enters from the Greek camp with news that Cassandra has been chosen as Agamemnon's concubine. Hecuba, after hearing further what is to become of Polyxena, Andromache, and herself, breaks into a lament for her cruel fate (278-91).

Suddenly Cassandra is seen, wreathed and robed like a priestess and carrying a lighted torch in her hand. The meaning of the torch becomes clear when she sings, not the expected lament, but her own weeding-song. The cry to Hymen — Ὑμὴν, ὦ Ὑμέναι', ἄναξ — rings out throughout the ode: blessed is the God of Marriage, blessed are they that are to wed, blessed is she, the bride! Since Hecuba can only weep for Priam and for Troy, Cassandra must bear the torch and lead the dance herself (attentions usually performed by the bride's mother) (315-24). In the antistrophe, she insists that the dance is sacred, since it celebrates her own marriage and her father's happy fortune. Hecuba must dance too, and the chorus must bless the marriage-bed prepared for her lord (332-41).

The significance of Cassandra's words, which are full of double meanings, emerges in the scene that follows. Hecuba is shocked: Cassandra should sing a lament, not a bridal-song, since the impending marriage is a union forced upon her, a far cry indeed from a mother's hopes (342-51). Cassandra explains, more lucid now, that her marriage will bring about the destruction of the Greeks. Then she realises that the axe that is to fall on Agamemnon will fall on her as well (362-4), but she dismisses the thought and turns again to the sufferings of the Greeks, dimly foreseeing Odysseus' wanderings, his homecoming, his live descent to Hades. The word brings her back to her own fate, too terrible to permit her to gloat over her enemies. As the full impact of her wedding-song is clear at last, the metre changes from iambic trimeter to excited trochaic tetrameter (444-50):

> But why do I proclaim Odysseus' woes?
> Lead me swiftly: in Hades let me lie wedded to my bridegroom.
> Yes, wretched shall your burial be, in darkness, not in light,
> commander of the Greeks, whose fortune now seems glorious.
> As for me, my body, naked and exposed in a mountain-cleft
> to raging winter rains, shall lie beside my bridegroom's tomb,
> I shall be a prey for beasts to feed on, I, Apollo's handmaid.

At this point the contrast between her vision of the future and her present attire, with its mocking reminders of a god's past love and her own hopes for marriage, becomes too much to bear. With a change of mood matched only perhaps by Jephtha's daughter in

Abelard's *planctus* [5], she tears the wreaths from her head. Calmly she turns to leave, her last words suggesting perhaps both a bride's farewell to her mother and home and a girl's lament for her own fate (458-61) [6]:

χαῖρέ μοι, μῆτερ, δαχρύσῃς μηδέν· ὦ φίλη πατρίς·
οἵ τε γῆς ἔνερθ᾽ ἀδελφοὶ χὠ τεχὼν ἡμᾶς πατήρ,
οὐ μαχρὰν δέξεσθέ μ᾽· ἥχω δ᾽ εἰς νεχροὺς νιχηφόρος
χαὶ δόμους πέρσασ᾽ Ἀτρειδῶν, ὧν ἀπωλόμεσθ᾽ ὕπο.

Mother, farewell. Do not weep. Oh beloved homeland,
and you, my brothers, beneath the earth, and you, father, who gave
us life,
soon you shall receive me. I shall come to the dead crowned with
victory,
having utterly laid waste the house of Atreus' sons, who now cause our
death.

Euripides has infused into this scene, which is full of allusions to the Cassandra scene in Aeschylus' *Agamemnon*, a new range of imagery drawn from the double parallel of death and marriage: the wedding which Cassandra celebrates in her *epithalamium* will be consummated in Hades; at the same time, as a bride, she will become a victim whose sacrifice will secure her enemies' downfall and her own glory in Hades [7].

2) *The Palatine Anthology*

Besides Attic tragedy we have evidence relevant to Seila's lament from three sides: the funeral epigrams for those who died

[5] See discussion below.

[6] Other tragic heroines who lament their own fate or death include the Suppliants and Cassandra in Aeschylus, Jocasta and Deianeira in Sophocles, Alcestis, Hecuba, Polyxena, Medea and Phaedra in Euripides. Their laments include a striking number of recurrent formulae and ideas.

[7] For allusions in Aeschylus' *Agamemnon* to Clytemnestra as officiating priest and to her impending murder as a holy mystery, with Cassandra as a candidate for initiation, see George Thomson, *Oresteia*, II (2nd. edition), Prague, 1966, pp. 86-7. Further reference to death as marriage with Hades is made in Euripides' *Orestes* (1109). E. W. Whittle has pointed out to us the possibility of an allusion to the theme in Aeschylus' *Supplices* (790-1), where the Chorus of Danaid women cries out that, rather than submit to an unholy marriage with their kinsmen, they will hang themselves at the altar of Zeus and so win Hades as their lord. The precise interpretation of the passage turns on whether πρόπαρ θανούσας δ᾽ Ἀΐδας ἀνάσσοι means, simply, "sooner may I die and may Hades rule over me", or, more specifically, "sooner may I die and may Hades be my husband", for which 905 possibly offers support.

young, from the seventh book of the Palatine Anthology; in a large number of funerary inscriptions; and in some uses of love-and-death *topoi* in the Greek romances. Although most examples are Hellenistic or post-Hellenistic, there is a sufficient number of earlier instances to establish that the theme of death as marriage was familiar outside tragedy from the late archaic and early classical periods.

To illustrate from only a few of the epigrams, the earliest example of the theme which can be dated with certainty is an epitaph by Simonides (sixth to fifth centuries B. C.). Tersely, the dead Gorgippos evokes the contrast between the marriage-bed and Persephone's *thalamus* (507) [8]:

Οὐκ ἐπιδὼν νύμφεια λέχη κατέβην τὸν ἄφυκτον
Γόργιππος ξανθῆς Φερσεφόνης θάλαμον.

Without having seen the marriage-bed, I, Gorgippos, descended
to the bridal chamber of blonde Persephone.

Erinna (late fourth century B. C.) has an epitaph for the betrothed girl Baucis, in which the gravestone speaks and evokes both the parallels and the contrasts between wedding and funeral (712):

"Βάσκανος ἔσσ', Ἀίδα." τὰ δέ τοι καλὰ σάμαθ' ὁρῶντι
ὠμοτάταν Βαυχοῦς ἀγγελέοντι τύχαν,
ὡς τὰν παῖδ', Ὑμέναιος ἐφ'. αἷς ἀείδετο πεύκαις,
ταῖσδ' ἐπὶ καδεστὰς ἔφλεγε πυρκαϊᾷ·
καὶ σὺ μέν, ὦ Ὑμέναιε, γάμων μολπαῖον ἀοιδὰν
ἐς θρήνων γοερῶν φθέγμα μεθαρμόσαο.

..."You are envious, Hades". The lovely inscription tells the beholder
of Baucis' most savage fate:
how with the very torch that accompanied her bridal song
her father-in-law lit the funeral pyre that consumed her.
And you yourself, Hymenaeus, transformed the harmonious
wedding-chant
into the sound of wailing threnodies.

---

[8] All our citations from the Palatine Anthology are taken from the edition of H. Beckby, *Anthologia Graeca* (4 vols.), München, 1957-8. Other poems in Book VII containing similar topoi and motifs are nos. 183-4, 186-8, 291, 486-7, 669. Cf. also R. Lattimore, *Themes in Greek and Latin Epitaphs*, Urbana, 1942, pp. 192-4, and, with special reference to the inscriptions, E. Griessmair, *Das Motiv der Mors Immatura in den Griechischen metrischen Grabinschriften*, Innsbruck, 1966, pp. 63-75. [In *A.G.* VIII, 51, Gregory Nazianzen compares the departure of the soul of his mother, who died at the altar, with the sacrifices offered by Abraham and by Jephtha].

In some other lines by Erinna in memory of the same girl (710), Baucis herself speaks, and invokes the objects that share in and testify to her death:

Στᾶλαι καὶ Σειρῆνες ἐμαὶ καὶ πένθιμε κρωσσέ,
    ὅστις ἔχεις Ἀΐδα τὰν ὀλίγαν σποδιάν,
τοῖς ἐμὸν ἐπχομένοισι παρ' ἠρίον εἴπατε χαίρειν,
    αἴτ ἀστοὶ τελέθωντ' αἴθ ἑτεροπτόλιες.
χὤτι με νύμφαν εὖσαν ἔχει τάφος, εἴπατε καὶ τό.

My gravestones and sirens, and you, pain-bringing urn
    that hold the paltry ashes which belong to Hades,
give greeting to those who pass beside my mound,
    whether they are native or of another city.
Tell them, I went into the tomb a bride...

Meleager (c. 140-c. 70 B. C.), in an epitaph for a girl Clearista (182), beginning, "No marriage, but betrothal to Hades", repeats and lightly elaborates the pattern of contrasts found in Erinna. Here the girl has died during the wedding-night itself. The flutes which serenaded her joyfully that evening accompany her funeral the next day; the epithalamium is exchanged for a threnody; the noise of slamming the door of the bride's bedroom is followed by Hymenaeus' silence; the torches that lit her way to bed accompany her to the grave [9].

The poetic conventions of such epitaphs for young girls continue to be present in the Byzantine period. Briefly and allusively in a poem of Paulus Silentiarius (sixth century A. D.), which according to two relatively ancient testimonies is in memory of his own daughter (604) [10]:

---

[9] Cf. *A. G.*, VII, 711; 185: the girl speaks her epitaph, and contrasts the fires of wedding and funeral. The contrast between marriage and tomb is already alluded to in *Odyssey* XX, 307. In Roman poetry Ovid (*Her.*, XXI, 172; *Fasti*, II, 561-2) and Propertius (IV, 11, 46) make swift allusions to the two kinds of torches (cf. Griessmair, op. cit., pp. 70-71).

[10] Cf. the excellent range of parallels adduced in G. Viansino's edition: Paolo Silenziario, *Epigrammi*, Torino, 1963, pp. 14-17. I would like to add one remarkable parallel from Renaissance literature: it is the exclamations of Capulet at the supposed death of his daughter Juliet (*Romeo and Juliet*, IV, 5):

O Sonne, the night before thy wedding day,
Hath Death laine with thy wife: there she lies,
Flower as she was, deflowred by him.
Death is my Sonne in law, Death is my Heire,
My daughter he hath wedded...
All things that we ordained Festivall,

Λέκτρα σοι ἀντὶ γάμων ἐπιτύμβια, παρθένε κούρη,
ἐστόρεσαν παλάμαις πενθαλέαις γενέται.

Instead of a bridal bed, a deathbed, innnocent girl,
   was decked for you by your parents' plangent hands...

In the same century, too, Agathias wrote an epitaph of particular interest in relation to Seila's lament: once more it is the girl herself who
speaks, but here with passionate invocations, and with a deep regret
that the joys of sexual fulfilment and of bearing children were denied
her (568):

ἆ Μοῖραι, τί τοσοῦτον ἀπηνέες οὐδ' ἐπὶ παστοὺς
   ἠγάγετ' οὐδ' ἐρατῆς ἔργα τεκνοσπορίης;
οἱ μὲν γὰρ γονέες με γαμήλιον εἰς Ὑμέναιον
   μέλλον ἄγειν, στυγεροῦ δ' εἰς Ἀχέροντος ἔβην.
ἀλλά, θεοί, λίτομαι, μητρός γε γόους πατέρος τε
   παύσατε τηχομένων εἵνεχ' ἐμεῦ φθιμένης.

... Ah Fates, why were you so harsh as not to lead me
   to joys of the bedroom, or the task of beloved childbearing?
My parents were about to bring me to Hymenaeus of the wedding,
   yet I descended to Acheron's hateful depths.
But you gods, I beseech, staunch my father's and mother's lamenting —
   they are wasting away on account of my death.

3) *Funerary inscriptions*

   The evidence of the funerary inscriptions is particularly important because it reflects an essentially more popular and less literary
tradition than the epigrams of the Anthology. It is not known precisely how these inscriptions were composed: the theory that the
stone-cutters used manuals from which the bereaved might choose
their themes remains only a hypothesis, with rather more evidence
to support it in Latin than in Greek [11]. The large number of common
ideas and formulae, many derived from classical literature, others

     Turne from their office to blacke Funerall:
     Our instruments to melancholy Bells,
     Our wedding cheare, to a sad buriall Feast:
     Our solemne Hymnes, to sullen Dyrges change:
     Our Bridall flowers serve for a buried Coarse:
     And all things change them to the contrarie.
Shakespeare here plays on the full Hellenistic range of conceit and paradox.
  [11] See Lattimore, *Themes*, pp. 19-20. For a more detailed discussion of the
problems, see R. Cagnat,*Sur les manuels des graveurs d'inscriptions*, in *Revue de
philologie*, XIII (1889), 51-65, and H. H. Armstrong, *Autobiographic Elements in Latin Inscriptions*, Baltimore, 1910, pp. 239-42.

found also in the epigrams, points to a fair degree of standardisation. Yet it would be a mistake to dismiss the evidence of the inscriptions as entirely derivative: within the bounds of the convention, ideas, language and style vary considerably according to the time and place of composition, and according to the status of the deceased. The inscriptions afford us a unique insight into a complete cross-section of society; and it may be the more humble, semi-literate examples which offer the most valuable evidence.

Among the inscriptions for those who died young, reference to death as marriage is extremely frequent, whether in the more general form of regret for one who has died before marriage, or of a more explicit allusion to marriage with Hades. The examples are too many to enumerate in full: all that can be attempted here is to outline the gradual emergence of the themes and images from the sixth century B. C. until the end of antiquity, to indicate their wide diffusion over the whole Greek-speaking world, and to illustrate how a single, traditional idea might be varied in countless ways for different poetic effects.

An early inscription from Attica (sixth century) illustrates the detached, almost serene dignity of the archaic style:

σμ̃εα Φρασικλείας· | κόρε̄ κεκλε̄́σομαι | αἰεί,
ἀντὶ γάμο | παρὰ θεο̃ν τοῦτο | λαχο̃σ' ὄνομα.

Phrasikleia's grave. I shall always have the name maiden,
  for the gods gave me this name instead of marriage [12].

The antithesis ἀντὶ γάμου... (τοῦτο λαχοῦσ' ὄνομα) is a common formula in later inscriptions [13]. Two centuries later, an inscription from Athens (second half of the fourth century) elaborates the same contrast in the more relaxed style of the late classical period:

οὔ σε γάμων πρόπολος, Πλαγγών, Ὑμέναιος ἐν οἴκοις
ὤλβισεν, ἀλλ' ἐδάκρυσ' ⟨ἐκτὸς⟩ ἀποφθιμένην·

Hymenaeus did not bless you in your home, Plangon, as attendant
  at your wedding; instead he wept (outside) for your death (GV,
                                                          1820, 1-2).

Young Simylis, in an inscription from Ikaria (third century B. C.), is

---

[12] The inscriptions are cited from Werner Peek, *Griechische Vers-Inschriften*, I, Berlin, 1955 [GV], and from G. Kaibel, *Epigrammata Graeca e lapidibus conlecta*, Berlin, 1878 [Kaibel]. This first one is GV, 68, Kaibel, 6.
[13] Cf. GV, 710, 5-6; 1263, 9-10; 1330, 5-6; 1437, 5; 1584, 5-6.

lamented in a series of negations comparable to those in the Palatine Anthology and in Seila's lament: she lies with her mother, leaving grief to her father, having known the lovely melody neither of marriage nor of wedding-songs — she is received instead in Hades' halls (GV, 1540). These negations frequently form a recurrent rhythmical pattern by means of incremental repetition, with the words οὐ γάμου, οὐδ' ὑμέναιου most commonly found at the beginning of a half-line [14]. Sometimes the negations introduce highly complex antitheses, as in this inscription from Karanis in Egypt (third to second centuries B. C.), where the details are strikingly similar to those in Meleager's epigram discussed above, which was written a hundred years later [15]:

δὶς δέκα γάρ μ' ἐκόμησε πατὴρ ἔτη, οὐδ' ἐτέλεσσα
νυμφιδίων θαλάμων εἰς ὑμέναια λέχη,
οὐδ' ὑπὸ παστὸν ἐμὸν δέμας ἤλυθεν, οὐδ' ἐκρότησαν
πάννυχ' ὁμηλικίη κεδροπαγεῖς σανίδας·
ὤλετο παρθενίη σειρὴν ἐμή· αἰαῖ ἐκείνην
Μοῖραν, ἰή, τίς ἐμοὶ νήματα πίκρ' ἔβαλεν.

For twice ten years my father tended me, yet I did not complete
  the rite of the marriage-chamber in the bridal bed,
nor has my body come beneath the nuptial curtain, nor has
  my friends' all-night knocking sounded at the cedar doors.
My allure as a girl is destroyed. Alas for that
  Fate, woe is me, who wove me such bitter threads (GV, 1608, 3-8).

In contrast to the occasionally rhetorical effect of these more elaborate series of negations, the stark simplicity of a mutilated and poorly-spelt fragment from Asia Minor (date uncertain) achieves a more intimate tone:

Ζ[η]τῖς, ὦ [παρ]οδῖτα, τίς | ἐνθά[δε κε]ύ[θε]τε τύμβω.|
Παρθένος ὧδε τέθαπτε | Σιμωνίδου ἀγλαΐη παῖς, |
οὔνομ[α 'Ιτα?]λίη· ταύτης | ὑμεν[αῖος ὅδ'] ἐστιν.

You ask, passer-by, who lies in this tomb.
  Here lies buried a maiden, Simonides' lovely child.
Italie is her name. This is her bridal song [16].

In two inscriptions widely separated in time and place, we find

---

[14] Cf. GV, 658, 9; 667, 3; 1243, 5-6; 1821, 1-2; 1826, 1; 1853, 1; 2038, 19; Kaibel, 373, 3-4.

[15] Cf. GV, 683, 3-5; 804, 5-7; 1162, 7-8; 1822, 1-3; 1823, 1-4; 1833, 7-8; 2026, 10-15; 2038, 12-13.

[16] *Monumenta Asiae Minoris Antiqua* [MAMA], III, 793. For a similar type of inscription, cf. *Corpus Inscriptionum Graecarum* [CIG], III, 4642.

the same formula as opened the second section of Seila's lament, *non sum saturata thalamo meo* —

[οὔπω] νυμφιδίων κραδίηι πεπληθότα λέκτρων...

not yet having taken his fill of the marriage-bed... (GV, 677, Ephesus, 3rd/2nd century B.C.)

οὐχὶ φίλων γονέων πεπλησμένος, οὐ συνε⟨ταίρων⟩,
τᾶς δὲ πικρᾶς Ἀΐδεω νῦν ἐπ᾽ ἐμοὶ κλισί[ας].

having taken my fill neither of my dear parents nor of my friends,
    but of the bitter couch of Hades that is now upon me... (GV, 434,
                                          Syros, 2nd century A. D.).

The contrast implied in Seila's formula, between the *thalamus* of marriage and the *thalamus infernus* prepared for her in Hades, is commonly found in the inscriptions, where the bright torchlight of the marriage-chamber is contrasted with the unlit darkness of Hades' dwelling. In an inscription from Smyrna (second century B. C.) Hymenaeus holds aloft the pine-torches, unlit and unconsumed, for the wedding that became a funeral [17]. All these threads are worked together in a late inscription from Cyrene (second century A. D.), with a new detail referring to the absence of nuptial oils, as in Seila's lament:

βαιόν σοι τὸ μετα|ξὺ βίου θανάτοιό | τ᾽ ἔθηκε
καὶ τύμβου, |Καπίτων, καὶ θαλάμοιο Τύ|χη,
νύκτα μίαν ψεῦστιν καὶ ἀνη|λέα, τὴν ἄνις αὐλῶν,
τὴν δίχα σοι πα|στῶν, τὴν ἄτερ εἰλαπίνης·
αἰαῖ | τὴν ἐπὶ πέπλα καὶ εἰς ἀμύριστα πε|σοῦσα[ν]
στέμματα καὶ βίβλους (σ)εῖ|ο, πρόμοιρε, ⟨τέ⟩φρην
οἳ θρήνοισι βο|ητὸν ὑμήναον, οἳ προχελεύθους|
λαμπάδας ὑστατίου καὶ κενεοῖο | λέχους.

Fortune allotted you only a short time, Capito, between life and death,
    between the tomb and the marriage-chamber:
a single night, cruel and deceitful, a night without flutes,
    a night without wedding-songs or marriage-feast for you.
Alas for your ashes, short-lived creature — they fell alike on
                                                  wedding-robes,
    on wedding garlands not steeped in unguents, and on your books.
Alas, wedding-song that is loud with lamentation, alas, torches
    that light the way to your last, empty bed [18].

---

[17] GV, 1148; cf. also GV, 704, 1-4; 719, 1-4; 947, 1-4; 949; 1472, 1-2; 1483, 1-4; 1801; 1944; *Inscriptiones Graecae* [IG], IX, 2, 316; MAMA, III, 8, 3.
[18] GV, 1522; cf. 1823, 1.

By an easy transference of thought, Seila moves in her lament from the lack of nuptial oils to the splendid line: *nec fronduit anima mea, oleo unctionis quod preparatum est mihi*. The point of her metaphor becomes tragically apparent in the last two lines, where she complains that her young years have been cut down (*abscisi sunt* — a metaphor from felling trees?) [19] by her premature death. This almost simultaneous flowering of love and withering of death finds more explicit expression in an inscription from Larisa (second to third centuries A. D.), where the imagery suggests imminent sexual fulfilment suddenly denied by death:

[παρ]θένος οὖσα τέθ[νη]κα Λε‖[ο]ντὼ ὡς νέον ἄνθος
ὥρης παντοθαλοῦς πρωτο‖[φ]ανὴ⟨ς⟩ καλύκων
καὶ μέλλου‖[σα] γάμῳ δεκαπεντaετὴς | μείγνυσθαι
ἐν φθι|μένοις κεῖμαι, ὕπνον | ἔχουσα μακρόν. |

I, Leonto, died a maiden, like a young flower
    when it bursts its bud and first shows its petals;
fifteen years old, just ready to be joined in wedlock,
    I have come to lie among the dead in a long sleep (GV, 988).

Expressed in another way, the full blossoming of youth denied to the girl in this life would be enjoyed by Hades in the next:

ἀκμὴν δ' οὐ γενετῆρες ἐμήν, οὐκ ἐσθλὸς ὅμαιμος,
οὐ πόσις, ἀλλ' Ἀίδης λυγρὸς ἐκαρπίσατο.

Neither my parents, nor my good brother, nor my husband have tasted
    my youth's fruit, but only cruel Hades (GV, 1162, 7-8, Lemnos, 2nd
                       century A.D.).

[19] The figure of Hades as one who plucks the souls of the young like trees, fruit or flowers is extremely common in ancient literature (see Lattimore, *Themes*, pp. 195-6). In the modern Greek folksongs, the flower of the soul, plucked and withered before its time by Charos, carries us at once by association of images to the familiar motif of the love-songs: love, caught in the eyes, descends to the lips and from there to the heart, where it takes root and blossoms like a plant that cannot be plucked out (cf. N. G. Politis, *Eklogai*, Athens, 1914, nos. 93, 4; 135, ιβ 2 and ιε 1; 98, 10; also, in the seventeenth century Cretan *Erophile*, I ii, 125, 185, 305, 343; III ii, 125-8). Further, in one type of wedding-song, sung as the bride leaves her home, her mother complains that the tender young plant she has nurtured for so long has been uprooted and stolen by a stranger, depriving her garden of its charm. Here the role of the bridegroom is equivalent to the role of Charos in the laments, and is expressed by means of the same formulae and imagery (cf. Politis, op. cit., nos. 141A and 187). Can the fusion of these two themes in the modern folk-songs throw light on Seila's choice of metaphor, with the imagery of the inscriptions providing perhaps a further link?

The idea of a young girl as bride of Hades finds varied expression in the inscriptions as in the Anthology's epigrams. Not only Hades, but Persephone and other cruel sprits of the underworld, are accused of ravishing men and women [20]. An inscription from Pantikapaion, belonging to the same period as the pseudo-Philo lament, develops this idea in a remarkably sustained and coherent way, rising to an almost mystical fervour in the final verse:

I, the maiden Theophile, short-lived daughter of Hekataios,
  was sought in marriage by young men.
But Hades came first and seized me, for he fell in love with me,
  seeing a Persephone fairer than Persephone.

  Even the letters inscribed on the stone column
  weep for Theophile, the girl from Sinope,
  whose bridal torchlight her father Hekataios
  lit for Hades and not for her wedding.

Maiden Theophile, not marriage, but the land of no return
  is yours: no longer the bride of Menophilos,
you share Persephone's bed; your father Hekataios
  has only the name of his poor dead one, and sees
your form in stone, while unjust Moira has plunged
  his hopes deep in the earth, unfulfilled.

You, whose beauty was the envy of mortals,
  Theophile, tenth of the Muses, a Grace
just ripe for marriage, unequalled in wisdom,
  it is not Hades who clasped you in his dark embrace,
but Pluto who has taken you as bride, kindling
  the marriage-torches in his chamber with light.
Father and mother, weep no more, lament no more;
  Theophile has gone to the bed of the immortal gods (GV, 1989).

4) Dream-books and erotic literature

The range and variety of poetic response to the idea of death as marriage in ancient literature cannot be explained purely in terms of literary convention. Most important, perhaps, was the sustained parallel in the ritual of the two ceremonies of wedding and funeral, which provided the poets with a wealth of comparisons and con-

---

[20] For references to Hades, see GV, 658, 8; 683, 5; 878, 1-2; 968, 1; 1151, 11; 1551, 7-8; *Inscriptiones Creticae*, I v, 41, 3-4. Thanatos is named in IG, IX, 2, 316, and a cruel spirit in GV, 228, 3; 1944, 3; 1976, 4; and Charon in 1976, 8-9. Persephone is sometimes accused, like Hades, as in GV, 1585, 1; but occasionally she may be requested by the mourner to guide the dead one to the land of the blessed (GV, 842, 5-6).

trasts: the solemn ablutions of bride and bridegroom, followed by the anointing with nuptial oils and perfumes, the elaborate dressing, usually in white, the wearing of the marriage-crown and a host of other details — all can be matched remarkably closely in the ritual preparation of the dead as he was about to depart on his last journey [21]. Nor do the parallels end here: a deliberate fusion is indicated by the custom of dressing those who died unmarried in wedding attire [22]. The correlation between marriage and death is drawn with extraordinary clarity by Artemidorus in his *Oneirocriticon*, the fullest surviving testimony of dream interpretation in antiquity [23]:

> If an unmarried man dream of death, it foretells his marriage; for both alike, marriage and death, have universally been held by mankind to be fulfilments (τέλη), and they are constantly indicated by one another; for which reason also if a sick man dream of marriage, it is a foreboding of death (II 49).

> If a sick person dream of sexual intercourse with a god or goddess..., it is a sign of death; for it is then, when the soul is near leaving the body which it inhabits, that it foresees union and intercourse with the gods (I 80).

> Since indeed marriage is akin to death and is indicated by dreaming of death, I thought it well to touch upon it here. If a sick man dreams of marrying a maiden, it is a sure sign of his death; for all the accompaniments of marriage are exactly the same as those of death (II 65).

---

[21] See J. C. Lawson, *Modern Greek Folklore and Ancient Greek Religion*, Cambridge, 1899, pp. 554-60; for a more detailed study of ancient and modern marriage and funeral customs, see N. G. Politis, in *Laographika Symmeikta*, Athens, 1931, pp. 232-322, and 323-62.

[22] For the custom of dressing the dead person in wedding attire, see Euripides' *Trojan Women*, 1219-21, and, more generally, Lattimore's *Themes*, p. 185.

[23] Translation from Lawson, op. cit., p. 533. There are some suggestive parallels in versions of the so-called *Somniale Danielis* that were edited by M. Förster, in *Archiv für das Studium der neueren Sprachen*, CXXV (1910), 39-70; CXXVII (1911), 31-84; CXXXIV (1916), 264-93. For instance: Nuptias facere, dampnum significat (*Archiv*, CXXV, 62).

Mulier que secum aliquem viderit nubere, gravem languorem significat (*Archiv*, CXXVII, 73).

Nuptias facere vel cantatrices videre, planctum et laborem significat (ibid., 75).

Further parallels may well come to light when some of the more important unpublished versions of the *Somniale* are printed (cf. A. Önnerfors, *Zur Überlieferungsgeschichte des sog. Somniale Danielis*, in *Eranos*, LVIII, 1960, 142-58). [Cf. Jutta Grub, *Das lateinische Traumbuch im Codex Upsaliensis C 664 (9. Jh.)*, Frankfurt-Bern-New York, 1984, p. 91: *Nuptias facere damnum significat*].

Further, there is some evidence that in mystical doctrine the initiate aspired, after death, to actual physical union with the deities of the Underworld, Pluto and Persephone, and that this "marriage" was foreshadowed in mystic ritual [24]. Such an idea is implicit in the long inscription from Pantikapaion. At the same time it would be a mistake to conclude, with Lawson, that this doctrine motivated a conscious transfer of ritual from marriage-ceremony to funeral: the aspirations of the initiated surely reflect a refinement and development of popular belief, which viewed death and marriage as fundamentally similar occasions, signalling the transition from one stage in the cycle of human existence to another. What emerges most clearly, perhaps, from the treatment of the idea of death as marriage in ancient literature is not a consistent religious doctrine, but a poetic response to a tradition which had remained rooted in popular belief and ritual.

Such a response could be highly individual in the finest dramatists and poets, yet it could also develop its own stereotypes. This is particularly noticeable when we turn to the Greek romances. Thus among the stylised *planctus* that occur in Achilles Tatius' romance, we perceive that certain expressions of the conjunction of love and death have become formulaic, and are repeated almost as refrains. In I 13 Charicles' father laments over his dead son:

> When, my child, shall the day of your wedlock be? When shall I perform at your marriage the rites that religion demands, horseman and bridegroom—bridegroom that shall never wed, most unfortunate of horsemen? Your bridal chamber is the grave; your wedlock is with death; the dirge your bridal song; these wailings your marriage lays. (γάμος δὲ ὁ θάνατος· θρῆνος δὲ ὁ ὑμέναιος· ὁ δὲ κωκυτὸς οὗτος τῶν γάμων ᾠδαί). A very different fire from this, my child, did I hope to kindle for you; but cruel fate has extinguished both it and you, and lit up in its place the torches of a funeral. A cruel illumination this! The tapers of your marriage rite have become the flambeaux of a requiem.

In similar language at III 10 Cleitophon bewails the capture and imprisonment of his beloved Leucippe:

> Here are fine trappings for a wedding! A prison is your bridal chamber, the earth your marriage bed (θάλαμος μὲν τὸ δεσμωτήριον, εὐ-

---

[24] An excellent summary of the evidence is contained in A. B. Cook, *Zeus*, Cambridge, 1914-40, II, 1162-9; further details may be found in L. R. Farnell, *The Cults of the Greek States*, Oxford, 1896, III. The existence of such a belief in the ancient mysteries of Eleusis is disputed by G. E. Mylonas, *Eleusis and the Eleusinian Mysteries*, Princeton, 1961.

νὴ δὲ ἡ γῆ), ropes and cords your necklaces and bracelets, a robber sleeps without as your bridesman, a dirge is your marriagehymn (ἀντὶ δὲ ὑμεναίων τίς σοι τὸν θρῆνον ἄδει).

And again in V 11, of Leucippe whom he now supposes dead, he exclaims:

> After death comes a wedding, after the dirge the marriage-hymn. (Μετὰ θάνατον γάμοι, μετὰ θρῆνον ὑμέναιοι). What sort of a bride is this that Fate gives me? Why, she has not even given her to me in the shape of a whole corpse.

The incantatory effect of the phrases we have cited in Greek is evident. To dismiss them as rhetorical clichés would be too easy. They retain some vestiges of their ritual origin, and the author, aware of this, exploits it for the sake of *pathétique* effects not unlike those aimed at in Seila's lament a century earlier [25].

One other parallel from the erotic literture of the Hellenistic period is worth considering. It occurs in the so-called "Alexandrian erotic fragment" (on a papyrus of the second century B. C.) discovered by Grenfell in 1896. This is a lyrical love-lament sung by a woman to the man who has abandoned her. In its creation of character and mood, with its swiftly flaring emotional transitions — romantic memory and longing, anger, resignation, abject pleas, threats, and at last attempts gently to humour the lover — this song seems one of the most thrilling love-lyrics of the ancient world. Its language has a passionate immediacy that sets it apart in Hellenistic poetry. It is not concerned with the theme of sacrifice or death, but the woman's invocations have a burning quality like Seila's:

> Ἄστρα φίλα καὶ συνερῶσα πότνια Νύξ μοι,
> παράπεμφον ἔτι με νῦν πρὸς ὃν
> ἡ Κύπρις ἔκδοτον
> ἄγει με χὼ πολὺς Ἔρως παραλαβών.
> συνοδηγὸν ἔχω τὸ πολὺ πῦρ
> τοὐν τῆι ψυχῆι μου καιόμενον.
> ταῦτά μ' ἀδικεῖ, ταῦτά μ' ὀδυνᾶι...

Dear stars, and you, Queen Night, who loved with me,

[25] Text and translation from S. Gaselee, *Achilles Tatius* (Loeb Classical Library), London-New York, 1917. Cf. also Xenophon, *Ephesiaca*, III, 6-7; Nonnos, *Dionysiaca*, XLVI, 303 ff. (Agave lamenting Pentheus' death, instead of his hoped-for marriage). On the religious background of the *topoi* in the Greek romances, see especially R. Merkelbach, *Roman und Mysterium in der Antike*, München, 1962.

escort me to him even now:
Cypris leads me to him
for our union, and the great love that seized me.
As companion on my way I have the great fire
that flames within my soul:
this injures me, this gives me pain.

The implicit images are those of the wedding-procession that she, abandoned, has been denied. She calls on the cosmic powers — the stars and the personified Night — to be her convoy, to light the bridal cortège that she will never know; it is Cypris (or her own sexual passion) that leads her as if to marriage; if she has no companions with wedding-torches, the fire of her longing blazing within her will be her torch-bearer. Again, as in the laments, a conceit transforms the language of love's deprivation into that of love's fulfilment. Similarly when, a moment later, she sees her desolation as the very condition that calls for garlands:

Μέλλω μαίνεσθαι,
ζῆλος γάρ μ' ἔχει
καὶ κατακάομαι
καταλελειμμένη.
αὐτὸ δὲ τοῦτό μοι
τοὺς στεφάνους βάλε,
οἷς μεμονωμένη
χρωτισθήσομαι.

I shall go mad,
for jealousy possesses me
and I still burn
in my abandonment.
Yet because of this,
deck me with garlands -
I want to be graced with them
in my loneliness [26].

5) Byzantine literature

The context where the parallels and contrasts of marriage and death are treated most fully in Byzantine literature is that of Abraham's sacrifice. It offers a significant parallel to the episode of Jephtha's daughter. Gregory of Nyssa (331-396 A. D.) includes in his sermon *De deitate filii et spiritus sancti* a lyrical *planctus*, although he

[26] Ed. U. von Wilamowitz-Moellendorf, *Des Mädchens Klage, eine alexandrinische Arie*, in *Nachrichten der kgl. Gesellschaft der Wiss. zu Göttingen*, Phil.-hist. Klasse, 1896, pp. 209-32.

is careful to point out that Abraham did not actually speak these words. As Mercati has demonstrated, the language, structure, themes and even the metrical qualities of Gregory's *planctus* are closely based on a passage in Ephraem's sermon *in Abrahamum*, which was translated from Syriac into Greek during the fourth century:

<table>
<tr><td align="center">Ephraem</td><td align="center">Gregory</td></tr>
<tr><td>Τοιοῦτον αὐτῷ πήξω
τὸν θάλαμον, εἰπέ μοι;
τοιαύτην εὐφροσύνην
γάμῳ παρασκευάσω;
'Ανάφω τε ἐπ' αὐτῷ
οὐ λαμπάδα νυμφῶνος,
οὐ φῶτα χαρμοσύνης,
ἀλλὰ πῦρ ἐντάφιον;</td><td>Τοιοῦτον αὐτῷ πήξω
τὸν θάλαμον;
τοιαύτην αὐτῷ εὐφροσύνην
παρασκευάσω τοῦ γάμου;
καὶ ἄφω ἐπ' αὐτῷ
οὐχὶ λαμπάδα γαμήλιον
ἀλλὰ πῦρ ἐπιτάφιον;</td></tr>
</table>

Is this the bridal chamber I shall make ready for him, [tell me]? Is this the rejoicing I shall prepare for his wedding? And shall I kindle for him not the nuptial torch [nor the light of rejoicing], but the funeral pyre [27]?

Later church fathers continue the tradition of this surprising fictitious lament. John Chrysostom uses the opportunity to inveigh against the pagan practice of lamentation, contrasting Abraham's exemplary fortitude with the futile complaints which common people would have indulged in. We cannot be sure that Abraham's *planctus* was Ephraem's innovation (although no hint of it can be gleaned from Philo, Josephus or the Talmud); but as Mercati has shown, parts of it bear a striking resemblance to some of the *topoi* recommended in a Greek handbook of rhetoric compiled in the previous century and attributed to Menander of Laodicea [28].

Romanos, in his *kontakion On Abraham and Isaac* [29], does not

---

[27] S. Ephraem Syri *Opera*, ed. S. I. Mercati, I, Roma, 1915, 57, 11.229ff.; Gregory of Nyssa, *P. G.*, XLVI, 468D. The phrases in square brackets are in Ephraem only. The parallels are fully listed and discussed by Mercati, ed. cit., p. 4ff.

[28] Menandri Rhet. Περὶ μονῳδίας, in *Rhetores Graeci*, ed. Spengel (Teubner), Leipzig, 1856, III 435: «If the man died young, then start off the *threnos* (by talking of) his youth, his fine looks, his hopes and prospects, and (speak) also of events, that soon the time would have come for the marriage chamber and the bridal room».

[29] S. Romani Melodi *Cantica, Cantica Genuina*, no. 41, ed. P. Maas and C. A. Trypanis, Oxford, 1963. The most recent discussion of this hymn is by J. Grosdidier de Matons, in *Romanos le Mélode, Hymnes*, I (Sources Chrétiennes), Paris, 1964, pp. 131-4. The *topos* of death instead of marriage occurs also in the *kontakion On Saint Tryphon*, attributed to Romanós but of doubtful authenticity, probably written in the seventh century (*Cantica Dubia*, ed. P. Maas and C. A. Trypanis, Berlin, 1970, no. 65, ι΄, ll. 6-10).

allude direcly to the marriage theme, but his treatment marks a significant advance. Following patristic tradition, he introduces Abraham's lament as fictitious; but Abraham himself goes on to imagine what Sarah would say if she knew of the intended sacrifice. A tense dialogue follows, in which the violence of Sarah's emotions reconciles Abraham with God's will. The lament has been transformed from an almost rhetorical conceit into a conflict of human passions no longer imagined but real, and this gives Abraham's eventual acceptance a new poignancy and validity.

The next important step in the treatment of this episode is made eleven centuries later, in an anonymous play from the period of the Cretan renaissance, *Abraham's Sacrifice*. In this play the theme of Isaac's death as marriage is closely integrated, dramatically and artistically, with the characterisation and plot. Sarah introduces the theme as she waits to awaken Isaac, referring to the journey he is about to make as a revelry, where he will meet not his father but Charos (433-40) [30]. As she dresses the boy she says that he is going to a wedding in Hades, and so he must be dressed immaculately (447-8). The theme is further extended by Abraham and Sarah, until Isaac, faced at last with his father's knife at his throat, cries out (834, 866-7):

κ' ἐγώ θὲ νὰ γενῶ τ' ἀρνὶ κ' ἐσύ, ἀφέντη, χάρος.

I am to be the lamb, and you, my father, will be Charos!

Καὶ ποῦ μὲ κράζεις, κύρη μου, νά 'ρθω νὰ γονατίσω;
'ς ποιὸ γάμο, 'ς ποιὰ ξεφάντωση καί θὲς νὰ προθυμήσω;

Where is it that you summon me to come and kneel down, father?
To what wedding, what revelry, that you think I'll come gladly?

It is possible, but not certain, that the author knew Romanos' *kontakion* [31]; since there is nothing comparable to this theme in the play's immediate source, Groto's *Lo Isach*, it seems clear that the poet was drawing on an unbroken tradition of laments, where the idea of

---

[30] The word for "revelry" (ξεφάντωση) is synonymous with "marriage" in the Cretan dialect, see edition of Ἡ Θυσία τοῦ Ἀβραάμ by G. A. Megas, Athens, 1954, p. 229, and A. Kriaris, Κρητικὰ Δημοτικὰ Τραγούδια (3rd. edition), Athens, 1969, p. 48, n. 23.

[31] See S. Baud-Bovy, *Sur un "Sacrifice d'Abraham" de Romanos*, in *Byzantion*, XIII (1938). Another example of the theme in Cretan drama occurs at the end of the *Erophile*, during the Nurse's lament: «I thought I would kiss the crown of marriage on your forehead, yet here I see you dead, and I fear to touch you» (V, 5, 581-2).

death as marriage in Hades has survived to this day in the folksongs [32].

In other respects the Byzantine tradition shows the survival of poetic conventions rather than their creative renewal. In elegiac poetry, a number of the *topoi* we have already traced in the ancient epigrams and funerary inscriptions are used again, as when Michael Psellos (1018-c. 1078), in his coldly and grandiosely rhetorical verses on the death of Skleraina, the mistress of Constantine IX, invokes the forces of the cosmos:

> Νῦν κοσμικὴ θύελλα, νῦν κοινὴ ζάλη,
> νῦν συμφορᾶς ἄπαυστος ἠγέρθη κλύδων.
> Νῦν, οὐρανέ, στέναξον ἐξ ὕψους μέγα
> καί, γῆ, κάτω βόησον, ὦ δεινοῦ πάθους.
> Νῦν ἀντὶ φωτὸς αἷμα πέμψον, φωσφόρε·
> νῦν, καὶ σελήνη καὶ χορὸς τῶν ἀστέρων,
> ἀντ' ἀκτίνων πέμποιτε κρουνοὺς δακρύων.
> Ἀὴρ δὲ καὶ θάλασσα κυματουμένη,
> ἀχλὺν ἐπενδύθητε καὶ βαθὺν ζόφον...
> ἡ τῶν Χαρίτων εὐπρεπὴς κατοικία
> ἡ πᾶν τὸ κάλλος τῶν ἐν ἀνθρώποις μόνη...
> φεῦ φεῦ, πρὸ ὥρας, ἐτρυγήθη ῥίζόθεν.

Now there is a cosmic whirlwind, now the ocean bursts its bonds,
now an endless sea of troubles has arisen.
Now, heaven, groan profoundly from above,
and earth, cry out below, oh dreadful sorrow!
Now, day's harbinger, send blood instead of light,
now, lady moon, and you, oh choir of stars,
instead of streams of light send streams of tears.
Oh air and storm-tossed sea,
shroud yourselves in gloom and in deep darkness...
She, the fair shelter of the Graces,
she who alone had all the beauty of mankind...
alas, alas, was harvested, uprooted before her time...[33]

When, on the other hand, one of the Byzantine romances takes up again the *topoi* of lament from the Greek erotic tales, it does so with a vivacity that outstrips Achilles Tatius. Rhetorical and over-laden with references to classical mythology, Eustathius Macrembo-

---

[32] For a general discussion, see Fritz Boehm, *Die neugriechische Totenklage*, Berlin, 1947, pp. 42 ff., and section 6 below.

[33] R. Cantarella, *Poeti Bizantini*, Milano, 1948, I 166, no. 2, ll. 1-9, 16-17, 21. Cf. also ibid. I 156, no. 6, esp. ll. 9-14 (Christopher of Mytilene, early eleventh century); I 211-14, esp. ll. 35-58, 76-82 (George Acropolites, 1217-82).

lites' prose romance *Hysmine and Hysminias* [34], written in the second half of the twelfth century, is nonetheless more than a mere imitation of the Hellenistic novel. It stands out among the Byzantine learned romances both for its bold eroticism (which, conveyed largely through the many dream-sequences of the narrator, Hysminias, has the effect of overshadowing the conventional intricacies of plot), and for its extravagant imagery, which has flashes of brilliance and power not unlike the imagery of the folksongs. In particular the dual themes of death and marriage are interwoven in the dreams and in the laments throughout the romance. When Hysminias hears of the marriage planned for Hysmine by her parents, he vows to kill himself, and breaks into a lament:

> ...But now your father, Sosthenes, ...has made ready your bridal chamber at Aulicomis; he has arranged besides your many wedding gifts; he has prepared your bridegroom... While I, your lover, will put on my head the virginal crown (for I am not ashamed of my love for you), and I will be escorted as bridegroom to Persephone and those who dwell in Hades. They shall prepare for me a splendid, virginal bridal chamber. But you will stand condemned for your faithlessness in love, — yes, the favours of my passion, and those very marks which your whole body bears from my hands and my lips shall accuse you: Plutus shall adorn you with riches, while Pluto shall escort me with pride (VI 6).

Later, the lovers escape, but their ship is caught in a storm. Hysmine cries out:

> ... The ship is my bridal chamber, the wave my bridal bed, the wind's song my bridal hymn, and I, a virgin, am the bride! Oh wretched bridal chamber, oh bitter marriage!

Then Hysminias joins her lament:

> ...Locked in your arms, with the waves as our marriage garland, I shall prepare for you a watery bridal bed... Yes, this very ship shall ferry us down to Hades, and it shall be the wedding chamber of both Aphrodite and Persephone (VII 9-10).

Later, a sacrificial victim is demanded by the captain to appease the

[34] *De Hysmines et Hysminiae Amoribus*, ed. P. Le Bas, in G. A. Hirschig, *Erotici Scriptores*, Paris, 1856. The passages cited below are on pp. 556, 564, 566. Similar topoi occur in Panthia's lament for her daughter Hysmine (VI 10, p. 558). The later and more popular Byzantine verse romances, however, do not develop the theme.

wrath of Poseidon: the lot falls on Hysmine, and she is thrown into the sea, leaving Hysminias to lament her loss:

> ...The sea is your wedding chamber and your tomb, and I am your bridal attendant. I shall sing no wedding songs for you, nor shall I applaud at the festivities; instead, with the sand as your cenotaph, I shall weave for you my bitter funeral songs, calling the whole band of Nereids to join my lament for this misfortune. Ah stormy sea, your waves have utterly destroyed my bridal chamber and my bride! (VII 17).

6) *Greek folksongs*

In the Greek popular laments, as in the ancient inscriptions and epigrams, a young person who died before or just after marriage was considered as particularly unfortunate. In a moving couplet from Kynouria, the dead man invokes the sky and the earth:

> Μή με σκεπάζης οὐρανέ, μή με πλακώνης, χῶμα,
> τ' ἀκόμα δὲν ἐφόρεσα στεφάνι κι' ἀρρεβῶνα.

> Sky, do not cover me, and earth, do not weigh down upon me!
> I have not yet worn the crown and ring of marriage.

In another couplet from Crete, the mourner asks the dead girl:

> Κοντὸ καὶ δὲν εὐρέθηκε γιὰ σένα παλληκάρι,
> μόνο νὰ σοῦ τὸ βάλουνε στὸν Ἅδη τὸ στεφάνι;

> Could no fine young man be found for you here,
> that only in Hades you should wear the marriage-crown [35]?

Sometimes the parallel is more sustained, as in a lament from Argos where the dying girl tells her family to sweep and tidy the house for her parents-in-law, who will come to take her as bride: they will bring a single crown and a single candle, for she will wed down in the church of Our Lady [36]. This extraordinary allusive technique is achieved only because of the close parallel in the preparation of a bride and a dead girl: the single crown, the single candle, and the deliberate ambiguity of the final line (the cemetery was within the chapel precincts) afford our only clues that this bride is prepared for a funeral and not a wedding [37].

---

[35] Texts from *Laographia*, III (1911), p. 489, 4, and from M. Lioudaki, Ἡ Τελευτὴ στὴν Κρήτη, in Ἐπετηρὶς τῆς Ἑταιρείας Κρητικῶν Σπουδῶν, II (1939), p. 414, respectively.

[36] *Laographia*, III (1911), 267, 1. 14.

[37] The language has a similar double potential in, for instance, a lament from

Sometimes allusion to marriage in Hades is a means of expressing the irrevocable finality of death, as in this limpid, moving dialogue between a girl newly dead and her parents:

— My daughter, down in Hades where you now think of going,
the cock never crows and the hen never clucks,
there is no water to be found, and the grass never grows.
There is no food when you are hungry, nor drink when you feel thirst,
and if you wish to take a rest, you cannot sleep your fill.
Stay at home, my child, stay here with your own kin.
— I cannot, dear father, I cannot, dearest mother:
Yesterday was my wedding-day, late last night I married.
Hades is my husband, the tombstone my mother-in-law [38].

The last line is a formulaic expression for death [39], found frequently in the Klephtic laments and also in the *Ballad of Evgenoula*, where the dying girl asks her mother to dress her as a bride, and leaves word for her betrothed to take another wife, just as she will take another husband:

Mani, where a mother's ritual duty had to be left unfulfilled: "for she never dressed a bridegroom / either alive or dead" (B. Petrounias, Μανιάτικα Μοιρολόγια, Athens, 1934, B. A8). In another lament, it is the dying girl who summons her lover to her bedside, and requests him to decorate her tomb as though for their wedding (A. Passow, *Carmina Popularia Graeciae Recentioris*, Leipzig, 1860, no. 378).

In a medieval Latin context, we can compare the beautiful little epitaph (probably late eleventh century) in the Schäftlarn MS (now in the Bayerische Staatsbibliothek) which has become famous for its collection of Regensburg love-verses:

Cur pater et mater, cur ploras, unice frater?
Non gemitu revocor, non lacrimis repetor,
Non flos etatis, non spes me posteritatis
Longius hic tenuit, quam Domino placuit.

(Anke Ebel, *Clm 17142: Eine Schäftlarner Miscellaneen-Handschrift des 12. Jahrhunderts*, München, 1970, p. 92).

That the language is spontaneously close to that of the popular bridal farewells is evident: only the phrase *spes posteritatis* establishes with certainty that the girl is bidding farewell to her family to go to her *Dominus* rather than *dominus*.

Dr. Ebel would date all the *Carmina Ratisponensia* to the year 1106 (op. cit., pp. 26, 34). But this depends on the implausible assumption that the whole corpus of verse was composed within a single year.

[38] Passow, op. cit., no. 374.

[39] Cf. A. Theros, Τὰ Τραγούδια τῶν Ἑλλήνων Athens, 1952, II 712, ll. 6-7; *Laographia*, III (1911), p. 489, 1-4, 7-10; Passow, no. 380, ll. 12-13, and especially no. 364, where the formula occurs at the end of a farewell addressed by the dying man to the days of his youth that can never return.

Σ' ἀφήνω, μάννα, τὸ ἔχε γειὰ καὶ ντύσε με σὰ νύφη,
κι' ὅταν θὰ σόρθη ὁ Κωσταντὴς νὰ μὴ μοῦ τὸν πικράνης,
μόν' στρῶσ' του γιόμα νὰ γευτῆ καὶ δεῖπνο νὰ δειπνήση,
κι' ἅπλωσε μὲς στὴν τσέπη μου καὶ πάρε τὸ κλειδί μου,
καὶ βγάλ' τόν ἀρραβῶνα του καὶ τὰ χαρίσματά του,
καὶ δῶσ' του τα τοῦ Κωσταντή, ἀλλοῦ ν' ἀρραβωνίση,
ὡσὰν κ' ἐγὼ παντρεύομαι, παίρνω τὸ Χάρον ἄντρα.

I bid you goodbye, mother: dress me as a bride,
and when Kostantis comes, take care not to grieve him,
but set a meal before him, and let him take his fill,
then go to my pocket and take out my key,
and bring his wedding-ring and the gifts he gave me.
Give them to Kostantis, that he may wed elsewhere,
for I shall marry Charos, he shall be my husband [40].

More rarely we see the macabre marriage as it is prepared in Hades. Lamenting her son, newly dead, a woman imagines the scene in Hades: her own mother is there, asking the springs for water, the gardens for apples and quinces, so that she can prepare the wedding of her grandson, newly arrived from the upper world (Passow n° 370).

These few illustrations, while far from exhaustive, may indicate something of the extent of the survival of ancient ideas and themes. As in antiquity, the parallels and contrasts of death and marriage are sustained through the ritual correlation. Certain details in ancient and modern examples tend to recur: wedding-crowns, torches and candles, elaborate preparation and dressing.

But in modern Greek the wealth of material enables us to trace an even closer link between the funeral-lament and the wedding-song: the laments sung for the dead girl before she departed for the Underworld have an exact counterpart in the laments sung for the bride before she left for her new home. The structural and formulaic correspondences may be illustrated by the following examples, the first a funeral-lament from Olympia, and the second and third wedding-laments from Crete and Epirus [41]:

Σήμερα μαῦρος οὐρανὸς κι' ἀραγνιασμένη μέρα,
σήμερα ξεχωρίζουνε ἀιτὸς καὶ περιστέρα,
σήμερα ξεχωρίζουνε παιδάκια ὀχ τὸν πατέρα.

---

[40] Politis, *Eklogai*, no. 217, ll. 14-20.
[41] Texts from *Laographia*, IV (1912-13), 183; P. Vlastos, Ὁ Γάμος ἐν Κρήτῃ, Athens, 1893, p. 74; A. Giagkas, Ἠπειρώτικα Δημοτικὰ Τραγούδια, Athens, 1958, no. 760, respectively.

Τέσσεροι στῦλοι τοῦ σπιτιοῦ, ἔχετε καλὴ νύχτα,
καὶ πέστε τῆς γυναίκας μου, δὲν ἔρχουμαι ἄλλη νύχτα.
Τέσσεροι στῦλοι τοῦ σπιτιοῦ, ἔχετε καλὸ βράδυ,
καὶ πέστε τοῦ πατέρα μου δὲν ἔρχουμ' ἄλλο βράδυ.

Today the sky is black and the day is gloomy,
today the eagle and the dove take leave,
today children take leave of their father.
Four walls of the house, I bid you goodnight,
tell my wife I'll come at night no more;
four walls of the house, I bid you good evening,
tell my father I'll come at evening-time no more.

Σήμερο μαῦρος οὐρανός, σήμερο μαύρ' ἡμέρα,
σήμερ' ἀποχωρίζεται μάννα τὴ θυγατέρα.
Ἄνοιξαν οἱ ἑφτὰ οὐρανοὶ τὰ δώδεκα βαγγέλια,
κι' ἐπῆραν τὸ παιδάκι μου ἀπὸ τὰ δυό μου χέρια.
Μισεύβγεις, θυγατέρα μου, καὶ πλιὸ δέ θὰ γελάσω,
σάββατο πλιὸ δὲ θὰ λουστῶ οὐδ' ἑορτῇ θ' ἀλλάξω.

Today the sky is black, today the day is black,
today a mother takes leave of her daughter.
The seven skies have opened the twelve gospels [42],
and have taken my child from out of my arms.
You are leaving, daughter — I shall never laugh again,
nor wash on Saturdays nor change for a festival.

Ἔχετε γειά, πατέρα μου, καὶ σὺ γλυκειά μου μάνα,
ἔχετε γειά ἀδερφάκια μου, καὶ σεῖς διχοὶ καὶ φίλοι,
ἐγὼ πάνω στὸ σπίτι μου καὶ στὸ πεθερικό μου,
πάνω νὰ μάθω γράμματα νά γράφω τὰ καλά μου.
Ἔχετε γειά, γειτόνισσες, καὶ σεῖς γειτονοποῦλες
κι' ἐγὼ πάνω στὸ σπίτι μου κ.λ.π.

I bid you goodbye, my father, and you, my sweet mother,
I bid you goodbye, brothers and sisters, and you, my friends and
kinsfolk,
I am going to my house and to my husband's kin,
I shall learn to read and write, to write down my good fortune.
I bid you goodbye, my neighbours, and my neighbours' daughters.
I am going to my house, etc.

[42] This line is apparently a confused intrusion from another song, possibly one of the *Laments of the Virgin*. For similar bridal farewells, see A. Giagkas, op. cit., nos. 760-75. Their relation to funeral laments has been analysed by Maria Ioannidu, *Untersuchungen zur Form der neugriechischen Klagelieder*, München, 1938, sect. III. The folklorist A. L. Lloyd has pointed out to us that similar structural and formulaic parallels between bridal farewells and funeral laments can be found in the folksongs of other Balkan countries. What appears to be characteristically Greek, however, is the emphasis on death as marriage in the Underworld.

As the bride makes these ritual farewells, her mother breaks down, addressing her daughter in a series of images customarily applied to the dead:

> You are leaving, my eyes have gone, my comfort has gone,
> the keys of my breast and the pillar of my heart have gone [43]!

When the priest arrives, the bride breaks into lamentation and hangs back. Sometimes she requires force:

> Drag me away, though I am weeping:
> if I weep, whom do I harm?
> Drag me away, though I weep still [44].

Or at the last moment she asks her mother to hide her. But this resistance — suggesting, beneath the convention, the bride's real fear of leaving girlhood — brings her mother to her senses:

> I had a pure white cotton-plant growing in my courtyard,
> I weeded it, I watered it, and it was all my own.
> But a stranger, yes a stranger came and took it from me.
> — Hide me mother, hide me, so the stranger cannot take me.
> — Why should I hide you, dear one, now you belong to him:
> Wear the stranger's clothes, wear the stranger's rings,
> for you belong to him, and he will take you now [45].

This wealth of parallels — which could easily be multiplied — suggests that the pseudo-Philo was familiar with the ancient and widespread wedding-and-funeral, bride-and-victim imagery of Greek tradition, and that he was relying on this tradition for his own remarkable innovation in the midst of his biblical material.

Can we be more precise about the nature of the poetic traditions the pseudo-Philo could have known? Here at least we have some basis for conjecture. The tone and style of Seila's lament are essentially popular: stylistically the closest affinities are not with the tragedies or the epigrams, but rather with the funerary inscriptions, the Grenfell fragment, and the much later recorded evidence of traditional poetry. At the same time, this later tradition of lyrical laments, together with the earlier evidence implied by some of the in-

---

[43] Vlastos, op. cit., p. 51.
[44] Ibid.
[45] Politis, *Laographika Symmeikta*, p. 281. Politis gives two other bridal farewells from Epirus, both in dialogue form, ibid. p. 280.

scriptions and epigrams, allows us to win an insight into what the un-
recorded popular laments of the Hellenistic period must have been
like. At all events, we can say with some certainty that the pseudo-
Philo knew a Greek tradition of laments for girls who had died
young, in which the elegiac language was deeply imbued with the
language of epithalamia. It is also possible that already in his time
there were traditional marriage-songs in which the language of wedding was suffused with that of lament — lament by the parents for
the loss of the bride, lament by the bride at leaving her parents'
home. The lateness of the recorded evidence here leaves this no more
than a possibility; yet the persistent poetic conjunction of the wedding and death imagery from the time of the tragedians onwards
strongly suggests that the wedding-lament too has an ancient tradition behind it, even if no archaic instances survive.

III
Abelard

It was to be eleven centuries before Jephtha's daughter again became the heroine of a *planctus*, in the song of Peter Abelard. In the
intervening ages only one poem, to our knowledge, hints that there
was something magnificent about her death: this occurs in the martyred saint Thecla's song in praise of virginity, with which
Methodius († 311) concludes his *Symposium* [46]. Here the beautiful
refrain — "I keep myself untouched for you, tending my gleaming
lamps: bridegroom, I come to you" — establishes Christ as the celestial νυμφίος and the young women as the wise virgins of the parable;
but the love-language throughout the hymn shows that the
bridegroom and bride are at the same time the protagonists of the
Song of Songs. By figura, the bride is identified with those men and
women who have longed for the mystic marriage: Abel, Joseph,
Jephtha's daughter, Judith, Susanna, John the Baptist and Mary, and
at last Thecla herself and her maidens. The strophe on Jephtha's
daughter is notable not only for bringing her into this context of the
heroines of divine love (of which we shall say more later), but also
for its swift double allusion to the sacrifice of Isaac and of Christ:

— Νεοσφαγῆ
ὁ Ἰεφθάε κόρην ἀνῆγε θυσίαν θεῷ,
ἄπειρον ἀνδρός, ἀμφὶ βωμὸν ἀμνάδος δίκην.
Ἡ δ' εὐγενῶς σου τὸν τύπον τῆς σαρκός, ὦ μάκαρ,

[46] Ed. Cantarella, op. cit., I, 3-7.

τελοῦσ' ἔκραζε καρτερῶς·
— ἀγνεύω σοι καὶ λαμπάδας φαεσφόρους κρατοῦσα,
νυμφίε, ὑπαντάνω σοι.

— The newly-killed one,
his girl, Jephtha led as sacrifice to God,
her who knew no man, like a lamb led to the altar.
And she, nobly fulfilling the image of your flesh,
blessed one, called out bravely:
— I keep myself untouched for you, tending my gleaming lamps —
bridegroom, I come to you [47]!

The prose tradition presents a very different picture. A number
of Jewish as well as Christian exegetes wrote about the Jephtha episode, either blaming Jephtha for his cruel vow or trying to find some
way to excuse him (and to excuse Yahweh for having condoned a human sacrifice). Yet it was always Jephtha who was the centre of discussion; the daughter was hardly mentioned, her thoughts and feelings never explored. Saint Paul (*Ad Hebr.*, XI, 32-33) spoke of
Jephtha as among those under the old covenant who were renowned
for their faith and justice, and this set a problem challenging the ingenuity of the Fathers. In the words of Wolfram von den Steinen,
who has valuably summarized this exegetical tradition:

> From the Epistle to the Hebrews onwards, the questions were
> concerned with how to judge the apparently holy Jephtha in his inad-
> missible vow and irreligious human sacrifice, and with what this event
> might mean in the doctrinal scheme of the Christian God: meanwhile,
> Jephtha's daughter was scarcely noticed... In the spiritual dimension
> of his poem, Abelard was in no way influenced by the Christian tra-
> dition [48].

What, then, was Abelard influenced by? In the first place, we would
say, by Seila's lament in pseudo-Philo [49].

---

[47] Ibid., 11. 78-84. Ephraem of Syria devotes stanzas to Jephtha and his daughter (*Carmina Nisibena*, no. 70, transl. Edmund Beck, *Corpus Scriptorum Christianorum Orientalium*, vol. CCXLI, Louvain, 1963, p. 102); Ephraem marvels at Jephtha's
steadfastness; of the daughter he says, "The dove saw that he was grieving, and she
encouraged him with her voice". In the early twelfth century, Theodore Prodromos,
a contemporary of Abelard, has two rather jejune tetrastichs on Jephtha and his
daughter (*P. G.*, CXXXIII, 1141).

[48] *Die Planctus Abaelards — Jephthas Tochter*, in *Mittellateinisches Jahrbuch*, IV
(1967) 136.

[49] We cannot wholly rule out the possibility that Abelard knew, not pseudo-
Philo himself, but some intermediate source as yet untraced. At all events it is clear

Abelard's *planctus* [50] has musically and poetically a four-part structure. The first and last parts are an opening chorus and a closing one; these are in strophes sung to the same melody, and are attributed to the girls of Israel. Between these two choruses, there is a re-enactment of the murder, in two scenes: one, of the girl's encounter with her father after his victory, and the other, of her last hours on earth. These parts of the work, unlike the choruses, have a variety of melodies (based on sequence forms) and are given to several speakers. We may set out the structure like this:

1) Prelude: the summons to the New Year commemoration
2) Scene 1: the encounter of father and daughter
3) Scene 2: the wedding-mime and murder
4) Finale: the judgement [51].

that he did not begin the imaginative presentation of Jephtha's daughter as romantic heroine *ex nihilo*. Moreover, it is possible to see some significant parallels between a passage about David and Jonathan in pseudo-Philo and Abelard's *Planctus* of David over Saul and Jonathan (parallels that have no counterpart in the Old Testament narrative). These in particular make Abelard's direct knowledge of pseudo-Philo highly probable:

Pseudo-Philo, LXII, 9 (ed. Kisch, p. 265)	Abelard, *Dolorum solatium* (ed. Dronke, *Poetic Individuality in the Middle Ages*, pp. 204-8).
Et respondens Ionathas, dixit ad David: Veni ad me frater meus David, et dicam tibi iusticias tuas. Tabescit anima mea in tris-ticia tua valde, quoniam separamur modo ab invicem, *et hoc coegerunt peccata nostra; ut non saturemur in alterutrum.* Sed memores simus dum vivimus, noctu et die in invicem. *Et si mors separat nos,* scio quia *anime nostre alterutrum se cognoscent.*	Plus fratre michi Ionatha, in una mecum anima, que peccata, que scelera nostra sciderunt viscera... et me post te vivere mori sit assidue, nec ad vitam anima satis sit dimidia... ut et mors nos iungeret magis quam disiungeret.

Von den Steinen (art. cit.) appears not to have known the pseudo-Philo; W. O. Sypherd, though beginning his book *Jephthah and his Daughter: a Study in Comparative Literature*, Newark, 1948, with extracts from both pseudo-Philo and Abelard, did not suggest any link between them.

[50] Ed. W. Meyer, *Gesammelte Abhandlungen zur mittellateinischen Rythmik*, I, Berlin, 1905, 347-52; G. Vecchi, *Pietro Abelardo, I «Planctus»*, Modena, 1951, pp. 48-55.

[51] (1) 11. 1-20 (ed. Meyer); (2) 11. 21-69; (3) 11. 70-106; (4) 11. 107-122. The melody of parts (1), (2) and (4) has been transcribed by Vecchi, ed. cit., pls. VII-XIV; for the problems involved in the transcription, see ibid., pp. 23-26.

It seems probable that in performance the two "scenes" would have been in some measure dramatic: that is, that we may imagine three soloists here, singing the lines of Jephtha, his daughter, and the narrator; possibly, too, the "wedding-mime" was acted as well as sung. But we have no direct evidence for these hypotheses; nor any evidence, external or internal, about instrumental accompaniment (such evidence is indeed rare for twelfth century lyric). If there are any who prefer to think of the entire composition as performed unaccompanied, and by a single voice or choir, they cannot strictly be refuted, though in the light of what scanty evidence there is in and about twelfth century lyrical texts and their performance, the "conservative" speculation would seem the more risky one.

The biblical account of the human sacrifice is brief and detached; austerely the author records what seems like a myth from a more archaic world, but a myth still too alive in the imagination of his time for him to ignore. It is the continued remembrance that he stressses at the close of his narrative:

> Exinde mos increbruit in Israel, et consuetudo servata est: ut post anni circulum conveniant in unum filiae Israel, et plangant filiam Iephte Galaaditae diebus quatuor [52].

This is Abelard's point of departure: his *planctus*, we might say, is an imaginative reconstruction of that commemorative rite. The girls are summoned to the rite, to mourn their heroine and cherish her, to re-enact the gruesome episode and reflect anew on its implications. There is a telling difference between the pseudo-Philo's montage and that of Abelard: in the first, the narrative is the framework, and at its centre is the lament of Seila herself; in the second, the entire framework is a lament *for* Seila [53], at the centre of which the narrative emerges. Artistically, this means a great advance in the portrayal and judgement of emotions: where pseudo-Philo had to express his judgements somewhat clumsily, through God's "asides", Abelard establishes perspectives that govern the work and shape its movement:

present - past - present
remembrance - drama - remembrance
valuation - involvement - valuation

[52] *Jud.*, XI, 39-40. Pseudo-Philo (XL, 8) has these details also, with the addition that the girls of Israel at that time *sepelierunt filiam Iepte, et planxerunt eam*. Further, his phrase *per singulos annos* (ibid.) is echoed by Abelard (1. 14).

[53] For brevity we use the name "Seila" also for Abelard's heroine, although in the *planctus* she is not named.

His form is intimately conjoined to the content, is an expression of the content itself.

The deep admiration Abelard's girls show for the way Seila confronted death takes its cue from God's words in pseudo-Philo — *et erit mors eius preciosa ante conspectum meum omni tempore*. In scene 1, the encounter between father and daughter, the significant expansions and divergences from the biblical account also reveal Abelard's stimulation by pseudo-Philo. He heightens his predecessor's effects: the girl's speech is already far fuller, more heroic and decisive in pseudo-Philo than in the Bible (note the ringing challenge in her first words — "And who is there who would be sad at dying, seeing her people freed?"); in Abelard's *planctus* the girl's answer to her father dominates the whole of scene 1, and her daring is taken further: she longs for the death that will be her immortal fame. In the Book of Judges and pseudo-Philo, Jephtha answers his daughter's speech, assenting to her departure for two months; in Abelard he says nothing: an answer would be superfluous, for she has taken control of the entire situation. The Bible shows her acquiescing in her father's vow; pseudo-Philo shows her boldly encouraging him; in Abelard, we have almost the impression that the father would fail to keep his vow if she were not compelling him to keep it. Both in pseudo-Philo and Abelard (and not in the Bible), the girl makes the explicit comparison and contrast between herself and Isaac, in both she voices the fearful doubt, will God find her death acceptable? The nuance of thought is different, however: in pseudo-Philo, "If God did not accept even Isaac's death, which he commanded, will I not be rejected and punished, who go to death spontaneously?". In Abelard: "If God did not accept the death of a boy, how much greater the glory if he accepts me, a girl!" Pseudo-Philo's sense of how far she surpasses her father in mind and character is expressed through God's words, *ipsam vidi magis sapientem pre patre suo*; Abelard *shows* us these surpassing qualities with every word she speaks. Unlike the Hellenistic Seila, his heroine does not indulge in the elegiac mood; her only allusion to lament — *plorans vacem planctibus quod sic me semine privet dominus* — records it almost rather as an objective fact.

Abelard's principal debt to pseudo-Philo is in his conception of the wedding-mime: in the whole notion, quite foreign to the Bible, of seeing Seila's sacrificial death in terms of a marriage-ceremony — in Abelard's words, *ut... tanquam nuptiis morti se preparent*. In both authors, the sense of her death as a grim parody of her wedding is evident, and decisive for the poetic structure. Yet Abelard's transformation of pseudo-Philo is also remarkable: threnody becomes drama. Instead of a girl lamenting, dreaming of every aspect of the wedding

on earth she will never know, we have a girl who is heroically silent
while all her attendants weep, while they give her every aspect of a
bride's preparation, every moment of which deepens her ordeal, in-
tensifies for her the contrast between the pretence of wedding and
the reality of dying.

At the opening of scene 2, a verbal echo sharpens this contrast
between pretence and reality: in the opening chorus the girls had
summoned their companions to come as mourners, to come without
golden robes or splendid jewellery (*aurate sint longe ciclades, et cultus
sint procul divites*). Now as Seila returns she casts off her robe of
mourning (*lugubris habitus deponit tegmina*), and is dressed in gold
and bridal splendour. The girls of the later generation are not martyr-
heroines — they cannot put on the golden robe with which she tri-
umphed in death — yet by treasuring her memory they are the true
inheritors of her robe of mourning; they have unburdened her of it
as much as if they had been her bridesmaids on that first occasion.

Thalamus is a key-word both in the Pseudo-Philo's lament of
Seila and in Abelard's wedding-mime. (There is naturally no equivalent in the Book of Judges). While Abelard has no phrase as stark
as *infernus thalamus meus*, his choice of language shows that he too
was conscious that the victim could also become the otherworld
bride. That is why in this part of the the *planctus* many words carry
associations of the Song of Songs: the girl's body is *languidum* —
overtly because of her weariness after her homeward journey, yet it
cannot help suggesting also the bride's voluptuous expectation of her
mystic marriage. The *unguenti species, pixides, monilia* of the victim
are also the gifts the divine lover of the Song of Songs lavishes on
his bride [54].

We have said that, unlike the earlier Seila, Abelard's heroine
does not lament. Yet at the climax of the second scene she who had
endured this ritual robing of the bride-victim in silence suddenly
flings away the remaining ornaments and cries out:

Que nupture satis sunt / periture nimis sunt!

It stands in sheer contrast to the earlier Seila's sustained lamenting,
though indeed inspired by it. This moment in which Abelard's stoic
heroine shows her naked anguish is perhaps one of the most moving
in medieval poetry. At once she conceals it again, wordlessly handing

[54] Cf. especially *Cant.*, I, 2-3, 9-10; II, 5; III, 6; IV, 10; VII, 1. (The closest
verbal correspondences are sometimes with Patristic renderings and paraphrases of
these verses rather than with the Vulgate text).

the sword to her father. Even Iphigenia and Antigone have no moment quite like this: Iphigenia, after first pleading for her life, moves on to an unshakeable resolve; Antigone is unwavering from first to last; only her incredible self-justification before she dies, arguing why she would not, even for husband or children, do what she did for her brother — is comparably unpredictable and disturbing in its truth.

In Abelard's finale, the chorus complete the narrative of the murder. Their fierce condemnation of the father's deed recalls God's anger at Jephtha in pseudo-Philo: only in these two authors is this attitude so unequivocal and unqualified. But Abelard, who in his ethical writings had so clearly distinguished between the rightness and wrongness of a deed and the motives — good or evil — of the doer, condemns the deed rather than the doer. Jephtha himself was insane; it was his deed that degraded his people [55]. The close of the chorus moves away from pseudo-Philo and is Abelard's individual development: the girls' ritual commemoration of Seila is an expiation for their predecessors' condonement of murder; by re-enacting that murder, they keep it alive in people's memories, to ensure that religious mania will not cause inhumanity again; by cherishing and admiring their heroine, they win something of her nobility of mind. Here in a sense we come closest to the archaic new-year rite: the ceremonial celebration of the death makes possible a "new year" of the spirit.

These comparisons will help to indicate the nature of Abelard's debt to the first lament of Seila, and the nature of his creative response. That he was imaginatively ready to respond, to give the passage buried in an old book a new kind of life, may be due to many causes. Some of them personal: that he could see the plangent Seila as a creature of fire and air must be in part because he had known such a gesture of reckless heroism in his own beloved Heloise: as he tells us in the *Historia Calamitatum*, she accepted being immured as a nun, at his command, explicitly as a sacrifice and a voluntary dying

---

[55] Referring to these lines (115-18 in Meyer's text), von den Steinen wrote (art. cit., p. 139): «Diese Anklage ist als letzte Steigerung der Klage an ihrem Platze richtig und lebensecht, will aber schwerlich, über die Stimmung der Weinenden hinaus, als abschliessende Verurteilung Jephthas gelten; denn das würde den Kern des Gedichtes aufheben». Previously (p. 138), he had even affirmed: «Ob Jephthas Gelübde so ganz richtig war, wird im "Planctus virginum" nicht zur Frage gestellt, weil das Lied ganz dem Opfer zugewandt ist». These comments seem irreconcilable with Abelard's text (*O mentem amentem iudicis...*). For a detailed discussion of the passage, see P. Dronke, *Poetic Individuality in the Middle Ages*, Oxford, 1970, pp. 119-20, 144.

for his sake (*P. L.*, CLXXVIII, 136; ed. Monfrin, p. 81). Yet there
was also, I believe, another stream of *poetic* inspiration, a stream
more elusive to trace than the direct literary link with pseudo-Philo.
The deaths of the heroines of the Christian world, the virgin martyrs, had long been celebrated in the love-language of the Song of
Songs. We saw a hint of this already in the early Byzantine hymn of
Saint Thecla; in the West, the literary and exegetic uses of the Song
of Songs before 1200 have been intensively studied in recent years,
in the monographs of Rosemarie Herde and Friedrich Ohly [56]. Yet
they are concerned exclusively with learned Latin traditions; was
there not perhaps also a tradition of popular, vernacular song in
which the imagery that conjoins love and death, the wedding and the
funeral, was used thematically? Was Abelard's stimulus purely
learned and literary, or could he too, like the pseudo-Philo before
him, draw inspiration from a living traditional poetry? The directness and sheer singable beauty of his *planctus* may be due to
Abelard's individual genius — yet we can go further in our attempt
to perceive what his genius was nourished by.

IV

A western vernacular tradition?

That the poetic and melodic forms of Abelard's *planctus* have
strong links with traditions of vernacular song has long been clear:
his *planctus* are indeed crucial evidence for the continued development of the *lai lyrique*, types of which existed, both in Latin and
French, already in the ninth and tenth centuries, and of which the
next dateable evidence does not occur till the twelfth [57]. The question of the relation between the French *lai lyrique* and the Breton *lai*
(which we know only through allusions and French adaptations) is
still fraught with difficulties [58]. At all events for Abelard we can say
that direct inspiration from Breton lyric is conceivable only on the
melodic side — he himself tells us (*Historia Calamitatum, P. L.,*

---

[56] F. Ohly, *Hohelied-Studien*, Wiesbaden, 1958; R. Herde, *Das Hohelied in der lateinischen Literatur des Mittelalters bis zum 12. Jahrhundert*, in *Studi medievali*, 3ª serie, VIII (1967), 959-1073; separate edition, Spoleto, 1968.

[57] Cf. H. Spanke, *Über das Fortleben der Sequenz in den romanischen Sprachen*, in *Zeitschrift für romanische Philologie*, LI (1931), 309-34; Id., *Sequenz und Lai*, in *Studi medievali*, N. S., XI (1938), 12ff., esp. 26-31.

[58] An excellent summary is given by Ursula Aarburg, *Lai, Leich*, in the ency-
clopaedia *Musik in Geschichte und Gegenwart*, VIII, Kassel-Basel-London-New York, 1960, 81-7; cf. most recently H. Baader, *Die Lais*, Frankfurt am Main, 1966, pp. 21-36.

CLXXVIII, 165; ed. Monfrin, p. 98) that though born in Brittany, he did not understand the Breton tongue *.

But we do have one remarkable poem in Provençal to show us what the *content* of a heroine's love-death could be in a traditional mode, and it is with a discussion of this that we should like to conclude. The poem is the *Chanson de Sainte Foy*, composed in southern France around 1060 — some two decades, that is, before Abelard's birth [59]. It is a song of nearly six hundred octosyllabic lines, in monorhymed strophes (*laisses*). It relates how, in the time of Diocletian and Maximian, a young Christian girl at Agen in Gascony was interrogated and put to death, and how in the end her persecutors were destroyed. We do not wish to suggest that Abelard knew this particular song, but indeed it gives us fascinating evidence of a *kind* of traditional vernacular song that he might have known.

The *Chanson de Sainte Foy* is exceptional in that we know precisely for whom and for what occasion it was destined, and how it was performed. Despite its length, it was not recited, but sung and danced — the poet himself calls it "fine for dancing" (*bella 'n tresca,* 14). The singing and dancing took place on the vigil of the saint's feast, after the liturgical office and the reading of the *Passio*; everyone who came to church — clergy and populace alike — participated in such vigils and such performances [60]. Thus although the poem clearly reveals that its author was not unlettered — was a *clerc* or monk — it is also a poem which beyond any doubt was "popular", that is, composed for the entire congregation, unlettered as well as lettered. What may cause surprise are the poetic subtleties in such a popular piece. What everyone could enjoy in it was a simple but exciting story of heroic martyrdom, sung in a simple strophic form, good to dance to. But this poet in fact created something capable of a far more sophisticated appreciation. His account of the victim's death has the poetic leitmotif of love; he relies on the bridal imagery of the Song of Songs, counting on the awareness, by some of his audience at least, of the echoes and associations, and at one moment indeed reversing this imagery in a way that demands an exceptional

---

[* It is, however, possible — and perhaps more plausible — to interpret Abelard's phrase, *Terra quippe barbara et terre lingua mihi incognita erat*, to mean that, having spent his childhood near Nantes, he did not know the region of Vannes or understand the (somewhat unusual) Vannetais dialect, which the monks of Saint-Gildas will have spoken. Cf. J. T. Muckle's note in his edition, *MS*, XII (1950), 163-213, at p. 203 n. 15.]

[59] Ed. E. Hoepffner and P. Alfaric, *La Chanson de Sainte Foy*, 2 vols., Paris, 1926. On the dating, ibid., I, 17-26.

[60] Ed. cit., II, 68ff.

imaginative agility from his listeners. To illustrate the easier thematic
uses first — when Sainte Foy affirms to her interrogator, Dacien:

> "De nostre don me voill aizir;
> Et en czo q'eu sei meils causir,
> Res mais non es qu'eu tant amir.
> Si llui non ei, non poiss guerir.
> Ren tant non am, non voill mentir.
> Ab lui voil ridre e gaudir".

> "I want to take my pleasure in my lord —
> in whatever I can choose that's best,
> there's nothing I admire so much.
> If I do not have him, I cannot get well.
> I love nothing else so much, I will not lie!
> With him I want to laugh and to have joy" [61].

she is recreating in herself the role of the girl in the Canticle, the girl
who abandons herself to the lover she has chosen out of thousands
(*electus ex milibus*), who languishes sick with love (*amore langueo*)
when he is away. Even the homely and delightful doublet *ridre e
gaudir* carries an echo of the Solomonic *exultabimus et laetabimur*. So
too in Sainte Foy's final profession of faith, immediately before her
execution, her dream is of the *dilectus... totus desiderabilis*:

> "Aqel volri' aver espos,
> Qualque plaid m'en fezess ab vos,
> Q'el si·m es belz et amoros".

> "It is him I wish to have as bridegroom,
> whatever quarrel it involves me in with you,
> for to me he is so fair, so lovable".

The love-language of the Canticle is present also in the last part
of the poem, when the author explains how the persecutors of martyrs themselves served God's design:

> Cist l'en trameiron aitals flors
> Q'en cel es bella lur colors,
> Dolcz' e suaus es lor olors,
> E qi la sent, pren l'en amors
> Et en sun corps creiss l'en vigors.

> They sent him such flowers as these,

---

[61] The lines cited are 231-6, and (in order of citation below) 311-13, 477-81, and
54-64. The Song of Songs references are to V 10, II 5, I 3, and V 16.

whose colour is fair in heaven;
sweet and soft is their perfume,
and whoever breathes it falls in love with it
and it makes his body grow in strength.

The innocents killed by Herod were traditionally known as the flowers of the martyrs, *flores martyrum* [62]; but the mention of the perfume, and especially of its erotic and vivifying effects, at once evokes the expressive and emotional sphere of the Song of Songs again. To make the poet's intention explicit (perhaps over-explicit) for a moment: as the *adolescentulae*, the bride's attendants in the Song, are lured and excited by the perfume of the bridegroom (*Cant.*, I, 2), so mankind can be lured by martyrs towards love of God.

But all these harmonies are already half-heard near the opening of the *Chanson*, where the Song of Songs imagery is used in a more unusual fashion:

Proverbi diss reiz Salamon
Del pomer qi naiss el boisson,
Cui clau la spina e·l cardon
E'll albespin in eviron.
Achi met flors sus el somjon
E pois las pomas de sazon.
Mal forun li pagan Gascon
Qi desconnogron Deu del tron.
Lur umbra streins aqest planczon
De cui cantam esta canczon,
E pres en Deus dolz fruit e bon.

King Solomon spoke a parable
of the apple-tree born in a thicket,
shut in by thorns and thistles
and hawthorn all around.
There, high above, it brings forth flowers,
and then apples, in due time.
Wicked were the pagan Gascons
who disavowed the throned God.
Their shadow closed in on the sapling
of which we are singing this song —
and yet God gathered sweet, fair fruit from it.

The echoes from the Canticle seem evident enough. When the bridegroom and bride praise each other's peerless excellence, he says:

---

[62] The most famous occurrence is in Prudentius, *Cathemerinon*, XII, 125, but it is also an ancient and widespread liturgical phrase.

As the lily among the *thorns,*
so is my beloved among the daughters.

And she:

As the *apple-tree* among forest-trees,
so is my lover among the sons of men...
I sat in the *shadow* of him whom I had longed for,
and his *fruit* was *sweet* to my throat [63].

Thorns, apple-tree, shadow, sweet fruit — all recur in the vernacular
song, yet none of them any longer means what it meant in the original. The thorns now do not simply offset the perfection of the lily:
they become menacing, they constrict and choke the newborn apple-
tree. It is not Solomon's apple-tree, full-grown and surpassing the
forest trees, but a frail sapling: not the lover, but the beloved. The
gentle shadow of the divine lover has become the baneful *umbra* of
death; the *dolz fruit* that this too tender tree could never bear on
earth is gathered by the bridegroom in the other world. The original
associations of the *umbra* and *dolz fruit* are reversed and rejected;
they are simultaneously reaffirmed for the otherworld experience.
The completeness of this fusion of negation and reaffirmation is
brought out by one other meaningful reversal: in the Song of Songs,
it was the lover who offered the sweet fruit of love's fulfilment, here
it is she who offers: in the otherworld, the unity of bridegroom and
bride is complete.

Thus an eleventh century vernacular poet in France, composing
a popular poem, was able to deepen the account of his martyr
heroine by a range of imagery that makes her a bride in death. Like
the Greek poets, he too was able to fuse the positive and negative
connotations of his imagery, conveying simultaneously the beauty
and the grimness of the heroic death. If we ask, then, why did
Abelard present Seila's death under the aspect of a wedding-mime?
what lay behind his imagery of the victim as bride?, the short answer,
"a passage in pseudo-Philo", may not be entirely adequate. Rather it
seems likely that, like the pseudo-Philo in his own age, Abelard too
was sensitive to a living vernacular tradition, a tradition that had absorbed much from a literary past, but could contribute an immediacy
and imaginative freedom of its own.

[63] *Cant.,* II, 2-3.

13

HECTOR IN ELEVENTH-CENTURY LATIN LYRICS *

The poetic vitality of the "matter of Troy" in the twelfth century has long been recognised. The most fecund imaginative achievements arise in vernacular poetry in the second half of the century —
Benoit's *Roman de Troie*, the *Roman d'Eneas* and Veldeke's *Eneide*.
Yet the Latin tradition of Trojan narrative, too, is many-sided and at
times innovative — from Hugh Primas's Trojan vignettes (ca. 1140)
to the epyllia of Simon Chèvre d'Or and the anonymous poet of the
Historia Troyana in the mid-century, to Joseph of Exeter's flamboyant
epic *Frigii Daretis Ylias* towards 1190 [1].

What remains less clearly perceived, on the other hand, is the
imaginative force that Trojan themes already had in several parts of
Europe in the period before 1100. While valuable work has been
done on particular compositions from this earlier time by scholars
such as Boutemy and Stohlmann, the sense that there was already a
many-sided burgeoning of Troy in the eleventh century is still largely
lacking: it is symptomatic, for instance, that in Margaret Scherer's
panorama, "Works of Literature and Music", arranged by centuries,
in her book *The Legends of Troy*,the eleventh century is left blank [2].
Yet it is to the later eleventh century that we must assign, among
other works, the verse epistle addressed by Godfrey of Reims (†
1095) to Bishop Hugh of Langres, that breaks off in the middle of
an ecphrasis *De excidio Troie* (vv. 395-481) [3], and the extensive lost

---

* *Scire litteras*, ed. S. Krämer, M. Bernhard (Bayerische Akademie der Wissen-
schaften, München 1988), pp. 137-148.

[1] Hugh Primas: *Die Oxforder Gedichte des Primas*, ed. Wilhelm Meyer (repr.
Darmstadt 1970), nos. IX and X (pp. 61-70), and *The Oxford Poems of Hugh Primas
and the Arundel Lyrics*, ed. C.J. McDonough (Toronto 1984), pp. 41-7; Simon Chèvre
d'Or: ed. André Boutemy, *Scriptorium* 1 (1946/7), pp. 267-88 and *Le Moyen Age* 52
(1946), pp. 243-56; Joseph of Exeter [Joseph Iscanus], *Werke und Briefe*, ed. Ludwig
Gompf (Leiden-Köln 1970); *Historia Troyana*: Jürgen Stohlmann, *Anonymi Historia
Troyana Daretis Frigii* (Beihefte zum Mittellateinischen Jahrbuch 1, 1968), who also
gives a helpful survey of related poetry and an extensive bibliography.

[2] Margaret R. Scherer, *The Legends of Troy in Art and Literature* (New York-
London 1963), p. 224.

[3] Ed. André Boutemy, "Trois oeuvres inédites de Godefroid de Reims", RMAL
3 (1947), pp. 335-66, at pp. 362-4.

Trojan poem by Odo of Orléans, the scope of which can be surmised from Godfrey's recollections of it in his own dream-poem dedicated to Odo [4]. Similarly, the anonymous *Heroides* epistle of Deidamia to Achilles [5], and the pair of *Heroides* by Baudri of Bourgueil—Paris to Helen, Helen to Paris [6] — probably belong to the late eleventh century; and the immensely popular virtuoso epitome of Troy's fall, *Pergama flere volo*, with its lament of Hecuba and lament for the city, is usually dated ca. 1100 [7].

But the eleventh century likewise sees the beginnings of the florescence of Trojan lyrical poetry, a poetry that culminates in the lament of Dido, the brilliant *lai lyrique*, *O decus, o Libie regnum*, composed in the northern French or perhaps Anglo-Norman world ca. 1130-50 [8]. It is on two Italian predecessors of this lyrical composition that I should like to focus in the present essay.

The first is a dramatic *planctus* for Hector, written in the margin of a text of the late-antique prose narrative, *Excidium Troie*, in a hand of the end of the eleventh century; the manuscript is of Italian, most probably of Roman, provenance [9]. The *planctus* was first printed by Ernesto Monaci (1897), who unfortunately took the refrain, *Heu, male te cupimus!*, which also serves as a heading for the song, to read *Heu male tecum*; his text, though generally faithful, contained five

---

[4] Ibid. pp. 344-51.

[5] Ed. Jürgen Stohlmann, in *Literatur und Sprache im Europäischen Mittelalter: Festschrift für Karl Langosch zum 70. Geburtstag*, ed. Alf Önnerfors et al. (Darmstadt 1973), pp. 195-231.

[6] Baldricus Burgulianus, *Carmina*, ed. Karlheinz Hilbert (Heidelberg 1979), nos. 7-8 (pp. 21-40).

[7] *Carmina Burana*, ed. Alfons Hilka — Otto Schumann — Bernhard Bischoff, I 2 (Heidelberg 1941), no. 101; cf. André Boutemy, "Le poème *Pergama flere volo* ... et ses imitateurs du XIIe siècle", *Latomus* 5 (1946), pp. 233-44.

[8] *Carmina Burana* I 2 (n. 7), no. 100. I have offered a discussion of this song, with a new text and translation and indications concerning its probable dating and provenance, in "Dido's Lament: From Medieval Latin Lyric to Chaucer", *Kontinuität und Wandel, Franco Munari zum 65. Geburtstag*, ed. Ulrich Justus Stache et al. (Hildesheim 1986), pp. 264-90 [*infra*, no. 15, pp. 431-56].

[9] Even if this MS may have been copied, as Maria De Marco suggests (*Aevum* 30, 1956, pp. 38-9), by a central Italian hand from a Beneventan exemplar, the codex must have been in Rome already very early in the twelfth century. This I would infer from the fact that in the gathering fols. 191-8, which originally came straight after fol. 166, fol. 191 continuing the Paulus Diaconus extracts from fol. 166 (see L. Duchesne, *Le Liber Pontificalis* II, Paris 1892, p. xxii), there is "un récit de l'arrestation et de la captivité du pape Pascal II (mars-avril 1111), dû à la plume d'un clerc de l'entourage du pape" (Duchesne, ibid.). The editors of the *Excidium Troiae*, E. Bagby Atwood and Virgil K. Whitaker (Cambridge, Mass. 1944), did not use this MS.

other minor slips. The lyric was edited again in 1955 by Maria De Marco, who believed it to be "still unknown (tuttora sconosciuto)". She read the refrain correctly, but introduced five new errors (in 17, 19, 25, and two in 32), as well as six classicising corrections (in 16, 35, 50, 55, 61, 62) which in my view are probably not justifiable, since the poet's Latin shows a markedly unclassical, vernacularising impulse. In a later article, De Marco attempted to argue that this *planctus* was intended for reading and not performance — a view that will be questioned below [10]. First a fresh text seems desirable; the accompanying translation may serve to indicate how some of the interpretative problems might be resolved, though, as the interpretation of the song has never yet been discussed, a number of detailed points must also be considered separately thereafter.

Heu, male te cupimus!	*Alas, we badly long for you!*

(Choraula)		(Precentor)
Hector, pugne victor Graie,		Hector, conqueror in the Grecian fight,
cum uxore de te age!		speak with your wife about your fate!
Eu, male t⟨e cupimus!⟩		*Alas, we badly long for you!*
Uxor Andromache tua		Your wife, Andromache,
mala tibi refert sua.	5	is telling you her woes.
Eu, male te cu⟨pimus!⟩		*Alas...*
(Andromache)		(Andromache)
Honor patrie, marite,		Honour of my land, my husband,
verba audi mea rite:		hear my words aright:
Eu, ⟨male te cupimus!⟩		*Alas...*
Bellum nobis sit in hostes,	10	Though there is war against our enemies,
ne Achilli, cave, hostes!		take care not to confront Achilles!
Eu, ⟨male te cupimus!⟩		*Alas...*

V: Vat. lat. 1984, fol. 14ʳ (Vat. lat. 1984 A, erroneously, De Marco p. 120)
M: E. Monaci, *Archivio della Società Romana di Storia Patria* 20 (1897), 460-2
D: M. De Marco, *Aevum* 29 (1955), 120-2
Punctuation and line-arrangement are mine; I have noted all divergences from M and D other than purely orthographic ones.
Heading: sic V Heu male tecum M *om.* D (*The spelling* Heu *occurs in* V *only here, elsewhere it is* Eu *throughout*)   7 Tecum honor p. m. M (*misreading the close of 6*)   10 sit: fit MD   11 hostes (*pro* obstes) V: *corr.* obstes D

<hr/>

[10] Ernesto Monaci, "Per la storia della *Schola cantorum* lateranense", *Archivio della Società Romana di Storia Patria* 20 (1897), pp. 451-63; Maria De Marco, "Un 'planctus' sulla morte di Ettore", *Aevum* 29 (1955), pp. 119-23; ead., "Cuius mortem defle lector", *Giornale Italiano di Filologia* N.S.3 (1972), pp. 372-7.

Ne cum illo, cave, certes:
dive fertur proles certe.
   Eu, ⟨male te cupimus!⟩   15

Marithetis dea mater,
Peleus sit eius pater, .
   Eu, male te cu⟨pimus!⟩

Subit et eum nec terror,
cuius feras adit terror.   20
   Eu, ⟨male te cupimus!⟩

Erudivit enim illum
ypocentaurus pupillum,
   Eu, ⟨male te cupimus!⟩

Est et ita eruditus   25
nobis ut refert auditus:
   Eu, ⟨male te cupimus!⟩

Lapithas ferit pugnando,
leones capit venando,
   Eu, ⟨male te cupimus!⟩   30

Cutis eius sic est dura
quod vix ferrum ibi durat.
   Eu, ⟨male te cupimus!⟩

Multum ergo, vir mi, ⟨c⟩ave,
ne illic eas! Nunc ave!   35
   Eu, ⟨male te cupimus!⟩

(Hector)
En cum illo dimicabo
solitaque vi necabo!
   Eu, ⟨male te cupimus!⟩

Cum Patroclo dimicavi,   40
sumptis armis quem necavi.
   Eu, ⟨male te cupimus!⟩

(Choraula)
Unde indignatus ille
ad campum venit Achilles,
   Eu, ⟨male te cupimus!⟩   45

Quem adorsus miles Hector —
cuius mortem defle, lector!
   Eu, ⟨male te cupimus!⟩

Postquam se iunxerunt ambo,

Take care not to engage with him:
he's surely said to be a goddess' son.
   Alas...

Divine Sea-Thetis is his mother —
though (mortal) Peleus be his father,
   Alas...

He (like his mother) is immune to fear;
fear of him even comes upon wild beasts.
   Alas...

For the centaur trained him
as his pupil,
   Alas...

And he has indeed been trained
as we have heard tell:
   Alas...

He wounds Lapiths when he fights,
he captures lions when he hunts,
   Alas...

His skin is so hard
that there iron can scarcely hold.
Alas...

So, my husband, take great care:
do not go there! Now farewell!
   Alas...

(Hector)
Look, I shall contend with him
and slay him with my usual strength!
   Alas...

With Patroclus I contended
and slew him, taking away his arms.
   Alas...

(Precentor)
Outraged at this, the great
Achilles came to the battlefield.
   Alas...

Hector, the knight, assailed him
— reader, weep for his death!
   Alas...

After they have joined combat,

---

16 Marithetis (*sic* V): *corr.* Mari⟨s⟩ Thetis D   17 sit: fit D   19 et eum:
enim eum D   25 et: enim D   31-3 *om.* M   32 quod vix: quam nec
D   34 Mutum M ave V: *corr.* cave D   35 illic: *corr.* illuc D   47 mortes M

mistis telis pugnant ambo.	50	both fight with weapons clashing.	
E⟨u, male te cupimus!⟩		*Alas...*	

Hectori fracta fit hasta,
illi tamen dixit "Asta!"
   Eu, male ⟨te cupimus!⟩

Hector's spear gets broken,
still he says to him "Stand your ground!"
   Alas...

Et Achille spata cedit —   55
set successus illi cedit.
   Eu, ⟨male te cupimus!⟩

And strikes Achilles with his sword —
but success yields to Achilles.
   Alas...

Ubi se sentit necari,
⟨ce⟩pit Hector deprecari:
   Eu, m⟨ale te cupimus!⟩   60

When he sensed he was being slain,
Hector started to beseech:
   Alas...

(Hector)
O Achille, scelus vita:
mihi misero da vita!
   Eu, male⟨ te cupimus!⟩

(Hector)
Oh Achilles, shun a crime:
give me my life, wretched as I am!
   Alas...

Per me patriam vicisti
et parentes subiecisti.   65
   Eu, ⟨male te cupimus!⟩

By (defeating) me, you have overcome my land
and have bowed my parents down.
   Alas...

Senex pater pro me plorat,
te Andromache implorat!
   ⟨*Eu, male te cupimus!*⟩

My old father laments for me,
Andromache is imploring you!
   Alas...

(Choraula)
Talia dum Hector dicit,   70
eum Achilles occidit.
   Eu, male te cupimus!

(Precentor)
While Hector says these words
Achilles kills him.
   Alas, we badly long for you!

50 mistis: *corr.* mixtis D   52 fit (?) V: sit (*recte?*) M   55 Achille: *corr.* Achilli
D   61 Achille: *corr.* Achille⟨s⟩ D   scelus: salus M   62 vita: *corr.* vitam D

The first remarkable feature of the form is that at line 7 Andromache appears to begin speaking (or singing) in person [11], and
that at 37, without any sign of introduction or narrative transition,
Hector answers her. Again at 43, without introduction, someone
who is neither Andromache nor Hector narrates what followed. This
narrator introduces Hector's final pleas to Achilles (61ff.) and concludes the composition (70f.).

    In round brackets set above the relevant strophes I have distin-
guished these three speakers, not in order to pre-empt the question,

[11] It is at least possible that Andromache is also speaking in the first two
strophes, but referring to herself in the third person. This was the way Monaci construed the opening strophes (p. 460).

in what sense is this *planctus* dramatic, but simply to show its articulation as clearly as possible. For the same reason I have distinguished the "narrative" moments from the refrain: while these could be assigned to the same speaker or singer, it may be helpful to underline that the refrain, "Heu, male te cupimus!", with its colloquial tone and its plural, shows kinship with traditional Italian vernacular *ritornelli*, which are lyrical and not narrative in orientation. Thus the refrain here can be imagined as sung by a chorus, or indeed by the whole of an assembled company, almost more readily than by a soloist.

According to De Marco, on the other hand, the existence of line 47 — "Cuius mortem defle, lector!" — is a clear proof that this *planctus* was intended for reading only, and not for performance [12]. (She appears to mean private reading, not public, and does not specify whether she means silent reading or reading aloud). Yet the clarity of this testimony seems to me deeply problematic, indeed illusory. First, because I know of not a single *planctus* in lyrical form in medieval Latin (or in any medieval vernacular) that was meant exclusively for reading and not for singing or chanting. Still less do I know of any songs with refrain that were meant for reading only. Was the poet perhaps tempted to use *lector* (rather than *auditor* or some equivalent) at 47 because it offered so convenient a rhyme for *Hector*? While this cannot be ruled out, the choice was by no means an inevitable one: verses auch as "Troie maximus protector", or "Miserere, celi rector!", would have been equally feasible for completing the couplet.

I would suggest a different solution. When in 1192/3 the Milanese "magister Humbertus de Balesma" gave his astonishing philosophical-astrological Advent sermon to the masters and students of Paris, taking as his text Isaiah VII 14, he began:

Audi, lector theologe, primi adventus et tue fidei argumentum,
secundi adventus et tui laboris remedium,
utriusque adventus et tue lectionis solatium [13].

He was addressing an audience each member of which was himself a *lector* of religious texts. Humbertus was in effect saying. "Listen, you who at other times read such things". Similarly I believe

---

[12] "Cuius mortem" (n. 10), esp. p. 374.

[13] Marie-Thérèse d'Alverny, "Humbertus de Balesma", *AHDLMA* 51 (1984), pp. 127-91, at p. 159. I have printed the lines so as to articulate the parallelism in Humbertus' rhythmic prose.

the Italian poet was summoning to emotional participation each member of an audience who at other times read about Troy's fall. That is, notwithstanding the popular ring of the refrain, his song will have been destined for, and sung for, a learned audience, one that could read about Hector as well as hear about him and mourn for him.

Was the *planctus* performed with separate singers for narrator, Andromache and Hector? While there may well have been occcasions when it was performed by a single soloist — for instance, if there was only one available who had mastered the words and music — the entrances of the two protagonists without explicit introduction would indicate that the poet at least conceived his *planctus* with three soloists in mind. Paradoxically, the hypothetical performance by a single soloist would have been possible only before an audience so familiar with dramatically sung dialogue that, because of this familiarity, they could also follow, making the necessary mental leaps between the characters, even when these were not physically distinguishable. The refrain is implicitly the lament of a chorus of Trojans; it could, as occasion suggested, have been sung either by a choir or by the audience; the narrator is likely to have acted as their precentor.

Songs composed in rhyming couplets followed by a refrain are not uncommon: the dirge for Charlemagne, *A solis ortu usque ad occidua* (814), and the love-song *Deus amet puellam*, copied in the early tenth century, are renowned examples [14]. It is relatively uncommon for these couplets to consist of octosyllabics with paroxytone, not proparoxytone, ending (in Norberg's notation, 8p lines, as against the 8pp ones so frequent in Latin hymnody). From tenth-century Italy there are the mocking couplets (2 × 8p) on Adalbertus, son of King Berengarius —

Age, age iam Alberte,
ultra Decium superbe [15]...

but these have no refrain; among more archaic religious lyrics, songs such as *Ama, puer, castitatem* and *Ab aquilone venite* consist of quatrains (basically 4 × 8p) followed by a refrain, yet the octosyllabics admit a number of irregularities [16]. The eleventh-century Italian

---

[14] *Poetae Latini* (MGH) I, pp. 434-6; V 2, 553f. On the authorship of the first, see the suggestion of Michael Lapidge, *Studi medievali*, 3a serie, 18 (1977), pp. 856ff., which is not in my view invalidated by the objections of Heinz Löwe, *Deutsches Archiv* 37 (1981), 3f.

[15] *Poetae* V 2, pp. 560f.

[16] *Poetae* IV 2, 573ff., 587f.

planctus poet, in short, availed himself of a simple but effective form, one that was not yet jaded (as forms confined to 8pp lines tended to be by his time).

His language has a freshness that is bound up with its unclassical features. It is not always easy to tell how far these are consciously present, or how far they may be due to his, or his copyist's, carelessness (such slips as 34 *ave* for *cave* make it unlikely that we have an autograph). Certain vernacularisms I believe should not be corrected: the form *Achille*, which is used in place of the classical accusative in 55, the form *vita*, used in place of the classical accusative in 62, or *mistis* for *mixtis* in 50. So, too, the use of *illic* for *illuc* is common in early medieval Latin [17], and in 35 *illic* should be allowed to stand. More problematic is *Marithetis* in 16: it is clearly written as one word, and Monaci's suggestion that it is the poet's attempted compound formation ("Sea-Thetis") still seems to me more attractive than De Marco's correction to "Mari(s) Thetis dea mater", which results in an awkwardly inverted word-order.

While the poet was familiar with the mythography of Hector and Achilles from several sources, the beauty and originality of his *planctus* stem in large measure from the way he transforms what I believe to have been his principal source, the 24th chapter in the *Historia* of Dares Phrygius. This might seem a singularly arid and unpromising fount for poetic inspiration, yet, as Margaret Scherer, referring primarily to some fifteenth-century elaborations of Dares, noted perceptively:

> As Hector's death draws near the romances make one of their most effective changes in the order of incidents. They combine the farewell to Andromache, which the *Iliad* places before the early combat with Ajax, with the scene near the end of the epic, in which the hero's parents plead with him not to fight. Then they place the combined action just before the fatal encounter with Achilles. It is rare to find the romances more dramatic than the *Iliad*, but from the modern

---

[17] Cf. Albert Blaise, *Dictionnaire latin-français des auteurs chrétiens* (Turnhout [2] 1962), p. 403, *s.v. illic*. For the previously mentioned vernacularisms, it is helpful to compare the language of a text such as the *Chronicon Salernitanum*, written shortly after 974 (ed. Ulla Westerbergh, Studia Latina Stockholmiensia III, 1956). There, as the editor notes (p. 226), "*s* and *ss* are repeatedly used instead of *x*" (cf. *mistis*, *Planctus* 50), and there too (p. 229) "the fact that final *s*, *m*, and *t* were not pronounced ... is reflected in the language of the chronicle". Westerbergh gives examples such as *cum Galli* (= -*is*) and *venusta forma* (= -*am* -*am*): compare *Achille* (= -*em*, 55, = -*es?*, 61) and *vita* (= -*am*, 62) in the lament.

point of view this change increases the suspense, quickens the action, and leads to the inevitable end [18].

But the poet of the *planctus* has done something more arresting than any of his successors in Trojan romances from the twelfth to the fifteenth centuries: he has simplified Dares' account, taking from the crucial chapter only what gave his song the highest concentration and force, and discarding all else. In *Heu, male te cupimus* all the to and fro in Dares' narrative is eliminated; Priam, Alexander, Helenus, Troilus, Aeneas, the infant Astyanax, the eight Greek heroes besides Achilles — all of whom Dares mentions in his brief chapter — make no appearance here. Instead of Dares' crowded scene, the poet, with masterly selectiveness, evokes only two moments of utmost intensity, in which two human beings encounter each other. To cite the passages he has chosen that are transmuted in his lament, setting those he has rejected in parenthesis alongside [19]:

But when the time for combat came, Andromache, Hector's wife, saw in her dreams that Hector must not go out to fight, and when she told him what she had seen, Hector rejected her words as womanish.

[Andromache in her sorrow sent word to Priam, that he should forbid Hector to fight that day. Priam sent Alexander, Helenus, Troilus and Aeneas into battle. When Hector heard of this, bitterly reproaching Andromache he demanded that she bring out his armour — there was no way to hold him back. Andromache, her long hair untied in grief, falling before Hector's feet holding out their son Astyanax, still could not call him back. Then with womanly lament she roused the town, raced into Priam's palace, told what she had seen in her dreams and that Hector was still determined to leap into battle, and, holding out Astyanax before Priam's

---

[18] *Legends* (n. 2), p. 82.

[19] I translate from *Daretis Phrygii de Excidio Troiae Historia*, ed. Ferdinandus Meister (Leipzig 1873), pp. 28-30.

knees, she bade him call Hector back. Priam commanded all to go into battle, but kept Hector behind. Agamemnon, Achilles, Diomede and Locrian Ajax, as they saw that Hector was not fighting, fought fiercely and killed many of the Trojan chieftains.]

When Hector heard the tumult, and heard the Trojans struggling wildly in the combat, he leapt into the fray.

[Immediately he slaughtered Idomeneus, wounded Iphinous, killed Leonteus, pierced Sthenelus' thigh with a spear.]

Achilles, when he saw that many leaders had fallen by Hector's hand, turned his spirit against him in order to confront him.

[For he thought that, unless he killed Hector, many of the Greeks would perish by his hand. Meanwhile there was the clash of battle. Hector killed Polypoetes, a very brave chieftain, and as he began to strip off Polypoetes' armour, Achilles advanced. The fighting intensified, a clamour arose from the town and all the army.]

Hector wounded Achilles' thigh. Achilles, despite the inflicted pain, began to pursue Hector all the more, and did not cease till he had killed him.

After further details (the flight of the Trojans, a combat between Achilles and Memnon in which both are wounded), the chapter concludes: "At night the Trojans lamented Hector, the Greeks their own dead". This is the Trojan lament that the eleventh-century poet creates, ignoring the mass of frantic detail in Dares and focussing only on the two essential, hopeless confrontations — Hector first with his wife, then with his enemy.

The refrain *Heu, male te cupimus!*, which dominates the piece, means that to the chorus of mourners Hector is already dead: they miss the hero who had been their greatest hope. Yet the words can equally evoke Andromache's tragic love-longing for her dead husband and the chorus's oneness with her in grief. The song is at once a dirge for Hector and a re-enactment of his death — just as half a century later Abelard, in his *Planctus virginum Israel super filia Iepte Galadite*, shows us both the ceremony of mourning for Jephtha's daughter and the dramatic recreation of her sacrifice by the maidens of a later time [20]. Here in the lament for Hector the narrator, or precentor, summons Hector to listen to the warnings and pleas of his wife. Andromache tells him of Achilles' reputed superhuman powers ("dive fertur proles certe") and of the inhuman terror he can inspire ("cuius feras adit terror"): Achilles has been trained for this since boyhood, he has absorbed both the cunning and the half-bestial nature of the centaur who fostered him. In the course of Andromache's words, the poet touches lightly on a number of the motifs concerning Achilles' youth, all of which he could have found for instance in Statius' *Achilleis*: not only the details of Achilles' nurture by the centaur Chiron (*Ach.* II 86 ff.), including his fighting of Lapiths (I 40f., II 112f.) and his capturing of lions (I 168 ff., II 125), but also that iron cannot penetrate Achilles' limbs, which Thetis had in his infancy dipped in the river Styx (I 480f.).

Hector answers his wife loftily: he does not chide Andromache's words as "womanish (*muliebria*)", as in Dares, but simply claims he cannot see why his "usual strength" should not prevail as it has done till now. Nonetheless, Andromache's awestruck portrayal of Achilles has goaded him to indignation. This is told by the narrator who, after his ominous warning to the audience, step by step recounts Hector's defeat. Then for three strophes comes the motif (as far as I know unparalleled in this form) of Hector begging Achilles to spare him. I would see it as the poet's individual transformation of the passage in the *Ilias Latina* (980-7) where Hector pleads with Achilles, not for his life, but that his corpse be returned to his parents:

> En concede meos miseris genitoribus artus,
> Quos pater infelix multo mercabitur auro:
> Dona feres victor. Priami nunc filius orat
> Te primus, dux ille ducum, quem Graecia solum
> Pertimuit: si nec precibus nec vulnere victi
> Nec lacrimis miseri nec clara gente moveris,
> Afflicti miserere patris, moveat tua Peleus
> Pectora pro Priamo, pro nostro corpore Pyrrhus [21].

---

[20] Cf. Margaret Alexiou, Peter Dronke, "The Lament of Jephtha's Daughter", *Studi medievali*, 3a Serie, 12 (1971), pp. 819-63, at pp. 851-9 [*supra*, no. 12, pp. 377-84].

[21] Ed. Aemilius Baehrens, *Poetae Latini Minores* III (Leipzig 1881), pp. 55f. Cf. Homer *Il.* 22, 338-43.

In this text we are told that Hector had "lost his strength (*amissis viribus*)"; the medieval poet introduces Hector's prayer more vividly: "When he sensed he was being slain (*Ubi se sentit necari*)..." Hector in his humiliation is no longer heroic: he pleads for his life in terms that contrast pathetically with the way he had set out for the duel. Then he had promised to slay Achilles; now what had seemed just to inflict on Achilles seems a "crime (*scelus*)" when aimed at himself. Hector's plea has a further import that the poet's source had not even hinted at: he claims that by defeating him the Greeks have won Troy itself — the war is over, why should Achilles sully the victory by a needless killing? Where in the Latin *Ilias* Hector ends by alluding to Peleus and Pyrrhus, Achilles' own father and son, in the *planctus*, with its greater emotional power, his last words and thoughts turn to Andromache.

The poet's final imaginative feat lies in another omission. The author of the Latin *Ilias* gives Achilles a harsh, vengeful reply of seven lines (989-95; cf. Homer, *Il.* 22, 345-54), and there are perhaps few other medieval poets who could have resisted the temptation to adapt and indeed amplify such a speech. How much more eloquent is the silence of Achilles in this *planctus*. Achilles himself is left featureless and remote: we have been shown him only through the eyes of Andromache. We are told nothing of his emotion as he cuts the now defenceless Hector down. The final occurrence of the refrain suggests that, even in Hector's weakness and helplessness at the last, the Trojans still feel tenderly towards him. The refrain here finds its profoundest meaning; the past, recreated and confronted, joins the present of lament; the song comes full circle [22].

A second song lamenting Hector's death is preserved in an Italian manuscript of the end of the twelfth century, but its language and rhymes suggest to me that it was likewise composed before 1100. Where *Heu, male te cupimus* (however it may have been performed) is akin to drama in conception, the other song, *Sub vespere Troianis menibus*, is akin to ballads. It moves swiftly, each moment recorded in staccato fashion; the poet does not linger over any instant long enough to generate an imaginative intensity comparable with that in the lyrical dialogue. Yet this balladlike song is remarkable too in its departures from hallowed classical tradition. As the only edition known to me, that of C. P. Bock in 1851 [23], is not easily accessible

[22] This is true also, even to the details of form and melody, of Abelard's *Planctus virginum Israel:* see "The Lament" (n. 20), loc. cit.

[23] "Lettres à Monsieur L. Bethmann sur un manuscrit de la Bibliothèque de Bourgogne intitulé 'liber Guidonis'", *Annuaire de la B.R. de Belgique* 12 (1851), pp.

and can be improved at several points, I give a new text below.

Sub vespere Troianis menibus prodit Hector, miles egregius,	At twilight from the Trojan ramparts Hector, the peerless knight, came forth.
quem ut vidit turba Myrmidonum, versis equis in castra fugiunt.	As the crowd of Myrmidons saw him, turning their horses, they fled to their camp.
Clamat simul "Achilles, propera! Arma cape et tuos libera!"	5 All at once they cried "Achilles, hasten! Take up your arms and free your own!"
Ait Hector "Fuga et saucia quem turpiter fugit Achagia!"	Hector said "Put to flight and wound (if you can) him from whom Greece is basely fleeing!"
Ad hec verba Achilles protinus arma capit, it ei obvius.	At these words Achilles forthwith 10 took up his arms, went out to face Hector.
Concurrerunt uterque Atrides,	Both the Atrides raced up to support him,
Diumedes, Aiax et Ulixes.	Diomede, Ajax and Ulysses.
Ait Hector "Viri, quo ruitis?	Hector said "Men, where are you rushing?
Mecum certat filius Thetidis!	With me (alone) is Thetis' son fighting!
Iam sentiet quid Hector valeat et si possit perfodi lancea."	15 Now he shall feel Hector's might — he shall feel if he can be pierced by lance!"
Pugnat Hector, pugnat nec dubitat,	Hector fights, he fights unhesitating,

B: Bruxelles, Bibl. Royale 3897-3919, fol. 119^v
A: C. P. Bock, *Annuaire de la Bibliothèque Royale de Belgique* 12 (1851), 61.
In B the couplets, apart from the first two, are written each on a separate line; punctuation and other verse-divisions are mine.
7 At, fugat, sauciat B   13 Ait (*sic* B): At A   15 Iiam B

41-212, at p. 61. On the MS see especially J. Van den Gheyn, *Catalogue V* (Bruxelles 1905), no. 3095 (pp. 27-30), and R. Calcoen, *Inventaire des manuscrits scientifiques de la Bibliothèque Royale de Belgique* I (Bruxelles 1965), pp. 79f., with a large bibliography. I am grateful to Albert Derolez for this last reference, and for his kindness in helping me obtain a photograph of the page containing the lyric. In Van den Gheyn's description of the MS he notes at fol. 173 "Fragment d'hymne notée, Inc. ... *lycheris iam rosam aspicis*": these words, however, stem not from a hymn but from the love-song, "Ver prope florigerum, flava Licori, /iam rosam aspicis ...", that I have attributed to Peter of Blois (see *The Medieval Poet and his World*, Roma 1984, pp. 319, 332). The fact that the other known MSS of this song lack musical notation makes this a particularly precious testimony; I hope to prepare an analysis and edition, together with the musicologist Susan Rankin, in the near future.

iacit astam, ensem evaginat.	he hurls his spear, unsheathes his sword.
Ferit hense Achillis clipeum,	With his sword he strikes Achilles' shield;
frangit eum mox prope capulum. 20	soon he breaks it near the hilt.
Fit certamen, set fit dispariter:	There is combat, but unequally:
unus obstat multis viriliter.	one man confronting many, manfully.
Leti duces ita desiliunt	Joyous, the princes thus dismount
et crudeli funere obruunt.	and assail him with a cruel death.
Sic cecidit nunc decus Asie, 25	Thus has Asia's glory fallen now,
sic occidit luctus Achagie!	thus he who was Greece's sorrow now lies low!

20 mox frangit eum B   23 desiluūt B   24 ut crudeli A

The song is in decasyllabic couplets, in a measure (4 + 6pp) that may derive from the refrains of some of the most archaic hymns (*In tremendo die iudicii*), and that is well attested in strophic forms, Latin and vernacular, in the later eleventh century and throughout the twelfth [24]. In *Sub vespere* there are no rhymes on stressed syllables: weak rhymes and half-rhymes (*manibus/egregius*) are used throughout, and twice (*Myrmidonum/fugiunt, valeat/lancea*) there is only assonance. These freedoms with regard to rhyming, and the complete absence of strong rhyme, suggest to me that the song stems from the eleventh century rather than the twelfth. *Sub vespere* may indeed be slightly older than the *planctus* of Oedipus composed in the same measure, *Diri patris infausta pignora* (s. XI ex.), which has quatrains with half-rhymes (*aspera/miseria/scelera/sidera*) alongside others with full rhyme [25].

From the outset the poet gives Hector the most heroic aura imaginable. He has nothing of the moving *hamartia* of the protagonist in *Heu, male te cupimus*. The Myrmidons, at the mere sight of him, scuttle back to the Greek camp and call upon Achilles for help (I punctuate and construe line 5 so that the subject is *turba Myrmidonum*). Line 7, as it stands in the manuscript ("At Hector fugat et sauciat"), is metrically defective, and would give a bizarre sense if it were combined in this form with 8 ("quem turpiter fugit Achagia")

---

[24] Cf. Dag Norberg, *Introduction à l'étude de la versification latine médiévale* (Stockholm 1958), pp. 152f. and 153 n. 1. To the examples Norberg mentions from the eleventh century should be added the bilingual play *Sponsus* (ed. D'Arco Silvio Avalle, Milano-Napoli 1965), in which the majority of the strophes, both Latin and vernacular, use this measure.

[25] Cf. Peter Dronke, *Fabula* (Leiden-Köln 1974), p. 128 n. 2.

— it would be saying that Hector was putting to flight and wounding someone on his own side. The solution I propose is to emend *At Hector* to *Ait Hector* (cf. 13, where this phrase is preserved correctly) for metre, and, by emending to *fuga* and *saucia*, to show Hector as issuing a challenge, daring Achilles to put him to flight and wound him, since the other Greeks are too cowardly to face him. The challenge is evidently one to single combat, and Achilles appears to accept it thus (the correctness of the emendation *Ait Hector* in 7 is confirmed by the complementary *Ad hec verba* in 9). But at once, as Achilles comes forth, five other Greeks (Agamemnon and Menelaus, Diomede, Ajax and Ulysses) rush out as well, leaving Hector badly outnumbered. Hector now reiterates that he wants to encounter Achilles alone (even though, in 16, he shows himself aware of Achilles' reputed invulnerability). But to no avail: the many Greeks set upon the one valiant Trojan (21-2). Joyful at their advantage in numbers, they even descend to the baseness of dismounting and dispatching him on foot (23-4), and the poet brings home the grief and the shame of it with the *Sic...sic* of his concluding couplet. It is this couplet that gives the succinct balladlike narrative the dimensions of *planctus*: only here do the poet's imaginative identification with his hero and his compassionate grief become explicit.

The notion that Hector was too great to be killed in fair combat, that the Greeks, including Achilles, had to use deceit to murder him, first occurs in the Trojan 'journal' of Dictys, notwithstanding this author's frequently pro-Greek attitude. There (III 15) we read:

> Not many days had passed before it was suddenly announced that Hector had set out with a few men to meet Penthesilea... So Achilles, taking a few loyal companions with him, hastened to lay an ambush. He cut off his unsuspecting enemy, and surrounded him as he was starting to cross a stream. Thus unexpectedly he killed Hector and all those comrades of the prince, who had never known this kind of deceit [26].

The detail that Hector and Achilles fought on foot is explicit in the *Ilias Latina* (956), where, as in Homer, Hector is less heroic and the deceit involved in his death is of a wholly different kind: Hector only takes courage to fight Achilles as he sees what appears to be his brother Deiphobus coming to help him, but it turns out to be Pallas Athena who, favouring Achilles, comes in Deiphobus' shape [27]. In a poem later than *Sub vespere*, the *Historia Troyana Daretis Frigii* (ca.

---

[26] I translate from Dictys Cretensis, *Ephemeris*, ed. Werner Eisenhut (Leipzig 1958), pp. 70f.

[27] Cf. Homer, *Il.* 22, 226ff.

1150), Stohlmann aptly observed that Achilles' fighting on foot is seen as an aspect of his deceitfulness ("It pede, quod fraudi via congruit ista latenti," 344), because in medieval combat leaders invariably fought on horseback [28]. This sense of an ignoble way of fighting would seem already to lie behind the expression "Leti duces ita desiliunt" in the lament *Sub vespere.*

While we can see what details in earlier accounts stimulated this eleventh-century lyrical poet, his specific way of forming the episode and interpreting Hector's death cannot, to my knowledge, be paralleled. The notion that Hector sought a duel with Achilles, but was forced instead to fight six of the major Greek heroes simultaneously, in an unfair contest, may well have been this poet's own invention — just as Achilles' silent cutting down of a Hector who dies with Andromache's name on his lips was the invention of the poet of *Heu, male te cupimus.* Far more than their contemporaries who used classical and leonine metres, the lyric poets assume as of right not only a freedom in the interpreting of emotion but, more startlingly, a freedom with long-established narrative facts. Thus the Dido of *O decus, o Libie regnum* takes her life in order to rejoin Aeneas (not Sichaeus!) in the otherworld; the Aeneas of *Superbi Paridis,* having reached Italy, rues his desertion of Dido and affirms he should never have believed or obeyed the gods' command to relinquish her [29]. The classical elements are compounded anew, in wholly unclassical ways.

---

[28] Jürgen Stohlmann, *Historia* (n. 1), p. 39; on the nature of Achilles' deceit in Benoit's *Roman de Troie,* see ibid. p. 170. Compare also the more summary declaration in *Carmina Burana* I 2 (n. 7), no. 102 (*Fervet amore Paris*), st. 9: *vite fraus Hectora demit.*

[29] *Carmina Burana* I 2, no. 99, st. 19 (p. 133):
Non semper utile est diis credere,
nec quicquid ammonent velle perficere-
nam instigaverant me te relinquere.

As I indicated long ago (PBB Tübingen 84, 1962, pp. 182f.), the editors' decision to remove ten of the twenty strophes of this song, relegating them to the critical apparatus, is misconceived. A further misconception underlies their notion that Aeneas in these strophes is mocking Dido — *voce ironica,* as their emended text declares. The MS reading, *yranica,* is, I submit, a semi-learned spelling of *uranica* (on which see *Lexicon Latinitatis Medii Aevi,* Turnhout 1975, p. 940, s.v.), perhaps influenced by Gk. OYPANIA. Aeneas, that is, speaks to Dido "with sublime voice (*voce uranica*)". Aeneas' blend of loving, compassionate addresses to Dido with self-accusations in this song is closely paralleled in Veldeke's *Eneide,* esp. at 2089ff. and 2169ff.: see "Dido's Lament" (n. 8), pp. 378f (*infra,* pp. 447 f.). In both poems the context precludes irony.

In conclusion, we can hazard a conjecture about the milieu in which at least the first of these Italian laments was performed. If Monaci was right in his tentative linking of *Heu, male te cupimus* with the papal *Schola cantorum*, we have a rich documentation of its festivities and songs in the eleventh century, in the *Polyptique du Chanoine Benoît* [30], and even earlier we know from John Immonides' own testimony the liveliness of the miming and singing and playing ("saltantem me Iohannem... cantantem... iocantem attendite: satiram ludam") with which John as compère presented his *Cena Cypriani* (876), which he dedicated to Pope John VIII and also intended for performance in the presence of Charles the Bald ("hanc exhibeat convivis imperator Karolus") [31]. It seems altogether possible that in the same Roman ambience where the biblical characters appeared in John's elaborate comic lyrical masquerade, Andromache and Hector entered and sang, presented as tragic figures, two centuries later. Something of the poetic freedom with which John had interpreted biblical moments as comedy will have extended to the classical moments, perceived freshly and tragically.

[30] Ed. P. Fabre (Lille 1889); see especially Ricarda Liver, "Cornomannia", *Vox Romanica* 30 (1971), pp. 32-43.

[31] See most recently Giovanni Orlandi, "Rielaborazioni medievali della 'Cena Cypriani' ", in *L'eredità classica nel Medioevo: il linguaggio comico*, Atti del III Convegno di Studi (Viterbo 1979), pp. 3-26.

ADDENDUM. While these pages were in proof, several valuable points of detail concerning the first lament came to me in a Latin seminar at Göteborg from Professors Tore Janson and Erik Wistrand, and also from Kimmo Järvinen, who suggested that *hostes* (11) should be taken as an unusual spelling of *obstes*, rather than as a copyist's slip, as I wrote originally.

14

THE PROVENÇAL *TROBAIRITZ* CASTELLOZA *

In medieval Europe, Provence is unique in preserving a small corpus of secular lyrical poetry composed by women. The names af twenty *trobairitz*, who flourished in the twelfth and thirteenth centuries, are still known to us; some five anonymous songs can likewise be plausibly ascribed to women poets [1]. Only two of the *trobairitz*, however, are represented in the manuscripts by more than a single composition. Four songs are well attested for the countess of Dia — though the exact dates and historical identity of this poet are still much debated [2]. I incline to follow those who see her as Beatritz, wife of a certain Count William of Poitiers in the third quarter of the twelfth century. Historical evidence is equally elusive with regard to Castelloza, of whom again four compositions survive: three are steadily ascribed to her in a group of manuscripts; but the fourth also — found alongside the others in a manuscript where all her lyrics are copied anonymously — seems to admit of no serious doubt [3].With

---

* *Medieval Women Writers*, ed. K.M. Wilson (The University of Georgia Press, Athens, Georgia, 1984), pp. 131-152.

[1] The majority of poems by *trobairitz* can be found collected in O. Schultz, *Die Provenzalischen Dichterinnen* (Altenburg 1888); Jules Véran, *Les poétesses provençales* (Paris 1946), and Meg Bogin, *The Women Troubadours* (New York 1976). Of these collections, only that of Véran includes the *sirventes* of Germonda (or Gormonda) of Montpellier, "Greu m'es a durar" (pp. 196-205), and the anonymous "Quan vei los praz verdesir" (pp. 64-67). None of the three collections includes Azalais d'Altier's "Tanz salutz e tantas amors," ed. V. Crescini, *Zeitschrift für romanische Philologie* 14 (1890): 128-132, or the piece "No·m posc mudar," attributed to Raimon Jordan in the unique manuscript, but more probably the work of an anonymous *trobairitz* (see the recent edition and translation by Martín de Riquer, *Los trovadores* [3 vols., Barcelona 1977], vol. 1, pp. 576-577).
Most important in the present context is that the three collections of *trobairitz* all exclude Castelloza's fourth song, "Per joi que d'amor m'avegna."

[2] There is an excellent text of the countess's songs, with notes and translation, in Riquer, vol. 2, pp. 791-802. The attribution to the countess of the anonymous woman's strophes in the *tenso* "Amics, en greu cossirier," where the partner is Raimbaut d'Aurenga, seems dubious: see most recently ibid., vol. 1, p. 452, vol. 2, pp. 791-793.

[3] Compare J. Boutière and A.H. Schutz, *Biographies des troubadours* (2nd ed.,

the melodies of the *trobairitz* we are less fortunate: music has survived for only one of the countess' songs, none remains for Castelloza's.

In the biographical note *(vida)* that in three manuscripts introduces her songs, Castelloza is said to be from the Auvergne, and her husband is named as Turc de Mairona. This Turc is also alluded to in a lyric of topical invective *(sirventes)* of 1212. Thus, if we can set Castelloza's compositions near that date, they may well be a generation later than the countess of Dia's. It seems to me likely, moreover, that Castelloza knew her predecessor's songs, though her own are keenly individual in their art; again, the songs of both *trobairitz* can be readily distingiushed from those of the trobadours.

Where the countess of Dia's four songs show a Cleopatra-like variety of attitudes to love and to the man she loves, Castelloza's show intense single-mindedness. The countess celebrates her joy in the lover whom she has chosen, a joy that also emboldens her to mock the slanderers and spies who menace love affairs. She can express her physical desires without reserve, in exultant erotic provocation of her beloved; and, in her only tragic song, she reflects on his unfaithfulness with the analytic ardour of one of Ovid's Heroides, still aware of her own desirability and beauty, still hoping to persuade him back to perfect mutual love.

Castelloza's songs, by contrast, are all meditations on her own anguished love, abasing herself and knowing — even while continuing to hope — that a future of constancy and oneness is not to be hoped for. Even if she is addressing her lover, and implicitly her audience, she utters soliloquies, in a depth of solitude. Where the countess's four songs create changeable perceptions, Castelloza's are facets of one unaltering perception.

Are her songs ordered to a particular design? In the manuscripts, their order (which is unvarying) is, as Dietmar Rieger pointed out, alphabetical [4]. This might of course be coincidence, or might reflect a mechanical ordering by an earlier collector. We also have some evidence, however, that — long before Dante's *Vita Nuova* — certain troubadours ordered their songs chronologically [5]. It is admittedly risky to entertain this notion for as small a sample of lyrics

Paris 1973), p. 334, and the judicious discussion by Dietmar Rieger, "Die *trobairitz* in Italien: Zu den altprovenzalischen Dichterinnen," *Cultura Neolatina* 31 (1971): 210-212.

[4] Rieger, "Die *trobairitz* in Italien," loc. cit.

[5] Compare D'Arco Silvio Avalle in *Geschichte der Textüberlieferung der antiken und mittelalterlichen Literatur* (2 vols. Zürich 1961-4), vol. 2, p. 292.

as Castelloza's. Yet I cannot easily escape the sense that with her we are in the presence not just of four songs but of a brief lyrical cycle, where an inner progression can be perceived, and where reverberations from one piece to the next heighten poetic meaning, so that the group as a whole is imaginatively richer than the four pieces considered separately. This is a point that cannot be demonstrated conclusively, yet the possible interrelatedness of Castelloza's songs seems worth bearing in mind in an attempt at reading.

In Spain and Portugal many love songs *(cantigas de amigo)* are put in the mouths of women, yet the manuscript tradition ascribes these songs exclusively to men. No *trovadora* is ever named. The reason that love lyrics composed by women survive from Provence, under the *trobairitz*'s names, must be bound up with the unusual degree of personal freedom that many women (at least in the higher reaches of society, and at least for three or four generations) there enjoyed. At the same time, while this freedom made possible some women's songs of marvellous directness, it is doubtful whether any of these were in a simple sense autobiographical. They are not truly comparable to private poetry by women, such as we know from the last two centuries: by their genre, they were intended for performance, in a cultivated, worldly society. This entailed from the outset certain stylizations, certain conventions of discretion, such as the use of fictive cover names *(senhals)*; it meant the creation of a dramatic persona which, even if based upon emotional realities, did not — like much of the topical poetry of the time — dwell on matters that were verifiable historically. Even the most intimate and harrowing moments of declared love in these songs are inseparable from elements of role-playing, elements of «craft» (in both senses of the term).

This is not to suggest that the content of songs such as Castelloza's should be taken lightly. There are indeed eminent scholars of troubadour poetry who see all *cansos* concerned with love in terms of a formal poetic game, a dispay of rhetorical and melodic skills in which content is mostly conventionalized and unimportant. It is true that in Provence (as everywhere in medieval Europe) there were many dexterous versifiers who were not poets. But for those who were poets, those whose lyrics are still worth reading and listening to as poetry today, I believe that what is said is at least as important as how it is said, and that content is fresh, not commonplace.

Castelloza, I would suggest, belongs with these poets, and does so in a way she could never have done if her lyrics were simply (as the older authorities claimed) exercises in a language of love that had been forged and refined by men. On the contrary, the singularity of her thoughts about love is grounded in what must have been a histor-

ically unusual situation. For a woman of Castelloza's time and milieu,
it seems there was no insuperable social obstacle or taboo to prevent
her from loving freely. And, whether it was a matter of poetic feign-
ing or experience, or of both intermingling, Castelloza could even
choose to love actively, rather than play the traditional part of waiting to be chosen. She could declare her feelings without a sense of
shame or guilt: if such a frank declaration from a woman still caused
surprise in her society, it did not of itself bring humiliation or moral
censure. And yet, if the preconditions for a woman's loving had become relatively easy, they did not make the turmoil of the emotions
easier. I am reminded of Ruth Finnegan's observations about
another, externally "permissive", society, where women compose
hauntingly beautiful love songs. Of the Gond women in the hill
forests of central India, Finnegan writes:

> The love-songs are the more heartfelt in that, among the Gond
> ..., the women enjoy much freedom and often live with two or three
> men before they finally choose with whom to settle down. But the
> corollary of this frequent changing of marriage partners ... is a deep
> experience of the sorrows as well as joys of inconstancy in love: the
> poems abound with references to heartbreak, betrayal, and the deceit-
> fulness of lovers ... [6]

Among the Gond women's songs we can find moments of heady
sensual invitation that have parallels particularly in the countess of
Dia:

> O come, my body is alone, come laugh with me, come talk with me.
> Bring mind to mind: clasp heart to heart.
> What of the future? I care not for the past.
> O come, beloved; come, laugh with me,
> Come, talk with me. My body is alone.

But we can also find a rending expression of the situation that
is essentially Castelloza's — a woman's realization that the man she
loves loves another woman better, and that this does not lessen her
love for him but only increases her wistful longing:

> Rust destroys the wheat
> She has destroyed your love for me
> How I long to cover you

---

[6] *The Penguin Book of Oral Poetry*, ed. Ruth Finnegan (London 1978), p. 14 f.;
the two songs are on pp. 20 and 30 respectively.

As the moon is hid by clouds
How I long to take you
All to myself
As a mother takes her child.

Castelloza's songs, like those of the Gond women, have a beauty that is bound up with a willed simplicity. The resources of language and syntax she wishes to draw on are not large: central in her four songs is the word *cor*, 'heart'; around it cluster the heart's oscillating sensations — the experience of disloyal and loyal love, sorrow and joy, dying and reviving, languishing and being healed. Against these, some rare audacious images and expressions emerge in sharp relief. Syntactically striking in the songs is the extraordinary frequency of causal connectives — especially *que* and *car*, 'for' and 'since' — which often seem to be pseudocausal, almost devoid of meaning. It is as if Castelloza were trying over and over to explain the reasons for her anguish, without ever arriving at a firm causal nexus — as if her many attempts at reasoning about her passion revealed themselves, through the syntax itself, as doomed.

The brief *vida* of Castelloza tells us, apart from her region of origin and the names of her husband and her lover, only that she was "very joyful and very well schooled and very beautiful". [7] Let us try to extend that *vida* a little, on the basis of the songs themselves — not in the hope of coming nearer to the historical Castelloza, but heuristically, so as to enter more fully into the imaginative situation she presents. We can say that the Castelloza of the lyrics, while not of lowly origin, is aware of being of lesser birth than the man she loves (let us call him Arman de Breon, as the *vida* does, even if no historical evidence about that name survives). Unlike the countess of Dia, Castelloza has not the confidence to regain confidence with reflections on her own beauty, merit, or position. She has loved Arman — it seems for a long time — and occasionally has felt her love returned by him; but of late he has abandoned her for another, more exalted woman; he has ignored her, or has responded to her signs of unabated love only with cold disdain.

What can she do? She can plead with him, provoke and challenge him, threaten him that she will die. All these impulses form part of Castelloza's emotional world and strategy; yet these are

---

[7] A fuller *vida*, published in 1701, allegedly from a manuscript of 1307, is now generally held to be a forgery: see especially the new edition of Castelloza by William D. Paden, Jr., et al., "The Poems of the *Trobairitz* Na Castelloza," *Romance Philology* 35 (1981): 158-182, at p. 159 f.

known from other lyrical contexts too. But there are far rarer elements in Castelloza's thoughts: a conviction that, because she has been bold enough to give her love so openly, she must abide by the consequences — that is, the love is her creation, and she must find its beauty and fulfilment in herself alone, in what she has fashioned, and in her own most beautiful memories of what had taken place. However keen the temptation for her to subside in sorrow, the love she has created can continue to sustain her, provided she can still hold to her belief in it. That is why, however disloyal Arman may be, Castelloza's affirmations of her own loyalty, of loving unswervingly and in perpetuity, are vital to the experience that she portrays.

The four songs are all in *canso* form: they consist of five or six strophes, in which the rhyme scheme of the first is maintained identically throughout the rest of the composition (*coblas unissonans*). Only the second song has an elaborate strophic form, with verses of several different lengths, and is followed by two four-line envois (*tornadas*), which echo the rhyme scheme of the later part of each strophe. Like many troubadours, Castelloza chose to create her own forms — each of her four is differentiated, at least in minor details, from all others that survive in Provençal lyric. Since close translations can convey almost nothing of the formal aspects of this poetry, I cite one strophe from each of her compositions in the original in the course of my discussion below. At the same time, I would suggest that Castelloza's forms are not among the most accomplished or most exquisite in troubadour lyric, and that she is not among the poets who lose most in a plain translation: what matters above all in her poetry is the meaning, and the movements of thought and emotion. While she has certain moments of spectacular expression, even the homeliest words take on depth by becoming part of her brooding contemplations; in the transitions among her griefs and fears and longings lies the essence of Castelloza's art.

What is unusual formally in the first song is the discrepancy between the opening line of each strophe (which has eight syllables) and the rest (which all have ten). This gives an effect of awkwardness, that may well have had its counterpart in the music: even though the melody does not survive, it is clear that the melodic line of the opening could not have been smoothly paralleled at any later point in the strophe. The poetic-musical form, that is, suggests a deliberate asymmetry, there is something jagged about it, that seems to mirror the protagonist's edgy hesitance — how is she to confront the man who has scorned her?

At first (1. 1), Castelloza seems to say that, for appearances' sake, to keep his reputation high in the world, she will accuse him only in private and speak nothing but good of him in her songs. Yet in this opening lurks an intrinsic irony and subterfuge, for the song, directed in the first place to Arman, is implicitly, like all troubadour lyric, directed to an audience too. The very insistence that she will present him, disloyal as he is, only in the most favorable light, undermines itself because she is already in principle proclaiming this to the world at large. The private occasion of the reproaches *is* the public one of the song. In a similar way, some two generations earlier, Heloise had written to Abelard reprehending his neglect of her, in a letter that, though initially addressed to him, was also consciously meant for posterity, to right misconceptions and present a testimony that was truthful and comprehensive [8]. Claiming that Abelard has forgotten her and fails to comfort her, Heloise writes, "If only I could make up some pretexts for excusing you!" — where the same ambivalence as Castelloza's, the same ironic disclosure that ostensibly is no disclosure but a wholly private rebuke, is at work.

In her next strophe (1. 2), Castelloza contemplates an alternative approach. Could she, who had made herself so vulnerable through giving love openly, not still gain an advantage, and recover Arman's love, by different tactics? Yet what kind of relationship would that lead to? —

> Ja mais no·us tenrai per valen,
> ni·us amarai de bon cor ni per fe,
> tro que veirei si ja·m valria re,
> s'ie·us mostrava cor felon ni enic...
> Non farei ja, qu'eu non vueill puscaz dir
> qu'eu anc ves vos agues cor de faillir —
> c'auriaz pois qualque razonamen
> s'ieu avia ves vos fait faillimen.

> I shall never think of you as deserving,
> or love you with all my heart, loyally,
> before I see if it might serve my turn
> were I to show you a heart hostile and rancorous...
> No, I shan't do it: I don't want to let you say
> that I ever had the heart to fail you —
> as then you would have some justification
> if in any of my acts indeed I failed you.

She raises the possibility of acting as a more calculating woman only to dismiss it instantly — such theatricality would be so out of charac-

---

[8] I have discussed this in detail in my *Women Writers of the Middle Ages* (Cambridge 1984), chap. 5.

ter for her that he would at once perceive her weakness through it, and might take advantage of her the more coldly and selfishly.

In the third strophe and the opening of the fourth, Castelloza reflects on how unconventional she has been in asking a man for love rather than waiting to be asked. In the world's eyes, she has played her cards badly: she has frightened off the man she cares about by her domineering, sermonizing manner. And yet, she affirms, the *bienpensants* are wrong — because (and here we have the first hint of one of Castelloza's pervasive themes) her fulfilment lies far more in herself, and in her poetry, than in her man. Even if he provokes harsh thoughts (*greu pessamen*) in her, because of his failure to respond lovingly, it is her own expression of her outgoing love (*preiar*) that revives her, the poet.

Not that this sublimation is all she seeks. In the moving close of the fourth strophe, she evokes a moment of blissful love experienced with her lover: the way he solaced her then was a revelation such as the uninitiated world can never know. But Castelloza's longing for such an exultant moment to return in reality is inseparable from her conviction that "even from saying this my heart takes joy" — that an imaginative recreation, while in a sense so much less than the real experience, can be preserved untarnished in a way that the real can never be.

Even if he grants her no more happiness of love in waking life, the imaginative realm is not diminished: "through my plaints and lais I'll always have joy in you, my friend" (1. 5). To express her constancy, Castelloza uses playfully the religious turn of phrase *no·m puesc convertir*, 'I can't become a convert'. The word *convertir* had been similarly used, and given special weight by being set at the close of a composition, by Almucs (or Almueis) de Castelnau, the lady to whom Castelloza address the *tornada* of her next song. Almucs had said, in reply to another lady's question, if she would forgive the man who had jilted her:

> Mas si vos faitz lui pentir,
> leu podes mi convertir.

> But if you can lead him to penance,
> you can convert me easily [9].

She would be "converted", that is, back to the role of the gracious beloved, who shows pity on her devotee. But where for Almucs "con-

---

[9] The complete text, with translation and discussion, is in ibid., chap. 4.

version" was conditional upon her lover's repenting, Castelloza affirms that she can never "convert" away from her one love, no matter what her lover's attitude may become.

The hint of a realm in which *convertir* means turning to God is taken up in the astonishing conclusion of Castelloza's song. This conclusion was so daring that it has survived intact in only one of the five manuscripts — in the rest, a tame, banal closing line has been substituted, perhaps because censorship had intervened. Alluding to the troubadour convention of sending songs to the beloved by a messenger, Castelloza declares, no, she will speak to her lover straight — as if to say, her message is too urgent and too grave to be entrusted to another. Men in love had often before Castelloza used the threat that the beloved's hardness will cause their death, and had argued that she would be responsible for that death in the sight of God. Thus, for instance, in some twelfth-century Latin verses a lover exclaims:

> If I die, how will you enter into heaven's delights —
> when the joys of heaven are barred to homicides? [10]

And in the story of Saint Basil, told in a lyrical mode in an early eleventh-century sequence in the Cambridge Songs, the infatuated daughter of Proterius threatens her father, who wanted to refuse her the marriage for which she craved:

> I'll die, father, if now
> I'm not united with that boy...
> If you delay,
> you'll no longer have a daughter,
> but on the day of Judgment
> you'll suffer torment
> as if you'd murdered me. [11].

Again, in Provence, Raimbaut d'Aurenga (d. 1173) had played with the conceit that God might be a rival in love, desiring his beloved and snatching her away from him [12]. But Castelloza's combination of a threat of otherworld torment for her lover with an outra-

---

[10] *Beiträge zur Kunde der lateinischen Literatur des Mittelalters* (2nd ed., Aarau 1905), ed. J. Werner, no. 117 ("Compar nulla tibi"), vv. 18-19 (p. 47).

[11] *Carmina Cantabrigiensia*, ed. Karl Strecker (MGH, 1926), no. 30a, st. 3a (p. 80).

[12] W.T. Pattison, *The Life and Works of the Troubadour Raimbaut d'Orange*, no. 22 (pp. 142-143).

geous, triumphant moment of bravado for herself — "at the Judgment I'll be the more desired" — would be hard to parallel. At the end of time, she claims, the reversal will take place: Arman will be punished for his lovelessness, while she, forsaken on earth, will be longed for supremely. She will be God's beloved — even if in life her intent had been to rouse a very different kind of desire. The song's muted lament here rises to a climax that is both irreverent and thrilling.

The next song again begins in melancholy. The self-sufficiency of the loving heart, finding its quietus in poetry, now seems a delusion — in reality this means only a resignation to disappointment and pain. As Castelloza, composing, recalls her amorous desires, she longs for a human response; while telling of her own state of feeling (2. 1), she suddenly, without a word of introduction, mentions "him": "if he does not accept me soon..."[13] The Provençal word, *retener*, has the specific feudal connotations of accepting as a retainer — Castelloza would gladly be in such a dependent, subservient relation to Arman, rather than be ignored by him.

The plea for his mercy, and the protestations of her own unfaltering loyalty, whatever he may do (2. 2-3), culminate in the pitiable avowal: he deserves a more exalted ladylove than me! This motif (which may well owe something, directly or indirectly, to the affirmations of Ovid's Briseis to Achilles in the *Heroides*) is made circumstantial in Castelloza's fourth song. Here she quickly reverts to a fierce recognition of how deeply — although her loving devotion had been perfect — she has been neglected.

The fifth strophe is perhaps the most difficult to interpret precisely, since none of the other lyrics by *trobairitz* offers a parallel that would help us gauge the tone. Is Castelloza's seizing her lover's glove, and then restoring it, touching, or comic, or both inseparably? —

Si pro·i agues, be·us membrera chantan —
　　aic vostre gan,
　qu'enblei ab gran tremor;
　　　pueis aic paor
　que·i aguesetz dampnage
　d'aicella que·us rete,
　amics — per qu'ieu dese
　l'i tornei; car ben cre
　que no·i ai podiratge!

---

[13] There is a comparable effect in the renowned eleventh-century Latin woman's love lament "Levis exsurgit Zephirus" (text and translation in my *The Medieval Lyric* [2nd ed., London-New York 1977], pp. 92 f.), where the man to whom the whole song is addressed is not mentioned before the final strophe ("Tu saltim, veris gratia...").

If it helped me, I'd remind you in my singing
    that I had your glove,
which, all trembling, I snatched away;
    then I was afraid
you would have trouble for that
from her who holds you as her dependent,
my friend — so that I afterwards
returned the glove; for I am sure
that I have not first claim on it!

The opening — "If it helped me, I'd remind you..." — confronts us with a public-private irony similar to that in the first song: even in half admitting that to recall the embarrassing episode to his mind will not help her regain his love (which should imply that she'll keep silent about it), Castelloza cannot — or pretends she cannot — prevent herself from reminding him: the song, as the conclusion makes explicit, is, after all, addressed to him. There seems to be an element of self-mockery in her account of the glove escapade; at the same time I would see it as linking with the strophe that follows (2. 6) — as a particular, involuntarily comic, instance of the woes that may befall ladies who in loving take the active part, the part that was mostly held to be the prerogative of knights. It is knightly to obtain a love token from a lady (though not to grab it from her, like the young, foolish Parzival, or to accept it and then lose it, like the troubadour Guiraut de Bornelh) [14] — but what if a lady wants a token from the man she loves? Castelloza tells how she deliberately flouted a social norm, and then suddenly felt afraid of having done so. At the close of the strophe, I have the sense that she has moved beyond comedy: the daredevil impulse, she acknowledges, was swiftly followed by humility. Her lover is a "retainer" in the service of another lady, whom she cannot hope to rival; it would be petty for her to discountenance him in that lady's eyes (and — as her allusion to her trembling fear may imply — if she did so, she could be sure of earning his scorn forever after).

The two *tornadas* diverge in tone: in the first, Castelloza may well recall Almucs' song, already mentioned, in which she sets down conditions for relenting to the lover who has been disloyal. Castelloza, by contrast, refuses to make conditions — her love is too absolute for that. And yet a censure of her lover, comparable to those which Almucs had once made, may also lurk behind her paradoxical mode of expression: for how can a man both be the "pillar of honour" and

[14] Guiraut de Bornelh, *Sämtliche Lieder*, ed. A. Kolsen (2 vols., Halle 1910), nos. 25-28.

be fickle to the woman to whom he had once promised lifelong love? In her second *tornada*, composed for him, Castelloza reaffirms that her own love can never become fickle: for her he will always be the "Fair Name" (Bels Noms — the *senhal*, in the customary way, conceals his real identity); and her power to continue living will always depend on remaining confident in the dignity of her ideal.

The third song begins, in its imaginative situation, at a later point in time. Now Castelloza looks back on the days, long since past, when Arman had promised her his unwavering faith. Her thoughts then turn to — in Juliet's words — "I should have been more strange, I must confess..." It was imprudent to have given her heart so candidly, to have been so palpably the seeker and not the sought, hoping to find in Arman a similar openness and refusal to be bound by conventions. The love — or is it simply longing? — becomes even more intense in disappointment: "Indeed I love you the more" (3. 2). And the absence of outgoing love from him creates within herself a space in which love strives for, and at times attains, self-sufficiency: "I consider myself healed, my friend, by my own devotion, when I implore you — for this is right for me" (3. 3).

This strophe closes with an impulse of humility, another intimation that her lover would deserve a more admirable beloved than she. This again points forward to the final song, where the thought becomes most poignant in its specific application, Castelloza affirming that she is willing to take second place to the other woman, to whom her lover has become irrevocably bound. This motif is, to my knowledge, without parallel in medieval love lyric.

Despite all her attempts to make her state of loving into something inwardly complete, that can dispense with solace from the lover outside her, Castelloza is again and again overcome by a sense that this is not wholly possible for her. She does need his comfort still, even if only rarely, in order to keep alive (3. 4); with a bitter irony she admits, her attachment may be only a "minor malady" — yet this too can, if she is neglected totally, bring about her death.

The final strophe of this song is the most problematic:

Tot lo maltrach e·l dampnage
que per vos m'es escaritz
vos fai grasir mos lignage —
e sobre totz mos maritz.
E s'anc fes ves mi faillida,
perdon la·us per bona fe,
e prec que veingnaz a me

depueis que aurez ausida
ma chanson — que·us faz fiansa,
sai trobetz bella semblansa!

All the affliction and harm
that have been my lot because of you,
my birth makes me thank you for these —
and my husband above all.
And if you have ever failed me,
I forgive you, in good faith,
and I beg you to come back to me
after you shall have heard
my song — for, I give you my pledge,
you will find a fair welcome here!

René Lavaud, taking *lignage* in the third line in the concrete sense of "kinsfolk", and emending the reading *vos* of the manuscripts to *me·l*, suggested that Castelloza means, Arman's rank is so high that her relatives, and most of all her husband, welcome her passion for him and approve of her unhappy love affair. William Paden, retaining the manuscript reading *vos*, translates: "My family makes *you* welcome, and especially my husband." Yet this complaisance of family and husband does not sound psychologically convincing, nor is it borne out by any indications elsewhere in the four songs. Should one not see *lignage* as referring to Castelloza's "ancestry" or "birth", which, as her other allusions make clear, is less distinguished than Arman's? Is she not saying: "since I am of lower birth than you, it is inevitable that I should suffer through loving you, and my husband is glad that you do not bring me unalloyed happiness through extramarital love"? This would accord well, also, with the way Castelloza's thought continues — "And if you have ever failed me, I forgive you, in good faith" — leading to the ardent invitation to him to return, with its implicit sensual promise.

The fourth song I would see both as the culmination of the thoughts expressed in the other three and as Castelloza's culminating poetic achievement. Here she adds also the technical refinement of *coblas capfinadas* — the device of echoing the close of one strophe in the opening of the next. The song begins with her melancholy acceptance that she has been deserted, and her thought of dying, since her own love cannot be quenched. Arman does not want to *leave* his new beloved (4. 1), so she herself, spurned, must *leave* this world (4. 2). But then Castelloza's thoughts turn to a very different solution of her woes, to a compromise: if he does not want her as his "dependent", can he not still use welcoming, friendly words to her, instead

of ignoring her disdainfully? His new lady need not be jealous if he
gives Castelloza such crumbs of comfort, and Castelloza in her turn
pledges never again to reproach Arman jealously about his new love-
service, never again to remind him that he had once promised this
service to her "all the days of your life" (compare 3. 1). She is now
ready to accept a subordinate share of his being:

> *Partir* m'en er, mas no·m degna,
> que morta m'an li conssir;
> e pos no·ill platz que·m retegna,
> vueilla·m d'aitant hobesir —
> c'ab sos avinens respos
> me tegna mon cor joyos;
> e ja a sidonz non tir
> s'ie·l fas d'aitant enardir,
> qu'ieu no·l prec per mi que·s tegna
> de *leis* amar ni *servir.*
>
> *Leis serva* — mas mi·n revegna,
> que no·m lais del tot morir...
>
> *Leave* I must, since he disprizes me,
> for troubling thoughts have put me to death;
> and since it does not please him to accept me,
> let him yield to me at least in this —
> that with ungrudging answers from him
> I may keep my heart lifted high;
> and let it not displease his lady
> if I encourage him so far,
> for I don't implore that for my sake he cease
> from loving or *serving her.*
>
> *Serve her* he shall — but return to me from her:
> let him not let me die entirely...

What alternatives could there be? Only to die, or to seek consolation in loving another man. While in 4. 3 Castelloza seems to conjure up this second thought, half beseeching, half threatening — "do
not will me to turn elsewhere" — in the next strophe she readily concedes it is out of the question, since of other knights "I desire not
a single one."

From this the fourth and fifth strophes rise to a climax of erotic
invitation, where Castelloza comes closest to some moments in the
countess of Dia's songs. Where previously (4. 2) she had hoped for
ungrudging responses (*avinens respos*) from Arman, and her assur-
ances that his new lady need have no jealous fears implied that such

respos were a matter of fair words only, now Castelloza admits that her thoughts had been more sensual: she wants no mere courtesies, she wants to embrace him again as a lover. The expressions in 4.4-5 all suggest that in lovemaking, too, hers is the passionately active part — she longs to enfold and embrace him (not to *be* enfolded and embraced) — and at last she arrives at a candid, deeply serious affirmation of her body's hunger, and of how she could be physically revived by his love.

These brief indications of the movements of mind and feeling in the four songs suggest, I think, that there is a dramatic progression extending over the four, and that they can, without forcing the texts, be perceived as an imaginative unity. From the stinging reproaches of disloyalty at the opening of the first song — as if she had an exclusive right to Arman — and from her realization of how foolhardy, in social terms, she has been in offering her love so unreservedly, without ever wondering "if thou think'st I am too quickly won," Castelloza works her way to a resigned recognition of the rival lady, as if to say "Let her have pride of place in your life, but don't shut me out altogether." The unfailing loyalty to Arman, that she has proclaimed throughout her songs, reveals itself at the last as inseparable from a never-ceasing sensual craving for him. In her last song Castelloza in effect invites Arman to share enjoying her love with enjoying that of the woman whom he loves more. She will not try to win him away completely or permanently, if only she can welcome him now and then. Here her motifs come closest to those of Briseis in Ovid (*Heroides* 3) — Briseis who pleads with Achilles to be allowed to remain his concubine, even if she has only the lowliest role in his life, rather than to be parted from him entirely. Castelloza may indeed be drawing upon Briseis' verse-epistle here, recreating it freely, though one cannot be sure from her words alone whether she had firsthand knowledge of the *Heroides* (as seems to me probable with the countess of Dia).

The countess and Almucs de Castelnau were women who (at least in poetry) had chosen their own style of behaviour in love, rather than acquiesce in the expectations of the men they loved. Castelloza also chooses, yet with a sense that in the last resort her mode of choosing is quixotic and fruitless. To be serenely, loyally accepted by the man she loves, on equal terms, is something she can dream about; but in waking existence the acceptance is only momentary, the serenity quickly changes into tormented uncertainty. Yet if on one occasion her lover solaced her in her sorrow (1. 4), even the thought that he might do so again helps to make existence bearable. I do not think, like the recent editor, Paden, that Castelloza's attitude "borders on masochism... in which satisfaction comes from suffering or humiliation apart from any sexual pleasure [15]". It is the respite from misery, however brief, that counts for Castelloza, as well as the sense that, even if she has been deserted, it is better to have known joy such as hers than to have shrunk away from giving her love spontaneously. And at the close of the fourth song, it is clearly in moments of sexual pleasure that Castelloza still seeks her contentment, though she is also aware, realistically, that this contentment will always be fugitive.

At the same time, Castelloza knows a satisfaction that is not directly sexual — yet again the source of this satisfaction is not in suffering or humiliation: it is in poetry. Composing helps make abandonment livable. To create something beautiful out of loneliness, to wrest some recollections out of the anguish — this the loving woman, the projection of the poet Castelloza, sees as her reason for existence. While often, in dramatic hyperbole or in threat, she speaks of dying, she is also aware that to languish irrevocably would be an admission of failure: it would cancel once and for all what she has proclaimed to be her poetic task — the affirming of her immutable devotion. So each thought of dying for love leads back to reviving thoughts — reproachful, or pleading, or magnanimous, or erotic.

As a poet, Castelloza is no virtuoso: her language is intently, even narrowly, concentrated; she does not create dazzling forms in the way, for instance, of her somewhat older contemporary, Raimbaut de Vaqueiras. Yet she makes articulate a range of thoughts and imaginings that no man among the troubadours had expressed; she uncovers new inner landscapes of the loving mind; and her voice has a timbre that, once one has listened to her attentively, could not be mistaken for that of any other poet of the age.

[15] Paden et al., p. 165.

Castelloza's Songs

In my translations, I have used as primary basis the new edition by William Paden and his collaborators. Paden has followed principally the manuscript N, which preserves some important readings unknown to the four other manuscripts and alone preserves Castelloza's fourth song. However, in the verses signalled below, I have reverted to the readings of René Lavaud (who kept chiefly to manuscript A for the first three songs), because I believe that they remain textually preferable. While Lavaud, in *Les troubadours cantaliens*, based his text of Castelloza's first three songs on Schultz's *Die provenzalischen Dichterinnen*, he added valuable corrections and a series of notes, and also gave the text of the fourth song. In my notes to the songs, where my translation is based on Lavaud's text and not Paden's, the lines in question are cited from Lavaud, with the initial L., and occasionally with a brief indication of why they have been preferred (a full textual discussion would exceed the scope of this essay). Punctuation in the strophes cited above and in the translations is my own; it does not always match either the Paden or the Lavaud edition.

1

[1]   My friend, if I found you welcoming,
modest ¹ and gracious and compassionate,
I'd love you well — whilst now I call to mind
that I find you bad to me, contemptible and proud.
And yet I make songs so as to let others hear
of your good character — for I cannot bear
not to have you praised by all the world,
even when you most hurt me and make me angriest.

[2]   I shall never think of you as deserving,
or love you with all my heart, loyally,
before I see if it might serve my turn ²

---

¹ It is also possible that *umil* is here used in the specifically courtly sense of "generous in feeling, capable of showing mercy, benign" (see the excursus "The Concept *umiltà*" in my *Medieval Latin and the Rise of European Love-Lyric*, [2nd ed., 2 vols., Oxford 1968], vol. 1, pp. 158-162).

² Tro que veirai si ja-m valria re, L.

were I to show you a heart hostile and rancorous...
No, I shan't do it: I don't want to let you say
that I ever had the heart to fail you—
as then you would have some justification [3]
if in any of my acts indeed I failed you.

[3]   I know well this way is right for me,
even if everyone says it is unseemly
for a lady to implore a knight on her own account
and to preach at him always, at such length.
But those who say this have no means to judge —
for I want to prove, rather than surrender by dying [4],
that in imploring I am sweetly refreshed,
when I implore the one who makes me think harsh thoughts [5].

[4]   Whoever reproaches me for loving you
is quite mad, since it accords with me so gently —
one who speaks thus does not know how it is with me:
he's never seen you with the eyes with which I saw you
when you told me not to sorrow any more —
for, any moment, it could come about
that once again I'd have the joy of that.
Even from saying this my heart takes joy.

[5]   I set all other love at naught,
and you must know that no joy ever sustains me
except for yours, that lightens me and revives
where most anguish and most harm beset me.
And I believe through my plaints and lais I will always
have joy in you, my friend — I can't become a convert —
nor do I have joy, or expect any solace,
save insofar as I'll gain it while I sleep.

[6]   I don't know how to confront you after this,
for by fair means and by foul I have probed
your impassive heart — mine does not weary of the probing.
And I send no messenger — it is I myself who tell you,
and I *shall* die, if you will not lighten me

---

[3] Qu'auriatz pois qualque razonamen, L.

[4] Qu'ieu vuoill proar, enans que-me lais morir, L.

[5] Quan prec cellui don ai greu pessamen, L. (the reading *greu* is corroborated by *douz* in the previous verse).

with any joy; and if you let me die,
you'll commit sin, and be in torment for it,
and at the Judgment I'll be the more desired!

2

[1] I ought not to have any desire to sing,
    for the more I sing
the worse it goes with my loving,
    as in me lament
and weeping make their lodging,
for I have pledged my heart and myself
to a thankless service,
and if he does not accept me soon,
I have waited overlong.

[2] Oh my fair friend, at least show a fair face
    to me before
I die of sorrowing,
    for those in love
accuse you of being barbarous,
since no joy comes to me
from you — though I don't recant for that
from loving in good faith,
at all times, heart unwavering.

[3] For you I shall never have a heart truant
    or full of wiles,
even if I find that makes you worse to me —
    as I hold this loyally
in great honour in my heart.
Yet more, I reflect — when I call to mind
the prized qualities that inform you —
and I realize that a lady
of higher station is right for you.

[4] Since I first saw you I have done your bidding,
    and in spite of all,
my friend, found you none the better inclined;
    no messenger of yours
ever implores me, or reports
that you're turning your bridle my way.
You do nothing at all, my friend!

And since joy does not bear me up,
the pain almost makes me rage.

[5] If it helped me, I'd remind you in my singing
   that I had your glove,
which, all trembling, I snatched away;
   then I was afraid
you would have trouble for that
from her who holds you as her dependent,
my friend — so that I afterwards
returned the glove; for I am sure
that I have not first claim on it!

[6] I realize that knights work their own undoing,
   for they beseech
ladies, more than ladies do them —
   they have no other
riches or sovereignty than in beseeching.
So, when a lady decides
to love, it is she who must beseech
the knight, if in him she sees
prowess and knightliness.

[7] Lady Almucs [6], I still
love the source of my hurt,
for he, pillar of honour,
has a fickle heart towards me.

[8] Fair Name, I don't recant
my loving you forever,
for in this loving I find good faith,
always, and steadiness of heart.

3

[1] A very long absence you will have made it,
my friend, since you parted from me,
and to me it seems cruel and barbarous,
for you swore to me and pledged

---

[6] The unique manuscript H of Almucs de Castelnau's song gives her name as
Almucs both in the *vida* and in the song; manuscript N of Castelloza's "Ja de chan-
tar" has Almurs. The other manuscripts have various forms; no manuscript gives the
form Almueis, which is an editorial conjecture.

that all the days of your life
you would have no lady but me;
and if you are caught up with another,
you have killed me and betrayed me —
for I had my hope in you,
that you would love me without need of doubting.

[2]   Handsome friend, with high longing
I loved you, since you delighted me,
and I know I committed a folly,
for you have recoiled from me the more for that [7],
since with you I never used subterfuge [8] —
and so you render me evil for good!
Indeed I love you the more — I do not recant that —
but love has seized me so fiercely
that I believe I can never have
well-being without your loving.

[3]   I shall have set a wretched precedent
for other women who love,
since it is usual that men send a message
and words that are sifted and chosen well.
As for me, I consider myself healed,
my friend, by my own devotion,
when I implore you — for this is right for me,
since even a worthier woman is enriched
if from you she wins some satisfaction
of kissing or close company.

[4]   Let me be cursed if ever I had a fickle
heart towards you, or behaved flightily!
No lover, however exalted,
was ever coveted by me.
No, I am pensive and filled with pain
as you do not recall my love —
if no joy comes to me from you,
you will soon find my life is finished:
for, with a minor malady,

---

[7] Que plus m'en etz escaritz, L. (the sense cannot support *encarzitz*, 'made dear').

[8] Qu'anc non fis vas vos ganchida, L.

a lady dies, if no one frees her from it [9].

[5]   All the affliction and harm
that have been my lot because of you,
my birth makes me thank you for these [10] —
and my husband above all.
And if you have ever failed me,
I forgive you, in good faith,
and I beg you to come back to me
after you shall have heard
my song — for, I give you my pledge,
you will find a fair welcome here! [11]

4

[1]   From now on I'll not care to exult
in joy that comes to me from love,
for I do not believe he cherishes me,
he who never wished to hear
my fair words or my songs —
and yet there never was a season [12]
that I could do without him.
No, I fear I shall have to die of it,
since I see he lives with another woman
whom, for my sake, he does not want to *leave*.

[2]   *Leave* I must, since he disprizes me,
for troubling thoughts have put me to death;
and since it does not please him to accept me,
let him yield to me at least in this —
that with ungrudging answers from him
I may keep [13] my heart lifted high;

---

[9] Mor dompna, s'om tot no-il lanssa, L. I am not happy about Paden's ingenious *s'om no cal lansa*, 'if no man apply a lancet' — less because of the conjecture that *lansa*, 'lance,' can also mean 'lancet' than because I know no parallel for *calar*, or *caler*, meaning 'to apply'.

[10] Me-l fai grazir mos linhatge, L. (compare his notes, vol. 3, p. 88 f.), but this emendation may not be necessary — see discussion above.

[11] Sai trobetz bella semblansa, L.

[12] Ni anc no fon la sazos, L.

[13] Grammatically, in this verse (*me tegna mon cor joyos*), *tegna* could be the first or third present subjunctive of *tener*; I prefer to take it as first person here (Lavaud and Paden take it as third).

and let it not displease his lady
if I encourage him so far,
for I don't implore that for my sake he cease
from loving or *serving her.*

[3]   *Serve her* he shall — but return to me from her:
let him not let me die entirely —
for I fear it will extinguish me,
that love of him, by which he makes me languish.
Ah, my friend, valiant and good
(for you are the best that ever was),
do not will me to turn elsewhere,
since you wish to do and say nothing to me —
so that one day I steel myself
against loving or *welcoming you.*

[4]   I *welcome you,* whatever may befall me —
all the affliction and cares;
and let no knight take an interest
in me, since I desire not a single one.
Fair friend, fiercely I long for you,
you on whom I keep both eyes fixed;
and it delights me to gaze on you,
for I could never single out another so fair.
I pray to God that with my arms I may enfold you,
for no other can make me *rich.*

[5]   *Rich* am I, if only you bring to mind
how I could come into a place
where I would kiss you and embrace you,
for, with that, new life could come
into my body, which you make yearn
for you greatly and covetously.
My friend, do not let me die:
since I cannot withhold myself from you,
give me a loving look, to revive me
and to kill my cares!

15

DIDO'S LAMENT: FROM MEDIEVAL LATIN LYRIC
TO CHAUCER*

In the earlier part of this study I should like to characterize certain medieval perceptions of Dido [1], using mainly twelfth-century sources, in order to show how far the Dido in these diverges from the heroine familiar through Vergil and Ovid. After that, I shall turn to the Dido whom Chaucer evokes in his "House of Fame" and "Legend of Good Women", and shall ask, to what extent does Chaucer in his presentations lay stress on medieval perceptions as against Vergilian and Ovidian ones?

Among the love-songs in the "Carmina Burana" comes a small group of poems that touch upon the matter of Troy. Outstanding among these is the lament put in the mouth of Dido [2]:

---

* *Kontinuität und Wandel. Lateinische Poesie von Naevius bis Baudelaire, Franco Munari zum 65. Geburtstag*, ed. U.J. Stache, W. Maaz, F. Wagner (Weidmannsche Verlagsbuchhandlung, Hildesheim 1986), pp. 364-390.

This essay is based on the first of the Matthews Lectures, that I gave at Birkbeck College, London, in February 1983. I am grateful to Margaret Alexiou and Jill Mann for some valuable comments.

When the essay was in press, Dieter Schaller kindly referred me to the article of I. Dauser, Pyrois circulus, in: ALMA 39 (1979) 95-102, who interprets the phrase in CB 100, st. 7, as "der Feuerkreis (der Unterwelt)".

[1] María Rosa Lida's "Dido y su defensa en la literatura española", in: *Revista de Filología Hispánica* 4 (1942) 209-252, 313-382, has a fine range of medieval reference and some outstanding insights; cf. also L.B. Hall, Chaucer and the Dido-and-Aeneas Story, in: *Mediaeval Studies* 25 (1963) 148-159, and M.L. Lord, Dido as an Example of Chastity: the Influence of Example Literature, in: *Harvard Library Bulletin* 17 (1969) 22-44, 216-232.

[2] The text of this "planctus" was last critically edited by O. Schumann (= Sn), *Carmina Burana I 2, Die Liebeslieder* (Heidelberg 1941), no. 100 (pp. 135-138), from three MSS — B: Codex Buranus (München Clm 4660), fol. 75ʳ/ᵛ; L: Linz Studienbibl. CCIII 6 (from Garsten), fols. 1ʳ/60ᵛ; M: München Clm 4598 (from Benediktbeuern), fol. 61ʳ/ᵛ (with neums). Textually, Sn attached most weight to M. The edition given below differs from his in taking B as the base MS, correcting it where necessary with the help of L and M, which have also been collated afresh. I believe

1	O decus, o Libie regnum, Kartaginis urbem —	Oh glory, kingdom of Libya, city of Carthage —
	O lacerandas fratris opes, o Punica bella!	a brother's wealth fated to be torn asunder, oh Punic conflicts!

2a   O *duces* Frigios, o dulces advenas — Oh Phrygian captains, gentle strangers
      quos, tanto tempore — whom, homeless
      dispersos, equore — so long, upon the ocean
       iam hyemps septima — seven winters
    iactaverat — had tossed,
      ob odium — because of Juno's
        Iunonis — — hate —
         Cillea rabies — the fury of Scylla,
         Ciclopum sanies, — the Cyclops' venom,
          Celeno pessima — most evil Celaeno
    transduxerat — had brought you
      ad solium — to Dido's
        Didonis — — throne —

2b   Qui me crudelibus exercent odiis, — they who now plague me with cruel hatred,
       arentis Libie — these shipwrecked men whom,
        post casum Frigie — after Troy's fall,
         quos *regno* naufragos — I'd welcomed in the kingdom
    exceperam: — of parched Libya:

it is desirable to emend B only in the following verses (the emendations are italicized in my text):
2a, 1 *O dulces* B (*O duces* LMSn); 2b, 4 *terre* B (*regno* LMSn); 3, 4 *de* B (*ue* LMSn); 4a, 3 *multo* BMSn (*uno* L); 7, 11 *desere swaves* (for *s.d.*) B (*desere suaves* LMSn). In 3,1, I have twice restored the Old French feminine form *dolant*(e) (*dolant* BLMSn). In the following verses I adopt the B reading, as against Sn's choice (orthographic variants are not mentioned here):
1, 2 *bella* B (*regna* LMSn); 3, 8 *ob* B (*propter* L *per* MSn); 4a, 5 *iam* B (*nam* LMSn); 4a, 11 *heu* B (*hai* MSn *prohdolor uixi nimis* L); 4b, 8 *fouet* B (*fouit* LMSn); 5b, 6 *abhorret* BL (*exhorret* MSn); 6b, 6 *fers* B (*fer* LMSn); 6b, 7 *tanti causa* B (*causa tanti* LMSn); 7, 16 *sis* BL (*sed* MSn); 7, 17 *et* B (*sis* LMSn).
(For a fuller statement of variants in LM, see Sn pp. 137-138).
Punctuation is my own (that at 2a, 2ff. is suggested by *Aen*. III 197, *dispersi iactamur gurgite vasto*: parallels in the surrounding verses bear out that the poet had this Vergilian passage in mind). My line-arrangement is intended to reflect the architectonics of the verse as precisely as possible. The neums in M, as my colleague Susan Rankin kindly confirmed for me, show that there is a certain amount of musical variation even in the symmetrical pairs of half-strophes. In 2a and 2b, moreover, it will be noted that there are light variations, or asymmetries, in the rhyme-scheme also, though the rhythmic and melodic form remains substantially the same.
In a letter of 11.4.83, Bernhard Bischoff (who generously lent me photographs of the L text) modified Sn's dating of the hands in L and M, setting L in s. XIII[1] and M "von der Schrift her s. XII[3/4] möglich, auf jeden Fall s. XII".

me miseram! —	woe is me,
quid feci,	what have I done,
que meis emulis,	subjecting men of Tyre
ignotis populis	and Sidon
et genti barbare	to my enemies,
Sydonios	to unknown peoples,
ac Tyrios	to a barbarous
subieci?	race?

3 Hai dolant⟨e⟩, hai dolant⟨e⟩,   Ah my grieving, ah my grieving —
iam volant carbasa: now their sails fly,
iam nulla spes Didonis!   now Dido's hope has gone!
Ve Tyriis colonis!   Woe upon you, Tyrians,
Plangite, Sydonii,   lament, Sidonians,
quod in ore gladii   that on the sword's edge
deperii,   I die,
ob amorem Frigii   for love of that Phrygian
predonis!   plunderer!

4a Eneas, hospes Frigius,   Aeneas, the Phrygian guest,
Iarbas, hostis Tyrius,   and Iarbas, the Tyrians' foe,
uno me temptant crimine,   assail me with the same wrong,
sed vario discrimine: yet with different perils:
iam sicientis Libie   now the queen of thirsty Libya
regina spreta linquitur,   is abandoned, spurned,
et thalamos Lavinie   and the Trojan guest
Troianus hospes sequitur!   sets out to wed Lavinia!
Quid agam misera?   What shall I, wretched, do?
Dido regnat altera!   Another Dido reigns!
Heu vixi nimium —   Ah I have lived too long —
mors agat cetera!   let death fulfil the rest!

4b Deserta siti regio   A land laid waste by thirst
me gravi cingit prelio: surrounds me with relentless war,
fratris me terret feritas   I am affrighted by my brother's fierceness
et Numidum crudelitas.   and the Numidians' cruelty.
Insultant hoc proverbio: With this byword they attack me:
'Dido se fecit Helenam —   'Dido has made herself a Helen —
regina nostra gremio   our queen warms a Trojan
Troianum fovet advenam!'   stranger in her lap!'
Gravis condicio,   It is a grievous plight —
furiosa ratio,   reason runs mad,
si mala perferam   if for my kindness
pro beneficio!   I suffer wrongs!

5a Anna, vides   Anna, do you see
que sit fides   what it means, the loyalty
deceptoris perfidi?   of this base deceiver?
Fraude ficta   By a false fraud
me relicta,   deserting me,

	regna fugit Punica!	he flees the Punic realms!
	Nil sorori	There's nothing for your sister
	nisi mori	left to do save die,
	soror, restat, unica.	one-and-only sister.

5b

	Sevit Scilla,	Scylla rages,
	nec tranquilla	and the ocean
	se promittunt equora.	does not roll calm —
	Solvit ratem,	he is setting sail,
	tempestatem	the Phrygian,
	nec abhorret Frigius!	he does not shudder before the storm!
	Dulcis soror,	Sweet sister,
	ut quid moror,	why do I delay,
	aut quid cessat gladius?	why does my sword hold back?

6a

	Fulget sydus Orionis,	Orion flashes out,
	sevit hyemps Aquilonis,	the North wind riots,
	Scilla regnat equore —	on the ocean Scylla reigns.
	tempestatis tempore,	In a time of tempest,
	Palinure,	Palinurus,
	non secure	your fleet can't safely
	classem solvis littore.	leave the shore!

6b

	Solvit ratem dux Troianus —	The Trojan captain frees his ship —
	solvat ensem nostra manus	let our hand free the sword,
	in iacturam sanguinis.	that the blood shall spill.
	Vale, flos Kartaginis!	Flower of Carthage, farewell!
	Hec, Enea,	Aeneas, this
	fers trophea,	is your victory's prize —
	tanti causa criminis!	you, the source of such great guilt!

7

	O dulcis anima,	Oh gentle soul,
	vite spes unica,	one-and-only hope of life,
	Flegetontis,	the abysm of Phlegethon,
	Acharontis	of Acheron,
	latebras	the horrendous
	ac tenebras	darkness
	mox adeas	shall soon be
	horroris,	your journey's goal,
	nec Pyrois te cyrculus moretur.	nor shall the fiery sun-disk[3] stay you.
	Eneam sequere,	Follow Aeneas,
	nec *swaves desere*	do not forsake
	illecebras	Amor's soft

[3] While in classical Latin *Pyrois* is used substantivally, as a name either for Mars, the "fiery" planet, or for one of the horses of the sun (Ovid, *Metam.* II 153), here it is used adjectivally (like Gk. πυρόεις), to qualify *cyrculus:* cf. Martianus Capella, *De Nupt.* II 194: *sublevatam [Philologiam] Pyrois circulus immoratur, in quo Iovis fuerat maximus filiorum.*

amoris,	allurements,
nec dulces nodos Veneris	do not destroy Venus's
perdideris:	sweet bonds:
sis nostri concia	aware of grief,
et nuntia	be herald
doloris.	of our grief!

The song is noteworthy not only for the poet's conception of Dido but for his imaginatively agile use of language and his mastery of an unusual lyrical form. It survives in three manuscripts: the Codex Buranus, copied probably in Southern Tirol in the decade 1220-30, and two codices of the later twelfth century and the first half of the thirteenth, one Bavarian, one Austrian. These, though frequently offering a less good text than the Buranus, can still help correct it in some readings. Yet, notwithstanding the exclusively Austrian and South German transmission, the song was composed in the French — or perhaps Anglo-Norman — world. This is clear from the strangely spelt words *hai dolant* (v.l. *achidolant*) that occur twice at the opening of the third strophe: these baffled all older scholars, but those responsible for the recent bilingual edition have accepted my suggestion (of 1965), that the words represent an attempt by German-speaking copyists to render Old French *ahi dolante* — where *ahi* is a vernacular exclamation of pain and *dolante* the feminine form of the participial adjective "grieving" [4]. The expression is found in several French romances, beginning with Chrétien de Troyes. The manuscript situation, as well as certain formal aspects, such as the poet's free conjunction of full and half rhymes, suggest to me that he was composing in the earlier twelfth century, probably in the decades 1130-50.

He was composing in the form that in French lyrical tradition came to be known as "lai lyrique" and in German as "Leich". Unlike the "classical" sequence, where each pair of half-strophes is syllabically parallel, the "lai lyrique" allowed freer developments: thus here the symmetrical pairs of half-strophes are varied by others that are left without formal counterparts. In such variation the "lai lyrique" rejoined the techniques of the so-called "archaic" sequences, which are well attested in Latin in the ninth century but only sparsely thereafter, and are also attested in a ninth-century vernacular, in the

[4] Cf. P. Dronke, The Beginnings of the Sequence, in: *PBB* (Tüb.) 77 (1965) 58, n. 39; *Carmina Burana: Zweisprachige Ausgabe* (Zürich/München 1974) p. 924; A. Tobler/E. Lommatzsch, *Altfranz. Wörterbuch* III 1992, s.v. *dolent*, F. Godefroy, *Lexique* IX, 404.

renowned Old French sequence about St. Eulalia [5]. Another significant link with the "archaic" sequences lies in Dido's passionate opening: it is in two classical hexameters, and moments in hexameters and other classical metres occur likewise in the ninth-century compositions in this form [6].

The number of surviving profane pieces in the form is small in Latin even in the twelfth century, and small in French and German before the thirteenth. Yet literary allusions to themes that were treated in the mode of "lai" or "Leich" enable us to fill some of the gaps at least in thought. To recall the allusion that is most relevant here: in Gottfried of Strassburg's "Tristan", what Tristan, disguised as a minstrel, plays for his beloved Isôt and for Gandîn is *den leich von Didône* [7]. Gottfried's use of the technical term makes clear that what Tristan played (or was thought to play) was in a form closely similar to that of our Latin "Leich". Through this Latin text, that is, we can almost recapture what Tristan performed for Isôt. The performance of the Latin piece, too, will probably have been by a soloist, accompanying himself or herself on harp or lute. (The melody, unfortunately, survives only in neums, and cannot be completely recovered).

The language of this Latin "planctus" shows a pervasive love of word-play of many kinds, from simple juxtaposition of words allied in sound and divergent in meaning (st. 2a *O duces... o dulces;* 4a *hospes... hostis*), or parallelism in which the same word is used with different senses (6b *Solvit ratem... solvat ensem*), to the use of "weighted" single words that have more than a single meaning. Thus at the close of 4a, in the words *mors agat cetera*, the final word, *cetera*, is one commonly used in twelfth-century Latin verse to apply to sexual consummation (the witty euphemism goes back to Ovid's "Amores" [8]). This sexual sense, which cannot but be present here, itself lends erotic colour to *mors*: Dido is bent upon a love-death. So,

---

[5] Cf. H. Spanke, *Studien zu Sequenz, Lai und Leich* (Darmstadt 1977), esp. "Sequenz und Lai" (pp. 146-202); J. Handschin, Über Estampie und Sequenz, in: *Zeitschrift für Musikwissenschaft* 12 (1929) 1-20, 13 (1930) 113-132.

[6] See P. von Winterfeld, Rhythmen- und Sequenzstudien, in: *ZfdA* 45 (1901) esp. p. 143. Hexameters also occur very frequently in the midst of syllabically free forms, in liturgical tropes from the ninth century to the eleventh: a fine range of instances can now be studied in "Corpus Troporum", I, III, and IV (Studia Latina Stockholmiensia XXI, XXV, XXVI, Stockholm 1975 ff.).

[7] *Tristan* (ed. Ranke-Krohn) 13347.

[8] I 5, 25 (*Cetera quis nescit?*); cf. e. g. *Die Lieder Walters von Châtillon in der Hs. 351 von St. Omer,* ed. K. Strecker, Berlin 1925, no. 17, st. 7 (*Sed quis nescit cetera?*), or Peter of Blois, *Carmina Burana* no. 63, st. 4b (*de cetero / ad alia / dum traducor studia*).

too, her words just before this — *Dido regnat altera* — can allude not
only to Lavinia, who (proleptically) has usurped Dido's rightful place,
but also to Dido's being beside herself — in madness, or the erotic
desperation that impels her into death. Again at the close, when
Dido bids her soul not to forsake Amor's soft allurements or Venus's
sweet bonds — that is, urges herself to be strong enough to affirm
her love unwavering till the last — Amor and Venus are at the same
time metonymies for love and dramatic reminders: for it was Amor
who took the shape of Aeneas' son Ascanius, to play sensually with
Dido and to arouse her, and Venus is not only the love Dido ex-
periences but also the divine mother, who brought Aeneas forth and
who helped to determine Dido's tragedy.

None of these subtleties in the language is mere virtuosity. The
artifices reflect and bear out the controlling paradox that underlies
the composition and lends the language its distinctive timbre: in this
Dido's thought, the victim of fate has become the persecutor. The
Trojans, so long exposed to Scylla, to the Cyclops and Celaeno, have
become in spirit like these monstrosities. They are the *barbari* — barbarous in their heartlessness. Aeneas, the guest (*hospes*) of Dido's
kingdom, and of her body, is also the plunderer (*predo*) of her kingdom and her body. Because of this, Dido will die, and the Tyrians
and Sidonians over whom she reigns will be rulerless. Through having sheltered victims, they themselves will become victimised, sub-
jected to Dido's nearer enemies and ultimately to the unknown race.

This poet was deeply familiar with Vergil's treatment of Dido
and with Ovid's; yet he felt free to develop her character afresh, crea-
tively, in ways that differ from — and even reverse — what he knew
from his sources. To begin with a small but revealing detail: neither
of the ancient poets had developed the imagery of thirst. In the "lai",
the insistence on the parchedness of Libya — *regnum arentis Libie*
(2b), *deserta siti regio* (4b) [9] — evokes an inner as well as an outer
landscape. Dido herself is the "spurned queen of thirsty Libya" (*sicientis Libie / regina spreta*, 4a): her land is thirsty, as she is athirst
for love. Her land, and she in her sexuality, are bereft of the life-
giving moisture that they need; Dido and her land are symbolically
one.

This Dido, unlike Vergil's, is compassionate. She has no sadistic
fantasies such as Vergil ascribes to her — of tearing Aeneas apart or
serving his little son as a banquet to him [10]. Here Dido, even while

[9] This phrase, admittedly, is from *Aen.* IV 42, but there it has purely geographi-
cal reference.
[10] *Aen.* IV 600-602.

she thinks of Aeneas as her betrayer, trembles for his safety on the ocean. She has no thought of vengeance on Aeneas or his descendants: insofar as she glimpses the future, it is not, as in Vergil, looking towards an endless hostility between her nation and that of her lover; rather, she sees Carthage as fated to yield to Rome, tragically, even as she was fated to yield to Aeneas.

The long final strophe is farthest of all from Vergil: Dido's only purpose at the moment of dying is to be reunited with Aeneas in the otherworld. In Ovid, where even more than in Vergil Dido dwells on the mortal danger to Aeneas of the storms at sea, she imagines the sea as punishing Aeneas with death because of his infidelity:

> it is not good for those who have broken faith to tempt the ocean — that is the place which exacts the penalty for perfidy... [11]

There is no such threat in the medieval "planctus". The poet, though he owes some of his atmosphere to Ovid, is prepared to discard whatever does not suit his own intent, and once at least he reverses Ovid's thought as audaciously as he does Vergil's. For him it is Aeneas whom Dido follows passionately, racing into death, whilst in Ovid it is to Sichaeus, her dead husband, that Dido cries out:

> *Nulla mora est: venio, venio, tibi debita coniux!* (VII 105)
> There's no delay — I come, I come! I, wife who am rightly yours.

And in the implacable underworld encounter depicted in the "Aeneid", Dido's shade refuses even to look at Aeneas when he pleads with her: she flees back (*refugit*) to Sichaeus, whose love — Vergil assures — still matches hers [12]. In the "planctus", Sichaeus is not once remembered.

Ovid evokes a softer emotional world for Dido than the Vergilian; yet in Ovid too it is Dido's *accusation* of Aeneas that remains dominant and that concludes the poem in the "Heroides". In the twelfth-century "lai", by contrast, Dido at the close is not accuser but "love's martyr": it is here that we can see why Chaucer could superscribe her tale, in the "Legend of Good Women", with the words *Incipit legenda Didonis martiris* — where *legenda* (a non-classical feminine singular) has the specific sense of "saint's life" [13].

The composer of this "lai", in his challenges to the Vergilian

---

[11] *Her.* VII 57-58.
[12] *Aen.* VI 469-474.
[13] Cf. *Lexicon Latinitatis Medii Aevi*, s.v.; *Novum Glossarium*, s.v.

narrative, was by no means an isolated innovator. A northern French poet who, inspired partly by his composition, produced another lament of Dido, *Anna soror*, in "lai lyrique" form [14], probably in the late twelfth century, again effects an amazing transformation. His Dido, at the moment of her suicide — a scene for which the principal source is Vergil — behaves in a way that wholly contradicts Vergil's account. In the "Aeneid", Dido has mounted her pyre and killed herself with Aeneas' sword before anyone, even Anna, can reach her. In the "planctus" *Anna soror*, by contrast, Dido is suddenly terrified of the pyre that she has built; she is afraid even to use the sword, much as she longs to; so she bids Anna — who must at this moment be beside her — to draw the sword and dispatch her:

Ipsa me perdidi —	I have destroyed myself —
quid Friges arguo?	why accuse Phrygians?
Merori subdidi	I have surrendered my life
vitam perpetuo.	to everlasting sorrow.
Heu me miseram:	Alas, wretched as I am,
ign*i* [15] credideram,	I'd trusted in fire:
*n*unc [16] uri metuo!	now, to be burnt, I am afraid.
Quanta sit sencio	I feel how grievous
mei [17] condicio	will be the state
supplicii,	of my torment,
ni gladii	if I do not enlist
fruar obsequio.	the service of the sword.
O luce clarior,	You, brighter than day's light,
Anna, pars anime,	Anna, half of my soul,
his quibus crucior	release me from these evils
me malis adime!	that torture me!
Quousque paciar?	How long shall I suffer?
Ne semper moriar	Lest I be forever a-dying,
me semel perime!	kill me once and for all!

Once more a dramatically central point is made by way of a word-play — *igni credideram*: Dido had trusted in love's fire, and she

[14] Ed. O. Schumann, Eine mittelalterliche Klage der Dido, in: *Liber Floridus [Fs. Paul Lehmann]* (St. Ottilien 1950) pp. 319-328; A. Wilmart, in: *Mediaeval and Renaissance Studies* 4 (1958) 35-37. In the strophes cited above, I have gone back to the MS — Oxford, Bodley Add. A 44, s. XIII[init.], fol. 30[r]/[v], noting my divergences from these two editions.

[15] *igne* MS, Schumann; *igni* em. Wilmart.

[16] *hunc* MS, edd.; *metuo: mutuo* em. Schumann.

[17] *mei* MS; *mea* Schumann, *mihi* Wilmart.

had trusted that the physical funeral-pyre would conclude her love-death splendidly. But then comes her moment of hesitation, of weakness, and precisely through that unheroic weakening this Dido is revealed in her most lovable aspect. Here her death is neither the terrible one evoked by Vergil nor the erotic consumation evoked in *O decus, o Libie regnum:* it is a release for Dido from the measureless, hopeless love that had become unbearable.

A third Latin lyric, *Troie post excidium,* also of the twelfth century but perhaps of German provenance [18], is again notable for its deliberate antithesis to what Vergil says. It is an exultant celebration of Dido's love; it concludes with the love-union in the cavern and does not look beyond. As in *O decus, o Libie regnum,* there is intellectual verbal play — but here so as to establish a witty complement to the poet's solemn intimation of universal love. He conjures up the love-making of Dido and Aeneas by scholastic-erotic metaphors, such as we know from Alan of Lille, or much later from Shakespeare's first comedies: Aeneas "shows his three propositions and makes his syllogism; she presses against it with opposing motions". Then suddenly these lighthearted allusions to the sexual act pass into an almost Boethian glimpse of cosmic love. The lyric concludes:

Et sic amborum in coniugio leta	And so, blissful in the conjunction of these two,
resplenduit etherea regia —	the palace of the ether grew resplendent —
nam ad amoris gaudia rident, clarescunt omnia!	for, at the joys of love, all things smile, grow radiant.

Where in Vergil Aeneas and Dido in the cavern sheltered from a thunderstorm — a storm which mirrored that love's turbulence, mirrored Dido's terror of dishonouring her husband's memory and the darkness of a union condemned to have no future — here in the Latin lyric the lovers in their bliss change the face of the heavens: it is they who re-establish an elemental serenity.

To return to the first of our Latin compositions, *O decus, o Libie regnum:* what is the secret of the way the Latin poet has transformed the classical materials?

By composing a "planctus", a lyrical lament in which Dido

---

[18] *Carmina Burana* no. 98 (Codex Buranus fols. 73ᵛ-74ʳ). In the verses cited above, I accept the MS reading *regia,* and arrange the lines differently from Schumann, who emended to *regio* (in fact an erased correction in the MS itself). Schumann did not note that in the MS there is a clear division-mark after *leta,* and printed this word as part of the following verse.

voices her own thoughts, and not a narrative in which she features, or where her thoughts are reported, he was able to concentrate on her rôle, on all the diverse impulses and the emotional transitions — from outbursts, to reasoning, to appeals to Anna, to the bitter address to the absent Aeneas, and finally the tender address to her own soul. Thus Dido's story becomes a lyrical-dramatic re-creation of the sorrows of a woman in love, in which all that is specific to her history becomes subordinate, worked in by way of allusions only, whilst the exploration of the state of grief and desire dominates. Such re-creations of a woman's love-longing or love-sorrow belong to one of the most archaic and most widespread genres in lyric: they are not dependent upon the classical heritage, nor upon a background of learned or aristocratic conventions, such as at times in medieval Europe poets and their audiences shared. Essentially, to use the phrase of the great pioneer scholar in this question, Ramón Menéndez Pidal, women's love-laments are a «poesía de tipo tradicional». They show certain qualities that one can, almost without exaggeration, call universal — poetic features that seem to be constants in the genre even outside European tradition, extending not only to the ways emotions are articulated but even to the use of specific expressive techniques. To give at least one illustration of this, I should like to cite a love-lament from those collected by Ruth Finnegan in her remarkable "Penguin Book of Oral Poetry". It is by a girl among the Gond in central India — a society where, as Finnegan notes, young girls are allowed much sexual freedom: they can choose to live with more than one man, before they finally settle; but this freedom also means that they can be freely left for another, and the sorrows of being left loom often in their songs [19]. —

> The wind and the rain are beating down.
> Take shelter or your clothes will be drenched.
> The rain is falling, falling.
>> In all my dreams I searched for you,
>> But I did not find even the echo of your steps.
>
> I have built a fence by the road-side,
> I have made a fence for my garden.
> Where have you hidden, thief of my heart?
>> In all my dreams I searched for you,
>> But I did not find even the echo of your steps.

[19] *The Penguin Book of Oral Poetry* (London 1978) pp. 14-15. The poem cited is on p. 25.

I have cut tall bamboos; I have cut short bamboos.
Large are the hollows of the dwarf bamboos.
The thief who crouched behind my fence has hidden in those hollows.
    In all my dreams I searched for you,
    But I did not find even the echo of your steps.

It would be possible to analyse this song, like Dido's lament, in the terms of medieval "artes poeticae". Both the medieval Latin poet and the Gond girl show subtle use of many rhetorical devices — "apostrophe", "anaphora", "antithesis", "parallelismus membrorum". But above all, central to both lyrics is the use of what Geoffrey of Vinsauf calls the "hidden comparison" (*collatio...in occulto*) [20] — in both, the outer and elemental world furnishes implicit images of the woman's state of being. The Gond girl, like Dido, is aware of the wind and rain as symbols of her abandonment, and, even in being abandoned, is, like Dido, still anxious for the lover who is exposed to them — "Take shelter, or your clothes will be drenched". In her song, the fence and the garden too form part of an inner landscape: they are her defence against love's grieving, a "hortus conclusus" to protect her from again being wounded. Yet for her as for the medieval Dido, all recourses are vain: the lost lover is still there, within her, and both songs conclude with the woman's sorrowful but resigned recognition of this.

    Rhetoric has multiple genesis: while it can be learnt from literary models or from treatises, it can as easily show itself as an innate poetic gift. Thus women's love-laments in a learned mode and an unlearned one can have a lot in common. While Dido's lament in the "Carmina Burana" owes much to Vergil and Ovid, in essence it does not belong to the world of classical "imitatio". There is a sense of liberation here, a capacity to create the portrait of the loving woman afresh, that has its closest affinities with the unlearned tradition of women's love-laments, with the expressive realm so beautifully typified by the song of the tribal girl from central India.

    Perhaps two decades after the first Latin lament of Dido, a poet who was probably composing for the court of Henry II and Eleanor of Aquitaine wrote the Old French "Roman d'Eneas" [21]. It is possi-

---

[20] *Poetria Nova* (ed. E. Faral, *Les arts poétiques du XIIe et du XIIIe siècle*, Paris 1924) 241 ff.

[21] The line-numbers that follow citations refer to *Enéas, texte critique*, ed. J. Salverda de Grave, Halle 1891. In 1971, R.J. Cormier gave a lively review of "The Present State of Studies on the *Roman d'Enéas*", in: *Cultura Neolatina* 31, 7-39; it was followed by his book about the poem: *One Heart One Mind* (Romance Monographs

ble that he knew the Latin lyrical lament, yet there is no need to assume it; what seems to me certain, on the other hand, is that this vernacular poet, apart from having Vergil's and Ovid's texts before him, was familiar with some traditional women's love-laments in his vernacular. He creates a "roman" — an extended verse narrative whose hero is Eneas. Thus the nature of his material and of his task meant that he could not present the Dido episode wholly from Dido's standpoint: he could not, without capsizing his story altogether, become Dido's partisan against his hero. And yet as artist the poet goes quite some way in this direction; to do so, his principal resource is to shape parts of his narrative to make them approach lyrical monologue.

Central to the poet's presentation of Dido are four extended "planctus", which, while they correspond in some measure to four of Dido's speeches in the "Aeneid", increasingly come to invent fresh thoughts for her, thoughts warranted neither by Vergil's matter nor by Ovid's. Her first "planctus" is the most Vergilian: it remains relatively close to her speech in "Aeneid" IV 305 ff., though at the climax the French poet extends his heroine's plea, heightening both the erotic tenderness and the anguished longing:

> If I could have a child by you,
> who might have even the least semblance of you,
> whom in place of you I could kiss
> and enfold and embrace,
> and who could solace me for you,
> I think it might go better for me;
> but it seems to me I shall have nothing
> to bring me solace or well-being;
> indeed I am certain I shall die
> when I see you part from me.
> Sire, why have you betrayed me? (1739-49)

Dido's second outburst of lamentation (1797-1856) again begins

---

3, University of Mississippi, 1973). For the Dido scenes, A. Pauphilet's *Le legs du Moyen Age* (Melun 1950), ch. 3, "L'antiquité et l'Enéas", esp. pp. 98-106, contains some sensitive comparisons between Vergil and the Old French text. The recent essay by D.J. Shirt, The Dido Episode in *Enéas*, in: *Medium Aevum* 51 (1982) 3-17, is unfortunately marred by the author's homiletic apprach: Dido, he claims, shows signs of "moral and mental disintegration... she shows herself as a wanton woman undeserving of sympathy" (p. 10). So too, Shirt's notion of "the author's wry, and even sardonic, attitude towards his heroine's predicament" (ibid.), and his constant attempts to see "irony", obscure many facets of the poet's narrative art.

with Vergilian notes, this time of vehemence: "You never belonged to the gods...you were nurtured by savage tigers..." [22]. But she goes on to analyse Eneas' inexorable resolve to leave her, in an original way, that leads her to project an ideal of shared love in which the partners are perfectly matched in feeling:

> We feel very differently:
> I die of love, he feels nothing —
> he is at peace; I have the pain.
> Love is not fair to me,
> since we do not feel as one [23].
> If he felt what I feel,
> so that he loved me as I love him,
> we would never part. (1823-30).

While even before this northern poet some troubadours in Provence had thought about mutual love in such a way, Dido's lines here, so simple in their words and logic, have the dramatic impact of someone discovering for herself a truth known only abstractly before.

In her third "planctus", Dido is alone. The incantatory quality increases, as a group of six verses begins each with *por quei*: "Why did I ever see or know him? Why did he come to this shore? Why did I welcome him in Carthage? Why did he sleep with me? Why did I transgress the loyalty that I promised to my lord? Why did my love vanquish me so?" (1984-90). Dido moves into bitter self-accusations, because of her own forsworn constancy to Sichaeus — as in Ovid (Her. VII 97 ff.), she resolves to die for shame at that disloyalty. Yet the French poet's emphasis is again unusual: his Dido thinks, how *little* is the brief affair with Eneas compared with her long devotion to her dead lord:

> por molt petit ai trespassee
> la fei qu'aveie tant guardee. (1993-4)

Yet this is not her ultimate conviction: in both Vergil and Ovid, Dido belongs to Sichaeus in death; in the French "roman", as in the Latin "planctus", her death becomes a total surrender to Aeneas. The

---

[22] Cf. *Aen.* IV 365-367.

[23] *Quant ne senton comunalment:* Cormier (note 21) 128 ff., who translates this verse "since we do not feel a community of souls", gives a suggestive (though in part over-ingenious) semantic analysis of all that may be implied by *comunalment* — compare the observations of E. Mickel, Dido's Epitaph in the *Enéas*, in: *Romance Notes* 21 (1980/1981) 240-242.

two medieval poets therefore exclude entirely all the Vergilian Dido's fantasies of wild and cruel vengeance on Aeneas, his son and his race (Aen. IV 590-629).

Dido's final "planctus" in the romance begins with a reminiscence of Vergil's *dulces exuviae* (IV 651), yet here the tone becomes one of renewed erotic ardour mingled with guilt: "Upon these sheets I want to end my life, / and on the bed in which I was dishonoured" [24]. Even while she believes she has lost her "entire glory" (*tote ma gloire*), Dido affirms she will never be forgotten: "people will speak of me in all ages, / at least among the Trojans". She sees her shame and her renown as a heroine of love inseparably, just as, in her closing words, a last accusation of Aeneas is inseparable from a surging impulse to forgive him. Momentarily the poet endows the pagan "amoureuse" with Christian saintliness:

> He has killed me most wrongfully;
> here I forgive him for my death;
> in the name of harmony, of peace,
> his garments and his bed I kiss —
> I forgive you, Lord Eneas (2063-7).

After Dido's death by Eneas' sword, the flame on her pyre is symbolically identified with the fervour of her love for him. As, in the Latin lament *Anna soror*, the words *igni credideram* evoke both the inner and the outer blaze, so here

> Dido remains, pierced mortally,
> and death afflicts and stabs her on one side
> and the flame on the other,
> the flame that kindles and sets alight her limbs.
> She cannot speak — nor high nor low —
> save to call out Eneas' name (2113-18)

The word *esprendre*, used of the flame, can — in medieval as in modern French — suggest both literal kindling of fire and human falling in love [25].

---

[24] *Enéas* 2049-2050: *Sor ces dras voil fenir ma vie / et sor le lit o fui honie.* While *dras* could mean "Gewänder, Kleider" as well as "Bettücher, Laken" (cf. Tobler/Lommatzsch [note 4] II 2060, s.v.), the second meaning seems to me poetically likelier here, since Enéas' *guarnemenz* have already been dwelt on three times in the preceding verses (2035, 2039, 2043).

[25] See Tobler/Lommatzsch III 1250-1252, s.v. (many examples); cf. also D. Shirt, (note 21) p. 14.

A detailed comparative "lectura" of the Dido episodes in the French "Eneas" and the free adaptation of it, "Eneide", composed a generation later by Heinrich von Veldeke [26], would be richly rewarding but would exceed the scope of this essay. Yet it seems hard to leave "Eneas" without adding at least one or two impressions, especially with regard to "planctus"-motifs, of how the Limburg poet responded to and modified the work of his predecessor. He has less of Vergil, but far more of "Minne". He discards nearly all allusion to the world surrounding Dido, the hostile neighbouring kingdoms and the hatred of her rejected suitors. Instead, his dialogues between Dido and Anna and Dido and Aeneas (which are longer than in the French), and even certain moments of elaborate symbolically weighted description that are his own — as of a peerless brachet with silken leash that Dido leads into the chase [27] — seem to direct us to an almost autonomous emotional sphere, a "Weltinnenraum" where love's pangs and fluctuations occur as if beyond time and place.

In Veldeke, Dido already utters a "planctus" on the evening of her enamourment, after Eneas has told the tale of Troy. She escorts him to his chamber (this too a scene more fully and tenderly developed than in the French), and then in the night lies alone:

"How long shall it go on like this?
What have I done to the day?
Who has brought day to bewilderment,
that he makes such long delay?
I have thought, again and again,
this is the longest night

---

[26] In the citations, line-numbers refer to the edition of G. Schieb/Th. Frings, *Henric Van Veldeken, Eneide* I (Berlin 1964). On the nature of Dido's love as depicted in the "Eneide" see esp. F. Maurer, "Rechte" Minne bei Heinrich von Veldeke, in: *Archiv für das Studium der Neueren Sprachen* 187 (1950) 1-9, and the cogent refutation of Maurer's sharp dichotomy between the loves of Dido and Lavinia, by W. Schröder, Dido und Lavine, in: *ZfdA* 88 (1958) 161-195 (reprinted in his "Veldeke-Studien", Berlin 1969). The comparison of the French and the German romance was broached in an acute pioneer study by Barker Fairley, *Die Eneide Heinrichs von Veldeke und der Roman d'Eneas* (Diss., Jena 1910). Nonetheless, Gabriele Schieb, in her bibliographic guide *Heinrich von Veldeke* (Stuttgart 1965), writes (52), "Trotz vieler Spezialuntersuchungen, die [Fairley] folgten, stehen wir aber im Grunde immer noch am Anfang eines wirklich befriedigenden Vergleichs". Certainly this is borne out by two more recent comparative essays that go into some detail about the Dido episodes — R. Zitzmann, in: *Euphorion* 46 (1952) 261-275, and J. Quint, in: *ZfdPh* 73 (1954) 241-267.

[27] On the symbolism of hound and leash, see M. Thiébaux, *The Stag of Love* (Ithaca 1974) pp. 178-181, who does not, however, discuss Veldeke.

there ever was in the world.
Woe is me — that journey,
that ever Paris went there
and seized Helen,
for which Troy was shattered —
it is being avenged on me,
un-gently and grievously.
Alas, where shall my honour go,
my prudence and my mind?" (1389-1403)

Figurally, day is Eneas, night is life without him, and Troy is the condition of being doomed. At the very start of her love-madness this Dido sees herself as victim on a scale larger than life.

At the same time, Veldeke anchors her passionate thoughts in a self-contained realm of "hohe Minne". We do not hear, as in the French or in Vergil, that she shows Eneas the splendours of Carthage, nor again that she neglects her tasks as queen, so that town-building stops and her enemies advance. Here, Dido gives Eneas *here dinest* (1636), as a courtly lover might to his lady, and fears *di merkare* (1644) — the spies that prey upon secret love in the world of Minnesang. Later, in the cave, she rues that her keen sensuality prevents her from showing perfect courtliness:

And yet she was sorrowing
that thus, so swiftly, she
did his will,
upon so little bidding.
But her great need caused it —
she would otherwise have died...(1881-6) —

For this overmastering physical love Veldeke's Dido feels a remorse that is in part courtly and in part (at least tacitly) Christian in prompting: her outpourings of grief to Eneas begin:

"Alas for the misdeed
that I did with you!
It must fare ill for me.
It is because of my guilt." (2034-7)

In Veldeke, Dido's lament, briefer than in the French, moves into a series of exchanges that are essentially still a dialogue between lovers (which cannot be said of the confrontation-scene either in the "Aeneid" or the "Eneas"): he protests (2089 ff.) —

"You are wholly without guilt.

No man was ever so fond of you
as I am and was."
"Alas, Lord Eneas,
if that were true,
it would be better news
than what shall cross the lands —
that I must slay myself."
"No," he said, "Lady,
in the name of the great loyalty
that you have shown me...
your life is still very precious,
you are a young woman still —
do not throw away your being...."

When at the end of her reproaches Dido swoons, this Eneas takes her in his arms till she revives, and once more speaks to her *minnelike* (2170-4):

"Because of my love for you
I must now live most joylessly.
In God's name forgive me
what here I do amiss:
necessity compels me to it."

In Dido's next words both to Eneas and to Anna, her expressions of her sense of guilt return, and it is her guilt — she tells them both — that makes it necessary for her to take her life. Her last "planctus" before Eneas is primarily a self-reproach:

"I must pay for it sorely.
I do not want to rail at you,
for you are without guilt.
You were as fond of me as was right,
I loved you to excess." (2361-5)

Veldeke intervenes in his own person to condemn Dido's "senseless" suicide and "unbalanced" love, as does Anna, echoing her sister's words: "You loved him to excess" (*ir mindet heme te unmaten*, 2473). Lack of courtly "mezura" and of Christian "temperantia" come to seem aspects of the same "particular fault".

In the "Eneide" as in the "Eneas", an element of Christian forgiveness dominates Dido's final words. Here she begins by recalling the grim fatality she had sensed in her first "planctus": "you were born to my undoing" (*ir wurdet mich te unheile geboren*, 2443). Then Veldeke outdoes his source: where before his Dido had raged against

Eneas, but had then said "I do not want to rail at you, for you are without guilt" — now, touchingly, she contradicts herself on both counts:

"I want to forgive you your guilt:
I cannot be angry with you". (2446-7)

Scholars have thought it probable that Chaucer knew the French "Eneas" [28]. I do not wish to argue that he knew one of the medieval Latin laments or celebrations of Dido, and indeed shall hardly touch upon the question of his direct sources here. It is clear at least that, whether by way of French texts or Latin ones or both, certain medieval, unclassical perceptions of Dido were alive in Chaucer's imagination.

For Chaucer as for the twelfth-century poets, Dido is love's saint, love's martyr. Both in the "House of Fame" and in the "Legend of Good Women" he outdoes the French "Eneas" poet in telling a keenly partisan, pro-Dido anti-Aeneas, version of the tale. Chaucer appears to be so deeply at one with Dido's attitudes and emotions that his narrative orientation comes close to that of the lyrical laments, in which Dido pleads her own cause.

And yet this is not Chaucer's only perspective. If in one sense he is Dido's unconditional champion, against a wholly base, perjured Aeneas, Chaucer also constantly compels us to look at his process of re-shaping the familiar narrative, and to ask: what kind of champion is this new poetic celebrant of Dido? What does his championing really signify?

Let me recall a few moments in both Chaucer's poems with these questions in mind.

In the "House of Fame", Chaucer dreams that in Venus' temple, the *temple ymad of glas*, he sees the story portrayed. His allusive recollections of it oscillate disturbingly between detachment and commitment, between dismissing many details offhandedly and fastening upon other details with hectic intensity. Near the opening and close, in particular, Chaucer uses the devices of "praecisio" and

---

[28] Cf.F.N. Robinson (ed.), *The Works of Geoffrey Chaucer* (London [2] 1957), p. 848. All my Chaucer citations are from this edition. Particularly illuminating on Dido in the "House of Fame" is W. Clemen, *Chaucers frühe Dichtung* (Göttingen 1963) pp. 106-116, and on Dido in the "Legend of Good Women", R.W. Frank, Jr., *Chaucer and the Legend of Good Women* (Cambridge Mass. 1972) pp. 57-78. The discussion below, however, partly because it takes a range of medieval Latin texts as its point of departure, is in many ways different in emphasis from that of Professors Clemen and Frank.

"occupatio" — cutting short, and passing over — with a frequency and seeming heavy-handedness that create an impression of self-parody: again and again, under the pretexts of length or inadequacy, Chaucer claims he will be silent about, or leave out, aspects of his tale. Thus when Venus arouses Dido's passion:

> And, shortly of this thyng to pace,
> She made Eneas so in grace
> Of Dido, quene of that contree,
> That, shortly for to tellen, she
> Becam hys love, and let him doo
> Al that weddynge longeth too.
> What shulde I speke more queynte,
> Or peyne me my wordes peynte
> To speke of love? Hyt wol not be;
> I kan not of that faculte.
> And eke to telle the manere
> How they aqueynteden in fere,
> Hyt were a long proces to telle,
> And over-long for yow to dwelle. (239-52)

The feigned embarrassment about speaking of the love-union, and the comic anxiety not to weary the audience, are inseparable from Chaucer the poet's habitually assumed stance of the outsider in matters of love, the emotionally stunted man. Whether we think of "Troilus and Criseyde" or the "Parliament of Fowls", the poet's persona always tends to be that of the man who does not himself know the heights of passion: he is half-envious, half-afraid of the experience; at moments he longs to come closer to the *gentil hertes* [29], then again he does not dare, or feels incapable.

All these disclaimers and "aposiopeseis" might suggest that Chaucer will go on to describe this "portreyture" as detachedly as if he were writing an entry for the National Gallery catalogue. Instead, he passes into fierce, excitable involvement and partisanship: Dido

> demed
> That he was good, for he such semed.
> Allas! what harm doth apparence,
> Whan hit is fals in existence!

---

[29] Chaucer's words in his invocation to love, *In gentil hertes ay redy to repaire* (*Troilus and Criseyde* III 5), appear to echo Guinizelli's *Al cor gentil rempaira sempre amore*, with perhaps also a hint of Dante's *Amor, ch'al cor gentil ratto s'apprende* (*ratto* possibly leading to Chaucer's *redy*).

For he to hir a traytour was;
Wherfore she slow hirself, allas! (263-8)

This thought is then given an unusual twist by being generalized and
made, as it were, exemplary: Dido's mistake, Chaucer claims, was
that of all women who "have no cunning to be strange" — who too
spontaneously give their love to a man whose genuineness they have
not yet tested. Only thus far does the poet suggest a hint of blame
for his heroine.

Dido herself, too, gives Aeneas' "most unnatural" treachery (*ful
unkyndely*, 295) a wider, exemplary dimension: for her it becomes an
instance of how all men exploit women, using women's love as a
means to diverse goals — to magnify their own name, to gain friendship, or voluptuousness, or selfish advantage (305-10).

At this point Chaucer interrupts Dido's plaints to affirm that
this is how he in truth dreamt that she lamented — *Non other auc-
tour alegge I* (314). Her lament then continues, and again it is as if
divested of all specificity: Dido's words here make of Aeneas' behaviour a simple, universal instance of male inconstancy, as in Ophelia's song:

Yong men will doo't, if they come too't,
By Cocke they are too blame.
Quoth she before you tumbled me,
You promis'd me to Wed:
So would I ha done by yonder Sunne,
And thou hadst not come to my bed.

When this Dido thinks of her loss of reputation, there is only the
faintest recollection of Vergil's Fama: uppermost in her thoughts is
the everyday slander by which the world humiliates women who
openly love — a slander she expresses not in Vergil's words, but in
words that Chaucer translates from a renowned medieval Latin poem
on the matter of Troy, *Pergama flere volo* [30]:

Loo, ryght as she hath don, now she
Wol doo eft-sones, hardely. (358 f.)

(This poem, which survives in nearly seventy manuscripts, in fact

---

[30] *Carmina Burana* no. 101, st. 17, 2: *Cras poterunt fieri   turpia sicut heri*. On
the MSS, see *CB* I 2, 141-4, I 3, 204-205. Robinson (note 28) p. 781, noted that
the MSS of the "House of Fame" cite this leonine verse, but was unaware of the
modern edition of *Pergama flere volo* and of the poem's vast diffusion.

stands next to Dido's lament in the Codex Buranus. It is possible
that Chaucer knew a similar collection of Latin poetry on Trojan
themes, in a manuscript now lost; but it may equally be a coincidence.)

The whole of Dido's "planctus" (315 ff.) is addressed to Aeneas
(*my swete herte...O Eneas...*), and yet Chaucer also intimates that
Dido is speaking *to hirselve* — that all is reverie and inner monologue. At the close, when she might seem to have convinced us both
of the magnitude and the banality of Aeneas' faithlessness, Chaucer
once more enters, to distinguish, with affected offhandedness, his
own account from the sanctioned, "classical" one:

> And al the maner how she deyde,
> And alle the wordes that she seyde,
> Whoso to knowe hit hath purpos,
> Rede Virgile in Eneydos
> Or the Epistle of Ovyde,
> What that she wrot or that she dyde;
> And nere hyt to long to endyte,
> Be God, I wolde hyt here write. (375-82)

A classical "imitatio", Chaucer claims, would be "to long", and
it does not interest him to attempt it [31]. This would not be his own
way of trying to make sense of the story. For Chaucer, its sense can
never be something static — it lies in the interplay between this diffi-
dent observer, ever unsure of his capacity to feel greatly, and the
heroine whose lamentations are great, and reach the observer, but
reach him as it were diminished. Yet it is precisely in this way that
they become meaningful to him and to an unheroic world — insofar
as they become universal or (to use a less exalted word) commonplace; insofar as the magnificent but remote queen of Carthage is
seen to have an experience no different from that of any woman
betrayed by any man.

In the "Legend of Good Women", the interactions between the
observer and the beautiful victim are even more troubling in their
alternation of hot and cold. The Legend of Dido begins with an invo-

---

[31] I cannot agree with J.A.W. Bennett's suggestion, that the reason Chaucer
calls Ovid's Epistle *to long to endyte* is "that he had already 'endited' it in the
'legend [of Good Women]'" (*Chaucer's Book of Fame*, Oxford 1968, p. 36). The
mention of *the book that hight the Hous of Fame* in the Prologue to the Legend (F
417, G 405) makes the relative dating of the two compositions clear; the assumption
that a particular legend, such as that of Dido, had been composed *before* the "House
of Fame" would be hard to make plausible.

cation to Vergil, and the poet's claim that he will *take / The tenor* of his narrative from Vergil and Ovid (928f.); it ends with a paraphrase of some verses near the opening of the "Heroides" epistle, and an almost insolently casual concluding reference:

> But who wol al this letter have in mynde,
> Rede Ovyde, and in hym he shal it fynde. (1366f.)

Here as throughout, each "aposiopesis" has something dismissive about it, as if Chaucer were saying he is not really involved in this narrative matter at all. In the course of sketching its background, the repeated pretexts of renouncing — *it acordeth nat to my matere* (955); *it were but los of tyme* (997); *it wolde lasten al to longe while* (1003); *What nedeth yow the feste to decrive* (1098); *it were to long to make rehersynge* (1185) — help to create the poetic persona of one who simply refuses to approach this tale in the hallowed and expected way.

Amid so much cool by-passing of the substance, come equally unexpected moments of exalted commitment. Dido is such

> That, if that God, that hevene and erthe made,
> Wolde han a love, for beaute and goodnesse,
> And womanhod, and trouthe, and semelynesse,
> Whom shulde he loven but this lady swete? (1039-42)

Who before Chaucer had evoked Dido by so daring a metaphysical conceit? If it has analogues, it is only in certain high-flying moments in Dante's early poetry and that of his friends, the "stilnovisti".

Yet the poet capable of seeing Dido in this way is also the one who, describing her love-torments, claims to know such matters only at second-hand — *As don these lovers, as I have herd seyd* (1167) — a poet who will leave his lovers alone in the cave with a facetious naïveté that is also a mockery of classical authority: into the cave

> with hire wente this Eneas also.
> I not, with hem if there wente any mo;
> The autor maketh of it no mencioun. (1226-8)

Yet these lines are at once followed by a perception of love's instability as sombre and lucent as comparable moments in "Troilus and Criseyde": the quip about what the author does not mention continues:

> And here began the depe affeccioun

Betwixe hem two; this was the firste morwe
Of hire gladnesse, and gynning of hire sorwe.

From here onwards, Chaucer's treatment of the love of Dido
and Aeneas is more radically un-Vergilian than any of the texts we
have considered till now. He invents a scene of cold-blooded perjury,
Aeneas kneeling before Dido *as a fals lovere*, swearing eternal constancy, so that Dido *becom his wyf / For everemo, whil that hem laste
lyf.* In Vergil, «she calls it marriage, drawing this name to veil her
guilt» (IV 172); in Chaucer a true, eternal marriage *is* contracted [32],
but the husband enters it in bad faith.

Now Chaucer the poet drops all pretence of dispassionateness:
in his own person he has a long apostrophe to all innocent, merciful
women who trust men and are deceived. If only they could learn
from a story such as this — or rather, from the amazingly loaded version of it that Chaucer conjures up to bring his point home:

This Eneas, that hath so depe yswore,
Is wery of his craft withinne a throwe...

Whilst for Chaucer love is *the craft so long to lerne* [33], his Aeneas
wearies as soon as he has achieved sexual possession and subjugation.

Chaucer, unlike earlier poets, imagines the last encounter between the two as taking place when they lie in bed together. Dido
senses that Aeneas is troubled, and asks solicitously what ails him;
and he, with *fals teres*, tells he has dreamt of Anchises and Mercury,
and of his need to depart. Chaucer makes Dido's stark outcry:

Have ye nat sworn to wyve me to take?
Allas! what woman wole ye of me make? (1304f.)

[32] On the learned tradition in which Dido "è espressamente indicata, contro
la narrazione di Virgilio, con l'appellativo di 'coniux' di Enea", see most recently C.
Villa / G.C. Alessio, Tra commedia e 'comedía', in: *IMU* 24 (1981) 1-136, at p. 29.
The marriage of Aeneas and Dido, mentioned by Dante (*Mon.* II iii, 14-16), was
given particular emphasis by Alfonso X in the 'Primera Crónica General', I, chs.
57-58 (ed. R. Menéndez Pidal, Madrid 1955, pp. 38f.). Before reaching Carthage,
Eneas "adormeciosse, e fuel dicho en suennos que primero casarie con la reyna
Dido, e depues irie a aquel logar o el cobdiciaua". The very day of Eneas' arrival
in Dido's palace, "fablaron de casamiento, e prometieron se un a otro ques tomassen
por marid e por mugier; e sobresso fizieronse grandes yuras segund ell uso de los
gentiles, e casaron luego, e fueron las bodas muy nobles e muy ricas. Y Eneas fico
por rey e por sennor de Carthago e de tod aquella tierra... E duro assi bien tres annos en esta bien andança".

[33] *The Parliament of Fowls*, line 1.

completely unclassical and unqueenlike. Suddenly we are back in the world of Ophelia's song, and of ballads — the world in which the common substrate of meaning in this story, as Chaucer conceives it, still rings true.

In Ovid, Dido says to Aeneas: «If you are ashamed to have me as your wife, let me be called not bride but hostess (*hospita*)» [34]. Chaucer transforms this, with his Dido, into an extreme of self-abasement: she *profereth hym to be / His thral, his servant in the leste degre*. Her words are closer indeed to what the captive slave, Briseis, writes in the "Heroides" to her beloved Achilles [35]. Here in Chaucer, it is deliberately, rendingly inconsistent with all that follows: Dido in desperation makes two more pleas, to an Aeneas whom she now pictures as an icy sadist — «if you marry me, you can kill me the same day, at least I'll then die bearing the name of wife»; and finally, «I am with child — let my child live!». This moment is inspired by a hint in Ovid, where Dido writes to Aeneas:

> Perhaps, you wretch, you are leaving Dido pregnant,
>   a part of you enclosed within my body.
> The hapless child will share his mother's doom —
>   you'll be the cause of death for a child that's not yet born..[36].

Here Dido passes from «perhaps» (*forsitan*, with subjunctive) to a simple future tense: Ovid as it were shows her in the course of convincing herself that the «perhaps» is true. Chaucer goes further: he not only discards Vergil's moment, where Dido wishes vainly that she could have had a child to remember Aeneas by, but also banishes all trace of Ovid's «perhaps»: he leaves us with Dido's shrill, and ultimately hopeless, appeal to the traitor's humanity. The language of the brief lament in which Dido utters these imprecations is Chaucer's homage to the realm of «poesía de tipo tradicional»:

> Have mercy! and let me with yow ryde!...
> And, so ye wole me now to wive take,
> As ye han sworn, thanne wol I yeve yow leve
> To slen me with youre swerd now sone at eve!
> For thanne yit shal I deyen as youre wif.
> I am with childe, and yeve my child his lyf!
> Mercy, lord! have pite in youre thought! (1316-24)

[34] *Her.* VII 167.
[35] *Her.* III 69 ff.
[36] *Her.* VII 133-136. For the notion that Dido was actually with child when she dies, cf. "Primera Crónica General" (note 32), p. 42, and Guillaume de Machaut, *Le jugement dou Roy de Navarre*, 2120-2121.

After that, Chaucer guides us back to his classical authorities — some final narrative details from Vergil, and the already mentioned concluding reference to Ovid. There is also one more use of "aposiopesis" — a particularly revealing one. Of Dido's lament to Anna, Chaucer says: «I cannot write of it, I feel so great a pity that I cannot compose it» [37]. Here the cool craftsman relying on his rhetorical device rejoins the fervent champion of forsaken women, whose heart dwells in their laments. The device can be used to pass over what is too long or too familiar — or what is too painful. Is it pretext or confession? Does this elusive observer not know, except by report, what the depths of sorrowing love are? — or does he know them only too well? The throw-away line at the close — «if you want to know more, read Ovid!» — is his refusal to answer further. He knows about the classical Dido from his books; he also knows about the medieval Dido, the martyr of love, tender and forgiving lover rather than relentless foe; he knows about the uncertainties of human feeling, and perception of feeling; and he has no single response — only a disconcerting, truthful relativism.

---

[37] *Legend of Good Women* 1344 f. (*...of which I may nat wryte, / So gret a routhe I have it for t'endite*). Cf. *Aen.* VI 32-33 (a parallel valuably suggested to me by E.A. Schmidt of Tübingen).

16

LAMENTS OF THE MARIES: FROM THE BEGINNINGS TO THE MYSTERY PLAYS *[1]

I

Around 1230 the *Carmina Burana* manuscript was enriched by the addition of a many-faceted Passion play [2]. The text, unfortunately, is defectively preserved. If, as I believe, it reflects — however imperfectly — a play that was coherently conceived by a single author, rather than an amalgam of materials from diverse sources, then the

---

* *Idee, Gestalt, Geschichte — Festschrift Klaus von See*, ed. G.W. Weber (Odense University Press 1988), pp. 89-116.

[1] This essay is in substance the second of the Matthews Lectures that I delivered at Birkbeck College (University of London) in February 1983. The sudden death of my father a few weeks earlier meant that the lecture had to be written in a village in New Zealand, where I did not have all the books I should have liked beside me. While I have added some references that I did not have then, a comprehensive documentation would have been out of all proportion, and has not been attempted. I hope, however, that these pages, while their discussion remains selective and at times provisional, may suggest certain fresh perspectives for the study of medieval *planctus* and medieval religious drama. The focus throughout is on the figures of Mary Magdalen and Mary the mother; for reasons of space, laments of the *three* Maries — such as those in the so-called "Ripoll" Resurrection play, from Vic (text and tr. in O.B. Hardison Jr., *Christian Rite and Christian Drama in the Middle Ages* [Baltimore 1965], pp. 240-4, 301-4) — have not been considered.

[2] *Carmina Burana*, ed. A. Hilka, O. Schumann, B. Bischoff (Heidelberg 1929-70), I 3, 16* (pp. 149-75). I cite the text from this edition, but retain the line-numbering of the older ed. by K. Young, in *The Drama of the Medieval Church* (2 vols., Oxford 1933), I, 518-33, which Bischoff also gives in parenthesis in the new text. On the date of the basic MS (ca. 1220-30), see especially my note in *PBB*, 84 (Tübingen 1962), 173-83. The rubricator of the Passion play — Schumann and Bischoff's "hand 11" — is the same as in the main MS, indicating that this is one of the early additions. The *Ludus breviter de passione* (CB 13*), by contrast, was added later, by "hand 21", which belongs to the second half or the end of the thirteenth century (CB I 3, p. 129). On the provenance of the MS, see most recently G. Steer, "'Carmina Burana' in Südtirol," *ZfdA*, 112 (1983), 1-37.

composition of the play belongs most probably to the later twelfth century, I would suggest to ca. 1180 [3].

It is still possible to glimpse some of the beauty of the play's design. Let us imagine a Gothic altarpiece, where a large central panel will portray one scene, and other scenes will be ranged around it in small self-contained panels; these panels will also often feature some of the same characters as appear in the main scene.

Let us imagine, further, that this particular altarpiece is a diptych, showing twenty scenes in all: on each *volet* the large central panel is surrounded by nine smaller ones. This I think gives a good approximation to the way the *Carmina Burana* Passion play is structured [4]. The two halves or "acts" each have a large, freely conceived

---

[3] While the lyrical lament *Planctus ante nescia* is already cited (anonymously) in a letter from Bec in the mid-twelfth century (cf. *CB* I 3, p. 131), it would in my view be difficult on stylistic grounds to date Mary's other Latin lament in the play, *Flete, fideles anime* (*CB* 4*), before 1150. This is especially clear from such strophes as 3a, 6a-b, which are not used in the play itself, and which show marked affinity in language to lyrics by Walter of Châtillon. On the other hand, there is no compelling reason to follow the older scholars who set this *planctus* in the thirteenth century; Salimbene's ascription of it to Gregory IX (1227-41) is clearly erroneous (cf. *CB* I 3, p. 115). The decades 1150-70 seem to me the likeliest for its composition.

[4] It may be helpful, for comprehending the structure, to distinguish the scenes as follows (other divisions could naturally also be suggested):

Act I
1 The entrance of the personages (first rubric).
2 While the first antiphon was chanted, the encounters it describes — between Christ, Pilate, the crowd and the chief priests — will have been mimed (1-6).
3 Flashbacks to Christ's ministry: (a) the calling of the apostles (7-9); (b) the healing of the blind man in Jericho, here combined with the calling of Zacheus (cf. Luke 18: 25-43; 19: 1-10) (10-16).
4 Christ's entry into Jerusalem (mimed during the singing of the antiphon) (17-25).
5 (Principal scene) Simon the Pharisee and Jesus (36-40); Mary Magdalen (41-120); Mary with Jesus in Simon's house (121-51).
6 The raising of Lazarus (152-8).
7 Judas with the chief priests (159-72).
8 A mime of the Last Supper (the rubric: *Interea Iesus faciat ut mos est in cena*).
9 The Mount of Olives (173-84).
10 Judas's betrayal (185-203).

Act II
11 Jesus before the chief priests (204-8).
12 Jesus before Pilate (209-13).
13 Jesus before Herod (214-15)
14 Pilate's pact with Herod (*Tunc conveniunt Pilatus et Herodes et osculantur invicem*) and renewed encounter with Jesus (216-25).

principal scene: the first has as its heroine Mary Magdalen, the second, Mary the mother. Before and after these great scenes come brief traditional ones, conceived hieratically, rich in biblical and liturgical words and music. If we imagine each "act" as about an hour's playing-time (allowing for such things as the mimed events and the *reprises* indicated in the manuscript), the scene which shows Mary Magdalen and her girl-friends, and which ends with her remorseful *planctus* at Christ's feet, will have occupied perhaps half an hour; so, too, in the second "act", the dominant scene is that of the complaints of Mary the mother: a brief hieratic scene of the crucifixion, concluding with Pilate's biblical words, "What I have written, I have written", is followed by Mary's three extended lyrics of lament. The first, the simplest, is in German, and may have been composed for this play; the other two (*Flete, fideles anime* and *Planctus ante nescia*) are virtuoso Latin *planctus*, of French provenance. One strophe of *Flete, fideles anime*, where Mary turns to John, her new son, is used by the dramatist as a refrain to bind the two Latin laments together. The three lyrics sung by Mary (again about half an hour's playing-time) are followed once more by swift incidents using almost wholly biblical words. The new bond between Mary and John, already dwelt on in the lyrical compositions, is re-enacted with the words *in illo tempore*: "Woman, behold your son" — "Behold your mother".

I should like to focus on certain moments in the two large scenes that have the Maries as their heroines. After an attempt at characterising these moments, I hope to illuminate them comparatively, looking both backward in time and forward. I shall try to trace certain traditions behind these scenes in texts that go back as far as the Patristic period; and I shall look at the *Nachleben* of these traditions in at least one medieval vernacular — the English. Laments of Mary the mother occur in all the English dramatic cycles, most beautifully in those of Towneley and "N-Town" (which was once identified with Coventry, but is now assigned to East Anglia). Such laments were part of a European *koinê*, and can also be paralleled in French, Provençal and Italian plays, as well as in religious lyrics, Greek, Latin and vernacular [5]. But the rarer lament of the sinful Mary, and her en-

---

15 The scourging and mocking (226-7).
16 Pilate's sentence of Jesus (228-39).
17 Judas's despair before the priests, and his hanging, led by a devil (240-3).
18 The way to Calvary and the crucifixion (244-7).
19 (Principal scene) Mary's lamentations (248-93)
20 Christ's last moments, Longinus, and the Jews (294-305).
    [5] While there are several studies of the figure of Mary Magdalen — see espe-

counters with lover, angel and demon, are also found in medieval English, in the Digby play, *Mary Magdalen*, which sheds unusual light on a largely submerged Continental tradition.

cially V. Saxer, *Le culte de Marie Madeleine en Occident* (Paris 1959) — I know of no systematic account of her laments. The laments of the Virgin Mary, by contrast, have been amply studied in a number of traditions. For the Greek, I would signal particularly M. Alexiou, "The Lament of the Virgin in Byzantine Literature and Modern Greek Folk-Song", *Byzantine and Modern Greek Studies* I (1975), 111-40, and *The Ritual Lament in Greek Tradition* (Cambridge 1974), pp. 62-78, 142-5, and, for the Modern Greek Good Friday songs, B. Bouvier, *Le mirologue de la Vierge* (Genève 1976). For the earliest Byzantine iconography, and its influence on western art till the eleventh century, see K. Weitzmann, "The Origin of the Threnos", in *De Artibus Opuscula XL: Essays in Honor of Erwin Panofsky*, ed. M. Meiss (New York 1961) I, 476-90; II, 161-6.

For the medieval West, E. Wechssler's *Die romanischen Marienklagen* (Halle a. S. 1893), a survey of texts in Latin and all the Romance vernaculars, is still in many ways unsuperseded. The Latin tradition has recently been the subject of a full-scale study by S. Sticca: *Il Planctus Mariae nella tradizione drammatica del Medio Evo* (Sulmona 1984). Sticca assembles a large range of materials, with vast bibliography. Unfortunately the texts are often cited with many inaccuracies (the quotation in the first note, p. 2, n. 1, for example, contains 9 errors in 8 lines), and there is little awareness of the problems regarding the dating and authenticity of the works mentioned. Thus for instance Sticca assumes that the laments of the Virgin in the fifteenth-century MSS of *Acta Pilati B* are "il più antico pianto o lamento della Vergine come motivo liturgico", and sets them "all'inizio del secolo quarto" (p. 46); or he calls the Latin *Threni* (discussed below) "il lamento della Vergine composto da Efrem Siro" (p. 48), even though no specialist today would claim this text for Ephraem, and it is uncertain whether a Syriac original ever existed. Similarly, Sticca presents the widely influential *Liber de Passione* as by St Bernard, unaware that already in 1893 Wechssler (pp. 17-25) had shown that this prose piece, ascribed variously in the MSS to Saints Augustine, Anselm and Bernard, plagiarises, among other texts, the lyrical lament *Planctus ante nescia*. To chart the complex Latin inheritance accurately, much work remains to be done.

For laments of the Virgin in medieval German, see esp. W. Lipphardt, "Studien zu den Marienklagen", *PBB*, 58 (1934), 390-444; on the Icelandic laments, the section "Die Marienklagen" in H. Schottmann's *Die isländische Mariendichtung* (München 1973), pp. 504-12. Schottmann's notions about the Latin tradition and its relations with the vernaculars (e.g. "wachsen seit dem Ende des 12. Jh.s auch im lateinischen Westen die Marienklagen, die bald von den Volkssprachen aufgenommen werden", p. 504) are, however, historically hazy, as the many earlier texts, Latin and vernacular, indicated below make plain.

Texts that were not yet available to Wechssler, and that are not discussed in the present essay, include the fourteenth-century *Passion provençale du Manuscrit Didot* (ed. W.P. Shepard, Paris 1928) and Jean Michel's *Le Mystère de la Passion* (ed. O. Jodogne, Gembloux 1959), which both contain extensive *planctus* for Mary Magdalen as well as for the Virgin; *La Passion du Palatinus* (ed. G. Frank, Paris 1922); F.J. Tanquerey, *Plaintes de la Vierge en anglo-français* (Paris 1921); and a few of the *laude* in V. de Bartholomaeis, *Laude drammatiche e rappresentazioni sacre* (3 vols., Florence

In the *Carmina Burana* play, Mary Magdalen enters singing of the world's delight (*mundi delectatio*). Her dedication to sensual bliss is expressed in the strophic form of the Archpoet's renowned "confession", *Estuans intrinsecus*, and in language notably close to the Archpoet's [6]:

> Pro mundano gaudio   vitam terminabo...
> nil curans de ceteris,   corpus procurabo.

> I'll pursue worldly joy to my life's end...
> I'll care for my body, caring naught for other things. (46-8)

With a group of girls she makes her way to the Merchant, to buy cosmetics and scent, and in a strophe that matches hers he offers her his finest wares.

Then she sings in German: these are her means "to compel young men, even despite themselves, to love". As Mary chants love's qualities, she touches on courtly values: "men of excellence shall love women capable of loving, for love makes you serenely joyful (*tuôt eu hoech gemüt*) and allows you to be held in high honour". While it should no longer surprise us that a playwright composing for an audience which extended far beyond a court could count on that audience's familiarity with the notions of "Hoher Mut" and the ennobling power of high love, it may still perhaps surprise that he attributes these thoughts to a woman whose own love is so far from "Hohe Minne", who plans to use her make-up and perfumes to arouse desire, not in one young man but in many.

After three strophes with refrain, Mary falls asleep. In her dreams an angel appears to her, telling her of Jesus who liberates from sin, and who at this moment is a guest nearby, in the house of Simon the Pharisee. But at once a demon appears with a dissuasive message [7], and as she wakes it is to this that Mary inclines: she sings

---

1943). The relation of Gonzalo de Berceo's *El duelo de la Virgen* to the pseudo-Bernardine *Liber de Passione*, fist signalled by Wechssler, has been set out more fully by B. Dutton: *Gonzalo de Berceo, Obras Completas* III (London 1975).

[6] Cf. *CB* 191, sts. 5-6:

> voluptatis avidus   magis quam salutis,
> mortuus in anima   curam gero cutis...
> morte bona morior,   dulci nece necor.

It seems to me altogether possible that the Archpoet's composition influenced the playwright.

[7] This devil's presence becomes explicit only in the rubric after 107 (*et amator recedat et diabolus*), but is presupposed also at Mary's other awakenings, as she turns back from the angel's message to the song *Mundi delectatio*.

her paean to the world's delight once more. A lover approaches her,
and then, again in German strophes, Mary summons her girl-friends
back to the Merchant — once more with a courtly aside for the
lover's benefit, stressing how necessary is joy to those who love: "he
who loves me must be free of cares".

The Merchant gives Mary a rouge which, he assures, will make
her not only beautiful but "absolutely joyful" (*vil reht wunecliche*).
Having accepted it, Mary again goes to sleep. A second time, and a
third, the angel sings his invitation to Simon's house, and the demon
— we can assume — mimes his contrary enticement. Suddenly, as
she awakes the third time, Mary bursts into strophes of lament and
renunciation:

> Heu, vita preterita,   vita plena malis...
> Hinc, ornatus seculi,   vestium candores!
> procul a me fugite,   turpes amatores!
>
> Alas for my past life, life full of wickedness...
> Away with you, worldly glamour, shining robes!
> Flee far from me, you ignoble lovers! (114ff)

Then, says the rubric, let her cast off her society clothes and put on
a black cloak, and her lover and the demon shall retreat.

Now Mary returns to the Merchant and asks for an unguent to
take to Christ, and he sells this to her. In Simon's house [8], her appeal
to Christ is couched in German strophes of utmost simplicity:

> Ich chume niht von den füezzen dein,
> du erloesest mich von den sunden mein
> unde von der grôzzen missetat,
> da mich deu werlt zuô hat braht...
> Awe, auve, daz ich ie wart geborn...
>
> I cannot leave your feet unless
> you save me from my sins,
> and from the great misdeed
> to which the world has brought me...
> Alas, alas that ever I was born... (125-8, 144)

Some other moments in this scene are chanted in Latin, in biblical words, some are again amplified in a Latin strophic form. The

---

[8] As the episode is based on Luke 7: 36ff (the *peccatrix* was commonly identified with Mary Magdalen), the MS rubric before 134, *Simon Petrus*, should clearly
be corrected to *Simon Phariseus*.

combination of Latin and vernacular in scenes such as these has been much discussed, and much misplaced ingenuity has gone into postulating pure, monolingual originals, and into arguing that these were in Latin, or (according to others) in the vernacular. I believe the dramatist conceived the strophes in the two languages deliberately in conjunction. Many among his first audiences will have known no Latin, or only a smattering picked up from church services. For them, hearing the Latin parts of the play being sung may well have been rather like hearing an opera today in a language that one hardly knows: as long as one has a notion of the plot in advance, and can understand the miming, not too much is lost. But it was the vernacular parts that brought such a lyrical drama most alive for the wider audience.

In the *Carmina Burana* play the Virgin's songs, unlike those of the Magdalen, begin in the vernacular. Her German lament, like that of the penitent in the first "act", is in limpid rhyming octosyllables of tender concentration, with a deliberate echo of the Magdalen in her opening cry:

Awe, awe, mich hiůt unde immer we!
awe, wie sihe ich nu an
daz liebiste chint, daz ie gewan
ze dirre werlde ie dehain wip.
awe, mines shoene chindes lip!

Alas, alas for me, today and ever!
Alas, how do I now see
the dearest child that ever any woman
in this world bore?
Alas for the body of my beautiful child! (248-52)

Mary appeals to the audience to note all the signs of his torture and to show pity at them; and at last she begs to die in place of her son:

Lat leben mir daz chindel min
unde toetet mich, die muter sin,
Mariam, mich vil armez wip.
zwiu sol mir leben unde lip?

Allow my little child to live
and kill me, his mother,
me, Mary, most wretched woman —
to what end should I have life and being? (261-4)

With this I should like to compare the articulation of thought and feeling in Mary's third lament in the play, the Latin *Planctus ante nescia*. This, composed latest in the 1140s, probably by Godfrey of Saint-Victor [9], became widely diffused throughout Europe outside as well as in dramatic contexts. Like the contemporary lament of Dido in the Codex Buranus, it is in the form of a *lai lyrique* [10], a form that, poetically and musically, allows great artistic and emotional range. Again as in Dido's lament, there is an almost baroque luxuriance, refined and at the same time ardent, in drawing out the details of grieving. Yet this luxuriance is also circumscribed by a meticulous structure [11]. After an exordium (1a-b), in which Mary tells the cause of her lament, the principal design of the *lai* is organised in a fivefold series of impassioned apostrophes: first (*a*) to her son, to the love he has shown and the cruelty shown towards him (2a-5b); then (*b*) an exclamation about Simeon's prophecy, now fulfilled (6a-b), is followed by (*c*) an apostrophe to Mors (7a), and (*d*) a long series of appeals to the Jewish people, in which pleas and menace mingle (8b-12b). At the close (*e*), Mary invokes the daughters of Jerusalem (13a-14), with whom she envisages a bond that at last calms her sorrows.

Mary addresses Christ in words that combine high love-language drawn from the secular world with sacred allusions [12]:

---

[9] The *planctus*, which is cited already as the work of *quidam* in a mid-twelfth-century letter (see above, n. 3), is included in the early thirteenth-century corpus of Godfrey's works in MS Paris Bibl. Mazar. 1002. My slight remaining hesitation about the authorship is connected with the generally accepted date of Godfrey's birth, ca. 1125-30. If this is correct, he must have been extremely young when he composed *Planctus ante nescia*, whereas its extraordinary verbal artistry suggests to me a poet at the summit of his powers.

[10] *O decus, o Libie regnum* (CB 100): I have given a new text with translation and detailed discussion in "Dido's Lament: From Medieval Latin Lyric to Chaucer", [*supra*, no. 15, pp. 431-56].

[11] The form is not clear from the numbering of the strophes of *Planctus ante nescia* in CB 14* (or in Young, *The Drama* II 496-8); but the music of 2 is repeated in 4, 11, and 12, that of 3 in 5, and that of 6 in 10. Whereas "classical" sequences avoid such repetitions, they were common in the "archaic" or *da capo* sequence, and later in the *lai lyrique*.

[12] Cf. the Latin text:

3a Flos florum,   dux morum,
   venie vena...

4a O quam sero deditus,   4b O quis amor corporis
   quam cito me deseris;   tibi fecit spolia;
   o quam digne genitus,   o quam dulcis pignoris
   quam abiecte moreris.   quam amara premia...

7a Parcito proli,

"Flower of flowers, prince of courtesy, stream of forgiveness..." The apostrophes extend from Christ's person to every aspect of his life and death: "Oh how lately given to me, how quickly you desert me! Oh how nobly begotten, how abjectly you die! Oh what love has despoiled your body, oh what bitter reward for so sweet a child!" In the strophes that dwell on the motif in the German *planctus*, "let me die in place of him", the first apostrophe is to Death personified: "Spare my son, Death, do not spare me — then alone do you heal me alone..." In the invocations to the Jews, this thought unfolds into an intense fantasy of longing: "I beseech you, spare the son, crucify the mother — or fasten us together to the cross-beam: it is bad to die alone! In my great sorrow give me back the body, even lifeless, that the torment may ease through kissing, through embracing! If

Mors, michi noli,
tunc michi soli
sola mederis...

8b Nato, queso, parcite,
matrem crucifigite
aut in crucis stipite
nos simul affigite!
male solus moritur.

9a Reddite mestissime
corpus, vel exanime,
ut sic minoratus
crescat cruciatus,
osculis, amplexibus!

9b Utinam sic doleam
ut dolore peream,
nam plus est dolori
sine morte mori
quam perire citius.

10a Quid stupes, gens misera,
terram se movere,
obscurari sidera,
languidos lugere?

10b Solem privas lumine,
quomodo luceret?
egrum medicamine,
unde convaleret?...

12b Quos fecisti, fontium
prosint tibi flumina:
sitim sedant omnium,
cuncta lavant crimina...

13b In amplexus ruite,
dum pendet in stipite;
mutuis amplexibus
se parat amantibus
brachiis protensis.

14 In hoc solo gaudeo,
quod pro vobis doleo.
vicem, queso, reddite,
matris damnum plangite!

only I could grieve so much as to die of grief — for there's greater grief in dying without dying than in perishing more swiftly".

This is followed by Mary's bitter warnings, and then by her begging Christ's persecutors to accept Christ, by whose wounds they could still be healed: "Why are you amazed, wretched race, that the earth quakes, the stars grow dark and the sick mourn? You deprive the sun of light — how should it gleam then? You take the medicine from the sick — how should they get well?... Let the streams of fountains that you have caused to run now give you aid: they slake the thirst of everyone, they wash away all guilt".

The concluding verses, appealing to the *filie Sion*, suggest a *peripeteia*, as Mary understands that the sorrow is not ultimately tragic or senseless: "Rush to embrace him as he hangs upon the beam: his arms outstretched, he is ready to exchange embraces with all who love him. I rejoice only in this, that I grieve on your behalf. Make exchange, I beg you: lament the mother's loss". A double mutuality is demanded: between the women who watch (implicitly this includes the audience) and Christ and Mary — a reciprocity of love with Christ, and of grief with his mother. With the thought of this, Mary passes from her passionate, almost erotic death-wish to acceptance and thereby to an inner composure.

This sketch of some of the movements of thought in the long, richly textured lyrical *lai* can suggest only a little of its psychological range; a performance such as that recorded by Andrea von Ramm [13] also shows how sensitively all these transitions of thought, tone and impulse are reflected in the music. Here is a twelfth-century matching of dramatic and melodic line in which we approach the art of Monteverdi's *Lamento della Vergine*.

II

The adventure, inner conflict, and lament of Mary Magdalen, and the triple lament of Mary the mother, not only constitute the dominant scenes in this early play but also use poetic materials quite alien to the rest of the play. These large scenes are not tied to biblical or even apocryphal sources. In my attempt to discuss their genesis,

---

[13] *Carmina Burana*, Studio der Frühen Musik, dir. Thomas Binkley (Das Alte Werk). There is also a recent recording of the complete *Carmina Burana* Passion play (much of the music reconstructed with the help of other sources), by the Schola Cantorum Basiliensis under Binkley's direction: *Das Grosse Passionsspiel* (Harmonia Mundi).

it will become apparent that in certain areas there is still little to guide us; hence some of my suggestions must remain tentative. Yet I believe that speculation here can be fruitful as well as challenging.

The presentation of both the Maries in this Passion play, each woman endowed with a vivid, highly emotional presence, the inner life of each showing a turning-point, or moment of full recognition, leads us back, I would suggest, at least as far as the prodigiously inventive Syrian poet Ephraem († 373), many of whose compositions were translated into Greek and Latin in late antiquity. Among the poetic homilies ascribed to Ephraem, I should like to pause at one on Mary Magdalen [14] and one on the Virgin.

In the first, [15] the heroine's opening words are a lament. The imagery of the sea, which pervades the composition, both introduces her soliloquy and receives new modulations in it:

> 19 Her thoughts whelmed up like the ocean, and her love seethed
>   like the waves.
>   She saw the ocean of mercy channelled into a single place...
> 29 "What did it avail me, this harlotry, this lasciviousness?...
> 37 I was like a tempest on the ocean, and sank many men's boats.
>   Why did I not marry one man alone, who could bridle my sen-
>   suality?..."
>
> 47 Soon her tears burst forth, staining her fatal make-up;
>   she took from her arms and flung away the flattering bracelets of
>   her youth;
>   she stripped her body of the linen robe of wantonness...
> 57 and she made her way towards the heavenly eagle's path.

Mary takes her gold and alabaster with her, in order to buy a splendid perfume:

> 75 The scent-merchant, seeing her, was amazed...
> 79 "What sort of clothes are these that you're showing your lovers
>   today?
>   In the past, when you came to me, you looked very different!...

---

[14] Strictly speaking, the "sinful woman" of Luke 7: Ephraem does not, like most medieval western writers, identify her explicitly with Mary Magdalen.

[15] *Sermo* II iv, ed. and tr. E. Beck, *Des heiligen Ephraem des Syrers Sermones* II (Corpus Scriptorum Christianorum Orientalium 311-12, Louvain 1970). In addition to Beck's German version, I have consulted the Latin one in T.J. Lamy, *S. Ephraemi Hymni et Sermones* (4 vols., Mecheln 1882-1902) I, 313-38. For the extracts cited in English below, Sebastian Brock has most kindly compared them with the Syriac original for me and has made a number of valuable suggestions.

93 You should wear things that go with your fine perfume — or else
    buy a cheap one, that matches your clothes of today..."

117 "Do not hinder me, sir, or disappoint me with your arguments.
    I've asked you for a perfume, but not for nothing: I'll pay the fair
    price.
    Take as much gold as you charge — give me the costliest
    perfume..."

135 Hearing her, Satan took it amiss, and was greatly troubled in
    mind.
    He was inwardly glad that she was carrying the perfume,
    but he looked anxious seeing the lowly clothes she wore...

143 He strained to catch her lip-movements, to make out the words
    she was saying,
    he looked into her eyes, to see where she directed them...

155 When Satan saw he could not change the sinful woman's resolve,
    changing his shape, he appeared as a young man
    resembling her former lover; he went up and stood in her path
    and began to address her: "Tell me, my lady, as you live,
    where are you walking to? Why so unusually hasty?
    What does it mean that you lower yourself like this?
    You are demeaning yourself as if you were a slave-girl. Instead of
    linen robes
    you've put on sordid rags..."

176 It's not than one of your lovers has died, is it,
    and that you're on your way to bury him? We'll come with you
    to the exequies, and join you in your mourning."

To these words of Satan's the sinful woman replied: "Yes, what
    you said was right:
someone has been snatched from me by death, and I am going
    to his exequies.
It is the wickedness of my thoughts that has died. I am going to
    bury them."
Satan answered the sinner with these words: "Let me tell you, my
    lady,
I am your former lover...

192 I'm again offering my gold to you — far more than ever before!"
    She answered Satan,
    she, the sinner: "I am tired of you, sir—
    you are no longer my lover. For I have gained a husband, in
    heaven —
    the God who rules over all..."

This poetic homily has virtually always been ascribed to
Ephraem; only Edmund Beck, who edited it in 1970, expressed

some doubts [16]. I would suggest that the text, whether or not by Ephraem, must be related at least indirectly to the *Carmina Burana* Passion play — and also, as will become evident later, to the English play, *Mary Magdalen*. While there are divergences of detail, Mary's vivacious exchanges of dialogue with the scent-merchant, her lament in which she casts off her finery, and the appearance to her of a devil, disguised as a lover or along with one or more lovers, are not likely to be the result of independent, fortuitously similar, poetic creation [17]. And yet, in the present state of research, it would be risky to affirm that the Ephraemic text itself was available anywhere in the medieval West; nor do I know any other, intermediate treatment of this matter in the early Latin Middle Ages. The free Greek adaptations of this homily that are extant include an encounter with the merchant, but not with a devil; no Latin version of the text has — at least till now — come to light. Much work on the manuscript tradition of "Ephraem Latinus" admittedly remains to be done. Only in 1971, for instance, a Latin adaptation of the Ephraemic verse homily on Joseph was published, and was shown to have been used by the Carolingian poet who composed the *Versus de Jacob et Joseph*. [18]

[16] Sebastian Brock, however, gives it to Ephraem without hesitation, in "Syriac Dialogue Poems: Marginalia to a Recent Edition", *Le Muséon* 97 (1984), 29-58, at p. 46. He adds that "The topic of the Sinful Woman and Satan was very popular among Syriac writers". On Ephraem's treatment of Mary the mother and Mary Magdalen, and especially on the fusion of the two women in his allusions to the garden scene after the Resurrection, see R. Murray, *Symbols of Church and Kingdom: A Study in Early Syriac Tradition* (2nd ed., Cambridge 1977), pp. 144-50, 329-35.

[17] The *CB* dramatist had certain western precedents for merchant scenes in other contexts: thus the eleventh-century southern French play of the *Sponsus* (ed. D'A. S. Avalle, Milan-Naples 1965) had featured an exchange of dialogue between the foolish virgins of the parable and the merchants — courteous but ineffectual — to whom they go for oil; and in the Vic Resurrection play (cit. n. 1 above) the three Maries converse with a merchant from whom they buy unguents to anoint the dead Christ. Neither scene, however, supplies any of the incidents in the German scene between Mary Magdalen, her girl-friends and the *chramer*.

Since writing these pages, I have learnt that an influence of Ephraem, by way of Greek adaptations, on Greek and Latin plays was already postulated by A.C. Mahr, *The Cyprus Passion Cycle* (Notre Dame 1947), pp. 36f. I have not been able to obtain his *Relations of Passion Plays to St Ephrem the Syrian* (Columbus 1942, cit. *ibid.*).

[18] L. Bailly, "Une traduction latine d'un sermon d'Ephrem dans le Clm 3516", *Sacris Erudiri*, 21 (1972/3), 71-80; C.E. Eder, "Ein dem Hl. Effrem zugeschriebener Sermo als Quelle zu den karolingischen Versus de Jacob et Joseph", *Frühmittelalterliche Studien*, 7 (1973), 223-7. [For the poem, ascribed to Paulinus of Aquileia, see

With the second branch of our laments, that of Mary the mother, the problem of transmission is rather the reverse: the so-called *Threni* — a lyrical homily, again ascribed to Ephraem — exist in a Latin version, but neither the Syriac original nor the presumed Greek intermediary has been found. There seems to be no serious reason, however, to dispute the verdict of Geerard in *Clavis Patrum Graecorum*, who, while admitting that "it still seems impossible to distinguish authentic, dubious and spurious" texts in the non-Syriac tradition of Ephraem, has no hesitation about assigning the *Threni* to the Patristic period. [19] As this text is not widely known or accessible, I shall cite a substantial portion — about a third of the whole, chosen so as to indicate the main elements in its composition. I have arranged the prose, both in Latin and English, in lines that may suggest a little of the poetic articulation which this *planctus* must have had.

> I   My sweetest son, my dearest son...
>   How can you hang on the wood, dead and denuded, my son, you
>   who cover heaven with its clouds?
>   How could you suffer thirst, you maker of all, who created the
>   oceans and all the waters there are?...
>
> II You impious Jews, murderers of Christ,
>   iniquitous against God and ungrateful to your Creator —
>   did he not sustain you with manna in the desert?
>   did he not, through Moses, open up the sea
>   and lead you into the promised land?...
>
> III Oh Gabriel, archangel and minister of God,
>   oh Gabriel, archangel, come now and look upon the cause!
>   Angel, where is that *Ave* now?
>   Herald, where is that blessed *Ave* which you spoke to me?...
>
>   Oh wondrous Simeon—look, here is the sword you foretold would
>   pierce my heart!
>   Look at the sword, look at the wound, my son and my God!
>   Your death has entered my heart: my inner being is rent,
>   my sight has darkened, and the dread sword has passed through
>   my breast.

---

the new ed. by D. Norberg, *L'oeuvre poétique de Paulin d'Aquilée* (Stockholm 1979), no. V.]

[19] M. Geerard, *Clavis Patrum Graecorum* II (Turnhout 1974), p. 366 and no. 4085 (p. 447). Geerard refers to J.S. Assemani's ed. of *S. Ephraem Syri Opera Graeca* (3 vols., Venice 1755), who, at I lxxxii, no. 41 gives the *Threni* as "Anonymo antiquo interprete", and indeed cites the incipits of two divergent Latin versions.

I behold your awesome passion, my son and my God.
I see your undeserved death, and cannot help.

IV Where now is your beauty and comeliness, my son?
Have mercy on your mother, my son, now I am desolate and
    bereft...
Give me some solace, my son:
I have nowhere on earth even to lay my head.
No other relative is left alive, father or mother, brother or sister,
    to revive my spirit.
To me you are father, you are brother, you are son;
to me you are life and spirit, hope and protection,
you are my consolation and my creation...

Incline to me now, holiest cross and blessed wood,
that I may kiss the wounds of my most beloved son and my God,
    and may greet my own son,
that I may embrace my son's body and his most gentle mouth,
his eyes and face, hands and feet, and may kiss the foully
    murdered body...

V My son, my gentlest and dearest son,
I honour these your afflictions,
I worship and adore your mercy and magnanimity.
I venerate the lance, the wound, the reed, the nails...
Through your death you have crushed death and trodden down
    destruction,
so that greater joy may lighten upon me, your lowly mother,
so that all those whom you love may rejoice with me,
and whoever are your enemies may blush and be confounded! [20]

---

[20] "Threni, id est Lamentationes, gloriosissimae virginis matris Mariae":
Ephraem Syrus, Opera, ed. A.B. Caillau, Collectio selecta patrum XXXVII (Paris
1842) 440-4 (the section-numbering is Caillau's):

I Mi fili dulcissime, fili mi carissime...
Quomodo in ligno pendes, mortuus ac denudatus, fili, qui caelum nubibus tegis?
Quomodo sitim tulisti, qui universorum es conditor, quique maria et aquas
    omnes creasti?

II O Judaei impii, Christique interfectores,
in deum iniqui et in creatorem vestrum ingrati —
numquid in eremo ipse vos manna aluit?
Numquid per Moysen mare diremit
et in terram promissionis vos traduxit?...

III O Gabriel, archangele et minister dei,
o Gabriel archangele, age iam et tuere causam!
Ubi illud nunc Ave, o angele?
Ubi Ave illud benedictum, quod ad me dixisti, o nuntie?...

The *Threni*, like *Planctus ante nescia*, are organised in terms of a series of apostrophes. Here Mary invokes first her son, then the Jews, then Gabriel and Simeon, then again Christ, then the personified Cross. At the close, as in *Planctus ante nescia*, comes a *peripeteia*: turning to Christ once more, Mary passes beyond the human anguish, protest and death-wish, to a comprehension of what his death signifies. After the fifth section, which ends the *planctus*, the poet concludes with his own prayer to the Virgin; the lament is also preceded by an opening sentence that establishes the setting.

It would be an absorbing task to relate the diverse elements in the *Threni* to later examples of the tradition in the medieval West. The motifs in the first two sections, for instance, show affinities with

> O Simeon admirande: ecce iam gladius, quo cor meum traiiciendum praedixisti!
> Ecce gladius, ecce vulnus, mi fili et deus meus.
> Mors tua cor meum subiit: dirupta sunt mea viscera;
> lumen meum obscuratum est, pectusque meum dirus gladius pertransiit.
> Tremendam tuam passionem intueor, fili mi et deus meus.
> Immeritam mortem tuam cerno, nec succurrere queo.
>
> IV Ubi modo forma tua ac decor, mi fili?
> Miserere iam desolatae atque orbatae matris, mi fili...
> Solatium mihi praebe, mi fili:
> non enim habeo prorsus ubi vel caput reclinem.
> Non alius mihi superest cognatus, pater vel mater, frater aut soror, qui animum
>   mihi reddant.
> Tu mihi es pater, tu frater, tu filius;
> tu mihi vita et spiritus, spes atque protectio,
> tu mea es consolatio et creatio...
>
> Tu mihi iam, crux sanctissima lignumque benedictum, decumbe,
> ut dilectissimi filii mei ac dei mei plagas exosculer propriumque filium salutem,
> ut filii mei corpus amplectar et os suavissimum,
> oculosque ac faciem, manus atque pedes, et caedem iniquissimam deosculer...
>
> V Mi fili, fili mi suavissime atque carissime,
> honoro tuas illas afflictiones,
> colo et adoro misericordiam et magnanimitatem tuam.
> Veneror lanceam, vulnus, arundinem, clavos...
> Mortem atque interitum tua morte protrivisti ac conculcasti,
> ut gaudium maius mihi humili matri tuae affulgeat,
> mecumque laetentur cuncti dilecti tui,
> erubescant autem et confundantur quicumque tui inimici!

(I have introduced minor modifications of spelling and punctuation, as well as the line-divisions). There are many notable parallels between the motifs and expressions in these *Threni* and those in some traditional Greek Good Friday songs collected in modern times: compare, for instance, in Bouvier's selection (cit. n. 5 above), the lament in the Kato Panya version, lines 192-217 (pp. 93-7).

the *Improperia* — Christ's reproaches to his people in the Good Friday liturgy, themselves composed perhaps in the sixth century. The invocation to the humanised Cross must relate to, and may even be the source for, Venantius Fortunatus' verse, in his hymn *Pange, lingua* [21] "Bend your boughs, tall tree" (*Flecte ramos, arbor alta*). The daring paradoxes in section IV — "to me you are father, you are brother, you are son" — echo Andromache's plea to Hector (*Iliad* VI 429f): "but you are father to me, and honoured mother, and brother, and you are the flowering husband by my side;" at the same time they point forward to Jacopone da Todi's *Donna de paradiso*, where Mary invokes Christ as *figlio, pat' e mmarito*. [22] But I cannot do more than touch on such parallels here. One detail has a particular bearing on the present discussion: in the *Threni* Mary's death-wish emerges, as in the twelfth-century *planctus*, with a quasi-erotic colouring: she laments her son's loss of beauty, she longs to kiss his lips and every part of his body; and then, without logical justification, comes the *peripeteia*: the intensely human longing is transformed into a comprehending worship of the merciful, redeeming godhead.

III

The literary context and the influence of the *Threni* still await investigation. For a picture of the laments of Mary in the Greek world, we are fortunate in now being able to rely on the work of Margaret Alexiou; but, since no Greek or Syriac version of these *Threni* has been traced, it is still difficult to relate them with precision to the fecund Greek tradition. There the earliest major text that can be dated at least approximately is the *kontakion*, *Mary at the Cross*, by Romanos (fl. 540), [23] that consists chiefly of a dialogue between Christ and his mother. While this is not far in time from the beginnings of Christian hymnody, it is also, in Alexiou's words, "structurally and poetically... one of the most exciting achievements of Byzan-

---

[21] *Opera Poetica*, ed. F. Leo (MGH, Berlin 1881), II 2.

[22] Jacopone da Todi, *Laude*, ed. F. Mancini (Bari 1974), pp. 201-6.

[23] *Hymnes*, ed. J. Grosdidier de Matons (Sources Chrétiennes, Paris 1964ff), IV 158-87. On the date of the tragedy *Christos Paschon*, which contains many laments by Mary, and which has been attributed to Gregory Nazianzen (s. IV²) not only by older scholars but also by A. Tuilier in the most recent edition (*La Passion du Christ*, Sources Chrétiennes, Paris 1969), see especially H. Hunger, *Die hochsprachliche Profanliteratur der Byzantiner* (2 vols., München 1978) II, 145, who sets it in the twelfth century, in the time of Prodromos (ca. 1100-1156/8).

tine literature" [24] Among medieval western laments of Mary, only perhaps Jacopone's *Donna de paradiso* — which again is in dialogue form — could be said to approach Romanos's composition in imaginative penetration and artistry. There are parallels between the Latin *Threni* and Romanos — in particular, the refrain that Romanos gives Mary, ὁ υἱὸς καὶ θεός μου, is the exact equivalent of *mi fili et mi deus*, that recurs so often in the Latin lament. It is possible that Romanos knew and was stimulated by the lines that lay behind the extant Latin, but more than this we cannot say.

While the Greek Marian laments have been finely charted, little has as yet been done to illuminate the early western evidence (which admittedly is far scantier). Indeed several scholars have claimed that the Passion play from Montecassino shows us the very beginning of the lament of Mary in the West. This south Italian play, which survives in a manuscript from early in the second half of the twelfth century, [25] is perhaps two to three decades older than its German counterpart among the *Carmina Burana*. [26] The Latin verses in the two plays are wholly unrelated. I believe the attempt to seek the origins of the Latin *planctus* of Mary in the Montecassino play can be shown to be mistaken: first and most obviously, because of the existence of the Latin *Threni* and of a number of other pretwelfth-century western texts, which are cited and discussed below. Yet there is a second reason, not capable of proof in the same ostensive way, since it turns on a literary argument, but one that seems to me likewise compelling. The *nature* of the texts we have suggests (as Alexiou has argued with the Greek evidence) that the lament of Mary was not primarily a learned invention at all. On the contrary, when these laments surface in the learned world, they still bear all

---

[24] "The Lament of the Virgin" (cit. n. 5), p. 113.

[25] Thus the editor, D.M. Inguanez, *Un dramma della Passione del secolo XII* (2nd ed., Montecassino 1939), p. 16.

[26] Inguanez does not discuss whether or not the MS is an autograph. Without seeing it, it is hard to tell how far the palpable errors in his text (e.g. 12 *nomine* for *numine*, 49 *sineatis* for *sinatis*, 67 *impletur* for *implentur*, 95 *testibis* for *testibus*, 112 *teste* for *testem*) are editorial slips, or could be due to an author's carelessness in copying, or if we must attribute some errors to a copyist who was not the author. This would appear to be Sticca's assumption, who claims, *Il Planctus* (cit. n. 5) p. 8, that the play was "composta nella prima metà del secolo dodicesimo", an even more confident dating than he asserted in his *The Latin Passion Play: Its Origins and Development* (Albany 1970), p. 57 ("the second if not the first half"). Till now at least, I have seen no good reasons advanced for setting the composition of the Italian play earlier than ca. 1150, or that of the German one later than ca. 1180.

the marks of a non-theological genre and lyric impulse, the marks of a traditional type of woman's lament.

The extant Montecassino play concludes with a three-line lament of Mary in the vernacular:

> Te portai nillu meu ventre.
> Quando te beio, ⟨mo⟩ro presente.
> Nillu teu regnu agi me a mmente!
>
> I carried you within my womb.
> When I behold you, I die here and now.
> In your kingdom, remember me! [27]

Inguanez, who discovered the text, printed this lament as a fragment, and thought it might be the translation of a Latin original. [28] I see no reason why it should not be complete in itself, [29] and no reason to postulate a Latin source; indeed I cannot see why this lament should not be older than the Latin play-text. Why do both the early Italian and German Passion plays, the one wholly and the other predominantly in Latin, include a lament for Mary in the vernacular? Is it not because there was a deep-rooted vernacular tradition of women's lyrical laments? Is not the *planctus* in the unlearned tongue in each case the clerical dramatist's tribute to the songs of the non-clerical world? (Whether he himself composed in the popular mode, or drew into his orbit something that was already circulating, is not demonstrable, and in any case is of secondary importance: it is the character of the vernacular inspiration that counts).

In the Gospels, as Alexiou notes, there is no reference to a lament by Mary. In the Apocrypha, the second Greek recension of the *Gospel of Nicodemus*, the *Acta Pilati B* (a recension apparently unknown in the Latin West), which survives in three manuscripts, none earlier than the fifteenth century, contains several laments of the Virgin, which in one manuscript (C) become particularly copi-

---

[27] Inguanez (p. 42) prints "... te portai", assuming the first line to be incomplete, but metrically there is no compelling reason for this. R. Edwards, *The Montecassino Passion and the Poetics of Medieval Drama* (Berkeley-Los Angeles 1977), p. 21, translates the first two lines as: "... Why did I carry you in my womb, when I see you dying now"; this is grammatically not possible.

[28] Inguanez p. 19 ("in volgare, una traduzione forse dal testo originale").

[29] Sticca, *Il Planctus* p. 169, cites Mancini's interesting attempt to complete the verses as a quatrain, on the basis of formulae known from later popular laments. While I would not exclude this possibility, I would also recall the very archaic presence in Italian traditional poetry of a three-line strophe, as in the *Elegia giudeo-italiana* (ca. 1200).

ous [30]. Scholarly controversy has focussed on whether these laments wer already an integral part of the original text, which is generally thought to go back to the fifth century, or were inserted in their varied forms only at a much later date, close to that of the extant manuscripts. Yet the debate may not have been altogether well-formulated. As is clear from Alexiou's discussion, even if in their recorded form and language (especially in C) these lamentations show signs of being late, they are in the manner of an age-old tradition, of Greek women singing ritual songs of lament at the deaths of their sons and husbands. For the people, to imagine Mary voicing such laments was the most obvious way to interpret the biblical and apocryphal scenes. Thus I would suggest there is no reason to suppose that the people would have failed to respond to those scenes in the fifth century, or that they would have responded to them quite differently then than in the fifteenth. In the fifth century, too, a reading of the *Acta*, for instance during Holy Week, might well have stimulated and been enriched by chants in the traditional mode, laments put in Mary's mouth, even if they differed in many details of wording from what the fifteenth-century manuscripts record.

In the West, the evidence for *planctus* of Mary is sparse before the twelfth century — not, I submit, because such laments did not exist, but because in their essential impulse and conception they were more at home in the non-literate world than in the clerical.

In Ireland a clerical poet, Blathmac, composed two verse homilies on Mary ca. 750, in simple rhymed Irish quatrains. One of these has many elements of *planctus* and allusions to *planctus* ("keening"):

> Come to me, loving Mary, that I may keen with you your very dear one. Alas that your son should go to the cross, he who was a great diadem, a beautiful hero.
>
> That with you I may beat my two hands for the captivity of your beautiful son...
>
> It would have been fitting for God's elements, the beautiful sea, the blue heaven, the present earth, that they should change their aspect when keening their hero...
>
> Tame beasts, wild beasts, birds had compassion on the son of the living God; and every beast that the ocean covers — they all keened him...
>
> Had I, being rich and honoured, power over the people of the world as far as every sea, they would come with you and me to keen your royal son [31].

[30] "The Lament of the Virgin", pp. 124-9.

[31] *The Poems of Blathmac Son of Cú Brettan*, ed. and tr. J. Carney (Irish Texts Society, Dublin 1964), pp. 2ff. I cite from Carney's tr. of sts. 1-2, 65, 129, 146.

Blathmac was composing for the people, and was playing upon archaic motifs of lament: not only the poet but the whole of nature joins in the song of mourning. Our next datable western testimony is, like Blathmac's, in a vernacular. It is the recently discovered and edited "Augsburger Passionslied", written in a tenth-century hand on a leaf that came from Strasbourg and is today in the municipal archive at Augsburg [32]:

A les ⟨es⟩pins batraunt sos caus
et ab ⟨l⟩es lan staudiraunt sos lad
et en la crux l'apenderaunt;

et ob l'acid lo potaraunt   (oblaeid MS)
— si greu est a pærlær —
et en la crux l'apendera⟨un⟩t.

With the thorns they will beat his head
and with the lances they will pierce his side
and on the cross they will hang him;

and with the vinegar they will slake him
— so grievous is it to relate —
and on the cross they will hang him.

In the manuscript the words are written as continuous prose. There are neumes over those that form the sixth line of the edited text. This helps to show that what we have are two three-line strophes (with variations in the number of syllables to the line, as in the Montecassino strophe), in which the third line functions as refrain. A number of word-forms remain problematic, and do not allow a precise localisation of the song, though to the editors the northern French area seems most probable.

In the fifth line — *si greu est a pærlær* — it becomes apparent that the song is a *planctus*. But who is the speaker who expresses the *com-passio* here? The question, as Heinrich Kuen saw in his stimulat-

---

[32] Ed. H. Berschin, W. Berschin, R. Schmidt, in *Lateinische Dichtungen des X. und XI. Jahrhunderts. Festgabe für Walther Bulst zum 80. Geburtstag* (Heidelberg 1981), pp. 251-79 and pl. VIII. The editors offer a diplomatic text; the text given here is much indebted to their linguistic discussion and incorporates a number of the suggestions advanced there. I have found a striking parallel to the refrain verse (3 and 6), *et en la crux l'apenderaunt*, with its future tense, in the Middle Breton *La destruction de Jérusalem* (ed. R. Hemon, Dublin 1969), fragm. 174: *En croas oz croucher acher mat* («En croix on vous suspendra de bon coeur»).

The neumes over the sixth Augsburg verse, my colleague Susan Rankin kindly informs me, are German and are of the eleventh century — that is, they are later than the text.

ing essay [33], is bound up with the remarkable use of future tenses in all the other five lines. They suggest dramatic immediacy, as if the events of the Passion were about to happen (or to be re-enacted). Kuen valuably compared the responsory sung — *ex persona Mariae*, as the rubric states — for the Adoration of the Cross on Good Friday in the tenth-century *Pontificale Romano-Germanicum*. There a similar vividness is achieved by the use of present tenses, which likewise presuppose that the crucifixion has not yet taken place:

> Vadis, propitiator,
> ad immolandum pro omnibus;
> non tibi occurrit Petrus qui dicebat:
> "Pro te moriar!"
> Reliquit te Thomas qui clamabat dicens:
> "Omnes cum eo moriamur!"
> Et nullus de illis,
> sed tu solus duceris,
> qui immaculatam me conservasti,
> filius et deus meus.

> You are making your way, atoner,
> to immolate yourself for all;
> Peter does not come to meet you, he who said:
> "For you I shall die!"
> Thomas has deserted you, who shouted saying:
> "Let us all die with him!"
> And none of them is there,
> but you are being led forth alone,
> you who kept me inviolate,
> my son and my God.

Kuen did not realise that this text, which the rubricator attributes fancifully to St Ambrose, is in fact a translation from Mary's opening verses to Christ in Romanos's dialogue, *Mary at the Cross*. It is a tribute to the imaginative power of Romanos's masterpiece that it was commemorated thus in early western liturgy. Kuen raises the possibility that the vernacular song, like the Latin responsory, was sung *ex persona Mariae*, perhaps as part of the Good Friday ceremony, and like the Latin with the strong sense that the crucifixion is imminent rather than past. It is this urgency that Jacopone too was to achieve in dramatic mode in *Donna de paradiso*, each new turn in his dialogue showing a new event in the Passion looming up. Jacopone

---

[33] "Das Futurum im Augsburger Passionslied", *Zeitschrift für romanische Philologie*, 95 (1979), 283-9.

likewise once uses future tenses, in the strophe where Mary cries out:

> O croce, e que farai?   el figlio meo torrai?
> e que ci aponerai,   chè no n'à en sè peccato?

> Oh cross, what will you do?   will you take my son away?
> and what will you accuse him of,   since he has no sin in him? [34]

Yet there is also one context where the Passion is of necessity
evoked in future tenses: it is the prophetic context, seen in the Christian passages among the Greek Sibylline prophecies, when the Sibyl
foretells the moments of Christ's sacrifice:

> Then Israel will give him slaps and the poisonous spittle
> on their polluted lips;
> gall for his food, and sheer vinegar for his drink
> will they impiously give him, whirled in an evil frenzy
> in breast and heart, not seeing with their eyes,
> blinder than moles, more dreadful than poisonous reptiles...
> but when he stretches out his arms and encompasses all things
> and wears a crown of thorns, they will pierce
> his side with lances... [35]

Like the speaker in the Augsburg song, the Sibyl intersperses her
predictions with lines that show her emotional involvement with the
sufferer. While I do not know of the appearance of the Sibyl as a dramatic personage in the West before the eleventh century (in the
Limoges *Ordo prophetarum*) [36], I do not feel we can altogether rule
out that the vernacular song was performed *ex persona Sibyllae*, even
though *ex persona Mariae* still seems to me on balance likelier. At all
events, the striking series of future tenses makes it improbable that
there was no dramatic element: it would be difficult to account for
these tenses if one tried to interpret the Augsburg lines simply as a
hymn, sung in the persona of a Christian praying and meditating.

The next two testimonies known to me are from the eleventh
century and are again in Latin. Though in the learned language, and

---

[34] Jacopone (n. 22), p. 203.
[35] *Sibyllinische Weissagungen*, ed. and tr. A. Kurfess (München 1951) I, 365-74.
Kurfess's translation of μυσαροῖς ἐνὶ χείλεσι in 366 as "auf *seine* gedunsenen Lippen"
(p. 51) gives an inappropriate sense. A briefer such prophecy of the Passion, based
on *SO* VIII 287ff., is cited in Latin prose by Augustine, *De civ.* XVIII 23, who himself was drawing on Lactantius, *Inst.* IV 18f. On other Latin adaptations of this
Greek text, see B. Bischoff, *Mittelalterliche Studien* I (München 1966) 130-163.
[36] Ed. K. Young, *The Drama* II.138-42.

by no means entirely popular in inspiration, they too reflect traditions and impulses that go beyond the learned world. Once more the
first example shows, like *Vadis, propitiator*, how close the Greek tradition of imaginative presentation of Mary could be to the Latin in the
early Middle Ages. An icon made around 1100, and presented by
Frederick Barbarossa to the cathedral of Spoleto in 1185, is inscribed
with a brief verse dialogue in Greek, between Mary and Christ, that
is known also from many later Byzantine icons:

> "Welcome your mother's plea, compassionate one".
> "What are you asking, mother?" "The salvation of mortals".
> "They have made me angry". "Have pity, oh my son".
> "But they show no change of heart". "Then save them freely".
> "They shall have their ransom". "Thanks be to you, oh Word" [37].

Bernhard Bischoff, discussing these verses, argued that they were imitated in the West in an even briefer epigrammatic Latin dialogue,
that survives (if we include variant versions) in some twenty
manuscripts:

> "Fili". "Quid, mater?" "Deus es?" "Sum". "Cur ita pendes?"
>   "Ne genus humanum tendat ad interitum".
>
> "My son". "What is it, mother?" "You are God?" "I am". "Why then
>   do you hang thus?"
>   "So that the human race should not go into death [38].

Some of the versions in twelfth-century manuscripts begin with the
theme of *planctus*, with verses such as *"Mater!" "Quid, nate?" "Cur
fles?" "Quia segregor a te"*. ("Mother!" "What is it, my son?" "Why
are you weeping?" "Because I am severed from you".) Yet these seem
to be later variations rather than the original nucleus.

The suggested dependence of the Latin verses on the Greek,
however, seems to me far from certain. The Latin dialogue, unlike the
Greek, centres on the cross, and on Mary's stupefaction — if Christ
is God, how can he die in this degrading way? Moreover, there is a
problem of chronology, in that the earliest known Latin version of
the distich, which I found on a drawing of the crucifixion in the St

---

[37] B. Bischoff, "Un riscontro latino dell'iscrizione della Santissima Icone del
Duomo di Spoleto", *Spoletium* XIX, 22 (1977), 13-16 (the Greek text on p. 13).

[38] *Deus es* should, I believe, be construed as an implicit question (rather than
as a statement or exclamation), because of the way it is linked in meaning with the
explicit question *Cur ita pendes?*

Simeon Psalter at Trier (MS Trier 14), stems, like the Spoleto icon, from ca. 1100 [39]. The fact that, as Bischoff himself notes, "the distich is here (in Trier) unrelated to the other inscriptions on the drawing" makes it unlikely that it was composed expressly for this page and indicates that it must be older. Rather than see the Latin as dependent on the Greek, I would suggest that the poets were both drawing on more ancient popular traditions familiar to them. In the case of the Greek text this has been made particularly plausible by the recent publication of a series of popular Italian verse dialogues, assembled by Lamberto Gentili, that have notable analogies with the text on the icon [40], and that, even if they are not wholly independent of it, show the forms of life that such a dialogue could assume in an unlearned milieu, forms of a more diffuse kind, such as may well also have lain behind the lapidary learned formulation. While there are no equally precise popular analogues for the Latin poet's verses, I believe it can be shown that he drew inspiration from a very early source in which Mary's experience was portrayed in a daringly human way, a way that later official theology either ignored or rejected as scandalous.

In the Latin distich Mary, as she sees Christ dying ignominiously, has a moment in which she doubts his divinity, even as she turns to him for reassurance: "You are God?" "I am". "Why then do you hang thus?" I know of only one source in which this doubt of Mary's is made explicit and analysed: in a homily on the Gospel of Luke by Origen, which survives in the Latin translation of Jerome. Origen interprets the sword that Simeon foretells will pierce Mary's soul (Luke 2: 35) as

> the sword of disloyalty: you will be struck by the blade of doubt, and your thoughts will lacerate you this way and that, when you see him, whom you had heard to be the son of God, and whom you knew to be generated without human seed, being crucified and dying, subject to human tortures, and at last tearfully lamenting, "Father, if it is possible, let this chalice pass from me". There were unworthy thoughts in human beings, which were disclosed so that (...) he who died for us might make those thoughts die: for as long as they were hidden and not brought into the open, it was impossible for them to be wholly annihilated [41].

[39] B. Bischoff, p. 14 and n. 4.

[40] L. Gentili, "Un riscontro popolare dell'iscrizione della Santissima Icone del Duomo di Spoleto", *Spoletium* XXIV, 27 (1982), 32-4.

[41] *In Lucam*, Homilia XVII (PG 13, 1842-7, at 1845-6). The last phrases cited — *quamdiu enim absconditae erant cogitationes, nec prolatae in medium, impossibile*

Origen's profound surmise — if Mary had never voiced her human anguish of doubt and had merely stifled it, the doubt could never have been laid to rest — is, I believe, what underlies the dialogue "*Fili*". "*Quid, mater?...*" Later theologians, to whom the very notion of Mary's entertaining an unworthy thought seemed blasphemous, unanimously interpreted the sword in Simeon's prophecy as Mary's sorrow, never as a doubt about her son's divinity. Yet they could not wholly suppress this rending dramatic insight which, even when it was no longer as explicit as in Origen and no longer directly indebted to him, left traces in Jacopone's *Donna de paradiso* — where Mary, in her lament, voices her fear that her son is, after all, a failure (*perchè t'à el mondo, figlio, cusì sprezzato?*) — and, as we shall see, in certain trenchantly non-theological moments in the English mystery plays.

It is again indirectly that our other eleventh-century Latin testimony suggests popular traditions lying behind a learned treatment. In the midst of the complex allegory and ornate language of the eleventh-century biblical epic, often known as *Messias*, by Eupolemius, there suddenly comes a passage of stark simplicity, and significantly, it is the Virgin's complaint:

> Illius adveniens planctu iam livida mater
> Et flavas disiecta comas his ethera pulsat:
> "O celi sacra stirps, o proles unica, tene
> Sic decuit pugnare tuis, ut te dare morti
> Non formidares et tanta subire pericla?
> Inspice me, tua sum genitrix! Heu cur mihi non das
> Responsum? Cur non "Dolor hic mihi, mater, et hic est"
> Te referente gemens doleo solorque dolentem?
> Me miseram! Quid agam? Quid dicam? Quid queror? Iste
> Inpius occidit, quodsi quid cordis haberet
> Humani — certe fera vel plus quam fera —, non hoc
> Patrasset facinus..."

> Now his mother, wan with lament, approaching,
> her golden hair awry, strikes heaven with these words:
> "Oh holy shoot of heaven, my only child, was it right
> for you to fight thus for your kindred, unafraid
> to give yourself to death and face such dangers?
> Look at me, I am your mother! Alas, why do you give me
> no answer? Why do you not, saying "Here is my pain, mother, and
>   here",

---

erat eas penitus interfici — allude to the continuation of Simeon's prophecy: *ut revelentur ex multis cordibus cogitationes.*

let me groan and grieve and console the griever?
Wretched as I am, what shall I do, what say, or what lament?
This impious one has killed you, who, if he had any spark
of human heart — that beast and more than beast — would not
have gone through with this crime...” [42]

These verses come so unexpectedly in the manneristic epic structure
that again the chances are that at least in part they reflect some
direct, poignant laments of the Virgin, whether Latin or German,
with which Eupolemius was familiar.

I would suggest that from an early period in each society — not
only in the Greek but also in the Celtic, Romance and Germanic —
laments of Mary were probably improvised in popular devotions, in
the manner in which, in the various societies, mothers traditionally
lamented for a dead son, wives for a dead husband. Occasionally an
exceptional poet — a Romanos, a Blathmac, or a Godfrey of Saint-
Victor — transformed the improvised songs into works of high artistry.

Many details regarding the genesis of the Passion plays remain
unclear. We cannot, for instance, say with certainty that the popular
Marian laments were their nucleus or even their point of departure;
nor do we know why fully-fledged Passion plays are not recorded before the twelfth century, or perhaps were not thought of till then. Yet
it seems safe to say that, while such plays owe their execution to
clerks, one important aspect of them was not clerical in inspiration,
but drew upon archaic kinds of women's lament.

IV

To me the special interest of the medieval English Digby play,
Mary Magdalen, is that it shows strikingly how, as with the traditions
implied by Mary the mother's song, what happens to be visible in
the learned world is little more than the tip of an iceberg. Here too
we can observe traditional motifs emerging, motifs of which scholars
till now have not taken note.

Thus the three editors who in 1982 republished *Mary Magdalen*
for the Early English Text Society write in their section, "Sources
of the Play":

---

[42] Eupolemius, *Das Bibelgedicht*, ed. K. Manitius (MGH, Weimar 1973) II,
746-57. The series of impassioned questions also owes something to those in the
planctus uttered by Euryalus' mother, *Aen.* IX 481-92: compare especially *tune... te,
sub tanta pericula missum* (481-3) with Eupolemius 748-50.

> In the story of Mary's weakness after the death of her father, the author has taken the three sentences from Jacobus de Voragine [these simply state that Mary was rich and beautiful and lived a sensual life] *and from this created* the allegorical structure of the temptation of Mary, the tavern scene... and her capitulation [43].

I cannot see how the English author could have created his structure from the sentences in Jacobus, since these carry not the slightest hint of that structure; nor, on the other hand, do I think that he was creating *ex nihilo*. He was working within a flamboyant popular tradition, of which only some traces have survived in literary form. The new editors do not know of the analogous development of Mary Magdalen's scenes in the *Carmina Burana* play, or the larger, cognate scenes in an early fourteenth-century Passion play from Vienna [44]; they do not know of Ephraem's verse homily on the Magdalen or of her vivid complaints and dialogues there. I am not, of course, suggesting that these works were known to the English dramatist, and indeed there are many points of difference among them [45]. But the variants themselves help to suggest how lively this scarcely recorded narrative-dramatic tradition must have been. Let me recall a few details from the English play that bring this out.

When Mary's father dies, three Kings — World, Flesh, and Devil — hold council on how to subjugate her and bring her to hell. They decide to send Lady Lechery and a Bad Angel to Mary's castle. Lechery addresses Mary in effusive courtly hyperboles — "Most debonarius wyth your aungelly delycyte!" (444) — and Mary in her answers shows herself a match for such aureate refinements. Lechery bids Mary not to mourn her father unhealthily long, but to come instead to Jerusalem. She accepts, leaving the family castle in Martha's and Lazarus' charge.

In Jerusalem she and Lechery visit a taverner: "I am a taverner, witty and wise" [46], he begins, and goes on to flaunt his choice and

---

[43] *The Digby Plays*, ed. D.C. Baker, J.L. Murphy, L.B. Hall Jr (Early English Text Society, Original Series, 283), p. xli (Parenthesis and italics are mine).

[44] *Das Wiener Passionsspiel* 279-506, ed. R. Froning, *Das Drama des Mittelalters* (1891/2, repr. Darmstadt 1964), pp. 302-24; cf. also the notes to *CB* 16*, passim.

[45] It would be a challenging and worthwhile task to compare and contrast the development of Mary Magdalen's character in the French Passion plays, particularly in that of Jean Michel (cit. above, n. 5). The French group does not, however, appear to use the distinctive details of the Ephraem homily or the *Carmina Burana* play.

[46] *Mary Magdalen* 470. From here, for greater ease of comparative study, the Middle English spellings have been lightly modernised; but the wording and the punctuation in the editions cited have been left unchanged.

extensive wine-list. He has a rôle similar to that of the Merchant in
the earlier texts — he too is asked for "the finest thou hast", he too
assures that what he is selling is worth the price, and, like the Merchant, the taverner helps to provide a transition to the appearance
of a lover. Here it is a Gallant, whose name (the taverner discloses
later) is Curiosity, itself an alias (according to the Bad Angel) for
Pride. The Gallant's opening speech reveals him as a fop, and his
wooing of Mary takes high-flown courtliness into burlesque. Mary at
first pretends to be offended by his advances. Then, as in the *Carmina Burana* play she can "compel young men, even despite themselves,
to love", so here, when she asks (523) "What cause that you love me
so suddenly?", the wooer answers:

> O needs I must, my own lady!
> Your person, it is so womanly,
> I cannot refrain me, sweet lily!

She replies: "Sir, courtesy doth it you lere!" At the same time, several
risqué double meanings signal deftly that we must not take the
elaborate façade too seriously. Thus Mary seems to promise the Gallant complete fidelity, yet her expression — "to die for your sake"
(546) — hints that sex is uppermost in her thought; and indeed
when we next see her (after an interlude between the Bad Angel and
the three diabolic Kings) Mary has more lovers than one: "Ah, God
be with my valentines!" Hoping that "some lover will appear", Mary
shall "lie down and sleep in the arbour".

   While she sleeps, Simon makes an entry ("I have ordained a
dinner of substance"): he is eager to lionise the prophet who has become so famous. Then, as in the *Carmina Burana* play, a Good Angel
appears to Mary in her sleep: "Woman, woman, why art thou so un-
stable?" (588). But here there is no triple alternation of Bad and
Good Angel: the Good Angel's speech suffices to bring about Mary's
remorse ("Alas, how bitterness in my heart doth abide!") and her
resolve to "pursue the Prophet... with sweet balms".

   Simon welcomes Jesus grandiosely, and bids his guests be seat-
ed. Then the rubric says:

> Here shall Mary follow along, with this lamentation:
>> Oh I, cursèd caitiff, that much woe hath wrought
>> Against my maker, of mightes most! (631f)

After two strophes of penitent complaint, she "shall wash the feet
of the prophet with the tears of her eyes, wiping them with her hair,

and then annoint him with a precious ointment". With this the play-text rejoins the biblical narrative.

Ephraem gave a rôle to the Merchant as well as to a Gallant (who in his version was Satan in disguise); but he did not present Mary's inner conflict as an appearance of angel and demon in her sleep. This conflict looms large in the *Carmina Burana* play, yet there the lover has a very minor part — at least if we go by the written play-text. (He might well have been allowed to flesh out his rôle by mime, or dance, or even an appropriate love-song). The English play replaces the merchant by a taverner (though with similar dramatic functions); here Mary's encounter with the lover is important, as in Ephraem, but so also is the appearance of the Good Angel to the sleeping Mary, as in the twelfth-century German play. In all three versions, Mary's lament is crucial: it shows her *peripeteia*, her turn from human to divine love, which must have seemed so impulsive, so inexplicable that, at least in popular imagination, even if not in the high art of Ephraem, the notion of Mary's being the plaything of angels and devils might well have seemed the best objective cor-relative — or "explanation" — of her behaviour [47].

V

I should like to signal, in conclusion, one or two notable aspects of Mary the mother's laments in the English mystery plays. In the Towneley play of Christ's *Scourging* [48], the traditional motif of lament — "let me die with you" — is given a startling modulation: Mary wants to carry the cross for Jesus, because she sees his shoulders have been gashed; and he answers her not theologically but in purely hu-

---

[47] In connection with these scenes, I would signal a problem to which I cannot yet suggest a precise historical solution. Caravaggio, in his renowned painting of Mary Magdalen (Galleria Doria-Pamphili), shows her sleeping, a tear running down her cheek. She has no halo, and, as neither the Bible nor the best-known legends tell of her sleep, one modern scholar at least has argued that the traditional title of the picture, "La Maddalena", may well be incorrect: see I. Toesca, "Observations on Caravaggio's 'Repentant Magdalen'," *Journal of the Warburg and Courtauld Institutes*, 25 (1962), 114f and pl. 17. Beside Caravaggio's figure is an elegant flacon of perfume and some jewellery. Does not her sleep give an image, as in the plays, of Mary at the crossroads of choice: what will she do with that scent and those gems? I think it likely enough that Caravaggio knew, and was drawn to, a dramatic motif of this kind, but cannot surmise in what form he may have known it.

[48] *The Towneley Plays*, ed. G. England, A.W. Pollard (Early English Text Society, Extra Series, 71), XXII (pp. 243-57).

man terms: the cross is too large and too rough for you — if you made the effort to lift it, you would fall to the ground (316ff). In the Towneley *Crucifixion* [49], Mary has a long lament interspersed by strophes given to John (309ff). She voices traditional motifs, but with vivid moments of physical perception:

> I see on either side
> Tears of blood down glide
>   Over all thy body bare.

John tries to console her by theological explanation:

> But lady, since it is his will
> The prophecy to fulfil,
> That mankind in sin not spill...
>   Thy weeping may not gain.

Yet to no avail: Mary does not listen, but launches into a lament over her son's lost beauty: "Thy eyes, as crystal clear, that shone as sun in sight... all dim". She appeals to Christ to say why he endures this: "Ah son, think on my woe!" (369). Christ does not answer: it is John who tells Mary of the promised resurrection. And she again pays no heed, but goes on: "Mourning makes me mad!" (383). In a moving and profound moment, she speaks of Christ's torn garment — "his robe... That of me was him given, And shaped with my sides" (387-9) — where the symbolic meaning, the inherited garment of human flesh, and the real handing on of worn clothes by those who are poor, seem to coalesce.

Mary then calls on the daughters of Jerusalem to weep — yet not, as in Godfrey's Latin *planctus*, with the sense that they can, through compassion, win salvation. Mary's bitterness is unrelieved, and further interventions by John do not lessen it. Then at last come two strophes invoking Death, comparable to those in Godfrey, and two that invoke Gabriel, comparable to the lines in the Latin *Threni*:

> Ah Death, what hast thou done? / with thee will I moytt soon,
> since I had children none but one / best under sun or moon...
> Gabriel, that good / some time thou gan me greet,
> And then I understood / thy words that were so sweet...
>   Where is that thou me hight? [50]

---

[49] *The Towneley Plays* XXIII (pp. 258-78).
[50] XXIII 430-40 (*moytt*: plead; *hight*: promised).

Mary's apostrophes to Death are frequent in the tradition; those to Gabriel are rare. Yet I would not venture to claim the Latin *Threni* as a direct source for the Towneley dramatist, any more than claim that he hit upon the idea of Mary's pleading with Gabriel spontaneously; rather, it is another small indication of how much wider this poetic tradition is than the written records can show.

The lament of Mary at the cross in the N-Town *Crucifixion* [51] has an unusual pair of strophes that may be this dramatist's individual alteration of a liturgical motif:

> Oh my son, my son! my darling dear!
> What have I defended thee?
> Thou hast spoken to all those that be here,
> And not one word thou speakest to me!
>
> To the Jews thou art full kind:
> Thou hast forgiven all their misdeed;
> And the thief thou hast in mind,
> For once asking mercy heaven is his meed [52].

In the *Improperia* of the Good Friday liturgy, it is Christ who reproachfully asks his people: "My people, what have I done to you? or in what way have I troubled you? Answer me!" Here, by a touching reversal, it is Mary who tries to elicit from Christ how she has offended him, and why he had not answered her earlier pleading and outcries, which had ended in her swooning. Christ then addresses her, commending her to John's care, and reminding her of his mission on earth. Then Mary Magdalen rebukes Mary the mother: Why do you have such sorrowful looks? It pains him more to see such pain in you! Again John's explanations and attempts to solace Mary are in vain:

> And through his death we shall have grace,
> To dwell with him in heaven place;
>   Therefore be merry in heart!

Mary replies:

> Ah! dear friend, well wot I this,
> That he doth buy us to his bliss;

---

[51] *Ludus Coventriae*, ed. J.O. Halliwell (London 1841), XXXII (pp. 311-28, without line-numbering).

[52] *Ludus*, p. 322 (*defended*: offended).

But yet of mirth ever more I miss,
When I see this sight! [53]

This is the nearest that the lamenting Mary of the English plays ever comes to admitting the truth of the Redemption — and still her human grief prevails over that truth. In all the four play-cycles, Mary's sorrowing remains unabated to the end. She never attains a moment of *peripeteia*. In the Towneley *Crucifixion*, Jesus himself bids her to cease weeping (447-64). Yet we are not shown that she does so: the dramatist leaves her without any word of acquiescence. In these plays, that is, we have a particularly forceful resurgence of the ancient non-theological traditions of women's laments. These could be harnessed to Passion plays, lending them intensity and imaginative depth. Yet they originate not in the Christian mysteries, where the *peripeteia* that brings cognizance of the Redemption is always present, but in the unredeemable grief of women who have never ceased to sing the loss of those they love.

[53] *Ludus*, pp. 326f.

INDICES

I - MANUSCRIPTS

---

* Though necessarily selective, this index is designed to make a range of themes and images accessible for comparative studies.

STORIA E LETTERATURA

biblica e patristica. 1952, pp. XLVIII-408.

43. *Epistolario di san Giuseppe Calasanzio,* edito e commentato da LEODE-GARIO PICANYOL. Vol. III: *Lettere dal n. 501 al n. 1100 (1626-1629).* 1951, pp. 490.

44. HYACINTHE DONDAINE, O.P., *Le Corpus dionysien de l'Université de Paris au XIIIe siècle.* 1953, pp. 164.

45. MASSIMO PETROCCHI, *Il problema del lassismo nel secolo XVIII.* 1953, pp. 136.

46. GEORGE B. PARKS, *The English Traveler to Italy.* Vol. I: *The Middle Ages (to 1525).* 1954, pp. 672, 19 tavv. f.t.

47. ARNALDO MOMIGLIANO, *Contributo alla storia degli studi classici.* 1979, pp. 416 (ristampa anastatica dell'edizione del 1955).

48.-49. *Epistolario di san Giuseppe Calasanzio,* edito e commentato da LEODEGARIO PICANYOL. Vol. IV: *Lettere dal n. 1101 e al n. 1730 (1629-1631).* 1952, pp. 450. - Vol. V: *Lettere dal n. 1731 al n. 2350 (1632-1635).* 1953, pp. 478.

50. FRANZ KARD. EHRLE, *Gesammelte Aufsätze sur englischen Scholastik,* herausgegeben von FRANZ PELSTER, S.J., 1970, pp. XXX-398.

51. B.L. ULLMAN, *Studies in the Italian Renaissance.* 1973, pp. 538, 38 ill. f.t. (second edition with additions and corrections).

52. ANNELIESE MAIER, *Studien zur Naturphilosphie der Spätscholastik.* IV. Band: *Metaphysische Hintergründe der spätscholastischen Naturphilosophie.* 1955, pp. VII-414.

53. AUGUSTO BECCARIA, *I codici di medicina del periodo presalernitano (secoli IX, X e XI).* 1956, pp. 508.

54. PAUL OSKAR KRISTELLER, *Studies in Reinassance Thought and Letters.* 1984, pp. XVI-682, 4 tavv. f.t. (second offset reprint of the edition of 1956).

55. *Le lettere di Benedetto XIV al card. de Tencin.* Dai testi originali, a cura di EMILIA MORELLI. Vol. I: *1740-1747.* 1955, pp. VII-502.

56.-57. *Epistolario di san Giuseppe Calasanzio,* edito e commentato da LEODEGARIO PICANYOL. Vol. VI: *Lettere dal n. 3000 (1635-1638).* 1954, pp. 456. - Vol. VII: *Lettere da n. 3001 al n. 3800 (1639-1641).* 1954, pp. 480.

58. *Epigrammata Bobiensia.* Detexit A. CAMPANA, edidit F. MUNARI. Vol. I: AUGUSTO CAMPANA, *«Heroicum Sulpiciae Carmen. LXX Epigrammata»: Storia della tradizione* (pubblicazione sospesa).

59. *Epigrammata Bobiensia.* Detexit A. CAMPANA, edidit F. MUNARI. Vol. II: *Introduzione ed edizione critica,* a cura di FRANCO MUNARI. 1955, pp. 156, 1 tav. f.t.

60. *Epistolario di san Giuseppe Calasanzio,* edito e commentato da LEODEGARIO PICANYOL. Vol. VIII: *Lettere dal n. 3801 al n. 4578 (1641-1648).* 1955, pp. 460.

61. TOMMASEO-VIEUSSEUX, *Carteggio inedito,* a cura di R. CIAMPINI E P. CIUREANU. Vol. I: *1825-1834.* 1956, pp. 424.

62. ROBERTO CESSI, *Saggi romani.* 1956, pp. 200.

63. GIORDANO BRUNO, *Due dialoghi sconosciuti e due dialoghi noti: «Idiota triumphans», «De somnii interpretatione», «Mordentius», «De mordentii circino»,* a cura di GIOVANNI AQUILECCHIA. 1957, pp. XXIV-72, 7 tavv. f.t.

116. CHRISTINE THOUZELLIER, *Hérésie et hérètique. Vaudois, cathares, patarins, albigeois.* 1969, pp. VIII-288, 2 tavv. f.t. (esaurito).
117. GAETANO DE SANCTIS, *Scritti minori.* Vol. II: *1892-1905.* 1970, pp. 524.
118. RAYMOND-JOSEPH LOENERTZ, *Byzantina et Franco-Graeca.* Articles parus de 1935 à 1966, réédités avec la collaboration de PETER SCHREINER. 1970, pp. XXX-634.
119. IVAN DUJČEV, *Medioevo bizantino-slavo.* Vol. III: *Altri saggi di storia politica e letteraria.* 1971, pp. XVI-736.
120. *La Chine au temps des lumières d'après la correspondance de la mission de Pékin:* JACQUES SILVESTRE DE SACY, *Henry Bertin dans le sillage de la Chine (1720-1892)* (pubblicazione sospesa).
121. HÉLÈNE WIERUSZOWSKI, *Politics and culture in medieval Spain and Italy.* 1971, pp. XX-684, 6 tavv. f.t.
122. GAETANO DE SANCTIS, *Scritti minori.* Vol. III: *1906-1919.* 1972, pp. 638.
123. GAETANO DE SANCTIS, *scritti minori.* Vol. IV: *1920-1930.* 1976, pp. 598.
124. GAETANO DE SANCTIS, *Scritti minori.* Vol. V: *1931-1947.* 1983, pp. 598.
125.-126. GAETANO DE SANCTIS, *Scritti minori.* Vol VI: *Recensioni-Cronache e commenti.* 1972. Tomi 2, pp. 1008.
127.-128. JOSEF KOCH, *Kleine Schriften,* 1973. Vol. I: pp. XVI-632; vol. II: pp. 504.
129.-130. LUDWIG BERTALOT, *Studien zum italienischen und deutschen Humanismus,* herausgegeben von PAUL OSKAR KRISTELLER. 1975. Vol. I: pp. XII-436, 17 tavv. f.t.; vol. II: pp. X-482, 8 tavv. f.t.
131.-133. HYGINI ANGLÉS, *Scripta musicologica,* cura et studio JOSEPHI LÓPEZ-CALO . 1975. Voll. 3, pp. VIII-1628.
134. NICCOLÒ TOMMASEO, *Un affetto. Memorie politiche.* Testo inedito. Edizione critica, introduzione e note di MICHELE CATAUDELLA. 1974, pp. 266. 4 tavv. f.t.
135.-136. ARNALDO MOMIGLIANO, *Quinto contributo alla storia degli studi classici e del mondo antico.* 1975. Voll. 2, pp. 1068 (ristampa anastatica 1988).
137. SCEVOLA MARIOTTI, *Scritti medievali ed umanistici.* 1976, pp. 288, 3 tavv. f.t.
138. ANNELIESE MAIER, *Ausgehendes Mittelalter. Gesammelte Aufsätze zur Geistesgeschichte des 14. Jahrhunderts.* III. Band herausgegeben von AGOSTINO PARAVICINI BAGLIANI. 1977, pp. XII-662.
139.-140. *Paleographica Diplomatica et Archivistica. Studi in onore di Giulio Battelli.* 1979. Voll. 2, pp. XXXII-1118.
141.-142. *Xenia Medii Aevi Historiam Illustrantia. Oblata Thomae Kaeppeli, o.p.* 1978. Voll. 2, pp. XV-918.
143. CHRISTINE MOHRMANN, *Études sur le latin des chrétiens.* Vol. IV: *Latin chrétien et latin médiéval.* 1977, pp. 456 (esaurito).
144. MATHEI VINDOCINENSIS *Opera.* Edidit FRANCO MUNARI. Vol. I: *Catalogo dei Manoscritti.* 1977, pp. 164.
145. RAYMOND-JOSEPH LOENERTZ, *Byzantina et Franco-Graeca.* 1977. Vol. II, pp. XIX-468.
146.-147. *Studi di poesia in onore di Antonio Traglia.* 1979. Voll. 2, pp. XXIV-1008.

148. ALFREDO RIZZO, *Scienza impura. Pagine di filologia ed umanità.* 1981, pp. XXVIII-238.

149.-150. ARNALDO MOMIGLIANO, *Sesto contributo alla storia degli studi classici e del mondo antico.* 1980. Voll. 2, pp. 890.

151. *Studi sul XIV secolo in memoria di Anneliese Maier,* a cura di ALFONSO MAIERÙ e AGOSTINO PARAVICINI BAGLIANI. 1981, pp. 560.

152. MATHEI VINDOCINENSIS *Opera.* Edidit FRANCO MUNARI. Vol. II: *Piramus et Tisbe - Milo - Epistule - Tobias.* 1982, pp. 270.

153.-154. *L'uomo e la storia. Studi storici in onore di Massimo Petrocchi.* 1982. Vol. I, pp. XX-374; vol. II, pp. 460.

155.-156. GERHART B. LADNER, *Images and Ideas in the Middle Ages. Selected studies in History and Art.* 1983-1984. Vol. I: pp. 428, 115 ill. f.t.; vol. II: pp. 429-1128, 66 ill. f.t.

157. ANGELO MERCATI, *Saggi di storia e letteratura.* 1982. Vol. II, pp. 590.

158. MIGUEL BATLLORI S.J., *Cultura e finanze. Studi sulla storia dei Gesuiti, da s. Ignazio al Vaticano II.* 1983, pp. 504.

159. MARIO SENSI, *Vita di pietà e vita civile di un altopiano tra Umbria e Marche (sec. XI-XVI).* 1984, pp. XX-536.

160. POMPONI MELAE *«De chorographia» libri tres.* Introduzione, edizione critica e commento a cura di PIERGIORGIO PARRONI. 1984, pp. 480.

161. ARNALDO MOMIGLIANO, *Settimo contributo alla storia degli studi classici e del mondo antico.* 1984, pp. 544 (esaurito).

162.-163. *Vestigia. Studi in onore di Giuseppe Billanovich,* a cura di R. AVESANI, M. FERRARI, T. FOFFANO, G. FRASSO, A. SOTTILI. 1984, voll. 2, pp. XXXVI-824, 15 tavv. f.t.

164. PETER DRONKE, *The Medieval Poet and his World.* 1984, pp. 500.

165. *Le lettere di Benedetto XIV al card. de Tencin.* Dai testi originali a cura di EMILIA MORELLI. Vol. III: *1753-1758.* 1984, pp. 504.

166. PAUL OSKAR KRISTELLER, *Studies in Reinaissance Thought and Letters,* Vol. II, 1985, pp. XVI-648, 15 tavv. f.t.

167. JEAN LECLERCQ, *Recueil d'études sur saint Bernard et ses écrits.* Vol. IV, 1987, pp. 430.

168. RICHARD TREXLER, *Church and Community (1200-1600). Studies in the History of Florence and New Spain.* 1987, pp. 630, 14 tavv. f.t.

169. ARNALDO MOMIGLIANO, *Ottavo contributo alla storia degli studi classici e del mondo antico.* 1987, pp. 476.

170. GABRIELE DE ROSA, *Tempo religioso e tempo storico. Saggi e note di storia sociale e religiosa dal Medioevo all'età contemporanea.* 1987, pp. XXXII-624.

171. MATHEI VINDOCINENSIS *Opera.* Edidit FRANCO MUNARI. Vol. III: *Ars versificatoria - Glossario - Indici.* 1988, pp. 386.

172.-174. SILVIO ACCAME, *Scritti minori.* Voll. 3. 1990, pp. 1550.

175. VITTORE BRANCA, *Tradizione delle opere di Giovanni Boccaccio.* Vol. II: *Un secondo elenco di manoscritti e studi sul testo del «Decameron» con due appendici.* 1991, pp. VIII-592.

176.-177. ARMANDO SAITTA, *Momenti e figure della civiltà europea. Saggi storici e storiografici.* Voll. 2, 1991, pp. XII-984.

178. PAUL OSKAR KRISTELLER, *Studies in Reinassance Thought and Letters*. Vol. III (in corso di stampa).
179. *Gli studi di filosofia medievale tra Otto e Novecento. Contributo a un bilancio storiografico*. Atti del Convegno tenuto a Roma il 21-23 settembre 1989, a cura di RUEDI IMBACH e ALFONSO MAIERÙ 1991, pp. VIII-436.
180. ARNALDO MOMIGLIANO, *Nono contributo alla storia degli studi classici e del mondo antico*, a cura di RICCARDO DI DONATO (in corso di stampa).
181. TULLIO GREGORY, *Mundana sapientia. Forme di conoscenza nella cultura medievale* (in corso di stampa).
182. JEAN LECLERCQ, *Recueil d'études sur saint Bernard et ses écrits*. Vol. V (in corso di stampa).
183. PETER DRONKE, *Intellectuals and Poets in Medieval Europe*. 1992, pp. 512, 8 tavv. f.t.

Tipografia Città Nuova della P.A.M.O.M. - Aprile 1992
00165 Roma - L. Cristina di Svezia, 17 - Tel. 5813475/82